Tokyo

The Complete **Residents'** Guide

Passionately Publishing...

EXPLORER

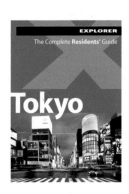

Tokyo Explorer 1st Edition ISBN 978-9948-8585-3-9

Copyright © Explorer Group Ltd 2008
All rights reserved.

Front Cover Photograph: Chūō Dōri – Victor Romero

Printed and bound by Emirates Printing Press, Dubai, United Arab Emirates.

Explorer Publishing & Distribution
PO Box 34275, Dubai
United Arab Emirates
Phone   +971 (0)4 340 8805
Fax   +971 (0)4 340 8806
Email   info@explorerpublishing.com
Web   www.explorerpublishing.com

Welcome...

Life in Tokyo has just become a lot simpler. This book is going to help you get to know the city, its people, their culture and customs, and much more. It's even got some Japanese words and *kanji* thrown in to help you get acquainted with the language. So no, it's not just another tourist guidebook. The *Tokyo Complete Resident's Guide* has been fully researched and written by a team of resident authors who have made Japan their home, and soon you'll know and love it just as much as they do.

The following pages are filled with everything you need to know to make the most of life in Tokyo. From local festivals to finding your dream home, we'll tell you how and where to do it.

Firstly, the **General Information** chapter (p.1) will bring you up to speed with Japan's history, geography and customs, and offer suggestions for places to stay and how to get around. The **Residents** chapter (p.49) will help get things off to a good start. It includes everything from choosing an area to live in, schools and colleges to enrol in, how to find work, a hospital or acupuncturist to getting a visa and all the other nitty gritty aspects of moving to a new country.

Next comes **Exploring** (p.145), which takes you through Tokyo's varied neighbourhoods, highlighting the bizarre and the beautiful, attractions, museums, parks, galleries and tours.

Turn to the **Activities** section (p.207) when you are feeling energised or have time on your hands. These pages are an A to Z of the most popular sporting activities, from the dōjō to the baseball field. When a little pampering is needed, the best spas and salons are just a phone call away.

For most, the **Shopping** chapter (p.271) will prove invaluable when settling in. This section tells you where to go for all you shopping needs. Finally, turn to the **Going Out** chapter (p.323) for a list of recommended bars, Michelin-starred restaurants and fun karaoke joints. For quieter nights, the theatre, cinema and comedy nights await.

To help you navigate, we've included a detailed Maps chapter (p.385) at the back. You'll notice coloured icons dotted throughout the book; these refer to the maps, and should help you find the bar, park, shop or company you're looking for. Turn to the inside back cover for a map of the metro system.

And if you think we have missed something (like your favourite drinking spot or a spectacularly good *cosplay* cafe), please let us know. Go to www.explorerpublishing.com, fill in the Reader Response form, and share the knowledge with your fellow explorers.

The Explorer Team

Explorer's Tokyo

Tokyo is made up of many separate 'cities', with distinctly different identities. All are worth visiting – see Tokyo Areas on p.153.

One must-see is the contrasting triangle that encompasses the cutting edge youth culture of Harajuku (p.154), the peaceful Yoyogi Kōen (p.186) and Meiji Jingū (p.178), and the glitz of Omotesandō (p.305), all within a few minutes of one another.

To see something a little different, head to areas like Shimokitazawa (p.166). Its maze-like streets are home to endless quirky shops, bars and restaurants.

For eating out (p.324), Tokyo is hard to beat. For one of the most convivial options, try an evening at an izakaya (p.327).

The views in Tokyo differ dramatically, from staggering skyscrapers (p.177) to the traditional temples and shrines (p.177).

Andy Sharp After eight years in Japan, British-born Andy is fluent in Japanese and works as a journalist and translator at a national English-language newspaper. When not at his keyboard, he likes to practise yoga and martial arts, kick a football about and explore *okonomiyaki* restaurants around the city. He is thinking of converting to the cult of Mount Fuji in the near future. **Ultimate Tokyo must-do:** a walk around the beautiful Imperial Palace (p.185). **Best city memory:** enjoying *hanami* (cherry blossom) season at Chidorigafuchi (p.44).

Beau Miller Beau first lived in Tokyo at age 4 (wearing a school uniform of short shorts, a blazer and a beanie) and has enjoyed a total of 17 years in the city. After four years studying at Claremont McKenna College in California and four months exploring China, he returned to Japan in 2005 and is currently the editor of weekly lifestyle magazine *Metropolis*. **Favourite restaurant:** Leroux (p.335). **Favourite cultural experience:** smashing open a keg of *sake* on New Year's Eve. **Best place to drink with the locals:** Costa Rica (p.366) in Harajuku.

Frank Spignese Living in Japan on-and-off for a decade, Frank spent three years in Saitama before migrating down to the city proper. He has written for the *Daily Yomiuri* since 2003, and his articles have also appeared in *Outdoor Japan* and *Tokyo Advocate*. His poetry and rants have been published in the expat literary anthologies *Faces in the Crowd* and *Jungle Crows*. **Best city memory:** first visit to Meiji Jingū (p.178). **Best place to drink with the locals:** Ueno Kōen (p.186). **Best thing about living in Tokyo:** being the tallest guy in the neighbourhood.

Jennifer Geaconne-Cruz Latin at heart, and New Yorker by nature, Jennifer arrived in Tokyo in 2001 and has already moved four times in her quest to be closer to the heart of it all. Starting as an intern teaching at university, she now works for *Harper's Bazaar Japan*, *Rolling Stone Japan*, *Oceans* magazine, among others. She's a sucker for fashion and is currently studying fashion design at Bunka Fashion Design University. **Favourite daytrip:** hiking in Kamakura (p.198). **Best view:** the city from Mori Tower (see the Mori Art Museum on p.171).

*Having trouble navigating your way around sprawling Tokyo? Look no further than the **Tokyo Mini Map**, an indispensable pocket-sized aid designed to help you get to grips with the roads, areas and attractions of this mega-metropolis.*

*Now that you're living in Tokyo, it won't be long before you're playing host to family, friends and long-lost relatives you've never even met. No problem – give them a copy of the **Tokyo Mini Explorer,** which is so packed full of fascinating information for tourists that you'll hardly see them at all.*

Julian Satterthwaite Julian came to Tokyo for 'two years, tops'. Seven years later, he's still there, seduced by a city that never stands still. A TV producer turned arts-and-entertainment writer, the native Londoner has covered every aspect of life in Japan for print and screen. **Favourite restaurant:** any branch of Ippudo *ramen* (p.343), especially after a few beers. **Best thing about living in Tokyo:** public transport that you can literally set your watch by. **Favourite experience:** climbing Mount Fuji (p.196).

Karryn Cartelle Karryn originally planned to stay in Tokyo for a year – three years on she is still there, and still amazed. She is a freelance writer who works for numerous publications in New Zealand and the UK, and regularly writes for Tokyo's *Metropolis* magazine. Karryn is passionate about yoga, and also loves meditation, photography and eating out. **Ultimate Tokyo must-do:** spend a summer Sunday in Yoyogi Kōen (p.186). **Favourite cultural experience:** checking out the pop culture at Jingū-bashi near Harajuku station (p.154).

Tamsin Bradshaw Tamsin has written for several guidebooks on Tokyo and Japan, and also contributes to *Time Magazine*, *The Japan Times* and *Metropolis*, covering everything from travel and lifestyle to bars and restaurants. Her love of exploring has helped her to get under the skin of Japan's amazing capital city. **Best thing about living in Tokyo:** the incredible selection of amazing restaurants. **Favourite cultural experience:** watching sumo wrestlers training early in the morning. **Favourite daytrip:** Minakami (p.195).

Thanks...

As well as the combined talent of our authors, whose expert local knowledge and incredible research have made this book what it is, there are a number of other people who have made great contributions. Big thanks go to Andy and Akane, Fujie and David, to Alistair for his stunning pictures, and to the O'Connell family (Nick, Hitomi, Mia and Miki) for all the help and tips, the guided tours and extra photography. Thanks also to Karryn Cartelle for the photographs on p.335 and p.331. A big *arigatō gozaimasu* to Miki and Nozomi for help with the Japanese, and to Helen, Jane, Jenny, Kathryn, Matt, Pamela and Richard for the proofing and fact checking. And last but not least, thanks to Stuart and Miki for putting up with having 'salarymen' as partners for a few months, and also to the mini explorers of Tokyo, Dan and Amy.

Where are we exploring next?

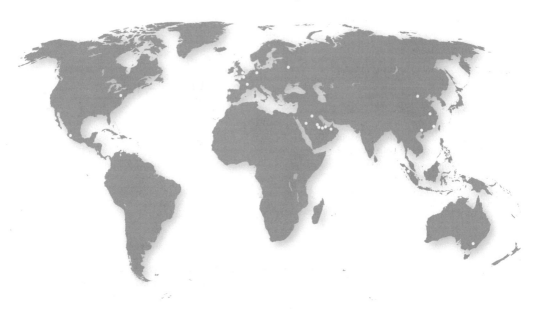

- Abu Dhabi
- Amsterdam
- Bahrain
- Bangkok*
- Barcelona
- Beijing
- Berlin
- Brussels

- Dubai
- Dublin
- Geneva
- Hong Kong
- Kuala Lumpur
- Kuwait
- London
- Los Angeles

- Mexico City*
- Moscow*
- New York
- New Zealand
- Oman
- Paris
- Qatar
- San Francisco*

- Saudi Arabia*
- Shanghai
- Singapore
- Sydney
- Taipei*
- Tokyo
- Vancouver

* Available 2008/2009

Where do you live?
Is your home city missing from our list? If you'd love to see a residents' guide for a location not currently on Explorer's horizon please email editorial@explorerpublishing.com.

Advertise with Explorer…
If you're interested in advertising with us, please contact sales@explorerpublishing.com.

Make Explorer your very own…
We offer a number of customization options for bulk sales. For more information and discount rates please contact corporatesales@explorerpublishing.com.

Contract Publishing
Have an idea for a publication or need to revamp your company's marketing material? Contact designlab@explorerpublishing to see how our expert contract publishing team can help.

Online

Life can move pretty fast, so to make sure you can stay up to date with all the latest goings on in your city, we've revamped our website to further enhance your time in the city, whether long or short.

Keep in the know...

Our Complete Residents' Guides and Mini Visitors' series continue to expand, covering destinations from Amsterdam to New Zealand and beyond. Keep up to date with our latest travels and hot tips by signing up to our monthly newsletter, or browse our products section for info on our current and forthcoming titles.

Make friends and influence people...

...by joining our Communities section. Meet fellow residents in your city, make your own recommendations for your favourite restaurants, bars, childcare agencies or dentists, plus find answers to your questions on daily life from long-term residents.

Discover new experiences...

Ever thought about living in a different city, or wondered where the locals really go to eat, drink and be merry? Check out our regular features section, or submit your own feature for publication!

Want to find a badminton club, the number for your bank, or maybe just a restaurant for a hot first date?

Check out city info on various destinations around the world in our Residents' info section – from finding a pilates class to contact details for international schools in your area, or the best place to buy everything from a spanner set to a Spandau Ballet album, we've got it all covered.

Let us know what you think!

All our information comes from residents which means you! If we missed out your favourite bar or market stall, or you know of any changes in the law, infrastructure, cost of living or entertainment scene, let us know by using our Feedback form.

Contents

Contents

COMFORT, ART AND CLASSIC SERVICE
HIGH ABOVE A DYNAMIC CITY

PARK HYATT TOKYO™

3-7-1-2 Nishi-Shinjuku, Shinjuku-ku, Tokyo 163-1055
TELEPHONE +81 3 5322 1234   FACSIMILE +81 3 5322 1288
tokyo.park.hyatt.com

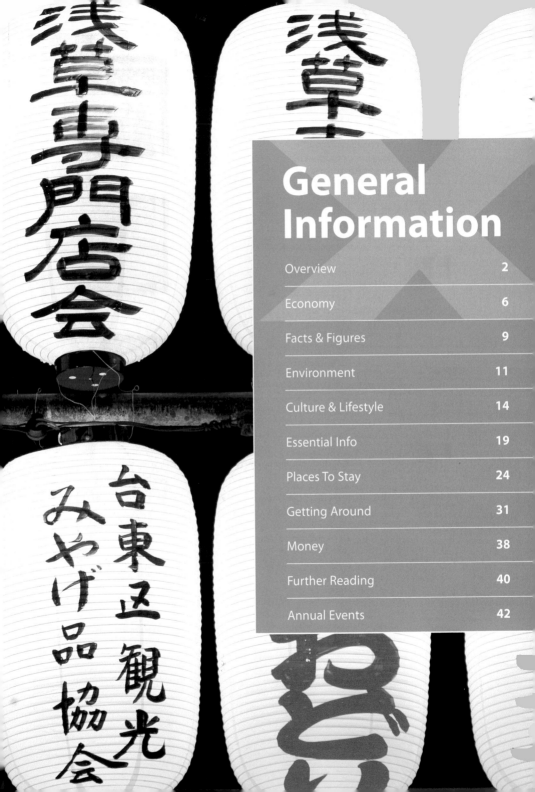

General
Information

Geography

Japan is an archipelago of over 3,000 islands lying off the east coast of continental Asia. Its only near neighbours are North and South Korea and Russia, all of which lie to the west, across the Sea of Japan. At their closest point, Japan and South Korea are separated by about 180 kilometres of sea. To the east lies the Pacific Ocean. Covering a total area of 377,835 square kilometres, Japan is comparable to California in size.

An island nation, it has no land borders, and no point is more than 150 kilometres from the sea. It has a total coastline of 29,751 kilometres distributed across thousands of isles and islets but the vast majority of the country's landmass is accounted for by four main islands: Honshū, Hokkaidō, Kyūshū and Shikoku (listed in decreasing order of size). Further-flung Japanese islands include the Ryūkyū group, centred on Okinawa. At their southernmost point, these islands are more than 1,900 kilometres from Tokyo, and far closer to Taiwan.

Japan's main islands all feature mountainous terrain, covering 76% of the total landmass, with numerous peaks above 2,000 metres. The country's highest point is the peak of the dormant volcano Mount Fuji, at 3,776 metres. The rugged topography means most of the populated areas lie along the coast, resulting in very high population densities. It also leaves little room for agricultural land, with only about 12% of Japan's area given over to farming. What agricultural land exists is often of marginal viability, being characterised by small plots, often in steeply sloping terrain. By far the most important crop is rice, and terraced paddies are a defining characteristic of rural Japan. Adding to the country's general congestion are large industrial centres; involved in heavy industries such as shipbuilding and steelmaking, consumer electronics and high technology. Politically, the country is divided into 47 prefectures (ken). The capital, Tokyo, lies approximately halfway up Honshū's Pacific coast, and crams about 10% of Japan's population into just 0.6% of its total area.

Tokyo Fact Box

Co-ordinates: 36° north of the equator, 138° east of the Greenwich Meridian
Bordering seas: Sea of Japan, Pacific Ocean
Total area: 377,835sq km (374,744sq km land, 3,091 sq km water)
Total coastline: 29,751km
Highest point: Mount Fuji (3,776m)
Lowest point: Hachiro-gata (4m below sea level)

History

With its relentless modernity and constant reinvention, it is easy to imagine that Tokyo's history spans no more than a couple of years. But the city today is the product of cyclical growth, destruction and rebuilding that dates back centuries. Archaeological evidence of human settlement in the Tokyo area dates from 300BC, with findings of pottery shards. The Japan as we know it began to take shape in the 5th to 7th centuries, with the advent of the imperial line to which the current emperor traces his origins. During this time, the capital was relocated following the death of each emperor. At the end of the 8th century, the capital settled in Heian-kyō (now Kyoto) and remained there until 1868.

Tokyo's story really begins in 1600s, with the victory of Tokugawa Ieyasu (see Top 'Gun on p.160) over rival warlords. Though the emperor in Heian-kyō remained nominal head of state, Tokugawa set up base in Tokyo, then called Edo, declared himself *shogun* (military administrator), and set about establishing strict control over the country.

The Birth Of Tokyo

Alarmed by the spread of Christianity following the arrival of the first Europeans in 1543, Tokugawa severed the country's links to the rest of the world, establishing a policy of seclusion that would be maintained by successive rulers. The seclusion lasted until 1853, when an American naval squadron led by Commodore Matthew Perry arrived off Edo, demanding that Japan open up to trade. Outgunned by the technologically superior Americans, the regime capitulated. The climb-down dismayed many in the samurai warrior class, who led a rebellion against the Tokugawa rulers and restored the emperor to power in 1868. The capital was moved to Edo, which was renamed Tokyo, and Japan embarked on a rapid programme of westernisation, introducing modern industries, western-style administration and a constitution. Openness led to prosperity and also growing military might: Japan signalled its arrival on the world stage with victory in wars against China (1894-1895) and then Russia (1904-1905).

Destruction, Rebirth, Destruction

Tokyo's growth and modernisation continued rapidly in the first two decades of the 20th century. But development was rudely interrupted in September 1923 by the Great Kantō Earthquake which levelled much of the city and left around 140,000 people dead or missing. Tokyo bounced back from the disaster with remarkable speed, however, with milestones including the opening of the first metro line in 1927. This came a year after the succession to the throne of Hirohito, whose reign coincided with the rise of militarism. The militarists continued to gain strength during the 1930s, with an increasingly aggressive Japan conquering large tracts of Asia. In 1940, Japan signed the Axis pact with Germany and Italy, paving the way for its entry into the second world war. In September 1941 the Japanese executed a surprise attack on Pearl Harbor, opening the Pacific theatre of the war. The conflict initially went well for Japan, but defeat at the Battle of Midway in 1942 marked the turning of the tide. Backed by overwhelming industrial might, US forces advanced steadily and invasion was averted only by Japan's surrender following the atomic bombing of Hiroshima and Nagasaki in 1945. Though Tokyo escaped atomic attack, it too was devastated. One raid alone, on the night of 9 March, 1945, is estimated to have killed around 100,000 people and destroyed around a quarter of the city's buildings. Just 22 years after the Great Kantō Earthquake, Tokyo was again in ruins.

Tokyo Metropolitan Government Building

Postwar Growth

Japan began to rebuild under US occupation following the second world war and growth really took off in the early 1950s. The country's role as a base for US forces involved in the Korean War gave the economy a huge boost, providing work for all kinds of suppliers to the military. A sustained period of growth ensued, and Japan went from poverty to wealth in the space of a generation. In the 1960s, growth averaged 10% a year. In 1964, Tokyo hosted the summer Olympics, marking Japan's full return to the community of nations. This was also the year in which the *shinkansen* (bullet train) began commutes between Tokyo and Osaka, offering the world the first evidence of Japan's burgeoning technological prowess.

Slump & Revival

Though Japan's growth was interrupted by the oil shocks of the 1970s, it resumed in the 1980s. Fuelled by booming exports, strong domestic demand and a rising yen, Japanese companies seemed set to conquer the world. In reality, the boom was storing up trouble in the form of an asset-price bubble.

When the bubble burst in 1990, growth came to an abrupt halt and Japan entered a decade of stagnation – its banks and industry were weighed down by unrecoverable debts accumulated during those bubble years. Recovery came post 2003, partly thanks to the dynamic leadership of then Prime Minister Junichiro Koizumi, whose government forced the banks to write off bad loans and resume lending. Since then, growth has continued, albeit tentatively. And while Tokyo has never quite returned to the extravagance of the 1980s, a spate of lavish new megadevelopments, such as 2007's Tokyo Midtown complex in Roppongi (p.156), indicate that the Japanese capital is once again on the up.

Sensōji

Japan Timeline

645	The government of Japan is organised along Chinese lines, establishing long dominance of Confucian philosophy.
794	After moving many times, the capital settles in Heian-kyō, now Kyoto.
1192	For the first time in history, Japan is united under one leader: Minamoto Yoritomo, the first *shogun*. The emperor remains nominal head of state, but has only figurehead status.
1281	Mongol invasion led by Kublai Khan is repelled, partly thanks to the destruction of the enemy fleet in a typhoon.
1543	A Portuguese ship brings the first Europeans to Japan.
1590	After a century of war, known as the Warring States period, Japan is fully unified under Toyotomi Hideyoshi.
1600	Power seized by Tokugawa Ieyasu, who establishes a strict policy of seclusion, banning almost all contact with foreigners (lasted over 300 years). Ieyasu sets up base in the Tokyo area, then called Edo.
1707	Mount Fuji erupts, then enters a period of dormancy that continues today.
1853	Commodore Perry leads a squadron of US naval vessels to Japan, demanding that the country open up to trade. Japan soon capitulates to the demand.
1868	Disenchanted samurai overthrow the *shogun* and restore power to the emperor. Edo, soon renamed Tokyo, becomes the new capital and government is reorganised along western lines.
1905	A rapidly modernising Japan surprises the world by defeating Russia in the Russo-Japanese war (1904-1905).
1923	An earthquake kills around 100,000 in the Tokyo area, and leaves the city in ruins.
1926	Emperor Hirohito succeeds to the throne.
1930	Militarists gain the upper hand in government. Japan seizes Manchuria the following year, and declares war on China in 1937.
1940	Japan signs Axis pact with Germany and Italy and enters the second world war.
1941	Japan conducts surprise attack on US naval base at Pearl Harbor, beginning a Pacific conflict that initially goes well for Tokyo. But defeat at the Battle of Midway in 1942 turns the tide, and Japan is soon pegged back.
1945	The first atomic bomb is dropped on the Japanese city of Hiroshima, with a second falling on Nagasaki a few days later. Japan surrenders, and is occupied by US forces until 1952. At around this time, Japan begins a period of rapid growth that transforms its economy.
1956	Japan admitted to United Nations.
1964	Tokyo hosts the summer Olympics, marking Japan's full return to the international community. Also in this year, the *shinkansen* (bullet train) starts up, linking Tokyo and Osaka and running at speeds of 210kmh.
1989	Akihito succeeds to the throne following the death of his father, Hirohito.
1990	Japan's economic bubble bursts, ending decades of growth and ushering in over 10 years of stagnation.
1993	After 38 years in charge, the Liberal Democratic Party is swept from power by an opposition coalition. But the new government proves fractious, and the LDP is back in charge by early 1996.
1995	The religious cult Aum Shinrikyo releases poison gas on the Tokyo subway system, killing 12 and injuring hundreds.
2003	Japan's economy shows signs of recovery from the post-bubble stagnation, though growth remains tentative in the ensuing years.
2007	Japan gets a new prime minister for the 48th time since the war when the LDP's Yasuo Fukuda takes the helm.

Japan Gross Domestic Product

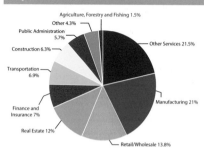

Source: Statistics Bureau

Japan Overview

Generally considered the world's second-biggest economy after the United States, it is easy to forget how far Japan has come, and how fast. In 1945, the country emerged from the second world war as a smouldering wreck, with most of its key cities flattened by US bombing. But Japan then embarked on several decades of rapid growth, averaging 10% a year in the 1960s, transforming itself into the prosperous, high-tech nation it is today. Though the 1990s saw a period of stagnation, Japan's economy is now growing again, albeit at a more modest rate: the third quarter of 2007 saw real annual growth of 1.5%. And although world attention is now on China's rapid growth, it is worth noting that Japan is still far ahead of its neighbour by most measures. While China's economy may seem bigger when measured using purchasing power parity, it is far smaller than Japan's at current exchange rates. In 2006, Japan's GDP grew 2.2% to an estimated $4.883 trillion, close to double that of China.

Trade & Industry

Japan's economic reputation rests on prowess in manufactured exports, with the country's big firms dominant in many sectors. In 2007, Toyota was poised to overtake General Motors as the world's number one automaker. Brands including Sony and Toshiba dominate consumer electronics. The country is a world leader in machine tools, semiconductors and chemicals. This knack for manufacturing makes up for a lack of natural resources, as Japan has virtually no oil or gas, and very little farmland. But exports actually accounted for only about 13% of GDP in 2006, with domestic consumption key to the overall health of the economy. Indeed, the consumer preference for saving over spending is what held Japan back in the 1990s. Spending is now growing again, however, amid signs of rising incomes. In 2006, the average monthly household income for working families stood at ¥525,719, fractionally up on the year before. Unemployment also remains low, standing at 4.1% in December 2007, compared with 4.7% in the US. Possible causes for concern include indebtedness and demography. At about 180% of GDP, Japan has the largest public debt of any major country, potentially putting public finances at risk. And with birth rates well below replacement levels, the country's population is forecast to shrink by about 15 million by 2040. Where will the next generation of workers and taxpayers come from?

Tokyo Overview

By any measure, Tokyo is big. While some cities in the developing world may have more people, there is no other single city on Earth that can match the Japanese capital for economic heft. According to a 2007 study by PricewaterhouseCoopers, Tokyo's annual output in 2006 totalled $1.19 trillion – or about the same as the whole of Canada. And though the city's growth is now outstripped by rivals in China and elsewhere, its sheer size means it won't be overtaken for long: the PwC study predicts it will still be number one in 2020, when it's economy will be worth an estimated annual $1.6 trillion. The city carries equally heavy weight domestically, accounting for about one-fifth of Japan's GDP and just under 40% of all retail sales. The city's growth has been broadly in line with the nation's over the past decade, dipping into negative territory from 2000 to 2002, before resuming tentative growth in 2003. Overall, Tokyo's prospects seem brighter than for Japan as a whole, not least because it is one of the few areas where the population is rising, mainly thanks to domestic migration. Analysts say the newcomers should help underpin the city's vital retail and real estate sectors.

Economy

Leading Industries

Tokyo has a significant presence in nearly every aspect of the Japanese economy, bar agriculture and other rural industries. But its dominance is most complete in service industries including finance, insurance, retailing and real estate. According to the Japanese government's 2007 breakdown of output by region, Tokyo's financial services industry was worth ¥12.1 trillion in 2004 (the most recent figures in the report), accounting for about an eighth of the city's output. Even that figure is dwarfed by the city's retail sector, which took in ¥18.3 trillion the same year, making it the capital's single biggest source of income. Tokyo is not Japan's leading industrial centre, that honour goes to the Osaka-Nagoya axis. But the city isn't far behind, and leads in some key areas. It is top in semiconductors and general electronics for example, and number two in chemicals.

New Developments

The biggest change in Tokyo's economy over recent years has been the advent and proliferation of the 'megadevelopments' – new urban complexes combining office, retail, leisure, hotel and residential units. The trend began with the Roppongi Hills development in 2003. The rival Tokyo Midtown complex opened in 2007, built around a tower just that little bit higher than Roppongi Hills, and together the two have begun to change a formerly sleazy part of town into a new commercial powerhouse. Other neighbourhoods are getting in on the act, too. The area around Tokyo station has seen a spate of new mixed-use towers. There are plans for a major redevelopment in Iidabashi. And, perhaps most ambitious of all, a second Tokyo tower is set to sprout in the east of the city. Almost twice as high as the existing tower, the new spike on the skyline is intended to be a focal point for a massive redevelopment of the Oshiage area, bringing jobs and development to a now down-at-heel part of town.

Tourism

Tokyo is among the world's leading tourist destinations – if you count domestic travellers, that is. It's a different story with regard to foreign tourists, with the capital hosting just 4.81 million overseas visitors in 2006, according to the metropolitan government. If that still sounds like a decent number, it's worth noting that Paris saw 15.9 million foreign tourists the same year. Nonetheless, both numbers were well up on the past, with foreign arrivals increasing 7.1% on a year earlier. In part this may be due to the country's 'Yokoso! Japan' tourist campaign, which has energetically promoted the country as a tourist destination, setting a goal of 10 million visitors per year by 2010. Though this campaign is intended to benefit the whole country, Tokyo is by far the biggest beneficiary, as nearly all foreign visitors to Japan spend at least some time in the capital. If Tokyo's foreign tourist numbers have traditionally been low, that is mainly down to its relative remoteness from other developed nations, and its perception as a high-cost destination. Those who do come tend to be drawn either by culture and history, or the exact opposite – Tokyo's reputation for living on the cutting-edge of technology and culture. Given the growing enthusiasm for Japanese pop culture in the US and Europe, prospects for more young visitors look bright. For now, however, tourism remains a medium-sized slice of the city's economy. For 2006, total spending by all tourists, domestic and foreign, amounted to ¥9.4 trillion, or 5.7% of Tokyo's total income.

Roppongi Hills

International Relations

Japan is generally considered a full and cooperative member of the international community, though the legacy of its wartime past continues to constrain its foreign policy in key respects. The country is a member of numerous international bodies, including the UN, the World Trade Organisation and the International Monetary Fund. While Japan plays a prominent role in all of these bodies, it is stymied whenever joint military action is proposed. The country's pacifist constitution forbids military action for any purpose except self-defence, largely due to shame over the country's militaristic expansionism during the second world war.

Recent years have seen a mounting debate over whether it is time to scrap such restrictions. Though a constitutional amendment is still some way off, successive governments have already shown willingness to allow modest overseas military deployments. After the second Gulf War, for example, Japanese forces were deployed to Iraq to help with reconstruction. Japan is generally considered one of the United States' most important allies, and is a key base for US forces in the Pacific. Its relations with its neighbours are more problematic however. South Korea and China feel Japan has shown insufficient contrition over its occupation of both countries. Japan is also involved in a dispute with China over fishing and mineral rights in the Pacific. Russia and Japan officially remain at war, never having concluded a peace treaty due to a dispute over the sovereignty of some islands now held by Moscow.

Hot Seat

Tokyo's controversial governor is Shintaro Ishihara. A writer-turned-politician, his conservative views regularly enrage liberals and foreigners, but his direct manner has won him a loyal following in the capital.

Government & Politics

Japan is a constitutional monarchy with a system of government that combines features of US and UK politics. Head of state is the emperor – currently Akihito, who succeeded his father, Hirohito, in 1989. As stipulated by the country's 1947 constitution, drawn up under the guidance of the occupying US forces, the emperor has no political power, but serves as a figurehead and symbol of Japan. Real power lies with the prime minister, who is also the head of the largest party in the country's parliament, the Diet. At the time of writing, the incumbent was Yasuo Fukuda of the Liberal Democratic Party, though Japan's habit of changing prime ministers with great frequency (the post has changed hands 48 times since the second world war) means this is likely to be out-of-date before long. The party in power changes much less frequently, however. The LDP has held office, on its own or in coalition, almost continuously since its founding in 1955. The only break came from 1993 to 1996, when an opposition coalition briefly seized power. A broadly conservative party, the LDP now holds office in coalition with New Kōmeitō, an even more conservative partner party. The principal opposition is currently the Democratic Party of Japan, which has been closing the gap on the LDP in recent years, without ever managing to win a general election. The DPJ is considered somewhat to the left of the LDP, but both parties are actually broad churches, embracing wide spectrums of opinion.

The prime minister presides over a cabinet, whose members are drawn from the *Diet*, and from both ruling parties. The parliament is composed of two chambers. The House of Representatives, or lower house, has 480 members: 300 elected from single-seat constituencies, 180 from multi-member seats using proportional representation. The House of Councillors, or upper house, has 242 members: 146 elected from 47 prefectural constituencies, 96 from a national list. The upper house only has the power to delay legislation, being the junior partner to the lower house. The judicial branch of government is headed by the Supreme Court, with member judges appointed by the emperor under the direction of the Diet. Locally, Japan is divided into 47 prefectures. Each is headed by a governor and has a significant degree of autonomy, though they depend largely on central government for finance. Of all prefectural governors, the most prominent is the one holding the top job, Shintaro Ishihara (see Hot Seat on the left).

Time Zones

Athens	-7
Bangkok	-2
Beijing	-1
Berlin	-8
Dallas	-15
Denver	-16
Dubai	-5
Dublin	-9
Hong Kong	-1
Johannesburg	-7
London	-9
Los Angeles	-17
Manila	-1
Mexico City	-15
Moscow	-6
Mumbai	-3.5
New York	-14
Paris	-8
Perth	-1
Prague	-8
Rio de Janeiro	-11
Rome	-8
Santiago	-12
Seoul	0
Singapore	-1
Sydney	1
Toronto	-14
Wellington	3

Population

Demography is a hot topic, and with good reason. With birth rates well below the replacement rate, the country's population is shrinking fast. In line with current trends, the government predicts the national population will fall from its current 127 million to approximately 90 million by 2055. The situation in Tokyo is rather different though. According to the 2005 census, the capital has 12.6 million inhabitants – 8.48 million in the 23 wards (*ku*) of Tokyo proper, and the rest in the rural west of the city – marking an increase of just over half a million since 2000. The Greater Tokyo Area includes Yokohama, Chiba, Kanagawa, Saitama and Tokyo proper and has a population of 35 million – making it the biggest city in the world according to some sources. The capital's status as a hub for most aspects of Japanese life continues to attract domestic migrants, while the city is also the focus for the country's limited immigration. Figures from the census show that women slightly outnumber men in Tokyo, accounting for 50.2% of the population. The average household size is 2.1 persons, down from 2.5 in 1990, a long way from the five-person norm of the 1950s and 60s. The average life expectancy for the city's Japanese residents is 82.6 years – higher than any major nation.

Japan Education Levels

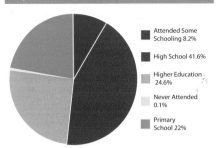

- Attended Some Schooling 8.2%
- High School 41.6%
- Higher Education 24.6%
- Never Attended 0.1%
- Primary School 22%

Source: National Institute for Population and Social Security Research

Japan Population Age Breakdown

Age groups (90+, 85-89, 80-84, 75-79, 70-74, 65-69, 60-64, 55-59, 50-54, 45-49, 40-44, 35-39, 30-34, 25-29, 20-24, 15-19, 10-14, 5-9, 0-4), axis 0% to 9%.

Source: National Institute of Population and Social Security Research

Foreign Population By Nationality

Korean	529,408
Chinese	253,096
Brazilian	188,355
Filipino	93,662
Other	93,048
USA	38,804
Peruvian	33,608
Thai	23,967
Other European	20,006
Vietnamese	12,965
British	10,411
Canadian	7,067
Australian	6,148

Source: Statistics Bureau, Ministry of Internal Affairs and Communications

National Flag

The Japanese national flag is among the world's most recognisable. A red circle on a white background, the design symbolises the rising sun. The exact origin of the motif is unknown, but it alludes to Japan's famous nickname – 'the land of the rising sun' – which was bestowed upon the country by the Chinese, who see the sun rise over their eastern neighbour. Known as the *hinomaru* in Japanese (red circle), the flag only became Japan's official standard in 1999. Sensitivity over any kind of nationalistic imagery, which some considered connected to wartime aggression, had precluded any official flag until then.

Local Time

The whole of Japan observes the same time as Tokyo: nine hours ahead of UTC (Universal Coordinated Time). Daylight saving time is not used, so the clocks never change. See table above for time differences with some key world cities, not incorporating daylight saving time.

Tokyo Tower at night

Social & Business Hours

The official working week in Tokyo is Monday to Friday, though many companies also operate on Saturdays. Standard office hours are generally considered 09:00 to 17:00, but this is really just the bare minimum for the dedicated office worker. Salarymen (or Japanese white-collar businessmen) regard long hours as the norm, with early starts and late nights – to midnight and beyond – far from unusual.

Banks generally open from 09:00 until 15:00, though some also offer evening and Saturday services. Post offices are mostly open 09:00 to 17:00, though some major branches (including the Central Post Office near Tokyo station) offer late hours, and even limited 24 hour service. Local government offices and other public offices typically open from about 08:30 to 17:00. Shop hours vary, but 10:00 to 20:00 is perhaps the most common pattern in major retail districts. The standard lunch hour during the working week is 12:00 to 13:00, with peak time for dinner between about 19:00 and 21:00. Drinking and dancing late is never a problem: bars and clubs in entertainment districts are open until dawn and after, and even the quietest neighbourhood is likely to have one or two spots for hungry and thirsty night owls.

Public Holidays

Japan has a generous 15 national holidays per year. Of these, the most significant are the three that fall between late April and early May, creating a 'Golden Week' of holidays. A popular time to go travelling, it can be difficult, and expensive, to get anywhere in or out of Japan during this period. The same is true during the first few days of January, when the whole country seems to shut down for New Year festivities. In mid-August there is the *Ōbon* festival, which is traditionally a time when Japanese return home to see their families. While there are no public holidays during this period, it is another popular time of the year for holiday and travel, again meaning high prices and low availability for any kind of transport. Japan's national holidays are all secular in nature, celebrating events and concepts including the emperor's birthday (23 December), culture (3 November), and the natural environment (4 May).

Public Holidays 2008	
New Year's Day	01 Jan
Coming-of-Age Day	second Mon in Jan
National Foundation Day	11 Feb
Vernal Equinox	20/21 Mar
Shōwa Day	29 Apr
Constitution Day	03 May
Green Day	04 May
Children's Day	05 May
Marine Day	third Mon in Jul
Respect for the Aged Day	third Mon in Sep
Autumn Equinox	23/24 Sep
Health & Sports Day	second Mon in Oct
Culture Day	03 Nov
Labour Thanksgiving Day	23 Nov
Emperor's Birthday	23 Dec

Temperature & Humidity

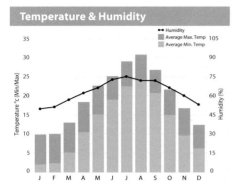

Rainfall

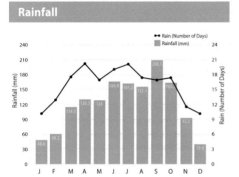

Climate

Tokyo enjoys a temperate climate with four distinct seasons. Spring (roughly April and May) is usually mild and fresh, with low humidity and temperatures in the low to mid 20s. Autumn (mid-September to mid-November) is similar, and most people would pick one of these two seasons as the time to visit. Winters are generally bright, dry and cold, with temperatures often dipping below 0°C in January and February. Light snow falls occasionally, but never really settles in Tokyo. Summer is the most uncomfortable time of year for most residents, with high humidity and temperatures up to 38°C.

There is officially a rainy season (*tsuyu*) in early summer, and when it does rain, it pours. Tokyo is a city of umbrella lovers for good reason. Late summer, usually September, is typhoon season, but such storms can arrive at any time during the warm months. Typhoons bring high winds and torrential rain (that can go on for days), but pose little danger in a city well prepared for their arrival.

Flora & Fauna

Tokyo is a greener city than its reputation allows. Parks abound, ranging from functional recreational spaces to exquisite landscaped Japanese gardens. Yoyogi Kōen (p.186) is popular for picnics and frisbee, and a weekend gathering place for Tokyo's musicians and tribe of rockabillies. For more refined surroundings, choose one of the city's traditional retreats, most famous of which is perhaps Shinbashi's Hamarikyū Gardens – a seaside square of green that was once home to a *shogun's* villa. But parks are only half the story of Tokyo's greenery. The western half of the city's administrative area, outside the 23 wards of Tokyo proper, is a land of forested hills and mountains. The highest point in the capital is Mount Kumotori (2,017 metres), but a host of different peaks offer hiking possibilities. Wherever you go, there is one tree that everyone stops to admire at least once a year. For a few days each spring, Japan goes crazy over cherry blossom (see p.44). Besides being beautiful, the short-lived pink blooms are considered symbolic of life's quick passing. On a brighter note, they are also an excuse for a serious party, with drunken gatherings under the blossom being very much the done thing.

Fauna

The undisputed king of Tokyo wildlife is the crow. Huge, menacing and prolific, the birds are accused of all sorts of crimes, both trivial (ripping open rubbish bags) and heinous (attacking pets and even small children). All efforts to reduce their numbers have come to naught, though perhaps that's really for the best. The city wouldn't be quite the same without the roguish birds. Smaller birds are less commonly seen, but lizards and – whenever it rains – frogs are to be found.

Travel out to the hills of western Tokyo and the wildlife gets a lot bigger. Japanese macaque monkeys are common, and an encounter with a brown bear or snakes is even possible. When hiking, wear a bell to warn of your approach and the bears will stay out of your way. There are no poisonous insects or snakes in the Tokyo area.

Marine Life

Home to one of the world's busiest ports, Tokyo Bay suffers from significant pollution, although water quality has improved enormously over the past 20 years. Marine life somehow survives, and seals are among its inhabitants. Other marine mammals include occasional dolphins and grey whales. Fishing is a popular pastime, despite pollution figures, and sea bass is one of the most popular catches, but you'll find everything from squid to deep-dwelling monkfish.

Environmental Issues

With over 35 million people crammed into the Greater Tokyo Area, it's not surprising that the megalopolis experiences environmental problems including air pollution. The metropolitan government estimates that the city's vehicles churn out enough particulate matter to fill 120,000 half-litre bottles every day. Measures to tackle the problem include compulsory exhaust filters for all diesel vehicles and, curiously, more roads. City officials say the extra roads will ease congestion and cut journey times, and thereby reduce pollution.

Vehicles are not the only source though. With lots of people and not much room, the city has nowhere to bury its rubbish. Incineration is seen as the answer, but with all sorts of plastics going up in smoke, the burning produces a toxic brew of emissions including dioxins. The emissions are blamed for cancer and other health problems, with campaigners particularly concerned by the way incineration plants are often located in the middle of densely populated areas. Proposed solutions include cleaner incineration technology and more rigorous separation of rubbish to ensure that toxin-producing plastics are not burned.

Overall, Japan's reputation on environmental issues is poor. Environmentalists accuse the country of crimes including overfishing, overpackaging and over-exploitation of natural resources such as tropical hardwoods. And then there is whaling, a perennial sore point in Japan's relations with the west. See also Environmental Groups on p.219. The country is, however, an enthusiastic proponent of the Kyoto Protocol on greenhouse gases, not least because the pact was signed on Japanese soil. Despite the enthusiasm, Japan's emissions continue to rise, though ministers are confident that the country will meet reduction targets by the 2012 deadline specified in the protocol. Those who wish to make their voice heard on environmental issues will find that Japan has branches of the major green campaign groups, such as Greenpeace, though environmental groups tend to be smaller and less influential than in western nations.

Mini Marvels

Explorer's *Mini Visitor's Guides* are the perfect holiday companion. They're small enough to fit in your pocket but beautiful enough to inspire you to explore. With detailed maps, visitor's information, restaurant and bar reviews, the lowdown on shopping and all the sights and sounds of the city, these mini marvels are a holiday must.

Imperial Palace

We're all over Asia

When it's time to make the next stop on your expat Asian adventure, be sure to pack an Explorer Residents' Guide. These essential books will help you make the most of your new life in a new city.

Explorer Residents' Guides – We Know Where You Live

Culture

It might seem like stating the obvious, but Japan is very Japanese. Even Tokyo, its most cosmopolitan city, is far from multicultural. Nationally, immigrants make up little more than 1% of the population. Add to this the fact that Japan has enjoyed centuries of independence, interrupted only by the post-war US occupation, and it's not surprising that it has a very strong sense of its own distinctiveness. This is both a strength and a weakness, with the country's foreign policy swaying between arrogance and insecurity regarding Japan's place in the world, and in a way, this distinctiveness is misplaced. Ethnically, the Japanese are mainly descendents of Chinese and Siberian migrants, and key building blocks of national culture, such as Buddhism and Confucianism, were originally Chinese imports, not to mention the fact that culturally, the country is a sponge for western influences. Nonetheless, any visitor is likely to find it genuinely distinct from continental Asia, and not just because it is richer and more developed. There's a tendency to put the needs of the group before those of the individual, strong bonds with family and friends, and an unrelenting expectation of modesty and politeness in all things. This is not to say that the Japanese are inscrutable. However, the reserved nature of most natives will seem more familiar to some foreigners (notably, the English) than to others. And not all Japanese fit the same mould – with the younger generations more likely to exhibit an individualistic streak. Culturally, the country's schizophrenic veneration of the old and fetishisation of the new makes for a glaring contradiction. But their most defining characteristic is probably their ability to embrace foreign influences, be it religion, technology or pop music, and adapt them. The country constantly moves forward, but it remains ever so Japanese.

The Cult Of Cute

In English, the word 'cute' is just another adjective. Its Japanese equivalent – kawaii – has almost religious status among Japan's youth. Once you have tuned in to the word, you will hear it everywhere, especially when teenage girls are around. Used to describe everything from people to pets, it is the highest form of approbation (as many foreign men have learned to their advantage). So next time you see a doe-eyed anime character or Hello Kitty pencil case, you know the perfect word to describe it: 'kawaii'

Race Relations

Tokyo has not been scarred by ethnic, racial or religious strife, largely because the city is so overwhelmingly and uniformly Japanese. But immigrant communities do experience consistent discrimination. Chinese and Korean communities feel that they are routinely portrayed as criminals by the country's media, and object to the attitude of Tokyo Mayor Shintaro Ishihara, who has described Asian immigrants in language considered derogatory. The origin of these tensions can be traced back to Japan's occupation of both countries; with China and Korea feeling Tokyo has shown insufficient contrition over its colonial past. Foreigners from other countries are also likely to experience discrimination at times – some bars and restaurants don't welcome foreign customers, though this may often be down to linguistic concerns. Long-term resident aliens also bemoan the impossibility of ever really fitting in – no matter how fluent your Japanese, you will always remain *gaijin*.

These anxieties were exacerbated in November 2007, when almost all foreigners, even registered residents, became subject to strict new immigration controls, including compulsory fingerprinting on entry. Concern over such issues is unlikely to be assuaged any time soon, which means the only answer is to accentuate the positive. The immigration controls are no tougher than those in the US, and resident foreigners get a dedicated line at the airport that can actually be quicker than that for nationals. Moreover, incomers can also benefit from reverse discrimination, often being seen as cool and sophisticated simply by virtue of their foreignness – a quirk that many learn to exploit.

Language

Other options **Language Schools** p.227, **Learning Japanese** p.138

For many people contemplating a move to Tokyo, the Japanese language can seem like a impossible barrier to enjoying life in the city. But there's no need to be intimidated.

Culture & Lifestyle

The city is actually fairly bilingual in key respects, not least in terms of public transport – most signs and ticket machines are in Japanese and English, making the system very easy to use, and many other aspects of everyday life also come with a little English, or at least a readable script. Restaurants serving foreign cuisine generally have bilingual menus and most road signs feature English, as do many building names. Better still,

Basic Japanese

General Words		Second	Niban me
Yes	Hai	Straight ahead	Massugu
No	iie	Close to...	...no chikaku
Please	Onegaishimasu	Traffic lights	Shingō
Thank you	Arigatō	Turning	Kado
You are welcome	Dō itashimashite	Left	Hidari
Excuse me	Sumimasen	Right	Migi
Sorry	Gomenasai	North	Kita
Greetings		South	Minami
Hello	Konnichiwa	East	Higashi
Goodbye	Sayonara	West	Nishi
How are you?	Genki desu ka?	Slow down	Yukkuri
Fine	Genki desu	Stop	Tomatte kudasai
Good	ii	**Calendar**	
Good morning	Ohayō gozaimasu	Date	Hinichi
Good afternoon	Konnichiwa	Next week	Raishū
Good evening	Konbanwa	Next month	Raigetsu
Good night	Oyasumi nasai	Next year	Rainen
Introduction		One day	Ichi nichi
What is your name?	Onamae wa?	One week	Isshūkan
My name is...	Watashi no namae wa...	This year	Kotoshi
Where are you from?	Doko kara kimashita ka?	Today	Kyō
I am from...	... kara kimashita	Tomorrow	Ashita
America	Amerika	Yesterday	Kinō
England/Britain	Igirisu	Year	Nen
Questions		**Accidents & Emergencies**	
How much?	Ikura desu ka?	Accident	Jiko
What?	Nan desu ka?	Insurance	Hoken
When?	Itsu desu ka?	Permit/Licence	Kyoka/Menkyo
Where is...?	... wa doko desu ka?	Police	Keisatsu
Which is...?	... wa dore desu ka?	**Numbers**	
Who is...?	... wa dare desu ka?	One	Ichi
Why is...?	... wa naze desu ka?	Two	Ni
Transport & Directions		Three	San
Airport	Kūkō	Four	Shi
Bank	Ginkō	Five	Go
Toilet	Toire	Six	Roku
Beach	Kaigan	Seven	Nana
Hotel	Hoteru	Eight	Hachi
Petrol station	Gasorin stando	Nine	Kyū
Restaurant	Resutoran	Ten	Jū
Road	Michi	Hundred	Hyaku
Avenue	Dōri	Thousand	Sen
First	Saisho	Ten thousand (unit)	Man

NB. For pronounciation of Japanese words, the line over a vowel (ō) means that the vowel sound is lengthened.

Japanese For Beginners

東京	Tokyo	Tokyo	警察	keisatsu	police
駅	eki	station	病院	byōin	hospital
電車	densha	train	右	migi	right
バス	basu	bus	左	hidari	left
タクシ−(空車)	takushii	taxi (for hire)	北	kita	north
入口	iriguchi	entrance	南	minami	south
出口	deguchi	exit	東	higashi	east
トイレ/便所	toire/benjo	toilet	西	nishi	west
女	onna	woman	上	ue	up/above
男	otoko	man	下	shita	down/below

Reading The Signs

Written Japanese has three scripts. The first two are phonetic scripts of 46 characters each; hiragana, which is used for the endings of verbs and adjectives and some Japanese words, and katakana, used for adopted foreign words. The third group is kanji, characters borrowed from Chinese and used for nouns, adjectives and verbs. While it is possible to learn the first two sets in just a few months (which can really benefit in reading signs and menus), there are many thousand kanji in use. A person needs an estimated 2,000 kanji for daily life or to read a newspaper, but if you start learning them, you'll soon start recognising some of the simple ones, which should encourage you to take on a few more.

most people speak at least a smattering of the language, since it's a mandatory subject in high school (although a strong focus on grammar often means they are better at reading and writing than speaking it). That said, there is no denying that language can be a problem for those who don't speak a word of Japanese. While the public transport system is fairly bilingual, taxis are not. You can get around this though by ensuring you carry a written copy of your address to show the driver. Other everyday aspects of life can be challenging, including dealing with officials, emergency services, or shop assistants, and many businessmen have little or no English, despite the fact that it is the second language of the city's commercial sector. The best way round the issue is to learn some Japanese, which is not as impossible as it sounds (see p.227 for language schools). Certainly, the *kanji* characters used in writing make complete literacy difficult, but spoken Japanese is no harder than any other language. Besides, you don't have to be fluent – a few well-chosen words can suddenly make those dreaded taxis, shop assistants and business associates seem perfectly friendly.

Religion

The Japanese have a pragmatic, flexible approach to religion that can seem puzzling to devout westerners. Nominally split between Buddhism and Shintō (the country's indigenous religion), Japanese people are actually happy to mix and match beliefs according to the occasion. Births and deaths are most often celebrated with a Buddhist ceremony, Shintō rites are often used to mark traditional weddings and the passing of the seasons, while Christian-style weddings are popular among the young (although of no religious significance). Underlying this flexibility is the fact that Japan is really among the most secular of nations, with religion playing no more than a ceremonial role for most citizens. The same is true at public level – though some of the country's political parties are affiliated with Buddhist organisations, it is rare to hear a politician invoke God in the way that would be considered normal in the US. The lines between religion and culture are often blurred, and praying for luck when visiting a temple or a shrine is a common practice.

An ancient religion of obscure origin, Shintō finds god in many things, living and non-living. Unusually for a major religion, it has no founding text or sacred document. The official state religion from 1868 until the end of the second world war, Shintō suffered somewhat from its association with the rise of militarism. Buddhism first arrived in the country about 1,500 years ago, but it has since splintered into numerous sects. Many of these survive today – the Jōdo Shin, Shingon and Nichiren versions of Buddhism said to have the most adherents. The divide between Buddhism and Shintō is, however, less than clear-cut. The two have had mingled beliefs and believers for centuries, often being celebrated as one and the same faith. A 2004 survey by the Agency for Cultural Affairs found that 50.7% of the population considered themselves primarily Shintō, while 43.6% were primarily Buddhist. But the same survey also found that followers of one faith generally accepted the other. The most important event in the Shintō calendar is *hatsumōde* – a person's first visit to a shrine in the New Year (see also Religious Sites p.177). Key Buddhist festivals include *Obon* – a few days in midsummer when the Japanese traditionally go home to visit their relatives (see p.42 for Annual Events). Christianity is estimated to have one to three million Japanese adherents. Other faiths are represented in tiny numbers, largely among immigrant communities.

Places Of Worship

Name	Area	Phone	Website	Type
Meiji Jingū	Harajuku	03 3379 9281	www.meijijingu.or.jp	Shintō
Sensōji	Asakusa	03 3842 0181	na	Buddhist
St Alban's	Kamiyachō	03 3431 8534	www.saintalbans.gol.com	Episcopalian
St Ignatius	Kōjimachi	03 3263 4576	www.ignatius.gr.jp	Catholic
St Paul Intl Lutheran Church	Iidabashi	03 3261 2390	www2.gol.com/users/alleluia	Lutheran
Tokyo Baptist Church	Shibuya-ku	03 3461 8425	www.tokyobaptist.org	Baptist
Tokyo Mosque	Yoyogi	03 5790 0760	http://islam3.hp.infoseek.co.jp	Muslim
Tokyo Synagogue	Hirō	03 3400 2559	www.jccjapan.or.jp	Jewish
Yasukuni Jinja	Chiyoda-ku	03 3261 8326	www.yasukuni.or.jp	Shintō
Zōjōji	Shiba Kōen	03 3432 1431	www.zojoji.or.jp	Buddhist

National Dress

A first-timer to Japan could be forgiven for thinking that the country's national dress includes dark suit and tie for men, and Gucci handbag for women. But while western clothing has long been dominant, traditional Japanese attire has not died out. Most often seen, and most famous, is the kimono. A deceptively complicated garment, the kimono essentially comprises a wraparound cloak secured with a sash called an *obi*. It is traditionally worn with wooden sandals called *geta*. Frequently highly decorative, good kimono are expensive to buy and so complicated to assemble that the wearer will require lessons to be able to dress properly. The best time to catch a glimpse of kimono-clad women is on a Saturday or Sunday, as kimono are a popular choice for weddings. Alternatively, the summer fireworks season sees many women dress up in their finest *yukata*, a lightweight cotton kimono intended for summer wear. It's less obvious to find a time when a man will don traditional garb (also called kimono), but the fireworks are probably a good bet, and men's *yukata* tend to be far plainer and simpler than the female versions.

Food & Drink

Other options **Eating Out** p.324, **Food** on p.272

Japan has one of the world's finest cuisines, but little of it is actually known outside the country. Sushi and sashimi are familiar to most, but delicacies such as *okonomiyaki* (a grilled pancake stacked with a mix of toppings).and *nabe* (a type of hotpot that you cook on the table) are not. Japanese food is also one of the world's healthiest, a fact perhaps reflected in the long life expectancy of its people.

Pride of place in Japanese cuisine goes to rice, which the locals treat with the same discernment the Italians devote to pasta. For the foreigner, it suffices to say that Japanese rice is short-grained and very sticky, making it easy to eat with chopsticks. If the carbohydrate doesn't come in the form of rice, it's likely to be one of three types of noodle: *soba* (made from buckwheat), *udon* (made from wheat), or *rāmen* (originally from China, and also wheat based). Whatever you order, it will most likely come with a bowl of soup made from either a *miso* or soy base. If the main dish comes with meat it will likely be beef, pork or chicken, but not lamb, which is not native to Japan, and

Ekiben
*Travelling around
Japan can be a
gourmet treat thanks
to ekiben lunch boxes
– a contraction of the
Japanese words 'eki'
(station) and 'bentō'
(packed meal). Every
large railway station
has its own variety,
usually featuring
regional delicacies and
priced at about ¥1,000.
Ekiben conventions
are held, and fans will
travel the length of
the country to try a
celebrated new variety.
Not surprisingly,
bustling Tokyo station
has various types of
ekiben, including
the country's most
expensive – a ¥3,800
extravaganza that
includes abalone and
other high-end treats.*

considered too smelly by many. And as the Japanese are the world's biggest consumers of seafood, you'll see plenty of fishy options. Some of this may be raw, although sashimi (raw fish on its own) is usually an appetiser, and sushi (raw fish on rice) a main, served only in specialist sushi restaurants. Other signature dishes include *tempura* (fish and vegetables deep-fried in batter), *yakitori* (grilled meat and veg on skewers), and various types of *nabe* (hotpot), usually cooked in a pan set in the centre of the table. The latter also includes *shabu-shabu* (a savoury version), and the well known *sukiyaki* (a sweeter version). Whatever you order, don't expect any elaborate, heavy sauces. Japanese food is more about good quality ingredients, prepared with just the right amount of seasoning.

Shopping For Food

Shopping for food has its ups and downs. On the plus side, the quality of produce on offer is usually superb, but prices are generally high, especially for fruit and veg (see Food on p.284). Also, the small size of most Tokyo supermarkets (p.314) means the variety is not what many foreigners would expect. This is doubly true if you are searching for your favourite treat from back home – your local supermarket is unlikely to have it. In these circumstances, there are two options: adapt to local produce or join the pilgrimage of expat shoppers heading to shops like National Azabu (p.315), a supermarket in the Hirō district that specialises in foreign foods. The chain of Meidi-ya delicatessens is also a good bet for overseas delicacies (p.315).

Dining Out

Tokyo is a great city for foodies. Embracing an enormous variety of ingredients, dishes, and regional variations (not to mention every type of world cuisine), the myriad dining options are united by one common thread: the best quality ingredients, simple preparation and elegant presentation. And it's not even expensive – or at least it doesn't have to be. There's a huge range of options that will cost you less than ¥1,000 – popular cheap eats include *tempura*, *gyūdon* (beef on rice), and every sort of noodle dish. Further up the scale, dinner in a nice restaurant fit for a date starts at about ¥3,000 per person including drinks. For a swanky meal in a popular part of town, budget ¥7,000 and upwards. That leaves newcomers with two problems – knowing where to start, and figuring out the menu. Helpful restaurant staff will generally do their best to help with the latter, and a few pointers can help with the former, see Eating Out on p.324.

Alcohol

Alcohol is consumed freely in Japan, but nearly always with food. The nation's most popular tipple is of western origin: beer. Introduced to Japan about 200 years ago, beer is now produced and consumed in huge quantities. The big four brewers are Asahi, Kirin, Sapporo and Suntory, with pale golden lager the standard. Local ales and stouts are also available, as are all foreign beers, wines and spirits. Japan's most famous indigenous drink is *sake* or *nihonshu*, a fermented rice wine. Dry or sweet, hot or cold, *sake* comes in as many varieties as normal wine. More robust, but just as Japanese, is *shōchū*, a spirit made from rice, wheat or potatoes.

Tea

If it's a non-alcoholic drink you're after, it has to be tea. Famously known for being the centre of a whole ceremony (p.357), Japanese green tea is also a staple drink for ordinary people, and is so common that it is often referred to simply as 'tea'. One of the most popular forms is *sencha*, a variety made from whole leaves, which is also said to have properties that aid in weight loss and general good health and well-being.

Essential Info

In Emergency

Tokyo has modern, comprehensive and high quality emergency services. For foreigners, the only problem is the ever-present language barrier, though translation services are available for medical emergencies (for a list of hospitals, see p.118).

Emergency Numbers

Ambulance	119
Coast Guard	118
Fire	119
Police	110

Embassies & Consulates

Country	Phone	Map
Australia	03 5232 4111	11 D4 **1**
Bangladesh	03 5704 0216	5 E3 **2**
Belgium	03 3262 0191	11 F4 **3**
Brazil	03 3404 5211	8 E1 **4**
Cambodia	03 5412 8521	11 B1 **5**
Canada	03 5412 6200	10 A4 **6**
China	03 3403 3388	11 A4 **7**
Denmark	03 3496 3001	5 E2 **8**
Finland	03 5447 6000	6 A2 **9**
France	03 5798 6000	6 A2 **10**
Germany	03 5791 7700	6 A2 **11**
India	03 3262 2391	10 C3 **12**
Indonesia	03 3441 4201	5 F3 **13**
Ireland	03 3263 0695	10 D2 **14**
Italy	03 3453 5291	6 B2 **15**
Laos	03 5411 2291	11 A3 **16**
Malaysia	03 3476 3840	5 E2 **17**
Myanmar	03 3441 9291	6 A4 **18**
Netherlands	03 5776 5400	11 D2 **19**
New Zealand	03 3467 2271	8 A3 **20**
Norway	03 3440 2611	11 A4 **21**
Pakistan	03 5421 7741	11 B4 **22**
Philippines	03 5562 1600	11 C3 **23**
Poland	03 5794 7020	5 F3 **24**
Portugal	03 5226 0614	10 C2 **25**
Russia	03 3583 4224	11 D3 **26**
Singapore	03 3586 9111	11 B3 **27**
South Africa	03 3265 3379	10 C3 **28**
South Korea	03 3452 7611	6 A2 **29**
Spain	03 3583 8531	11 D2 **30**
Sri Lanka	03 3440 6911	6 A3 **31**
Sweden	03 5562 5050	11 D2 **32**
Thailand	03 3441 1386	5 F3 **33**
UK	03 5211 1100	10 D2 **34**
USA	03 3224 5000	11 D1 **35**
Vietnam	03 3466 3313	3 D4 **36**

Police

The police maintain a strong presence on the streets. They are generally friendly and approachable, but do not usually speak English. In the event of a crime-related emergency, call 110. If you are the victim of crime while out and about, look for a *kōban* (police box) – these can be found at most major intersections.

Hospitals

Tokyo has some of the world's best medical facilities and high-quality treatment is available for every conceivable accident or disease. But dealing with medical institutions can be a daunting experience. Though all Japanese doctors have to pass English exams as part of their training, few are comfortable using it as a working language. However, the metropolitan government run a telephone translation service (03 5285 8185), which offers assistance in English, Chinese, Korean, Thai and Spanish. The Tokyo Metropolitan Health and Medical Information Center (03 5285 8181) offers advice in the same selection of languages. Alternatively, there are a variety of clinics and hospitals where English and other foreign languages are spoken (see table p.120). In a medical emergency call 119 for an ambulance. But if you can get to the hospital on your own, do. Tokyo hospitals can be both public and private, but the distinction isn't hugely important. In all cases you will need to show ID, and be prepared to pay for your treatment. Foreign residents working for Japanese companies will generally have Japanese public health insurance, which covers 70% of the cost. If you have public health insurance, make sure to take your *hoken* insurance ID card with you as you will be expected to present it.

Lost Property

Tokyo is probably the best city in the world in which to lose something. Nearly every resident can tell a tale of a lost wallet, phone or other valuable, only to later get it back. In a testament to the city's safety, you will probably even find that any money you had is still there too. If you lose something on the street, report the loss to the nearest police station or *kōban*. The Tokyo Metropolitan Police also operate a lost and found department (03 3814 4151). The loss or theft of passports should be reported immediately to the police on 110. Next, report the same at your embassy or consulate who will arrange temporary travel documents. For a list of embassies see the table, left. If you leave something on a train, go to the lost property office at any station on that line.

Earthquakes

Sitting on the Pacific's 'ring of fire', Tokyo is one of the most earthquake-prone cities on Earth. Small-to-moderate quakes occur frequently, but pose little or no danger to life

Drinking Outdoors

*Tokyoites love an
excuse to celebrate
outdoors – and there
are no laws prohibiting
public drunkenness. In
April, companies and
friends gather under
the cherry blossoms
to have a few drinks,
eat sushi and sing
impromptu karaoke. In
late summer, couples
don yukata robes
and toast impressive
firework displays over
Tokyo Bay or around
the Meiji Jingū Outer
Gardens. In December,
the city's bars are
jammed with groups
looking back on a fun-
filled year, fuelled with
a lot of alcohol.*

or property. The city is hit by a major quake once every 70 years or so, and the next big one is overdue, which means it pays to be prepared (and Tokyo certainly is). All homes should have an emergency survival kit including torch, non-perishable food and first aid supplies. Keep essentials such as passports somewhere where they can be retrieved quickly in an emergency. Familiarise yourself with the evacuation routes and rallying points in your neighbourhood, which will be shown on information provided to all households by ward governments, and above all, don't panic. The Tokyo International Communication Committee website (www.tokyo-icc.jp) contains a useful guide to preparing for an earthquake.

Gay & Lesbian
Other options **Gay & Lesbian** (Going Out) p.373

Tokyo is a relaxed and friendly place for the gay or lesbian city dweller, and there's a thriving bar and club scene (see Going Out on p.324). The place to start is the 2-chōme district of Shinjuku, which is home to a host of gay- and lesbian-friendly bars, cafes and bookshops. Other gay and lesbian venues can be found in the city's key entertainment districts, including Shibuya and Roppongi. That said, things get a little more complicated when living and working in the city, particularly if your employer is a traditional Japanese firm. Many gay and lesbian people choose to be discreet about their sexuality in the workplace, for fear of lingering discrimination in a society where conformity is considered a virtue, but this is entirely down to the individual. After office hours however, anything goes.

Women
Tokyo is among the safest of all major cities. Crime is low, and women can generally feel safe anywhere in the city, at any time. That said, common sense precautions should be observed, and caution is required when walking alone late at night in quiet parts of town. The city's public transport is also very safe, but with one proviso: Japan has a bad and well-deserved reputation for aggressive gropers. Made possible by the overcrowding of trains in the morning rush, any groping can usually be stopped with a firm response. To be on the safe side, use the women only carriages that many lines provide during rush hours. There are no set dress codes or requirements for women, but be warned that some of the older generation are prejudice against women eating or drinking alone in bars and restaurants.

Children
Tokyo is generally a friendly and easy city for travellers with children, not least because of the low crime rate and a superb public transport system. Most shops and stations have baby changing facilities, though some of these are located within ladies' toilets, posing a problem for solo dads. Children are indulged and doted upon by the Japanese, but there are limits. Snazzy restaurants aren't overly welcoming, and restaurants in general don't usually offer children's menus. One exception are the family restaurants where children are welcome all day long (p.329). The city is also short on babysitting services, as Japanese mums are loathe to leave their offspring with a stranger – for visitors, the bigger, newer hotels are the best bet but for resident families, it's usual to hire domestic help or to go through one of the Babysitting and Childcare agencies (see Setting Up Home on p.104 for more information).
Popular attractions for parents with children in tow include Ueno Zoo (p.182), Shinagawa Aquarium (p.168), Tokyo Sea Life Park (p.169), Tokyo Disneyland (p.226) and Disneysea. By far the city's best-known toyshop is Kiddy Land in Harajuku, but there are many great toyshops in the city (see p.303).

Photography

As the centre of the world's camera industry, Japan is unsurprisingly a nation of shutterbugs. Serious enthusiasts abound, and no one leaves home without at least a camera-equipped mobile phone. Perhaps because of this, people are generally relaxed about having their photo taken, but standard rules of courtesy still apply. If in doubt, ask permission first, and observe particular care at temples or other locations where good manners are expected. Locations where photography is banned are generally clearly signposted as such. For photography classes, see p.234 and for cameras and equipment, see p.278.

Tokyo Tower

People With Disabilities

Tokyo's accessibility is pretty good, and getting steadily better. This is partly thanks to the city's continual redevelopment: all new buildings are generally constructed to the latest accessibility standards, with most modern hotels, shops and public offices adapted for people with disabilities. Older buildings will prove almost impossible though, with narrow stairwells being the norm for much housing, as well as steep stairs down into many restaurants and bars.

Public transport is generally wheelchair-friendly. Most stations have lifts to platform level, or wheelchair lifts running alongside stairs. Train doors open level with the platform, and staff can provide ramps where the gap between platform and door is wider than usual. As the city's stations are all permanently staffed, it should not be a problem finding assistance. All trains have a few spaces set aside for wheelchairs – look out for the wheelchair logo by the appropriate doors. Buses are also improving. Newer models with low entry are being introduced steadily. The Japanese Red Cross has a slightly dated but still useful guide to Tokyo accessibility at http://accessible.jp.org. Pedestrian crossings have buzzers when it's safe to cross and many of the city's pavements have raised, studded tiles to guide the blind.

What To Wear

With a temperate climate and liberal attitudes to the display of flesh, Japan is a free and easy place when it comes to clothes. If there is an exception, it is in the business environment, where smart and sober dress is de rigueur. Men are definitely expected to wear a tie, while dark suits are a good idea for both genders. At most other times, it's a case of come as you are, though Tokyoites are a chic bunch and it's worth dressing to impress when heading to a posh restaurant or formal occasion. Temperatures are mild for most of the year, but can touch 38°C in midsummer, and hit below zero in midwinter so a year-round wardrobe will require outfits for both warm and cold weather. Heavy rain also makes a good coat and umbrella essential – umbrellas can be picked up everywhere, even in *hyaku-en* (¥100) stores or convenience stores.

Dos & Don'ts

Tokyo lacks the strict and specific taboos found in more religious parts of the world.

However, it is worth remembering that this is a society that values courtesy and consideration for others and good manners are highly appreciated. Smoking on the street has been banned around Chiyoda-ku (the business district around Tokyo station) since hot cigarette tips are a hazard for children. Make sure to use the designated smoking areas only. If going swimming, make sure to hide any tattoos. Public pools ban people with decorated skin, which is seen as the insignia of *yakuza* gangsters. Avoid eating on the street or on a train, which is considered rude and unsightly, as is blowing your nose. If you are invited to someone's home, don't wear shoes beyond the entrance hall (a custom that means nice socks are a must).

Crime & Safety

Other options **In Emergency** p.19, **Legal Issues** p.65

Among Tokyo's biggest selling points is its low crime rate. One 2006 study showed the Japanese capital to have a murder rate of just 1.4 people per 100,000 residents, comparing favourably with over two in London, about six in New York, 18 in Moscow, and around 38 in Washington. That said, it's a dangerous game to compare international crime statistics, as different countries have different ways of reporting and recording the data. But anecdotal evidence backs up the stats. Ask any long-term resident about crime and safety and you will probably be regaled with tales of honesty and happy endings (lost wallets are regularly found with money intact, see Lost Property on p.19). Though common sense and vigilance are always advisable, low crime makes life a lot less stressful here than in many other cities. No-go areas simply don't exist and taxis and public transport are safe – though women should watch out for gropers on crowded trains (see p.36). And while Japan's famous *yakuza* gangsters are a high-profile presence in some parts of town, they generally pose little or no danger to foreigners.

Traffic Accidents & Violations

If you acquire a Japanese driver's licence, you can lose it through accidents and traffic violations, all of which attract demerit points. If you have 15 points or more, your licence may be suspended. More serious offences attract fines and even jail sentences. Accidents involving fatalities are treated with great severity, whether it is your fault or not. For more detail on the tariff of points for traffic offences and other road-related laws, contact the Japan Automobile Federation (www.jaf.or.jp). Among their publications is the useful *Rules of the Road*, available in six languages. See Transportation on p.139 for more on this.

Getting Arrested

Japan may be a low-crime country, but it isn't forgiving of criminals and the treatment of detainees would be considered unacceptable in many western nations. If arrested, you can be held for up to 23 days while police investigate. Bail is rarely granted to foreigners, and police interrogation can be long, demanding, and unrecorded. Foreign embassies advise against signing anything in these circumstances; you may not understand what you are signing, and retracting it later will be difficult. Whatever you do, contact a lawyer (see p.67). Ask the arresting police officer to get you a duty lawyer, and they will contact the Japan Bar Association on your behalf.

Prison Sentences

If you end up in prison, be prepared for a pretty strict regime, often including labour. The system aims at the rehabilitation of offenders, with a system of rewards for good behaviour, and a network of volunteers to help those on probation and parole. Inmates are allowed visits by family members and other specified persons, with each visit usually lasting 30 minutes. Foreign prisoners are allowed to exchange letters with their relatives in their native language. Visits by foreign relatives may require the attendance of a translator to monitor the conversation. Prisoners can be released on parole, with the period of supervision equalling the remaining jail time. Japan is one of the few developed countries that still enforces the death penalty, and its system of capital punishment is the subject of regular complaints by Amnesty International and other organisations. Those on death row experience much harsher conditions than ordinary prisoners, including minimal exercise and very limited visiting rights. Executions may be carried out at short notice, with family members only notified after the event.

Victims Of Crime

If you are the victim of a crime in Japan it is always worth reporting the incident to police, even where petty offences are concerned (call 110 in an emergency). The police take reports of crime seriously and are duty bound to follow up on any incident. Victims of crime may be entitled to compensation with regard to injuries, damage to property and loss of earnings, thanks to recent revisions to the criminal justice system. Contact a lawyer (see p.67) for details of eligibility (embassies can often provide details of bilingual lawyers, see p.19). Japan is lacking in dedicated bilingual organisations or helplines for crime victims, but a good starting point for practical advice is the general purpose Tokyo English Life Line (see Support Groups on p.131). Low-cost counselling in English is also available from the Tokyo Bar Association (03 5367 5280, www.toben.or.jp), though a Japanese speaker will need to make the initial reservation by phone.

Traffic Accidents
If you are involved in or witness an accident, call the police on 110.

Police

Tokyo's police maintain a strong street presence, mainly through a network of *kōban* (mini police boxes). With about 1,200 *kōban* throughout the city (usually located at major intersections), you are never far from uniformed assistance should the need arise. The city has about 42,000 police, approximately one for every 300 residents (this is well below the one per 230 in London, but so are Tokyo's crime rates, see Crime & Safety on p.22). Don't expect the average officer to speak English, but they are generally approachable, and will do their best to help. Officers can be recognised by their dark blue uniforms, and are for the most part armed. Police cars have a black and white livery. Call 110 in an emergency.

City Information

The city government operates tourist information centres at three locations: Shinjuku, Haneda Airport, and Ueno. The Japan National Tourist Information Organization (JNTO) in the Tokyo Kōtsū Kaikan building in Yurakuchō, near Ginza, is also worth checking out. All centres (see table below) offer comprehensive information on sights and accommodation in the city, and have English-speaking staff, but the Yūrakuchō office is the only one that offers an accommodation booking service. It is host to the Welcome Inn Reservation Center, which specialises in booking affordable, foreigner-friendly hotels. The International Tourism Center of Japan provides an online accomodation booking service, see www.itcj.jp for more. There are also Tourist Information Desks in each ward – see the official Tokyo Tourism website (www.tourism.metro.tokyo.jp) for locations and other useful information. Foreigners arriving at Narita Airport can check the JNTO-run Tourist Information Centers in each terminal (Terminal 1: 0476 30 3383; Terminal 2: 0476 34 5877). For more general information about travel in Japan, see the JNTO website (www.jnto.go.jp).

Tourist Information

Name	Location	Area	Telephone	Website
Asakusa Cultural & Sightseeing Center	Asakusa station, Ginza line	Taitō-ku	03 3842 5566	na
JNTO Tourist Information Center	Tokyo Kōtsū Kaikan Bldg, 2-10-1 Yūrakuchō (10F)	Chiyoda-ku	03 3201 3331	www.jnto.go.jp
Odakyū Sightseeing Service Center	Shinjuku station (west side)	Shinjuku-ku	03 5321 7887	www.odakyu.jp
Tokyo Tourist Information Center	Keisei Ueno station	Ueno	03 3836 3471	
	Tokyo Metropolitan Govt Bldg, 2-8-1 Nishi-Shinjuku	Shinjuku-ku	03 5321 3077	
	Haneda Airport Terminal1	Haneda	03 5757 9345	www.tourism.metro.tokyo.jp

Places To Stay

Love Hotels

Spot a gaudy-looking hotel with a strangely discreet entrance and you've probably found a love hotel – Japan's answer to the lack of privacy for young couples in a crowded land. Rooms often feature extravagant theme decor, and can be booked for two-hour 'rests'. Overnight stays are also possible. Costs and amenities vary: three hours will set you back around ¥5,000 to ¥6,000, while an overnight stay can be anywhere from ¥8,000 to ¥15,000. These establishments are known to be pretty unwelcoming to foreigners. Homosexual couples, Japanese or foreign, are also often turned away.

Love Hotel

Places To Stay

Tokyo has an enormous variety of accommodation, though prices are relatively high compared to the rest of Asia. The city is not on the backpacker trail, meaning super-cheap hostels (p.30) and guesthouses (p.29) are in short supply, but affordable options include the famous capsule hotels (p.30). Those on higher budgets have the full range of normal hotels to choose from, as well as a variety of uniquely Japanese options. Whatever price you pay, it's not hard to find accommodation that is clean, safe and stylish.

Hotels

Other options **Landmark Hotels** p.26

Hotels range from utilitarian value options to high-end luxury that can match any city in the world. Standards of service, cleanliness and safety are generally good, but prices are higher than in the rest of Asia. Hotels are located all over the city, with rooms starting at about ¥8,000 and rising to ¥15,000 to ¥20,000 for a midrange three-star hotel. In the four- to five-star categories there is the full range of western-style hotels. Prices range from ¥25,000 to ¥80,000 for standard rooms. Hotels with star ratings are up to international standard so there won't be any nasty surprises. While Tokyo does not officially have any six-star establishments, off-the-scale indulgence is far from impossible. Want a private swimming pool in your room? Try the Grand Hyatt in Roppongi (see p.26), just as long as your budget runs to at least ¥500,000 per night. Language-wise, don't expect English-speaking staff at anything less than a four-star hotel. More modest establishments will generally be Japanese speaking only, but if you made the booking through an English-language website you can assume that they will at least be expecting to deal with foreign customers.

Budget Hotels

Among the cheapest accommodation options in Tokyo are the so-called 'Business' and 'City' hotels. These are basic, utilitarian places aimed at the travelling salaryman. They offer few amenities, and accommodation varies in size from small to tiny – don't be surprised if you can touch both sides of the room with your arms outstretched. But while they may be basic, they are generally safe, clean and comfortable, and a good option for the budget traveller.

Business hotel standards do vary quite a bit, but a good tip is to look for the newest one you can find – the older hotels may not have been refurbished since they opened. Business hotels can be found in every part of the city, and range in price from ¥8,000 to ¥14,000 per person per night. As is standard with Japanese budget hotels, prices are per person, not per room, which actually makes single occupancy better value than sharing. Among the well-known reliable budget hotel chains is the Sunroute brand (see table opposite for contact details),

which has branches in Asakusa, which is convenient for the nearby sights, and Shinjuku, a happening shopping and entertainment hub. More celebrated is the Hotel Villa Fontaine Shiodome (see table below), which manages to combine economy with a little style. For further cheaper options, see also Hostels and Guesthouses on p.29.

Hotels

Deluxe

Cerulean Tower	Shibuya-ku	03 3476 3000	www.ceruleantower-hotel.com	8 B4	40
Conrad	Shinbashi	03 6388 8000	www.ConradHotels.com	15 B1	42
Dai-ichi Hotel Tokyo	Shinbashi	03 3501 4411	www.daiichihotels.com	11 F1	43
Four Seasons Hotel Tokyo at Chinzanso	Bunkyō-ku	03 3943 2222	www.fourseasons.com	9 A1	46
Four Seasons Hotel Tokyo at Marunouchi	Marunouchi	03 5222 7222	www.fourseasons.com	14 B2	47
Grand Hyatt	Roppongi	03 4333 1234	http://tokyo.grand.hyatt.com	11 B3	49
Grand Prince Hotel Akasaka	Akasaka	03 3234 1111	www.princehotelsjapan.com	10 C2	50
Hilton Tokyo	Shinjuku-ku	03 3344 5111	www1.hilton.com	7 A1	52
Hotel New Otani Tokyo	Chiyoda-ku	03 3265 1111	www.newotani.co.jp	10 B3	55
Hotel Okura	Toranomon	03 3582 0111	www.okura.com	11 D1	56
Hotel Seiyo Ginza	Ginza	03 3535 1111	www.seiyo-ginza.com	14 C2	57
Imperial Hotel	Yūrakuchō	03 3504 1111	www.imperialhotel.co.jp	14 A2	61
Keio Plaza Hotel	Shinjuku-ku	03 3344 0111	www.keioplaza.com	7 A1	62
Le Meridien Grand Pacific Tokyo	Odaiba	03 5500 6711	www.meridien-grandpacific.com	6 C4	63
Mandarin Oriental	Nihonbashi	03 3270 8800	www.mandarinoriental.com	13 C4	64
Marunouchi Hotel	Marunouchi	03 3217 1111	www.marunouchi-hotel.co.jp	13 B4	65
Palace Hotel	Otemachi	03 3211 5211	www.palacehotelstokyo.com	13 A4	68
Park Hyatt ▶ p.xii	Shinjuku-ku	03 5322 1234	www.tokyo.park.hyatt.com	7 A2	69
The Peninsula	Yūrakuchō	03 6270 2888	http://tokyo.peninsula.com	14 A2	70
Tokyo Prince	Shiba-kōen	03 3432 1111	www.princehotels.co.jp	11 E3	71
Rihga Royal	Waseda	03 5285 1121	www.rihga.com	3 F2	72
The Ritz-Carlton	Roppongi	03 3423 8000	www.ritzcarlton.com	11 B2	73
The Westin	Ebisu	03 5423 7000	www.Westin.com	5 F3	77

Midrange

Arimax Hotel Shibuya	Shibuya-ku	03 5454 1122	www.arimaxhotelshibuya.co.jp	8 A3	37
Asakusa View Hotel	Asakusa	03 3847 1111	www.viewhotels.co.jp/asakusa	4 E2	38
Claska	Meguro-ku	03 5773 9667	www.claska.com	5 E2	41
Excel Hotel Tokyu	Shibuya-ku	03 5457 0109	www.tokyuhotelsjapan.com	8 C4	45
Grand Prince Hotel Takanawa	Shinagawa-ku	03 3447 1111	www.princehotels.co.jp	6 A3	51
Hotel East 21	Toyocho	03 5683 5683	http://tokyo-east21.okura.com	4 F4	53
Hotel Excellent Ebisu	Ebisu	03 5458 0087	www.soeikikatu.co.jp	5 F2	78
Hotel Ibis	Roppongi	03 3403 4411	www.ibis-hotel.com	11 B2	54
Mercure Hotel Ginza Tokyo	Ginza	03 4335 1111	www.mercure-asia.com	14 B2	66
Royal Park Hotel	Suitengumae	03 3667 1111	www.rph.co.jp	4 D4	74
Sunroute Plaza Shinjuku	Shinjuku-ku	03 3375 3211	www.sunroutehotel.jp	7 B2	76

Budget

Asia Center of Japan	Akasaka	03 3402 6111	www.asiacenter.or.jp	11 A1	39
Day Nice Hotel	Kiba	03 3642 0011	www.daynice-hotel.com	6 E1	44
Ginza Capital Hotel	Ginza	03 3543 8211	www.ginza-capital.co.jp	14 C4	48
Hotel Sunroute Asakusa	Asakusa	03 3847 1511	www.sunroute-asakusa.co.jp	12 F2	58
Hotel Universe	Nihonbashi	03 3668 7711	www.hotelu-kayabacho.com	14 E1	59
Hotel Villa Fontaine Shiodome	Shinbashi	03 3569 2220	www.hvf.jp/shiodome	14 A4	60
New Koyo Backpacker's Hotel	Minowa	03 3873 0343	www.newkoyo.jp	4 E1	67
Sakura Hotel	Chiyoda-ku	03 3261 3939	www.sakura-hotel.co.jp	3 D4	79
Shinjuku Washington Hotel	Shinjuku-ku	03 3343 3111	www.wh-rsv.com	7 A2	75

Landmark Hotels

Cerulean Tower

26-1 Sakura-
gaoka-chō
Shibuya-ku
🚇 *Shibuya*
Map 8 B4 40

03 3476 3000 | *www.ceruleantower-hotel.com*
The biggest, poshest hotel in the Shibuya entertainment district, the Cerulean Tower is notable for its exceptional views across the whole city, not least from the 40th floor bars and restaurants. Rooms are spacious and modern, and an onsite Noh theatre offers cultural distraction.

Conrad Tokyo

1-9-1 Higashi-
Shinbashi
Minato-ku
🚇 *Shinbashi*
Map 15 B1 42

03 6388 8000 | *www.conradhotels.com*
Among the most stylish of the city's recent crop of new hotels, the Conrad features cutting-edge contemporary decor. Equally impressive are the views, but be sure to ask for a room overlooking Tokyo Bay if you really want to be impressed. The Gordon Ramsay restaurant wins plaudits from gourmets.

Four Seasons Hotel Tokyo at Chinzan-so

2-10-8 Sekiguchi
Mejiro
Bunkyō-ku
🚇 *Edogawabashi*
Map 9 A1 46

03 3943 2222 | *www.fourseasons.com*
A little off the beaten track in north central Tokyo, the Four Seasons at Chinzan-so features elegant, spacious rooms and is set in a beautifully landscaped Japanese garden. Rooms are available in a variety of western and Japanese styles. The spa is lovely and is a popular spot to relax and detox.

Four Seasons Hotel Tokyo at Marunouchi

Pacific Century Place
1-11-1 Marunouchi
Chiyoda-ku
🚇 *Tokyo*
Map 14 B2 47

03 5222 7222 | *www.fourseasons.com*
The newer of the Four Seasons hotels in Tokyo, the Marunouchi branch is located in a landmark tower, and features rooms marked by understated, stylish and contemporary decor. It's walking distance from Tokyo station, Tokyo International Forum and Ginza and Ōtemachi.

Grand Hyatt

6-10-3 Roppongi
Minato-ku
🚇 *Roppongi*
Map 11 B3 49

03 4333 1234 | *http://tokyo.grand.hyatt.com*
Part of the landmark Roppongi Hills development, the Grand Hyatt replaced the Park Hyatt as the celebrity hotel of choice. Highlights for high rollers include a suite with its own private pool. Maduro is the bar to be seen in, while The Oak Door is a popular restaurant for quality meat dishes.

6-6-2 Nishi-Shinjuku
Shinjuku-ku
Tochōmae
Map 7 A1 **52**

Hilton Tokyo

03 3344 5111 | www1.hilton.com
Set among the skyscrapers of west Shinjuku, the Hilton is well situated for the surrounding business and entertainment districts. Reasonably priced for a luxury hotel, it features understated contemporary styling and comprehensive facilities, including the full range of business services.

2-10-4 Toranomon
Minato-ku
Kamiyachō
Map 11 D1 **56**

Hotel Okura

03 3582 0111 | www.okura.com
Among the oldest of Tokyo's western-style hotels, the Okura is a slice of 1960s Modernism that you will either love or hate. The period detail is consistent inside and out, though rooms are being progressively updated. Sober style, impeccable service, and very convenient should you need the US embassy as it's next door.

1-1-1 Uchisaiwai-chō
Yūrakuchō
Chiyoda-ku
Hibiya
Map 14 A2 **61**

Imperial Hotel

03 3504 1111 | www.imperialhotel.co.jp
A Tokyo landmark, the Imperial is being refurbished to bring it right up to date. Work is due to be completed in 2008, but many of the new rooms are already completed, featuring a modern take on the Imperial's traditionally sober style. The hotel is just a few minutes walk from the Ginza shopping district.

2-1-1 Nihonbashi
Muromachi
Chūō-ku
Mitsukoshimae
Map 13 C4 **64**

Mandarin Oriental

03 3270 8800 | www.mandarinoriental.com
One of several Tokyo newcomers, the Mandarin Oriental opened in 2007 in the Nihonbashi business district, a short walk from Tokyo station and Ginza. A stunning 38th floor lobby is the prelude to equally impressive rooms furnished in luxurious, muted tones. The spa rivals any in town.

1-1-1 Marunouchi
Ōtemachi
Chiyoda-ku
Ōtemachi
Map 13 A4 **68**

Palace Hotel

03 3211 5211 | www.palacehoteltokyo.com
One of the grand old names in Tokyo hotels, the Palace has fallen behind western rivals but is reasonably priced and well located for the Ōtemachi business district and Ginza shopping. The 10th floor bar offers superb views over the Imperial Palace and grounds.

Park Hyatt ▶ p.xii

3-7-1-2 Nishi Shinjuku
Shinjuku-ku
🚇 *Shinjuku*
Map 7 A2 69

03 5322 1234 | www.parkhyatttokyo.com
Long the reigning king of Tokyo hotels, especially after it provided the setting for *Lost in Translation*, the Park Hyatt has been overtaken by newer arrivals, but remains a chic, stylish choice. There are commanding views from all rooms, and it's home to one of the city's best restaurants, The New York Grill (p.331).

The Peninsula

1-8-1 Yūrakuchō
Chiyoda-ku
🚇 *Hibiya*
Map 14 A2 70

03 6270 2888 | http://tokyo.peninsula.com
Since opening in 2007, the Peninsula has rivalled the Grand Hyatt for swankiest digs in town, though its clientele tends more toward business than celebrity. Rooms are notably spacious, and offer some of the best views over the Imperial Palace and central Tokyo. Strategically located for Ginza and Ōtemachi.

Rihga Royal

1-104-19 Totsuka-machi
Shinjuku-ku
🚇 *Takadanobaba*
Map 3 F2 72

03 5285 1121 | www.rihga.com
A landmark to the north of the city centre, the Rihga Royal is traditional rather than funky, but offers reliable quality and comfort. It's also notable for one of the most elegant landscaped gardens in the city. Situated next to the prestigious Waseda University, the hotel is convenient for the Shinjuku shopping, entertainment and business hub.

The Ritz-Carlton

Tokyo Midtown 9-7-1 Akasaka
Minato-ku
🚇 *Roppongi*
Map 11 B2 73

03 3423 8000 | www.ritzcarlton.com
Among the newest hotels in Tokyo, the Ritz-Carlton is part of the prestigious new Tokyo Midtown development in Roppongi, guaranteeing a great selection of dining, drinking and partying options. The 46th floor spa is a spectacular place to unwind. Interior design is upscale conservative, with Japanese-style rooms also available.

The Westin

Ebisu Garden Place 1-4-1 Mita
Meguro-ku
🚇 *Ebisu*
Map 5 F3 77

03 5423 7000 | www.westin.com
Located in leafy Ebisu Garden Place, the Westin is a good bet for business or pleasure, being a short hop from Shibuya, Shinjuku and Shinagawa. Furnishings have an antique European flavour, as does the newly opened Spa Parisien. Ebisu station on the Yamanote Line is a short walk away.

Places To Stay

Hotel Apartments

Tokyo has an increasing number of serviced apartments on offer, but don't expect any bargains. Starting at a minimum ¥250,000 per month, such apartments may be cheaper than a luxury hotel room, but are most likely smaller too. For that sort of money expect no more than about 30 square metres. Prices rise roughly in line with floor space, with a 50 square metre apartment likely to cost ¥500,000 or more. Opt for a three-bed apartment suitable for a family and the monthly fee can easily head towards ¥1,000,000. Facilities vary from one block to another, but range from basic (concierge and maid) to hotel-like, including gyms, dry cleaning and babysitting services. Serviced apartments in Tokyo can sometimes be booked daily or weekly, but many require a one month stay, with discounts offered for longer bookings.

Hotel Apartments

Luxury			
Oakwood Premier Tokyo Midtown	Roppongi	03 5412 3131	www.oakwood.com
Deluxe			
Court Annex Akasaka	Akasaka	03 3583 7544	www.asahihomes.co.jp
Ebisu W	Ebisu	03 5420 8765	www.executivesuite.jp
Marriott Executive Apartments	Kamiyachō	03 6402 1800	www.marriott.co.jp
Nishi-Azabu Vierge	Azabu	03 5420 8765	www.executivesuite.jp
Oakwood Apartments Shinjuku	Shinjuku-ku	03 5338 3131	www.oakwood.com
Pacific Tower Roppongi	Roppongi	03 3511 8051	www.tokyoapartments.jp
Prudential Tower Residences	Nagatachō	03 6406 6654	www.moriliving.com
Takanawa Executive Suite	Shinagawa-ku	03 3445 2805	www.apartments33.co.jp
Standard			
Court Annex Roppongi	Roppongi	03 3583 7544	www.asahihomes.co.jp
Tokyu Stay Higashi-Ginza	Ginza	03 5551 0109	www.tokyustay.co.jp
Tokyu Stay Shibuya	Shibuya-ku	03 3477 1091	www.tokyustay.co.jp
Tokyu Stay Shinbashi	Shinbashi	03 5401 1109	www.tokyustay.co.jp

Ryokan & Minshuku

The Japanese equivalent of the B&B is the *ryokan* or *minshuku*. Small, family-owned hotels, these generally offer Japanese-style rooms – *tatami* mat flooring and futon mattresses. Breakfast is included in the price, and often dinner too. Quality and style vary enormously, as do prices, but they offer a good taster of real Japanese living. Don't bank on English-speaking staff however, and be ready for a the full Japanese experience at breakfast time – likely to be fish, rice and the pungent fermented beans known as *natto* (p.). The words *ryokan* and *minshuku* essentially describe the same concept, but *ryokan* are the more upmarket of the two, and will generally include en suite facilities and better quality food. The richest concentration of *ryokan*

Ryokan & Minshuku

Andon	2-34-10 Nihonzutsumi, Taitō-ku	03 3873 8611	www.andon.co.jp
Homeikan	5-10-5 Hongō, Bunkyō-ku	03 3811 1187	www.homeikan.com
Kangetsu	1-2-20 Chidori, Ōta-ku	03 3751 0007	www.kangetsu.com
Kikuya	2-18-9 Nishi-Asakusa, Taitō-ku	03 3841 6404	http://homepage2.nifty.com
Sadachiyo	2-20-1 Asakusa, Taitō-ku	03 3842 6431	www.sadachiyo.co.jp

and *minshuku* can be found in the Ueno area. Bookings can be made through the International Tourism Center of Japan website (www.itcj.jp).

Capsule Hotels

Tokyo is an expensive city but there is one cheap option that's uniquely Japanese. For between ¥3,000 to ¥4,000, capsule hotels offer 'rooms' that are about two metres long, and about one metre high and wide. If you can cope with small spaces, and the snoring of your fellow residents, these are safe and surprisingly comfortable places to stay. Each capsule is high enough for most people to sit up, and comes with free cable TV. Bathing facilities are communal but usually pleasant enough (and a good place to figure out Japanese bathing rituals ahead of a visit to a proper hot spring). Most capsule hotels are for men only, but the ones listed here also accept women.

Capsule Hotels			
Capsule Hotel Asakusa Riverside	03 3844 5117	www.asakusa-capsule.jp	4 E2
Capsule Inn Akihabara	03 3251 0841	www.capsuleinn.com	13 D1
Hotel Siesta	03 3449 5255	www.siesta-en.com	5 F2

Hostels

Tokyo's reputation as a high-cost destination creates a bit of a vicious circle. Budget travellers avoid it because they think there is nowhere to stay and hostels are few and far between because there are no patrons to stay in them. The Tokyo International Youth Hostel in Iidabashi is the best known of the limited options. Hostels in Tokyo provide clean, basic facilities. Some are affiliated with Hostelling International, but none require any kind of membership. For other cheap options see Budget Hotels on p.24.

Hostels				
New Koyo Backpacker's Hotel	Minowa	03 3873 0343	www.newkoyo.jp	4 E1
Sakura Hostel	Asakusa	03 3847 8111	www.sakura-hostel.co.jp	4 E2
Sumidagawa Youth Hostel	Asakusa	03 3851 1121	http://sumidagawayh.com	13 F1
Tokyo International Hostel	Iidabashi	03 3235 1107	www.tokyo-ih.jp	9 D3
Yoyogi Youth Hostel	Yoyogi	03 3467 9163	www.jyh.gr.jp/yoyogi/	7 B4

Campsites

Other options **Camping** p.214

Unsurprisingly, Tokyo central doesn't offer many camping options, but you don't have to go far out to find a place to pitch your tent. Most central is Wakasu Kaihin-Kōen campsite, which offers year-round camping by Tokyo Bay, and a variety of attractions to keep the kids amused (note that the website is in Japanese only). Further out again, there are several sites in the Tama hills in rural western Tokyo. This area is only an hour or so from central Tokyo by train, but a world apart in atmosphere. Hiking trails abound, and you can easily find a solitary spot to explore.

Most campsites have tents to rent if you don't want to bring your own, but check this before you go. Camping is possible year-round, but be warned that nighttime temperatures can plummet to below zero in January and February. For where to go to stock up on equipment, see Outdoor Goods on p.295.

Campsites			
Hikawa Campsite	Western Tokyo	0428 83 2134	www.okutamas.co.jp/hikawa
Ina Camping Village	Western Tokyo	042 596 1775	www10.ocn.ne.jp/~inacamp/
Wakasu Kaihin-Kōen Campsite	Wakasu	03 5569 6701	www.tptc.or.jp

Getting Around

Other options **Transportation** p.139

Other options **Transportation** p.139

Cheap Travel
The Japan Rail Pass (www.japanrailpass. net) is available for short-term visitors to Japan and allows unlimited travel on all JR networks including shinkansen, (except the express 'Nozomi' trains). Ideal for tourists and new residents looking to see a lot of the country, an ordinary one week pass costs ¥28,300, which you can easily spend in just two days travel (Tokyo to Hiroshima and back is ¥36,000), making them great value! You can't get one once you've got a resident's stamp in your passport, but they don't always check if you look more like a visiting tourist than a resident gaijin.

Train is king in Tokyo, and most people get around the city on its extensive and reliable overland and underground trains. While services can be jam-packed during peak hours, making for uncomfortable journeys, trains are nearly always bang on time and stations are well signposted in English. Circling the heart of Tokyo is the JR (Japan Rail) Yamanote line that passes through the major hubs – Shinagawa, Shibuya, Shinjuku, Ikebukuro and Ueno stations. Residents will regularly find themselves making short hops along this line. The city also has a number of private lines stretching out from these major hubs.

Spiralling through the city in what may initially seem an illogical pattern is Tokyo's subway system. Once figured out, it is easy enough to get around the 12 lines – run by two separate companies Tokyo Metro and TOEI – thanks to clear colour coding. Just make sure you know which exit you need to take or you could be in for long walk. Driving in Tokyo can be very difficult if you are not familiar with the roads and a navigation system can be really useful. Traffic jams, although at times dreadful, are not as bad as in other major cities and driving can be a viable option if you can afford to rent a parking spot at or near your home. Many of the country's expressways feed into the tolled Shuto Expressway. Other major roads include Kannana Dōri and Kanpachi Dōri, which circle the city in a huge loop and Route One, that connects the major cities along the old Tōkaidō road to Osaka. Motorbikes and scooters can be a great way to skip past cars stuck in traffic and enable you to see more of the city than you would sat on a train.

While buses may take you closer to your door, they tend to have signs in Japanese only and are often slower and more expensive than the trains. Commuting by foot or by bicycle (p.33) is relatively common, and not too tough a slog in a city of few hills. Taxis are on the expensive side and you may need to give directions to some drivers. Extensions and improvements to the roads and railway systems are constant, despite an already comprehensive transport network.

Air Travel

Narita Airport is the international gateway to Japan, and Haneda Airport is the domestic airport. Domestic flights are the quickest way to travel around the country, but the *shinkansen* may be more convenient as the train takes you into the heart of cities without the security checks. Narita has direct flights to most major international cities, and planes fly from Haneda to nearly every airport across the country. Major routes are to Osaka, Sapporo and Fukuoka, but a quick search will find you a flight to pretty much anywhere in the country.

Japan has two major carriers, Japan Airlines (JAL) and All Nippon Airways (ANA). They have what amounts to a duopoly of the market and serve many Japanese and overseas cities. While JAL is the bigger airline, there is little difference between them in terms of price and service. Work is underway to extend the second runway at Narita Airport to accommodate bigger aircraft, and a fourth runway is due for completion at Haneda Airport in 2009. Security at the airports is tight and all foreigners entering the country are now photographed and fingerprinted (see Say Cheese on p.53 for more).

Flights out of Japan are more expensive than flying in, and travel agents collude on prices to keep them that way. Low fare deals are quoted without taxes and are not so cheap when it comes down to it. Try to shop around and buy tickets as early as possible – discounts are available if you book in advance or fly in the month of your birthday. For domestic flights, a one-way flight to Fukuoka costs about ¥20,000, while a single trip to Hiroshima will set you back about ¥18,000.

Airlines

Aeroflot Russian Airlines	03 5532 8781	www.aeroflot.com
Air Canada	03 5405 8800	www.aircanada.ca
Air China	03 5251 0711	www.airchina.com.cn
Air France	03 3570 8577	www.airfrance.com
Air India	03 3508 0261	www.airindia.in
Air New Zealand	03 7634 8388	www.airnz.com
Alitalia	0476 32 7811	www.alitalia.it
All Nippon Airways (ANA)	0120 02 9709	www.ana.co.jp
American Airlines	03 4550 2111	www.aa.com
British Airways	03 3570 8657	www.ba.com
Cathay Pacific Airways	03 5159 1700	www.cathaypacific.com
China Airlines	03 5520 0333	www.chinaairlines.com
Delta Air Lines	03 3593 6666	www.delta.com
Emirates	05 7000 1008	www.emirates.com
Garuda Indonesia	03 3240 6161	www.garuda-indonesia.com
Japan Airlines (JAL)	03 5460 0511	www.jal.co.jp
KLM Royal Dutch Airlines	03 3570 8770	www.klm.com
Korean Air	03 7632 7561	www.koreanair.com
Lufthansa	03 5750 5713	www.lufthansa.com
Malaysia Airlines	03 5733 2111	www.malaysiaairlines.com
Northwest Airlines	03 7631 8000	www.nwa.com
Philippine Airlines	03 3593 2421	www.philippineair.com
Qantas Airways	03 3593 7000	www.qantas.com.au
Singapore Airlines	03 3213 3431	www.singaporeair.com
Thai Airways International	03 7634 8329	www.thaiair.com
United Airlines	03 3817 4411	www.ual.com

Narita Airport

Narita Airport is the biggest international air hub in Japan and handles nearly all international flights out of the Kantō region. The airport has two terminals, both of which are easy to navigate, and the new electronic check-in system is very smooth with helpful staff to assist. Travellers leaving customs can get to buses, trains or the car park in less than five minutes. The airport is located in the Chiba-ken, about 60 kilometres from central Tokyo. The fastest train links to the city take about 50 minutes. Airport facilities are of a good standard with everything you would expect at a major international airport. A minor criticism would be the lack of places to eat and drink near the boarding gates. For flight information, call 0476 34 8000. You can contact the Narita Customs and Lost Property Office in Terminal 1 at 0476 32 2105 and in Terminal 2 at 0476 34 5220.

Airport Transport – Narita

The JR Narita Express (N'EX) takes passengers from the airport to Tokyo station in 53 minutes on trains that leave about every half hour. It also connects to major hubs such as Shinagawa, Shibuya, Shinjuku and Yokohama. The ordinary fare to Tokyo is ¥2,940. Local JR train services and metro lines connect with the city. A cheaper option is the Keisei Line to Ueno or Nippori station. The Skyliner takes 51 minutes and costs ¥1,920, and the slower, but more frequent, limited express costs ¥1,000.

Buses leave from in front of the departure lobbies of both terminals. A number of companies run convenient services to many locations in central Tokyo for about ¥3,000. Airport Limousine Bus and Keisei Bus are the main operators.

Taxis are an expensive option given the distance to the city and have fixed prices to different areas ranging from ¥14,000 to ¥20,000.

Haneda Airport

Haneda is the busiest airport in Japan carrying over 60 million passengers annually. The majority of flights from Haneda are domestic, but there are also some international flights to nearby Asian countries. The two domestic and one international terminals are geared to make things simple for passengers and ground transport facilities take you right into the heart of the airport. The airport is located in the south of the city and is easily accessible by public transport. Departures and Arrivals are filled with *omiyage* (souvenir) shops and plenty of free food samples. For flight information call 03 5757 8111 and for lost property call 03 5757 8107.

Airport Transport – Haneda

The Tokyo Monorail takes 21 minutes to JR Hamamatsucho station and costs ¥470 with services leaving every few minutes. Limousine buses take about 40 minutes to get to Tokyo station. Buses leave every 30 to 60 minutes to many locations and cost around ¥900.
The express train on the Keikyū Airport line gets to Shinagawa station in 18 minutes.
A journey into central Tokyo by taxi should cost between ¥4,000 and ¥6,000.

Where's My Bike?

Watch out for the elderly gents who act as bicycle parking attendants (they actually work for the council). They might shift your cycle somewhere nearby or even transport it to a lot, where you have to pay about ¥3,000 to have it returned.

Bicycle

Other options **Cycling** p.217

Cycling is a relatively safe way to get around the city and is convenient for skipping past cars in traffic jams. While there are few designated cycle paths, many Tokyoites use pedal power to transport themselves around the city – some on extremely cool bikes, others on *mama-chari* (shopping bicycles with baskets). You can cycle to your nearest station and leave your bike in a secure bicycle park, or else leave it on the street.
If your bicycle is stolen, you should report it to the nearest *kōban* (police box) and give them the registration number you were given when you purchased your bike.
Motorists, with the exception of some truck drivers on busy routes, generally leave room for cyclists. Theft is relatively common and the police regularly stop people to check that the registration number matches the cyclist's ID. The wearing of a helmet is not compulsory, but the law as to whether you can ride on pavements is very grey. It leans towards sticking to the roads – few people, however, adhere to this. The law on liability for accidents is also grey, and much is dealt with on a case-by-case basis – most drivers will prefer to settle out of court.

Boat

Boats are not generally used as public transport, but there are a number of cruises along the Sumida River towards Tokyo Bay to various tourist attractions (see Boat Tours & Charters on p.188).
Car ferries are also available from the Ariake Ferry Terminal to Tomakomai in Hokkaidō (about ¥26,000 for car and driver) or Tokushima and Kitakyūshū (about ¥14,000 for a passenger ticket to Kitakyūshū). The trip to Tomakomai takes 20 hours.
High-speed ferries go from Takeshiba Terminal near Hamamatsucho station to the Izu and Ogasawara islands. Of the Izu islands (see p.201), Ōshima is great for a quiet weekend getaway, and Niijima has tremendous beaches and is perfect for camping (see p.214). A trip to Ōshima on a high speed ferry (make sure you take this rather than the normal slow ferry) takes about 90 minutes and costs about ¥5,000 one way.

Cycling in the city

The No.99

One bus that almost every foreigner will have to take at some point is the No.99 from Shinagawa station to the Tokyo Regional Immigration Bureau. Your local ward office should have a map or information on services and routes in your area.

Bus

Using buses can be daunting to newcomers as destinations and stops are often only given in Japanese, but the network is comprehensive with routes winding off from most train stations into the suburbs and beyond.

In general, buses tend to complement train services and are less frequent, but some areas can only be reached by bus. Buses can get very crowded during peak hours, but are relatively quiet during the day. Tourists will rarely need to jump on a bus, as most attractions are easily accessible by train. For a map and timetable of the bus routes, go to your local ward office (see Residents on p.49).

Fares differ depending on the route, but tend to be about ¥200. Buses run by the Metropolitan Government offer a ¥500 day ticket that allows unlimited travel.

On buses with flat fares, you have to put the correct fare into a machine next to the driver when you board. On buses where you board at the rear, you pick up a ticket with a number and check the board at the front of the bus for the fare that corresponds with the number on the ticket. This is the fare you put into the machine next to the driver as you get off – it is usually able to give change. Don't worry, it gets easier with practice.

Bus companies include Tōbu Bus (www.tobu-bus.com), Tōkyū Bus (www.tokyubus.co.jp) and Odakyū Bus (www.odakyubus.co.jp), but all the websites are in Japanese.

Take The Bus

Some bus lines save you the hassle of swapping from JR to metro lines and offer a more direct route than taking the metro. A particularly useful one is the Toei green bus Shibuya to Roppongi route.

Car

Other options **Transportation** p.139

The idea of driving around Tokyo may sound daunting, but many people do it. Roads are smooth and well maintained, and nearly all road signs have English written below the Japanese. Just beware the many traffic lights, narrow roads, and the price of parking in some areas. People usually drive conservatively giving consideration to others, but be aware of the occasional young petrol-head whizzing across a junction as the traffic lights are turning red.

Driving is on the left in Japan and most cars are right-hand drive automatics – people are sometimes astonished if you tell them you can drive a car with manual gears.

Drivers must have a valid international driving licence or a Japanese driving licence.

The legal minimum driving age is 18 and speed limits range from 100kph on expressways to 30kph on narrow city streets.

Traffic conditions depend entirely on the day or time of day. Morning rush hour into central Tokyo is between 07:00 and 09:00 on weekdays, and evening rush hour heading out is between 18:00 and 22:00. National holiday weekends are also mayhem as this is when many people head out to the countryside.

The Japan Automobile Federation (JAF) has an English language version of its *Rules of the Road* available for ¥1,000. You can pick up a copy from any of the city's JAF offices (www.jaf.or.jp). Road signs follow international standards with a few minor exceptions and should not cause difficulties.

City transport

Drivers should note the revision of the Road Traffic Law made in June 2006. Cars parked illegally, even momentarily, are liable to receive a ticket from an army of private sector traffic wardens, so it's best to make use of the many carparks in the city. Parking fees vary depending on the area and time of day and range from ¥100 per hour to up to ¥200 per 10 minutes in central districts. 24 hour rates are also available. The city has no congestion charges and there are presently no plans to introduce them. If you do not have a parking space at home, you can rent private lots nearby starting at about ¥20,000 per month. In central areas this figure can hit ¥60,000.

A number of expressways feed into the city, among these are the Tōmei-Meishin expressway, coming in from Kōbe via Nagoya, Osaka and Kyoto, the Tōhoku Expressway from Sendai in the north and Chūō expressway from Nagano and Nagoya. In Tokyo, all these expressways are joined up in the rather difficult to navigate Shuto expressway system. It helps to know exactly where you want to get off the Shuto, as a slight misjudgement can mean a long and expensive journey back. Beware also that the normally sedate drivers in Japan can rev up to break-neck speeds on these roads. Expressways are tolled and long distance journeys can be pricey. A trip from Tokyo to Aomori costs about ¥14,000 (700km), to Kyoto about ¥10,500 (500km), and to Kagoshima in the south of Kyūshū, a whopping ¥27,500 (1,400km). Many expressways now use an electronic toll collection (ETC) system alongside tollbooths.

Major roads coming in from the suburbs include Route 1, Aoyama Dōri (R246), Kōshū Kaidō (R20), Ōmekaidō, Kawagoe Kaidō (R254), Naka Sendo (R17), Nikko Kaidō (R4), Mita Kaidō (R6), Keiyō Dōri (R14) and Harumi Dōri. The city also has a series of ring roads, Sotobori Dōri that circles the Imperial Palace, Meiji Dōri, Yamate Dōri and the huge looping Kannana Dōri and Kanpachi Dōri. Traffic can get very heavy on these roads. Owning a car is Japan is not cheap. As well as tolls and soaring petrol prices, getting insurance is mandatory, as is car tax, which can range from ¥10,000 to ¥50,000 per year depending on engine size. You must also pay an acquisition tax on purchase and take your car in for *shaken* every two years (a compulsory inspection that can cost up to ¥250,000). On top of this, there's a mountain of paperwork. If all of this seems too much, you can always rent a car. See also Transportation on p.139.

Metro

At first glance the metro map (see inside back cover) resembles a bowl of spaghetti but after a few weeks getting to know the different lines, it's easy to plan routes using the colour-coded lines and numbered stations.

Two companies operate 12 metro lines, mainly within the central area, encompassed by the JR Yamanote Line. Public-private Tokyo Metro runs the Ginza, Marunouchi, Hibiya, Tozai, Chiyoda, Yūrakuchō (including the new Fukutoshin Line), Hanzomon and Nambuku lines, while public entity Tokyo Metropolitan Bureau of Transportation (TOEI) presides over the Asakusa, Mita, Shinjuku and Ōedo lines. One thing to note is that the two operators have separate ticketing systems. However, the PASMO or Suica prepaid cards (see right) can be used on both. Otherwise, a single ticket can be bought on journeys combining the two systems, but you will

Route Planners

As with trains, few people refer to written timetables due to the efficiency and frequency of services. Many people log onto online sites via mobile phone to plan their trip – www.jorudan.co.jp is a good one in English.

All For One

The PASMO and Suica prepaid cards can be used on all rail lines and buses and are the easiest way to travel. They can even be used in vending machines, shops, kiosks and restaurants. To use, just swipe them over the card reader and the fare or cost of the item being purchased will automatically be deducted. The cards are available from vending machines and ticket counters and require a refundable deposit of ¥500. PASMO must initially be credited with ¥500 to ¥9,500 and Suica cards with ¥1,500. Credit can be topped up at machines and at station ticket desks up to a maximum of ¥20,000.

need a special transfer ticket and you will be charged ¥90 to ¥100 for the pleasure. Fares start at ¥160 for Tokyo Metro and ¥190 for TOEI. Day passes are also available. The Tokyo Free Kippu gives unlimited travel on all metro lines and JR trains in Greater Tokyo and costs ¥1,580. The TOEI and Tokyo Metro one-day economy pass costs ¥1,000. A Tokyo Metro one-day pass costs ¥710 and ¥980 for a two-day pass. TOEI day passes cost ¥700.

Taxi

Taxis are the most expensive way to get around Tokyo. This was compounded in December 2007 when the minimum fare for the first two kilometres was bumped up to ¥710 – fares cost about ¥80 for every 274 metres after that. An approximate daytime fare for a ride in a standard cab from Tokyo station to Shinjuku would be ¥2,500, and ¥6,000 to Haneda Airport.

Taxi Companies	
Nihon Kotsu	03 5755 2336
Odakyu Kotsu Taxi	03 3406 7171
Outech	03 3599 6740
Tokyo Yellow Cab	03 3521 8880
Tomin Kotsu	03 3317 6333
Toto Taxi	03 3590 1010

Except for some services to and from the airports, nearly all taxis are metered and run by independent operators where you just pay the displayed fare. Available taxis will have a red light (green is when they're taken), displaying the word 空車 (kūsha) – literally 'empty car'. They can be easily flagged down from the side of the road by putting out your arm and waving your hand, palm down, towards you (just mimic any Japanese nearby), but places such as train stations have a rank and queue system. When getting in and out, be warned, the doors open automatically so keep your hands clear. Taxi drivers tend to be honest so they will take you the most direct route – if they know it. Not all have encyclopaedic knowledge of the city so if you don't know where you're going check to see if the car has a navigation system before hopping in.

Train

Tokyo's rail network is the envy of the world. Clean, punctual, and frequent, very few people have an axe to grind over the excellent train service. Notices and announcements on nearly all stations and trains are in both English and Japanese. The biggest downside is travelling between 07:00 and 09:00 or out of the city between 18:00 and 22:00, when you will probably find yourself packed in like sardines, that and the drunks catching the last train home and the occasional *jinshin jiko* (accidents caused by people jumping in front of trains).

Japan Rail (JR) lines include the circular Yamanote Line that has trains every two or three minutes, the Chūō Line that cuts through the city centre, the Keihin-Tohoku Line that links Yokohama to Saitama, and the Saikyo/Rinkai Line, a fast service that runs parallel to the western side of the Yamanote down to Daiba.

Several other rail companies run services departing from major stations on the Yamanote line out to the suburbs.

While you can pick up timetables at JR Midori-no-Madoguchi ticket counters, most residents either don't bother checking due to regular and efficient service or tend to use internet sites or mobile phones to check train times and connections. One great site that gives quick reliable information in English and Japanese is www.jorudan.co.jp. If you travel regularly, it may be worth investing in a monthly, three-monthly, or six-monthly *teiki-ken* commuter pass. Suica and PASMO prepaid travel cards (see p.35 for more) can also be used on any train or metro service and most bus services in the Greater Tokyo area. These allow you to just swipe your card as you go through the gates, and the fare is automatically deducted. To charge them, go to any of the ticket machines located at most stations.

Plan Your Route Online

Hyperdia's website (www.hyperdia.com) provides up-to-the-minute information on the fastest route, as well as timetables for the Tokyo area and all of Japan. Just type in your start point and your destination and away you go.

Pleasure Train

Two rail trips worth taking are the driverless New Transit Yurikamome service, departing from Shinbashi station, crossing Tokyo Bay through Odaiba, and terminating at Toyosu; and the Tokyo Monorail, which connects Hamamatsucho station with Haneda Airport. The former is rarely crowded and offers amazing elevated views of the urban sprawl.

There are also several different types of train. These range from the *futsū* (normal) trains that stop at all stations and the faster *kyūkō* ordinary express that only stop at certain stations, to the *tokkyū* limited express services that only serve main stations. Watch out if you mistakenly catch a faster train when you only need to go one or two stops on a *futsū* train, as you could end up backtracking quite a distance.

Finally, the *shinkansen* bullet train is the pride of Japan's rail network. To head west toward Osaka, Kyoto, Hiroshima or Fukuoka catch the 'shink' from Tokyo or Shinagawa, or board at Tokyo or Ueno to head north to Sendai, Aomori or Niigata.

Tram

The Toden Arakawa line is Tokyo's only tram, which runs along the northern part of the city. Two other rail services worth taking for the views alone are the driverless New Transit Yurikamome service departing from Shinbashi station through Odaiba and terminating at Toyosu and the Tokyo Monorail, which runs along the western shore, connecting Hamamatsucho station with Haneda Airport. The former offers amazing elevated views of the urban sprawl.

Not technically a tram, the Tōkyū Setagaya Line is a light rail transit line that passes through the leafy suburbs of wealthy Setagaya and has the same feel as a tram, offering pretty residential views.

Walking

Other options **Hiking** p.223, **Walking Tours** p.194

Many pockets in central Tokyo are close together, making your feet a viable option for traversing the city. The numerous pedestrian crossings, bridges, underpasses and often wide pavements make Tokyo a safe place to walk. Stay alert, however, as many cyclists also use the pavements and tend not to let you know when they are trying to pass from behind.

Harajuku, Omotesandō, Shibuya, Aoyama and Roppongi are short walks from each other and there is much of interest in these areas (see p.154). Ginza becomes a pedestrian paradise on Sundays, allowing shoppers to leisurely stroll along the normally congested roads. For spectacular views of the Tokyo waterfront, try taking the Yurikamome Line to Shibaura-Futo station and walking across the Rainbow Bridge to Odaiba (for more ideas, see Walking Tours and Walk This Way in Exploring on p.145).

Loop The Loop

2009 will mark the Yamanote line's centenary. Of the 30 stations on the line, only 29 are operational. The one near Harajuku was used only once, to shuttle members of the imperial family to the Olympic Games in 1964. The tracks measure roughly 34.5 kilometres in circumference, but the inside (uchimawari) line is 70 metres shorter than the outside (sotomawari).

Tokyo metro

Money

It is not uncommon for people to walk around Tokyo with wallets stuffed full of ¥10,000 notes. While this may be partly due to the low crime rate in the city, it is more likely because cash is the preferred mode of payment. Credit cards can be used in most upscale or foreigner-friendly restaurants and shops but it's wise to have cash on you just in case. Cheques and debit cards are generally not accepted, nor are foreign currencies. For bureaux de change, see Money Exchanges below.

Local Currency

The currency in Japan is the yen (¥) or *en*. Notes come in denominations of ¥10,000, ¥5,000, ¥2,000 and ¥1,000 – although the ¥2,000 bill is still relatively rare and will draw gasps of glee whenever you pull one out of your wallet. ¥500, ¥100, ¥50, ¥10, ¥5 and ¥1 coins are in circulation. The yen is not pegged to any other currency. For exchange rates, see the table below.

Banks

Other options **Bank Accounts** p.65

For a country renowned for its high-tech prowess, Japan's banking services, while improving, seem to lag behind those in many other countries and visits to the bank can be lengthy. The Marunouchi financial district houses the head branches of most national banks, while there are hundreds of smaller branches in convenient locations across the city.

Well-known banks include Mizuho Bank, Sumitomo-Mitsui Banking Corporation and The Bank of Tokyo-Mitsubishi UFJ (United Financial of Japan). Shinsei Bank is a foreign-owned newcomer to the Japanese banking world, and offers longer business hours, free use of ATMs and online banking in English. Japan Post also offers post office accounts (www.post.japanpost.jp).

All banks are internationally recognised so it is easy transfer funds overseas. The usual services are offered, such as current and savings accounts (see Bank Accounts, p.65), internet banking (usually only in Japanese) and loans and financing. You can exchange money into major currencies such as the US dollar and euro at most branches, but for other currencies you may have to go to a branch in Marunouchi. Banking hours are generally from 09:00 to 15:00, Monday to Friday, and banks stay open over lunch.

ATMs

Up until just a few years ago, ATMs used to close in the early evening. Thankfully things have changed and many ATMs operate around the clock. ATMs can be found at banks and also in supermarkets, shopping centres, department stores, and more recently in many convenience stores. Cards from certain banks can be used in the ATMs of other banks. Unfortunately, foreign credit and debit cards can only be used at the international ATMs, mostly found in post offices and a few other locations, making it imperative to have a card issued from a Japanese bank.

Recent news reports have highlighted incidents where crooks standing behind people using ATMs have noted their pin code, robbed the person, and gone back to withdraw cash from their account, but such crimes are still extremely rare in Japan.

Exchange Rates

Foreign Currency (FC)	1 Unit FC = ¥ x	¥100 = x FC
Australia	97.2	1.03
Canada	112.7	0.87
China	15.32	6.53
Euro	162.8	0.61
Hong Kong	14.5	6.89
New Zealand	85.5	1.17
Singapore	77.5	1.29
Switzerland	98.3	1.02
UAE	29.07	34.4
UK	228.4	0.44
USA	113.2	0.88

Money Exchanges

Aside from the major hotels and banks, money exchanges are pretty scarce in Tokyo. Travelex exchanges can be found in several places including Tokyo station, the Tokyo Midtown tower in Roppongi and on the east side of Shibuya station. Banks tend to offer slightly better rates than hotels. US dollars, euros and sterling tend to be the easiest currencies to exchange, but lesser currencies such as the New Zealand or Australian dollar will be difficult to change. Independent money exchanges tend to operate from 09:00 or 10:00 through to the early evening.

Online Communities

There are numerous expat-focused websites offering advice and advertising services specially for expatriates. See p.41 for a list. And check out www.explorerpublishing.com, where you can join an online community for your city, share tips, get updates, ask questions and make friends.

Credit Cards

Credit cards account for just 10% of total transactions; so do not expect to be able to survive in the city entirely on your credit card and always carry cash. Visa, American Express and Mastercard can be used in department stores, high-end shops and most decent hotels, but anywhere smaller or less frequented by foreigners will probably not accept them. Few places charge a transaction fee for credit cards.

Restaurants and shops tend not to ask for a signature or PIN when you pay by credit card, nor do they check signatures against cards, so make sure you keep your card safe as anyone could make purchases on it with little difficulty. If you lose a credit card or suspect you are a victim of online fraud, contact your bank immediately.

In the last few years, several other methods of electronic payment have appeared. Goods can be purchased in and around train stations from kiosks, vending machines, combinis and some shops with Suica or PASMO integrated travel cards (see All For One on p.35) and some mobile phones are also equipped with IC chips that can act like a credit card to make purchases (see Mobile Phones on p.112 for more). Debit cards are rare.

Although the Japanese were once known as savers rather than spenders – in 1975 they saved 23.1% of total household disposable income – credit card and other debt is increasingly becoming a problem and the savings ratio fell to 3.1% in 2005.

Tipping

People rarely tip in Japan. In many situations offering a tip could cause embarrassment and should be avoided unless you absolutely feel that the service deserves at tip. Do not worry about not leaving one, because unlike in some countries, the service staff do not depend on tips to live. The exception is taxis, as rounding your fare up to an easy-to-handle amount will help the driver out. Some restaurants may add a service charge of about 10% to your bill.

City skyline at night

Newspapers & Magazines

Newspapers are sold at station kiosks, book shops and convenience stores, and can be purchased in some major hotels. English-speaking residents in Tokyo can take their pick from three local English language dailies. *The Japan Times* (¥180), founded in 1897, is the oldest English language daily in Japan and the only independent. It sends its own journalists out to cover domestic events and has a useful classified section on Mondays. The *Daily Yomiuri* (¥120), Japan's largest English-language newspaper is the sister paper of the conservative *Yomiuri Shinbun* – the newspaper with the largest circulation in the world, selling more than 10 million copies a day. It includes translations of domestic news reports from the Japanese language paper, world news reports, and features original arts and sports writing. Pages from western newspapers such as the *Los Angeles Times*, *The Times* and the *Observer* appear in these papers on a regular basis. The more liberal *Asahi Shinbun* is affiliated with the *International Herald Tribune* and a joint *Asahi/IHT* (¥150) is printed daily, with the *IHT* at the front and the *Asahi* at the back.

Weekly versions of the above, and of the left-leaning *Mainichi Shinbun (Mainichi Weekly)*, are also available, but tend to be geared to Japanese learners of English. The financial daily *Nihon Keizai Shinbun* also prints a weekly paper – *The Nikkei Weekly*. *Kanji* readers can pick up Japanese versions of all of the above (bar the *Japan Times)*, as well as other Japanese papers such as the *Sankei Shinbun* and the *Nikkei Shinbun*. While newspapers are not censored as such, a lot of domestic news is sourced from *kasha* or reporters' clubs and coverage is often limited to what journalists are told, which can sometimes mean a bland read.

A number of glossy English language magazines on Tokyo can be picked up for free in many shops, restaurants and bars. *Metropolis*, *Tokyo Weekender*, *Tokyo Journal* and *Japanzine* feature entertaining articles and are filled with ads for restaurants and bars for *gaijin* (foreigners). The *Hiragana Times* is aimed at those learning Japanese and can be found in bookshops (see Books on p.278).

Foreign newspapers such as the *Wall Street Journal* and the *Financial Times* are available a day late at larger bookshops. Die-hard news junkies can go to branches of FedEx Kinko's (www.english.fedexkinkos.co.jp) and get same-day copies of publications from around the world – for a price.

Blogs

Search for 'Tokyo blog' on Google and thousands of entries appear, making it difficult to find truly interesting and informative reads. A good start is Kurashi, *where you can check out Martin J. Frid's angle on the local news, or try* Tokyo Daily Photo. *Another recommendation is the long-running* Sake-drenched Postcards; *it covers a range of interesting topics. There are also loads of blogs in which people have taken a snap of their dinner, illustrating what a foodie city it is –* Pigoutdiary *is a good example and will get gastronomes slavering.*

Books

Other options **Books** (Shopping) p.278

All the usual travel guide publishers have books on Tokyo, all of which can be found in foreign language sections of the city's mammoth-sized bookshops. Explorer Publishing also produce the *Tokyo Mini Explorer* – a guidebook that's small in size but packed full of all the information visitor's need on Tokyo. Michelin recently released their first Tokyo guide and stirred up controversy by giving stars to all 150 restaurants in the book – far more than Paris or any other major city (see Gourmet Gobbles on p.325). A number of other restaurant and entertainment guides such as the *Zagat Survey* and *Time Out Tokyo* are also available.

For a deeper insight into the workings of the city, *Tokyo: A View of the City* by Donald Richie, an American author who has spent more than 50 years in Japan, is a short entertaining work that delves into the more hedonistic side of the city. Edward Seidensticker's *Tokyo Rising: The City Since the Great Earthquake* takes a detailed look at the city since the Great Kantō Earthquake in 1923, and takes the reader through the second world war and the city's subsequent boom.

The lives of normal Tokyo folk are brilliantly portrayed in Haruki Murakami's *Underground: The Tokyo Gas Attack and the Japanese Psyche*. The work comprises interviews with victims of the Aum Shinrikyō cult's March 1995 sarin gas attack on the subway system, and with members of the cult, past and present. Many of Murakami's fictional works are also set in the city.

Websites

Tokyo expats have a wealth of online information at their fingertips. You can get domestic news stories on the national dailies websites, search for a job on a classifieds site, see what bands are playing in the listings of one of the free entertainment magazines or read the rants and raves of fellow *gaijin* in an online forum. See the table on p.41 for some of the most popular sites.

Websites

Business	
www.japaninc.com	Online version of business magazine
www.tokyo-business.jp	Metropolitan government business information
City Information	
http://tokyo.asiaxpat.com	Expat info, jobs and accommodation ads
www.blacktokyo.com	Information for black people in Tokyo
www.daijob.com	Jobs in Japan
www.fewjapan.com	Foreign Executive Women
www.frugaljapan.com	A guide to making the most of your financial resources in Japan
www.gaijinpot.com	Jobs, classifieds and forums for foreigners
www.japan-guide.com	A comprehensive guide to living and traveling in Japan
www.jnto.go.jp	Japan National Tourism Organisation
www.jobsinjapan.com	Jobs in Japan
www.metro.tokyo.jp	Official site of the Tokyo Metropolitan Government
www.tcvb.or.jp	Maps and other info from the Tokyo Convention and Visitors Bureau
www.tfemploy.go.jp	Information centre for foreigners in Tokyo
www.tokyo1.org	Archive of over 100,000 images of Tokyo
www.tourism.metro.tokyo.jp	Tokyo Tourist Information Center
Culture	
www.kabuki21.com	Kabuki information
www.metropolis.co.jp	Magazine focusing on entertainment with thorough listings
www.sumo.or.jp	Official Grand Sumo homepage
www.tokyoartbeat.com	Bilingual art and design guide
Directories	
http://english.itp.ne.jp	Online telephone directory
http://tokyo.geoexpat.com/directory	Useful Tokyo directory
www.yellowpage-jp.com	Yellow Pages
News & Media	
http://mdn.mainichi.jp	Mainichi Daily News
www.asahi.com	Asahi Shinbun
www.japantimes.co.jp	Japan Times
www.japantoday.com	Japan Today news site with readers' comments
www.yomiuri.co.jp	Daily Yomiuri
Nightlife	
http://tokyo.to/city/index.html	Wining and dining options
www.bento.com/froth.html	Links to sites on clubs and bars
www.hotpepper.jp	Gourmet listings (in Japanese)
Online Shopping	
www.amazon.co.jp	Books, CDs and DVDs
www.japan-shop.com	Links to online shopping resources in Japan

Annual Events

1 January
Various Locations

New Year

There are numerous midnight 'Countdown' parties, but for a more traditional celebration, most temples toll their bells around midnight and people gather to ring in the New Year. The next day, some people get up to see *hatsu-hinode* (the first sunrise of the year). Most people have several days off work at this time, and a popular custom is to go with friends and families to visit a shrine to make wishes for the year and receive *omamori* charms (burning last year's 'expired' charms on bonfires).

2 January
Imperial Palace
Chiyoda-ku
🚇 **Tokyo**
Map 10 E 2

Ippan Sanga – Emperor's New Year's Message

This is only one of two days when the public may enter the grounds of the Imperial Palace – the other being on the emperor's birthday. Large crowds gather below the palace balcony to hear the monarch and the imperial family come out seven times to wish them a happy New Year.

**Late January
– early February**
Yokohama
Map 2 A4

Chinese New Year

Experience an explosive lunar New Year in the Chinese heart of the Kantō region. Firecrackers – officially banned in some places – are let off on the streets after midnight on New Year's Eve while New Year's Day features daytime dragon and lion dances along streets lined with restaurants, teashops and stalls selling hot Chinese snacks and booze.

3 February
Various Locations

Setsubun

Say goodbye to winter and in with the spring by hurling soybeans at an *oni* (devil) at temples across the capital. After you have purified yourself destroying the eyes of the *oni* with the beans, eat a bean for every year of your life and an extra one for good fortune. Crowds swarm to Sensōji in Asakusa (see p.178) to take part in the fun.

Mid February
Various Locations

Tokyo Marathon

www.tokyo42195.org

The 25,000 entrants run a course from the Tokyo Metropolitan Government Building in Shinjuku, around the Imperial Palace, up to Asakusa and back down to finish at Tokyo Big Sight in Odaiba. Join the masses waving *Hinomaru* national flags and shouting *gambatte*! (keep going!) to the athletes and fun-runners.

**Late February to
early March**
Various Locations

Tokyo International Arts Festival

03 5428 0337 | http://tif.anj.or.jp

This is a festival of music, dance and theatre performed by artists from across the globe that aims 'to get rid of biases which are unconsciously attached to everyday life in Japanese society.' In recent years the event has featured prominent artists from the Middle East, the former Soviet Union, Asia, Europe and the United States. It takes place at various venues across the city.

3 March
Various Locations

Hinamatsuri (Doll's Festival)

Most Japanese families with daughters will decorate their house with *hina* dolls, often elaborate multi-stepped platforms with many dolls representing the Emperor, Empress and members of the court from the Heian Period (794-1185) around mid-February until Girl's Day on 3 March. See an impressive display of the wonderfully crafted dolls and visitors sporting traditional kimono at several shrines, including Meiji Jingū (p.178).

Annual Events

Marunouchi reflections

Hankyū Seibu Ginza

Fuji Building

Tokyo International Forum

Ginza architecture

Japan Fashion Week in Tokyo

Spring & Autumn
Various Locations

03 3242 8551 | www.jfw.jp

Tokyo is one of the world centres of fashion and the Japanese are known for sporting some of the most outlandish outfits. Anyone with an eye for style will love this. The week includes designer' and textile exhibitions, many special events and, of course, the eagerly-awaited new collections.

Hanami (Cherry Blossom Viewing)

Late March
Various Locations

Cherry blossom is seen as significant in Japan as a metaphor for life, in that it is beautiful yet fleeting. These days, however, it is a great excuse for people to drink, feast and have good-natured fun under the trees. Popular *hanami* spots include Ueno Kōen (p.186), Chidorigafuchi (Imperial Palace p.185), Yoyogi Kōen (p.186) and Inokashira Kōen (p.181).

Tokyo International Anime Fair

Late March
Tokyo Big Sight
Koto-ku
Map 6 E3

03 5403 7840 | www.tokyoanime.jp

The world's largest anime exhibition is chaired by the governor of Tokyo, Shintaro Ishihara, and attracts over 100,000 visitors a year to exhibits by more than 250 companies. A major attraction is the cosplay outfits of popular anime characters worn by attractive girls and *otaku* (nerdy) gentleman.

La Folle Journee au Japon

Late April / Early May
Chiyoda-ku
🚇 **Yūrakuchō**
Map 2 B2

www.t-i-forum.co.jp/lfj_2008/

This event is composed of a series of 300 or so 45 minute classical music performances based around Tokyo International Forum (www.t-i-forum.co.jp) and other venues in the Marunouchi area. Artists from around the world bring classical music to the masses with shows reasonably priced between ¥1,500 and ¥3,000.

Golden Week

29 April – 5 May
Various Locations

Four national holidays, (Emperor) Shōwa Day, Constitution Day, Greenery Day and Childrens' Day make up what is known as Golden Week. It is also a time of mass exodus from Tokyo, either overseas or to towns and cities across Japan, making it unadvisable to travel unless it is absolutely necessary. Childrens' or Boys' Day is marked by the flying of *koinobori* (carp) flags from people's homes, and Greenery Day sees a number of environmental events.

Kanda Matsuri Festival

Mid May
Chiyoda-ku
🚇 **Ochanomizu**
Map 13 B1

03 3254 0753 | www.kandamyoujin.or.jp

This biennial event reaches its climax at the weekend when 200 *mikoshi* (portable shrines) are carried from the Kanda Myōjin by suitably lubricated parishioners of the shrine around the area. Traditional music using *shamisen* instruments can be heard, recreating a sense of old Edo (the old name for Tokyo) at an event that marks the 400th anniversary of the Edo Shogunate.

Sanja Matsuri

Third weekend in May
Asakusa
🚇 **Asakusa**
Map 4 E2

www.asakusajinja.jp

Sanja Matsuri is Tokyo's largest festival. Based in Asakusa, this is a frenetic event in which the participants and spectators get caught up in a heady atmosphere that recreates times gone by. The colourful parade goes on over a few days, in honour of the founders of the Sensōji (p.178). Floats carry musicians and drummers, accompanied by traditional dancers and geisha. On the final day, *mikoshi* (portable shrines) are carried by *happi* coat-clad folk from the Asakusa shrine around this traditional quarter.

Life in the fast lane?

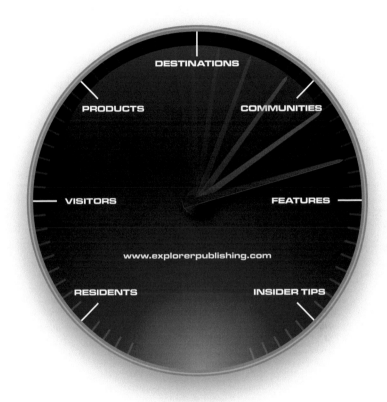

Life can move pretty quickly so make sure you keep in the know with regular updates from **www.explorerpublishing.com**

Or better still, share your knowledge and advice with others, find answers to your questions, or just make new friends in our community area

www.explorerpublishing.com – for life in real time

EXPLORER
www.explorerpublishing.com

7 July
Various Locations

Tanabata (Star Festival)

According to a Chinese legend, the two stars Orihime and Hikoboshi, who are normally separated by the Milky Way, get a chance to meet on this day. Children tie colourful strips of paper bearing their wishes to bamboo branches and there are usually stalls selling food and drink. Many places in Tokyo hold small Tanabata festivals (which vary from place to place), but it may be worth jumping on a train and going to the real thing in Hiratsuka.

Late July
Niigata-ken
Map 1 B3

Fuji Rock Festival

www.fujirockfestival.com

Japan's biggest rock festival is held in the Naeba ski resort in the mountains of Niigata, about two hours on the *shinkansen* from central Tokyo. Held in the last three days of July every summer, it is likened to Britain's Glastonbury Festival and attracts the biggest names in rock to the main stages. It also provides a platform for emerging and cult artists to play away until the early hours around the stunning site.

Mid-August
Various Locations

Obon

While not an official national holiday, this is the time of year when many Japanese head back to their *furusato* (hometown) to spend time with their families and visit the graves of their ancestors. In Japanese Buddhism, it is believed that during *Obon*, ancestors' spirits return to this world. Many areas hold colourful *Obon* dancing on the streets. People usually get about three or four days off work (normally from around 13 August).

Last Saturday in August
Asakusa
🚇 *Asakusa*
Map 4 E2

Sumida River Fireworks Festival

http://sumidagawa-hanabi.com

No summer is complete without a night of fireworks. The grandest of Tokyo's displays is at the Sumidagawa when over 20,000 *hanabi* are launched from two platforms in the river creating a tremendous spectacle. Small stalls sell festival food and drink such as beer, *kakigōri* (flavoured crushed ice), candy-floss and *takoyaki* (fried octopus dumplings) to the *yukata*-wearing crowds (see p.17 for more on traditional dress).

Last weekend in August
Kōenji
Map 2 A2

Kōenji Awa Odori

www.koenji-awaodori.com

About 12,000 dancers from more than 180 groups dance through the streets near Kōenji station, wearing brightly coloured costumes during this festival, which is the second biggest of its kind in Japan. The dance, which attracts more than half a million spectators, originated in Tokushima in Shikoku over 400 years ago and is great to watch or join in.

Mid-September
Chiba-ken
Map 2 C2

Tokyo Game Show

http://tgs.cesa.or.jp

With more *otaku* (nerds) here than in Akihabara, this show at Makuhari Messe gives gamers plenty to slaver over during the two days it is open to the public. All of the major game producers – bar Nintendo, which does its own thing – show off their latest software and hardware.

Late September
Chiyoda-ku
🚇 *Yūrakuchō*
Map 14 B2

Tokyo Jazz Festival

03 5777 8600 | *www.tokyo-jazz.com*

2007's festival featured an eclectic mix of international and homegrown artists ranging from the wild Japanese jazzsters Soil and 'Pimp' Session to the sax of Candy Dulfer, and a Big Band and Standard Night. While not a cheap affair, all jazz fans should find something to their taste. The festival is held in the International Forum.

Annual Events

Late October
Various Locations

Tokyo International Film Festival
www.tiff-jp.net

Independent movie buffs should find this festival stimulating. It showcases films of various genres from around the world, each one competing for the Tokyo Grand Prix, awarded for best film. 2007's line-up featured screenings from up-and-coming Chinese directors, as well as the international set, and it's anyone's guess what will be featured in years to come. Be warned – non-English language films are subtitled in Japanese only.

Late October – early November
Chiba-ken
Map 2 C2

Tokyo Motor Show
www.tokyo-motorshow.com

The motor show is a massive biennial event held in Makuhari Messe that is as popular for the race queens as it is the cars. Given the stunning array of vehicles on display it is no surprise that it gets incredibly crowded – 1,425,800 people visited the show in 2007.

Early December
Various Locations

FIFA Club World Cup
www.fifa.com/clubworldcup

The Yokohama International Stadium and the Tokyo National Stadium have hosted matches over the past four years between the champions of the various continental tournaments. These matches are popular as they give fans a chance to see teams such as AC Milan, Boca Juniors and Liverpool in action.

Festivals around Tokyo

Our mission is to help you succeed overseas by providing you with a first-stop website to share stories, network globally, develop personally and find the best resources!

Visit Now: www.ExpatWomen.com

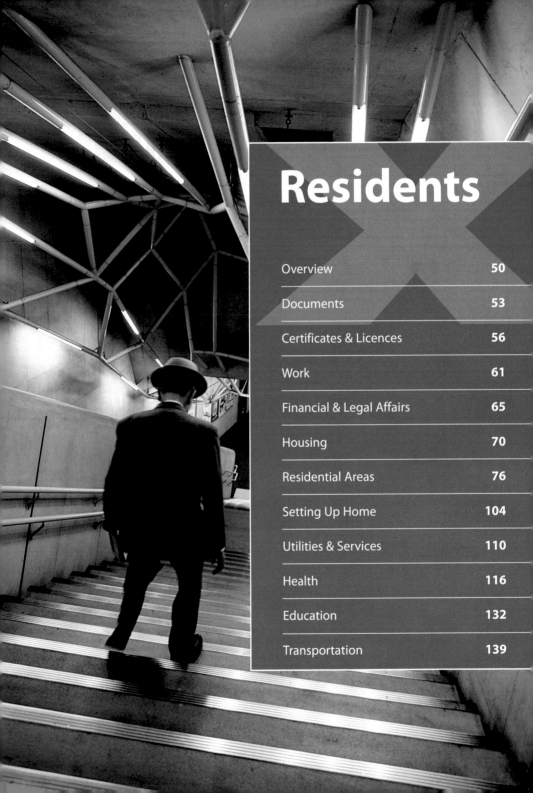

Residents

Residents

Overview

Each day, Tokyo wages within itself a battle between east and west, and between tradition and modernity. This identity crisis, these growing pains, are a large part of what makes this city so appealing to the spectrum of people who call it home. Tokyo lives up to its reputation as a 24 hour city that only takes a break three times a year – around New Year (p.42), Golden Week (p.44) and *Obon* (p.46) – before it resumes its frenzied ebb and flow.

The city is home to most of Japan's biggest companies and foreign business people often serve short stints here. English teaching is big business and many westerners are employed as language instructors.

Tokyo is said to be expensive, but the city has plenty of places to visit (p.145) eat (p.324) and shop (p.272) on the cheap. There are loads of free sights, including shrines, temples and museums, as well as the observatory from the 45th floor of the Tokyo Metropolitan Government Building (*Tochō*) in Shinjuku. When shopping, keep a lookout for ¥100 stores, which sell products (and even groceries) for a fraction of what you'd pay in regular shops. Inexpensive restaurants and budget business and capsule hotels abound. Even in the ritziest districts, like Ginza (p.153) and Omotesandō (p.88), you'll find bars where beer rings in at around the same as you'd pay in a convenience store. One thing is for sure though, living in Tokyo means you'll never have to pay for tissues again, as they are handed out on street corners throughout the city. But like the saying goes, 'life is what you make it', and life in Tokyo can be just as cosmopolitan and fast-paced, or as calm and relaxing, as you would like it to be.

Online Communities

There are numerous expat-focused websites offering advice and advertising services especially for expatriates. See p.41 for a list. And check out www.explorerpublishing.com, where you can join an online community for your city, share tips, get updates, ask questions and make friends.

Considering The City

Many people arrive in Tokyo thinking they know what's in store: robotic office workers and foreign English teachers, quirky techno gadgets and a gazillion vending machines that hawk everything and anything. But there is so much more to this evolving, international city than quirky stereotypes. It is one of the most westernised cities in Asia, offering a cosmopolitan lifestyle on a par with (and possibly far exceeding) that of many other great capitals. Tokyo is made up of 23 wards (*ku*), 26 cities (*shi*), five towns and eight villages.

Jobs exist in nearly every sector, from banking and IT to arts and entertainment. English teaching is still an option – but with the Enron-style downfall of Nova (a language school chain that employed 4,000 foreign instructors), the demand for language teachers with little training, experience or Japanese language ability has lessened. Finding work outside the classroom often requires an appropriate work visa. In other words, the toughest step is getting your foot in the Japanese door. Once you've got one in, there are a host of job-hunting resources, including English websites like Gaijinpot.com (www.gaijinpot.com) and Daijob.com (www.daijob.com), as well as temp agencies and recruitment firms.

Tattoos Mean Trouble
Whereas body ink and sunglasses were once an immediate giveaway that the wearer was mixed up in organised crime, today they signify little more than an attempt to look cool. That said, some public baths won't accept people with tattoos (see Onsen on p.264 for more).

The cost of living is not as high as it is often portrayed. Yes, there are probably a few ¥10,000 melons on offer at your neighbourhood grocery store, but it still only costs ¥160 to catch the metro across town. For expats, the city currently ranks fourth in the list of the world's most expensive cities, according to *Mercer Worldwide Cost of Living Survey 2007*, but this is all relative to salary and expat packages, and residents of the city enjoy one of the highest standards of living in the world.

Before You Arrive

So you've decided to give Tokyo a go. There are a few things you can do to ease into your new life in Japan before you even get on the plane.

Ward Offices

To find your local ward (ku) office, visit the Tokyo Metropolitan Government's website: www.metro.tokyo.jp. All ward offices have an English language guide to living in each ward, which is available for free. This is a useful thing to pick up when you first arrive as it lists everything from facilities to rubbish disposal.

- **Visa:** visit the Ministry of Foreign Affairs website (www.mofa.go.jp), which provides answers to most questions. To check the status of a visa application, call 03 5501 8431 on weekdays between 10:00 to 12:00 and 14:00 to 16:00 (Tokyo time). If you plan to arrive on a tourist visa and hope to find sponsorship and change your status of residence to allow you to work, bring all the documents you may need, including your university degree (not a copy).
- **Passport:** check it won't be expiring anytime soon and has plenty of blank pages.
- **Pets:** pets must be quarantined before entering Japan, during which time the owner is responsible for all food and care. See www.maff-aqs.go.jp for details. Also note that many landlords refuse tenants with animals.
- **International driving licence:** apply for one in your home country before you leave. It allows you to drive for up to one year without having to apply for a Japanese one (p.56).
- **Medicine:** stock up on over-the-counter drugs and prescriptions (including items such as stronger fluoride toothpaste and birth control pills), as these may be hard to find.
- **Electronics:** Tokyo uses NTSC, 100 volts and 50hz, so leave behind anything that is 240 volts or PAL, or buy adaptors.
- **Credit card:** sign up for a card abroad, if only for emergency use, as Japanese banks are notoriously picky about who they lend to.
- **Bank account:** there's no need to close bank accounts back home. In fact, keeping them open makes it easier to receive and remit money.
- **Change of address:** notify all relevant financial institutions, tax authorities, and the postal service of your new address.
- **Phone:** sign up for a voice-over-internet (VOIP) service before you leave, bring the modem and plug it into your internet connection once in Tokyo for international calls on the cheap.
- **Dress appropriately:** be prepared for hot and humid summers, crisp, sunny autumns and springs, chilly, dry winters, and 40 days of rain in June and July.
- **Travel insurance:** make sure to get it before you set off for Tokyo.
- **Money:** bring local currency. Plastic hasn't gone mainstream yet, and you'll need to be able to at least get into the city, and ATMs do not operate 24 hours (see Money on p.38).

When You Arrive

The first thing to avoid on arrival is getting a taxi from the airport. Narita is over an hour from the city centre, and the fare runs to about ¥30,000. Instead, hop on an orange Limousine Bus or grab a seat on either the Japan Rail (JR) or Keisei express trains into town. See Getting Around on p.31.

If you still need to sort out your visa, gather all necessary documents and head down to the Tokyo Regional Immigration Bureau in Shinagawa (p.53). Get there early, and be prepared to spend several hours waiting for your number to be called – resist the urge to start throwing things when all staff break for lunch for an hour, despite a room full of waiting foreigners.

If you are fortunate enough to have already secured permission to work in Japan, the first step to getting settled in is registering with your local ward or city office (www.metro.tokyo.jp). This is where to apply for an alien registration card (*gaikokujin torokushō*), also called a *gaijin* card. The Tokyo Metropolitan Government Building also has English literature about everything from local parks to how to divide up your rubbish (2-8-1 Nishi-Shinjuku, Shinjuku-ku, 03 5321 1111). It's also worth letting your embassy know you're in town (p.19).

Inkan

Inkan (or *hanko*) are name stamps used in place of, or as well as, signatures on official documents. *Inkan* are given more weight than just a signature and although foreigners are not required to have one, getting one will speed up the processing of bank and other official documents. They can be purchased at stationery and speciality shops, and most will be the *katakana* form of your last name. Your stamp can be officially registered at your local ward. Once used for official business, an *inkan* must be used from then on in place of a signature.

Once you've found somewhere to live (p.78), you may need somewhere to sit, eat and sleep (see Setting Up Home on p.104). For day-to-day items, it's worth checking out your local *hyaku-en* (¥100 store), see p.300. For second-hand goods, check out the classifieds in weekly magazines like *Metropolis* (www.metropolis.co.jp) or see p.297. Expats moving on elsewhere often hold 'Sayonara Sales' (p.309) where you'll find furniture and appliances for a fraction of their value.

The next step is getting a mobile phone and opening a bank account. There are a few mobile phone service providers to choose from (see p.112 for where to go). Knowing where to open a bank account can be difficult. Shinsei Bank (www.shinseibank.com) is one of the most foreigner-friendly and progressive banks in Japan. They offer online banking, as well as a 24 hour, toll-free English help line. For other popular banking choices, see p.65.

If you want to get a car, be prepared to pay exorbitant parking fees, high tolls and congested traffic. Many people forego cars and opt for automatic scooters, which start at 50cc but also come in 90cc, 125cc and 250cc models. Besides, Tokyo's efficient train and bus network means most residents get by perfectly well on their own two legs. If it's all too overwhelming or stressful, call the Tokyo English Life Line (03 5774 0992), which offers free and anonymous help and counselling daily between 09:00 and 23:00. Groups such as the Tokyo Women's Group (03 4588 0691) and Welcome Furoshiki (03 5472 7074) run orientation programmes to help you settle in to your new home. See Support Groups on p.131 for more.

When You Leave

- The Japanese equivalent of a garage sale, the sayonara sale is a great way of getting rid of unwanted goods.
- Decide what you'll be shipping and what you'll be carrying. Find out the baggage limitations well before your departure date. Take the rest to the post office in boxes, or call a shipping company for a free estimate. If you plan early, opt for surface shipping and you can save money.
- For the things you won't be selling, shipping or carrying, call one of the city's many private rubbish removal companies (p.104). Tell them how much you need to dispose of and they'll bring a truck, load it up and take it away – just make sure to agree on a price beforehand.
- Security deposit: Japanese landlords are notorious for trying to keep deposit money. Be sure to ask for it back, and try not to be surprised by unannounced deductions.
- Taxes are computed in June. If you leave before then, you are legally required to appoint someone to pay on your behalf.

Another Man's Treasure

Getting rid of your unwanted worldly possessions can be expensive and exhausting. Whereas charities in many countries are happy to accept donations of undamaged clothes and other items, in Japan it's a different story. While there are certainly people who could use warm clothes and food, a lack of efficient distribution channels makes it difficult to give to those in need. Still, be persistent and try The Salvation Army (03 3237 0881), the Franciscan Chapel Center (03 3401 2141) or even a vintage clothing shop (see p.298).

Shiodome terrace views

Documents

Bureaucracy in Japan is confusing, inconvenient, inefficient and slow – as most tend to be. Thankfully though the bureaucrats tend to be polite, helpful and understanding. There are special windows for foreigners at ward offices (*kuyakusho*) and city halls (*shiyakusho*), where you will need to go to register as a resident alien. To apply for a visa, visa extension or re-entry permit, you will need to go to the Tokyo Regional Immigration Bureau in Shinagawa (03 5796 7112). To avoid lengthy waits or being sent back to any counter, bring all the relevant documents, fill in every form thoroughly and get a number as soon as the booths open.

Say Cheese

Since 20 November, 2007, controversial new legislation requires the majority of non-citizens (exceptions include diplomats and those under 16) entering the country to be photographed and fingerprinted. Though aimed at combating terrorism, critics of the policy say xenophobia may be in play, pointing out that the only terrorists Japan has experienced to date have been homegrown.

Entry Visa

If you come from one of the 62 countries and regions that have a visa waiver agreement with Japan (see left), you can apply for short-term landing permission on arrival, which will allow you to stay for 14 days (countries such as Brunei) up to six months (countries such as Austria, Germany, Ireland, Lichtenstein, Mexico, Switzerland and the United Kingdom). Those from countries that do not have a visa exemption agreement with Japan are eligible to stay in the country for up to 90 days and will need to contact a Japanese embassy or consulate to apply for a visit visa before travelling.

If you arrive with your visa already sorted out, entering the country should be relatively quick and painless. It is difficult to arrive as a tourist and then try to change a visa. This requires a sponsor (such as an employer) and lots of paperwork. If the immigration date stamped in your passport is about to expire, you will need to leave and re-enter the country to renew it.

There are no required health tests, but following the SARS scare, a non-invasive thermal body scanner was put into use at Narita Airport. There is also an office where you can report any worrying symptoms that started while travelling.

Residence Visa

If you wish to work and reside in Japan, you will need an appropriate visa (see overleaf). Those with temporary visitor, transit or general visas are not permitted to work (p.61). For a list of immigration offices and to download application forms, see The Ministry of Justice website (www.immi-moj.go.jp). The Tokyo Regional Immigration Bureau Office (5-5-30 Konan, Minato-ku) also has an information centre, open Monday to Friday from 09:00 to 12:00 and 13:00 to 16:00, as does the Shinjuku Foreign Resident Information Center (03 3209 6177).

Come On In

Countries with a visa exemption agreement with Japan include: The EU, Australia, Canada, Chile, Hong Kong (BNO, SAR passport), Israel, Lesotho, Macau (SAR passport), Mauritius, Mexico, New Zealand, Norway, Republic of Korea, Singapore, Switzerland, Taiwan, USA and UK. For the full list of countries and further information, visit the Ministry of Justice website at www.immi-moj.go.jp.

Essential Documents

Passport: you will need to have it handy, but are not required to carry it at all times.

Gaijin Card: your certificate of alien registration proves you're in Japan legally, and must be carried at all times.

Driving Licence: international licences expire after one year, after which time you'll need to switch over to a Japanese one.

University Degree: to get a work visa, you will need to prove you have significant work experience (usually 10 years) or a four-year degree. A photocopy of the diploma may not be accepted, so make sure to bring the original.

Bank book: if you have a Japanese bank account, this book is a record of all transactions. It may be required as proof of salary to a potential landlord.

Tax report: keep your end-of-year tax and earnings statement – you'll need it if you apply for a visa extension.

Profit and loss reports (or for new businesses, a detailed business plan): these are required to self-sponsor a visa.

Inkan/hanko: The personalised ink stamp is still preferable to a signature for official documents.

To make life easy, you can contact an English-speaking visa consultant (see table below) who can assist with immigration and visa issues, establishing permanent residency, starting a business, as well as other legal and administrative processes.

Visa Consultants

Ishizaka Immigration Lawyer's Office	Shinjuku-ku	www.ishizakaoffice.com	03 5269 3977
Niitsu Legal Visa Office	Hirō	www.niitsu-law.jp	03 3443 5112
Kazumi Nakayama Administrative Scrivener Office	Takadanobaba	n_kazumi77@yahoo.co.jp	03 5330 0651
Ando Administrative Office	Kasai	www12.ocn.ne.jp/~office41	03 5658 2276
Azuma Legal and Business Support Center	Tsukiji	www.azuma-law.com	03 6226 5105

Permanent Residency & Citizenship

Those in Japan for the long haul may choose to pursue permanent residency or even citizenship. The most common way to become a permanent resident is to apply after five years of marriage to a Japanese citizen. Alternatively, you can apply after a period of five to 10 years of residence and stable employment. The main benefits of permanent residency include not having to renew your visa every one to three years and being able to borrow money more readily.

Citizenship is another story. It is considerably more difficult to become a citizen (see also Blogging It left). There is no dual nationality system, and family checks, translation of documents, and the examination of your home, your suitability to become a Japanese citizen and other intrusive checks, as well as the lengthy decision-making process by the Japanese authorities, are not for the fainthearted.

Blogging It
Debito Arudo (former US citizen David Aldwinckle) has a good blog on becoming a citizen with useful insights, tips and anecdotes (www.debito.org).

Spouse & Dependent Visas

If you're working in Japan, you can sponsor your spouse and children for a visa. You or your employer will need to apply for Certificates of Eligibility for the family. For this you will need the application form (downloadable from The Ministry of Justice website at www.immi-moj.go.jp), marriage certificate, birth certificates (for each child), a letter of employment from your company and a 4cm x 3cm photo of each applicant. If you are in Japan, and wish to bring family into the country, you must also submit tax certificates from your city or ward office.

If you have a baby in Japan, you must apply for dependent status within 30 days, for which you will need a birth certificate (see Maternity on p.122 for more information). There is no age limit for dependents, though the older they are, the more likely it is that you will need to certify that the child is still your dependent. Dependents are able to work part-time (up to 28 hours per week), but must first seek special permission at the immigration office. To sponsor retired parents and same-sex partners, you need to apply for a special visa, as the law currently does not classify them as dependents.

Marrying A Japanese Citizen

Marriage to a Japanese citizen makes you eligible for a spousal visa. If already in Japan, you will need to apply for a Change of Status at immigration. Fill out the application form and take your original passport and copies, alien card, two different photos of you and your spouse together, an eight-section questionnaire, your spouse's Family Register (*koseki tōhon*) and certificate of residence (*jyūminhyō*) to the immigration office. You will need to prove financial stability (this can be done by submitting tax returns – both *jyūminzei kazei shōmei* and *jyūminzei nōzei shōmei*) and a letter of employment from an employer (either yours or your spouse's). You can also send a proxy (often a Japanese in-law) to immigration to apply on your behalf.

Self-Sponsoring

To apply for a Certificate of Eligibility as an investor or manager (self-sponsor), you will need to first register your company and employ more than two people (who must be either Japanese, the spouse of a Japanese or a permanent resident). If the company is young and no profit and loss report is available, a detailed business plan with projections for the next year may be substituted.

Student Visas

To apply for a student visa, you may need to include a copy of the acceptance letter from the university you intend on studying at, as well as proof that you can pay for tuition, along with your application. Proof of an adequate level of Japanese language may also be required. Some universities may apply for a visa on your behalf. Student visa holders are not usually permitted to work.

Working Holidays ◄

Japan has working holiday agreements with Australia, Canada, Denmark, France, Germany, Ireland, New Zealand, the Republic of Korea and the United Kingdom. Country-specific details are available on the website of the Ministry of Foreign Affairs (www.mofa. go.jp). For further information or to answer any questions, The Japan Association for Working Holiday Makers has a very good website, visit www.jawhm.or.jp.

Work Visa

Only four visas allow the holder to be employed: special, diplomatic, official and working. Visas are valid for six months, one year or three years, after which the holder must apply for an extension. If you plan to leave the country and come back, you will need to purchase a re-entry permit (one time ¥3,000 or multiple ¥6,000).

To apply for a work visa, you must first apply for a certificate of eligibility (*zairyū shikaku nintei shōmeisho*), a process usually handled by your employer before you arrive. There are 14 types of work visas: professor, artist, religious activities, journalist, investor/ business manager, legal/accounting services, medical services, researcher, instructor, engineer, specialist in humanities/international services, intracompany transferee, skilled labourer and entertainer. If you switch fields, you may need to apply for a Change of Status.

To apply, you will need your CV, university degree (original, not a copy) and employment agreement (this must specify position, salary, job description and length of contract). The employer will need to supply an official registration form (*tōkibo tōhon*), a recent profit and loss report (*son-eki keisansho*) and company literature. Fill out the application form, attach a photograph (4cm x 3cm), and include a return envelope with ¥430 postage affixed and addressed to your employer. There is no application fee. The process takes one to three months.

Normally, the employer will forward the certificate of eligibility on to the employee, who can then apply for a work visa at a Japanese embassy or consulate overseas. If the applicant is in Japan, and their period of temporary landing permission (*zairyū kikan*) has not passed, they can apply for a Change of Status (*zairyū shikaku no henkō*) at the immigration bureau. If the Certificate of Eligibility does not arrive before the visit visa date stamped in your passport expires, you will need to leave and re-enter Japan. For a list of immigration offices and to download application forms, see the Ministry of Justice website (www.immi-moj.go.jp). For more information on immigration see p.54, and for visa consultants, see table opposite.

ID Card

Upon receiving a visa, all foreigners must register with their local municipal office and apply for a Certificate of Alien Registration (*gaikokujin torokushō*). This ID card, issued by the Ministry of Justice, lists your name, nationality, birthday, address, occupation and visa status and must be carried at all times. You are not legally required to show it to anyone other than government or law enforcement personnel, though you may be asked to show it in hotels, video rental shops, health clubs, and any other business that requires a photo ID. To replace, renew or update your *gaijin* card, visit your local ward (see Ward Offices on p.88), city office or police station.

Driving Licence

Other options **Transportation** p.139

Thanks to the efficient, cheap and convenient public transport network, the motivation to drive is minimal. Many Japanese wait until after university or until they get married to get a driving licence, despite the legal minimum age being 18, as driving schools are notoriously pricey, charging between ¥250,000 and ¥500,000 for lessons.

For foreigners, it's best to get an international driving licence (IDL) before arriving in Japan or else to transfer to a Japanese licence (a process called *gaimen kirikae*). If you use an IDL, you won't be covered by Japanese insurance and the licence is only valid for one year. If you decide to get a Japanese licence, you may or may not have to take a road test, depending on what country your licence is from.

If you have not got a licence, the other option is to buckle up and take the test (see Transportation on p.139). JapanDriversLicense.com offers consultation, study material for the written tests, and can arrange practice times and instruction. Visit their website at www.japandriverslicense.com. For licensing centres, see the table below.

Transferring A Foreign Licence

To transfer to a Japanese licence, your licence must be at least three months old. To apply, bring an official Japanese translation of the licence from the Japan Automobile Federation (www.jaf.or.jp), a valid passport, alien registration card, the foreign driver's licence, two 3cm x 2.4cm photos, as well as the relevant application form, to one of three testing and issuing centres (see table). You are also required to take an eye test on site. The transfer fee is around ¥4,000.

JapanDriversLicense.com (03 5575 6321) can help you prepare the paperwork and acquire a licence at one of the Licensing Centres (see table below). They can also help you to prepare for the road test preparation and provide translators for written exams. If the foreign licence was issued by one of the 22 countries (see Compatible Licences above) with reciprocal agreements with Japan, you are exempt from the road test and need only pass a short, straightforward exam. If your licence is from the US or another country not on the list, you will need to schedule a driving test. You can do the test in a manual or automatic car. If you do the test in an automatic, your licence will not be valid for a manual car.

Licensing Centres	
Fuchu	042 334 6000
Koto-ku	03 3699 1151
Samezu	03 3474 1374

Driving licences must be renewed every three years. If you have no points on your licence (p.143), go to the relevant police station with your licence and alien registration card to renew it. To check which police station you should go to, call your local licensing centre. If you have points on your licence, you'll have to renew it at one of the licensing centres.

Driving School

Before getting a learner's permit that allows you to practise on the open road (accompanied by someone with three years of Japan driving experience), you will need to pass an eye test and undergo psychological screening, spend 10 hours in a classroom, 12 hours driving on a course and pass a written exam. This is followed by 14 theory classes, 20 driving sessions and a final written test.

Koyama Driving School (www.koyama.co.jp) is a good option for foreigners as it offers full English support. It has four schools in Greater Tokyo, see the Driving Schools table opposite for contact details.

Going It Alone

To avoid going through a driving school, you can try and go it alone. Submit an application for a learner's permit to a licensing centre (see table left) and take both an eye exam and a 50 question, true or false test. If all is good, you will take two road tests at the test centre. If you pass these, you will need to sit a 90 question, true or false exam, followed (if you pass) by yet another driving test. Clear that hurdle, and all that's left is a mandatory class about what to do in emergencies. If you fail, keep practising (perhaps with a private instructor), and take the test again when you're ready.

Motorcycle Licence

Scooters are incredibly popular as they are cheap and a quick and convenient way to get around. You can drive a 49cc bike (*gentsuki*) on a moped licence (available from age 16) or a standard driving licence (Japanese or IDL). For small (50-124cc), mid-size (125-400cc) and large bikes, you need a special licence. If you go through a driving school, expect to pay at least ¥100,000. A valid, foreign-issued licence is transferable (see Transferring A Foreign Licence, left).

Driving Schools			
Akitsu	3-15-18 Akitsu-chō, Higashi-Murayama-shi	Western Tokyo	042 396 7070
Futako-Tamagawa	3-43-1 Tamagawa	Setagaya-ku	03 5716 5888
Shakujii	1-4-4 Yahara	Nerima-ku	03 3996 0671
Tsunashima	2-48-13 Ōsone, Kōhoku-ku	Yokohama	045 531 6461

Who Am I?
If your child has dual nationality they can keep two passports up until age 20, by which time they must decide their nationality. However, poor communication between countries means many dual citizens keep both passports and the authorities in the respective countries will be none the wiser.

Birth Certificate & Registration

When your baby is born, you'll need to inform your local city or ward office within 14 days. If you are away from your residence, you can submit the notification form at the city office of the birthplace. The application should also include the hospital birth certificate (signed by the doctor and including the baby's full name), the Mother and Child Health Handbook (*boshi kenkō techō*) that you will have received when registering the pregnancy (p.122) and your National Health Insurance certificate (if applicable). If you have a personal seal (*inkan*), bring that as well. Either parent can register the child, or an agent can do it on your behalf. Ask for additional copies of the registration certificate, as you will need them for immigration procedures.

You will also have to notify your local public health centre (*hokenjo*). Inside your Mother and Child Health Handbook you will find a birth report, which needs to be filled out and given to the centre. Once received, they will send you information about a home-visit check-up, free health check-ups and a vaccination schedule.

The next step, if you are single or

Dressed up for the 'Shichi-Go-San' Festival

neither parent is Japanese, is to apply for a dependency visa (p.54) within 30 days of the birth. For more information, contact the Tokyo Regional Immigration Bureau's Civil Affairs Department, Nationality Section on 03 3214 6231. This process requires a passport. Embassy policies vary for passport applications but the process will usually take three to four weeks.

> **Family Register**
> The Family Register (*koseki*) is a precious book. Every family has one and it records everything from a citizen's registered address and family genealogy to each birth, death, marriage, divorce and adoption.

Baby Passports

Christening
Getting your child christened is fairly straightforward and there are a number of churches to choose from (see p.17).

Passport applications generally require the physical presence of the child and both parents (or a notarised consent from the non-appearing parent), both parents' passports, the original proof of the child's birth from the ward or city office (see p.88), an original marriage certificate (if applicable), proof of termination of all prior marriages (if applicable), two identical photos of the child, the application fee – and sometimes evidence of the couple's physical presence together at conception.

Adoption

Adopting a child in Japan is not an easy process for foreign parents (or when one of the parents is non-Japanese). It is best to be prepared for a few hurdles along the way, and to try to be patient with the process. If you plan to adopt, contact The Child Guidance Center (03 3208 1121) or any of the adoption agencies based here.

Once you have found a child you wish to adopt, you will have to go through the family court. The process will take a minimum of nine months and will cost you upwards of ¥2 million, depending on the agency you choose. Visit www.myadoptionlinks.com/japan for a comprehensive guide, including agency contact information. See also Adoption under Financial & Legal Affairs on p.65.

Marriage Certificate & Registration

Christmas Cake
There is a lot of pressure on Japanese women to get married before 30. Unmarried ladies over 25 are often known as 'Christmas Cake,' – referring of course to how hard it is to sell a christmas cake after 25 December.

Getting married can be as simple as going to your local ward office and signing the necessary papers, or as extravagant as hosting a traditional Shinto wedding at a shrine. Other popular options include Western-style, Buddhist, Christian and non-religious ceremonies. A foreign couple can also get married in Japan, or choose to just do the paperwork in Japan and wait and have the ceremony back home. Popular venues include shrines such as Sensōji (p.178), which will cost around ¥70,000, Kanda Myōjin (www.kandamyoujin.or.jp) and Meiji Jingū (p.178).

The Paperwork

The procedure for both foreign and mixed foreign-Japanese weddings is similar. To file a marriage registration, go to the local city office of your permanent address or of your Japanese partner's address. A foreigner will need to present their passport and a Certificate of No Impediment from their embassy (cost

> **Shotgun Weddings**
> Wedding halls in the city have recently started to cater to shotgun weddings – where the bride to be unexpectedly grows a baby bump. The term for these, *omedetakon*, combines the words for 'celebratory occasion' (*omedeta*) and marriage (*kekkon*). A more colloquial term, *dekichatta kekkon*, is a euphemism for a wedding after 'something's been done.'

Traditional marriage ceremonies

varies by country), an alien registration card and personal seal (*inkan*) if they have one, otherwise a signature will suffice. A Japanese person should supply a copy of their Family Register (*koseki tōhon*) and their *inkan*. In both cases the marriage notification form should be signed (in advance) by two witnesses over the age of 20. Once these documents are approved you are officially married. Once married, a Japanese citizen can open their Family Register to a foreigner and apply for a spouse visa (p.54). A Japanese woman can change her name and record it in her Family Register, but this must be done within the first six months of marriage, otherwise it will go through the courts and the request may be denied.

> **Fake Priests**
> It's considered a novelty to have a foreign priest perform the wedding ceremony in fake chapels. Some Westerners take full advantage by moonlighting as men of God on weekends, pocketing a good chunk of change in the process.

Death Certificate & Registration

The death of a family member or a friend in Japan means you will need to follow local protocol. This means paperwork, and lots of it. The first step is to notify the authorities, which can be done by calling 110. You should also immediately contact the embassy of the deceased, which can assist with the process – starting with locating and notifying the next of kin.

Registering A Death

If the death occurred in a hospital, a local death certificate will be prepared by the doctor and the family, friend or person in attendance. In all other cases, it will be issued by the authorities. If the cause of death is unknown, an additional report from either the doctor or the medical examiner's office may be required.

Once the paperwork is in order, either the next of kin or an authorised agent (usually an undertaker) must present it to the city or ward office. If everything is in order, they will issue a Notification of Death and permission for cremation or burial. There is a nominal fee of around ¥350, and the process must be carried out within seven days of the death. The alien registration card of the deceased must be returned to the city or ward office within 14 days, so it is best to bring it at the same time as the death certificate, or give it to the undertaker to hand over.

The embassy of the deceased should be notified immediately and can assist with locating and notifying the next of kin, provide guidance, and assist with arrangements. When you call, try to have as much information as possible, including the deceased's full name, date and place of birth, passport number, details about the time and cause of death, the location of the death and the location of the remains.

Keep Your Chopsticks To Yourself

If you've ever tried to pass food to someone chopsticks to chopsticks, you've made a serious cultural taboo. Tradition dictates that the only time two pairs can be used to hold one item is during cremation rituals, when the bones are passed between grieving relatives and placed in an urn.

Investigation & Autopsy

By law, cremation or embalming cannot take place within 24 hours of death. If police determine foul play may be in order, they may request that an investigation or autopsy be carried out.

Returning The Deceased To Country Of Origin

Local companies offering mortuary services, and the repatriation of remains, include Shinjuku's Sanyu Life (03 3341 6664, www.sanyu-life.co.jp), the nationwide Air Mortuary Service (0120 06 5191), and Saitama's International Mortuary Services Japan (048 261 3302). The embassy of the deceased can provide additional options, and may be able to facilitate arrangements. Cremation before repatriation costs around ¥500,000 and embalming costs about ¥1.5 million.

Business Etiquette

The complicated world of Japanese business etiquette is a minefield of potential dangers even for natives. Business Japanese is very different from everyday use, and those new to the working world often need coaching from seniors. Other strict rules relating to hierarchy and form such as how deep to bow, for how long, and to whom are just the icing on the cake. Happily, the foreign worker does not have to worry about these too much, as politeness goes a long way and mastering every rule of Japanese etiquette is not expected of gaijin.

Working In Tokyo

With little more than 1% of Japan's population composed of immigrants, the country's foreign workers are few in number, but it doesn't feel that way in Tokyo. There's a thriving international community and a superb standard of living for foreign workers. Pay levels are comparable to western countries, but taxes are much lower, particularly compared to Europe, and the cost of living is lower than you might think if you're prepared to adapt a little (it's at least comparable to that of London and New York). The largest immigrant groups are from South Korea and China, but the biggest expat communities are the major English-speaking nations: the USA, UK, Canada and Australia. Expats can be broadly divided into three categories: English teachers, business people and a miscellaneous group including IT specialists, recruitment consultants, journalists, teachers and language assistants.

The Anglophone dominance of these sectors isn't a coincidence, with English universally accepted as the second business language. Few Japanese speak it fluently, but nearly all can understand at least a bit. A native English speaker is sure to find work but any non-natives with poor English are likely to struggle. And then there's Japanese. Many local firms won't look at foreigners who don't have near-fluent Japanese and many recruitment agencies will only take on bilingual job seekers. Japan is a major trading nation so focusing on firms with an international outlook is a good idea. Also, as the years go by and with a rapidly falling population, there's a growing shortage of nationals working on home soil. Japan is reluctant to see immigration as the answer, but for the foreigners who do come to work in Japan, the good news is that there are plenty of jobs to be had.

Business Culture

Whatever job you do, expect to work hard. Japan is famous for its strong work ethic and long hours and diligent effort is expected of every employee. Other aspects of the Japanese working world, such as 'jobs-for-life', are gradually eroding. While there used to be a stigma attached to changing jobs, it is less and less the case, with recruitment firms and headhunters proliferating, and the concept of the mid-career change of direction becoming almost fashionable. In any event, it is accepted that foreign workers inevitably come and go.

Benefits For Workers

If you find work with a Japanese firm, the job will most likely come with a package of standard benefits, including entitlement to Japanese public health services. This is a worthwhile perk, as it means the government will cover about 70% of medical costs (see Health on p.116).

You will also have to pay into the Japanese public pension system but partial refunds of pension contributions are available to foreigners leaving Japan and you may (depending on your home country), be able to transfer your contributions to your domestic public pension – see the Social Insurance Agency website (www.sia. go.jp) or p.67 for more. Most big Japanese firms will also have a staff perks such as large biannual bonuses, private health cover, a transport allowance or company car, weekend breaks and gym membership.

Networking

Once you are established in the Japanese working world there is a wealth of networking opportunities to enhance your contact book and lay the foundations for that next career move. Organisations exist to bring people together by nationality, profession and gender, including the Entrepreneur Association of Tokyo (www.ea-tokyo.com), Foreign Executive Women in Japan (www.fewjapan.com) and the Foreign

Correspondents' Club of Japan (www.fccj.or.jp). Other good bets include groups aimed at expats of different countries, of which the Tokyo American Club (p.242) is the most prominent. See table below or Social Groups in the Activities section (p.242) for more.

Business Councils & Groups

American Chamber of Commerce	www.accj.or.jp
Australian & New Zealand Chamber of Commerce	www.anzccj.jp
British Chamber of Commerce	www.bccjapan.com
Canadian Chamber of Commerce	www.cccj.or.jp
French Chamber of Commerce & Industry	www.ccifj.or.jp
German Chamber of Commerce	www.japan.ahk.de
Japan Business Federation	www.keidanren.or.jp
Japan Chamber of Commerce & Industry	www.jcci.or.jp
Tokyo Chamber of Commerce & Industry	www.tokyo-cci.or.jp
Foreign Women Lawyers' Association	www.fwla.net

Working Hours

Standard working hours in Japan are 09:00 to 17:00, Monday to Friday, but this has little bearing on the hours people actually work. The salaryman is expected to show his dedication to the company by putting in very long hours and working until the last train at midnight, and even doing overnight stints is not uncommon. Japanese firms do pay overtime, but workers are likely to feel pressure not to claim every last hour. The law stipulates a minimum 10 days' annual leave, and many firms offer 15 to 20, but employees are expected not to take their full entitlement. Foreign workers are often exempt from these expectations. Outside the office sector, long hours are also the norm – shops generally open from 10:00 to 20:00. However, a generous 14 annual public holidays (p.10) somewhat makes up for this extreme work ethic.

Finding Work

Tokyo offers a wealth of job opportunities but strict visa requirements and the language barrier mean it isn't always easy to find work. Most foreigners who work in the city had a job to come to before leaving home. Turning up without a work visa and finding employment is tough, and working on a tourist visa is strictly forbidden.

Finding Work Before You Come

Finding work before you come is advisable. All jobs require a valid work visa, and getting one requires a job offer. If you can't get a job transfer, the best option is to scour ads for openings. Unfortunately, the employment sections of the country's major papers are in Japanese only and recruitment agencies invariably want people who are in situ and have a work visa already. Japan's two best-known English job-search websites (www.daijob.com and www.gaijinpot.com) are a good place to start, as is the English-language *Japan Times* website (www.japantimes.co.jp), and www.jobsinjapan.com. The American Chamber of Commerce Japan lists jobs (www.ecentral.jp) on its website, as does *Metropolis* magazine (http://jobfinder.metropolis.co.jp). See also Useful Websites on p.41. Opportunities vary according to sector. Finance, IT and education have the most jobs, followed by work as a teacher or a language assistant. See English Teachers to the right.

English Teachers

There is always a need for English teachers in Tokyo. Following the bankruptcy of the Nova school in autumn 2007, two of the biggest schools are Aeon (www.aeonet.com) and Gaba (www.gaba.co.jp). Both recruit in the US, UK, Canada, Australia and New Zealand. A degree in any discipline is usually the only qualification needed, and even if it's not your career, it can still be good fun and very rewarding. The JET Programme (www.jetprogramme.org) provides opportunities for language assistants in public schools.

Finding Work While You're Here

Few employers will bend the rules and employ someone without a visa, with the exception perhaps of some bars and clubs, who are always on the lookout for international staff – a good bet is the happening Roppongi area (p.156). On the downside, even if you do find work here, it's unlikely that your employer will sponsor an official visa.

Job hunters that have a visa and wish to change job are in a much stronger position. The procedure is the same as for finding work before you come (p.62), but employers will be far keener to meet you if you're in the country and legally available for work. Check out the *Japan Times* classifieds every Monday. Networking is also a good idea, so keep an eye out for any meetings and events in your industry sector. The Foreigners Employment Service Center in Roppongi (03 3588 8369, www.tfemploy.go.jp) can offer good general advice.

Recruitment Agencies

Recruitment agencies used to be few and far between due to the stigma associated with changing jobs. This has changed over the past decade or so, and Japan is gradually losing its fixation with jobs for life. If you are bilingual, there is now a wealth of agencies to choose from, with registration possible online. An interview will also usually be required. For the monolingual, try the English speaking recruitment agencies Daijob and Gaijinpot (www.daijob.com and www.gaijinpot.com). Finance and IT professionals are more likely to be headhunted. Big international job

Recruitment Agencies		
Adecco	03 5220 6765	www.adecco.co.jp
Korn/Ferry	03 3560 1400	www.kornferry.com
Michael Page	03 5733 7166	www.michaelpage.co.jp
Recruit Agent	0120 05 0454	www.r-agent.co.jp
Robert Walters	03 4570 1500	www.robertwalters.co.jp
The Specialized Group	03 4520 6800	www.specialized-group.com

agencies such as Robert Walters and Michael Page have offices in the city (see table), while local specialists can be found with a web search.

Voluntary & Charity Work

Opportunities for voluntary and charitable work are relatively limited for non-Japanese speakers. Websites for groups such as Foreign Executive Women in Japan (FEW), the only English-language directory of charitable and voluntary organisations in the city, are a good place to start (www.fewjapan.com). Options listed include everything from branches of the Guardian Angels and Amnesty International to environmental and social charities. Working for these organisations on a paid basis requires a valid work visa. English-speaking volunteers are always welcome with organisations such as the prominent Tokyo English Life Line (see Support Groups on p.131).

Working As A Freelancer Or Contractor

Read It Or Weep
Big firms that regularly employ foreigners will provide a contract in English and Japanese. Smaller companies may only provide one in Japanese. If you can't read Japanese, get a lawyer or a reliable bilingual friend to look it over before signing anything.

Many foreigners freelance in fields such as journalism, teaching and IT. But the usual catch applies: you need a valid work visa. There is no specific freelance work visa so many people freelance as a sideline to a regular job that provides the visa and a stable income. Another popular route is to get a regular job first, then quit and go freelance. You won't lose your work visa if you leave the company that first sponsored it; though you may need to show the immigration authorities that you have a source of income to support yourself so try to have some freelance contracts lined up.

Employment Contracts

Employment contracts operate in much the same way as any western country, but the offer letter can have its quirks. To the consternation of many westerners, offer letters are sometimes frustratingly vague on one key point: your salary. Many will only indicate a salary range, rather than a precise figure, and attempts to press your prospective employer on this can cause affront. Agree to take the job and the pay will be specified in the contract.

By law, all employers must provide a written contract spelling out standard terms and conditions including pay, working hours, holiday entitlement, overtime procedures and notice periods. One standard benefit is a commuting allowance. This is calculated in accordance with the cost of a monthly train ticket between an employee's home and the office. Most contracts will feature a probation period of three to six months and will need to be renewed annually. Japan attaches great prestige to permanent contracts, and those joining a company mid-career generally won't get one. Pay rises are another controversial aspect. Most Japanese firms award salary increases in line with age and length of service and attempts to haggle are unlikely to be productive. Maternity leave should pose no problem and legal entitlement is one year (p.123). To leave a company before the contract ends, give notice (in writing) as specified in your contract.

Labour Law

Employees in Japanese companies are covered by a variety of legal standards. The working week is legally described as eight hours a day, up to a maximum of 40 hours a week. However, employers must pay overtime for any extra hours worked, and must provide holidays to all employees who have been with the company for more than six months. Sick leave is not guaranteed and many Japanese firms expect employees to take sick leave out of their holiday entitlement. Maternity leave entitlement is up to one year. Commuting costs are also covered. If you become involved in a dispute with your employer, they must provide at least 30 days' notice of dismissal. If you need advice or assistance, there

Labour Lawyers		
Haraguchi International Law Office	03 5774 9434	www.haraguchi-law.com
Hayabusa Law	03 3595 7070	www.halaw.jp
Sakuma Law Office	03 3354 0561	www.skmlaw.jp
Satsuki Law Office	03 5261 8291	www.satsukilaw.com

are several options. Unions are common and are present in nearly all workplaces. They may be able to help you if you are a member or if you are prepared to become one. However, some may not allow contractors to join and the language barrier will be a problem if you don't speak Japanese. If you need legal advice, the Tokyo Bar Association (www.toben.or.jp) can provide advice in English at low cost, or for free if you can show you are facing financial hardship. The metropolitan government's Labor Consultation Center (03 5211 2346) also offers advice in English for limited periods in the afternoon. For general advice on employment matters, and an overview of Japanese labour laws, contact the Foreigners Employment Service Center in Roppongi (03 3588 8369, www.tfemploy.go.jp).

Changing Jobs

Changing jobs used to be stigmatised in Japan. The goal was to secure work with a good company and stay there until retirement, gradually inching your way up the corporate ladder. Such sentiments linger on, but changing jobs is now more socially acceptable, and the norm for foreigners. Moving companies is relatively easy. A company cannot ban you from working elsewhere and you can keep your visa – just make sure that your new employer is willing to renew it when it expires. If your former employer guaranteed your apartment, ask whether your new company will be prepared to take over the guarantee.

Company Closure

If the company you work for goes out of business, you have no legal guarantee of receiving overdue pay. However, all taxpayers are entitled to unemployment benefit (the amount and duration depends on how long you have been working). For details, contact the Tokyo Employment Service Center for Foreigners in Shinjuku (03 3204 8369, www.tfemploy.go.jp). Losing your job will not cost you your visa. For other sources of advice, see the labour law section (above).

Bank Accounts

Postal Savings Accounts

Japan Post, the official Japanese postal service, also provides banking and insurance services. ATMs are located in most post offices, as well as in free-standing kiosks and convenience stores. In most cases, you don't need a Certificate of Alien Registration card to open an account, just bring a passport and a contact address. Application forms are in Japanese but a separate guide in English will show you what to fill in where.

Domestic banks such as Bank of Tokyo-Mitsubishi UFJ, Sumitomo Mitsui Banking Corporation, and Mizuho Bank are the most visible, although some banking services are available from international banks such as Citibank and HSBC. Most banks offer services from basic accounts to foreign currency accounts and retirement schemes. Japan Post Bank (the banking section of the recently privatised postal service) also provide banking services that are popular and easily accessible via the JP-Bank ATMs in post offices. Japan is traditionally a cash-based society, but ATM cards are now standard, credit cards are becoming more common, and IC and e-cash cards are gaining popularity. Cheque-based transactions carry hefty fees of up to several thousand yen per transaction and are rare. Instead, most people use a standard account to send and receive electronic transfers for salary and bill payments. Most banks do not require a minimum balance to open a standard account, though there may be a monthly fee if the balance falls below a certain amount. You will need to bring your Certificate of Alien Registration card, and some banks may require additional identification such as a passport with visa, or *inkan* (p.151) stamp. ATM transactions often carry nominal fees for weekend or holiday transactions, or transactions made at an ATM of another bank. The main domestic banks offer online and telebanking, though these services are usually only offered in Japanese. Banking hours are Monday to Friday, 09:00 to 15:00. ATMs can be found at banks and also in supermarkets, shopping centres, department stores, and more recently in many convenience stores, and most operate round the clock. Unfortunately, foreign credit and debit cards can only be used at the international ATMs, mostly found in post offices and a few other locations, making it imperative to have a card issued from a Japanese bank. Banks are closed on national holidays and weekends, and virtually all banking is halted and ATMs are closed from 1 to 4 January for New Year.

Banking Comparison Table

Name	Phone	Web	Online Banking	Tele-Banking
Bank of Tokyo-Mitsubishi UFJ	03 3240 1111	www.bk.mufg.jp	✓	0120 11 0330
Citibank	03 5568 1653	www.citibank.co.jp	✓	0120 41 0956
HSBC	03 5203 3111	www.hsbc.co.jp	✓	0120 77 7268
Japan Post Bank	0570 04 6111	www.post.japanpost.jp	✗	No
Mizuho Bank	03 3596 1111	www.mizuhobank.co.jp	✓	03 3211 6324
Resona Bank	03 3287 2111	www.resona-gr.co.jp	✓	0120 24 3839
Shinsei Bank	03 5954 7530	www.shinseibank.com	✓	0120 45 6007
Sumitomo Mitsui Bank	03 3230 0840	www.smbc.co.jp	✓	03 5745 5051

Financial Planning

Keep It Close

Most people have domestic savings accounts and don't expect to earn interest on them. Some foreign banks offer limited off-shore banking.

Tokyo was rated as the fourth most expensive city in the world to live in for 2007, according to the *Mercer Cost of Living Survey*. Depending on your job and where you live, saving is not an impossible goal, but it does take some planning. Though Japanese households boast a savings ratio much higher than that of many other industrialised countries, interest rates can put a limit on how much that money can grow while in a bank account. Unlike the 5% interest rates in the US and 3% rates in Europe, Japan has maintained interest rates below 1% for investments and savings since 2003. Consulting an independent financial planner is the easiest way of gaining access to a broad range of investment options. Most recommend starting by keeping three to six month's monthly living expenses in savings; check out members of the Japan Association for Financial Planners (JAFP). Many banks offer financial planning, though they will most likely steer you towards their own products. Off-shore accounts and investing

Cost Of Living

Apple	¥98
Aspirin (24 tablets)	¥683
Bread (loaf)	¥138
Bus ticket	¥210
Cappucino	¥580
CD	¥2,250
Chocolate bar	¥157
Cigarettes (20)	¥320
Cinema ticket	¥1,500
DVD (new release)	¥3,500
Eggs (10)	¥138
Golf (18 holes)	¥19,250
House wine (glass)	¥630
Local bus	¥210
Local stamp	¥80
Milk (1L)	¥197
Orange juice (1L)	¥198
Postcard	¥157
Rice (2kg)	¥740
Salon haircut (man)	¥4,500
Salon haircut (woman)	¥6,500
Soda (1 can)	¥110
Strawberries (1 punnett)	¥698
Sugar (1kg)	¥198
Taxi fare (10km)	¥3,522
Toothpaste	¥254
Water (1.5L supermarket)	¥198

are not common, but foreign exchange investments and foreign currency accounts have gained popularity. It's best to maintain an active bank account in your home country, and a Japanese account is strongly recommended.

Pensions

Japan has a national pension scheme that was devised as a social safety net for residents aged 65 and older. It is mandatory for all residents aged 20 to 59, including foreigners. There are two types of pension: national and employee. The national pension scheme is meant to provide the most basic benefits, which can be collected under disability benefits, bereavement benefits, and those for seniors and the elderly.

Your employer may also have a pension scheme, which offers additional payments and benefits. If this is the case, you will still automatically be enrolled in the national scheme. Your monthly payments will be higher (deducted automatically from your salary), but you will receive more benefits in the long run. Private companies may provide pension plans, but in general foreign employees are not eligible.

If your employer does not provide you with a pension or you are self-employed, you must register for the national pension scheme independently at your ward office. You will receive a bill by post each month that you can pay at banks and post offices. As of 2007, the average national pension payment is set to rise 0.354% each year until 2016 due to pension reforms in 2004. Most expats do not stay in the country long enough to collect their benefits, which kick in at the age of 65 and after 25 years of payments, but you are eligible to receive a lump sum refund of your pension payments, which is variable depending on the length of time you've paid into the system. This is provided you no longer reside in Japan, have paid into the system for at least six months and did not receive any pension payments during your residency. Just submit a form to the pension agency by mail within two years of your departure and payments will be remitted to your bank account abroad.

Get Smart ◀
Countries such as the UK and US have pension agreements with Japan, allowing expats from those countries to switch their pension payments to the Japanese system for the duration of their stay. Check with your embassy and enquire about any pension or taxation agreements your home country may have with Japan; it may save you money in the long run.

Taxation

Residents are subject to two kinds of tax: national and local. National taxes comprise a mix of direct and indirect taxes, including personal income tax, consumption tax on goods and services (5%), alcohol, tobacco, and petrol, inheritance tax, gift tax on gifted property, vehicle weight tax, stamp duty, and customs duty on imported goods. Local taxes are a combination of a metropolitan tax for living in the Tokyo area and municipal taxes paid to your ward or city office.

Financial Advisors

Banner Financial Services Japan K.K.	03 5724 5100	www.bannerjapan.com
Magellan Tresidder Tuohy	03 3769 5511	www.magellantt.com
STAR Financial Management	03 5427 7700	www.starfml.com

Expats are subject to the same tax laws and rates as nationals, with some conditions. Residents of one year or less are only taxed on income received in Japan. If personal annual income within the tax year amounted to less than ¥1.95 million, a rebate can be claimed. Residents of one to four years and 364 days are taxed on income received in Japan and abroad. Residents of five years or more are taxed on all income sources in Japan, transferred to Japan from abroad or held in a foreign bank account.

Personal income tax rates vary according to income bracket. It is usually deducted at source by your employer before payday. Your employer will also file all your tax returns on your behalf. Failure to pay taxes in Japan can result in fines, penalties, and seizure of assets so it's best to keep up to date.

If you have additional sources of income or are self-employed, you will have to file all or part of your tax returns on your own. Tax forms are available at your local tax office (in Japanese only). Most ward tax offices offer help (some in English) during the tax season (mid-February to March 15). Be prepared for a long wait, and bring all travel and expense receipts, your Certificate of Alien Registration card, bank account information, and withholding tax statement (*Gensen Chōshū-hyō*). Depending on what your employer covers, you may also be eligible to claim transport, teaching materials, or other such items as expenses.

Rebates are the same for every taxpayer, regardless of occupation. The majority of employers deduct income tax at source so it's quite likely that most taxpayers will get some kind of rebate as estimates are usually slightly higher than the total actually due. Any rebate due will be paid into the same account as your pay, usually within a few months following the end of the tax year.

In 2007 prefectural and local tax was upped from 8% to 10% of taxable income, with 4% going to the Tokyo prefecture and 6% to the respective ward or city office. For the self-employed, Prefectural Enterprise Tax is 3% to 5%. This is levied on a quarterly basis, and bills are sent by post. It is payable at most banks and post offices. If the quarterly payment is more than your budget can handle, you can negotiate smaller, more frequent payments through your local ward.

Seeing Double?

Some countries have tax treaties with Japan which allow their citizens to pay both their Japanese and home countrys taxes and Social Security through the Japanese system. Check with your embassy to see whether your country has a tax treaty with Japan, or you may end up paying more than you need to.

Legal Eagles

There are three basic types of lawyers: *bengoshi*, *gyoseishoshi*, and *shihoshoshi*. *Bengoshi* cover almost every legal service and are the only lawyers qualified to negotiate and handle lawsuits. *Gyoseishoshi* work primarily with documentation law and related representation, such as licences and visas, certification, wills, and court claims. Their fees are generally lower than for *bengoshi*. *Shihoshoshi* are similar to scriveners. They handle documents for court procedures, as well as company and real estate registration.

Legal Issues

Japanese law is divided into six codes: a democratic Constitution, civil code, civil procedure code, penal code, criminal procedure code, and the commercial code. These codes are maintained and carried out by a tiered court system, which involves a Supreme Court, high courts, district courts, family courts and summary courts. In general, lawsuits in the Japanese court system are more likely to result in out of court settlements.

Law Firms

Baker & McKenzie GJBJ	03 5157 2700	www.taalo-bakernet.com
Blakemore & Mitsuki	03 3503 5571	www.blakemore.gr.jp
Haraguchi International Law Office	03 5774 9434	www.haraguchi-law.com
Hibiki Law Office	03 3297 0720	na
Hijikata Law & Accounting Office	03 3545 6750	www.hijikata.com
Maekawa Law Office	03 5207 6315	na
Masayuki Honda Law Office	03 3464 0778	na
New Tokyo International	03 6721 3111	www.newtokyolaw.or.jp
Tokyo Bar Association	03 5367 5280	www.toben.or.jp

Drink-Driving

Japan's drink-driving and DUI/DWI laws are among the strictest in the world. The minimum legal blood-alcohol content is 0.03%. If you're caught, you could be facing up to five years in jail with hard labour or a fine of up to ¥1 million. Being a passenger with, providing alcohol, or lending a vehicle to someone later convicted of a DUI or DWI, can land you in jail for up to three years with hard labour or a maximum fine of ¥500,000.

Court proceedings are carried out exclusively in Japanese – interpreters should be arranged by the parties involved. There is no pre-trial discovery or jury system, and the judge's decision is final. Legal documents are written in Japanese, and all non-Japanese legal documents must be translated and notarised. The law applies to all citizens and non-citizens.

Japan has remarkably low reported crime rates, and police have a visible presence in Tokyo, with police boxes *kōban* all over the city. Neighbourhood patrols are common. Serious crime is rare, but theft and burglary occur as in any big city. Bag snatching from motorbikes or bicycles (*hittakuri*) is a regular complaint, as is data theft at ATMs. Crime is treated seriously and there are very strict laws on drug possession, gun possession, drink-driving, and overstaying visas.

Individuals that are arrested can be detained for three to 23 days and will be questioned by the authorities or prosecutor. Translators can be requested, but the quality and availability varies. Everyone has a right to legal counsel, with the option of going public or private. In the case of serious offences however, reports have been made of individuals being held without legal counsel or communication with their embassy until indictment. Prisons are run on a rules-based system where inmates are expected to engage in work and social reform activities. Solitary confinement is not unusual for routine infractions, and medical care is generally limited to emergencies. Better accommodation is provided for good behaviour, but parole is usually not considered until at least 60% of a sentence has been served.

Common legal issues that face expats range from labour disputes, traffic violations, divorce proceedings and child-custody disputes, to visa and immigration procedures. In popular nightlife areas such as Roppongi or Kabuki-chō in Shinjuku, arrests for public disturbances brought on by drunk or rowdy behaviour are not unheard of.

Divorce

To be a granted a divorce while living in Tokyo, at least one of the parties involved must be a legal resident. The most basic type of divorce is by mutual agreement, known as a 'ward office divorce'. This is possible if your spouse is a Japanese national and can be applied for at your local ward office. The form must be signed and/or stamped by both parties and accompanied by the marriage certificate and resident card (for the non-Japanese party) and family register (for the Japanese side). Only one party needs to be present to submit the application.

In cases where neither party is Japanese, there is no mutual agreement, or it involves child-custody or alimony payments, it will go to the family or district court. If a mediated consent cannot be arrived at through the family court, the district court will make the decision. Both parties need to complete and sign a Divorce Registration Form, along with two witnesses over 20 years of age, and present a Resident Register, a copy of the marriage certificate, original passport, Certificate of Alien Registration card, and the required revenue stamps. If children under 20 years are involved, you must also provide their birth certificates, and in some cases those of both parents. All non-Japanese documents must be translated. Check with your embassy if Japanese divorces are valid or if they need to be registered in your home country.

There are many qualified divorce lawyers in Tokyo and it pays to hire one. A good lawyer well versed in international law will be able to tell you if it is more beneficial for you to get divorced outside of Japan and can help with visa concerns. In general, child-custody is awarded to one parent, usually the mother. If one parent is a Japanese national the courts tend to award custody to them, unless proven that this is not in the child's best interests. Maintenance payments are generally awarded to wives.

Making A Will

A person can write their own will, but it's better to consult a *gyōseishoshi* lawyer to make your wishes as clear as possible and to ensure legality. Property and the inheritance of assets can be of particular importance. Any special requests regarding medical care in the event of an accident or terminal illness should also be mentioned. Once written, a will must be notarised. Check with your embassy to see if it needs to be registered in your home country.

Adoption

Traditionally, the importance placed on blood relations and family in Japanese culture made adoption a rarity. Today, it is more common, but not as widespread as in other countries. To adopt in Japan, you must be a long-term resident. If you are looking to adopt from outside Japan, you will need to consider the adoption laws in Japan, those of the country you wish to adopt from, and those of your home country. In general, the Japanese authorities will not consider the adoption until the adoption eligibility requirements have been met in the child's home country.

The Family Court and the Child Guidance Center (CGC) of your local ward office can give you information about the procedure as well as listings of children's homes and adoption agencies (all agencies are privately owned). Adoption can also be arranged though missionaries.

Adoption begins with the filing of a petition in family court; wherein the child is determined to be eligible for adoption in Japan, and in their home country. The judge then appoints a date for the next hearing. This is followed by a six-month trial period, when the family and child will be visited by a court-appointed observer (usually three times). The family, child, and observer must all be present at the next hearing, and as long as no further hearings are deemed necessary by the judge, a decision will be made within two to three weeks. If the adoption is approved, the court issues a certificate and the adoption must be registered at the family's ward office. If no objections are made in the next two weeks, the adoption is final.

Adoption fees vary with each agency, and can run into millions of yen. The time needed to complete the adoption procedure can be nine months or more and it is wise to seek the advice of a lawyer (see Law Firms table on p.67). For more information, see also Certificates on p.58.

Adoption

There are two kinds of adoption in Japan: 'regular' and 'special'. 'Special' adoption severs the child's ties with their biological family, while with 'regular' adoption the child still has ties to their biological family. In 'special' adoptions, one of the prospective parents must be over 25, and the other no younger than 20. Depending on your home country, the Family Court may allow single-parent adoption, but this is rare.

Rainbow Bridge

Housing

Tokyo is no longer just the domain of small apartments. New buildings and housing options appear weekly, and the face of Tokyo living is changing rapidly. The size/price ratio of an average apartment might be shocking at first, but with a bit of planning you can easily find something to suit your needs, whether you're a student looking for a cheap room or a family seeking a luxury apartment. Renting is the most popular short-term option but if you are planning a family or want to stay a while, buying a house or an apartment might be a better bet. Location is everything but the huge availability means you're sure to find something good. Choosing a place to live can seem like an overwhelming task. There are so many areas to choose from, and depending on your situation many factors can come into play. If you have a limited budget, then Ginza (p.153) will not be for you. Do you have a family? If so, then you might want to check out Meguro-ku (p.84) or Setagaya-ku (p.92). If you're younger or single, it might be important to you to maintain your social life by sticking to areas with lots of entertainment options like Azabu (p.88) or Shibuya (p.94). If your job is in Nihonbashi, then neighbourhoods in Chiyoda-ku (p.80) might be convenient. If you're looking for a truly Japanese living experience you might want to look outside these areas too (see Outer Tokyo on p.102).

Ebisu

Rooms To Rent

Free weekly magazines like Metropolis *and* Tokyo Notice Board *– available every Friday in shops like Tower Records (p.278), or Kinokuniya (p.278) and websites like* Craigslist *(http://tokyo.craigslist. jp) post ads for apartments to rent and houses to share.*

Renting In Tokyo

Some employers provide accommodation, but it's more likely you will be provided with a housing allowance. Rent is usually paid monthly, by bank transfer. Utilities will need to be set up independently (see Utilities & Services, p.110), however serviced apartments or business apartments often include this in the rent – parking may or may not be included. Occupants are responsible for keeping their apartments in basic working order but most buildings will have a maintenance man. Any costs resulting from repairs are the responsibility of the tenant. Rental contracts usually range from one to two years, after which there is a renewal fee. Rents are not usually negotiable.

Housing Abbreviations	
jyō	size equal to 1
(example 5 jyō)	*tatami* mat, approx. 1.65 sqm
1,2,3	number of rooms
Br	bedroom
DK	dine-in kitchen
K	kitchen
L	living room
SK	system kitchen
Sqm.	square metre
UB	unit bath
eg. 1K = I bedroom with kitchen	

Finding A Home

Most expats use an agency when looking for a home (despite the fee), as agents are a one-stop solution for finding an apartment, drafting contracts, and overcoming the language barrier. Some landlords are reluctant to rent to foreigners, so an agent makes life easier. If going it alone, you'll need some Japanese language skills. Note that some places may ask for references and/or a guarantor. If you need a guarantor, your employer may be able to act as one for you. 'Hiring' a guarantor from the agency is costly and not recommended. Once your application has been approved you will be asked to pay a security deposit (*shikikin*). You may also be required to pay a form of non-refundable 'thank-you' or 'key' money (*reikin*). This, with the deposit, can add up to three to six months rent.

Gaijin *Houses*

Gaijin *Houses* (see *Guesthouses* on p.29 and p.72) are popular with low income and temporary residents (including Japanese) as they don't require a deposit or 'key money'.

Shared apartments are not common given the small size of the average apartment. If you want to share a house, check out the ads in weekly magazines such as *Tokyo Notice Board* or *Metropolis*, or one of the many expat-focused websites (see Useful Websites, p.41 for more).

Space in Tokyo is at a premium and apartment walls can be thin. Many buildings have informal but highly encouraged guidelines against loud noise late at night and some buildings prohibit pets and instruments like pianos. Any conditions will be listed on the property's information sheet provided by the agent.

Rents are greatly influenced by location and in general, the newer the building, the more expensive it will be. Apartments in trendy, central areas such as Shibuya, Omotesandō, or Daikanyama are more expensive than in older or less central areas like Nakano-ku or Takadanobaba. Corner apartments and those on the upper floors also tend to go for higher rents. The time of year you begin renting may also be reflected in the rate, as the influx of students and new company employees in the spring can sometimes turn cheap apartments into premium properties.

Real Estate Agents

Name	Phone	Web	Type
Century 21 SKY Realty	03 3585 0021	www.century21japan.com	expat focused
Ken Corporation Ltd	03 5413 5666	www.kencorp.com	luxury rentals
Kimita Estate Plan	03 5770 4649	www.kimita.co.jp	renting, buying
Koei Kanri	03 5485 7600	www.tokyoapartment.jp	buying, selling, apartments, offices
Plaza Homes	03 3585 8611	www.realestate-tokyo.com	rental, purchase

Freehold Property

Freehold is the only kind of property ownership in Japan. Land is considered a separate asset from buildings, which means that when you buy property, you only own the building and not the land. This is called 'land lease'. This is only possible when the landowner and buyer are not the same person.

The Lease

Always read the lease carefully before signing. If in doubt take a Japanese-speaking friend with you when you go to sign. Knowing exactly what you're getting and what's expected of you will save you time, money, and prevent any nasty surprises down the line.

Most leases will be in Japanese. If you are dealing with an agency or landlord that caters to expats you may get a copy in English too. The lease should be signed by the tenant and the landlord. Occasionally, a guarantor's signature is required as well.

A landlord will usually ask for a copy of your Certificate of Alien Registration card, proof of employment (such as an income statement from your employer), basic bank information (such as a copy of the front page of your bankbook), and possibly a copy of your passport and visa.

Leases are usually a two-year commitment. If you choose to move before then, you are normally required to give one or two month's notice. Moving out early may mean losing a big chunk of your security deposit, and/or a penalty fee.

'Key money' and the security deposit are usually paid before moving in. Rent is usually paid monthly by bank transfer.

Most landlords will remind you several weeks in advance that your lease is up. If you choose to renew, this is the time to negotiate any rent hikes. Most accommodation requires a renewal fee equal to one month's rent. Your landlord will send you a copy of the new lease, and you will have to fill out everything again, including any forms that need to be signed by a guarantor.

Tenants are expected to keep their apartment or house in good working order. This includes maintaining the garden, cleaning air-conditioning filters, and keeping plumbing free from obstruction. Any repairs are usually at the cost of the tenant.

On moving out, most leases require that you leave the apartment as it was when you moved in. This means that it's best not to make improvements or renovations without your landlords consent. Some landlords may strike a deal with you regarding additions such as extra air-conditioning units and reduce your rent on renewal or offer a bigger refund when you move out.

Main Accommodation Options

Housing options range from one-room lofts to luxury apartments. As with most accommodation, if it's newer, trendier, larger, or sunnier, it's probably more expensive. Being close to the station is a particularly important point, as this can shorten your commute by up to 30 minutes. Japanese-style apartments and houses with *tatami* mats will often be cheaper than western-style wooden floored ones.

Studios & Lofts

Lofts and studios are perfect for students, singles or those looking to save money. They are also a means of living in a trendy part of town on a budget. Expect minimal floor space though, which can be anything from 4.5 *jyō* (approx. 7.5 sqm) to 6 *jyō* (approx. 9 sqm).

Apartments

Apartments can be in standalone towers, or in smaller apartment buildings known as *manshon*. The average size of each room is about 6 *jyō*. Living room and kitchen areas are typically 7 *jyō* (11.5sq m) to 10 *jyō* (16.5sq m). Apartments offer more storage space than studios and lofts, and if they are located in a *manshon* building, they may come with extra storage space in a common storage area. Parking may or may not be included in the rent.

Online Communities

There are numerous expat-focused websites offering advice and advertising services especially for expatriates. See p.41 for a list. And check out www.explorerpublishing.com, where you can join an online community for your city, share tips, get updates, ask questions and make friends.

Guesthouses

If you are looking for the communal experience, a *gaijin* house might be just the ticket. Your roommates will most likely be a mix of young, single expats or Japanese. They are a great money saver if you just want your own room and don't need a fancy kitchen or bathroom and they're really social (see *Gaijin* Houses on p.71 and Guesthouses on p.24).

Luxury Apartments

Luxury apartments are just that. Rooms are larger with more light and there'll most likely be a concierge. Other services and amenities may include a gym, swimming pool, parking and even car rental. These can be found in new high-rises such as Mori Tower, or the equivalent in high-end downtown areas like Azabu or Ginza.

Houses

Houses vary in size from small two room niches to spacious five bedroom affairs. You may have space for a garden, and it's more likely that you will be able to have a pet.

Serviced Apartments

Serviced apartments are good if you are only planning to stay short-term, are on an extended business trip, or are too busy to do housework. Typically, they are located near large international companies in areas like Shinjuku or Nihonbashi. The options are endless, and can include everything from cleaning services to food.

Other Rental Costs

Utilities are usually provided but you are expected to set up an account in your own name. Forms from the electric, gas, and water companies can be found either in your apartment or house, or in your mailbox. Most leases include a monthly maintenance fee added on to or included with the rent. This covers the upkeep of common areas such as the lobby, stairwells, elevators, and hallways. Some upmarket apartment buildings may also have parking, swimming pool, gym and maintenance fees. If you have a garden, there may be an extra maintenance fee. Basic maintenance costs such as replacing light bulbs or air-conditioning filters are up to the tenant. If major repairs are needed, discuss it with your landlord but be prepared to bear the cost yourself.

Buying Property

Anyone can buy property or purchase a home in Japan. There are no formal limitations as to what you can buy, but securing a loan or mortgage could be a problem if you are not a long-term resident with proof of intention to stay in Japan or to become a permanent resident. If you can pay cash, or are able to secure a mortgage, then it's fairly straightforward.

Property price (known as 'land price') is calculated taking the price of the land and adding on that of the building. Land prices fluctuate with the market and the government sets price indices. The average lifespan of a Japanese mortgage is 35 years, and buildings are typically torn down and rebuilt every 30 years so land is seen as a sound investment. New housing areas are constantly being developed so keep your eyes open and consult a qualified development agency if you're keen to buy.

Property Developers

Century 21 SKY Realty	03 3585 0021	www.century21japan.com
James Takahashi Real Estate	na	www.jamestakahashi.com
Kimita Estate Plan	03 5770 4649	www.kimita.co.jp
Koei Kanri	03 5485 7600	www.tokyoapartment.jp
Plaza Homes	03 3585 8611	www.realestate-tokyo.com

The Buying Process

First you need to submit a purchasing application to the selling party. This opens your negotiations.

Legal issues regarding the property, method of payment, contract signing and closure dates are explained and reviewed with you by a real estate agent.

On the contract signing day, the legal details of the property and the payment schedule is once again reviewed with you by the real estate agent. You then sign and stamp the contract with your *inkan*. At this point, you pay a deposit to the seller (usually about 10% of the value), and any commission fees to the real estate agent. Apply for a mortgage, which must be approved and completed by the contract closing date. If you are rejected, the deposit and commission may be refundable.

Once your loan is approved, you will need to pay off any remaining fees, for which you will get a receipt. This includes the price of the sale, the agent's commission, and any taxes incurred. A *shihoshoshi* lawyer then prepares all the registration documents, confirms the transaction with a legal bureau, pays the registration fee and gets a receipt.

The seller will then give you the keys, and the *shihoshoshi* will prepare and hand over the deed in your name.

If you pull out of the negotiations between the contract signing day and the contract closing day, you are usually required to pay the seller another 10% on the value of the property as penalty. Agent commissions are set by the government at 3.15% of the value of the property, plus ¥63,000.

Buying Into It
Expats can invest in property or buy land. However, considerable documentation and guarantors may be necessary, particularly if you are trying to secure a loan or mortgage. Conditions vary widely but it's wise to consult an estate agent based in Japan who can help you with the particulars and offer legal counsel.

Property Shopping List

If purchasing property, you will be expected to have: an *inkan/hanko* registered with your local ward office, a certificate of the *inkan/hanko* registration, a certificate of signature, Certificate of Alien Registration card, Certificate of Tax, Tax Notice, proof of visa (usually your passport), stamp duty (a stamp you buy to put on the contract) and any documents that your bank has required for you to secure the loan or mortgage.

Buying To Rent
Buying to rent follows the same process as buying a property to live in. Once purchased, you will have to use an agent to rent out the property on your behalf. Don't forget to calculate agent commission fees into the budget (see p.74).

Selling
Selling follows a similar process to buying. The seller can go it alone or list the property with an agent, who will complete the process and do all negotiations along with a *shihoshoshi* (real estate lawyer, p.67 for more). The bonus of using an agent is that any legal or bureaucratic oversights that might delay the process can be avoided. There are no penalties for selling before the mortgage term is up.

Mortgages

Getting a mortgage as an expat poses a particular problem: the majority of banks are unwilling to approve a mortgage for anyone who is not a permanent resident. Getting a mortgage requires a guarantor (preferably Japanese), proof of income for up to five years, five years of tax returns, and proof of visa status. You may also be required to provide proof of 'ability to pay off the loan'. Mortgages are typically for 35 years, but they enjoy a characteristically low interest rate. Mistubishi-UFJ Bank has been known to provide mortgages to long-term expat residents with a Japanese spouse and in full-time employment. Alternatively, try looking into getting one from the Public Housing Loan Corporation (03 5800 8000). Their interest rates are higher but they seem to be more open to lending to expats.

Mortgage Providers		
Bank of Tokyo-Mitsubishi UFJ	03 3240 1111	www.bk.mufg.jp
Citibank	03 5568 1653	www.citibank.co.jp
Shinsei Bank	03 5954 7530	www.shinseibank.com
Sumitomo Mitsui Bank	03 3230 0840	www.smbc.co.jp

Other Purchasing Costs

In addition to the price of the property, there are other costs involved when buying. Whether you are building, selling, or getting a property loan, you'll have to pay stamp duty. Depending on the value of the property it can be anything from ¥400 to ¥200,000. *Shihoshoshi* legal fees for preparing the registration and deed can easily run into a few hundred thousand yen, depending on the complexity of the transaction. Insurance fees will cost up to a few hundred thousand yen as well. The agent fee is 3.15%, plus ¥63,000 for both the seller and the purchaser. Finally maintenance fees for the property can range from ¥1,000 up to ¥10,000 per month for high-end properties.

Real Estate Law

When buying property, there are some basic legal proceedings that need to be taken into account (see The Buying Process, p.73). The purchase application is the first step. The buyer must submit a purchase application to the seller (or the seller's agent) to open negotiations. The legal background of the property must then be disclosed to the buyer. At the conclusion of the purchasing contract the buyer must pay a deposit to show that their interest is in earnest. After the contract closure, the property must be registered by a *shihoshoshi* lawyer (p.73).

It is not required that you draw up a new will when buying property, but it is advisable in line with the inheritance regulations in Japan and those of your home country. Since a *shihoshoshi* lawyer must register the property, you are obliged to hire one. If you wish to renegotiate any of the terms of contract or have any doubts about the process, speak to your lawyer. For any further legal proceedings or lawsuits, you will need to hire a *bengoshi*. See Legal Eagles on p.67 for clarification.

Suburban Tokyo

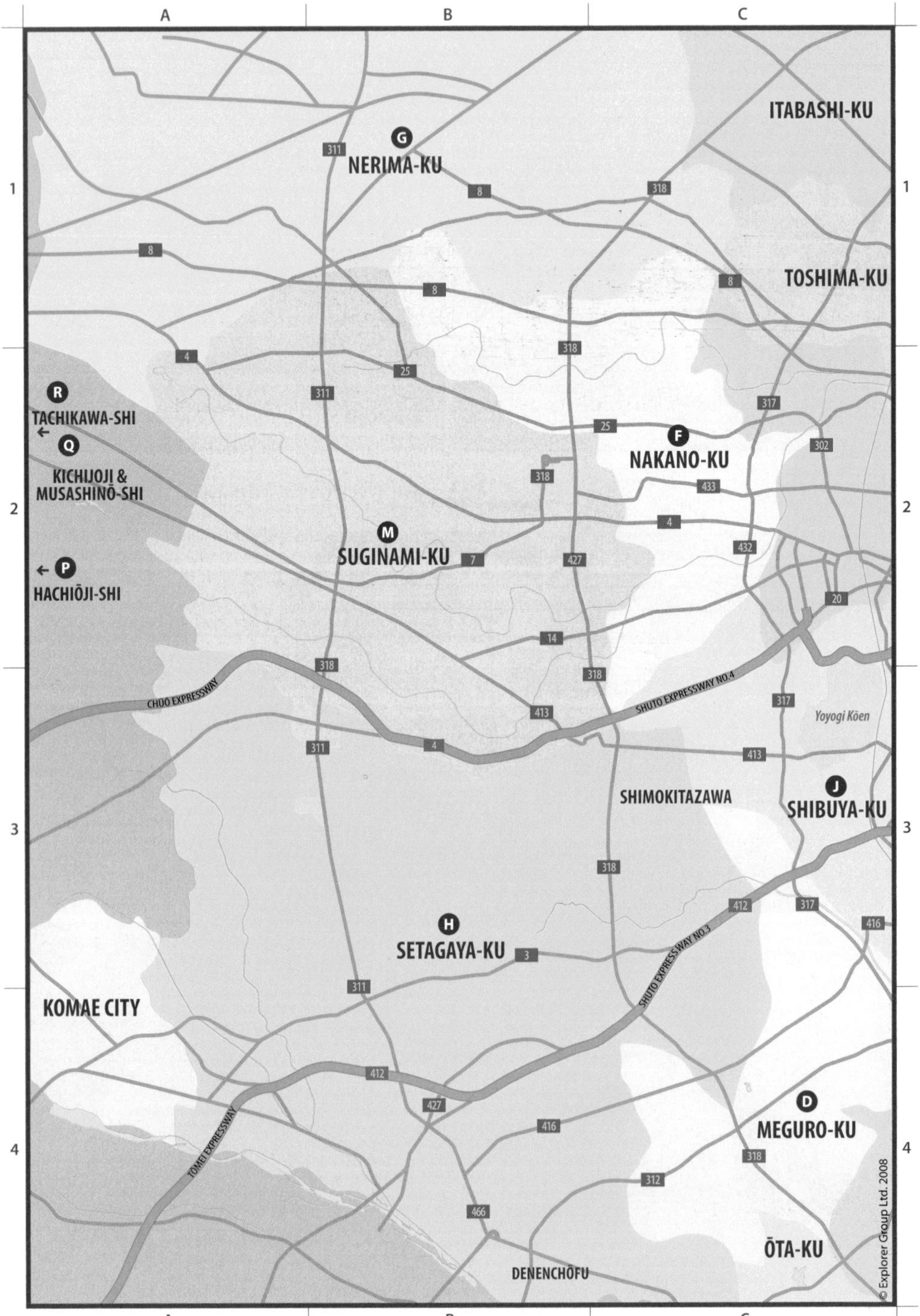

ITABASHI-KU

G
NERIMA-KU

311

8

318

TOSHIMA-KU

8

8

8

318

4

25

R
TACHIKAWA-SHI
←

311

25

317

Q
KICHIJŌJI &
MUSASHINŌ-SHI

318

F
NAKANO-KU

302

433

M

P
← HACHIŌJI-SHI

SUGINAMI-KU

7

4

20

427

432

14

318

20

318

413

SHUTO EXPRESSWAY NO.4

317

CHŪŌ EXPRESSWAY

311

4

413

Yoyogi Kōen

SHIMOKITAZAWA

J
SHIBUYA-KU

318

412

317

416

H
SETAGAYA-KU

3

SHUTO EXPRESSWAY NO.3

KOMAE CITY

311

412

D
MEGURO-KU

427

416

318

312

ŌTA-KU

466

TŌMEI EXPRESSWAY

DENENCHŌFU

© Explorer Group Ltd. 2008

Tokyo Explorer 1st Edition

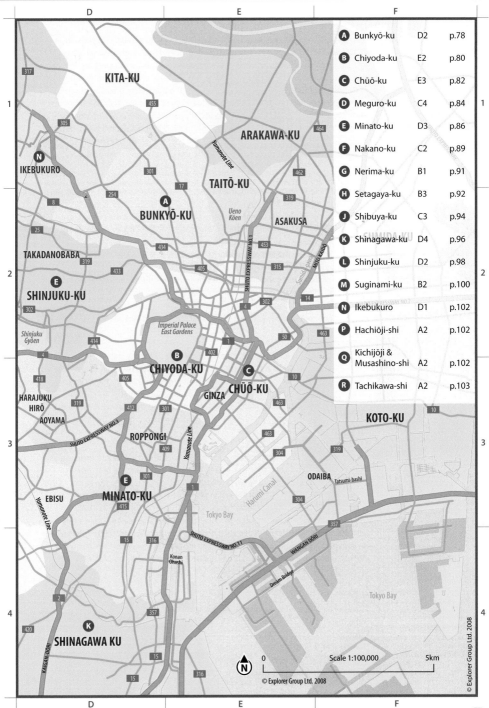

A	Bunkyō-ku	D2	p.78
B	Chiyoda-ku	E2	p.80
C	Chūō-ku	E3	p.82
D	Meguro-ku	C4	p.84
E	Minato-ku	D3	p.86
F	Nakano-ku	C2	p.89
G	Nerima-ku	B1	p.91
H	Setagaya-ku	B3	p.92
J	Shibuya-ku	C3	p.94
K	Shinagawa-ku	D4	p.96
L	Shinjuku-ku	D2	p.98
M	Suginami-ku	B2	p.100
N	Ikebukuro	D1	p.102
P	Hachiōji-shi	A2	p.102
Q	Kichijōji & Musashino-shi	A2	p.102
R	Tachikawa-shi	A2	p.103

© Explorer Group Ltd. 2008

Scale 1:100,000

Area **A** *p.77*
See also Map 4 B2

Bunkyō-ku

Bunkyō-ku is one of Tokyo's most historical central areas. Bordered by Chiyoda-ku and Shinjuku-ku in the south, it completes a triangle of residential areas popular with expats for its downtown accessibility and atmosphere. The main residential areas are Sengoku, Hakusan, Honkomagome and Sendagi. These areas are mostly serviced by the Toei Mita and Namboku metro lines in the northern part of the ward. More urban areas can be found in the south near Korakōen and Suidōbashi stations on the JR Chūō-Sobu line and Marunouchi metro line. Tokyo University, Nippon University and Chuo University all have campuses in the area, adding to the welcome mix of modern attractions, bustling activity, and traditional splendour. This area is popular with expat families who have ties with the Lycée Franco-Japonais and the British Council, both located in Iidabashi.

Best Points
The best of both worlds is available here. It's a quiet residential area with plenty of greenery, but there are also amenities, things to do and great medical care.

Accommodation

Originally the domain of established Japanese-style homes, this area has now become more balanced and also has a variety of 1K *manshon* buildings, apartments and even luxury high-rise apartments. Prices for rented apartments are relatively reasonable, with studios and 1Ks in older buildings starting at ¥100,000 and four and five bedroom houses with gardens going for up to ¥1 million per month. Cheaper places, such as 1Ks for as little as ¥60,000 per month, can be found in the Sendagi area near Honkomagome and Edogawabashi, near the southern border with Shinjuku-ku. The areas of Uguisudani and Okachimachi have a number of cheap apartments and guesthouses. The area is comparatively cheap as it is not as hip and happening as other high-end addresses. Many train lines pass through Ueno station, making it an ideal locale for commuters. It's a great place for expat families and kids will be content.

Worst Points
If you have kids, it might be a bit far from some of the international schools. The Shuto expressway may bring unwelcome traffic if you live in the southwest of the ward, and weekend crowds might cramp your style if you live near the Kasuga area.

Shopping & Amenities

You'll be able to buy your basic daily needs at the shops near the stations; Korakōen and Suidōbashi are usually relatively busy, and there is a good selection of bookshops, convenience stores, cafes and pharmacies in the vicinity. With Tokyo Dome City located in the south of the ward, there is no lack of shopping opportunities. One station west of Suidōbashi, in Iidabashi, is another enclave of shops and cafes, and you can find a few Starbucks and a Miuraya international supermarket in the station shopping mall.

Entertainment & Leisure

Bunkyō-ku is packed with things to see and do. It's hard not to get caught up in the weekend crowds heading for the thrills at Korakōen amusement park or to take in a concert or sports game at the Tokyo Dome. Ueno Zoo (p.182) is just to the east in Taito-ku, a short train ride away. If you are looking for more cultural pursuits, you can make your way to the Bunkyō Civic Center, Sanbyakunin Theatre or the Yayoi Art Museum. For some relaxation, check out LaQua, one of the largest spa complexes in Japan. Koshikawa Botanical Garden in Hakusan or Rikugien Garden in Honkomagome will delight you with their greenery; the plum blossoms in February are particularly well known. If you are interested in traditional Japanese culture, the area also has some notable shrines and temples, such as Yushima Shrine, Kichijo Temple, and Gokoku Temple.

Healthcare

There are a number of large hospitals in Bunkyō-ku. Near the Toyko University campus is the University of Tokyo Hospital. In Sendagi there is the Nippon Medical School Hospital, Komagome Hospital is near Honkomagome, and Nittsu Hospital is on Kasuga Dōri close to Ōtsuka in the west. There are also some independent clinics dealing with everything from dentistry and general medicine to dermatology located in the Korakōen and Suidōbashi areas.

Education

There are several Japanese high-schools and universities in Bunkyō-ku, but no international schools. The closest is Lycée Franco-Japonais in Iidabashi.

Transport

Bunkyō-ku is well serviced by public transport, with bus lines running from the main stations and also to Shinjuku, Shibuya and areas in Minato-ku. It's easy to catch a train to most parts of the city, either via JR lines or the metro. JR lines include the central Yamanote, Chūō and Chūō-Sobu lines, but they can get crowded during the morning and evening rushes and at the weekends. The Toei, Mita, Ōedo, Namboku, Tozai and Marunouchi metro lines pass through Bunkyō-ku, allowing access to areas like Roppongi, Ginza and Nihonbashi.

Along the main roads, such as Kasuga Dōri, Hongo Dōri, and the Shuto Expressway on the extreme southwest border of the ward, traffic can get heavy, especially in the rush hours and at the weekend. This is also true near the stations, especially Korakōen and Suidōbashi. However, moving away from the stations, the roads become quieter.

Safety & Annoyances

During sporting events and concerts, the area near Korakōen and Tokyo Dome may pose problems for some people, as crowds, sometimes a bit tipsy, gather there after games. Roads can also become especially congested and noise can be an issue.

Mori Tower

Apartments

Tower blocks

Area **B** *p.77*
See also Map 4

Chiyoda-ku

With Tokyo station at its heart, Chiyoda-ku is truly the centre of Japan. It's one of the greener places in the Tokyo metropolitan area thanks to the presence of the Imperial Palace and the tree-lined Yasukuni Shrine area. It hosts many governmental bodies such as the *Diet* (Japan's parliament), the Supreme Court and the Metropolitan Police Headquarters. More recently, with the development of the Marunouchi and Yūrakuchō areas, it has taken on a new modern feel, with high-end shops, boutiques and eateries. The east is dominated by the palace and government buildings, so the most popular residential areas are in the western part bordering Shinjuku-ku, near Iidabashi and Ichigaya. This area includes the Bancho area (Bancho 1-6), and Kioicho.

Best Points
This is the centre of it all. Green spaces, exciting places with good shopping and quiet neighbourhoods.

Worst Points
Housing can be a bit pricey and it may be hard to find smaller apartments. Kids will have a bit of a commute to school.

Accommodation

Most of the accommodation is concentrated in the west of the ward, and depending on the area, types of housing can vary. There is a good mix of apartment blocks, *manshon* buildings and homes with gardens.

Shopping & Amenities

There is an abundance of shopping in Chiyoda-ku. In the residential areas you are likely to find local greengrocers, butchers, convenience stores and supermarkets – for major shopping head to the east of Chiyoda, closer to the major stations. The areas around Tokyo, Yūrakuchō, Iidabashi, Ochanomizu and Yotsuya stations all have major shopping opportunities with a mix of shops, cafes and shopping complexes. Iidabashi has a Miuraya international grocery store in the station.

Akihabara is the place to go to fill your electronic needs, and the Kanda/Jimbocho zone is famous for it's hundreds of new, used and antique bookshops. Jimbocho also has a high concentration of sports shops, and the main street leading from Jimbocho to the west exit of Ochanomizu station is lined with music and instrument shops. The Yūrakuchō/Hibiya area in the southeast is now stocked with new upscale shops, as well as old favourites like Bic Camera and Seibu department store. Head closer to the Hibiya metro station for Hibiya Shante.

Two jewels in the Tokyo station area shopping crown are the Marunouchi Building and Shin-Maranouchi Building, which house upscale shops and gourmet restaurants. For more fine dining, the Iidabashi area running into Kagurazaka in Shinjuku is well known for its excellent French restaurants. And if you're in the mood for even more fine dining and luxury shopping, Ginza is just a few train stops away.

Entertainment & Leisure

Chiyoda-ku has a staggeringly high concentration of leisure and cultural opportunities, mostly found near the Imperial Palace complex (p.185). Tokyo is a city known for its concrete expanses, so the greenery of the area is a welcome breath of fresher air to often tree-deprived Tokyoites. The area surrounding the palace is no doubt the greatest attraction here. Surrounded by a moat, picturesque bridges, like Nijubashi, and gardens, it's an oasis of peace right next to the bustling Tokyo station area. Just to the south of the palace in the Hibiya area, close to both Kasumigaseki and Yūrakuchō stations, is Hibiya Kōen, which has a traditional garden-style space that's a popular place to stretch out and relax, and also a more active and park-like area.

Yasukuni Jinja (p.178), in the Kudan-Kita area near Kudanshita station, also has beautiful stands of trees. For a change of pace, check out Kanda Jinja, known for it's lively festivals. There are several theatres in the ward, of which the Budokan and the National Theatre are the most notable. The National Museum of Modern Art (p.172) borders the palace, and you can find a science museum just at the south edge of Kitanomaru Kōen. The Tokyo International Forum makes up a significant portion of the Yūrakuchō area.

Marunouchi Building

Healthcare

There are no major public hospitals in the area, but the hospital of the Tokyo Medical and Dental University is nearby, just over the border in Bunkyō-ku. Nihon Dental University has a large dental hospital just a minute from Iidabashi station. Stand-alone clinics for various specialities can be found in most of the neighbourhoods and near major stations.

Education

There are no English-speaking international schools in the area. The Lycée Franco-Japonais is in the Fujimi neighbourhood, just to the north-east of Yasukuni Jinja near Iidabashi station. Sophia University has its campus in the Kioicho area. Chiyoda Library is located in the Kudan-Minami neighbourhood, along with several other branch libraries located around the ward. Check with the branch to see if they have English books, as some may not. The National Archives Headquarters are here.

Transport

This area is one of the most easily accessible areas due to Tokyo station's status as the largest transfer hub in the city. As well as being serviced by the JR Chūō and Chūō-Sobu lines and the Yūrakuchō, Hanzomon, Tozai, Namboku, Marunouchi and Shinjuku metro lines, Tokyo station is a gateway station to all Shinkansen routes moving from the Kanto region, and to the Keio line moving towards Chiba and Tokyo Disneyland. Bus services allow access to major stations in the north such as Ueno, and to Shinagawa in the south. The highway bus service runs out of Tokyo station to other cities.

Traffic levels around Tokyo station and the palace are often very high, and it can get really congested around Iidabashi and Yūrakuchō stations. However, in the residential areas things quiet down significantly, but watch out for a profusion of one way streets. If you don't have parking at your house or building, parking is limited to rented parking spaces or small pay parking lots costing up to ¥2,000 per day.

Safety & Annoyances

With the presence of the police headquarters and palace, most of Chiyoda-ku is pretty safe. Cars and crowds may get a bit noisy near Tokyo station, but the residential areas are very quiet.

Districts In Chiyoda-ku

Bancho (1-6) – This is one of the densest areas for expat living, and is a famous place for local politicians. Not quite as green as other parts of the ward or some other residential areas, but close to the west side of the Imperial Palace in Bancho-3 is Chidorigafuchi Kōen, which greens up the area a bit. The area is rather pricey with mostly larger homes with gardens or luxury apartments running in excess of ¥1.3 million per month for a four bedroom. Closer to Hanzomon station you can find smaller apartments with options for studios and 1K in the ¥170,000 to ¥200,000 per month range. The British Embassy is located in Bancho-1.

Kioicho – This slightly more urban area, located close to Sophia University and just south of Bancho, is a little pricey, with three bedroom apartments costing ¥800,000 to ¥900,000 per month. In the area is Sotobori Kōen, as well as the facilities of the New Otani (www.newotani.co.jp) and Akasaka Prince (www.princejapan.com) hotels.

Area **C** p.77
See also Map 4, 6

Chūō-ku

Chūō-ku is located east of Chiyoda-ku and is bordered by Minato-ku to the south-west. The Sumidagawa flows through the east of the ward, giving this very urban and active ward two distinct atmospheres. The main areas of Chūō-ku are Ginza and Nihonbashi, just to the east of Tokyo station, and to the east of that, the riverside district. This area is not quite as popular as others because of the prices, but it can be a beautiful place if you're looking for very urban or exclusive riverside living.

Best Points
Easy access, very lively, and right in the thick of things.

Worst Points
Not so many options for daily needs in Nihonbashi's northern and eastern areas, and kids will have to commute to school.

Accommodation

Ginza and the riverside district are almost exclusively the domain of high-rise apartment developments. These exclusive addresses can cost as much as ¥1.5 million per month for a three bedroom space overlooking the Sumidagawa. One bedroom apartments are hard to come by, and even then they are in excess of ¥400,000 a month. Towards the Nihonbashi area, which is mostly office and banking buildings, there are some more modest apartment blocks to be found mostly with one and two bedroom spaces. 1K apartments in the area cost about ¥80,000 to ¥120,000 per month, 2DK properties cost ¥160,000 for older buildings and up to ¥350,000 for new buildings with a gym and parking space.

Shopping & Amenities

The Ginza area, which runs up to Nihonbashi and down to the Shiodome complex on the southern tip of Chūō-ku bordering the port, is one the main shopping sectors in Tokyo. It has a prestigious history of being the home base for many luxury Japanese brands and department stores, as well as for international luxury brands in Japan. There are several famous department stores like Mitsukoshi, Wako and Matsuya in the stretch of shopping wonder between Ginza and Nihonbashi. International grocery and food brands can be found in their basement food-halls. You'll find status brands like Van Cleef and Arpels, and Prada alongside more affordable brands such as Adidas, Zara and Gap. Ginza has its fair share of gourmet dining mixed with more affordable options.

Away from the station, the Nihonbashi area turns into a forest of office buildings and convenience stores, so daily shopping needs might be difficult to meet, but Nihonbashi station has a Precce international market and some little cafes and shops. Closer to the riverside there is Harumi Island Triton Square at Kachidoki station, which makes for a pleasant riverside shopping experience.

Entertainment & Leisure

For a taste of traditional theatre, the Kabuki-za Theatre (p.383) is located in Ginza. There are also some clubs that cater mostly to the domestic business crowd. Hamarikyu Garden is located near the Shiodome complex, next to Tsukiji Fish Market (p.310).

Healthcare

St Luke's Hospital (p.120) and The National Cancer Center are both located in Chūō-ku. Ginza has a few independent clinics catering to foreigners, and various clinics near the major stations.

Education

There aren't any schools for expat families in the area, but nearby Minato-ku has a good selection, with the Montessori School of Tokyo, Tokyo International School, and Nishimachi International School (p.135). The Tokyo YMCA International School (p.135), and the K International School (p.134) are a bit further away in Koto-ku to the north-east, while the Canadian International School (p.134) is in neighbouring Shinagawa-ku.

Transport

Chūō-ku is mostly serviced by the metro, with Ginza being the converging point for the Ginza, Maruonouchi, Hibiya, Tozai and Ōedo lines. These lines can be a bit packed during the working week, especially during the morning and evening rush hours. Local bus services are available at all major stations, running to points north and south. The Shuto Expressway loops into Chūō-ku near Shiodome, and there can be a lot of traffic between Ginza and Nihonbashi. Nihonbashi and the surrounding areas are very congested during the week, however some area turns into virtual ghost towns on the weekends. As there is no street parking in Tokyo, a space will either be provided by your building or you will have to rent it.

Safety & Annoyances

There are no particular concerns to safety, but the weekend shopping crowds in Ginza and Shiodome, or weekday work crowds in Nihonbashi may be an annoyance for some.

Views of Chūō-Dōri

Area **D** p.76 ◄
See also Map 5

Best Points ◄
*The laid-back feeling
makes it an ideal place
for young families and
singles alike. Close to
Shibuya and Roppongi,
there's plenty of
choice for places to
go and things to do.
It's also close to many
international schools.*

Worst Points ◄
*If you have a car, this is
probably not the best
area for you. Housing
can be pricey in some
areas, and train access
in many cases needs a
transfer in Shibuya.*

Meguro-ku

Meguro-ku is one of the most popular areas for expat living in Tokyo. With 12 embassies, good accessibility and perfectly situated between the heart of the city and the outer edges, it's a great place to live if you are looking for a slower place of life. From Meguro station (which actually lies just outside the ward in Shinagawa) Meguro-ku fans out west and south-westwards until it reaches Setagaya-ku. It's within easy reach of Shibuya, Shinjuku and Roppongi. The main residential areas are Meguro, Kamiōsaki, Aobadai, and Naka-Meguro. The area is primarily residential housing, with some urban pockets near Meguro station. The Megurogawa runs through the Aobadai, Naka-Meguro and Meguro areas, which are a hybrid of slightly developed and semi-suburban quiet.

Accommodation

Kamiōsaki is a popular expat area, characterised by larger apartments and stylish semi-detached houses. In the areas closest to Meguro station, there are a mix of new and older mid-size apartment blocks and semi-detached houses. Further out, you can find detached homes with gardens. Depending on the neighbourhood, budget options may be hard to come by as some of Toyko's trendiest areas are located in Meguro-ku.

Shopping & Amenities

Around Meguro station, there are quite a few options in terms of shopping and food. You can find the usual fast-food joints and chain cafes alongside slightly more fashionable cafes and restaurants. There is a shopping centre in the station with Body Shop and HMV Records. Heading towards Naka-Meguro, you can find a profusion of small shops, boutiques, *izakayas*, and cafes. This area is known for its relaxed shopping atmosphere and the streets are dotted with small vegetable shops and neighbourhood grocery stores. The Naka-Meguro GT Plaza also offers a variety of shopping and cafe options at the station including Kaldi Coffee Farm (p.287), an international market, and Tsutaya video rental shops.

Entertainment & Leisure

Naka-Meguro is known for its cafe culture, and there are plenty of bars and pubs with live shows at the weekend. Meguro also has a few popular museums, most notably the Meguro Parasitological Museum, and the Sculpture Museum of Modern Art further out in Meguro-ku towards Sangenjaya. The relaxing Megurogawa provides the perfect backdrop for cherry blossom viewing in April. Himonya Kōen, located just outside of Gakugeidaigaku station on the Tōkyū-Toyoko line is a lovely retreat.

Healthcare

In addition to the independent clinics found near the local stations, the National Hospital of Tokyo Medical Centre (p.118) is located in Higashigaoka on Jiyū Dōri.

Education

One of Meguro-ku's draws for the expat community is it's proximity to international schools and good kindergartens. There are two international schools within its borders, GREGG International School (www.gis-j.com) and the International Secondary School (www.isstokyo.com). It's also well situated for families who send their kids to international schools in Minato-ku or Setagaya-ku.

Transport

The area is serviced by the Yamanote Line (at Meguro station), the Tōkyū-Toyoko Line, and Tōkyū-Denentoshi line. The Yamanote line offers the convenience of complete access to major stations around town, all within an hour or less. However, it is also one of the busiest lines in Tokyo and can be difficult to manoeuvre if you have a stroller or need to sit. The Tōkyū-Toyoko line heads out towards Yokohama and is a bit quieter, although it can get busy during rush hour. This line has an express service to major stations on the way to Yokohama for commuters. The Tōkyū-Denentoshi line, another high-traffic line, goes through Setagaya-ku, also with express stops for commuters. Although it may not have the myriad of transport options that other areas of the city offer, these three lines offer convenient connecting points for major stations within Tokyo and quick access to the Yokohama area. In addition, bus services run from most stations into areas such as Setagaya, Nakano and Suginami wards.

Closer to Meguro station, you'll find that the streets are more urban and full of traffic, and in general it's made more for pedestrian traffic. Further into the neighbourhoods however, there are fewer cars and narrower, one-way streets. Parking is pretty much limited to that provided by your housing or to the few paid parking spaces.

Safety & Annoyances

The area is mainly semi-suburban, so there are few safety issues. Traffic near Meguro station may cause some noise concerns, but for the most part expats families choose this area for its quiet atmosphere.

Districts In Meguro-ku

Aobadai & Naka-Meguro – Running adjacent to the Megurogawa, the neighbourhoods of Aobadai are quiet, and as you get closer to Naka-Meguro the buildings get more stylish and expensive. This area is best suited for young professionals, singles and couples who are looking for one bedroom, two bedroom and 1K apartments. One bedroom and 1K apartments run from ¥150,000 to ¥200,000 per month, depending on the age of the building and how close it is to the river. You can also find some Japanese-style wooden homes if you look hard.

Gakugeidaigaku – This area, which includes Himonya Kōen, is a more affordable option, with two bedroom units averaging ¥300,000 a month.

Jiyūgaoka – This is a main shopping hub for Western Tokyo with a wide variety of small boutiques, larger international shops, and relaxing cafes. The streets around the station are small and quaintly paved in some spots, and it's popular with artistic types, singles, and young couples. It's only 15 minutes from Shibuya on the Denentoshi line and is home to GREGG International School (www.gis-j.com). Accommodation is mostly one and two bedroom apartments, with prices ranging from ¥170,000 to ¥300,000 per month. More upscale designer homes go for upwards of ¥1 million per month.

Kamiōsaki – This area joins Ebisu in Shibuya-ku, and is well known for being an area with established families and a rich and moneyed history. Accommodation is generally in three bedroom or larger houses, and apartments which are considered prime property, costing millions of yen per month. Many of the homes have gardens or courtyards and some even have pools. This area is a favourite with embassy families and business people. The Nature Study Kōen nearby offers some welcome greenery.

Meguro – Although mostly in Meguro-ku, this area also commonly includes the area around Meguro station, slightly inside Shinagawa-ku. With detached and semi-detached homes, it's known as one of the places where the local embassy expats live. There are more shops and businesses near the station and quieter pockets in the neighbourhoods. You can find lofts as cheap as ¥70,000 a month, and detached homes with three bedrooms, a garden and a pool for upwards of ¥1 million a month.

Sangenjaya – Just outside Meguro-ku, Sangenjaya is still somewhat pricey to live in, but you can find good value for money. It's surprisingly quaint and offers a number of fine restaurants.

Area ❸ p.77
See also Map 6

Minato-ku

Minato-ku is one of the most popular, and most expensive, areas for expats in Tokyo. It runs up against and almost blends into Shibuya-ku on its western side, Chiyoda-ku in the north, Chūō-ku and Tokyo Port in the east, and Shinagawa-ku in the south. This relatively small ward is densely populated, but has beautiful pockets of trees and the potential for a relaxed lifestyle. At its heart is Tokyo Tower, the symbol of the spirit of the city. Depending on the area, you can find the pulse of the city's nightlife, exclusive shopping and apartments, or spacious family living.

The key to its attractiveness lies in its diversity. It houses a wealth of embassies, private clubs like Tokyo American Club (p.242), the newly dubbed Roppongi Art Triangle, high-end retailers, the sprawling entertainment and shopping complexes of Odaiba, and more traditional delights like the greenery of Aoyama Cemetery. The main neighbourhoods for residents are Akasaka, Aoyama, Omotesandō and Roppongi in the north and Azabu, Shirokane and Takanawa in the south.

Best Points
You get everything here: an international lifestyle, good access, shopping, entertainment and culture, all within easy reach of international schools.

Worst Points
It's quite expensive and can be very crowded in certain areas. Waits for housing can be a bit long.

Accomodation

Depending on the area you want to live in, accommodation and prices vary. However rents here are among the highest in Tokyo and much of the accommodation is geared towards high-end and luxury homes. The central location makes even the most humble studio apartment a big investment, but it's worth it if you want to take advantage of this international and eclectic area.

Roppongi, despite its night owl reputation, has many housing options. Just don't expect many bargains. Living in the heart of Roppongi is unheard of, but just outside the main crossing are quiet residential areas. This is a good place for those who are susceptible to homesickness, and many business people sent to Tokyo for work set up home here. You'll never pine for a cheeseburger and there are always some friendly fellow expats at the local bar. However, those looking for a more authentic Japanese experience might want to live elsewhere.

Harajuku and Aoyama have a number of apartment options right in the heart of the action but it is one of the pricier areas to live. Guesthouses (p.72) are few and far between in these parts and the expats who settle here are either successful artists or young urban professionals. It's a good place for foreign residents with children as there are many international schools and Yoyogi Kōen is nearby. Minami-Aoyama and Kita-Aoyama are particularly desirable addresses.

Shopping & Amenities

This is one of the best places in the city in terms of amenities and shopping. Omotesandō and Aoyama both have an endless array of shops, boutiques, international markets, cafes and restaurants. Omotesandō Hills is a recent addition to the area with exclusive wine and tea bars, boutiques and event spaces. The Roppongi and Azabu area is home to the world-famous Roppongi Hills, a complete and self-contained lifestyle complex that is seen as a revolution in architecture and urban living. It's a hotspot for shopping, culture, and even has a large cinema complex.Tokyo Midtown (p.313) is a development project that was completed in 2007 in the Nogizaka neighbourhood. Here you'll find upscale boutiques, restaurants, and a large Precce international grocery store. For more everyday needs, the National Azabu Supermarket (p.315) is a favourite among expats for grocery shopping.

Further out in Takanawa/Shirokane, there's the Platinum Street shopping area. Finally, out near Tokyo Port and serviced by the Yurikamome monorail line, is Odaiba (p.88), which is home to Venus Fort (p.313) and Palette Town shopping megaplexes. Palette Town is home to a huge ferris wheel that affords great views of the city. Closer to hand is the Shiodome area, yet another lifestyle complex.

Entertainment & Leisure

In the shadow of Tokyo Tower, the Roppongi Art Triangle has taken shape. It's two largest attractions are Mori Tower and The National Museum of Modern Art (p.172). Between Azabu, Roppongi and Nogizaka there are hundreds of opportunities for live music, bars, and events. Zepp Tokyo, a large concert complex is located in Odaiba, as are amusement parks and event halls. For some natural beauty, Arisuga Kōen, which borders Azabu, is a stretch of trees that offers a popular escape.

Healthcare

This area has no lack of clinics and hospitals, and some cater especially to expats. St Luke's Hospital (p.120) in Tsukiji has a well-known obstetrics department. The Tokyo Midtown Clinic and Roppongi Hills Clinics are located in the eponymously named lifestyle complexes. Akai Medical Clinic (p.126) in Omotesandō is a favourite for those looking to improve their complexions.

Education

The majority of Tokyo's international schools are conveniently located in Minato-ku, which has secured it's place as one of the top areas for expat families in Tokyo. These include Montessori School of Tokyo (p.132), Nishimachi International School (p.135), Shirokane International School and Tokyo International School (p.135). It's also just a short commute to The British School in Tokyo (p.133) and the International School of the Sacred Heart in Shibuya (p.134). There are also several libraries, most notably Minato Library and the Art Library in the National Museum of Modern Art. Roppongi Hills also operates Academy Hills, a members-only learning and education complex and library located in Mori Tower.

Transport

Easily accessible from virtually any major point in central Tokyo, Minato-ku is serviced by the Ōedo, Asakusa and Mita lines, and the Tokyo Metro Namboku, Hanzomon, Ginza, Chiyoda, and Hibiya lines. Bus services are limited however, because of the easy connections between the metro and train systems in Shibuya, Meguro and Chiyoda. The Ōedo line is particularly convenient as it allows a straight shot from the waterfront of Chūō-ku all the way west to Shinjuku and even northwest into Toshima-ku. The metro lines tend to get crowded during rush hour, but because access is more evenly spread between several lines, the traffic tends to thin out during the mid-mornings, afternoons, and other off-peak hours.

On the roads, Minato-ku is one of the most traffic-heavy parts of the city. The streets around Roppongi, Omotesandō and Aoyama Dōri tend to be congested. There are often large crowds and people in the Roppongi and Omotesandō areas, especially at the weekend. Parking is restricted to private parking for residents.

Roppongi Hills

Safety & Annoyances

The greatest concern in this area lies around the Roppongi district. There is the potential for rowdy crowds in the evenings and weekends as it's a favourite nightspot. As you move into the neighbourhoods, like Shirokane and Aoyama, it's much quieter.

Districts In Minato-ku

Akasaka & Takanawa – The Akasaka area, dominated by foreign companies and the ARK Hills complex, is easily serviced by the Marunouchi, Ginza, and Namboku metro lines. It's characterised by high towers, upscale apartments, and serviced apartments. Things can get expensive with older one bedroom spaces running up to ¥300,000 per month and newer 3 bedroom spaces in excess of ¥600,000. This is the perfect place for young, single professionals and those looking to live close to work. Takanawa, in the south of the ward near Shinagawa station, has a similar atmosphere and is popular with the executive set.

Aoyama – This area commands the highest rents in all of Tokyo. You won't find so many larger properties here, and it's generally a quieter commercial district dotted with design studios and luxury boutiques. The streets are narrow and have a quaint backstreet feel. It's got lots of greenery and hosts Aoyama Cemetery, one of the leafiest spots in the metropolitan area. Mostly one and two-bedroom spaces, these are located in exclusive boutique apartments with long waiting lists. Apartments here are at a premium and the prices show it. Older one bedrooms start at around ¥380,000 per month and go up from that. The 'cheaper' two bedroom apartments can go as high as ¥600,000 per month.

Azabu – Some international families prefer Azabu because of it's proximity to Arisugawa Kōen. This lush area is home to a number of embassies as well as luxury homes. Known to be expensive, rare one bedroom spaces start at ¥400,000 per month, while the more common four and five bedroom homes with gardens and pools run in excess of a ¥1 million per month.

Shirokane – Bordering Shibuya-ku and Shinagawa-ku, this is a popular neighbourhood with embassy families. There is excellent shopping, quiet green neighbourhoods and many large, luxury homes. Accomodation is particularly expensive, with predominently three and four bedroom units costing from between ¥700,000 to more than ¥1 million per month.

Omotesandō – This area is often called the Champs Elyseés of Tokyo, lined with designer boutiques of every persuasion, and centred around the new Omotesandō Hills development. Weekends are crowded with window shoppers and style hunters, and the area runs right into Harajuku's Jingūmae district. Like Aoyama, it's mostly one and two bedroom apartments that range from ¥350,000 to ¥450,000 per month. The draw here is all the shopping and amenities, with hundreds of shops, galleries, cafes and salons right at your fingertips.

Roppongi – The classic heart of Minato-ku has been undergoing a gentrification in the last few years. Previously the domain of clubs and shot bars, it's now taken on an air of cool, modern style. The majority of offerings are one and two bedroom apartments, often in older buildings. The Nogizaka area has become hot property and prices there are quickly rising due to the recent opening of the Toyko Midtown project and the elegantly curved National Museum of Modern Art. One bedroom flats start at around ¥250,000 per month and the odd 3 bedroom can run to about ¥450,000.

Odaiba – Few expats live in Odaiba. It is extremely expensive and most living quarters are of the corporate apartment variety. The commute to and from the mainland can be taxing and the sterile environs could become depressing after lengthy exposure. There is also a sense of detachment, and expats might feel cut off from downtown Tokyo.

Ward Offices ◄

To find your local ward (ku) office, visit the Tokyo Metropolitan Government's website: www.metro.tokyo.jp. All ward offices have an English language guide to living in each ward, which is available for free. This is a useful thing to pick up when you first arrive as it lists everything from facilities to rubbish dispoal.

Area **F** *p.76*
See also Map 3

Best Points
Close to some of the main downtown areas, yet you have a bit more freedom and space. Easy to access trains and metro for most of the popular destinations.

Worst Points
Aesthetically, it's not as nice as some other places. It's a no-nonsense area where what you see is what you get.

Nakano-ku

Only a stone's throw from Shinjuku is Nakano-ku, the bridge from the urban clamour of central Tokyo to the quieter suburban regions in the western part of the metropolitan area. Ranging from the busy shopping hub around Nakano station to the quieter streets of Nakano-Sakaue, Nakano-Shinbashi and Ochiai, if you want to be close to the city centre, but not to pay the high prices, then Nakano-ku is a good option. It's becoming more popular with those who work in Shinjuku and want to live close to work and the area is serviced by the JR Chūō and Sobu lines and the Tozai, Marunouchi and Ōedo metro lines.

Accommodation

In recent years, the Nakano-ku area has started to become more developed with quite a few new high-rise apartment complexes near Higashi-Nakano and Nakano-Sakaue stations. Ochiai and Nakano-Shinbashi are relatively quiet in comparison and have a few new mid-sized apartment blocks with mostly one and two bedroom units. Modestly aged one bedroom units (1DK) run to about ¥80,000 per month in the Nakano-Sakaue area, Higashi-Nakano has older units that can be cheaper, but it's being gentrified a bit.

Shopping & Amenities

The Nakano and Higashi-Nakano station areas are filled with shopping opportunities. There are some major supermarkets like Peacock and Seiyu, in addition to smaller greengrocers and butchers. Near Nakano station is Sun Mall, a packed shopping arcade, and Sun Plaza with shops and restaurants. Ochiai, Nakano-Shinbashi, and Nakano-Sakaue are a bit more limited for shopping, but there are smaller neighbourhood shops and groceries.

Entertainment & Leisure

Since Nakano-ku is so close to Shinjuku, many people just hop on a train and head there. However, if you want to stay closer to home there are always the local pubs and watering-holes, and a good place to start is in the area just north of Nakano station, where there's a small web of Chinese, *ramen*, *yakitori* and *yakiniku* restaurants. Check out Aoba Ramen for one of the area's most popular bowls of *ramen*. Sun Plaza has bowling lanes, a fitness centre and a well-known concert hall. Nakano-ku also has an excellent public library with a large English selection.

Healthcare

Nakano General Hospital is located just a couple of blocks from Nakano station, and there are several independent clinics scattered about the area. There are also more healthcare options closeby in Suginami-ku and Shinjuku-ku.

Education

The closest international schools are found in Mitaka-shi, Musashino-shi, Suginami-ku, Setagaya-ku and Nerima-ku. This maybe a bit of a commute for some families.

Transport

Nakano-ku is serviced by the JR Chūō and Chūō-Sobu lines, as well as the Seibu-Shinjuku line in its northern reaches. The Marunouchi, Tozai and Odeo metro lines also pass through the area on the way to Shinjuku. The Chūō line and Marunouchi lines tend to be the most crowded, especially during the rush hours, and Nakano-Sakaue station can be particularly busy late at night, bringing back and transferring party-goers and office workers from Roppongi and Shinjuku on the Ōedo and Marunouchi lines. The local bus service is a great way to get to places in Shibuya-ku and Setagaya-ku, and services run from most major stations with stops on Yamate Dōri and Okubo Dōri. These are both major thoroughfares and carry heavy traffic, and around the Nakano and Nakano-Sakaue station areas there is often congestion. There is no street parking and the streets are often very narrow.

Safety & Annoyances
As with much of Tokyo, there are few reasons for alarm. The Nakano area has a noted fire department.

Districts In Nakano-ku
Nakano – A relatively built-up area on the Chūō line that provides the convenience of easy shopping and commuting along one of the major train lines in Tokyo, Nakano is suitable for single people, students and couples. Buildings tend to be a bit older, but you can get some good deals on smaller apartments. 1K apartments start from ¥80,000 and run up to the ¥150,000 range. Larger apartments cost around ¥140,000 for two bedrooms and ¥300,000 for three.

Ochiai – This area is much quieter and more residential than Nakano. You'll find mainly *manshon* style apartments, apartment blocks and some semi-detached houses. The neighbourhoods can be a bit tightly packed and less inviting than other areas of the city, but its location is a plus. There are mainly 1K and 2K apartments available here ranging from ¥90,000 to ¥200,000.

Nakano-Sakaue – This is a great spot to be if you want to live in a high-rise building overlooking the skyline of Shinjuku. The buildings are newer, sleeker, and taller, but there are also some smaller apartment blocks. There isn't much in the way of shopping so you'll have to travel a bit, but Shinjuku is just a couple of stops away on the metro. Yamate Dōri can be a blessing with a good bus service to Shibuya. 1K apartments generally start at ¥80,000 per month in some of the smaller, older buildings and can go as high as ¥280,000 for a new high-rise with a view of Shinjuku. Larger spaces can cost in excess of ¥500,000 for a three bedroom in some of the newly developed areas.

Housing in Hibiya

Area ⒢ p.76
See also Map 3

Best Points
You can get apartments with great views that won't be blocked by buildings. The living is quiet, but not too far from the centre of town.

Worst Points
The Ōedo line can get crowded, and there isn't much in the way of exciting shopping.

Nerima-ku

Nerima-ku may seem like it's in the farthest reaches of Tokyo, but it's a good option for those who want to get away from the bustle of the city. The main residential area is around Nerima station, which is a 20 minute ride from Shinjuku via the Ōedo metro line. The area has large, modern buildings, which become smaller as you move into the neighbourhoods. New buildings going up are a mix of smaller designer apartment *manshons* and larger apartment towers. There's more greenery than in other parts of the city, simply because it's not quite as densely developed. The streets are quiet, and there's little traffic once you leave the immediate station area. Nerima is ideal for young couples or people who don't want to be hemmed in by buildings.

Accommodation

Housing is a mix of established detached and semi-detached houses and *manshon* blocks. Most non-Japanese opt for the apartment blocks, some of which are designer. Some of the buildings are garden style apartments, which are at the higher end of the price range, going for as much as ¥400,000 per month for two beds. For smaller budgets, there are studios, 1K and one-beds starting from ¥80,000 up to ¥250,000 a month.

Shopping & Amenities

The area around the station has shops, cafes and a shopping centre with a grocery store. In nearby Toshimaen, there is a United Cinema and a few cafes.

Entertainment & Leisure

For most leisure opportunities, you'll have to go outside the main Nerima area to places like Toshimaen, one stop away on the Ōedo line. There you'll find an amusement park popular with the kids, as well as a quiet, affordable garden-style spa, Niwa No Yu (five minutes from the Toshimaen Ōedo line station), that has both mixed and single-sex bathing. Hop on the Ōedo line to Hikarigaoka, about 20 minutes away, and you'll find Hikarigaoka Kōen, a large green space located on a former military base.

Healthcare

The Nerima Hikarigaoka Hospital and Nerima General Hospital are relatively close by. Seibo Hospital has English-speaking staff and is a maternity hospital popular with expats.

Education

The Santa Maria International School (03 3904 0517) is located in Nerima-ku and the New International School in Toshima-ku (p.135) isn't far away. Commutes to international schools in Musashino-shi and Suginami-ku are much easier than to those in Setagaya-ku, however the Ōedo line goes right into Minato-ku, which may make a difference.

Transport

Nerima-ku is not accessible via JR lines, but is serviced by metro lines such as Seibu-Shinjuku, Seibu-Ikebukuro, Yūrakuchō, and Tobu-Tojo lines. The Yūrakuchō and Ōedo lines also service the area. In general, expect to make up to two changes to get into the city centre, and last trains depart early. The bus service is more dependable and will bring you to main stations like Ikebukuro, Takadanobaba, Nakano, Kichijōji and Mitaka. For drivers, the station area is busy and some of the streets further out can get rather narrow. For parking, it's best to get a space through your building or to rent one.

Safety & Annoyances

There are few safety concerns in this tranquil area. However, as it's a prime route for people commuting into the city, trains are often crowded during rush hour.

Area **H** p.76
See also Map 5

Setagaya-ku

Setagaya-ku is a truly special district because of its uniquely suburban personality, but convenient location. Located near Meguro in the southwest of the city, it is one of the largest kus and has become the centre of expat family life in Tokyo due to excellent access to international schools, affordable accommodation, greenery and space, and short commutes to the city centre. The quiet Tamagawa is a feature attraction here, and it's banks play host to summer barbecues and fireworks. If you're looking for a truly suburban experience with opportunities to spend time outdoors, then Setagaya-ku may be for you. It's easily accessed via the Tōkyū-Toyoko, Tōkyū-Denentoshi and Ikegami lines.

Best Points
If you have kids going to international school, want more space for your money, or like spending time outdoors, Setagaya's suburban splendour is perfect.

Accommodation

One of the more attractive points about Setagaya-ku is that it's more affordable than many other districts. For the price you might pay for a two bedroom apartment elsewhere, you can have a multi-bedroom detached house with a garden. Apartments run the full gamut from one room studio-style apartments in the Jiyūgaoka area starting at ¥70,000 per month, right up to the more spacious 4 bedroom dwellings in Futako-Tamagawa going for as much as ¥800,000. Rents and housing types vary according to area, and some are more exclusive than others, but on the whole more space for your money is easier to come by here.

Worst Points
You might need a car to get around from north to south, as the two main train lines are set a bit far apart. If you don't live in Jiyūgaoka or Denenchōfu, shopping may not be what you are used to, and you might have to travel to find the more exciting shops.

Shopping & Amenities

There are plenty of smaller local shops around stations; Jiyūgaoka, Denenchōfu, and Futako-Tamagawa will have more choices than others. Jiyūgaoka is particularly known as a shopping destination, with international grocery stores, cafes and clothing boutiques large and small. British clothing chain Next is a popular choice, as is the main branch of The Garden Jiyūgaoka, an international gourmet grocery. The Futako-Tamagawa area is also of note, and has a large Takashimaya department store complex.

Entertainment & Leisure

Setagaya-ku is the perfect choice for people who want to spend time outdoors or exercising, or for families with kids. There are several large parks in the ward, such as Baji Kōen and Komazawa Olympic Park, which houses various sports and swimming facilities. Sogo Undojyō can be found at Ōkura station towards Denenchōfu. Cycling or running along the banks of the Tamagawa is a pleasure, and it's a great picnic and fishing spot. If you're looking for more excitement, hop on the train; you're rarely more than 20 minutes away from Shibuya or Meguro.

Healthcare

There are several hospitals servicing Setagaya-ku, most notably Komazawa Hospital, Tamagawa Hospital, Kanto Chuo Hospital and St Françoise Hospital.

Education

One of the biggest draws in Setagaya-ku is its international schools. Not only is it home to many of the best schools in Tokyo – GREGG International School (www.gis-j.com), Seisen International School (www.seisen.com) and St Mary's International School (p.135), but it also has relatively easy access to schools in Shibuya-ku, Musashinno-shi, Mitaka-shi, Meguro-ku and Minato-ku. Denenchōfu is a good location for the Deutsche Schule Tokyo Yokohama (www.dsty.jp).

Transport

Setagaya-ku is generally considered outside the main Tokyo area, but it has easy access to Shibuya and Western Tokyo, and also Yokohama. You can get to Shibuya via the

Tōkyū-Toyoko, Tōkyū-Denentoshi and Ikegami lines further south from Meguro-ku. Commuter express trains to Shibuya, Meguro and Ebisu are often packed in rush hours, but if you aren't in a rush the local trains are a less-crowded alternative. The Keio and Odakyu lines also offer access to central Tokyo via Shinjuku. A bus service runs into Shibuya and Shinjuku, as well as Nakano-ku, Suginami-ku and Yokohama.

Streets tend to be wider than in other areas, traffic is generally lighter and parking is easier to find, as much of the accommodation includes parking. Traffic is a bit heavier along major routes like Setayaga Dōri, Tamagawa Dōri and Kananna Dōri, but it shouldn't pose much of a problem.

Safety & Annoyances

There are few concerns here, as this is one of the quietest parts of town. Stations like Shimokitazawa might get a bit rowdy with students and Jiyūgaoka can get a bit crowded at the weekend, but in general things are safe.

Districts In Setagaya-ku

Denenchōfu – Bordering Setagaya-ku and Ōta-ku, this is a decidedly more luxurious and attractive area. Housing costs are higher and smaller options are not so readily available. It's especially popular with families associated with the American School in Japan. Most accomodation options consist of three and four bedroom houses for around ¥500,000 to ¥600,000 a month.

Fukazawa & Sakura-Shinmachi – Situated close to Seisen International School and Komazawa Olympic Park, this area is a quiet, green neighbourhood. Mainly four and five bedroom houses, and they are on the pricier side.

Kaminoge & Seta – This area includes Ōyama and Todoroki neighbourhoods, and is close to St Mary's International School (p.135).

Senzokuike – Close to Senzoku Kōen, just outside Setagaya-ku, this area is popular with families with kids at the Deutsche Schule Tokyo Yokohama.

Shimokitazawa – Shimokitazawa is one of the most foreigner-friendly neighbourhoods around. This is one of its endearing aspects, with open-minded Japanese and expats living in relative harmony. That young kid sidling up to you at the bar is interested in genuine conversation, not merely free English lessons. Exotic eateries have flourished in the past 10 years – particularly Southeast Asian restaurants – and there's a bar on every block. Shimokitazawa has a number of housing options but it's not as cheap as it once was. Most of the apartments available around the station are cramped and claustrophobic.

Housing in Setagaya-ku

Look a kilometre away from the heart of the main neighbourhood however, and you'll find much more spacious flats. This area is popular with students, and the atmosphere reflects it. It's only a few minutes from Shibuya on the Keio Inokashira line and is famous for its young and quirky shopping. Housing is mostly one and two bedroom apartments and semi-detached houses. Depending on the building's age they can be quite affordable compared to other places in Setagaya-ku. Nearby Daita and Ikenoue are more residential and are quickly becoming popular places to live, with easy access to both Shinjuku and Shibuya.

Area ❶ p.76
See also Map 3, 5

Best Points
The perfect mix of bustling life and potential for quiet. Lots to see and do, so if you are young or single this can be a great place to live. Also plenty of greenery for so close to the centre of town.

Worst Points
Harajuku and Shibuya proper have limited housing choices. Accommodation can be rather expensive.

Housing in Hirō

Shibuya-ku

Shibuya-ku is well known for being a retail district where shoppers from all over the world mingle at Hachiko Square, but it's also a place with some great living options. Located just to the east of Meguro and Shinjuku wards, and at some points merging with Minato-ku, the area has easy access to the city centre. Focused around Yoyogi Kōen (p.186), there are plenty of accommodation choices. The Shibuya residential areas are mainly found in Daikanyama, Ebisu, Jingūmae, Harajuku, Hirō, Yoyogi-Uehara and Shōtō.

Accommodation
There are several types of housing available. Closer to the centre, it's mostly apartments for singles but as you move out towards Ebisu, Daikanyama, Shōtō, Yoyogi-Uehara and Hirō there are more spacious options. The area around Shibuya station is extremely noisy and not recommended for those who like a little peace and quiet.

Shopping & Amenities
There is excellent shopping potential in Shibuya-ku. Most stores are only a short walk away, and there are some very good international shops as well as the ubiquitous department stores. Shibuya station houses scores of shops, cafes and has three deparment stores attached directly to it. Daikanyama boasts some of the hippest designer boutiques, as well as shops by the likes of Calvin Klein and American Apparel. The area is full of notable restaurants, hip clubs and relaxing cafes. Yoyogi-Uehara is more about charm, however there are also some good shopping options here, mostly in the form of small boutiques. Hirō also is an enclave of cafes, boutiques, and international markets like the National Azabu Supermarket (p.315). Takeshita Dōri is just a taste of what the funky Harajuku district offers.

Entertainment & Leisure
Yoyogi Kōen is the largest green area in Tokyo, and is a great place to walk or relax. There are usually groups of people holding live concerts, events and just posing around near Harajuku station. This area also has Shibuya Ax concert hall and the Yoyogi Event Hall, where Cirque du Soleil used to perform. Bunkamura Orchard Hall, Bunkamura Museum and its related cinema are a great place to take in some culture. There are dozens of cinemas, bowling alleys and theatres in the area around the station. Hirō and Daikanyama have a cafe and people-watching culture unparalleled in Tokyo.

Healthcare
The Hirō Hospital and Japanese Red Cross Medical Centre (p.119) are the two main healthcare facilities in the area. Also of note is the Higashi Healthy Plaza, a healthcare and health-welfare complex located between Shibuya and Ebisu.

Education
The British School in Japan (p.133) and Horizon International School (www.horizon.ac.jp) are in located in Shibuya-ku. It's also easy access to most schools in Minato-ku, and the American School in Japan (p.133) in Chofu. The National Children's Castle (p.232) is a 15 minute walk from Shibuya station towards Omotesandō.

Residential Areas

Top Dog ◀

Hachiko was the beloved pooch of Eisaburo Ueno and he is honoured with a bronze statue near Shibuya station. Legend has it that the dog would accompany his owner to the station every morning, and be waiting there when he returned from work. Even after Ueno died, Hachiko continued to wait there every day for the next 11 years. Though seemingly a moral tale of unflinching loyalty, the plot thickened when an autopsy later revealed wooden skewers in the dog's stomach – suggesting that the generous proprietors of the food stalls nearby had something to do with his loyalty.

Transport

Shibuya-ku is one of the most eclectic areas in terms of transport. It's easily accessible from the JR Yamanote and Saikyo train lines, as well as the Ginza, Chiyoda, Hanzomon and Hibiya metro lines. In addition, the Tōkyū-Denentoshi and Tōkyū-Toyoko lines run from Shibuya and Ebisu stations, heading towards Meguro-ku, Setagaya-ku and Yokohama. The Keio and Odakyu lines also pass through Shibuya on the way from Shinjuku to Setagaya-ku. Bus services are reliable, running through to Meguro-ku, Minato-ku, Setagaya-ku and Western Tokyo areas like Nakano-ku and Suginami-ku.

By car, depending on the area, you shouldn't get many traffic problems. The zones just around Shibuya and Ebisu station are usually fairly congested, but places like Daikanyama, Hirō and Yoyogi-Uehara are less busy.

Safety & Annoyances

The area around Shibuya station is crowded and can be a safety concern, but it's not overtly dangerous. Practice a healthy dose of awareness and common sense as you might in any other city centre location. Other areas in the ward, such as Harajuku, are simply crowded and noisy.

Districts In Shibuya-ku

Daikanyama – Just a few minutes from Shibuya on the Tōkyū-Toyoko line, Dainkanyama is known for its artists, design professionals and celebrities. The buildings are a mix of some smaller, older Japanese-style houses, apartment blocks and larger, brand new designer homes. It's a wonderful spot if you're interested in architecture. The streets are wide and lined with trees, and the neighbourhoods are far quieter than other parts of Shibuya, but they are also among the most expensive. Expect to find mostly one to three bedroom apartments starting at ¥300,000 and running to upwards of ¥2 million for a designer four-bedroom place.

Ebisu – Just north of Meguro-ku and east of Daikanyama, Ebisu is a popular choice for executives. The housing here is quite expensive heading towards Ebisu Garden Place, however closer to the station there are mostly one and two bedroom units that are a bit more affordable. Options range from ¥180,000 for a well-lived in two bedroom to ¥550,000 for a three bedroom flat.

Harajuku – Most of the accommodation here is in the Jingūmae area. There is not much in terms of choice and often limited availability. A two bedroom will typically cost about ¥580,000. Nearby, Horizon International School (www.horizon.ac.jp) is popular with expats.

Hirō – Bordering Azabu with easy access to the International School of the Sacred Heart and Nishimachi International School (p.135), housing in Hirō is at a premium. This is one of the most popular areas for expats to live in, as it's got greenery and it's close to international supermarkets like National Azabu (p.315), and it's not far from the Tokyo American Club (p.242) for a bit of social and sporting activity. Expect to see apartments that are mostly two to four bedrooms with rents from ¥400,000 to more than ¥1.6 million a month.

Shōtō – One of the oldest Shibuya neighbourhoods, Shōtō is a favourite of families with kids at either the American School (p.133) or the British School (p.133). The area consists of mostly upscale homes and larger multi-room apartments with hefty price tags – a four bedroom apartment can cost as much as ¥900,000 per month.

Yoyogi-Uehara – A great place for people with kids at the American School in Japan, it's a peaceful area with a semi-suburban atmosphere. Among trees, wide streets, small shops and cafes, houses are mostly detached with gardens, and a three bedroom can easily run to as much as ¥900,000. There is a beautiful mosque in the area.

Area **K** *p.77*
See also Map 6

Shinagawa-ku

Located in the southeast of Tokyo, Shinagawa-ku is an alternative to living in the more typically expat areas. East of Minato-ku and south of Chūō-ku, Shinagawa is nestled in the crook of Tokyo Bay, allowing for some surprising waterfront opportunities and beautiful views of the Rainbow Bridge and Odaiba. It's convenient for families associated with the Canadian International School and is home to the immigration arm of the Ministry of Justice. The main residential areas are in Higashi-Gotanda, Ikedayama and the seaside zone, Shinagawa. The area is a knot of high rise buildings, bridges, and canals, but if you venture out further, there's a decidedly different feel.

Best Points

Being by the water and having convenient access to the centre of Tokyo's shopping and culture make this an attractive area.

Worst Points

Prices are high and it may be difficult to find smaller, more affordable apartments.

Accommodation

Prices vary greatly depending on the area, however it's the domain of mostly one to three bedroom apartments and homes. Ikedayama is exclusive and offers luxury, high-end stately homes. In Higashi-Gotanda and Shinagawa Seaside, one-beds start at ¥200,000 and three-beds cost from ¥340,000 to ¥450,000.

Shopping & Amenities

The Shinagawa station area has several shopping opportunities, including the Shinagawa GC building and Shinagawa Intercity. There is a large Dean and Deluca deli and grocery located in the station along with other boutiques and restaurants, and all around the station there are cafes, shops, karaoke venues and cinemas. It's an easy trip to some of the city's major retail centres such as Roppongi and Ginza, and Odaiba shopping megaplexes and Shiodome lifestyle complex are just a few minutes away.

Entertainment & Leisure

The biggest attraction is the Shinagawa Aquarium (p.168) – kids love it. Nearby is Shinagawa Kumin Kōen, a park that makes a good play area for children. There are amusement centres in Odaiba's Palette Town, as well as the popular Hamarikyu Garden, just off of Hinode Pier in the bay. The water-bus from Hinode goes north to Asakusa and is a lovely afternoon trip up the Sumidagawa. For artistic inspiration, try the Hara Museum of Contemporary Art. The Tokyo American Club (p.239) is near Shinagawa station, until 2010.

Healthcare

In addition to the local independent clinics, St Lukes Hospital is conveniently placed in the east of Shinagawa-ku close to Tsukiji Fish Market.

Education

The Canadian International School (www.cisjapan.net) is in Kita-Shinagawa, near Gotanda station. The area also offers convenient access to the international schools in Minato-ku.

Transport

Shinagawa station is one of the major stops on the JR Yamanote line. It is also a major travel hub into Kanagawa and is a stop for *shinkansen* trains. Haneda Airport is 15 minutes away. The Tokyo Monorail and Rinkai lines provide transport to the waterfront and island stations in the bay, as does the nearby Yurikamome line in Minato-ku. Buses run north and south from most major stations in the area, as well as down to the waterfront areas from Shinagawa station. The area surrounding Shinagawa and Gotanda stations is a bit congested, but the residential areas are less busy.

Safety & Annoyances

Although traffic in the Gotanda and Shinagawa areas may be a bit annoying, there are no major safety concerns.

Dry Cleaners p.74
Divorce Lawyers p.108

Written by residents, these unique guidebooks are packed with insider info, from arriving in a new destination to making it your home and everything in between.

Explorer Residents' Guides
We Know Where You Live

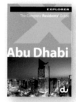

Area **L** *p.77*
See also Map 3, 4

Best Points
Easy access, great shopping, and the beauty of Shinjuku Gyōen all in one area. If you want a home with both quiet and excitement, this may be for you.

Worst Points
Housing options are limited if you have a smaller apartment and budget in mind.

Shinjuku-ku

Shinjuku is one of the major hubs for transport and shopping in Tokyo. And while it is not quite as green or quiet as some other areas, it has some charm that attracts expats to live there. Bordered by Shibuya in the south and Bunkyō and Chiyoda wards in the north and east, the main residential areas are concentrated closer to Chiyoda-ku and Bunkyō-ku, with the western area being primarily commercial. This means it has limited housing options, but great shopping. It's serviced by the JR Chūō, Sobu and Yamanote lines as well as the Seibu Shinjuku line and the Ōedo, Shinjuku and Marunouchi metro lines.

Accommodation
There's not much in the way of accomodation around Shinjuku station. Single bedroom and smaller apartments are available, but they will take some hunting down, especially if you want a reasonable price. But further afield there are many options. Shin-Okubo is a popular place for expats to secure an apartment. There are also many guesthouses in this area that cater exclusively to foreigners. Rents in Shin-Okubo are reasonable as many Japanese consider the area to be dangerous. This is partly due to all the Chinese and Koreans living here. However, it's actually very safe and you'll be as comfortable here as in any other Tokyo neighbourhood. Shinjuku itself is not a particularly nice place for expat families to set up shop. Some areas can be somewhat seedy and there isn't much for children to do.

Shopping & Amenities
There is no lack of shopping opportunities, and the best ones are found close to Shinjuku station. Hundreds of shops, department stores and luxury boutiques make it a one stop destination for shopping. Major electronics outlets like Bic Camera (p.295) and Yodobashi (p.282) are favourites. You can also find decent shopping around Iidabashi and Yotsuya stations, but don't expect the variety found in Shinjuku.

Entertainment & Leisure
Shinjuku has several cinemas and hundreds of bars and cafes. There are a few large karaoke boxes, and the Kabuki-cho entertainment district is often packed. Opera City is a favourite for performances and exhibitions. Nearby you can also access the northern reaches of Yoyogi Kōen (p.186) and Shinjuku Gyōen (p.186), a small oasis of peace in the bustle of Shinjuku. If you want more, Shibuya, Harajuku and Roppongi are just a few stops away.

Healthcare
Koseinenkin Hospital (03 3269 8111) is in the area, as well as many independent clinics. Seibo International Catholic Hospital (p.119) is nearby, and has a good obstetrics ward and English-speaking staff. Keio University Hospital (p.120) is opposite Shinanomachi station.

Education
Shinjuku-ku holds special appeal for French expats sending kids to the Lycée Franco-Japonais (p.134). It is also a manageable commute to the international schools in Minato, Shibuya and the western wards of Tokyo.

Transport
Shinjuku is a very busy area, with many major train lines and roads running through it, and traffic is heavy at most times of the day, except weekend mornings. Parking is limited to pay parking lots and rented spaces. Shinjuku is the busiest station in Japan, with the highest number of passengers passing through its platforms on any given day. It is the nexus of not only most of the major train lines in Tokyo, but also

Shinjuku lights

some of the most important metro lines in the city. JR lines include the Yamanote, Chūō and Chūō-Sobu lines cutting east-west through the city, and the Shonan-Shinjuku and Tokkaido lines heading towards Chiba and Yokohama. Seibu lines go north into Toshima and Nerima wards, and both Keio and Odakyu lines head west and southwest into Setagaya-ku and Meguro-ku, then all to the Yokohama area. Narita Airport is about 90 minutes away via the Narita Express, leaving from Shinjuku station.

Shinjuku-ku is also accessible via the Marunouchi, Shinjuku, Chiyoda and Ōedo metro lines. Highway buses out of the Kanto region leave from Shinjuku station, while local bus services run west into Nakano and Sugnami wards, south into Shibuya, and east into Chiyoda and Bunkyō wards.

Safety & Annoyances

Life in Shinjuku-ku can be rather noisy if you are close to the major stations. Get into the neighbourhoods, and things quiet down. Kabuki-cho is an area that is frequently cited by police as a not-so-safe area (in relative terms in Japan), however it's quite far from the usual residential areas and doesn't post a threat to most people.

Districts In Shinjuku-ku

Ichigaya & Iidabashi – This area is close to the Lycée Franco-Japonais (p.134). Walk a bit south from Iidabashi and you come to Yasukuni Jinja (p.178), a very green spot. This area is mostly three and four bedroom apartments and semi-detached houses going for about ¥400,000. Closer to Akebonobashi, things can get more expensive with some newer luxury homes for over ¥1 million per month.

Kagurazaka – Well-known for its small French bistros, this area is a favourite for families with the Lycée Franco-Japonais. There are small, leafy streets, little shrines and tiny shops. There isn't much in the way of shopping (it's mostly down the road near Iidabashi), but it's a lovely place if you don't mind walking a bit to stock up on groceries and other bits and bobs.

Expect to see more single room apartments here, mostly in older buildings. These are balanced with newly constructed luxury towers with a good view of Shinjuku since they are the tallest things in the area. 2DK spaces start at a reasonable ¥120,000 per month, and luxury units can go for as much as ¥900,000 for a two bedroom penthouse in one of the new towers.

Takadanobaba – The closest thing that Tokyo has to a college town, Takadanobaba (or Baba) is a jumping community with lots of good food and low-key, late night entertainment. Sandwiched between Shinjuku and Ikebukuro, it has slowly gained itself a reputation as a desirable place to live.

Housing in Baba can be very cheap if you are willing to share some amenities. Due to the number of students in the area, there are numerous guesthouses and shared apartments. Most of these are geared towards young Japanese, so you may want to keep that in mind. Apartments can be found near the main station, but living a brisk 20 minute walk away will greatly reduce the rent.

Yotsuya – A comparatively urban area, this has more in the way of affordable and smaller options. Despite the packed-in and built-up feel, the streets can still be pretty quiet. You can find a lot of one and two bedroom apartments for ¥120,000 to ¥300,000 per month.

Area p.76
See also Map 3

Best Points
*Convenience of being
close to Shinjuku
without the high prices.
You can have a quieter
lifestyle with some
welcome distractions.
It's an easy commute
to most international
schools and
commercial districts.*

Worst Points
*Some of the buildings
are a bit old and
the development
isn't quite as quick
as in neighbouring
Nakano-ku.*

Suginami-ku

Just 10 minutes west of Shinjuku is Suginami-ku, a lively and vital part of the Tokyo metropolitan area. The Suginami area is bordered by Nakano-ku in the east, Nerima-ku in the north and Setagaya-ku in the south. The main residential areas of Suginami-ku are Kōenji, Asagaya and Ogikubo. These neighbourhoods are slightly more city-like than most residential neighbourhoods in other parts of Tokyo, however it still has its fair share of greenery.

Accommodation

This area is mostly for singles, couples and students attending nearby universities. Both houses and multi-room apartments are available, but newer accommodation is getting pricier. Houses are closer together than in some other wards popular with expats, but neighbourhoods are quiet enough to let you relax.

Shopping & Amenities

Good shopping abounds around the main neighbourhoods in Suginami-ku. Kōenji is well known for its second-hand shops and small vintage toy stores, while Asagaya has various shopping streets, and Ogikubo has a Lumine department store and Town Seven shopping building. There are two international markets, Kaldi Coffee Farm and The Garden Jiyūgaoka, in the Lumine in Ogikubo, as well as several organic markets from there to Asagaya.

Entertainment & Leisure

Life is a bit slower on this side of Shinjuku, and the fun tends to be found in the *izakayas* lining the streets near the stations. Asagaya and Ogikubo are known for their classical and jazz bars, small *izakayas*, French bistros and winebars. Kōenji is home to many live houses specialising in blues, punk and rock, and favourite local restaurants such as Rose-tei (for giant pork cutlets) and Dachibin (for Okinawan food). Most of the cafes are centred in the Asagaya and Kōenji station areas, and Planet 3rd, about three blocks south of Kōenji station is worth a visit.

There are several traditional shrines and temples in the area, allowing it to maintain a more natural feel. Zempukuji Kōen is located in Ogikubo, just on the border with Musashino-shi and Kichijōji.

Healthcare

Kawakita Hospital is located in Asagaya and offers various specialities. There are numerous clinics in the area, and Musashino hospital is not far from Suginami-ku.

Education

Although the commute to the international schools of Minato-ku might be a bit long, Suginami-ku has Aoba-Japan International School (www.a-jis.com). In addition, international schools located in Musashino-shi, Mitaka-shi and Setagaya-ku will be close by. There is also Santa Maria International School (2-2-4, Minami Tanaka, Nerima-ku, 03 3904 0509) and the New International School (p.134) in Toshima-ku.

Transport

Suginami is serviced mainly by the JR Chūō and Sobu lines, and the Tozai and Marunouchi metro lines. Bus services are available southeast to Shibuya and Setagaya-ku, and take about 30 minutes.

There are two main thoroughfares running through the ward into the centre of the city, Ōmekaidō and Itsukaichi-kaidō. These roads are often busy, regardless of the time of day. In the neighbourhood backstreets, the roads are a complex maze of narrow one-way streets. Parking is hard to come by if you don't have a permanent spot, and there is no kerbside parking.

Safety & Annoyances

Suginami-ku is rather well policed, as in the past there have been complaints of break-ins. The traffic around the stations might pose a noise problem, as might the noise from trains as some houses can be quite close to the tracks. It can also get crowded during the summer festival season.

Districts In Suginami-ku

Kōenji – This area is a well-known spot for music and vintage lovers. The area is best suited to young singles and couples who don't mind living in an older apartment. Prices range from ¥60,000 per month for a studio a few minutes walk from the station, to two and three bedroom apartments further away that go for ¥250,000 to ¥350,000. The Awaodori festival (p.46) each summer is the second largest dance festival of its kind in Japan.

Asagaya – Nakasugi Dōri is a beautiful, tree-lined avenue just near the station. There are a few upscale mid-size apartment buildings here, but most of the area is older *manshons* and one and two bedroom semi-detached and detached houses. 1K rents start around ¥70,000 per month in the older buildings and two bedroom semi-detached houses can run to as little as ¥120,000. The Tanabata Festival (p.46) in the summer is a popular event.

Ogikubo – A favorite residential area for famous Japanese comedians and up and coming sumo wrestlers, this area is a bit more urban than Asagaya, and traditional *ramen* shops abound. Newer buildings seem to be constructed here a bit more often, so if you're looking for a newer place this might be for you. IYC yoga centre (p.269), the first major yoga school in the country, is located here and draws enthusiasts from all over Tokyo and Japan. This area is perfect for young professionals and singles looking for convenience and a less expensive alternative to Shibuya or Shinjuku. 1K apartments range from ¥80,000 to ¥120,000 per month, and two bedrooms average between ¥120,000 and ¥160,000.

Bustling nearby Shinjuku

Outer Tokyo

Central Tokyo isn't the only place where you can find a great place to live. There are also some interesting and often quieter areas to the west of Shinjuku that still have excellent access to the heart of the city. It is possible to commute into the city from Chiba, Kanagawa, Saitama and Yokohama prefectures and Kawasaki city. It may mean a longer commute, but housing is likely to be a lot cheaper, and can open up options for larger houses in quieter areas rather than just apartments. Depending on what you're looking for and your commute, the areas below might be worth considering.

Area **N** *p.77*
See also Map 3

Ikebukuro

Ikebukuro borders the northern prefecture of Saitama. The area only really came into its own in the 1980's, and 50 years ago it was just rice fields. There are numerous bars, shops (it's home to department stores Seibu and Tobu, and the fashionable Sunshine Street boutiques) and good spots for cheap eats. Sunshine City has an aquarium and a planetarium and the Tokyo Metropolitan Art Space (p.164) is on the west side. However, other amenities may be slightly lacking: it's extremely urban and the pockets of green that flourish in other parts of town are clearly missing. The parks that exist are grey concrete plazas with a few blades of grass, and litter and homeless people seem more prevalent than other areas. However, foreign urbanites with a penchant for bright lights and big cities will live comfortably.

Ikebukuro is one of the cheaper places to live on the Yamanote Line. Decent sized apartments can be found in the immediate area for under ¥100,000 and those willing to live a 10 minute walk from the station will pay considerably less. Ikebukuro station is book-ended on the Yamanote line by Mejiro and Ōtsuka and a number of friendly guesthouses cater to foreigners. The Tobu Toju and Seibu Ikebukuro lines have terminuses in Ikebukuro and apartments can be found very cheaply along these lines.

Area **P** *p.76*

Hachiōji-shi

A modern and bustling out-post of Tokyo, Hachiōji is like a smaller version of Shinjuku, located about 40 minutes west by the JR Chūō line. The closest major station to the American military base at Fussa, this area is a popular playground for young people from surrounding universities as well as mainly American expats associated with contracted business in the area. Around the station are some taller commercial buildings and a Sogo department store. Moving away from the station area, the neighbourhoods quickly become quiet but retain a light urban feel. 1K apartments in recently-built buildings can start from as low as ¥30,000 per month. Houses are a steal, with 4 bedroom houses with gardens for as little as ¥380,000.

Hachioji Gastrointestinal Hospital and Tokai University Hachioji Hospital are located in the area. The main international schools are bit of a hike, but schools that service Musashino-shi may be a manageable commute. Hachiōji may be further from Tokyo than some people would like, but it represents an excellent opportunity for anyone interested in living closer to the natural areas surrounding the city.

Area **Q** *p.76*

Kichijōji & Musashino-shi

This semi-suburban area is centred around Kichijōji station and has plenty of shopping, including Parco and Marui department stores. Crafts mecca Yuzaway is attached to the station, and across the road is a cinema. Isetan has an annexe store, and about two blocks from the station you can find a Tokyu Hands (p.308) department store. There is also a Yodobashi Camera (p.321), plenty of small boutiques and cafes, and several shopping streets which have small blocks that run the gamut of specialising in used records, second-hand clothes, Pan-Asian goods, cosmetics, handmade knits, one-of a kind design items by local artists, as well as more upscale shopping. The area is rich

Tokyo Metropolitan Art Space

in history and is famous for its popular Inokashira Kōen. This park is well renowned for its swan-shaped boats and beautiful cherry blossoms in April, and has a small zoo. The Jindai Botanical Gardens (p.184) is a must-visit. There is also Kichijoji Art Museum and Ghibli Museum (p.175). Most of the accommodation in Kichijōji and Musashino-shi is a mix of suburban detached and semi-detached homes, as well as smaller apartment complexes and *manshons*. If you are looking for a more Japanese-style home, this is a good place to find it. Prices range from ¥50,000 per month for an older 1K to ¥500,000 for a 4-bedroom house. The range of prices and the potential for both slow and faster-paced lifestyles make Musashino-shi a location that is growing in popularity with expats in Tokyo. Musashino Hospital is easily accessible. The Inter Pacific High School is located in Musashino-shi, and the Tokyo International Learning Community is also close by in Mitaka-shi. Kichijoji 0123 is well-known nursery located in a very quiet area only an eight minute walk from Kichijōji station. There are also a few international schools in Meguro-ku, Setagaya-ku, and Chofu-shi to the south that can be easily accessed from Musachino-shi. Most noteable of these is the American School in Japan. The Aoba International School is close by in Suginami-ku.

The weekends can get a bit crowded, as can 'leaf-viewing' season in autumn and *hanami* (cherry-blossom viewing) season in spring. In general, however, the area allows for a relaxed lifestyle away from the typical noise of the city.

This area is about 15 minutes west of Shinjuku on the Chūō and Chūō-Sobu lines, and from Shibuya station on the Keio-Inokashira line. It also receives limited service by the Tozai metro line.

Area **R** *p.76*

Tachikawa-shi

Just a 30 minute train ride from Shinjuku, Tachikawa-shi is a blend of urban and suburban co-existence. The station area has some high rise commercial buildings, being one of the main stops and hubs on the JR Chūō line. The Tama monorail also stops in Tachikawa. The expat community doesn't have quite as strong a presence as in other areas of Tokyo, so this might give you a more unique Tokyo living experience.

You can find convenient shopping choices such as Isetan, Marui, and Takashimaya department stores. Electronics giant Bic Camera also has an outlet, as does HMV Records. The Cinema City movie complex has a karaoke box to maximise your entertainment choices. Just 10 minutes from the station is Showa Kinen, which provides a nice green space to relax. The park also puts on spectacular fireworks over the summer months.

There are plenty of one, two and three bedroom apartments located close to the station that may be more affordable than in other places closer to the city centre. One bedroom units start from as little as ¥70,000 a month in a modestly aged building to as high as ¥300,000 a month for something in one of the newer apartment blocks. Houses can be found further from the station, usually in slightly older but quiet, and inviting neighbourhoods. Prices start at ¥200,000 per month for a two bedroom unit. Tachikawa Hospital is located a short distance from the station. The international schools in Musashino-shi are close by, so school commutes may not be too long. The station area is rather built-up, so shopping crowds and noise from the station may be a concern, however in the neighbourhoods peace and quiet are the norm.

Setting Up Home

Now that you've found a place to hang your hat it's time to set up house and enjoy life in Japan. Settling in needn't be difficult and there are a range of foreigner-friendly services in the city to help you make a house a home. If you've come to Japan for a job you may have had everything organised for you, but there will still be those little things that you'll need to find on your own like where to rent a movie, hire a cleaner or babysitter, and who to call when you come across that first nasty cockroach.

Moving Services

Relocating is not an easy task, especially if you're downsizing from a roomy, western-style place to a smaller Japanese apartment. However, there are a number of reputable international movers such as Crown Relocations, Allied Pickfords, and Santa Fe Relocation Services (see tables) who can take the hassle out of the shift.

If you're moving locally, well-priced removal companies like Sekine offer their services for around ¥10,000 to ¥20,000 per half or full day. Many companies offer full packing services but you can opt to do it yourself and save some cash.

Cars and mini vans can also be rented for a day but prices are often comparable to hiring professionals, and the latter offer the added peace of mind that your goods are insured against damage during the move.

There are a number of furnished apartments available, as well as places were you can pick up cheap furnishings. If you want to ship your own furniture over, or take it with you when you leave, make sure to check the shipping restrictions in both your port of departure and arrival. You can bring in household effects free of duty and/or tax within a reasonable limit. Restricted items are pretty standard and cover a range of illegal and inappropriate articles, visit www.customs.go.jp for more.

Smooth Moves

To make your move as painless as possible, here are some tips:

- Create a list of all the people who you need to notify of your change of address and send them a letter with the details. Also change your address with your local post office. They will forward your mail to your new address for up to a year.
- Pack each room one by one and label each box so you know where to take it to unpack.
- Check the weight of each box as you are packing it to make sure it's not getting too heavy to move.

Removal Companies

Economove	0120 98 1862	www.economovejapan.com
Econoship	0120 22 2111	www.econoship.net
Quoz	03 5932 7777	www.quoz.biz
Seino Transportation	0120 75 4754	www.seino.co.jp/seino
Sekine	03 5313 3910	www13.plala.or.jp/sekine-/
XPS Tokyo	03 5438 7631	www.xpstokyo.com
Yamatane Corporation	03 3820 1130	www.yamatane.co.jp

Relocation Companies

A-CROSS	03 5449 7621	www.a-cross.jp
Allied Pickfords	03 5549 6200	www.alliedpickfords.co.jp
Asian Tigers Premier Worldwide Movers	03 6402 2371	www.asiantigers-japan.com
Crown Relocations	03 5447 2301	www.crownrelo.com
H&R Consultants	03 5575 2340	www.JapanHomeSearch.com
MKC Properties	03 5485 7781	www.mkc-properties.com
Santa Fe Relocation Services	03 3589 6666	www.santaferelo.com

Furnishing Your Home

A number of real estate agencies offer fully furnished and semi-furnished apartments. Semi-furnished apartments typically include basic fixtures, curtains, and some electrical appliances. Some removal companies, such as XPS Tokyo (above) sell new and used furniture. Alternatively, H&R Consultants (above) will lease furniture, linen, crockery, and electrical items for short or long periods, as will May's Corporation (www.mays.co.jp) and Tokyo Lease Corporation (www.furniture-rental-tokyo.com). For new goods,

IKEA (www.ikea.com) is a low-cost option. HH Style (www.hhstyle.com) has more stylish choices and Ma by SoShiTe (www.mabysoshite.com) sells Japanese-style furniture.

Second-Hand Items

There are a number of flea markets (p.309) selling second-hand items but if you're looking for second-hand furniture or electronic equipment, visit *Tokyo Notice Board* (www.tokyonoticeboard.co.jp) or *Metropolis* (www.metropolis.co.jp). Notice boards at places like the National Azabu supermarket (p.315) also list items for sale. Don't hesitate if you see something you like as goods tend to go quick. '*Sayonara* Sales' (organised by residents who are leaving) often off-load goods for free or on the cheap (p.308).

Tailors & Furniture Restoration

Other options **Tailoring** p.302

Most tailors only do dressmaking and alterations. Mado Mado (04 2255 4181, www.mado-mado.com) makes curtains to order and has a huge selection of fabrics to choose from (no English is spoken though). IKEA (www.ikea.com) is also good for curtains, you can choose the fabric and have them made-to-measure. Cibone (03 3475 8017, www.cibone.com). Department store Tokyu Hands (p.308) sells everything you might need to do your own stitching and designs. If your much-loved furniture is in need of some TLC, call Restore Repair Service (03 3455 8866, www.restore.co.jp). They can repair furniture and restore antiques. Daniel (0120 49 7669, www.daniel.co.jp) can also help with items in need of attention.

Household Insurance		
Fuji Fire & Marine Insurance	0120 228 386	www.fujikasai.co.jp
Nipponkoa Insurance	0120 258 110	www.nipponkoa.co.jp
Nissay Dowa Insurance	0120 950 055	www.nissaydowa.co.jp

Household Insurance

Japan may be a relatively safe country but it is still wise to have some form of house protection, especially considering the high earthquake risk. A real estate agency will sort an insurance package for you, for which you will have to pay a premium. Try foreigner friendly ones like Monthly Apartment Tokyo (03 5772 3919, www.monthly-apartment-tokyo.com) and Tokyo Rent (03 3265 6363, www.tokyorent.com). If you leave before the term expires you may be entitled to a partial refund (if you have paid upfront). Insurance policies vary but the average cost is ¥20,000 to ¥40,000 for two years cover. Earthquake coverage is separate and costs an additional ¥10,000 to ¥20,000 for two years. Always check what is included in the policy before signing.

Laundry Services

There are numerous launderettes dotted throughout the city. Coin Laundry (www.coinlaundry.co.jp) is a large chain with a number of branches in Western Tokyo while Shimizuyu Laundry (3-12-3 Minami Aoyama and 1-17-5 Minami Aoyama, Minato-ku, Map 8-E2) near exit A4 of Omotesandō station covers the city centre.

To wash a load will cost from ¥150 to ¥300 – cold water washes are the cheaper option. Many people put on a load and leave, returning just as it finishes, but be warned, the launderette will not take responsibility for stolen clothes.

Kimono

Most apartments have their own washing machine (often found on the balcony due to limited space).

Drycleaning is cheap and there are drycleaners all over the city. It usually takes a couple of days and some places will deliver for an additional fee. Prices vary but on average expect to pay around ¥700 for trousers, ¥1,900 for coats and ¥600 for skirts. Well-known chains like Hakuyosha (www.hakuyosha.co.jp) offer a range of additional services such as curtain and carpet cleaning, and pick up and delivery.

Domestic Help

Other options **Entry Visa** p.53

Finding domestic help is fairly simple and there is a range of reputable and reliable agencies (see table below). Using an agency offers the added bonus of having a middleman to go through if you're not happy with the service but hiring independently will be cheaper. Duskin Merry Maids don't speak much English over the phone but you should be able to communicate fine in person. If you want to hire yourself, ask around for recommendations, check out supermarket noticeboards in shops like National Azabu (p.315) or Nissin (p.315) or look for ads at the Tokyo Union Church (www2.gol.com/users/tuc). The going rate for non-agency help is around ¥1,500 an hour.

Full-time and part-time housekeepers usually return home at the end of the day rather than living with the family and you will have to pay their transport costs. Part-time maids cost around ¥2,000 an hour and normally have to be hired for a minimum of three to four hours. If you're looking for someone permanent, expect to pay ¥190,000 to ¥240,000 (live-in help prices will be slightly lower).

Domestic Help Agencies		
Chez Vous	0120 69 9100	www.chezvous.co.jp
Duskin Merry Maids	0120 89 2949	www.duskin.cleans.jp
Tokyo Maid Services	03 3291 3595	na

Sponsoring A Maid

If you sponsor a full-time maid, you are guaranteeing their employment and they must be paid a set wage each month. Not just anyone can sponsor though and you'll have to go to the immigration office to see if you are eligible (they usually only consider high-flying professionals).

A contract needs to be drawn up, outlining the working hours and payment (the minimum wage is ¥150,000 per month), the number of paid holiday days (normally around 10 days, but may be up to a month), health insurance benefits (covered by you), and an annual paid ticket to their home country. Most maids come from the Philippines and Thailand, or other South-East Asian countries.

Babysitting & Childcare

There are a number of babysitting companies and domestic help agencies specialising in childcare. Most are Japanese but there are some foreigner friendly services like Chez Vous and Poppins. Sitter credentials vary from trained childcare professionals to bubbly young adults (with childcare experience). The going rate is just under ¥2,000 an hour. However, factors like time of day, additional services such as pick-up from school, the age of the child and whether or not you need a regular service or just someone for the odd day affects the price. Agencies normally charge a registration fee (which can be anything from ¥5,000 to ¥50,000) and an annual fee (usually around ¥10,000).

Babysitting & Childcare		
Chez Vous	0120 69 9100	www.chezvous.co.jp
Family Support	03 3377 3177	www.familysupport.co.jp
Kinder Network	03 6415 8271	www.kinder-network.com
Poppins	03 3447 2100	www.poppins.ne.jp

Tokyo New Mothers (www.phpbbplanet.com/tokyonewmothers) is a support group and a great forum for finding out useful information. You can also ask at your local school whether any of the teaching assistants are looking for extra work – check with the principal first though rather than directly approaching a teacher. Hotels like the New Otani (www.newotani.co.jp) and Grand Hyatt (http://tokyo.grand.hyatt.com) also provide babysitting services for guests.

Domestic Services

If you're in need of some household repairs, speak to your landlord or rental agency – they should organise for someone to come round. Foreigners in need of a handyman to help with

Domestic Services		
Name	Phone	Type of Service
Apex	03 3455 6474	Pest control
Benry	0120 84 0052	Handyman
Chez Vous	0120 69 9100	Handyman
Duskin	0120 10 0100	Pest control

the general cleaning of vents and air-conditioning units and odd jobs like furniture assembly can hire help through Chez Vous or Benry (see table). Expect to pay upwards of ¥15,000 for a half-day's work. Benry also has a pest control service. Many agencies have several branches but they will all take on jobs citywide.

DVD & Video Rental

From ordering online, picking up a DVD at your local train station, or the traditional approach of visiting your neighbourhood video shop, you'll never be far from Hollywood. DVDs are cheap to rent at only a few hundred yen each and there are a number of smaller video shops as well as chain stores where you can pick up a movie. One of the best known and convenient (with stores near most major stations) is Tsutaya (www.tsutaya.co.jp), which sells and rents DVDs and has a great selection. Once you have been a member of your local branch for a month you can use your membership card at other branches across the city. Geo (www.geogp.com) is another well-known DVD rental chain with over 60 locations citywide.

Under Tsutaya's umbrella is Tsutaya Discas (www2.discas.net/cgi-bin/netdvds), an online video shop. If you can read Japanese there are a number of online shops like Discas where you can rent DVDs online. They will ship movies for free within one to three days and you can keep for as long as you like – although the next title on order won't be sent out until the last one is returned. Expect to pay a monthly flat fee of at least ¥2,000 – prices vary depending on the package. Posren is another online option but the website is in Japanese only (http://posren.livedoor.com).

A good English option is Astala Vista who distribute DVDs through machines at major stations (at 30 locations). DVDs cost ¥350 for 24 hours, paid for by credit card.

Pets

Other options **Pets** (Shopping) p.297

In this city with a declining birth rate, dogs seem to have taken on the role of the pampered child. Don't be surprised to see pooches being wheeled about in prams and buggies, or to find them in the chair in the local hair salon, being groomed in the latest style. Be wary of where you shop when looking for a pet, and it's probably wise to steer clear of the pet shops in the Roppongi area. Animal lovers can adopt cats and dogs through non-profit organisations like ARK (see Pet Refuge on p.108) and from international noticeboards at foreign supermarkets, where you'll find ads placed by expats leaving town that can't take their pet with them when they leave.

Puppy love

Cats & Dogs

Dogs must be registered at your local ward office within 30 days of becoming the owner, after which you will be issued a licence tag for its collar. Your dog must have an annual rabies vaccination, which should take place between 1 April and 30 June. It is compulsory for dog owners to clean up after their dog and they must be kept on a leash in crowded areas. Cats must be neutered and should be kept inside. All cats and dogs must wear a collar stating the owner's contact details.

Fish & Birds

There are a number of petshops selling fish throughout the city. Most are small but have a decent selection. Aqualine (www.aqualine8.com) in Arakawa-ku has an extensive range of tropical fish, priced between ¥8,000 and ¥600,000. Aqua Forest in Shinjuku station (www.a-forest.co.jp) also has a good supply. Alternatively, check out An Aquarium (www.an-aquarium.com) at the top of the Matsuzakaya department store in Ginza.
Bird lovers should try the pet shop on the top of the Seibu department store (p.308) in Shibuya. If you have a bird and it's in need of a vet, there is a specialist clinic for birds in Ebisu (see Veterinary Clinics table below).

Grooming & Training

There's no shortage of pet salons, and many could rival top human ones. Grooming doesn't come cheap though; a trim and shampoo can hit ¥20,000 for a big dog at some of the more upmarket places. Dog Days also provide superior dog treats – including vegetarian and organic meals. Some cafes offer dog meals on the menu and many are pooch-friendly. If you've just acquired a new puppy and need some training, Canine Unlimited offer private and group obedience classes in English.

Pet Grooming & Training

Name	Phone	Website	Type of Service
Canine Unlimited	03 5768 9915	www.canine.jp	Obedience training
Cradle	03 6408 0707	www.cradle-inc.com	General grooming, trimming, washing
Dog Days	03 5413 0050	www.dogdays.co.jp	Grooming, pet products, dog spa and boarding
F by Design f	03 5775 6773	www.designf.co.jp	Grooming
Pampered Paws	0422 76 6878	www.pamperedpaws.com	Animal Hairdressing

Vets & Kennels

There are a number of veterinary clinics in the city where some English is spoken. These clinics cater for all animals and services include everything from vaccinations to surgery and behaviour therapy. Akasaka Animal Hospital provides the regular veterinary services as well as nutritional management, obedience training, boarding and grooming services. Emergency services are available for after office hours. Angell Memorial Hirō Central Hospital can be contacted on a 24 hour basis but you will be charged an additional consultation fee of ¥6,000 to ¥15,000 depending on the time.

Veterinary Clinics

Akasaka Animal Hospital	Akabishi Bldg 4-1-29 Akasaka	Minato-ku	03 3583 5852
American Animal Hospital	1-13-1 Kami Ishihara	Chofu-ku	0424 821441
Angell Memorial Hirō Central Hospital	5-24-1 Hirō	Shibuya-ku	03 5420 0012
Animal Wellness Center	1-27-8 Yato-cho	Western Tokyo	0424 38 7811
Ebisu Bird Clinic	1-27-3 Ebisu-nishi	Shibuya-ku	03 3461 8005
Komazawa Animal Hospital	3-16-2 Komazawa	Setagaya-ku	03 3421 7009
Small Animal Clinic	6-5-2 Roppongi	Minato-ku	03 5786 2928

Most places charge a low consultation fee of between ¥1,000 and ¥3,000, but any further tests and treatment are at an additional cost. Blood tests cost in the range of ¥12,000 to ¥18,000.

If you need to go out of town, try Bow Wow Gardens (see table below). Kennel rates vary according to the size of the pet and start at ¥3,000 a night, upwards to ¥8,500. The more centrally located Dog Days charges between ¥7,000 and ¥12,000 a night and has some rather luxurious sleeping options. Daytime dog sitter fees are usually around half of what you'll pay for overnight care. Online noticeboards, such as Tokyo with Kids (www.tokyowithkids.com), are another means of finding someone to care for your pet while you're away.

Pet Boarding & Sitting		
Name	Phone	Type of Service
Bow Wow Gardens	042 380 8200	Boarding services (night and day)
Cradle	03 6408 0707	Daycare
Dog Days	03 5413 0050	Dog Hotel
Dogs Day Care	0120 412 312	Daycare and overnight stays
Pet Royal Inn	0120 223 011	Boarding service at Narita Airport

Pets Out
Most apartments do not allow pets. Check with the real estate agency or landlord before you think about bringing home a four-legged friend.

Bringing Your Pet To Japan
Visit the Japanese Animal Quarantine Service website (www.maff-aqs.go.jp) for up-to-date information on bringing your pet to Japan as regulations vary depending on where you are coming from. You will need to notify the Animal Quarantine Service at least 40 days before you arrive, stating the number of animals you are bringing into the country. If all the paperwork is in order and the animal has an ISO compliant microchip, quarantine can be less than 12 hours. The animal must be in good health, have an up-to-date vaccination card and have had its rabies vaccinations in order to be admitted. Regulations for transporting your pet vary between airlines so check these with your carrier. Animals will be sedated for their comfort during the flight.

Dog grooming

Taking Your Pet Home
When taking your pet out of Japan, they must meet the entry requirements of the country you are moving to, and pass Japan's final quarantine check. Animals must be checked, and test negative, for rabies at the Animal Quarantine Station (AQS) to be cleared to leave. This is a fairly straightforward procedure but you should contact the AQS several days before you are due to leave to arrange the tests. Visit the AQS website for more information at www.maff-aqs.go.jp.

Utilities & Services

As you would expect, Tokyo has the full range of modern utilities, including mains gas. Electricity and gas are provided by private utility firms, while water and sewerage are the responsibility of the metropolitan government's Bureau of Waterworks. For all these utilities there is no choice of suppliers, and connection will usually be handled by your landlord or letting agent. Service is reliable and high quality in all respects, with power cuts all but unheard of.

When it comes to telephone and internet, Tokyoites are among the world's most favoured residents. Mobile phone networks offer cutting edge technology and services, often ahead of other nations, while broadband access is the norm for internet users, who get to enjoy the fastest average connection speeds in the world. Charges for all utilities are generally separate from the rent, but there are exceptions to this rule – check with your landlord or letting agent before taking a property.

Cold Comfort

Although the standard of construction is very high, the city's apartments are notoriously badly insulated – meaning they get painfully cold in winter. Cut your winter bills and avoid seasonal blues by picking a south-facing property, guaranteeing warming sunshine all through the day.

Electricity

Electricity in Tokyo is provided by the Tokyo Electric Power Company (TEPCO), a private utility firm. Connection will usually be arranged by your landlord or letting agent when you move into a new apartment, but you may have to arrange disconnection yourself when the time comes to leave. This and many other services can be done online in English on the TEPCO website (www.tepco.co.jp). If you do need to call TEPCO, English-speaking operators are available toll free on 0120 995 001/005 (the number varies according to which ward of Tokyo you are in, check the website for more details). TEPCO also has branch offices located all over town, mostly open 09:00 to 17:00.

The easiest way to pay your bill is by automatic direct debit, but it is also possible to pay by cash at any post office or convenience store. In either case, billing is monthly. The cost of electricity naturally varies according to size of home and personal habits, but a couple living in a small to medium sized apartment can expect bills of approximately ¥4,000 to ¥6,000 per month in the milder spring and autumn months, rising to ¥8,000 to ¥12,000 per month in the heat of summer and the cold of winter. Electricity is supplied at 100 volts and 50Hz (eastern Japan only, the west is 60Hz), and uses two-pin plugs with flat pins. All appliances are sold with the right plugs. Items from most countries outside Japan will need adaptors for current and plugs.

Water

Water and sewerage in Tokyo are the responsibility of the metropolitan government's Bureau of Waterworks. As with other utilities, connection to the water supply will be arranged by your landlord or letting agent when you move into a new property. If that is not the case, you can arrange to start and stop the water supply in English using the Bureau's website (www.waterworks.metro.tokyo.jp), or they can be contacted by phone on 03 5326 1100. As they say on the website, service in English is offered, 'but please put up with some inconveniences caused by the language barrier'.

Tokyo tap water is safe and drinkable, although filters are popular and widely available. Your water charges also cover sewerage, which is by sewer pipe. Charges vary according to the quantity of water supplied. Bills come every two months, with an average for a single person or couple being about ¥4,000. Bills can be paid by monthly direct debit (which gets you a small discount), or in cash at any post office or convenience store.

Gas

Gas is supplied by Tokyo Gas, a private utility firm (www.tokyo-gas.co.jp). As with other utilities, your gas connection will usually be arranged by your landlord or letting agent when you move into a new property. If not, contact Tokyo Gas on 03 5722 0111 (from a mobile) or 0570 00 2211 (from a landline). English-speaking operators may be available. Gas is generally used for cooking, and often water heating too. Monthly bills for a couple in a moderate apartment are likely to be between ¥3,000 to ¥8,000.

Rubbish Disposal & Recycling

Rubbish disposal in Tokyo is complicated and can vary from ward to ward, and building to building. Much of the city's waste is incinerated, meaning rubbish must be separated into burnable and non-burnable. In addition, bottles, cans and paper should be separated for recycling. Each type of waste will then be collected separately, at least once a week, sometimes twice. If your apartment building has a rubbish room, there will be a notice, usually in Japanese and English, specifying the collection schedule for your area. If there is no notice, or if you live in a house or apartment building with no rubbish room, look for similar notices at the rubbish collection point on the street or contact your ward office for a copy of the collection schedule (usually available in English on request).

There is no fee for standard rubbish collection, but large non-electrical items (furniture) must be collected by the ward, which will charge according to the size of the item. Contact your ward office for details. Under Japanese law, large electrical items (fridges, televisions, etc.) must be recycled. The cost of this is borne by the consumer, with fees varying according to appliance – a fridge will cost about ¥5,000. Again, contact your ward office for details. You can avoid the charge when replacing an old item by asking the retailer to take away the old goods when delivering the new. The shop will then take care of disposing of the discarded goods.

However you dispose of your rubbish in Tokyo, think carefully before breaking the rules: many a foreigner has come to grief with their neighbours or building superintendent after getting caught failing to separate their rubbish, or putting it out on the wrong day, which can mean it is not collected.

Telephone box

Telephone

Other options **Mobile Phones** p.294

The dominant telephone company in Japan is NTT, a former state monopoly that has now been privatised. Getting a landline from NTT is usually quick and easy, thanks to their efficient English-language services – call toll free on 0120 364 463 for all enquiries. But it won't necessarily be cheap: new users must normally pay a one-off subscription fee of ¥37,800 to get connected. In practice, however, there are ways around this. Most popular is the 'lite' line, under which NTT waives the one-off fee in return for a small monthly premium (about ¥250) on top of your monthly line rental (about ¥1,600 to ¥2,900). This makes lite lines (which offer identical service to normal lines), much better value, unless you are sure to be in Japan long term. After you have your line, you need to choose a provider for local, national and international calls. A useful English guide to these so-called My Line providers can be found online at www.myline.org. In theory, it's possible to choose different providers for each different type of call. In practice, picking one provider for all three will save you hassle, and probably money, too. For example, if you choose NTT sister company NTT Communications as your provider for all calls, you can register for their 'sekaiwari' discount international call plan. This costs nothing extra, but slashes international call rates: calls to the US drop from a standard daytime rate of ¥53 per minute to ¥9 per minute; calls to the UK go from ¥140 per minute to ¥20. Other providers, such as KDDI and Softbank, offer similar discount plans. Whichever provider you choose, all local calls will be charged at rates of about ¥8 to ¥9 for three minutes.

Telephone Service Providers		
KDDI	0077 780081	www.kddi.com
NTT Communications	0120 506 506	www.ntt.com
NTT East	0120 106 934	www.ntt-east.co.jp
Softbank Telecom	0800 919 0808	www.softbanktelecom.co.jp
Verizon Japan	0120 610 071	www.verizonbusiness.com

Tariffs get cheaper in the evening from 20:00, and then again from 23:00 to 08:00. Assorted extra services are offered, including call waiting, call forwarding and caller ID display. A nuisance-call blocking service is also offered, allowing users to block any caller simply by punching a code into their handset after receiving a call from the phone pest in question.

Nowadays, it is also possible to get your phone through your cable TV operator (see Television, p.115), or through your broadband internet service provider (see Internet, p.113). Whichever option you choose, you are likely to enjoy reliable and high-quality lines that are not noticeably different from regular lines. Call rates can also be very competitive through these alternative providers.

Pay phones are widely available in Japan, and accept both cash and prepaid cards, which can be bought at convenience stores.

Foreigner Friendly
Newcomer to the market, Softbank is the most foreigner-friendly mobile provider, with its main branch in Harajuku. It emplys dozens of 'gaijin' staff. Softbank is also at present the only operator to offer unlimited calls between subscribers.

Mobile Phones

Japan is a world leader in mobile phone technology, with some of the most advanced handsets and services. The country has three mobile phone network operators: NTT DoCoMo, au by KDDI, and Softbank Mobile. There isn't much to choose between the three, with handset and call costs all very similar, and the myriad of different price plans on offer can make it hard to know which one to pick. Mobile phone numbers start with either 090, 080 or 070.

Your best bet is to head down to one of the major electrical retailers, such as Bic Camera (p.282) or Yodobashi Camera (p.282), where they will be able to talk you through the options (there will usually be an English speaker on hand) and sign you up there and then to any plan on any network. All three networks also have their own dedicated shops, with branches dotted all over town, but these are less likely to feature English-speaking staff. Monthly contract fees generally range from about ¥4,000 to ¥8,000, with a number of free calls included. New subscribers can often get a handset for a token ¥1, or even free, although the latest models go for about ¥30,000. Whichever network you choose, the phone will be offered with various data, language options and voice services. Some of the latest 'One-Seg' phones also come with TV reception capability. All mobile phones can make overseas calls, but make sure this is permitted under the particular price plan you choose. Taking the

Mobile Operators		
au by KDDI	See p.294	www.au.kddi.com
NTT DoCoMo	0120 005 250	www.nttdocomo.co.jp
SoftBank Mobile	See p.294	http://mb.softbank.jp/mb

handsets overseas is more complicated, however, as Japan uses different mobile phone technology from most other nations. Until recently that meant that Japanese handsets didn't work abroad, but multiband phones with international roaming capability are now available – if this is important to you, make sure to specify it when choosing a handset. Getting a regular mobile phone will require a resident's ID. For non-residents, rental handsets are available from the major networks and specialists including PuPuRu

Useful Numbers & Area Codes

Area Codes

Country Code – Japan	+81
Chiba	043/ 047
Hakone	0460
Kawaguchiko	0555
Kobe	078
Kusatso	0279
Kyoto	075
Nagano	0261
Nara	0742
Nijima Island	04992
Nikko	0288
Osaka	06
Oshima Island	04992
Tokyo	03
Western Toko	042
Yokohama	045

Useful Numbers

Toll Free Numbers	0120
International Access Number – Cable & Wireless	+61
International Access Number – Japan Telecom	+41
International Access Number – KDDI	001
KDDI Enquiries (English)	0077
NTT Directory Enquiries	104
NTT Information Service (in English)	0120 36 4463

(www.pupuru.com), Telecom Square (www.telecomsquare.co.jp) and Rentafone Japan (www.rentafonejapan.com). Prepaid phones can also be bought at electrical retailers.

Cheap Overseas Calls

Decreases in rates for standard landlines has seen the relative decline of alternative means to make cheap international calls. Callback services are no longer used much, but discount prepaid phonecards are still competitive. Brastel (www.brastel.com) and KDDI (www.kddi.com) are among the most widely available prepaid cards. These can be purchased online, and recharged either online or at certain convenience stores. Internet voice and video calling using Skype and Microsoft Messenger is available, and works well thanks to Japan's high-speed internet links. It's also free between users of the same provider.

Internet

Other options **Internet Cafes** p.362, **Websites** p.41

Japan is heaven for any keen internet user. With broadband as standard, and connection speeds of up to 100 Mbps, nowhere else on Earth does it better, faster or more reliably. Tokyo offers a plethora of connection options, but while dial-up and ISDN services are still available, the vast majority of users now opt to get online using ADSL, which shares your regular phone line, cable or optical fibre. All three offer reliable high-speed connections, with speeds of 30 to 40 Mbps now considered average. Choosing from the variety of providers and price plans can be bewildering. As with picking a mobile phone, the best place to start is to head to a major electrical retailer such as Bic Camera (p.282), Yodobashi Camera (p.282), Sakuraya (www.sakuraya.co.jp) and Laox (www.laox.co.jp) as they will be able to talk you through the options and sign you up to any plan from any major provider. Take ID and proof of address with you if hoping to sign up on the spot.

Internet Service Providers

@nifty	www.nifty.com	0120 50 2210
AOL	www.jp.aol.com	0120 26 5265
ASAHI Net	http://asahi-net.jp	03 3569 3522
au one net	www.auone-net.jp	0077 78 0081
BIGLOBE	www.biglobe.ne.jp	0120 56 0962
Fusion GOL	www.gol.com	0120 98 7700
OCN	www.ocn.ne.jp	0120 50 6506
ODN	www.odn.ne.jp	0088 22 8850
So-net	www.so-net.ne.jp	0120 11 7268
Yahoo!BB	http://bbpromo.yahoo.co.jp	0120 33 4546

The most popular options are now those offering unlimited online time (such as Yahoo!BB), with packages ranging from about ¥3,000 to ¥8,000 per month, depending on the speed of connection and the services selected. It is also becoming increasingly popular to get telephone services through an internet service provider. Whether by ADSL or cable, such phones provide you with a regular telephone number from which you can make and receive calls in the usual way. The audio quality is just as good as with normal lines, and you can use the internet while making a call.

Whatever internet option you choose, billing is monthly, with charges usually debited directly from your bank account or credit card. Japan has no internet censorship or other restrictions, meaning all sites and services will be available – and may well function faster and better than at home. But visitors to Japan may find that internet cafes are not as common as they are in their home country. The Japanese are keen users of mobile-phone based email and internet, which has reduced the need for internet cafes. There are still plenty throughout the city, and rates are reasonable, ranging from ¥300 to ¥400 per hour. For more on internet cafes, see p.362.

Postal Services

Postal services in Japan are provided by Japan Post (www.post.japanpost.jp), a former state monopoly that is now in the early stages of a decade-long privatisation process. Post offices can be found all over town and are generally open 09:00 to 17:00, Monday to Friday, though some major branches offer limited 24 hour service.

Postal service is generally quick and reliable by global standards. Standard airmail letters reach the US in five to eight days, the UK in about four days, and Australia in about seven days. Sending a 1 kilogram parcel to any of these countries will cost from ¥1,860, with prices rising if you choose express delivery options. Express mail services are available with contents insurance of up to ¥2 million. Mail within Tokyo will generally arrive the next day. Mail to other parts of Japan will take a day or two. Japan Post boxes can be found on the street all over the city and also in convenience stores. Letters are delivered to your door. Stamps can be bought at post offices and most convenience stores.

Courier Services

All the major international courier companies are represented in Tokyo, with Federal Express, UPS and DHL all widely available. The range of services on offer is the same as in other developed countries. Delivery fees are also broadly similar. For example, a 1 kilogram package sent from Japan to the US with FedEx will cost from around ¥10,000. Delivery to the US or Europe takes two to three days.

There are also several domestic courier firms, including Sagawa Express and Kuroneko Yamato. These are less foreigner-friendly than the international firms in terms of bilingual services, but offer the invaluable 'takkyubin' domestic delivery service. Ideal for sending bulky or heavy items around Japan, the takkyubin service is particularly popular with golfers and winter sports fans. Rather than lugging your clubs or snowboard around, send them in advance – it only takes two or three days to anywhere in Japan, and costs as little as ¥2,000. It is also common for people travelling inside Japan, or to an airport to fly abroad, to send luggage a day or so earlier, and pick it up at the airport, hotel or the house of friends or relatives. Items for delivery by takkyubin can be dropped off at any convenience store, but you will need someone who can write Japanese to fill in the form for you (try the staff).

Courier Services		
DHL	0120 39 2580	www.dhl.co.jp
Federal Express	0120 00 3200	www.fedex.com/jp
Kuroneko Yamato	03 3541 3411	www.kuronekoyamato.co.jp
Nippon Express	0120 22 0202	www.nittsu.co.jp
Sagawa Express	03 5764 3117	www.sagawa-exp.co.jp
UPS	0120 27 1040	www.ups.com/jp

Radio

Radio is less influential in Japan than in many other countries, with both music and talk stations very much overshadowed by their television rivals. Nonetheless, there is a variety of stations for Japanese speakers, on both FM and AM, with public broadcaster NHK the biggest player in both genres. Those looking for specialist music channels

TV Asahi Building

are likely to be disappointed, however; a scan of the airwaves will turn up one J-Pop station after the other. English speakers also have few options. Best known is Inter FM 76.1, which features a mix of talk and pop in English and Japanese. But listeners in Tokyo can also catch US armed forces' radio station Eagle 810 (AM). Though this channel does feature a lot of material solely of interest to the military, it also carries general content including syndicated programmes from National Public Radio in the US. Satellite radio is not available in Japan, though many overseas stations are freely available on the internet.

Television

There are seven main terrestrial channels available in the Tokyo area: TV Asahi, Fuji Television, TV Tokyo, Tokyo Broadcasting System, NTV, and the two channels of public broadcaster NHK. All channels are in Japanese, but there is some bilingual broadcasting. Many western films and TV series are shown with both Japanese and English audio, and the main news programmes on NHK and TV Asahi feature English translation of all stories. To receive the English audio you will need a bilingual TV capable of receiving and selecting between the two audio channels. Check with the retailer when purchasing your set, although all but the very cheapest TVs now have this function.

Tokyo residents can also get a wide variety of satellite and cable channels. The main satellite provider is Sky PerfecTV, which offers a wide variety of news, sports and entertainment channels, including many familiar western names such as BBC World, CNN International, Discovery Channel and Animal Planet. Also available by satellite is WOWOW, which is popular with expats for movies and TV series. Receiving satellite broadcasting will require a dish, which some households may find impossible to

Satellite & Cable Providers		
Cable TV Shinagawa	03 3788 3811	www.cts.ne.jp
j:com	0120 99 9000	www.jcom.co.jp
Minato Cable	0120 03 7109	www.cabletv.co.jp
Shinjuku Cable	0120 03 7109	www.cabletv.co.jp
Sky PerfecTV	0570 03 9888	www.skyperfectv.co.jp
Tokyo Cable Network	03 3814 8349	www.tcn-catv.co.jp
Tokyo Cablevision	03 5155 1350	www.tcv.or.jp
WOWOW	0120 58 0807	www.wowow.co.jp
Yahoo!BB	0120 33 4546	http://bbpromo.yahoo.co.jp

install as a south-facing site is required. Companies may send a technician to visit your home to establish whether installation is possible. If it isn't, much the same content is available via a wide variety of cable channels. The many permutations are impossible to summarise here, as the channels tend to be very local, varying from ward to ward. Ask your landlord or inquire at one of the major electrical retailers (see Electronics & Home Appliances p.282) to find out which one serves your area. Whichever one it is, the line-up of international channels is likely to be similar to that featured on satellite. Sports fans can also rest assured that they won't have to go without a fix of their favourite action: both cable and satellite show a good selection of popular western sports including football from the English, Spanish and Italian leagues, and US Major League baseball. Whether you pick cable or satellite, billing will be by automatic monthly payment, with fees typically about ¥4,000 to ¥8,000 per month depending on the mix of content chosen.

General Medical Care

Things are done differently in Japan, so expect to hit a few roadblocks on your path to good health. These days more doctors are studying abroad and bringing a more global approach to their practice, but tradition still reigns, especially in the public sector, and you'll find there are a number of rules and restrictions that make for some inflexible treatment.

Due to the better standard of care and the higher frequency of medical professionals who speak English, most foreigners go private here. Foreign clinics have regular clientele, and having a 'family doctor' is important for keeping your health record all in one place. If you have a child, these clinics can also follow the immunisation schedule of your home country, making the transition smooth between Japan and abroad. If you ask around, you'll find that a lot of people visit the same clinics and they will be able to point you in the right direction of who they think is best.

Maternity care and cosmetic surgery are viewed as extras and are not covered by the National Health Insurance (NHI) scheme, but they may be covered by private plans. NHI covers some dental care but orthodontics is not included, and once again, what is and isn't covered varies among private insurance providers. Some people have NHI but since most foreign clinics don't accept it they also have their own private insurance (see Health Insurance opposite).

The standard of living is high in Japan and you'll find there are no pressing health risks different to those you would find in any other developed nation. However working long hours is typical here, which can take its toll and may result in stress-related problems.

Public Healthcare

The government's National Health Insurance plan (NHI) covers those who are not covered by their company. Once enrolled you will receive an NHI card, which must be taken to any hospital or clinic you visit. This entitles you to 70% off your medical costs, while the remaining 30% of the fee should be paid on the day.

Private Healthcare

The standard of care here is high, but it does pay to ask around before undergoing any treatment or registering for a birth at a hospital. A useful tool is the Tokyo Metropolitan Health and Medical Information Center (03 5285 8181), who can provide any specific information you need on health providers in Tokyo.

Emergency Services

Call 119 if you need an ambulance. If you don't have a phone, public telephones can be used for free by pressing the red button on the front. If you don't speak Japanese, remember to speak slowly when talking to the operator. The Japan Helpline (0120 461 997) also provides English emergency telephone assistance 24 hours a day. Ambulances are free but don't expect the level of care that you may be used to back in your home country. Hospitals have emergency departments but not every person in need of care is accepted. In the event of an emergency your ambulance will call hospitals in the vicinity to see if they can admit you – don't be surprised if a number of calls are made before you find a place. A good place to try is the Japan Red Cross Medical Center (p.119), as they have English-speaking staff.

Pharmacies

Pharmacies sell a full range of medicine including cold and flu pills, pain relief, antihistamines, antibiotics, antifungal cream, antacids and more – all of which are available over the counter. You may have fun explaining your symptoms if you don't speak Japanese – to make the process smoother try find out the Japanese name of

---

Health Checkups

Annual health check-ups are common and many employers will pay for a comprehensive medical check-up. These can be done at various clinics or hospitals, but if your company is not paying, check that it is covered by your insurance plan before booking in, as these exams can be rather pricey. At the Tokyo Medical and Surgical Clinic (see table on p.125), expect to pay upwards of ¥57,000.

A Word Of Warning

It is not compulsory for a hospital to accept you if they are busy, and even in emergencies they can turn you away if they don't have the resources available. Ambulances will call hospitals in their area to see which one can take you, and it is not uncommon to be rejected by a number of hospitals before finding one.

your problem before you go. Although many people seek treatment when they are sick, they also tend to continue to work through their sickness, taking medicine to cure the symptom but not treating the cause. For a listing of pharmacies, see p.293.

Health Insurance

Am I Insured?
Foreign clinics in Japan typically don't accept National Health Insurance, so check before going for a consultation.

If you live in Japan you're required to have some form of health insurance. Some companies will provide this as part of their employment package – although they are not obliged to do so. If they don't, you will have to choose between the Japan National Health Insurance (NHI) scheme or private health insurance.

To register for NHI, you will need to contact your local ward office (p.88). Fees are calculated per household, payable by the head of the household, and you will be invoiced three times a year, in January, July and October. This insurance covers 70% of your costs at a medical facility, with the remaining 30% payable at the medical facility before you check out. Most procedures are included, but expenses that are not are health check-ups, cosmetic surgery, orthodontics, normal childbirth, abortions and non-compulsory vaccinations.

Private health insurance companies provide different packages from basic to premium. At the higher end of the market expect to pay around ¥15,000 a month for full coverage, which will give you 100% of your money back on most medical claims. When choosing a provider look carefully through their coverage plan as there are some questionable insurance agencies out there. One popular and reputable choice, Global Health Insurance, has a range of special packages for expats, teachers and groups. Their prices depend on age, benefits, and whether you want to pay extra to remove

Health Insurance Companies

Global Health	0120 36 0422	www.globalhealth.jp
Medone	03 4580 1711	www.medone.jp
Pacific Prime (Hong Kong)	+852 3113 1331	www.pacificprime.com

the excess that must be paid for each claim. You could end up paying ¥16,000 a month, or the same amount quarterly – depending on what you are after. See insurance companies (above) for more details. If your company or your spouse's company does not offer health insurance and you stay for longer than a year in Japan, you will be applicable for NHI (regardless of whether you already have cover with another company). In general though this is not enforced and is not well-known.

Donor Cards

A Good Heart
The Japan Organ Transplant Network has a comprehensive website in English (www.jotnw.or.jp) with useful information, including recent laws and how to become a registered donor.

If you would like to become an organ donor, visit the Japan Organ Transplant Network website (www.jotnw.or.jp) for information on organ donation and how to become a donor. Email support@jotnw.or.jp to request an organ donation decision card (in English), on which you can circle the appropriate option for what you would like to donate in the event of an accident. Donor cards are also available at city halls, public health centres, post offices and driving schools.

Giving Blood

The Japan Red Cross Society (www.jrc.or.jp) works with the local government to ensure there is a constant supply of blood donated. Their goal is achieved through blood drives held in the city and surrounding prefectures, and through blood collection centres. There are a number of centres near Shinjuku station including Shinjuku West Exit (03 3348 1211) and Shinjuku East Exit (03 5269 1431), one in Shibuya (03 3770 0820) and in Ikebukuro (03 3988 9000). When donating blood you will have to fill out a questionnaire and application form (written in Japanese), although some places have an English copy of the form that you can use as guidance, but in most cases you have to speak and read Japanese, or bring someone along with you who can. Blood from certain nationalities such as British, French and nationals of other European countries is

Like star signs, blood types are considered good personality indicators and it is common to see a field for 'blood type' on everything from application forms to dating websites. Some hairdressers will even list their blood type to help you decide who you want to cut your hair.

not currently accepted, so it may pay to call and check before going to donate. You will also need to be resident for at least four weeks before giving blood.

Giving Up Smoking

The Tokyo British Clinic (www.tokyobritishclinic.com) takes a novel approach in helping their patients stop smoking. They provide a one-on-one (or couple) session where the reason why a person smokes is pinpointed, and they are taught how to control the desire to smoke. Once this is done (which is typically figured out within one 90 minute session), they claim that patients will find it easy to quit. One session is ¥60,000 (¥80,000 for a couple). There are also some English-speaking hypnotherapists based in Tokyo who can help with quitting smoking (see Alternative Therapies p.126).

Hospitals

The government-run hospitals offer a comprehensive range of medical services and are well-staffed with hundreds of nurses and (depending on size) around a hundred doctors. The most foreigner-friendly places are the National Center for Child Health and Development (p.118) and the Tokyo Metropolitan Hirō Hospital (p.119). Others include National Tokyo Hospital Organization Medical Center (p.118) and Tokyo Metropolitan Otsuka Hospital (p.119). If you want to talk with an English speaker once at the hospital, call the Tokyo Metropolitan Health and Medical Information Center (03 5285 8181) between 09:00 and 20:00. They have English, Chinese, Korean, Thai and Spanish speakers available to provide information about medical institutions. They can also answer questions about the medical and health insurance system.

The fee to see a doctor at a general hospital or clinic is around ¥10,000, slightly more at some of the larger hospitals such as St Lukes (p.120). Appointment fees (as well as any other fees incurred) have to be paid at the time of the visit. If you have National Health Insurance (NHI) you will pay 30% of the total amount on the day and if you have private insurance you will have to pay the full amount and claim it back later. When visiting a hospital, you should have your health insurance details with you, or if you have one, your NHI card.

Emergency services are available at government-run hospitals but you or the ambulance will have to call ahead to see if they are free to accept you. The Japan Red Cross Medical Center (p.119) is your best option if you have an emergency at night as they have English-speaking staff there.

Main Public Hospitals

2-10-1 Okura
Setagaya-ku
🚇 **Soshigaya-Okura**
Map 5 C2 **1**

National Center for Child Health & Development
03 3416 0181 | www.ncchd.go.jp

If your child is in need of serious medical attention, this is the place to come. The service is good and some English is spoken. Departments include general paediatrics, maternal and perinatal services and emergency care, and they have exceptional paediatric critical care. Within each department is a comprehensive range of divisions. Among the general services they offer are two special divisions specifically for adolescents: adolescent medicine and adolescent psychological medicine.

2-5-1 Higashigaoka
Meguro-ku
🚇 **Komazawa Daigaku**
Map 5 C4 **2**

National Hospital Organization Tokyo Medical Center
03 3411 0111 | www.ntmc.go.jp

There are 25 departments at this medical centre, including internal medicine, psychiatry, cardiology, paediatrics, orthopaedics, neurosurgery, plastic surgery, obstetrics and gynaecology, dermatology, urology, ophthalmology, dental, and oral surgery. They also have specialised facilities for cancer and AIDS patients. There are emergency services, but you'll need to call ahead to see if a doctor is free. Also, if possible, you should come with a Japanese speaker to help with the paperwork. Visiting hours are 15:00 to 19:00 Monday to Friday and 13:00 to 19:00 at weekends.

2-34-10 Ebisu
Shibuya-ku
🚇 *Hirō*
Map 5 F2 **3**

Tokyo Metropolitan Hirō Hospital

03 3444 1181 | www.byouin.metro.tokyo.jp/Hirō

With its convenient location, this is a good choice from the government hospitals in the city. They have a large number of well-trained staff – around 100 doctors and well over 400 nurses. Their departments include internal medicine, respiratory medicine, cardiology, neuro-psychiatry, paediatrics surgery, cardiovascular surgery, orthopaedic surgery, rehabilitation, neurosurgery, plastic and reconstructive surgery, dermatology, urology, obstetrics and gynaecology, ophthalmology, radiology, dentistry and oral surgery. Visiting hours are 11:00 to 21:00 daily.

2-8-1 Minami Ōtsuka
Toshima-ku
🚇 *Shin-Ōtsuka*
Map 4 A1 **4**

Tokyo Metropolitan Otsuka Hospital

03 3941 3211 | www.byouin.metro.tokyo.jp/ohtsuka

There are around hundreds of trained professionals employed here, with over 80 doctors, more than 350 nurses and 36 midwives. Departments include internal medicine, respiratory medicine, cardiology, neuro-psychiatry, paediatrics, orthopaedic surgery, rehabilitation, neurosurgery, plastic and reconstructive surgery, dermatology, urology, obstetrics and gynecology, ophthalmology, rehabilitation, rheumatology, radiology, dentistry, and oral surgery. Visiting hours vary between wards, but are typically from 15:00 to 20:00 on weekdays and 13:00 to 20:00 on weekends.

Main Private Hospitals

5-6-8 Minami Azabu
Shibuya-ku
🚇 *Hirō*
Map 11 A4 **5**

Aiiku Hospital

03 3473 8321 | www.aiiku.net

A convenient hospital, centrally located in Minami Azabu, many foreign mothers choose to give birth in its maternity and child health centre, and they are well-equipped to meet mothers' pre and postnatal needs. Within the hospital they have a neonatal intensive care unit, obstetrics and gynaecology department, paediatric department, paediatric surgery facilities, as well as dermatology services to treat a number of skin conditions in children and adults.

2-5-1 Naka-Ochiai
Shinjuku-ku
🚇 *Shimo-Ochiai*
Map 3 E2 **6**

International Catholic Hospital

03 3951 1111 | www.seibokai.or.jp

This international hospital has English, French, and Spanish speaking staff on hand for those in need of assistance in other languages. They are well-known for their maternity services, but they also provide a range of other medical care. The hospital has ophthalmology, dermatology, radiology, orthopaedic, neurology, and urology departments as well as ear, nose and throat specialists. The radiology department can provide breast exams and other treatment relating to breast cancer.

4-1-22 Hirō
Shibuya-ku
🚇 *Hirō*
Map 8 F4 **7**

Japan Red Cross Medical Center

03 3400 1311 | www.med.jrc.or.jp

If you're in an emergency (and don't speak Japanese) this is the best place to go. They have English-speaking staff and their location in Hirō (an expat area), means it's convenient for many. Besides their well-known emergency department they offer a host of other medical services including allergology, cardiology, dermatology, neurology, orthopaedic, obstetrics, ophthalmology, paediatric, radiology, rehabilitation and urology, among specialised medical services.

35 Shinanomachi
Shinjuku-ku
Shinanomachi
Map 7 F3 8

Keio University Hospital

03 3353 1211 | www.hosp.med.keio.ac.jp

This large hospital has a comprehensive list of departments as well as a school of medicine and faculty of nursing and medical care. Their list of specialists cover cardiology, Chinese medicine, dermatology, nerve problems, neurosurgery, geriatrics, plastic surgery, obstetrics, ophthalmology, urology, psychiatric, radiology, rehabilitation, HIV counselling, gynaecology, paediatrics, orthopaedics, ear, nose and throat, and they also have a sports clinic.

9-1 Akashi-cho
Chūō-ku
Tsukiji
Map 14 D3 9

St Luke's International Hospital

03 3541 5151 | www.luke.or.jp

Established in 1902 as Japan's first modern hospital, this place is something of an institution in Tokyo and a good choice for English speakers. The original building fell prey to the Great Kanto Earthquake and a more modern version of the hospital was built on the same site. Since then the place has continued to flourish and they have a vast selection of medical care available, covering gynaecology, maternity, emergency, ophthalmology, neurosurgery, dental and oral surgery, ear, nose and throat, internal medicine, orthopaedic, psychiatry and radiation therapy.

Dermatologists

Azabu Skin Clinic	Hagiwara Bldg 7F, 1-3-1 Hirō	Shibuya-ku	0120 005 327	www.azabu-skinclinic.com
Minami Aoyama Skin Care Clinic	Avant Minami Aoyama (B1F), 5-14-7 Minami-Aoyama	Minato-ku	03 5464 1656	www.minami-aoyama.info
National Medical Clinic	5-16-11 Minami Azabu	Hirō	03 3473 2057	www.nmclinic.net
Tokyo Midtown Medical Center	Tokyo Midtown 6F, 9-7-4 Akasaka	Roppongi	03 5413 7911	www.tokyomidtown-mc.jp
Tokyo Skin Clinic	3-1-24 Roppongi 2F	Minato-ku	03 3585 0282	www.tokyo-skin-clinic.com

Health Centres & Clinics

Tokyo has a selection of clinics for foreigners, with both foreign doctors and doctors who speak English on the medical team. A visit to one of these is a much less stressful experience than visiting a local hospital, and most have a comprehensive set of services covering general health checks, internal medicine, obstetrics and gynaecology, STD screenings, immunisations, paediatrics, ear, nose and throat problems, and minor surgery. You need to make an appointment before visiting a clinic and at most places appointment fees are around ¥8,000 to ¥10,000, with any additional tests, such as X-rays and blood tests, costing extra. Fees are typically paid at the time of the appointment, but some allow invoicing monthly. The new kid on the block, the Tokyo Midtown Medical Center is leading the way when it comes to providing an international standard of policies and procedures, and it is worth visiting their website to see if they can meet your needs before going.

Health Centres & Clinics

Hirō International Clinic	Hirō	03 5789 8861	www.hiroo-ic.com
International Clinic	Roppongi	03 3583 7831	na
International Medical Center Of Japan	Shinjuku-ku	03 3202 7181	www.imcj.go.jp
The King Clinic	Jingūmae	03 3409 0764	www.thekingclinic.com
National Medical Clinic	Hirō	03 3473 2057	www.nmclinic.net
Roppongi Hills Clinic	Roppongi	03 3796 0066	www.66clinic.com
Tokai University Hospital	Kanagawa	03 3370 2321	www.tokai.edu
Tokyo British Clinic	Shibuya-ku	03 5458 6099	www.tokyobritishclinic.com
Tokyo Medical & Surgical Clinic	Minato-ku	03 3436 3028	www.tmsc.jp
Tokyo Midtown Medical Center	Roppongi	03 5413 7911	www.tokyomidtown-mc.jp
Tokyo Women's Medical University Hospital	Shinjuku-ku	03 3353 8111	www.twmu.ac.jp

Small but indispensable…

Perfectly proportioned to fit in your pocket, this marvellous mini guidebook makes sure you don't just get the holiday you paid for but rather the one that you dreamed of.

Tokyo Mini Visitors' Guide
Maximising your holiday, minimising your hand luggage

Maternity
Other options **Maternity Items** p.292

Maternity Mark
*The Maternity Mark
is a key chain for
pregnant women that
can be attached to a
bag to show you are
pregnant. It is meant
to encourage the
general public to be
more courteous, such
as seated passengers
on trains giving up
their spot. They can be
picked up for free from
the stationmaster's
office and at
information offices in
Tokyo Metro stations.*

Giving birth in a foreign country can be scary, especially when you don't know the language. However, a large number of foreign women choose to give birth in Japan, and are pleasantly surprised by the resources available; although a lot of research may be needed to find the information you need.

Once the doctor has confirmed you are pregnant, you will be given a confirmation slip that you need to take to your ward office (p.88) and exchange for the Maternal & Child Health Handbook, or *Boshi Kenkō Techō* in Japanese. This is used to document all appointments, measurements and vaccines.

You'll have to decide early on in your pregnancy what kind of birth you would like. Whether you want a waterbirth, have a midwife deliver your baby (with no doctor present), or create your own birthing plan complete with scented candles, all these options are available – you just need to research and find out where. Once you've decided on the method, it's advisable to choose the place and caregiver, as some doctors and midwives may not be willing (or have the time) to take you on at a later date.

If you want a hospital birth, be sure to ask a lot of questions about what will happen on the day as some places won't allow your husband to be in the delivery room or may separate you and your baby for most, if not all, of your hospital stay. These regulations vary with each birthing place. Also check what pain relief is available, as if you want to have an epidural most places do not offer this.

The best people to talk to are the various support groups such as Tokyo Pregnancy Group (http://tokyopregnancygroup.blogspot.com) and the Childbirth Education Center (www.birthinjapan.com). The Childbirth Education Center runs a number of classes including Birth Preparation, Baby Basics, a Birth Refresher class and a Choosing a Caregiver class.

Once you've delivered, you have to register with the city, your embassy, and immigration. Each embassy has a different policy so check details before the birth (see Birth Certificate & Registration p.57). After the birth you can leave the hospital whenever you decide but most women stay 4 to 5 days. New mums, who have National Health Insurance, will also receive a lump sum of ¥350,000 once the baby is born.

Abortions
*The abortion rate
is high and many
believe this is due
to the government
restrictions on
contraception. A
person can have an
abortion for socio-
economic reasons. The
policy does not allow
for abortions based
on the early detection
of birth defects, but if
you are in a low socio-
economic category you
will be entitled to one
under this clause.*

Hospitals

Most expats choose to deliver in a private hospital rather than public, and the most foreigner-friendly maternity hospitals tend to be private and their prices higher – Aiiku Hospital (p.119) is popular. This normally ensures you get the level of care you want, more privacy, and the pain relief you need. You will also find that more doctors in the private sector speak English. There are a few places that are part public, part private, but going private gets the majority vote.

At the cheapest expect to pay around ¥300,000 at a small private clinic and at the top end of the market it could cost ¥1 to ¥2 million. This price includes an epidural, and the potential birthing complications that could result in an emergency caesarean. When choosing a hospital it is important to do so early on in the pregnancy, as you will need to register in order to deliver there. Even if you are considering going home for the birth, as a cautionary procedure consider signing up just in case. Also note that although cheaper (costing around ¥300,000), most public hospitals do not offer the option of epidurals.

Antenatal Care

Japan has one of the lowest infant mortality rates in the world, with only 2.8 deaths per 1,000 live births, and these figures reflect a very high level of care throughout pregnancy and birth. There is no requirement to see the obstetrician at the hospital you plan to give birth in, and when it comes time to deliver, most hospitals work on an 'on-call' system so you can't be sure which doctor will be at the birth.

Maternity Hospitals & Clinics

Private				
Aiiku Hospital	5-6-8 Minami Azabu	Hirō	03 3473 8321	www.aiiku.net
Aqua Birth House	4-16-21 Sakuragaoka	Setagaya-ku	03 3427 1314	www.aqua-birthhouse.com
International Catholic Hospital	2-5-1 Naka-Ochiai	Shinjuku-ku	03 3951 1111	www.seibokai.or.jp
Japan Red Cross Medical Center	4-1-22 Hirō	Shibuya-ku	03 3400 1311	www.med.jrc.or.jp
Matsugaoka Birth Center	1-10-13 Matsugaoka	Nakano-ku	03 5343 6071	www2.odn.ne.jp/~cdk23230
National Medical Clinic	5-16-11 Minami Azabu	Hirō	03 3473 2057	www.nmclinic.net
Sanno Hospital	8-10-16 Akasaka	Minato-ku	03 3402 3151	www.sannoclc.or.jp
St Luke's International Hospital	9-1 Akashi-cho	Chūō-ku	03 3541 5151	www.luke.or.jp
Tokyo British Clinic	Daikanyama Y Bldg 2-13-7 Ebisu-Nishi	Shibuya-ku	03 5458 6099	www.tokyobritishclinic.com
Tokyo Medical and Surgical Clinic	3-4-30 Shiba Kōen	Minato-ku	03 3436 3028	www.tmsc.jp
Public				
National Center for Child Health and Development	2-10-1 Okura	Setagaya-ku	03 3416 0181	www.ncchd.go.jp

Postnatal Care

If you have National Health Insurance, you are entitled to one free home visit from a midwife. This will take place one to two weeks after the birth and she will provide a standard check-up of the baby and answer any questions you may have. Services after the baby is born vary between wards but typically free medical check-ups are given for babies at three to four months, a dental check-up at 18 months, and another free medical exam at three years of age. All these services are provided in Japanese. If after the birth you decide to breastfeed, support groups like La Leche League of Tokyo (www.llli.org/Tokyo.html) can provide advice. Breastfeeding in public is accepted, but a little modesty will go a long way. If you are looking for a lactation consultant, Iona Macnab is the only private International Board Certified consultant (www. blueskytokyo.com) who is not affiliated with any hospital.

Maternity Leave

Women are entitled to one year of maternity leave, but many resign when they have a baby. Leave is paid for up to six weeks before and up to six weeks after the birth, although eight weeks of post-natal leave is typically taken. Paternity leave is also available (but is rarely taken – statistics show the rate of paternity leave is only 0.56%). You will need to check with your employer about maternity leave (including how long you need to be working there to qualify – especially if it is a foreign company.

Breast Cancer

The Run for the Cure foundation (www.runforthecure.org) has made excellent inroads in raising the awareness of breast cancer here and they are very active in the foreign community. If you would like a mammogram take a look at their list of clinics and hospitals. One other good place, which is not yet on their list, is the Tokyo Midtown Medical Center (www.tokyomidtown-mc.jp).

Gynaecology & Obstetrics

Many of the foreign clinics have either a male or female gynaecologist on their team, so be sure to double check who your doctor is if you have a preference. Word of mouth is one of the best ways to find a doctor who's right for you. If you want the contraceptive pill you'll also need to have a check up with your local gynae, and many clinics are weary of giving pill prescriptions for longer than a few months (maximum) without conducting standard tests first.

Limerick County Library

Contraception & Sexual Health

Oral contraception was only legalised in Japan in 1999 and has been slow to catch on. Research undertaken by the Japan Family Planning Association revealed the morning-after pill is a more popular birth control choice than preventative measures. However, this pill is not available over the counter and people need to visit a doctor in order to get it. The regular birth control pill can be picked up from international clinics, but there is limited choice with some clinics only offering the standard Japanese brand. Some dermatologists prescribe foreign brands of the pill for skin problems. Condoms are readily available, and can be picked up in convenience stores and pharmacies.

Gynaecology & Obstetrics

Aiiku Hospital	5-6-8 Minami Azabu	Hirō	03 3473 8321	www.aiiku.net
International Catholic Hospital	2-5-1 Naka-Ochiai	Shinjuku-ku	03 3951 1111	www.seibokai.or.jp
Kato Ladies Clinic	7-20-3 Nishi-Shinjuku	Shinjuku-ku	03 3366 3777	www.towako-kato.com
Odawara Women's Clinic	2-11-6 Ebisu-Nishi	Shibuya-ku	03 3447 0369	http://fert-tokyo.jp
Parkside Hirō Ladies Clinic	5-16-13 Minami-Azabu	Hirō	03 5798 3470	www.ladies-clinic.or.jp
Tochigi Clinic	2-19-8 Sanno	Niijima-ku	03 3777 7712	www.hospita.jp/000161.shtml
Tokyo Medical and Surgical Clinic	3-4-30 Shiba Kōen	Minato-ku	03 3436 3028	www.tmsc.jp
Tokyo Midtown Medical Center	6F Tokyo Midtown, 9-7-4 Akasaka	Minato-ku	03 5413 7911	www.tokyomidtown-mc.jp
Yoga Ladies Clinic	3-8-11 Kamiyoga	Setagaya-ku	03 5491 5137	http://ylc.cool.ne.jp

Fertility Treatments

Word of mouth is the best way to go when it comes to finding out the best fertility treatment on offer and although places do come recommended, ask around first to save any frustration later. The Odawara Women's clinic has become quite well-known among foreign women in Tokyo for their skills in fertility treatment. Other options are Kato Ladies Clinic and the Tokyo Medical and Surgical Clinic. Despite the low birth rate in Japan, National Health Insurance does not cover fertility treatment. If you have a low income, however, the National Health Insurance may provide some monetary support – call them to see if you qualify.

Paediatrics

Foreign clinics, like the Tokyo Medical and Surgical Clinic (p.120), can follow the vaccination schedule of your home country and they use a mix of imported and local vaccines. Generally in Japan, there are optional and regular vaccinations and parents can decide which ones their children should have – these are free unless you go privately and then you may have to pay the doctors standard fee. The vaccination schedule includes the optional vaccinations of DPT, DT, MR and Japanese encephalitis. The chickenpox vaccination is also available.

The city provides free medical check-ups for babies and medical exams for three year olds at public health centres and approved medical facilities at set times throughout the year. Parents are informed when the vaccination is due via a notice in the post. Whether a visit to a paeditrician is covered depends on your

Children With Disabilities

If you have a child under 18 years with a severe physical disability who requires an operation, the government may subsidise it. Factors that influence this are your income level and your ward's policies on the matter. If your child has other special needs and you're looking for some English support there are online support groups like Special Kids Japan (http://lists. topica.com/lists/SKJ), monthly parent meetings through the Tokyo English Life Line (p.131) exceptional parenting programme (email tellparentgroup@ hotmail.com to join the mailing list) and the Tokyo International Learning Community (www.tilcjapan.com) – an international school for children with special needs.

insurance, and under National Health Insurance, subsidies are given for medical expenses for children.

When choosing your paeditrican ask around first and make sure you have a good talk with your health care provider about their immunization schedule before making a decision – especially if you plan to leave Japan part-way through the schedule.

Paediatrics

Aiiku Hospital	5-6-8 Minami Azabu	Hirō	03 3473 8321	www.aiiku.net
Endo Clinic	2-24-13 Kamiōsaki	Shinagawa-ku	03 3492 6422	na
International Catholic Hospital	2-5-1 Naka-Ochiai	Shinjuku-ku	03 3951 1111	www.seibokai.or.jp
National Medical Clinic	5-16-11 Minami Azabu	Hirō	03 3473 2057	www.nmclinic.net
St Luke's International Hospital	9-1 Akashi-cho	Chūō-ku	03 3541 5151	www.luke.or.jp
Tokyo Adventist Hospital	3-17-3 Amanuma	Suginami-ku	03 3392 6151	www.tokyoeisei.com
Tokyo Medical & Surgical Clinic	3-4-30 Shiba Kōen	Minato-ku	03 3436 3028	www.tmsc.jp

Dentists & Orthodontists

The best way to get dental care in Tokyo is to visit an English-speaking clinic that caters specifically for foreigners. A check-up will cost around ¥5,000, and any treatment needed will be extra. Prices do vary, but for a professional clean expect to pay upwards of ¥8,000. Whether your visit be covered by insurance depends on your individual plan. Under National Health Insurance normal treatment is covered, but orthodontics and cosmetic treatment for your teeth are not. Young children may be entitled to a free check-up – contact your ward office to find out if this is available in your area. Different private clinics also offer child dentistry which they promote through their website.

Dentists & Orthodontists

Arisugawa Parkside Dental Office	Suite B-104 Arisugawa Residence, 5-14-1 Minami-Azabu	Hirō	03 5475 3312	www.tokyodentist.com
Eto Dental Clinic	6-5-1 Nishi Shinjuku (2F)	Shinjuku-ku	03 5323 4288	www.eto.or.jp
Fujimi Dental Clinic	4F Chūō Bldg 21, 1-8-21 Ginza	Chūō-ku	03 3563 4022	www.fdclinic.com
Hillside View Orthodontic Office	3F Daikanyama Plaza, 24-7 Sarugaku	Daikanyama	03 3780 8177	www.hillsideview.com
Hirō Orthodontic Office	4F Nagatsu Bldg, 5-15-16 Minami Azabu	Hirō	03 5449 7700	www.smiline.or.jp
Nakashima Dental Office	4F Roppongi U Bldg, 4-5-2 Roppongi	Minato-ku	03 3479 2726	www.dentist-nakashima.jp
Nishieifuku Dental Clinic	2F Union Trois Bldg, 4-19-10 Eifuku	Suginami-ku	03 5378 2228	www.iihani.com
United Dental Office	1F 2-3-8 Azabudai	Minato-ku	03 5570 4334	www.uniteddentaloffice.com

Opticians & Ophthalmologists

If you're looking to buy glasses there are a number of options available; from low-cost glasses chains like Zoff (www.zoff.co.jp) through to having tests done at a more sophisticated eye clinic. If you already wear contact lenses you'll find they are readily available from outlets inside shopping malls, online, or through optometrists, but you will need your prescription handy. When you're short on contact solution you can pick some up from pharmacies and convenience stores. For more, see Eyewear on p.282. Eye laser surgery is cheap here and some Japanese lasik clinics offer the surgery for as little as ¥100,000. Places that speak English tend to have higher prices – up to double

– so it pays to shop around with the help of a Japanese friend first. The surgery is only a few minutes long but you will need to take it easy for a few days afterwards.

If you want to take your child to see someone, there are opthalmologists and opticians available at hospitals and clinics who can perform any necessary tests. One recommended doctor is Dr Hiroyuki Arai at the Queen's Eye Clinic.

Expect an eye test when you go for your driving licence in Japan. This is done on the spot to check your vision and to check for colour blindness.

Opticians & Ophthalmologists

Ginza Lasik Clinic	Fugetsudo Bldg, 6-6-1 Ginza	Chūō-ku	0120 049 765
Kobe Clinic Hirō	Prime Tower 7F, 1-1-39 Hirō	Shibuya-ku	0120 049 315
Minamiaoyama Eye Clinic Tokyo	Round-Cross Aoyama Bldg 8F 2-27-25 Minami-Aoyama	Minato-ku	0120 893 810
National Hospital Organization Tokyo Medical Center	2-5-1 Higashigaoka	Meguro-ku	03 3411 0111
Nozaki Eye Clinic	3-16-16 Shiroganedai	Minato-ku	03 3461 1671
Queen's Eye Clinic	Queen's Square, 2-3 Minato-Mirai	Yokohama	045 682 4455

Latest Treatments

If you want to keep abreast of the latest cosmetic surgery trends in Japan visit www.imaic.org. The IMAI centre provides foreigners with information on aesthetic plastic surgery in Japan.

Cosmetic Treatment & Surgery

Cosmetic surgery is common in Japan and it's fairly easy to find an English-speaking surgeon if you're after a nip and tuck. The popularity of treatments vary depending on the customer; with the Asian population the non-cutting eyelid procedure is a popular choice, while among women in general, breast augmentation, liposuction, face lifts, botox and the treatment of scars to make them less noticeable are regular options. Non-surgical treatments like chemical peels, laser treatments, and hair removal are also widely available. Clinics also cater for men and the Plaza Plastic Surgery offers treatment for erectile dysfunction and male baldness.

Cosmetic Treatment & Surgery

Akai Medical Clinic	KNK Bldg (3F), 3-5-17 Kita-Aoyama	Minato-ku	03 5771 4114	www.akaiclinic.com
	Katsuyuki Bldg (4F), 1-2-8 Horai-cho, Naka	Yokohama	045 252 9455	
Azabu Skin Clinic	Hagiwara Bldg (7F), 1-3-1 Hirō	Shibuya-ku	0120 005 327	www.azabu-skinclinic.com
Daikanyama Clinic	1-10-2 Ebisu-Minami (4F)	Shibuya-ku	03 3760 6800	www.daikanyama-clinic.jp
Masaki Clinic	101 Daikanyama Parkside Village, 9-8 Sarugakucho	Daikanyama	0120 120 454	www.dr-masaki.com
Plaza Plastic Surgery	5-5-1 Hirō (4F)	Shibuya-ku	03 5475 2345	www.plazaclinic.net
Shonan Cosmetic Surgery Clinic	Shinjuku Island Tower (12F)	Shinjuku-ku	0120 256 999	www.s-b-c.net
Town Plastic Surgery Clinic	Takayama Land Bldg (6F), 1-20-16 Jinnan	Shibuya-ku	0120 107 286	www.keisei.ne.jp

Alternative Therapies

The alternative therapy scene is well established in Tokyo, with forms of energy healing such as reiki and shiatsu originating in Japan. Some foreigners also practise their various therapies here. The Natural Healing Center promotes foreign healers based in Japan. To see what treatments are on offer and for a list of practitioners, you can check out their website at www.naturalhealingcenter.com. Some foreigners choose to study alternative healing in Japan. The Kimura Shiatsu Institute is a popular choice for those looking to heal themselves and family and friends.

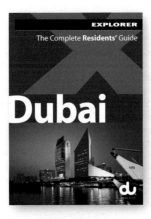

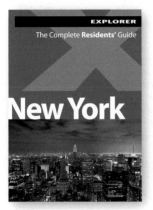

Turn to the team page and ask yourself…

…would you like to see your face?

Explorer has grown from a one-man operation a decade ago to a 60+ team today and our expansion isn't slowing down. We are always looking for creative bods, from PR pro's and master marketers to daring designers and excellent editors, as well as super sales and support staff.

So what are you waiting for? Apply online at www.explorerpublishing.com

Acupressure & Acupuncture

The healing touch of shiatsu, a form of pressure massage, is perfect for those looking for balance – physically, spiritually, emotionally, and mentally. It works well for those with tense shoulders and back, as well as chronic illnesses such as problems with internal organs. In Tokyo you'll find places to both experience and learn shiatsu techniques. There are also a number of English-speaking acupuncturists based here who can work with you on specific problems. As acupuncture continues to become more accepted in the west it has also become more accepted among the foreign population here.

Aromatherapy

Relaxing with an aromatherapy massage is a popular way to unwind and the more up-market Health Spas (p.258) offer delectable aromatic massages designed to invigorate, harmonise, or relax the body. If you want to buy your own oil blends, visit the Tree of Life on Omotesandō in Shibuya (6-3-8 Jingūmae) for a full selection.

Homeopathy

The Japan Homeopathic Medical Association (www.jphma.org) is the governing agent for homeopathy practitioners, and if you want to be sure you're visiting a quality provider, check if they are registered with them. You may need the help of a Japanese friend if you really want to find out more as most services are currently only available in Japanese. Homeopathy Japan has three English-speaking practitioners and they charge ¥10,000 for a session (¥8,400 for children), plus a remedy fee.

Reflexology & Massage Therapy

If you're in need of some quick stress relief, try reflexology. This hand and foot pressure massage helps release tension in the body, and with numerous places in the city offering cheap reflexology services, it's one therapy that is easy to find and affordable. Queensway is a reflexology chain with a number of branches (see table below) throughout Tokyo.

Massage therapy is more expensive here but you won't be short on variety. From shiatsu to aromatherapy, or even rolfing (see table below), Tokyo has it all. For more on other massage services, see Massage in Activities on p.208.

Alternative Therapies

Acura Acupuncture Clinic	Shibuya-ku	03 5469 0810	www.acuraclinic.com	Acupuncture
Edward Obaidey Acupuncture Clinic	Setagaya-ku	03 3418 8989	www.edwardshinkyu.com	Acupuncture, Moxibustion & Shiatsu
Homeopathy Japan	Shibuya-ku	03 5352 7750	Homeopathy	
Kimura Shiatsu Institute	Shibuya-ku	03 3485 4515	www.shiatsu-k.com	Shiatsu
Maholo Healing	Minato-ku	03 5484 3450	www.maholo.co.jp	Aromatherapy & Flower Counselling
Queensway	Aoyama	03 6419 2777	www.raja.co.jp	Foot Reflexology
	Yūrakuchō	03 5220 2477		
	Marunouchi	03 3504 2227		
Rolfing Studio Nobicyouth	Shibuya-ku	090 6163 1017	na	Rolfing
Roppongi Osteopathy	Minato-ku	03 3401 3544	na	Massage
Yamate-st. Acupuncture Clinic	Naka Meguro	03 3792 8989	www.yamate-st.com	Acupuncture

Physiotherapy

If you're suffering from an injury and are in need of help with your recovery there are a range of Japanese options available, as well as some foreigner-friendly choices. A good option is Tokyo Physio, who work from head to toe healing aches and pains. They also work specifically with running injuries, can help restore flexibility to joints after post-operative surgery, and treat a range of problems children may encounter such as delayed functional development. Care in clinics and hospitals here may be combined with other forms of treatment to help speed up your recovery.

Physiotherapy			
Manomedica	Chūō Iikura Bldg 2A, 3-4-11 Azabudai	Azabu	03 5570 2270
Tokyo Midtown Medical Center	Tokyo Midtown (6F), 9-7-4 Akasaka	Roppongi	03 5413 7911
Tokyo Physio	Atrium Shirokane 104, 5-12-27 Shirokane	Minato-ku	03 3443 6769

Back Treatment

In a city where everyone is as overworked as in Tokyo you're bound to have a high number of people who suffer from back pain. As a result, there are a number of specialist clinics that can help cure you. The standard treatment here is chiropractic and you'll find some good English-speaking practitioners. Expect to pay around ¥8,000 for an initial visit, or slightly more for a more comprehensive assessment.

The Tokyo Midtown Medical Center has taken things a step further by opening a comprehensive back care clinic. Here you can follow a treatment plan that combines chiropractic, osteopathy, acupuncture, Chinese medicine, and a fitness program. Lionel Gougne offers craniosacral therapy for ¥15,000 per hour session. He also works with children and charges slightly less for this, but a child session typically only lasts 10 to 20 minutes.

Back Treatment				
Craniosacral Therapy & Osteopathy Clinic	Oak Terrace (3C), 10 Samoncho	Shinjuku-ku	03 6657 1999	www.craniosacral-therapy.net
Manomedica	Chūō Iikura Bldg (2A), 3-4-11 Azabudai	Azabu	03 5570 2270	www.manomedica.com
Star Chiropractic	103 A&D House, 2-15-10 Jiyūgaoka	Meguro-ku	03 3725 7731	www.star-chiro.com
Suto Healing Center	701 Azabu Sendaizaka Res, 1-5-1 Minami-Azabu	Minato-ku	03 3402 1654	www.shc.gr.jp
Tokyo Midtown Medical Center	Tokyo Midtown (6F), 9-7-4 Akasaka	Roppongi	03 5413 7911	www.tokyomidtown-mc.jp

Nutritionists & Slimming

It's hard to walk into a pharmacy in Japan without being bombarded by the sight of shelves piled high with diet pills and slimming shakes, and these quick fixes are a popular choice for many Japanese women. For a a more lasting approach to weight-loss, nutritionist Erica Angyal is a glowing example of how to treat your body right and currently works as a nutritionist and health consultant in Tokyo. She is the author of *Gorgeous Skin in 30 Days* and the official nutritionist for Miss Universe Japan.

Healer Sainoor Premji helps bring a person's body into balance in many different ways. Among other services, she provides nutritional counselling, where eating habits are discussed along with how certain foods affect your moods, and your well-being will be examined. If you're a member of Weight Watchers you'll need to seek your support online, as although there are many people interested in getting together, there are no English meetings here yet.

Nutritionists & Slimming	
Nutritionists	
Erica Angyal	www.gorgeous-skin.com
Sainoor Premji	www.healthizarnaturalhealing.ca
Personal Trainers	
Bryon Gibbens	090 1407 9013
Heather Kandawire	090 6500 8507
Robert Daoust	090 8444 8509
Steve Terada	080 3092 8271
Travis Johnson	03 3443 2357

There are a number of foreign personal trainers who can work with you in and out of the gym as well as providing nutritional advice. Those suffering from more serious problems such as IBS are advised to go to a medical clinic, and the foreign clinics here can help with these types of problems.

Counselling & Therapy

The International Mental Health Professionals Japan organisation (www.imhpj.org) is a great resource, which allows you to search for mental health professionals in your area. Many of the English-speaking psychologists have either trained abroad or are foreign, and they deal with a range of issues including individual, family and couple therapy, stress management, sexual problems and addictions. There are also places like the Ikebukuro Counselling Center that deal with stresses that relate to being a foreigner in Japan.

Being new in a country can often lead to culture shock, and in turn, may result in depression. The clinics here are skilled at dealing with this and the Tokyo English

Psychiatrists		
Doug Berger	Shibuya-ku	03 3716 6624
Masafumi Nakakuki	Minato-ku	03 3280 5776
Ryuko Ishikawa	Ginza-ku	03 5524 7670

Life Line (TELL) can provide needed support and advice about what you should do. Try to minimise culture shock, and its effects, by learning as much as you can about Japan before arriving here. When you arrive, try joining new activities or networking events to make new friends.

Counselling services also cover marriage, and sessions can be catered specifically to cross-cultural couples, as well as couples from the same culture. These services can be extended to include family counselling or counselling for children. Among kids, common behavioural problems encountered in Japan include learning disabilities, loss of self-confidence, depression, eating disorders, and Attention Deficit Disorder (ADD). If you have a more serious psychiatric issue to contend with, government hospitals such as Matsuzawa Tokyo Metropolitan Hospital and Toshima Tokyo Metropolitan Hospital (see table below) offer care and treatment for those suffering from severe psychosis and other related illnesses.

Counsellors & Therapists				
Name	Area	Phone	Website	Type
Family Center Japan	Chūō-ku	03 5524 7670	www.familycenterjapan.com	Individual, family and couple therapy
Ikebukuro Counselling Center	Toshima-ku	03 3986 8316	www.hozumiclinic.com	Personal problems, social relationships, work issues and culture shock
TELL Community Counseling Service	Shibuya-ku	03 3498 0231	www.telljp.com	Psychotherapy services – children, family, couple and individual therapy
Tokyo British Clinic	Shibuya-ku	03 5458 6099	www.tokyobritishclinic.com	Psychotherapy for personal, marital, sexual problems, and other addictions
Tokyo Meguro Counseling Center	Minato-ku	03 3716 6624	www.megurocounseling.com	Mental health, marriage and couples, children family counseling and group therapy
Tokyo Metropolitan Matsuzawa Hospital	Setagaya-ku	03 3303 7211	www.byouin.metro.tokyo.jp /matsuzawa	Severe psychotic problems
Toshima Tokyo Metropolitan Hospital	Itabashi-ku	03 5375 1234	www.toshima-hp.metro.tokyo.jp	Severe psychotic problems

Addiction Counselling & Rehabilitation

You'll never be far from support in Tokyo, with some mainstay addiction support groups, such as Alcoholics Anonymous, having regular English meetings at various locations throughout the city. The classified section in *Metropolis* magazine (www.metropolis.co.jp), under 'Help', has listings for a number of groups with contact details or details of when and where they meet. The Tokyo British Clinic also provides help for alcoholics, as well as treating other addictions.

Addiction Counselling & Rehabilitation			
Alcoholics Anonymous	Various locations	03 3971 1471	www.aatokyo.org
Overeaters Anonymous	Roppongi	03 5605 9325	www.oatokyo.org
Tokyo British Clinic	Ebisu	03 5458 6099	www.tokyobritishclinic.com

Support Groups

Being far away from home can be challenging, especially when you have a pressing problem that you need support with. Luckily many foreigners have trodden the path before you and a number of groups have been set up; ranging from supporting those affected by breast cancer or AIDS, to lifelines designed to offer any kind of support you need. For what's available, see the table below. More comprehensive listings can be found in *Metropolis* magazine (www.metropolis.co.jp), under 'Support' in the Help section of its Classifieds. Some groups that are worthy of a special mention include Tokyo English Life Line (TELL), the AIDS Hotline and The Tyler Foundation.

Support Groups	
AIDS Hotline	0120 461 995
International Social Services Japan	03 3760 3471
Japan Helpline	0120 461 997
Run for the Cure (Breast Cancer)	03 3466 4798
Tokyo English Life Line	03 5774 0992
Tokyo Rape Crisis Center	03 3207 3692
Tokyo Women's Group	03 4588 0691
The Tyler Foundation for Childhood Cancer	090 8852 8128
Welcome Furoshiki	03 5472 7074

TELL (www.telljp.com) is a non-profit group providing phone support for a broad range of problems, and is one of the most comprehensive support networks in Tokyo. They have a vast pool of knowledge to draw from, and are able to recommend people and organisations to see if you have a specific problem. Talking about AIDS is kind of taboo in Japan and you may feel you have limited support. But with the AIDS Hotline, a 24 hour, free phone information number (for foreigners), you'll always be able to reach someone. They provide counselling and information, and even if you don't have AIDS they can answer any questions you may have. They also have a website, visit www.jhelp.com. If your child has cancer and you need someone to talk to, contact the Tyler Foundation (www.tylershineon.org). They support both children with cancer and their families.

Rainy day in Shibuya

Education

Choosing a school can be difficult, particularly when you have a number of different factors to consider, from location and curriculum, to cost and the length of the waiting list. Try to visit as many as possible, set up appointments with admissions staff and speak to other expat parents to get the inside track.

Nurseries & Pre-Schools

Nursery and pre-schools accept children aged between 18 months and 5 years. This is not compulsory education but it does allow your child to get used to the routine of going to school and offers you a few hours off. Most schools open Monday to Friday on a half-day basis, usually from 09:00 to 14:00 or 14:30, but many offer extended care until 16:30; shorter weeks of two, three or four days are possible, depending on your child's needs (recommended for children under 2 years). A five-day week on a half-day basis will cost around ¥155,000, while a full-day programme will cost around ¥2,270,000 a term. In most cases, you will have to enrol your child for a full term and pay for this block period.

Teaching approaches vary, with everything from Montessori schools to those focusing on the mother and child bond and peer group interaction (Maria's Babies Society) or those geared towards child development (Grace International Learning Center). Many of the private kindergartens have affiliated primary schools. Needless to say, if your child has attended the pre-school, it'll be easier to get them into the affiliated primary. Demand is high so think about contacting your school of choice 12 months in advance to secure a place. See also Primary & Secondary Schools on p.133 as some of these also have pre-school facilities.

Katsu Court 101
2-7-25 Moto-Azabu
Minato-ku
🚉 *Azabujuban*
Map 11 A4 **10**

ABC International School

03 5793 1359 | *www.abcinternationalschool.com*

ABC International School has several branches in Minato-ku offering English language pre-schooling for children aged 15 months to 5 years. Classes are divided by age group, with 15 months to 2 year olds together, and 2 to 3 year olds, 3 to 4 and 4 to 5 year olds grouped together. Classes are four hours long, two to five days a week. Hours vary with each age group. Children aged 4 to 5 years go for five hours, five days a week.

2-13-11 Seta
Setagaya-ku
🚉 *Futako-tamagawa*
Map 5 B2 **11**

Grace International Learning Center

03 5716 3100 | *www.grace-learning.com*

GILC is an English language school that was founded in the US. It accepts children aged 1 to 6 years. Children learn by playing and exploring with a variety of learning materials, and from interaction with their peers and adults. Half-day programmes are available for children under 2 years. For all other ages, full days are from 09:00 to 14:30. Extra nursery hours are possible.

3-36-20 Tomy's Hse,
101 Jingūmae
Shibuya-ku
🚉 *Harajuku*
Map 8 D1 **12**

Maria's Babies Society

03 3404 3468 | *www.mariasbabies.co.jp*

Maria's offers pre-school for children between the ages of 1 and 6 years. Programmes include half days for tots who are walking to full days for 5 year olds and under. Afternoon extension programmes and a Little Diplomats Programme for two hours twice a week for 3 to 5 year-olds are also available.

3-5-13 Minami-Azabu
Minato-ku
🚉 *Azabujuban*
Map 6 A2 **13**

The Montessori School of Tokyo

03 5449 7067 | *http://montessorijapan.com*

This school is open to 1 to 14 year olds. The focus is on children learning by hands-on experience, whereby they must think and problem solve for themselves, all the while developing their self-esteem and confidence. Sunshine Programmes are available to children under 6. Under 3s can take part in the Sunshine Morning Programme for four hours five days a week, while 3 to 6 year olds can enjoy the Sunshine Full Day option, five days a week. Extended care is also available.

Primary & Secondary Schools

Primary school starts just after your child turns 6 for both public and private schools. The children of expats and international parents can attend an international school if they wish, but they can also go to Japanese schools if they like, or parents can even home school their children. More and more often Japanese parents want to send their children to international schools and there is quite a demand for high quality international schooling.

Programmes vary from school to school. You can find anything from bible studies or progressive athletics and fine arts programmes to integrated Japanese language and cultural learning. Education at this age tends to be co-educational, and school sizes, while they vary from 150 to 2,000, are most often around 400 or 500. Class sizes vary; with some, such as the British International School, as small as six students.

Likewise, fees vary. It's not uncommon to pay between ¥1,000,000 and ¥2,000,000 a year, plus an application fee of several hundred thousand yen. Many Tokyo schools are open, accepting anyone, but several of the international schools – including the Tokyo International School – take English language ability into account.

Schooling in Tokyo is generally based on a three-term system, from August to December, January to March and April to June. However, there are exceptions among the international schools, which often function on the same term system their home country uses. For example, the Canadian International School runs on two terms.

Most international schools start accepting applications in the autumn, a year in advance of the actual start date so it's important to apply early and to more than one school. You will generally need to supply the following:

• Application form
• Application fees (where required)
• Child's birth certificate
• Copy of your child's passport (the photo page)
• Child's most recent report and transcripts for the last year of schooling

1-1-1 Nomizu,
Chofu-shi
🚇 *Tama*
Map 2 A2

American School in Japan

04 2234 5300 | www.asij.ac.jp
This is the oldest and best-known international school in Tokyo, serving 1,500 students aged 3 through to grade 12, across two different campuses in Roppongi and Chofu. Students hail from 40 different countries. ASIJ is accredited with the Western Association of Schools and Colleges and the curriculum is largely drawn from the United States system of education. The school hosts several open days a year. Call their office or visit their website for dates and further information.

1-21-18 Shibuya
Shibuya-ku
🚇 *Shibuya*
Map 8 C3 **14**

British International School

03 5467 4321 | www.bst.ac.jp
Class sizes at the British International School are small, with as few as six students per class, and only 500 students in the whole school, catering to children aged 3 to 13 years. While students are predominantly British, all nationalities are welcome. The school follows the English National Curriculum, focusing on basic literacy and numeracy skills, and supplemented with a wide range of specialist subjects, including music, drama, Japanese, French and science. Extra-curricular activities such as football, tennis and swimming give students a chance to spend time outdoors. There are

two campuses, in Shibuya and Showa. Tours of the Shibuya campus are possible on Mondays and Wednesdays at 09:30 during term time, while the Showa campus can be viewed at 14:00 on Thursdays.

Canadian International School

5-8-20
Kitashinagawa
Shinagawa-ku
🚉 *Shinagawa*
Map 6 A4 **15**

03 5793 1398 | *www.cisjapan.net*
CIS accepts children from kindergarten age through to grade 12. The school functions on a two-term year, to allow students to study intensively for a whole term without interruption. The school is accredited with the Department of Education of the Province of Prince Edward Island, Canada.

International School of the Sacred Heart

4-3-1 Hirō
Shibuya-ku
🚉 *Hirō*
Map 5 F2 **16**

03 3400 3951 | *www.issh.ac.jp*
ISS first opened in 1908, and is affiliated to the Society of the Sacred Heart. It provides a Catholic education to girls from grades 1 to 12 but offers co-educational classes for 3 to 5 year olds. In all, there are around 550 students. While it is a Catholic school, students of all denominations are welcome. The curriculum is based on a mix of the education systems of the United States, United Kingdom, Australia and Canada. Students in grades 11 and 12 can choose to take part in the Advanced Placement Programme, whereby they can undertake college-level courses. These courses can count towards college credits for most colleges and universities in the United States, and are recognised as entrance qualifications for universities in the United Kingdom, Canada and Australia.

K International School

1-5-15 Shirakawa
Koto-ku
🚉 *Morishita*
Map 4 E4 **17**

03 3642 9993 | *www.kist.ed.jp*
The focus at K International School is on creativity, leadership and communication skills. There are 350 students from kindergarten to the final year, of 52 different nationalities. The primary school curriculum (ages 3 to 12) is based on the International Baccalaureate Organisation's (IBO) Primary Years Programme. Grades 6 to 10 follow the IBO's Middle Years Programme and grades 11 and 12 follow the IBO's Diploma Programme. The school is a member of the Council of International Schools.

Lycée Franco-Japonais de Tokyo

Various Locations

03 3261 0137 | *www.lfjt.or.jp*
This French school has 900 students across two campuses for primary and secondary students. The campuses are located in Fujimi (kindergarten and primary school classes) and Ryogoku (secondary school classes). The curriculum follows the International Baccalaureate programme. Students learn French from kindergarten, and English and Japanese from grade 1. In secondary school, they can also study German or Spanish. The academic year runs from September to June.

New International School

3-18-32
Minami-Ikebukuro
Toshima-ku
🚉 *Ikebukuro*
Map 3 F1 **18**

03 3980 1057 | *www.newinternationalschool.com*
This school opened in 2001, and caters to 160 students, from pre-kindergarten age through to grade 9. Students are taught bilingually in English and Japanese (Mandarin is optional). Students are taught in multi-age groups and there can be up to a three-year age gap among students in each classroom. Students learn and participate as a group, individually, or on a project basis. One benefit of this bilingual education is that students can easily make the transition onto Japanese, English and overseas high schools. For more information on multi-age teaching, visit the website.

Education

Nishimachi International School

2-14-7 Moto-Azabu
Minato-ku
◉ **Azabujuban**
Map 11 B4 **19**

03 3451 5520 | *www.nishimachi.ac.jp*

Nishimachi is a small, intimate school with a total of 440 students from kindergarten to grade 9. Conveniently located in Moto-Azabu, a popular residential area, Nishimachi is respected for its unique teaching methods. All classes are taught in English and Japanese. The school tries to ensure a balanced mix of students, with a good English to Japanese native speaker ratio, an equal split of boys and girls and a diverse mix of nationalities. It's popular with many expat families, as well as with well-to-do Japanese parents who want their children to learn English. The application procedure involves a strict professional assessment – this school likes to be exclusive.

St Mary's International School

1-6-19 Seta
Setagaya-ku
◉ **Kaminoge**
Map 5 A4 **20**

03 3709 1411 | *www.smis.ac.jp*

This boys' school is relatively large, with 930 students from kindergarten age up to grade 12. The school offers a Readiness Program for 5 year olds to prepare for entry into the school. At high school level, St Mary's offers a four-year college preparatory programme under the International Baccalaureate curriculum. St Mary's is a Catholic school, but students from all denominations are welcome. Admissions are based on previous school transcripts and standardised test results, as well as an interview with prospective students and their parents.

Tokyo Chinese School

14 Gobancho
Chiyoda-ku
◉ **Ichigaya**
Map 10 B1 **21**

03 3261 4993 | *www.tcs.or.jp*

One of Tokyo's few non-English international schools, the Tokyo Chinese School runs classes in Chinese at both the primary and secondary levels, from grade 1 to 12. There is no Chinese language kindergarten. Classes are taught in Mandarin and children study Chinese culture and language, and take Japanese language classes. English is studied at primary level only. The school has approximately 360 students, with the majority of its pupils coming from China, Taiwan and Japan.

Tokyo International School

3-4-22 Mita
Minato-ku
◉ **Mita**
Map 6 B2 **22**

03 5484 1160 | *www.tokyois.com*

TIS encourages students to learn by being inquisitive and through leadership. It is a co-educational, international school, with students from 45 different countries. It offers primary and middle school education, and uses the International Baccalaureate system. There is a strong emphasis on language, including Japanese language skills.

School children crossing

University & Higher Education

Japan has over 700 universities, although not many of these offer courses in English. Look out for the international universities with branches in Japan, such as McGill University (p.136) and Temple University (p.137). Tokyo International University (p.137) offers an English language masters in its Graduate School of Economics. Many Japanese universities also have international exchange programmes with recognised universities abroad. There are five types of tertiary institution that foreign students can enrol in. These consist of universities, graduate schools, junior colleges, special training colleges (post-secondary courses) and institutes of technology.

Courses & Other Stuff
The Japan Student Services Organisation (www.jasso.go.jp) provides comprehensive information on undergraduate degrees, while the Asian Students Cultural Association (www.jpss.jp) is a good source of information on graduate courses.

Student Life

Studying overseas can be a rewarding experience, particularly given the cultural richness of a city like Tokyo. Japan's economic prowess and advanced technological know-how make study in related fields a fascinating experience, just as studies such as fashion or design can offer a unique perspective on the industry.

University life in Tokyo doesn't have to be expensive. There are plenty of cheap eats in the university areas that cater specifically to the student population. For more on eating out, p.324. Getting around is also easy, thanks to the highly efficient service run by Tokyo Metro and JR trains (p.35), with stops close to most colleges . Taxis on the other hand charge extortionate rates and are best avoided.

In leisure time, the city's vast rail network (p.36), gives students the opportunity to easily explore the country (see Day Trips on p.197) and there are many city attractions that can be viewed for free (p.168). When the sun goes down, it's time to party, and there are plenty of options from bars (p.364) and clubs (p.375) to cinema (p.378), comedy shows (p.379) and theatre (p.383).

For more information, Japan Study Support has a comprehensive website (www.jpss.jp) on living and studying in Japan.

Student Accomodation

Many universities provide inexpensive accommodation – such as dormitories – on campus, or can assist you in finding reasonably priced digs off campus. Accommodation will cost upwards of ¥50,000 a month. Remember, if you decide to live off campus, you may find you have to pay a hefty security deposit, and sign a two-year rental contract. Guesthouses (p.29) are also a good cheap option.

Red Tape
Be prepared for vast amounts of paperwork when enrolling in a Japanese university. Study in Japan has a very good, informative website that will take you through the stages step by step, visit www.studyjapan.go.jp.

University Entrance Requirements

Universities in Japan will admit you to an undergraduate programme if you have completed 12 years of primary and secondary education. If you haven't done so but have passed the International Baccalaureate or Abitur and are over 18, you can still be admitted. Students with neither of these qualifications can undertake MEXT's college preparatory course (www.mext.go.jp). Admission to a post-graduate course requires 16 years of education. For more information on applying for a student visa, visit the Ministry of Foreign Affairs' website (www.mofa.go.jp).

In order to enrol in a university, you will need:
• A valid passport
• A certificate of admission from your university
• Proof that you can pay all living and educational costs while in Japan

Adult Education

Universities like Temple University Japan (p.137) offer adult education options, like diplomas which carry some value, or programmes which are for self-improvement but have no accreditation. Temple University Japan's non-credit Continuing Education programme offers a mix of courses; from academic skills and business to culture and the arts. These courses are held at night and on weekends. They tend to run for ten weeks and are open to anyone.

Sophia University
7-1 Kioi
Chiyoda-ku
🚇 Yotsuya
Map 10 B2 **23**

McGill Univesity

03 5215 1383 | www.mcgillmbajapan.com

Montreal's McGill University offers a two-year, English-language MBA programme in Japan. The course is a 60-credit course to the same standard as the MBA programme on the Montreal campus, but it allows students to work full-time as they study. Classes contain up to 40 students.

Sophia University

Various Locations
Chiyoda-ku
🚇 **Yotsuya**
Map 10 B2 **24**

03 3238 4018 | *www.fla.sophia.ac.jp*
This university was first set up by the Society of Jesus and has been a full-blown university since 1928. Sophia University has 10,000 undergraduate students and 1,000 graduates. All courses at its Faculty of Liberal Arts (FLA) are taught in English, with the exception of the Japanese language courses.

Temple University

2-8-12 Minami-Azabu
Minato-ku
🚇 **Shirokane-Takanawa**
Map 6 A2 **25**

03 5441 9800 | *www.tuj.ac.jp*
Established in 1982, Temple University's Japan campus has a range of English-language degrees and postgraduate diplomas to cater to the needs of the adult English-speaking population in Tokyo. It recently set up an Executive MBA programme, which allows executives to study part time while working. This course is ranked 14th in the world for

Tokyo University of Science

quality and performance. The university is affiliated with Philadelphia's Temple University.

Tokyo International University

1-13-1 Matoba-Kita,
Kawagoe
Saitama-ken
🚇 **Matoba**
Map 2 A1

049 232 1111 | *www.tiu.ac.jp*
This university's Masters in Economics programme, through the Graduate School of Economics, is a two-year course. Twenty students are accepted each year, with a focus on small group classes. Scholarships are available for international students.

University of Tokyo

Various Locations

03 3812 2111 | *www.u-tokyo.ac.jp*
It may not offer English-language degrees, but it does offer a range of Japanese language courses and it is the most well known university in Japan. If you want to study here, make sure you master Japanese first. The university has campuses all over the city, in Komaba, Kashiwa, Shirokane, Nakano and Hongo.

Special Needs Education

Several schools cater to children with special needs (see below). Teachers are specifically trained to work with children with learning difficulties or disabilities. Some regular schools such as the American School in Japan (p.133) accept special needs children, but you should check the facilities and discuss teaching options with the principal before enrolling your child. The level of assistance available depends on the school and the individual's needs. Harvey and MacLaurin's provide counselling to parents and will help parents to locate the most appropriate school for their child's needs. There are also various groups that provide support to parents, including the Exceptional Parents Program run by Tokyo English Life Line Communications Counseling Service (tellparentgroup@hotmail.com). See Support Groups on p.131 for more.

Harvey & MacLaurin's School

3-19-23-1003
Takanawa
Minato-ku
🚇 **Takanawa**
Map 6 A3 **26**

03 3473 6896 | *www.harvey.co.jp/maclaurin*
This is a very small school catering to students with developmental disabilities (ADHD, PDD, LD), autism and cerebal palsy. It offers classes to a very small number of students working on motor skills, art, communication and social skills, and speech therapy. They

also offer an after-school programme working on individual learning, art and motor skills. Family counselling, occupational therapy and psychology sessions can be included if necessary.

2-51-7 Tama-cho
Western Tokyo

Tokyo International Learning Community
042 401 0585 | *www.tilcjapan.com*
This school accepts children with very mild disabilities through to those with multiple disabilities and developmental delays. It follows an Individualised Education Programme (IEP) model as followed in the USA. Home schooling is also possible in cases of developmental delays from birth. It accepts students from the age of 3 to 21. A range of therapy is offered, from music, speech and drama therapy to occupational and psycho-educational therapy.

Japanese signs

5-15-15 Mita
Minato-ku
🚇 Mita
Map 6 A2 27

Yamato International School
03 5488 7888 | *www.yamato-is.jp*
Yamato International School's teachers are trained to work with children with special needs. Students and teachers come from various international backgrounds and individual needs are considered, as well as age appropriateness and social and cultural appropriateness. Students are taught reading, writing and maths, as well as how to take the bus and train safely. Swimming lessons and language classes are also offered. Hug play care is offered for children aged 6 months to 2 years and play care times can be extended between 07:30 and 08:30 in the morning and from 15:00 to 19:00 in the afternoon.

Learning Japanese
Other options **Language Schools** p.227, **Language** p.15

Tokyo is a difficult place to get around if you don't speak at least some basic Japanese (see p.15 for some basic words to get you started). There are plenty of language schools offering one-on-one or group classes during the day or in the evenings. Some of the best language schools run on a term basis, with classes commencing just three times a year, so make sure to sign up well in advance of the date you would like to start. It is worth sitting in on a class, if possible, before signing up so that you are sure it is what you're looking for. For those of school-going age, most international schools offer Japanese classes; either as part of the compulsory curriculum or as an elective.

Language Schools		
Berlitz	0120 510 923	www.berlitz.co.jp
Human Academy	03 5348 8951	www.athuman.com
Shinjuku Japanese Language Institute	03 5273 0044	www.sng.ac.jp
The Tokyo School of the Japanese Language (Naganuma)	03 3463 7261	www.naganuma-school.or.jp
Yamano Japanese Language School	03 5772 5111	www.aikgroup.co.jp/j-school

Transportation

Other options **Car** p.34, **Getting Around** p.31

Tokyo's public transport system is incredibly efficient, reliable and punctual. For this reason, most residents travel by metro (p.35), train (p.36) bus (p.34), or bicycle (p.33). Taxis are expensive. Scooters are popular for travelling short distances and for commuting to and from work. Cars on the other hand can be expensive and frustrating to run, with high petrol costs, heavy traffic, expensive toll roads and traffic lights every 50 metres (p.139 for more on driving in the city) but then again, you have the freedom to go where you want, when you want, and there's nothing like jumping in a car and hitting the road to escape the city on the weekend.

Jaunts Behind The Wheel

Kanetsu Expressway north of the city takes you to Gunma, Nagano, and other neighbouring prefectures – these are all good for a weekend on the slopes in winter and to see some countryside in summer.
Tomei Expressway heads towards Nagoya along the coast, and the Tohoku expressway heads north to Aomori through Sendai.
The Metropolitan Expressway around inner Tokyo passes through Ueno, Asakusa, central Tokyo, Odaiba and Yokohama.
The Chuo Expressway links Meguro and Shinjuku and also heads south out of the city to Nagoya. It also connects with the Kanetsu Expressway, allowing drivers to avoid inner city traffic.

Driving Habits

The Japanese people's impeccable manners extend to their driving. People are always polite, you will never be sworn at, rarely will you be honked at, and people will often give way to you, and dim their lights at night when waiting behind you in a queue. On the down side, drivers often speed through intersections, even when the lights are red and they also have a habit of stopping on the corner of a street, in a way that blocks the traffic.

Driving In Tokyo

Driving in Tokyo can be both a pleasant and a frustrating experience. The (main) roads are wide and well sign-posted in English and Japanese, but traffic is heavy and there are endless traffic lights to contend with. Buying a car is surprisingly inexpensive, especially second-hand, but they can be expensive to maintain. Petrol is expensive, as is parking (see below).

You need a Japanese driver's licence to drive in Japan (p.56) but you can use an international one when you first arrive and then switch over (within the year).

Expect to be behind the wheel for an hour or two if travelling from one side of the city to the other. For journeys to neighbouring wards, count on 15 to 30 minutes. To get out of Tokyo city, you're looking at a minimum of 90 minutes, with most places of interest around three hours away.

Petrol Stations

ENEOS, JOMO and Cosmo are the main petrol stations. Attendants will fill up the tank for you and clean your windows for free. Other services available include car wash and, depending on the station, repairs. Some petrol stations close in the evening from 18:00 to 20:00 so it's best to refuel during daylight hours. Petrol is expensive and costs approximately ¥120 per litre. Unleaded and diesel are available.

Parking

Despite the lack of available space in the city, parking is plentiful, whether in car parks or at metered spaces. Many car parks use a stacking system, stacking cars one on top of the other with the use of clever electronics. If your car has a GPS system, finding a space is easy as it will locate car parks and highlight them with a small 'P' on the screen. When parking in a metered space, make sure to place the car's wheels over the metre flap – this operates mechanically once you park and the metering will kick in. Payment is in cash – notes only – at the nearby machine. Not paying will incur a fine. Some car parks offer monthly rates, usually around ¥50,000, but otherwise it's pay as you go.

Traffic Rules

Speed cameras are dotted throughout the city. If caught speeding, you will receive a court summons in the post. If you don't speak Japanese, you will need to hire a translator to go with you. Speed limits vary depending on the road: Expressways – 80 to 100kph, urban areas – 40kph, side streets – 30kph, all other roads – 50-60kph. In terms of lane discipline, undertaking and overtaking is permissible.

Drinking & Driving

Japan has a zero tolerance policy when it comes to drinking and driving and the police are cracking down on this. If you're caught driving under the influence your licence will be confiscated and you may face imprisonment for up to three years, mandatory labour and a fine of up to ¥500,000. Passengers will also be held responsible, receiving a fine and possible imprisonment. If you are caught driving while intoxicated, again you will lose your licence and you can face five years imprisonment and a hefty fine of up to ¥1 million. Similarly, any passengers will be subject to large fines and the threat of imprisonment. The penalty for injuring a third party is severe.

Non-Driving Pests
Pedestrians and cyclists can be a liability for the driver. Cyclists in particular can be a menace and often cycle up the wrong side of the road and ignore traffic lights.

Traffic Accidents

If you are involved in an accident, no matter whose fault it is, both parties will be held responsible, proportionately to whose fault it is. So one party may be 70% at fault and the other 30%. Cyclists and pedestrians, as well as faulty car parts through dodgy dealers are the main cause of accidents. In 2004, the number of traffic accidents (injury or death) was 952,191, the highest to date.

Vehicle Leasing

If you don't have a resident's visa, your only option is to lease a vehicle. For this you need an international driving licence. There are plenty of leasing companies in the city, and some will allow those leasing with resident visas to buy the car at the end of the lease period, usually between two and four years. If you think you might want to purchase your lease car further down the line, look at companies like Occidental Corporation who offer finance leasing options.

A wide variety of cars are available, from Nissans and Volvos to Hummers (see table opposite). While cars like Hummers are popular among Tokyo's young and wealthiest, they are not so practical for Tokyo's narrow side streets. Japanese cars can be the best option, as they are well made, efficient and easily serviceable.

Vehicle Leasing Agents		
Gaijin Inc.	0475 72 1355	www.gaijininc.com
Hertz	03 3325 6480	www.hertz.com
Japan Automobile Federation	03 6833 9100	www.jaf.or.jp
Lease Japan	052 973 3953	www.leasejapan.com
National	03 3475 1839	www.nationalcar.com
Nippon Rent a Car	03 3485 7196	www.nipponrentacar.co.jp
Nissan Rent a Car	0120 004 123	www.nissanrent.com
Occidental Corporation	03 5768 6022	www.occidental.co.jp
ORIX Rent a Car	0120 000 543	http://car.orix.co.jp

Lease rates can be calculated on a variety of different bases – from one day or one week to one month or six months. Shop around for the best deals for the duration you are looking at. Expect to pay around ¥9,000 a day for a Toyota Corolla, with any additional days at a slightly discounted rate. Luxury sedans start at around ¥15,000 a day. Insurance and 24-hour roadside assistance are often included in the cost, along with basic maintenance, vehicle inspection test and taxes. If your Japanese skills are not so hot, it's best to use a company that has an English-language helpline.

Buying A Vehicle

Buying a vehicle – particularly a second hand one – is quite affordable. In most cases you will need an alien registration card, an international driver's licence, proof of address, proof of valid employment, and a parking space certificate (to prove that you have a car park). You may also need an *inkan* and a personal seal certificate if buying from a Japanese dealer.

Japanese-made cars such as Toyota, Nissan, Honda and Mazda are the most affordable, with brand new *kei*-class, the smallest available, for less than ¥1 million. All the international brands from BMW and Audi to Porsche and Ferrari are available. If you are after a high-end sports car, Tokyo is the place to get one (especially if you don't mind a second-hand car) as the vehicle financing options are favourable.

For new cars, you can go directly to the brands themselves, as they provide English-language services. The advantage of going through a manufacturer's dealership rather than a local dealer selling all different types of cars is that they will speak English, and can assist you with all the Japanese-language forms. This is not the case with small, localised dealers. For second hand cars, try companies like Gaijin Inc. or Occidental Corporation. They will handle most of the paperwork – including transfer of ownership forms if you're buying a used car.

For private sales, cars are advertised in English-language magazines like *Metropolis* and in newspaper classifieds. Get the car checked over by an independent, third party garage before buying if possible.

Car Costs

Owning and operating a car involves various expenses. You are obliged to put it through compulsory inspections (*shakken*) every two to three years. For new cars, this is only necessary after three years. *Shakken* costs somewhere between ¥100,000 and ¥200,000, along with a weight tax (between ¥8,000 and ¥50,000) and mandatory insurance payments of about ¥30,000.

Annual automobile tax costs between ¥10,000 and ¥50,000. When you first buy the car, you will also have to pay an acquisition tax.

New Car Dealers

Aston Martin	Aston Martin Akasaka	Minato-ku	03 3411 2332	www.astonmartin-akasaka.com
Audi	Audi Japan	Minato-ku	03 3584 4323	www.audi.co.jp
Bentley	Bentley Tokyo Shiba Kōen	Minato-ku	03 5730 1610	www.bentleymotors.com
BMW	BMW Tokyo	Minato-ku	03 3443 2291	www.bmw-tokyo.co.jp
Cadillac	Gaijin Inc.	Chiba-ken	0432 68 8700	www.gaijininc.com
Citroën		Koto-ku	03 3599 7870	www.citroen.co.jp
Ferrari	Gaijin Inc.	Chiba-ken	0432 68 8700	www.gaijininc.com
Honda		Various Locations	03 3467 2151	www.honda.co.jp
Hyundai	Hyundai	Chiyoda-ku	03 5532 8134	www.hyundaicorp.com
Jaguar		Various Locations	0120 050 689	www.jaguar.co.jp
Land Rover	AutoCraft Tokyo	Minato-ku	03 5460 2055	www.autocraft.co.jp
Lexus		Various Locations	0800 500 5577	http://lexus.jp
Mazda		Oyama-ku	03 3973 8119	www.mazdatokyo-g.co.jp
Mercedes Benz		Minato-ku	0120 009 927	www.mercedes-benz.co.jp
Mitsubishi		Various Locations	0120 324 860	www.mitsubishi-motors.co.jp
Nissan		Various Locations	03 3265 7211	www.nissan.co.jp
Peugeot	Gaijin Inc.	Chiba-ken	0432 68 8700	www.gaijininc.com
Porsche		Meguro-ku	03 3719 6221	www.porsche.co.jp/dealers/meguro
Rover	AutoCraft Tokyo	Taito-ku	03 5826 7885	www.autocraft.co.jp
Subaru		Various Locations	0422 33 7000	www.subaru.jp
Toyota		Various Locations	03 3817 7111	www.toyota.co.jp
Volkswagon		Various Locations	03 5706 9920	www.vw-tokyo.com
Volvo		Roppongi	03 3585 2627	www.volvocars.co.jp

Exporting & Importing A Vehicle

Provided you have owned and used a car for more than a year, you can import it duty free. You will need proof of ownership, including the local registration, licence number and Vehicle Identification Number, as well as a Japan Customs Declaration.

Used Car Dealers

Auto Direct	Minato-ku	03 5573 8776	www.autodirect.jp
Gaijin Inc.	Chiba-ken	043 268 8700	www.gaijininc.com
Occidental Corp	Meguro-ku	03 5768 6022	www.occidental.co.jp

Exporting a car is also possible. Make sure you are aware of the requirements in the country you are exporting to. Most countries require you to have owned the car for at least a year if not two before exporting it. Exporting to the US is not advisable, unless the car originated there and you have all the documentation to prove it. Companies that can help you with exporting include Gaijin Inc (if you purchase through them) and A-CROSS (03 5449 7621, www.a-cross.jp), who can help you with both import and export. A-CROSS mainly deal in relocation and will export cars only as a part of a relocation package.

Vehicle Finance

Vehicle Finance

Gaijin Inc.	043 268 8700	www.gaijininc.com
Mercedes Benz	0120 009 927	www.mercedes-benz.co.jp
Occidental Corp	03 5768 6022	www.occidental.co.jp

Japan's low interest rates mean that most people tend to go directly through dealers rather than take a loan out with their bank when buying a car. The added bonus of going through a dealer is that they will assist you with the whole process, and they usually offer English language services. Rates vary but expect to pay anywhere between 2% and 4%, depending whether it's a new or second-hand vehicle.

Vehicle Insurance

Automobile Liability Insurance is obligatory. You will have to pay for this at the time of the

Vehicle Insurance

ACE Insurance	03 5740 0666	www.ace-insurance.co.jp
AXA Non-Life Insurance Co	03 5444 2001	www.axa-direct.co.jp
The General Insurance Association of Japan	03 3255 1439	www.sonpo.or.jp
Japan Insurance.Net	0120 467 873	www.japaninsurance.net
Mitsui Sumitomo Insurance Group	03 3297 1111	www.ms-ins.com

vehicle inspection (*shaken*), which will probably work out at around ¥30,000 a year. Your insurance is valid until the next inspection date. It is also advisable to get voluntary insurance, as damage compensation can be quite expensive. If you are in an accident you will have to bear part of the cost and voluntary insurance will help to minimise these costs.

Registering A Vehicle

When transferring ownership of a vehicle, the responsibility for registering the change will fall with the buyer, unless you go through a dealer. To buy and register a vehicle you need to follow this procedure:

• Arrange for the car to undergo a compulsory inspection (*shaken*). Make sure you receive the Compulsory Insurance document (CALI or JCI). Keep your CALI or JCI in your vehicle at all times.

• Obtain a notarised signature or *inkan* (p.51) from the seller.

Registration Service

Auto Direct	03 5573 8776
Gaijin Inc.	043 268 8700
Lease Japan	052 973 3953
Occidental Corp	03 5768 6022
Tokyo General Agency	03 5786 6770

• Prepare a Power of Attorney in Japanese if necessary, and ensure the seller has one.

• Prepare a Certificate of Transfer (Bill of Sale). This form should be completed in Japanese. The seller's signature must match the notarised signature provided.

• Obtain a Certificate of Vehicle Tax Payment. Normally the seller will provide this. You will receive a bill each May, which is payable at most banks and post offices. Keep the receipt as proof of payment.

Breakdowns

Recovery and towing services through companies like Japan Automobile Federation (03 6833 9100, www.jaf.or.jp) are usually only available in Japanese, but they offer a 24-hour service. Dealers like as Occidental Corporation (03 5768 6022, www.occidental. co.jp) and Gaijin Inc. (043 268 8700, www.gaijininc.com) have an English-language service.

- Obtain a certificate of permission for a parking space. This states that you have a valid parking space. Make sure it is stamped with the *inkan* of the owner of the space as you will need it to apply for a parking permit at the police station.
- Make sure you get a map showing the location of the parking lot and the position of your parking space. Your real estate agent or the building management company should be able to provide this. This should show the dimensions of your parking space and its location relative to other spaces. The police will check the space before they issue a parking permit.
- Visit your local police station with four signed copies of the police parking application approval form. You also need to bring the documents listed in points above.
- Getting your permit will take five business days and costs roughly ¥2,500.
- Once you have received your permit, get the car registered in your name at your local Land Transport Office (*Rikunkyoku)*. Make sure you also bring a receipt for the payment of the vehicle weight tax, automobile tax and automobile acquisition tax.
- You need to have an international drivers licence to register a car. Bring your alien registration card, and all documents relating to the steps listed above.
- Once done, make sure your vehicle registration is up to date and has not expired; otherwise your insurance will not be valid. Contact the Ministry of Land, Infrastructure and Transport (www.mlit.go.jp) for further assistance.

Boozy Bike Rides

After a few beers it may seem like a good idea to ride your bike home but be warned, drink-driving laws apply to bicycles too.

Traffic Fines & Offences

You need an international driving licence to drive in Japan. If you don't have one, you may be subject to fines, arrest or imprisonment and your insurance will be invalid. The international licence must be transferred to a Japanese one within 12 months. Again, failure to do so may result in fines, imprisonment or arrest, and points on your licence. There is zero tolerance for drink driving and driving under the influence of drugs (p.140). If you are caught speeding you will be fined and will lose points on your licence. More severe punishments result if you are caught driving well over the speed limit (p.140 for speed limits). The Japanese police have the authority to contact financial institutions to check on your financial status in the event of non-payment of an offence, so there's no point trying to avoid it.

For severe offences, your licence may be suspended or cancelled. Contact the Japan Automobile Federation (03 6833 9100, www.jaf.or.jp) for more infromation. They produce a *Rules of the Road* booklet in five languages, which costs ¥1,000.

Traffic Accidents

If you are involved in an accident, move your vehicle out of the way of traffic (if possible) to a safe place. Administer whatever first aid you can and call the police emergency service on 110. If it is serious or if in any doubt as to who is to blame, wait until the police arrive. Make sure to always carry your drivers licence, registration and insurance on you.

Vehicle Repairs

Most dealers provide repair services, so if you buy through them they will be able to do any necessary repair work. Basic maintenance and repairs will be included in the warranty for new cars, and for some used cars. Auto Sport Iwase is an independent repair shop good for full servicing and repairs, but they don't speak much English.

Vehicle Repairs		
Autosport Iwase	Adachi	03 3857 1826
Gaijin Inc.	Chiba-ken	043 268 8700
Occidental Corporation	Meguro-ku	03 5768 6022

Exploring

Exploring

Tokyo is a megalopolis like no other. You could live in the city for years and still not know it inside and out, which of course adds to its charm. There are always new places to explore and unknown enclaves waiting to be discovered. Most residents have a handful of favourite haunts and are unfamiliar with the rest of the city – people who spend a lot of time in Ginza and Roppongi are probably not that hip to Ikebukuro. And denizens of Harajuku and Shibuya don't spend much time hanging out in Ueno. Tokyo is not a major tourist destination. It's a bit too overwhelming for globetrotting retirees to navigate, and backpackers tend to steer clear due to the steep costs. However, recently Taiwanese, South Korean and well-to-do Chinese have started coming over on package tours.

A city of contrasts, Tokyo is a mishmash of the old and the new. Sacred temples are sandwiched between mile-high skyscrapers, sprawling public parks offer respite from the hustle and bustle of the metropolis, and hidden residential enclaves look the same as they did 50 years ago.

The majority of the city's most impressive buildings are in west Shinjuku (p.158). Most of these were built at the height of the Bubble Economy and offer an overwhelming glimpse of the space age architecture the city is known for.

Destructive fires, earthquakes and bombings during the second world war have forced Tokyo to rebuild itself numerous times. Surprisingly, the layout of the streets and roads remains virtually the same as it was a century ago. Construction is big business and old buildings are constantly being torn down and replaced with ultramodern ones. Talk of moving the seat of government out of Tokyo proper has come and gone. Rumours of relocating Tsukiji Fish Market (p.156) have yet to come to fruition. Still, changes abound. Roppongi and Omotesandō have both recently been the sights of gargantuan architectural projects and Shinjuku seems to have a new building every other month. Roppongi and Shibuya are the main areas for going out and partying (see Bars & Pubs on p.364). Ginza is more upscale, popular with those with cash to spend. Shinjuku and Ikebukuro are full of restaurants (see Restaurants on p.330), and are home to the city's seedier establishments. Ueno has a number of parks and the outlying area sports an antiquated vibe. The surrounding prefectures are suburban sprawls and of little interest, although Chiba has some attractive beaches (p.183) and Gunma is famed for its *onsen* (p.264) natural hot springs.

JR's Top Tip

When first getting acquainted with the city, stick to the JR Lines. These above ground trains give you stellar panoramic views and will allow you to marvel at the overpowering expansiveness of the capital. Tokyo Metro is a characteristically claustrophobic underground system with zero natural light and zero soul.

Sensōji

West Shinjuku p.158

Take a trip to outer space without leaving planet Earth. The skyscrapers of west Shinjuku are a futuristic trip that even those with no interest in architecture can appreciate. The free vistas from atop any of these buildings (see the Tokyo Metropolitan Government Building on p.177) are far more encompassing than the more well-known views from Tokyo Tower or Landmark Tower.

Tsukiji Fish Market p.156

The enormous epicentre of the Japanese fishing industry has to be seen to be believed. Sea creatures from all over the world are sold and auctioned off, while the rest of the city is still snug in bed. Get here bright and early or you'll miss the action. Better yet, after a night out cavorting, head to Tsukiji and indulge in a sushi breakfast.

Kabukichō p.158

When the sun goes down, the vampires come out... and Kabukichō is the place to see them. Hustlers, hipsters and hostesses strut their stuff in Asia's more renowned Red Light District. But there's more happening here than just sleaze and sin. Kabukichō has a number of back alley watering holes, live houses and cheap *ramen* shops.

Meiji Jingū p.178

A trip to Kyoto is nice but Tokyo has its own slice of spiritual serenity in the heart of the city. Meiji Jingū is a Shintō shrine originally built in 1920 and is one of the city's most memorable landmarks. No high-rises are visible once inside the grounds and you'll forget that you're in a big city. Head here on a weekend and you may spy a traditional Japanese wedding (or ten).

Shibuya p.157

To see Tokyo's young and wannabe young head to Shibuya. What eventually becomes hip in the rest of the country has its genesis here. The fashionistas all try to out do each other and its great place for people watching. Start with the obligatory meeting at the Hachikō (p.95) statue and let the fun begin. Bars, clubs and cheap eats abound.

Sensōji p.178

Visiting Sensōji (also known as Asakusa Temple) is like taking a trip back in time. It is Tokyo's oldest temple and possibly the most important. This Buddhist structure is busy every day of the year with burning incense and praying visitors. The imposing Thunder Gate is one of the most photographed sights in all of Japan. Stalls hawking religious goods line the streets and there isn't a bad restaurant in the area.

Live Music p.380

Tokyo is a music lover's paradise and every area has a few live houses. There are venues for every budget. Swanky supper clubs feature the biggest names in jazz. Discos of all sizes run the gamut of electronic music. Underground foreign punks and local indie-rockers share the stage at cramped live houses. Free open-mic nights are a good chance to hear some up-and-coming amateurs.

Shin-Ōkubo p.158

Tokyo is by no means a melting pot but for a bit of non-Japanese culture shock, make your way to Shin-Ōkubo. The city's Koreatown, it's more than just a tourist trap. It's a functioning Korean neighbourhood that boasts numerous *yakiniku* restaurants and you can smell the *kimchi* in the air. Chinese and other Asian residents also make their home here and Japanese is rarely spoken.

Kamakura p.198

A short train ride out of the city, Kamakura is home to the awe-inspiring Great Buddha statue. This gigantic bronze temple stands over 30 metres and weighs 95 tonnes. It is one of the most iconic images in the country and it's easy to see why. Bring your camera, snap away, and then take a leisurely stroll down Yui or Zaimokuza Beach.

Imperial Palace p.185

Situated in what traditionalists consider the true heart of Tokyo, the Imperial Palace and its environs are a great place for some laid-back exploration. Though the actual palace is closed to the public, views can still be gleamed, particularly of the impressive bridge, Nijūbashi. The placid East Garden (p.185) features a tea pavilion and rolling lawns. Queue up on New Year's Day or on the emperor's birthday to inch further inside.

Ueno Museums

Tokyo is a cultured city and the sophisticated museums that dot Ueno Kōen attest to that. The National Museum of Western Art (p.172) has an impressive permanent collection with great special exhibitions. While the Tokyo Metropolitan Art Museum (p.172) and the Ueno Royal Museum (p.177) house more cutting edge works. Lastly, the Tokyo National Museum (p.177) is treasure chest of traditional Japanese art.

Onsen p.264

Tokyo's natural hot springs, known as *onsen*, range from a room with a simple bath to a massive complex offering bathing facilities, saunas, massage and beauty treatments, restaurants, karaoke and a plethora of relaxation rooms. As well as these natural springs (*onsen*) there are also many 'artificial' bathing centres known as *sento* located throughout the city.

Food

With more Michelin stars than you can shake a chopstick at, Tokyo is the new food capital of the world. From sushi and *tempura* to *okonomiyaki* and noodles, *nabe* (hotpot) in the winter and *unagi* (grilled eel) in the summer, local cuisine has to be sampled to be appreciated in its full splendour. To learn more about Japanese food, see p.341. For suggestions about where to eat out, see Restaurants on p.330.

Buskers

In the past 10 years, busking has taken off in a big way, and it is all the more entertaining to see the Japanese, who are generally a reserved people, let it all hang out. Full bands will rock out near Yoyogi Kōen (p.186) on the weekends. Folkies can be found around Ikebukuro, Ebisu and Shibuya stations. And you'll even catch the occasional jazz trio in Shinjuku.

Takao Mountain p.187

Before trekking way out to the overcrowded Mount Fuji, climb a peak a bit closer to home. Mount Takao in Hachiōji is one of Tokyo's best-kept secrets. A quick train from Shinjuku, Takao stands 600 metres tall and is a good way to get away from it all. Lovers beware: superstition dictates that couples that hike here together will soon break up.

Akihabara p.283

Put Istanbul's grand bazaar in Tokyo and replace porcelain and carpets with computers and *manga* and you have Akihabara. Pick up electronic goods at warehouse prices in this labyrinth of stores crammed with everything from video games, cameras, DVDs, computers and anime. 'Akiba' is known as *otaku* (nerd) heaven and the streets are filled with bespectacled gents and girls in all manner of costume advertising the ubiquitous maid cafes.

Edo-Tokyo Museum p.175

To get a taste of what Tokyo was like long before you arrived, head to this educational museum. Sadly overlooked by many expats, the Edo-Tokyo is a window into the past with exhibits recreating Edo era and post-Meiji Tokyo. With six floors, it is almost as overwhelming as Tokyo itself. The building it is housed in resembles a UFO landing and is worth the trip alone.

Baseball p.211

Japan is baseball mad and Tokyo has five pro teams. The Giants and Lions play in ultramodern domed stadiums, while the Swallows, Marines and Bay Stars play in more homey conventional ballparks. The synchronised cheers and general noisemaking is a spectacle in itself. Non-North American sports fans will also get wrapped up in the ceremony, regardless of their knowledge of the game.

Sumo p.250

There's more to sumo than fat guys in nappies pushing each other around, and viewing highlights on television simply can't do justice to actual sport. Sumo must be witnessed first hand and Ryōgoku Kokugikan Stadium is the place to be. Two-week tournaments take place in January, May and September. An intricate, ritualised sport, Sumo is a quintessential Japan experience.

Yoyogi Kōen p.186

Tokyo is rife with parks but there is something extra special about Yoyogi Kōen. A rolling mass of green, it is the place to be on a clear sunny day. Isolated from the hubbub of the city's epicentre, you can momentarily imagine that you are lost in the countryside. With tonnes of free music, various international festivals and a congenial vibe, it is the precious emerald jewel of the metropolis.

Roppongi p.156

Roppongi lives up to the hype. It's a non-stop party town and doesn't let up until the wee small hours of the morning. Ageism is not practised and revellers of all ages can find a place to tie one on. Start out at any one of its many bars and then boogie down until the crows start to caw.

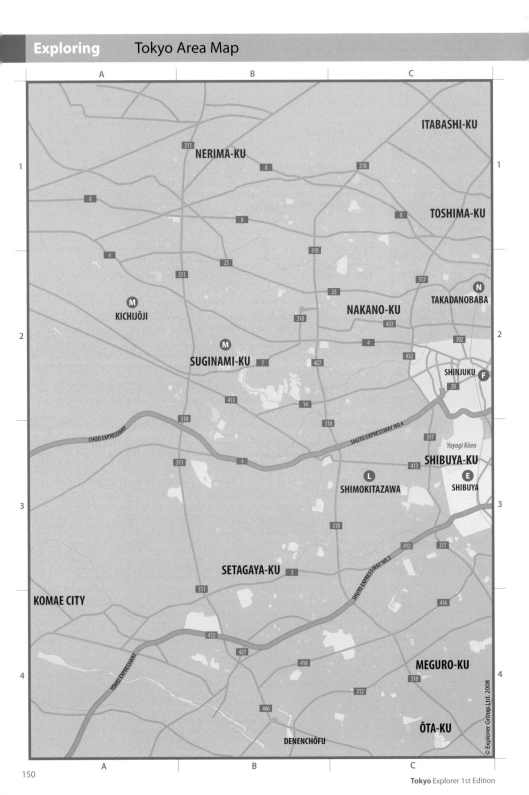

Tokyo Area Map

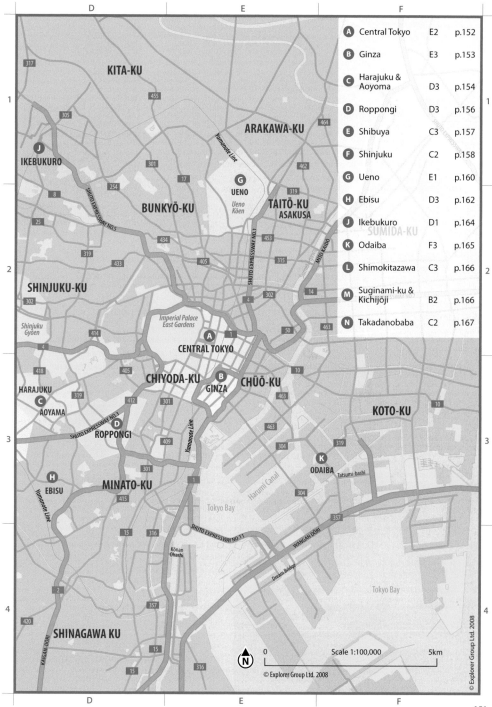

A	Central Tokyo	E2	p.152
B	Ginza	E3	p.153
C	Harajuku & Aoyama	D3	p.154
D	Roppongi	D3	p.156
E	Shibuya	C3	p.157
F	Shinjuku	C2	p.158
G	Ueno	E1	p.160
H	Ebisu	D3	p.162
J	Ikebukuro	D1	p.164
K	Odaiba	F3	p.165
L	Shimokitazawa	C3	p.166
M	Suginami-ku & Kichijōji	B2	p.166
N	Takadanobaba	C2	p.167

KITA-KU

ARAKAWA-KU

IKEBUKURO

BUNKYŌ-KU

UENO
Ueno Kōen

TAITŌ-KU
ASAKUSA

SUMIDA-KU

SHINJUKU-KU

Shinjuku Gyōen

Imperial Palace East Gardens

CENTRAL TOKYO

CHIYODA-KU

GINZA

CHŪŌ-KU

KOTO-KU

HARAJUKU

AOYAMA

ROPPONGI

EBISU

MINATO-KU

ODAIBA
Tatsumi-bashi

Harumi Canal

Tokyo Bay

Kōnan Ōhashi

Dream Bridge

WANGAN DŌRI

SHINAGAWA KU

KAIGAN DŌRI

Tokyo Bay

Yamanote Line

MITO KAIDO

SHUTO EXPRESSWAY NO.5

SHUTO EXPRESSWAY NO.1

SHUTO EXPRESSWAY NO.3

SHUTO EXPRESSWAY NO.11

0   Scale 1:100,000   5km

N

© Explorer Group Ltd. 2008

© Explorer Group Ltd. 2008

Area **A** p.151
See also Map 4

The Lowdown
*The old city centre exudes
a grandfatherly aura,
reminding residents of
how it was when Edo
(now Tokyo) began.*

The Good
*Sensōji (p.178) can be
found here and is one of
the most sacred shrines
in all of Japan.*

The Bad
*The nightlife is limited, and
few expats visit.*

Must-Do
*Take in some classic sights
like the Imperial Palace
and Sensōji (p.178). Then
head to Jinbochō and
window-shop in
antique book shops.*

Imperial Palace Gardens

Central Tokyo

What was once the proper heart of Tokyo has lost some of
its prestige over the years. Western Tokyo has expanded
and blossomed as the old centre has stayed true to its stoic
roots. Marunouchi, Chiyoda, Kanda – call it what you will
– the areas have gradually blended into one immense mass
of office buildings and briefcases. This area is more orderly
than other skyscraper districts in Tokyo and the streets are
not as congested.

However, the quarter is by no means dead. By day it's a
thriving financial district, home to big name companies
like Bloomberg and JP Morgan. Lunchtime is hectic as
office workers scurry about and many restaurants have
reasonable afternoon set menus so it's a great place to
grab lunch. By night, the sparkling new Marunouchi
Building and Marunouchi Oazo are trendy dating spots.
There are shops and boutiques of every variety and many
choice restaurants, and the clientele is less youth obsessed
than Shibuya (p.157) and not as snooty as Ginza (p.153). The Jinbochō district in
Chiyoda-ku is famed for its used book shops (see p.298).

Tokyo station is a sight for sore eyes. Functioning in its present state since 1914, the
building in which it is housed is far more attractive than the typical Japanese train
station. The Marunouchi side, with its red brick facade, is rumoured to have been
inspired by Amsterdam's main station. Fans of contemporary architecture can check
out the many sleek office buildings outside the Marunouchi exit.

There are some attractive gardens and parks sandwiched between the office buildings,
giving pencil pushers a break from corporate life. And the mysterious Imperial Palace
(west of Tokyo station) undyingly holds a special place in the hearts of Tokyoites, just
a short walk form Tokyo station. The original palace was destroyed during the second
world war after heavy Allied bombing. The present incarnation was completed in
the late 60s and is symbolic of Japan's re-emergence as a world power. The Imperial
Palace East Gardens (p.185) are also worth visiting. The nearby National Museum of
Modern Art (p.172) is often overlooked, but comes highly recommended, and was the
first official art museum in the country. Kitanomaru Kōen is a gorgeous park that is
rarely crowded. Much more low-key than other big parks in the city, it only really gets
busy during *hanami* (cherry blossom) season. Nippon Budōkan (03 3216 5100) is a
concert hall that will be familiar to music fans. Bob Dylan, Cheap Trick and Blur have all

recorded live albums at the legendary venue.
Originally built for martial arts exhibitions, its
fate changed when The Beatles arrived in 1966.
Many angry traditionalists protested the 'Fab
Four's' concerts, claiming that it would tarnish
the sanctimony of the Budōkan but the angry
masses lost out and the rest is rock history. Big
names still play here, with the cheapest tickets
starting at around ¥7,000.

North of Central Tokyo is the electric town
of Akihabara (p.283). Tech-geeks and fans of
manga and video games will love it. Further
north-east is Asakusa, home to the must-see
Sensōji (p.178) – the surrounding streets are a
reminder of what old Edo was once like.

Area **B** *p.151*
See also Map 14

Ginza

Omotesandō and Roppongi may be the new shopping hotspots, and Harajuku and Shibuya may be the fashion trendsetters, but Ginza is the true heart of consumerism. Ginza was ultramodern when the rest of the city still resembled a collection of backwater villages. The area, which is named after a Japanese silver coin mint that thrived here from the 17th to 19th centuries, has always been associated with money. After the Great Kantō Earthquake of 1923, city planners took the opportunity to rebuild the municipality into a modern marvel. Department stores, boutiques and chic eateries soon flourished and it became the city's original shopping Mecca, and its broad streets and spacious pavements give it a Manhattan-like air. Though other hip upstart neighbourhoods have tried to steal some of its fire, Ginza still radiates a shop-til-you-drop snootiness that makes it one of the city's quintessential destinations.

A number of train lines run throughout the city and getting around is never a problem. The area is also unexpectedly quiet at night – there's none of the raucous traffic and late night revellers that are in other parts of town.

Mitsukoshi (p.307) and Matsuya (p.307) department stores have gargantuan shops that you could literally get lost in. For those with a proclivity for the finer things, there's Wako (p.308). Inside you'll find top-end jewels and handbags, while outside, the building's clock tower is one of Tokyo's most iconic images. Don't be embarrassed to window-shop; Japanese staff make everyone feel welcome.

For those who don't wish to part with their lifesavings, there are other attractions. The ever-popular Sony Building (5-3-1 Ginza, Chūo-ku, www.sonybuilding.jp) displays the newest gadgets from the electronics giant. It's a hands-on environment and button pushing is thoroughly encouraged – kids will have a blast with the latest Play Station games, despite the queues on weekends. Kabuki-za (p.383) is the most distinguished *kabuki* theatre in all of Tokyo. There are two shows a day, usually lasting four to five hours. Those with only a minor interest can pop in for an act or two. The building is impressive in its own right and English language audio guides are available. Ginza is full of art galleries (try Gallery Koyanagi, p.171 or Tokyo Gallery, p.172) and you won't have to look hard to find them. These range from cutting edge avant-garde design displays to the hokey sunset and puppies variety. The greatest concentration of galleries is just south of Harumi Dōri.

The Lowdown
Tokyo's original shopping centre maintains its original majesty and will bring out the consumer in everyone.

The Good
Wide streets and hordes of art galleries make this a great place to explore on foot.

The Bad
The wealthy, dolled-up, middle-aged women who shop this area might make you feel self-conscious if you're a T-shirt and jeans kind of person.

Must-Do
Buy something! Shop, drop, pick yourself back up and hit some galleries.

Chūō Dōri

Area C p.151
See also Map 7

Harajuku & Aoyama

Harajuku is where the city's teens come out to play. The shops and boutiques cater to them and their weekly allowances, and weekends are buzzing with kids sporting the latest fashions. Adults will not feel excluded; it's one of the best places for people watching, and it attracts an older crowd once the sun goes down. Neighbouring Aoyama is geared towards upwardly mobile thirty-somethings and it is often hard to tell where one area ends and the other begins. Aside from consumer craziness, there are some must-see sights in these parts. Meiji Jingū (p.178) is one of the most sacred Shintō shrines in the nation and Yoyogi Kōen (p.186) is a never-ending expanse of greenery. Harajuku is bisected by two main streets – Meiji Dōri and Omotesandō. Omotesandō is one of the widest streets in the city and the trees that line it make it an oddity in Tokyo city planning. Heading east down Omotesandō, you'll eventually reach upmarket Aoyama, where locals have more of a penchant for Gucci sunglasses and Louis Vuitton bags, than mohawks and black eyeliner.

Harajuku and Aoyama are great places to shop. The Japanese are shopping-obsessed and you'd be hard pressed to find a better place to witness them in all their consumer glory. Takeshita Dōri (see Areas To Shop on p.304) is where the hip teens buy all their clothes and accessories. It is a narrow road that runs parallel with Omotesandō. Follow the kids out the Omotesandō exit of Harajuku station and you're there. Dotted with fastfood joints and gaudy boutiques, this is where the action is if you're under 20. Regardless of your age though, it's a scene to behold. It's hard to believe that the breathtaking Meiji Jingū (p.178), a sacred Shintō shrine, sits so close to all this juvenile consumerism.

The area where Meiji Dōri and Aoyama Dōri intersect is chock full of shops. And the recently opened Omotesandō Hills (p.313) is giving Roppongi Hills a run for its money. The famed Oriental Bazaar (p.300) is geared more towards tourists than residents, but kitschy Japanese goods can be found here, and it's a good place to head if you're redecorating.

Leafy Yoyogi Kōen is the place to be on a sunny Sunday afternoon. It opened in 1967, soon after the Summer Olympics, and has been one of the city's premier relaxation spots ever since. On weekdays it is pretty much deserted, except for cherry blossom season. At the main entrance you'll often encounter the Tokyo Rockabilly Club. These modern greasers, with their slicked-back pompadours and retro-leather duds, dance and prance to 1950s rock'n' roll. Feel free to take their picture, but don't try to dance with them – they take their performances seriously. On weekends, bands perform on the streets surrounding the park and you'll hear everything from Dixieland jazz to death metal.

Yoyogi Kōen is a great place to picnic, but bring own your food and drink, as the stalls surrounding the park charge a fortune. Bike paths wind their way through the heart of the green expanse and bicycles can be rented cheaply.

The pavilion hatch shell off Inokashira Dōri often hosts international festivals. The Thai (mid-May) and Jamaican festivals (late May) are particularly popular and expats come from all over the Kantō Plain. Check out *Metropolis* (www. metropolis.co.jp) or *Japanzine* (www.seekjapan.jp) to stay abreast of upcoming festivals. These two-day affairs are well worth attending.

The Lowdown

Teen shoppers run amok and dolled-up Goths make the scene, as sacred Meiji Jingū and placid Yoyogi Kōen sit quietly smack-dab in the middle of the juvenile chaos.

The Good

This is a lively area and the energy is contagious, you'll never want for something to do here.

The Bad

Harajuku can get overly crowded on weekends, especially in the summer, and upscale Aoyama can be a bit snooty.

The Must-Do

Check out all the Gothic Lolitas hanging out near Harajuku station.

Lolita Goths & Harajuku Girls

Harajuku is the place to see the infamous Lolita Goths and Harajuku Girls. The small plaza that links Harajuku station to Yoyogi Kōen is rife with youngsters decked out in their baby doll dresses and *kabuki* makeup and on weekends it's mayhem. Buskers and street performers congregate here as well and it's a good chance to check out some free entertainment.

Goths and girls near Harajuku station

Area **D** *p.151*
See also Map 11

The Lowdown

The party centre of the city, this is where to drink and dance until the sun comes up.

The Good

The area is teeming with friendly Japanese and party goers looking to meet new people, so it's a great social hub.

The Bad

As party central as it might be, Roppongi makes for an expensive night out. An evening of full-on revellry will set you back between ¥10,000 and ¥20,000.

Must-Do

Get down and party with the best of them in the area's multiple bars and clubs.

Roppongi

The city's all-night party heart never stops beating. Roppongi rocks from sundown until sunrise, with endless options for revellry. With the recent addition of Roppongi Hills, the area is trying to revamp its hedonistic image, but this doesn't fool anyone. This is where people come to get down, get wild and dance their troubles away. Roppongi caters very much to expats, but the Japanese have also caught on, and on a weekend night it is hands down the most multicultural place in the city. Like most entertainment hotspots, it exudes a youthful vibe and the kids run wild. But don't let that deter you. Ageism is not practiced here and people of all ages can get their groove on. It can get rowdier than other parts of Tokyo, but it's by no means dangerous. Long-time residents will often scoff at the idea of heading to Roppongi, but they're just trying to feel superior. Almost every foreign resident has some fond memories of their Roppongi days and secretly wish that they still had the constitution to carry on there all night long. The most common patrons are foreign executives and off duty American military personnel, but English teachers will make the trek out from Saitama and Chiba to tie one on. There was once a big *yakuza* presence here, but that has slowly faded.

Until the opening of Roppongi Hills and Tokyo Midtown (p.313), this was not a big shopping area, but these mammoth additions have quickly changed all that. These cities unto themselves will satisfy all your shopping needs. You can shop until you drop. And just before you drop, you check into one of their many hotels and get some sleep. Aside from the aforementioned malls, there's not much to do during the day. All of the bars will be closed and only a few of the restaurants will be open. The Mori Art Museum (p.171) in Roppongi Hills has great special exhibits and is recommended. Gaudy Tokyo Tower (p.177) rises high above the city streets and has a decent observation deck. Night time is the right time to be in Roppongi. Almond Café (corner of Roppongi Dōri and Gaien Higashi, Exit 3 from Roppongi station) on the main crossing is the place to meet and you'll see hordes of people here waiting for friends and dates on weekend nights. From there, head to any of the local watering holes, but be prepared for rooms full of cigar smoke and lecherous would-be Casanovas. Dancing options abound. Those looking for something more intellectually stimulating should head to Super Deluxe (p.382). This cavernous club promotes performance art and avant-garde music nights.

Shop Life

For the Japanese, shopping is as vital as eating and breathing. The recently constructed Roppongi Hills is a testimony to mass consumption. A mini-city unto itself, it sees 100,000 visitors on weekdays and up to 300,000 on weekends. Swank boutiques rub shoulders with four-star restaurants, while pristine gardens give weary shoppers a chance to rest their feet.

Tokyo Tower

Roppongi

Area ⑤ p.150
See also Map 8

Shibuya

Japan is very much a youth-based culture and nowhere is that more evident than in Shibuya. Those past their teens will not feel excluded, but it undeniably caters to the kids. Famed for its hip shopping centres and with its finger firmly on the pulse of contemporary fashion, this is where all trends are born.

The Lowdown
The hip, hopping epicentre of everything that is cool, Shibuya is where the chic and wannabe chic come to shop, drink and go clubbing.

The area is a sprawling mess though. Its streets are continually swarming with people and the centre is a labyrinth, high atop a hill. Shibuya Crossing is renowned for being the most crossed streets on Earth and its one of the few places where you have to wait in line to simply walk down it. Weekends between 12:00 and 21:00 should be avoided if hordes of people are not to your liking. The recent addition of upmarket hotels and department stores have attempted to bring a more mature element to the area, but it doesn't seem to be working. Japanese over the age of 30 avoid it like the plague. By day it's shop 'til you drop, and by night it's a boogie-down disco Mecca.

The Good
Shibuya is a rocking good time and is alive and kicking regardless of the hour.

Shibuya is one of the most famed shopping areas in the country. Slick urban fashion is all the rage and dolled up teens and twenty-somethings can be seen scuffling about with armloads of shopping bags on daily basis. However, those over 25 won't find much here in the way of clothing. Shibuya 109 (p.281) is where all of Tokyo's *gyaru* get accessorised. *Gyaru* are the fake tanned, wobbly high heel wearing fashionistas that simultaneously follow and set the trends. The adjacent 109-2 store sells similar clothing for the pre-teen market. Big name department stores Parco (p.308) and Seibu (p.308) have branches in Shibuya. The Tokyu Hands (p.308) store is particularly impressive. This household goods emporium sells knick-knacks and appliances for every room and it's also a great place to buy gifts and Halloween costumes. Tower Records (p.278) has a huge English-language book section on the top floor and sells foreign magazines and newspapers.

The Bad
On weekends, it's a mob scene and even the queues have queues.

Shibuya is not all empty-headed consumerism. If shopping is not your cup of tea, there's still plenty to see and do. Shibuya station has five exits, but the Hachikō exit is where everyone meets, and it has to be experienced at least once. On weekend nights all the hipsters gather and wait for their friends to arrive. The exit is named after the most famous dog in Japanese history, Hachikō, for whom a statue was erected in 1934. He was an Akita dog who used to wait here for his owner to return from work every day – for the full story, see Top Dog on p.95.

Must-Do
Spend some of your hard earned yen at any of Shibuya's many shopping centres.

There are a few worthy museums off the beaten path. Bunkamura (p.170) is one of the most exciting galleries in the city and hosts many big name exhibitions. Owned by the Tokyu Hands department store (p.308), its sleek interior is far more airy than other museums in the city. Recent artists exhibited include Picasso and Renoir. There is also a concert hall that showcases ballet and classical music and a small art house theatre that screens European and Asian films. Two of Japan's more peculiar museums are also in Shibuya. The Eyeglass Museum (2-29-18 Dōgenzaka, 03 3496 3315) and the Tobacco and Salt Museum (1-16-8 Jinnan, 03 3476 2041) are far more interesting than they sound and are easy on the wallet. The former is free and the latter costs just ¥100.

Just up the hill, past the 109 building is the infamous Love Hotel Hill. Clustered together on these dingy side streets are too many Love Hotels to name. These dens of the flesh offer rooms to rent by the night or by the hour. They are popular places to escape for twenty-somethings (many of whom live with their parents) and with couples in the throws of adultery (for obvious reasons). The insane designs of the buildings are well worth a look. Some are modelled on medieval castles, while others have a Romanesque theme and feature Doric columns.

Shibuya has its fair share of music venues and some cool watering holes. Try Insomnia Lounge (p.367), CoZmo's Café (www.cozmoscafe.com) or The Pink Cow (www.thepinkcow.com). Womb (p.377), Club Asia (03 5458 2551, 2-21-7 Dōgenzaka) and Ruby Room (03 3780 3022, Kasumi Bldg 2-25-17 Dōgenzaka) are popular clubs open all night. Live music can be found at the Shibuya AX concert venue in Yoyogi Kōen.

Area **F** p.150
See also Map 3

Shinjuku

Shinjuku is the pulsating urban heart of contemporary Tokyo. It has the *Blade Runner-like* cityscape the city is famous for and vertical neon lights scream from every building. Shoppers and commuters barrel down the street like stampeding cattle, and this part of the city never sleeps. Shinjuku's two most famous sections are very different universes. Kabukichō (see below) is the sleazy Red Light District, full of gangsters, wannabe gangsters and drunk middle-aged perverts. In the eyes of the Japanese, it is the most dangerous place on the planet, but any foreign resident with an iota of street smarts will be fine here. West Shinjuku is the modern architectural Mecca of the city. Its mind-boggling skyscrapers shoot into the sky and point the country firmly towards the future. As hustle and bustle as Shinjuku is, there are actually many pockets of quietude tucked away. Parks and back alley cafes offer some respite and the areas away from the main train station are rather relaxed. In terms of culture, Shinjuku has the insightful Shinjuku Historical Museum (p.176) and galleries such as Wako Works of Art (p.173) and the Kenji Taki Gallery (p.171).

Department stores Mitsukoshi (p.307) and Isetan (p.307) are in Shinjuku and can get packed on the weekends. The branch of Kinokuniya (p.314) at Takashimaya Times Square has one floor of foreign-language books and is popular with expat bibliophiles. This area is also famed for its electronics shops and has a mini-Akihabara feel. Prices don't vary much from shop to shop, but look around for some occasional bargains. East Shinjuku is famed for its numerous record and CD shops. Audiophiles could get lost wandering these backstreet stores; bootlegs and rare import shops are everywhere. The bargain Don Quixote (1-16-5 Kabukichō, www.donki.com) store has two branches in Shinjuku and is a good place to buy household goods when setting up shop. The Kabukichō store is five storeys, however the aisles are very narrow and can be congested. The Shin-Ōkubo location is far more comfortable and the staff are much more helpful.

Shin-Ōkubo itself is a good place to get local produce and imported Asian food – if you have a penchant for kitschy Korean pop culture goods you'll be in heaven. It is also as close to Seoul as you can get without leaving Japan. There are many speciality stores here, selling imported Korean food and K-pop CDs. *Yakiniku* (grilled beef), *kimchi* (spicy pickles) and *bibimbap* (mixed vegetable, meat and rice) restaurants are everywhere, though dinner can be pricey. Lunch sets are usually available and offer good food for reasonable prices. Menus are almost always in Japanese and Korean and any attempts to speak English will fall on deaf ears.

For other nightlife options, Shinjuku has masses of bars and nightclubs (see Bars & Pubs on p.364). One drinking option is the Golden Gai adjacent to Kabukichō. This jumble of tiny alleyways is home to many rustic stand-up bars, but the customers can be somewhat territorial and many places only welcome regulars. For a foreigner-friendly bar, try Bar Plastic Model (p.364).

Shinjuku Gyōen (p.186) is a green oasis on the east side (not to be confused with Shinjuku Central Park). The grounds are immaculate and the staff take great pride in keeping riff-raff out. Entry is ¥200 (there's a ticket machine at the main gate).

The Lowdown
Shinjuku is the vivacious, electrifying contemporary heart of the city, with sleazy back alleys, soaring skyscrapers and endless entertainment options.

The Good
Heaps of watering holes, the most impressive contemporary architecture in the country and dodgy – though relatively harmless – characters will keep you coming back for more.

The Bad
Shinjuku station is as confusing as an upside-down roadmap and everyone eventually falls prey to its labyrinth of exits and entrances.

Must-Do
Make your way to Kabukichō's Red Light District and immerse yourself in its complete and utter wantonness.

Kabukichō

Even if you're not interested in complete debauchery, Kabukichō is a good time. You'll see *yakuza* everywhere, but they generally have no interest in foreigners and you'll most likely be left totally alone. A lot of the more sleazy businesses are only open to Japanese, though foreigners are guaranteed to be flagged down by touts with offers of overpriced strip joints. The bars are barebones and the drinks are comparatively cheap. Some establishments don't allow foreigners, and attempts to change their mind are futile. Scope out the bar before entering and you'll save yourself some aggravation. There are also a number of chain *izakayas* (p.328) in Kabukichō. These are a good place to finish a night and they stay open very late.

Tokyo Areas

A stroll through the towering business area of western Shinjuku is a cheap way to spend a day and see some of the city's most impressive architecture. Most of these uber-modern skyscrapers were built at the height of the Bubble Economy and echo the easy spending ways that characterised the times. The Tokyo Metropolitan Government Building (p.177) is particularly spellbinding. Its airy Romanesque piazza lies in stark contrast to the futuristic towers that surround it and is a good place for a cup of coffee after taking in the views of Tokyo from the 45th floor observatory. Like Roppongi Hills and the Sunshine Building in Ikebukuro, Shinjuku Sumitomo Building (p.177) prides itself on being a self-contained mini-city. The view from the 51st floor is highly recommended. Down the street is the high-tech Shinjuku NS Building. It is a hollow structure with a massive plaza and a transparent roof. At 100 metres there is a skywalk that offers a nice overview of the building. In the lobby you'll find an enormous 30 metre pendulum clock, considered the world's largest by the *Guinness Book of Records*.

Tokyo Metropolitan Government Building

Kabukichō bar

Nightlife in Kabukichō

Area **G** *p.151*
See also Map 4, 12

Ueno

Ueno is an anomaly to the rest of the city. There are no mile-high skyscrapers, it is comparatively easy to navigate, and it retains an old world charm that other parts of the city are quickly forgetting.

Since the end of the second world war, businesses and residents have been setting up shop in the east side. Culturally speaking, Kanda, Nihonbashi and the area immediately around Tokyo station have incrementally gone the way of the dodo, but Ueno keeps on going. Home to some of the most famed museums in the country; it exudes a quasi-cultured air that is by no means snooty. Originally, this was one of the more blue-collar neighbourhoods, and the notion of building highfalutin art museums here raised a few eyebrows. Ueno Kōen (see below) may be scruffy around the edges, but it is still one of Tokyo's highlights.

Ueno was made for strolling. The open-air markets that thrive outside the main gate of Ueno station are like a trip back in time with fishmongers and produce salesmen hawking their goods at top volume. There's not much nightlife, but during the day it's hectic. Starting at the station, one good way to explore the area is to follow the self-guided walk around 'Ueno Onshi Kōen and Vicinity' on the *Tokyo Walks* leaflet available from the JNTO Tourist Information Centre (see p.23).

The main place to shop is Ameyoko Market (p.309). This outdoor emporium began after the second world war as a black-market where Japanese could buy hard-to-come-by goods. It's no longer quite so seamy but it still retains a hustle and bustle vibe that most other shopping districts have long forsaken. It's also the only place in place in the city where haggling occurs, but in Japanese only. Ueno is one of the least English-language friendly parts of town. And for long time residents, that's half of its appeal. Luggage, dried squid, baseball caps – everything under the sun is available and designer goods are usually the real McCoy. For those who crave air conditioning and bar codes, there are a few big name department stores in the area as well.

Ueno has a number of attractions and it is somewhere people return to again and again. Ueno Kōen (p.186) is by far the most urban of all Tokyo's parks, the concrete far outweighing the greenery. Yet, there is something undeniably charming about the place. With numerous museums, temples and a zoo, it offers a cornucopia of entertainment possibilities. Ueno Zoo (p.182) is nothing to write home about, but it's somewhere to while away a few hours, especially for kids. The elephants are chained to the ground and the bears are housed in cages the size of walk-in closets, but the penguins are free to waddle and the ever-popular panda has roomy digs. The predatory bird and reptile exhibits are particularly impressive.

Speaking of predatory birds, watch out for the crows. Crows are everywhere in Tokyo, and Ueno Kōen is full of them. These clever birds are pretty sizeable and can be quite intimidating. Be careful when walking small dogs and never leave food unattended.

The park has many museums and they can get quite crowded on weekends and holidays. Weekdays are the best time to go, but all of them are closed on Mondays. The National Museum of Western Art (p.172) opened in the late 1950s and is the only museum in Tokyo devoted solely to western art. The permanent collection is impressive and the special exhibitions are usually very good and are extremely popular. The Tokyo Metropolitan Art Museum (p.172) was constructed underground and is one of the architectural oddities of Ueno. The permanent collection has some wonderful Japanese art and the special exhibitions are very cutting edge. It

The Lowdown
Ueno is a slice of old school Tokyo, eschewing the skyscrapers and gaudy neon lights that infest the rest of the city. Flat and easy to navigate, its back alleys offer endless opportunities for exploring.

The Good
Ueno Kōen (p.186) is home to Tokyo's own Museum Mile. The National Museum of Western Art (p.172), Tokyo Metropolitan Art Museum (p.172) and Tokyo National Museum (p.177) all demand repeat visits.

The Bad
There is not much in the way of nightlife here. Once the sun goes down, so do energy levels.

Must-Do
Make your way to any of Ueno Kōen's excellent museums. In the spring, splay out on the grass and take in the blooming cherry blossoms with a load of inebriated office workers.

Top 'Gun
Tokugawa Ieyasu is one of the most venerated *shoguns* in Japanese history. He has been immortalised in numerous *manga* and films. Novelist James Clavell based his famous novel *Shogun* on Ieyasu's life story. For more on the part he played in Japan's history, see p.2.

occasionally displays paintings by local art students and is well worth a look. Tokyo National Museum (p.177) is a treasure trove of traditional Japanese art and culture. The oldest and largest museum in the country it has an overwhelming 25 rooms and will require repeat trips to take it all in. Housing nearly 90,000 items, including samurai swords, *kabuki* costumes and woodblock prints, it is not to be missed. Another museum worth a visit is Ueno Royal Museum (p.177), which showcases Japanese paintings and sculptures.

Tōshōgū Shrine is dedicated to *shogun* Tokugawa Ieyasu (see Top 'Gun, left). Built in 1627, it holds the distinction of being one of the few major structures in Tokyo to survive the second world war. The shrine is similar to the shrine in Nikko where he is interred and is famous for its intricate dragon carvings.

Many homeless people live in Ueno Kōen and the makeshift abodes that they have constructed are fascinating – the blue tarp lean-tos are a testament to ingenuity. They pose no threat and don't panhandle, never mind accost. Most of them lost their jobs after the Bubble Economy burst in the 1990s and are a sobering reminder that Japan's financial miracle left a few people behind.

Lion in Ueno Zoo

Ueno Kōen

Tokyo National Museum

Other Areas

Area ⓗ p.151
See also Map 5

Ebisu

Despite being encircled by frenzied Shibuya and Roppongi, Ebisu exudes an unperturbed manner. Easily accessible, it can be taken in on foot with relative ease. The west exit of Ebisu station is rather unassuming and a great place to do some exploring. Tiny streets twist and turn, dotted with cool restaurants and bars. The east exit is more pronounced with the pleasant Ebisu Garden Place drawing the crowds.

The Lowdown
Cool but low-key area that's a popular hangout for the over 25s.

Ebisu is centrally located, yet slightly removed from the hustle and bustle that infests other big neighbourhoods and there are many imported food shops (see Food on p.284). Bordering Daikanyama and Hirō have heaps of shopping options. A trip to Ebisu wouldn't be the same without a visit to the most beloved Good Day Books (p.298), one of only two shops in the city specialising in second-hand English-language books.

The Good
One of the most uncrowded, relaxed spots in Tokyo.

The main areas of interest are mostly on the east side. Ebisu Garden Place frequently features free art displays at its entrance. Nearly all exhibitions last for about a month and are worth a look. The structural design of the Garden Place gets mixed reviews. With its faux European construction, it has a Disney-like feel to it. However, there are often extraordinary sculpture exhibitions on display for free and the courtyard is a nice place to stop and smell the roses. The patio is rather picturesque and is popular for a coffee and romantic moments with your significant other. The Yebisu Beer Museum (p.189) celebrates the fine art of brewing and will even interest teetotallers. Exhibitions cover the history of beer in Japan, classic advertising and brewing techniques. Admission is free, but sampling the suds will cost you ¥200 for each little glass. The Tokyo Metropolitan Museum of Photography (p.176) hosts great exhibitions. Most of them are either about Japan or feature the work of Japanese photographers. It's a fantastic window into the Japanese mindset and is never crowded. Recent exhibitions have focused on 1970s Tokyo and world religious sights. On the west side there are two excellent entertainment options, Milk and What the Dickens. Both housed in the same building (ROOB 6 Building, 1-13-3 Ebisu-Nishi), they are off the beaten Tokyo nightlife map, but are always hopping. Milk is an underground DJ bar that focuses on trance and hip-hop. The even have a chill-out lounge for those who want to take a break from dancing. The Dickens is a comfy British-style pub that has many imported beers on draft. There is music nightly and seldom a cover charge, and the first Sunday of the month heralds a popular poetry open-mic night.

The Bad
Little in the way of historical buildings.

Must-Do
Explore Ebisu Garden Place at your leisure.

Ebisu Garden Place

Great things can come in small packages…

Perfectly proportioned to fit in your pocket, these marvellous mini guidebooks make sure you don't just get the holiday you paid for, but rather the one that you dreamed of.

Explorer Mini Visitors' Guides
Maximising your holiday, minimising your hand luggage

Area ❶ p.151
See also Map 3

Ikebukuro

Ikebukuro is the black sheep of Tokyo. Disowned by residents in more affluent neighbourhoods, it is short on history but full of its own unique energy. It borders the northern prefecture of Saitama. Shopping is big business and consumers commute down from Saitama in hordes. Big name department stores Seibu and Tobu have branches

Tokyo Metropolitan Art Space

The Lowdown
A jumbled urban maze, Ikebukuro is one of the least pretentious neighbourhoods in the capital.

The Good
Cheap restaurants, great bars and a youthful vibe that isn't as fashion obsessed as other parts of town.

here and Sunshine Street has many fashionable boutiques. The Seibu (p.308) is the company's largest and has an excellent art museum on the 12th floor. The Tobu branch is also huge and it's popular with expats for its imported food emporium. Junkudo book shop (p.278) is a favourite destination for readers. The top floor of this mammoth building is full of English-language books and magazines. It has more of a library astrosphere and the staff won't bother you if you simply want to leaf through some periodicals. Sunshine City (p.226) has tonnes of stores and avid shoppers will be overwhelmed.

The Bad
Litter, grey concrete parks and staid architecture make this one of the least aesthetically pleasing areas in town.

The vivacious heart of Ikebukuro lies on the east side. Here you'll find all the hustle and bustle, bright lights and swarms of people. The very Japanese architectural notion of massive shopping complexes that are cities unto themselves started with Sunshine City. Inside you'll find Sunshine International Aquarium (p.169), a planetarium and an Asian arts museum. It's also home to the fastest elevator in the world – a thrilling free ride. There's an observation deck on the 60th floor, though the free views from Shinjuku's skyscrapers are more impressive. Nearby is the Toyota Auto Salon Amlux (www.amlux.jp). This showcase centre with more than 80 automobiles will entertain even those with little interest in cars. Sunshine Street is great place to stroll and take in the energy of the city. Many Nigerians have set up hip-hop clothing and record shops and touts patrol the street trying to get the kids to check out their wares.

Must-Do
Check out either the Sunshine International Aquarium (p.169) or the planetarium.

There are a number of watering holes in both east and west Ikebukuro, with *izakayas* and pubs everywhere. Popular local bars, The Black Sheep (1-7-12 B1, Higashi-Ikebukuro, 03 3987 2289) and King George Sankei Building (B1), 1-22-5 Higashi-Ikebukuro, 03 5952 4134), have a cosy ambience. There is also a minor Red Light District on the east side. Like Kabukichō (p.158), most of these establishments are off limits to foreigners, though you may get the occasional tout trying to drag you off to some high-priced strip joint. The main attraction on the west side is Tokyo Metropolitan Art Space (p.172). This gigantic art emporium consists of 14 floors and hosts local exhibitions as well as avant-garde performance art. The escalator at the main enhance is the world's largest and you can ride up and down it for free. The plaza outside the building is a popular place to grab lunch or down a can of beer on a hot summer night. Fledgling hip-hop dancers practise their moves here and buskers serenade passersby.

Street Tunes
The area around Ikebukuro station is full of street musicians; the most popular places are just outside the west and Metropolitan exits.

Steamy Baths

For an authentic *onsen* (p.264), there's no need to hightail it into the mountains. The Oedo Onsen Monogatari (p.265) pumps water from 1,400 metres and has baths of varying temperatures. Modelled on an Edo-era village, it's less cheesy than it sounds and offers quality baths. Unlike most *onsen*, it is also foreign friendly. There is a mixed-gender bath area as well, but don't get too excited – bathing suits are mandatory.

Area **K** p.151
See also Map 11

Odaiba

Odaiba divides Tokyoites right down the middle. For some it is a testament to Japanese ingenuity and one of the primo date spots in the city. For others it is an antiseptic destination, as fake as plastic trees and lacking any real soul. Regardless of the great debate, there is a lot to do and see here and it is a uniquely Tokyo experience.

An island in the middle of Tokyo Bay, Odaiba is built on reclaimed land and only came into its present steel-and-glass incarnation in the mid 90s. Evidence of Japan's onward-and-upward mentality, it is host to some of the most far out sci-fi buildings the city has to offer. It has spectacular views of mainland Tokyo as well the most picturesque waterfront in town. Sheltered by the enormity of the metropolis, Tokyoites often forget how integral the ocean is to the city's existence – Odaiba is a subtle reminder.

There are some shopping options but you'll find better bargains and more variety elsewhere. The gaudy Palette Town has heaps of shops and boutiques, mostly of them fairly upmarket. Housed within Palette Town are Venus Fort (p.313) and Sun Walk. Venus Fort is a screaming example of Japanese kitsch. This shopping mall features an open-air court in the style of an 18th century Mediterranean villa. European eateries are everywhere and some of them have outdoor seating. Beneath Venus Fort is the more generic Sun Walk shopping centre. The Fuji TV headquarters is as ultramodern as they come. You won't need a map to find it; thanks to the space age pinball machine motif, you'll spot it with your eyes closed. Inside you'll find exhibitions hyping up the networks' current TV programmes and a worthwhile observation deck. But the real attraction is the building itself; wander around it and bask in its innovative architecture. If heights are not an issue, take a ride in the gigantic Ferris wheel adjacent to Palette Town. The Japanese will brag that it's the biggest in the world but this is not true. However, standing over 100 metres, it's still impressive. Tickets cost ¥900.

Tokyo Big Sight is another architectural mind-boggler. With its enormous inverted pyramids, it is well worth a look. Boasting two huge exhibition halls and a 100 seat conference room, there is always something happening. Check local listings for the popular Design Fiesta. This mammoth undertaking takes place periodically throughout the year and gives local artists a chance to display and sell their work. The Museum of Maritime Science (p.175) and the National Museum of Emerging Science & Innovation (p.176) are great for the kids. The waterfront is nice for a stroll, and a miniature Statue of Liberty is worth a few snaps, as is the Rainbow Bridge. Swimming is prohibited but young kids still jump into its murky waters on the dog days of summer.

The Lowdown
Space-age architecture and over-the-top garishness make Odaiba one of the most Tokyoesque destinations.

The Good
Wacky buildings, a seaside vibe and a great place for a date.

The Bad
The area attracts a strange mix of teenagers and middle-aged women who don't seem to care for each others' existence.

Must-Do
Stroll by the water, check out the views and then take a spin on the Ferris wheel.

Odaiba

Area ❶ *p.150*
See also Map 5

Shimokitazawa

The Lowdown
The only
neighbourhood in
Tokyo that is as hip as
it thinks it is. Shimokita
is youthful without the
air-headedness that
permeates other parts
of the city.

While unwisely overlooked by tourists breezing through, Shimokitazawa has much to offer long-term expats. A few stops from Shibuya on the Keiō Inokashira line, it is laidback and personable, without losing any of that funky Tokyo swagger. Shimokita – as the locals call it – is imbued with a youthful energy and is less commercial than the teen shopping districts of Shibuya and Harajuku. Dreadlocked hippies, thoroughly pierced punks and bookish intellectuals make their home here and the alternative aura is tangible the moment you step out of the station. Buskers and street performers jostle for space on the narrow alleyways, further cementing its bohemian reputation.

The Good
Cool cafes, bars and
restaurants dot
every street.

There is a bevy of second-hand and vintage clothing shops immediately around the station. These are not Salvation Army-type shops though so don't expect to save money. Faded American T-shirts and classic dungarees are big business. Most cater to younger Japanese though and sizes may be too small for westerners. Local records shops specialise in rare vinyl and bootleg albums. Music fans could wander around the back alleys for days, discovering tiny music shops. On weekends, Japanese kids will often set up shop on the side streets, hosting mini-garage sales. This is good way to pick up some household items or kitschy pop culture goods (see Village Vanguard on p.305).

The Bad
Gigantic scavenging
crows make a bleary-
eyed walks home in
the morning even
more unpleasant.

Shimokita is short on must-see sights; its groovy vibe is the main attraction. A good way to get a feel for the area is to go out the north exit, wander the side streets and then follow the tracks around to the south exit. Strangely, the area's disposition changes distinctly from day to night. In the afternoon and early evening, it's full of Japanese teens and twenty-somethings. Once the sun goes down, older expats come out to play and head to the bars. Two of the most venerable institutions are Heaven's Door (Takimoto Building (2F), 2-17-10, Kitazawa, 03 3411 6774) and Shelter (p.382). Heaven's Door is a long-standing expat watering hole that serves imported English and Irish beers. They have an interesting English-language library and some comfy couches. As well as showing the obligatory Premiership matches, they also host meetings by local leftist political groups and workers' rights parties. Shelter is one of the most historic punk clubs in the city. No frills, it's a dingy cellar joint where everyone is focused solely on the music. It can fill up quickly on weekends, so be sure to arrive early if you want to get in.

Must-Do
Take in some street
performers in the
early evening.

Area Ⓜ *p.150*
See also Map 3

Suginami-ku & Kichijōji

The Lowdown
These residential
districts have taken on
a life of their own and
are excellent places for
expats to live and play.

Slightly off the beaten path, Suginami-ku and Kichijōji have slowly become popular with expats. The Chūō Line, running out from Shinjuku, hits all the main areas and binds these disparate neighbourhoods. Kōenji, Asagaya, Ogikubo and Kichijōji form one elongated link that offers respite from inner Tokyo, while still retaining an air of urbanity. Foreigners first began to settle out here in the late 1980s and incrementally a number of bars and clubs have opened to cater to them. Artists and musicians have also made their home here and there is a bohemian underground that will not be discernible on your first visit. Kōenji has really blossomed in the past few years and Japanese youth have also grown fond of it. Lots of records shops and tiny punk clubs have put it on the map. If you're looking for funky clothes or some silly J-pop culture goods, this is the place.

The Good
Less pricey than other
parts of town, a night
out around here won't
break the bank.

Asagaya was the original expat hangout. Its alleyways full of miniature bars make it a great place to drink and take in some local music. After exiting the station, turn left and follow the small street that follows the train tracks. This cluster of tiny alleyways and closet-sized bars is always full of characters but most people are extremely welcoming and it's a good chance to meet locals. Gamuso (03 3223 4041) is a hip, expat watering

A well-kept secret at first, Shimokita experienced an influx of students and hipsters when the late 80s Bubble Economy made living in the heart of Tokyo more expensive. Clued-up expats followed suit and have slowly, but surely, made it one of the most foreigner-friendly neighbourhoods around.

The Bad

During peak hours, the Chūō Line is one of the most uncomfortably packed in Tokyo. Sadly, its tracks are often the sites of suicides. Not a nice way to start the day.

Must-Do

Finish a night with a few frosty beverages in Asagaya, where you can sample some local jazz for free.

hole that often has free music and DJs. For live jazz head to Manhattan (2-2-7 Asagaya-Kita, Suginami-ku, 03 3336 7961). This tiny club somehow manages to squeeze a full jazz quartet into what little space is available.

Ogikubo is famed for its *ramen* and people flock from all over the city to slurp soup. Head out the north exit and pick any of the shops that line Omekaido Dōri. *Ramen* lovers often queue up on weekends, so be prepared to wait, or better yet, come for lunch on a weekday and avoid the masses.

Kichijōji is a city unto itself and has many big name department stores, great restaurants and friendly bars, as well as a gorgeous park and many grocery shops selling imported foods. Inokashira Kōen is one of the city's best-kept secrets. With peaceful lakes, endless trees and a quaint zoo (p.181), it is a great place to head on a sunny day. It's also home to the wonderful Ghibli Museum (p.175), a must-visit that features the highly acclaimed animated works of Miyazaki Hayao. Street performers and artists take over on the weekends, giving the park a mini-festival feel. If you are looking to picnic, get here early as it can get busy quickly. The lane that connects the park to Kichijōji station is a great place to amble and take in the neighbourhood. There are many local craft shops and Asian restaurants, attracting a healthy crowd.

Takadanobaba

*Area 🅝 p.150
See also Map 3*

Sandwiched between Shinjuku and Ikebukuro, Takadanobaba (also known as Baba) was once the centre for all things equine. Horse tracks, horseback riding schools and abattoirs specialising in horsemeat were its claim to fame. The equine set have long left town though, and today Baba is as modern as any other part of the city.

The Lowdown

A chilled-out vibe pervades in this college town, offering oodles of cool restaurants and drinking options.

The Good

Unprejudiced college students and working south Asian families will make you feel less like a foreigner.

The Bad

Drunken college students.

Must-Do

Spend a relaxing Sunday morning at Ben's Café (p.358), leafing through the newspaper and enjoying some of the best coffee in Tokyo.

Nearby, Waseda (www.waseda.jp) and Gakushuin (www.gakushuin.ac.jp) universities give it a tangible collegiate aura. Frugal students have given rise to many cheap restaurants and this is a great place to grab lunch or dinner. In the past five years, a number of South Asian eateries have sprung up. Indian, Nepalese, even Burmese food can easily be found and restaurants are often open late. Ben's Café (p.358) is a Baba institution and has been serving homesick westerners good coffee and authentic bagels for over 10 years. Poetry readings are held on the third and fourth Sunday of every month as well as occasional short fiction readings. Another establishment that endears the area to expats is the Blue Parrot English bookstore (p.278). Used DVDs, magazines, as well as books, can be picked up dirt cheap. There is also an online shop. Shopping choices are greatly overshadowed by the plethora of options in neighbouring Ikebukuro and Shinjuku, but there are a few places of interest. Big Box is a shopping centre directly outside the Waseda exit. No building in the history of architecture has ever been so aptly named. Big, boxy and windowless, this centre has a number of clothing and bric-a-brac shops as well as a sports club. There are not a lot of must-see sights in Baba. The main attraction is the laidback vibe that is often missing in other parts of town. It's a great place to stroll, get lost down winding roads and stumble upon something new. Go with an open mind and a sense of adventure to experience the true heart and soul of Takadanobaba.

Autumn leaves

Pachinko parlour

Amusement Centres
Other options **Theme Parks** p.180

Where else in Japan can you be a rock star, a footballer, a martial artist, a warlord or a commando for only ¥100? Game centres (*geisen*) can be found near virtually every train station in Tokyo and come in all shapes and sizes from the massive Joypolis in Odaiba (1-6-1 Daiba, Minato-ku, 03 5500 1801, www.sega.jp/joypolis/tokyo_e) and flagship SEGA centres in Shibuya (Maruhan Pachinko Tower, 258-6 Udagawachō, 03 3780 2667) and Akihabara (1-15-1 Soto-kanda, Chiyoda-ku, 03 3252 7528) to dingy smoke-filled basements in less salubrious areas of town.

Walk into a game centre and you'll be faced with hordes of giggling schoolgirls laughing at photographs taken on Print Club machines and young men trying to catch cuddly toys for their dates on crane games. There will also be a crowd of youths cheering on a flexible dancer gyrating to music on a dancing stage game, or a budding Dave Grohl knocking out the rhythm on a drumming game. Delve deeper and you'll find typical arcade games such as shoot-em-ups, sports games and kung fu battles. At the back of many centres are the very popular and overpriced multi-player card games such as WCCF football, Derby Owners Club and Sangokushi. For more on the very Japanese type of game centre, Pachinko parlours, see Gambling on p.378.

Aquariums & Marine Centres
There are few nice aquariums. All of them are family oriented and ideal for a day out with the kids. Most offer discounts for children and seniors and are much more reasonable than museums, amusement parks or cinemas. The majority have been built in the past 15 years and feature state of the art facilities. English-language accessibility varies but looking at fish swimming about shouldn't require too much input and Japanese language skills. Most aquariums have the obligatory sea lion shows, but seats go quickly on weekends and national holidays. Starfish petting and other activities are popular and will keep the little ones occupied.

4-10-30 Takanawa
Minato-ku
🚉 **Shinagawa**
Map 6 A3 🚊

Epson Aqua Stadium
03 5421 1111 | www.princehotels.co.jp
Found in the Shinagawa Prince Hotel, the Epson Aqua Stadium is an excellent aquarium with many attractions and a wide variety of sea life. Housing over 300 species, there is also a sea lion and dolphin show. The real attraction is the Submarine Tunnel, which allows you to walk through a pool full of sharks and stingrays. Long-time residents will enjoy the enlightening Life in Tokyo Bay exhibition. Entry costs ¥1,800 for adults and ¥1,000 for kids.

3-2-1
Katsushima-ku
Shinagawa-ku
🚉 **Shinagawa**
Map 2 B3

Shinagawa Aquarium
03 3762 3433 | www.aquarium.gr.jp
The Shinagawa Aquarium in southern Tokyo has a walkthrough tunnel that takes you deep inside a 500 tonne tank full of nearly 3,000 fish. The tunnel is 22 metres long and offers an under-the-sea vantage point that will have you awestruck. One of the more academic exhibitions reproduces the watery environs of the world's greatest rivers, while kids will love the sea lion and porpoise shows that run throughout the day. For a dose of ecological reality, check out the Shinagawa Bay tank. It reproduces the polluted bottom of present-day Tokyo Harbour. Entry costs ¥1,100 for adults and ¥600 for children.

Sunshine International Aquarium

3-1 Higashi-Ikebukuro
Toshima-ku
🚇 *Ikebukuro*
Map 3 F1 2

03 3989 3466 | www.sunshinecity.co.jp

Sunshine International Aquarium displays sea creatures from all over the globe. Home to more than 60,000 fish, it is surprisingly compact and ideal for children with short attention spans as it can be covered in just over an hour. Situated on the 10th floor of Sunshine City, it purports to be the highest aquarium in the world. The sea lion show is especially notable and the creatures have been taught to politely bow Japanese-style. There are also non-aquatic animals on display if you get tired of looking at fins and scales. Entry costs ¥1,800 for adults and ¥900 for children.

Tokyo Sea Life Park

6-2-3 Rinkai-chō
Edogawa-ku
🚇 *Edogawabashi*
Map 2 C2

03 3869 5152 | www.tokyo-zoo.net

With its humungous glass dome beckoning from afar, Tokyo Sea Life Park is one of the best aquariums in the country. Sitting in Tokyo Bay, on the borders of Chiba, it has a tangible living and breathing aquatic aura. Collecting species from all four of the world's oceans, it is the largest aquarium in the country. Hammerhead sharks, enormous blue-fin tuna and blue-spine unicorn fish are some of the more eye-catching creatures on display. There is also a popular penguin and puffin exhibition just outside the main hall. Tickets cost ¥700 for adults and ¥250 for children.

Archaeological Sites

There are a number of small archaeology collections in Tokyo. Most are in inconspicuous neighbourhoods or outlying prefectures. These museums lack the pizazz of the hip art houses in the city, but that's the way the curators like it. Most only have permanent collections and rarely show special exhibitions. Think Edo-era pottery and Meiji-era lacquer ware. They tend to have a library feel and often co-exist with academic institutions or municipal government agencies. There should be enough to interest real history buffs, and while staff are not used to foreign faces, they'll be welcoming. Just expect limited information in English.

Fuchu City Museum

1-3 Sengen-chō
Fuchū-shi
🚇 *Higasi-Fuchū*
Map 2 A3

0423 68 7921 | www.art.city.fuchu.tokyo.jp

Near the banks of the Tamagawa, the Fuchu City Museum is made up of eight restored buildings from the Meiji period, among which there is an elementary school, farmhouse and government office building. There is also an exhibition showing archaeological remains from the Jōmon period, excavated around Fuchū city. The museum is surrounded by a beautiful plum tree orchard and features over 1,000 specimens. Adult tickets cost ¥200 and children's entry is ¥100.

Funabashi Tobinodai Archaeological Museum

Funabashi
Chiba-ken
Map 1 C3

0474 95 1325 | www.city.funabashi.chiba.jp

Located in Chiba, Funabashi Tobinodai Archaeological Museum showcases excavated earthenware, and has recreations of ancient pit dwellings. The museum concentrates on the Jōmon period, with collections of pottery and other archaeological remains from the Funabashi area. It will most likely appeal to adults rather than children. Housed in an unspectacular building, there's no park or garden and it can easily be covered in under an hour. The entrance fee is ¥100.

Matsudo Museum

Matsudo City
Chiba-ken
🚇 *Kōen Chūō-guchi*
Map 1 C3

0473 84 8181 | www2.city.matsudo.chiba.jp

The Matsudo Museum is one of Chiba's more interactive archaeological centres. Many of the exhibitions are hands-on and it's a good place for inquisitive kids. Earthenware and tools from the Jōmon and Yayoi periods are on display, while a huge screen shows historical documentaries. The museum is located in a massive 50 hectare park which is perfect for strolling. Adult entry is ¥300, while entry for children is ¥100.

Tama-shi
Western Tokyo
🚇 ***Tama Center***
Map 2 A3

Tokyo Archaeological Research Centre
042 373 5296 | www.tef.or.jp
Located in Tama city, the Tokyo Archaeological Research Centre is actively involved in the excavation of ancient remains. They have a permanent collection of artefacts as well as temporary exhibitions that change annually. Adjacent to the museum is a garden park with restored Jōmon period houses. Lectures are held three times a week on the quest for fire in ancient Tokyo. The research centre is close to the Sanrio Puroland theme park. Admission is free.

Art Galleries
Other options **Art** p.275, **Art & Craft Supplies** p.276

Art is big business and every major district in the metropolis has an abundance of galleries. Art in Japan is universally appreciated, eschewing the bourgeois stigma that is associated with it in the west. You'll see people from all walks of life strolling through museums and art workshops. Curators tend to be unpretentious and don't mind people coming in for a look around.
The art displayed in the city often reflects the neighbourhood in which it is found. Ginza in particular is noted for its numerous galleries. Wander about the area and you can't help tripping over them, though the greatest concentration is just south of Harumi Dōri. Indeed, the area is so resplendant in art galleries and the Japanese have even coined an expression for meandering through Ginza's art galleries; *ginbura*. The galleries in Ginza and Omotesandō often feature upmarket works and are aimed at serious art collectors with money to burn, while those found in Shinjuku and around are far more audacious, exhibiting the makings of those struggling to make a name for themselves.

1-10-1 Kyōbashi
Chūō-ku
🚇 ***Tokyo***
Map 14 C1 4

Bridgestone Museum of Art
03 3563 0241 | www.bridgestone-museum.gr.jp
Set amidst the offices and high-rise buildings around Tokyo station, this gem is well worth seeking out. The founder of the famous tyre company, Shojiro Ishibashi, opened his private collection to the public in 1952. While not in the most cultured of neighbourhoods, the emphasis is on contemporary European paintings with a healthy dose of French impressionists. Renoir, Monet and Cézanne all feature but the true treat is the western-influenced works by Japanese artists from the Meiji Era. While some cynics may write them off as mere imitators, these artists are indicative of the Japanese ability to ingeniously reinterpret anything and everything. The gallery is open from 10:00 to 18:00 and admission costs ¥700.

24-1-2 Dōgenzaka
Shibuya-ku
🚇 ***Shibuya***
Map 8 A3 5

Bunkamura
03 3477 9111 | www.bunkamura.co.jp
Set in the shopping mania of Shibuya, this fine gallery is owned by the Tokyu Hands department store. It hosts excellent exhibitions with an emphasis on modern art and the European masters. The building is extremely spacious and surprisingly conducive to wandering at leisure and there's also a cinema that shows underground, art-house foreign films. The bookstore on the basement floor is far more engaging than those found in most gift shops and is a great way to while away an hour or two. Entry to most exhibitions is around ¥1,000.

Mori Art Museum

Carre MOJI

5-11-24 Minami Aoyama (3F)
Shibuya
Map 8 E3 6

03 5766 7120 | *www.carremoji.jp*

Those looking to adorn their homes with slick-contemporary Japanese calligraphy should head to Carre MOJI. This gallery is indicative of the ilk that dominates the Omotesandō vicinity; uber hip and hawking fine art to well-oiled buyers. Displaying the most time-honoured of Japanese art forms in a modern setting, they have lucratively been cashing in on the western infatuation with eastern *kanji* characters. Even non-buyers and mono-linguistic expats will appreciate a stroll through this glossy gallery. Carre MOJI employs a dozen distinguished Japanese calligraphy artists and they all wilfully accept special projects. The gallery is open daily except Sundays.

Gallery Koyanagi

Koyanagi Bldg (8F)
1-7-5 Ginza
Chūō-ku
Ginza
Map 14 B2 7

03 3561 1896 | *www.gallerykoyanagi.com*

One of the most respected galleries in Ginza, Koyanagi attracts big name art dealers and displays works by some of Tokyo's most celebrated artists. With an emphasis on photography, Koyanagi also occasionally showcases multimedia installations and glass works. Recent exhibitions by Japanese artists Mariko Mori and Rei Naito have been especially impressive. The gallery also brings in international talent, particularly from Europe and North America. French conceptual artist Sophie Calle and German photographer Thomas Ruff have both displayed their work here.

Kenji Taki Gallery

3-18-2-102
Nishi-Shinjuku
Shinjuku-ku
Nishi-Shinjuku
Map 7 A2 8

03 3378 6051 | *www2.odn.ne.jp/kenjitaki*

This happening Shinjuku gallery made its name showcasing uber hip Japanese artists, but it has lately opened its doors to fledgling western talent. Situated in a grey, concrete district of Shinjuku, its vivacious exhibitions stand in stark contrast to its environs. The success of the Shinjuku joint has lead to another gallery opening in Nagoya. Recent exhibitions have displayed the works of conceptual artist Eiji Watanabe and local legend Isamu Noguchi.

Mori Art Museum

Roppongi Hills
Minato-ku
Roppongi
Map 11 B3 9

03 5777 8600 | *www.mori.art.museum*

Those who believe that Roppongi Hills is merely a soulless shopping centre need to take the elevator up to the 53rd floor. The Mori Art Museum features exhilarating temporary exhibitions that are always fresh and exciting. The focus is on contemporary, cutting edge works and has quickly become one of the most popular art hotspots in the city. Recent exhibitions have displayed modern African art and works from the thriving Berlin underground. There is no permanent collection and most exhibitions last for about three or four months. Idyllically situated at the top of Mori Tower, it offers great city panoramas after dark. Admission is around ¥1,500. Open from 10:00 to 22:00 Wednesday to Monday, and closing at 17:00 on Tuesdays.

The National Art Center

7-22-2 Roppongi
Minato-ku
Nogizaka
Map 11 A2 12

03 5777 8600 | *www.nact.jp*

The National Art Center is home to the largest exhibition space in Japan. The 14,000 square metres of temporary exhibition space heavily feature Japanese art and how

Japan is viewed by the world; with some international collections and great social commentaries thrown in, such as a recent exhibition on fashion and architecture. The third floor is home to a comprehensive art library, with a special collection of over 38,000 Japanese exhibition catalogues. Lectures and volunteer schemes form part of the educational programme. For refreshment, three cafes and a French brasserie are at hand. Admission prices vary. Open daily from 10:00 to 18:00, and until 20:00 on Fridays. Closed on Tuesdays. Exit 6 of Nogizaka station is directly linked to the centre.

Tokyo Metropolitan Art Museum

3-1 Kitanomaru Kōen
Chiyoda-ku
🚇 **Takebashi**
Map 9 F4 10

National Museum of Modern Art
03 5777 8600 | www.momat.go.jp

Though overshadowed by better known museums, this was the first official national museum of art in Japan and is highly recommended. Exhibits include works by modern Japanese masters. Considering that it was originally run by the Ministry of Education, it has an audacious permanent collection. The rooms dedicated to the Humanism movement of the Taishō era are particularly interesting. The National Film Centre wing screens alternative art films by Japanese and non-Japanese auteurs, though without English subtitles. Admission is ¥420 for adults, ¥130 for students and ¥70 for others. Closed on Mondays.

7-7 Ueno Kōen
Taitō-ku
🚇 **Ueno**
Map 12 D2 11

National Museum of Western Art
03 3828 5131 | www.nmwa.go.jp

Japan's largest western art museum is a magnificent collection that begs repeat visits. Its sleek building was designed by illustrious Swiss architect Le Corbusier with Rodin's *Gates of Hell* standing forebodingly at the entry. Other impressive Rodin works are housed inside, including *John the Baptist* and *The Kiss*. There is a wealth of Renaissance and French impressionist paintings, as well as more modern works. Jean Dubufett's *Cow with a Beautiful Tail* and Chaim Soutine's *Mad Woman* are particularly noteworthy. Special loan exhibitions cost extra and are wildly popular. Admission is ¥420, open from 09:30 to 17:00. It is closed on Mondays.

8-10-5 Ginza (7F)
Chūō-ku
🚇 **Ginza**
Map 14 A4 13

Tokyo Gallery
03 3571 1808 | www.tokyo-gallery.com

This Ginza institution features cutting edge exhibitions, displaying works by both established and up-and-coming artists. Claiming to be the first modern art gallery in Japan, Tokyo Gallery has helped to create artistic ties with young talents from other East Asian nations. They continually exhibit contemporary art by artists from China and South Korea and in 2002 they opened a sister gallery in Beijing. Some of the works can be somewhat raucous and are not for the timid. Recently, photography and contemporary sculpture have been the main focus. The online gallery is extremely moving and worth a look.

8-36 Ueno Kōen
Taitō-ku
🚇 **Ueno**
Map 12 C2 14

Tokyo Metropolitan Art Museum
03 3823 6921 | www.tobikan.jp

There's always something worth seeing here. This Ueno museum houses an intriguing permanent collection of modern Japanese works on its first floor and reserves its other floors for up-and-coming local artists. Art collectives, newspapers and schools regularly rent out the exhibition halls, where you can get a chance to see some unheralded talent. Art lectures and workshops are held frequently, although these are predominantly in Japanese. They also have an extensive library. Admission varies depending on the exhibit, but the permanent collection is free. The museum is closed on Mondays.

Wako Works of Art

3-18-2-101
Nishi-Shinjuku
Shinjuku-ku
🚉 *Nishi-Shinjuku*
Map 3 D4 **15**

03 3373 2860 | www.wako-art.jp

Buried between the giant skyscrapers of Nishi-Shinjuku lies this idiosyncratic gallery. Wako Works of Art focuses on young Japanese talent as well as showcasing renowned western artists. They also coordinate shows at larger venues and have their own art-book publishing company. Recent exhibitions have showcased German photographer Wolfgang Tillmans and provocative American multimedia artist Mike Kelley.

Forts & Castles

Castle aficionados will have to head out to the hills as Tokyo proper has none. The Imperial Palace (p.189) is technically a castle, but the only way you'll get close to it is if you're an ambassador. Due to massive Allied bombing during the war, many of the city's castles were destroyed. Luckily, many castles in the surrounding prefectures of Saitama and Kanagawa have survived, albeit with a fair amount of reconstruction. Entry is free to most castles and are a pleasant way to spend a day outside the buzzing metropolis.

Hachigata Castle

Yorii
Saitama-ken
Map 2 A1

www.town.yorii.saitama.jp

Built in 1476, Hachigata Castle has been remarkably preserved and is well worth a look. It sits in an area of Saitama that was once an important trading junction and has formidable defences to keep out would be invaders. The adjacent museum costs ¥200 and gives a thorough overview of the castle's history. Catch the Tōbu Tōju Line from Ikebukuro and get off at Yorii station. It's a good half hour hike through this pleasant town to reach the castle, otherwise a taxi will cost about ¥1,000.

Keep Up Kiddo

If you're friends with any older Japanese, taking in some castles is an excellent activity to do together. Retirees rue the younger generation's lack of interest in history and would be happy to share their knowledge with you. Older Japanese are also surprisingly spry and love to get out and stretch their legs.

Kawagoe Castle

Kawagoe
Saitama-ken
Map 2 A1

www.city.kawagoe.saitama.jp

The distinguished town of Kawagoe in Saitama was once a major trading depot and features many worthy sites of interest to history buffs. Kawagoe Castle is one of its most eminent edifices. Originally built in 1457, the castle has undergone major renovations in recent years and the lord's quarters are now the only original structure. Kawagoe was once known as 'Little Edo' and was an important defensive position for the Tokyo warlords. After viewing the castle, walk around the old town and take in the antiquated atmosphere. Catch the Tōbu Tōju Line from Ikebukuro to Kawagoe station. There is a tourist bus outside the main ticket gate that is a 15 minute ride to the castle.

Odawara Castle

Odawara
Kanagawa-ken
Map 2 A3

www.kanagawa-kankou.or.jp

This four-storey castle in the neighbouring prefecture of Kanagawa was originally built in 1495 and then reconstructed in 1960. Made of white concrete and situated in a lovely mountain park, it's a short walk from Odawara's main train station. The Enoura coastal area near the castle is famed for its clean waters and has a wealth of marine life that is popular for scuba diving. To get here, take the Tōkaidō line from Tokyo station.

Heritage Sites

Other options **Art** p.275

Saitama-ken
Map 2 A1

Kawagoe

049 224 8811 | *www.city.kawagoe.saitama.jp*
Of all the prefectures surrounding Tokyo, Saitama gets the least respect. At first glance it may seem a suburban sprawl devoid of class, but the significant city of Kawagoe offers visitors a trip back to Japan's colourful past. Once known as 'Little Edo' for its eminence as a trading post between the capital and the outlying countryside, Kawagoe has held fervently onto its past. The city's old town is well preserved, the storefronts' awnings shielding shoppers from the sun. Unlike some recreated, faux heritage towns, Kawagoe smacks of authenticity. Its trademark bell tower stands strapping and still clangs three times a day. A brief walk from the old town is the venerable Kita-in temple. This sanctified structure is housed in a wide-open expanse that challenges its bland suburban surroundings. The 500 holy Rakan statuettes that dot its grounds are well preserved and each one exudes an individual air. Kawagoe is a short trip from Ikebukuro on the Tōbu Tōju Line. Once at the station, go left out of the ticket gate and head down the main shopping street. At the end of the street, turn left and you'll be on the cusp of the old town. For more information, visit the tourist centre just outside the ticket gate (open daily). The city has a website with an English section and is very informative. Most expats never make the trip up to this allegedly lacklustre area, but they are truly missing out.

Tochigi-ken
Map 1 C3

Nikko

0288 54 2496 | *www.nikko-jp.org*
Nikko is a UNESCO World Heritage Site. Spiritual and quasi-spiritual pilgrims from all over the country come to bask in the divine brilliance of this historic town. It's significance dates to the 8th century, when Buddhist monks founded a sanctuary. The burial chamber of the shogun Tokugawa Ieyasu (p.160) and his grandson are the foremost attractions, and even those with zero interest in history will be captivated by this splendid shrine. While most shrines in Japan are minimalist, Tōshō-gū gallantly boast a colourful quality that at times is giddying. But there are many highlights. Sanjiko is a peculiar storeroom that features a depiction of an elephant by an artisan who had never actually laid eyes on one. Nikko has many other attractive holy sights, as well as natural wonders such as the serene Chūzenji lake and impressive Kegon waterfall. But perhaps its most charming characteristic is the free-and-easy air that is conducive to strolling about without a worry in the world. Package tours are readily available (see p.196), though coming here independently is recommended. There are several *onsen* in the area and the *soba* restaurants are particularly noteworthy.

Historic Houses

7-1-1 Masugata
Tama-ku
Kanagawa-ken
Map 2 B4

Japan Open-Air Folk House Museum

044 922 2181 | *www.city.kawasaki.jp*
Sadly, there are not many remnants of traditional residential architecture in Tokyo proper. Luckily, just south in Kanagawa-ken is the absorbing Japan Open-Air Folk House Museum. This interesting collection of old Japanese houses features many barns and merchant dwellings. Realising the importance of saving part of Japan's quickly dwindling cityscape, the Kawasaki city government began restoring fading buildings and there are now more than 20 rustic abodes. Far from hokey, you'll temporarily be

transported 200 years into the past. Craft workshops and storytelling seminars are held occasionally, but only in Japanese.

Museums

Tokyo has more museums than most cities, and you could spend a lifetime taking them all in. Ueno Kōen alone has a cornucopia, and almost every *ku* has something to offer art lovers. Everything from antiquated Asian arts to cutting edge avant-garde exhibitions is on offer. The availability of English-language information varies, though the ubiquitous 'do not touch' signs will subtly remind you not to get too close to the Picassos. Try to avoid the bigger museums on weekends, especially when they have special exhibitions of the classic European variety. These are always mobbed and attract gaggles of retirees who move like molasses. Weekdays are the best time to go if you can swing it and remember that almost all major museums are closed on Mondays.

1-3-61 Kōraku
Bunkyō-ku
🚇 *Suidōbashi*
Map 9 F2 **16**

The Baseball Hall of Fame & Museum

03 3811 3600 | *http://english.baseball-museum.or.jp*

The Japanese Baseball Hall of Fame & Museum gives an overview of the history of the nation's adopted national pastime. Housed within the Tokyo Giant's stadium, it takes you through how the game was introduced in Japan and chronicles the early ballplayers that made it so popular. Chockfull of memorabilia, you can see caps, jerseys and bats that once belonged to some of Japan's biggest stars. The entire collection can be viewed in an hour or two and is a nice place to visit before or after taking in a game at the Tokyo Dome (p.180). Entry costs ¥500 for adults and ¥200 for children.

1-4-1 Yokoami
Sumida-ku
🚇 *Ryōgoku*
Map 4 E3 **17**

Edo Tokyo Museum

03 3626 9974 | *www.edo-tokyo-museum.or.jp*

Edo Tokyo is one of the most mesmerising museums in all of Japan. It opened in 1993 and extensively covers the history of old Edo in a hands-on environment that keeps it from becoming staid. Detailed replicas of old neighbourhoods give visitors a trip into the past. The tour starts with a reproduction of the Nihonbashi Bridge and then gives you a peek into the lives of shoguns, tradesmen and everyday labourers. However, the two most moving exhibitions touch on darker times, and displays depicting the massive Allied bombings of the second world war and the Great Kantō Earthquake of 1923 are testimony to the city's perseverance. The space age building in which the museum is housed is an event in itself. Entry is ¥600 for adults and ¥300 for students. Group rates are available. It is closed on Mondays.

1-1-83 Inokashira Kōen
Kichijōji
🚇 *Kichijōji*
Map 2 A2

Ghibli Museum

042 240 2211 | *www.ghibli-museum.jp*

This wonderful museum features the revered, animated works of Miyazaki Hayao. It's a great day out for the whole family, with giant robots, the Cat Bus, and strange buildings all part of its huge appeal. Be warned, tickets are like gold dust and must be purchased a few weeks in advance. The website has a step-by-step guide to buying them from machines in Lawson convenience stores. Each ticket is for a designated time only, and ticket holders will be asked to present ID. Entry fees start at ¥100 and run to ¥1,000. The museum is open from 10:00 to 18:00, except Tuesdays and public holidays.

3-1 Higashi-Yashio
Shinagawa-ku
Odaiba
🚇 *Fune-no Kagakukan*
Map 6 C4 **18**

Museum of Maritime Science

03 5500 1111 | *www.funenokagakukan.or.jp*

This museum provides a comprehensive history on the importance of seafaring in Japan. It is housed in a structure replicating an ocean liner, with observation decks that allow a perfect view of the city. There are meticulous models of submarines, ferries and

battleships and there is a pond with radio-controlled boats for the kids. Close by is the moored Soya, which conducted Japan's first venture to Antarctica in 1938. Regrettably, all of the exhibition information is in Japanese, but you can still have a great nautical experience without actually taking to the deep blue sea.

National Museum of Emerging Science & Innovation

2-41 Aomi Odaiba
Koto-ku
 Tokyo Teleport
Map 6 D4 19

National Museum of Emerging Science & Innovation

03 3570 9151 | www.miraikan.jst.go.jp

Don't be put off by the antiseptic name, this place is actually rather entertaining. The exhibits are split up into four different areas: Earth Environment and Frontiers, Innovation and the Future, Information Science and Technology for Society, and Life Science. All are educational without being staid. There are lots of hands-on activities for the youngsters and the young-at-heart. The museum opened in 2001 and is one of the centrepieces of the fledgling Odaiba district. Spearheaded by Japanese astronaut Mamoru Mohri, it's housed in one of the most off-the-wall buildings in the city (just 15 minutes on foot from Tokyo Teleport Station. There are some English explanations, but knowing a bit of Japanese will greatly enhance your experience. Entry is ¥500 for adults and ¥200 for kids. It is closed on Tuesdays.

Shinjuku Historical Museum

22 San'eichō
Shinjuku-ku
Akebonobashi
Map 10 A1 3

03 3359 2131 | www.regasu-shinjuku.or.jp

The Shinjuku Historical Museum will be of interest to both history buffs and Tokyoites looking to get a clearer insight into the history of the metropolis. Excavated relics range from the Jōmon to the Edo period, with an emphasis on Shinjuku and its environs. There are displays recreating everyday life during the Edo and early Shōwa periods, as well as a small cinema explaining the history of the city. Historical dramas are sometimes staged, though only in Japanese. Entry is ¥300 for adults and ¥100 for children.

Sumo Museum

1-3-28 Yoko-ami
Sumida-ku
Ryōgoku
Map 4 E3 20

03 3622 0366 | www.sumo.or.jp

Dedicated to documenting the rich history of sumo wrestling, this museum offers little in the way of English explanations but is still recommended for fans of either sport or Japanese culture. It's inside the sumo stadium Kokugikan. Memorabilia such as old referee costumes, paintings and sculpture take you back in time and famous bouts are memorialised on woodblock prints. The most eye-catching displays are of the elaborate *keshō mawashi*, the ritual aprons the wrestlers wear entering the ring. Entry is free and it is closed on weekends.

Tokyo Metropolitan Museum of Photography

1-13-3 Mita
Ebisu
Meguro-ku
Ebisu
Map 5 F3 21

03 3280 0099 | www.syabi.com

The Tokyo Metropolitan Museum of Photography is an often overlooked art space found inside the Ebisu Garden Place complex. The museum houses some 20,000 photos, although not all are on display at the one time. The museum also has a thorough animation collection. The temporary exhibitions on the second floor are always worth a look. The permanent collection can be found on the third floor. Recent exhibitions have focused on surrealism in photography, Tokyo in the 1970s and world religious sights. Admission fees vary.

12-9 Ueno Kōen ◀
Taitō-ku
🚇 *Ueno*
Map 12 D1 **22**

Tokyo National Museum
03 3822 1191 | *www.tnm.go.jp*
If you were to visit only one museum in all of Japan, this should be it. Housing more than 90,000 pieces, this museum is an overwhelming testament to the country's rich cultural history. Samurai swords and woodblock prints are abundant and there are also impressive displays of lacquer ware and calligraphy. The room devoted to the arts and crafts of Hokkaidō's indigenous Ainu gives an all encompassing view into the true soul of the Japanese spirit. Entry is ¥600 for adults, ¥400 for students and children get in for free. Open from 09:30 to 17:00, except Mondays.

1-2 Ueno Kōen ◀
Taitō-ku
🚇 *Ueno*
Map 12 C3 **23**

Ueno Royal Museum
03 3833 4191 | *www.ueno-mori.org*
Formerly known as the Japan Art Association Museum, Ueno Royal Museum has a number of exhibition halls that have continually showcased some of Japan's pre-eminent painters and sculptors. Opened in 1972, the museum underwent massive renovations in 1992, giving it a more spacious atmosphere. There is also an art school and lectures take place routinely. There is also a public space reserved for artists to get together, exchange ideas and meet friends. There is no permanent collection, only temporary exhibitions. Check the website for details. Entry fees vary.

Other Attractions

4-2-8 Shibakōen ◀
Minato-ku
🚇 *Minato*
Map 11 E3 **44**

Tokyo Tower
03 3433 5111 | *www.tokyotower.co.jp*
Despite its gaudy appearance, and being a little past its prime, the views from the observation deck on the 52nd floor of one of Tokyo's major landmarks are still worth a look, especially at night. Ticket prices vary, allowing you access to different attractions inside, including a wax works museum.

2-8-1 Nishi-Shinjuku ◀
Shinjuku-ku
🚇 *Shinjuku*
Map 7 A2 **45**

Tokyo Metropolitan Government Building
03 5321 1111 | *www.metro.tokyo.jp*
Climb these towers for great views out over the futuristic skyline of Shinjuku. Visits to the observatories on the 45th floors of these towers are free and offer some of the city's best vantage points. If visiting during the day, head to the south tower, when you may even be lucky enough to catch a glimpse of Mount Fuji. Once the sun goes to sleep, it's best to go up the north tower for the bright lights of Tokyo's buzzing nightlife.

Religious Sites
At first glance, you could be forgiven for assuming that the city lacks any tangible spirituality. But indistinctly obscured amid the carbon-copy apartment complexes and massive skyscrapers, there is intense evidence of the once-pious core of the Japanese spirit. Around every corner there are tiny temples and unpretentious shrines, which are living breathing societies, with small congregations and dutiful parishioners. And then there are the awe-inspiring paeans to a higher power that draw the tourists and dare the sceptics not to believe. These days, most Tokyoites subscribe to a chaotic religious mishmash, combining elements of Shintoism, Buddhism and Christianity (see p.16). But, get out the electronic dictionary; type in 'agnostic' and most of them will be nodding their heads in self-realising concurrence. Regardless, Tokyo is rife with houses of worship that both the spiritual and the secular will marvel at. For what to do at shrines and temples, see p.195.

Panoramas
For more fantastic vistas of the city, try the observation platform on the 51st floor of the Shinjuku Sumitomo Building (near the Tokyo Metropolitan Government Building, above) or Mori Art Museum in Roppongi (p.171). The Fuji TV headquarters in Odaiba (p.165) is another futuristic wonder with a good observation deck, and you can't beat a go on one of the world's largest ferris wheels.

Meiji Jingū

1-1 Kamizono-chō
Harajuku
🚇 **Harajuku**
Map 7 B4 24

03 3379 5511 | *www.meijijingu.or.jp*

It's hard to believe that one of the most sanctified sights borders the consumer crazy Harajuku shopping district. Meiji Jingū and its grounds are surprisingly simple, but they emanate an awe-inspiring grandeur. The shrine was built by volunteers in 1920 and is dedicated to the memory of the Emperor Meiji and his wife, Empress Shoken. Emperor Meiji was devoted to keeping peace during his reign and the shrine is extremely still, as if lulling visitors with its serene charm. Destroyed during the second world war, it was rebuilt in the late 1950s. On Sundays you will usually spy weddings of young couples dressed in traditional garb, with full processions. Another good time to go is on a Thursday. Parents come with their newborn babies to have them blessed on its hallowed grounds.

Sensōji

2-3-1 Asakusa
Taitō-ku
🚇 **Asakusa**
Map 4 E2 25

03 3842 0181

A visit to Sensōji (also known as Asakusa Kannon) is one of the most culturally gratifying experiences in all of Tokyo. This Buddhist structure dates from the seventh century and it is the city's oldest temple. The existing incarnation is a post-war restoration, but it still retains an antiquated holiness. Sensōji has three entrances, but for the full experience be sure to enter via the Kaminarimon Gate, which has the imposing God of Thunder and the God of Wind on either side. From here, head down the effervescent Nakamise, the main shopping lane where spiritual goods, snacks and tourist knick-knacks can be purchased. On entering the main grounds you will see travellers and religious pilgrims wafting incense smoke into their faces. This allegedly brings good fortune; so don't be bashful about sharing in the smoke. Next to the temple is a towering five-storied pagoda. It's one of the few pagodas in Tokyo proper and stands at over 50 metres tall.

St Ignatius

6-5-1 Koujimachi
Chiyoda-ku
🚇 **Yotsuya**
Map 10 B2 26

03 3263 4584 | *www.ignatius.gr.jp*

There are more churches in Tokyo than might be presumed. However, these offer nothing in the way of aesthetics and exist purely as houses of worship. Most are inconspicuous buildings with little to alert passers by to their religious functions. St Ignatius in Yūrakuchō is an exception. This Catholic parish has been rebuilt three times, most recently in 1995. An airy rotunda with divine stained-glass windows, it's suffused in natural light, giving the impression of infinite space. Outside there's a lush green lawn where parishioners congregate to chat after mass. Many of the worshippers are Filipinos and on Sundays, the sidewalk is lined with makeshift stalls selling Filipino treats.

Yasukuni Jinja

3-1-1 Kudan-kita
Chiyoda-ku
🚇 **Kudanshita**
Map 9 D4 27

03 3261 8326 | *www.yasukuni.or.jp*

A visit to Yasukuni-Jinja is as loaded with moral landmines as a holiday in Myanmar. This striking Shintō shrine was originally built in 1869 to memorialize Japan's war casualties. During the second world war many Japanese soldiers claimed that if they died in battle, they would meet their families and fellow soldiers here. Yasukuni, which roughly translates as 'peaceful nation' was controversy free, until after the second world war, when 12 reputed war criminals were interred here. Any time a Japanese prime minister pays a visit to the shrine there is great uproar across east Asia, particularly in China and South Korea. Adding to the controversy is the adjacent Yushukan museum. This building paints a revisionist tale of the war, with the Imperial Japanese military attempting to free its Asian neighbours from the grasp of western colonisers. Aesthetically, it's a thing of beauty. The *torii* gate at the entrance is a staggering 26 metres tall and there are more statues than usually found at a Japanese religious site. Regardless of your political views, a trip to Yasukuni is both fascinating and frustrating.

Japan's shrines and temples

Theme Parks

Other options **Water Parks** (below), **Amusement Centres** p.168

Many Japanese go crazy for theme parks and even cold winter weekdays will bring mobs of people. Almost all of these parks were built during the Bubble Economy when people had money to burn and many closed down in the early 90s. The ones listed here are still going strong though. All of them are conveniently located near major train stations and finding them will not be a problem. Both youngsters and the young at heart will enjoy them. While many of the attractions are geared towards children, they are also popular spots for dates and can be a romantic escape for couples.

Tama-shi
Western Tokyo
🚇 **Tama Center**
Map 2 A3

Sanrio Puroland

www.puroland.co.jp

Sanrio Puroland is a theme park based around the characters made famous by the Sanrio Company. Hello Kitty is their main ambassador and those with a fondness for the friendly feline will enjoy it. Located in the Tama district, just outside of the city centre, it first opened in 1990. Kitty's House and the Tome Machine of Dreams are two of the most popular attractions. It's very much a place for the kiddies and there are no heart-stopping roller coasters but if *kawaii* (all things cute) is your thing, you'll be in paradise. Entry for adults is ¥3,000, juniors (12-17 years) ¥2,700 and children ¥2,000.

1-1 Maihama
Chiba-ken
🚇 **Maihama**
Map 2 C3

Tokyo Disneyland

045 683 3333 | *www.tokyodisneyresort.co.jp*

When talking to Japanese people about Tokyo Disneyland, never ask them if they have been. Rather, ask them how many times. One of the most beloved sights in the country, it is the most visited theme park in the world and people flock here 365 days a year. It opened in 1983 and was the first Disney theme park outside of the US. It is almost an exact replica of the original Disney in California, though considerably more orderly. Long lines are a fact of life and summer weekends greet mobs. Other insanely busy times are Christmas, Halloween and Valentine's Day. All the beloved Disney characters are on hand and favourite attractions like Space Mountain and Big Thunder Mountain are always a thrill. Entry for adults is ¥5,800, juniors (12-17 years) ¥5,000, children ¥3,900, and seniors ¥5,100. Entry after 18:00 receives a discount.

1-3-61 Kōraku
Bunkyō-ku
🚇 **Kōrakōen**
Map 9 F2 **28**

Tokyo Dome City

03 5800 9999 | *www.tokyo-dome.co.jp*

You don't have to travel far to get some top-notch amusement park action in this city. In the heart of the metropolis is the ever-popular Tokyo Dome City. The Liner Gale and Skyflower are fun rides that are not for the timid, while the scream-inducing Tower Hacker is even more intimidating. This behemoth ride drops shrieking passengers straight down from 80 metres. There are also more pedestrian rides for toddlers and there's a large bowling alley. It's located next to the Tokyo Dome baseball stadium and is a great place to go before or after a game. Entry is ¥4,000 for adults and ¥3,000 for children.

Water Parks

Other options **Theme Parks** (above)

Water Parks are a relatively new phenomenon. In the painfully humid summer they are a perfect way to cool down. They are family oriented and have activities and pools suitable for young children. Parents need not worry about safety; there are plenty of lifeguards. Be prepared for mobs of people during summer weekend and over the

August school holiday. Water parks can be fun, but jumping, screaming hyperactive-schoolkids don't make for a particularly relaxing time.

Akiruno ◀
Akiruno
🚇 **Akikawa**
Map 1 B3

Tokyo Summerland

042 558 6511 | www.summerland.co.jp

Tokyo Summerland is centrally located and is a great way to beat the heat. This massive park gets really busy in the summer, especially during mid-August. While there are pools to just chill out and relax in, most of the attractions are of the thrills and chills variety. The Screamer Water Slide lives up to its name, and Looping Star Ship and Free Fall are two other exciting rides. To unwind, try the more soothing Adventure Lagoon. The entrance fee is ¥3,500 for adults and ¥2,500 for children.

3-25-1 Mukōyama ◀
Nerima-ku
🚇 **Toshimaen**
Map 2 A2

Toshimaen Pool

03 3990 8844 | www.toshimaen.co.jp

Just outside of Ikebukuro is this wonderful water park. It's a bit of a trek, but well worth it. Not as over-the-top and full of screaming kids as the other big water parks, Toshimaen Pool is just a great place to jump in the water. There are a few different pools of varying depths as well as the obligatory water slides. But there are also hot tubs and saunas, giving mums and dads a much needed chance to relax. The pricing system is a little peculiar. Adults get in for ¥3,800, while children over 110cm get in for ¥2,800 and children under 110cm get in for ¥1,500.

3294 Yanoguchi ◀
Inagi-shi
🚇 **Yomiuriland-mae**
Map 1 B3

Yomiuri Land

044 966 1111 | www.yomiuriland.co.jp

The Yomiuri Land amusement park has the typical rollercoasters and Ferris wheels, but it's the water park that they are most famous for. Only open from July through September, it's well worth splashing about during the dog days. They have many wave pools varying in depth and wave strength and there is also a special diving pool that actually encourages kids to plunge from 5 metres up. Two mega-slides, Slalom Slider and Straight Slider, will get your heart racing. Some rides are off-limits to younger children. Adult tickets cost ¥3,200 and children's tickets cost ¥2,000.

Zoos, Wildlife Parks & Open Farms

The Japanese are an animal loving people and there are some praiseworthy zoos in the Tokyo area. All of them have some form of English-language map and navigation should not be a problem. These are great places to take the kids as Japanese zoos tend to focus on the cutest animals. Ueno Zoo (p.182) is the oldest and will require repeated visits to take it all in. Inokashira Zoo is in the park of the same name and features a picturesque botanical garden. Ōshima Kōen Zoo is on a small island south of Tokyo and features animals in a pastoral setting.

Seibo Kitamura

The sculpture museum connected to Inokashira Kōen is a recommended visit. It exhibits selected works by renowned sculptor and industrial artist Seibo Kitamura (those familiar with Peace Park in Nagasaki will know his works). His iconic image of a Herculean figure warning against the slaughter of innocents is known throughout Japan. One hoisted arm points toward the peril of nuclear weaponry, while the extended arm represents peace. A smaller version of this statute is on display at the museum.

1-17-6 Gotenyama ◀
Musashino-shi
🚇 **Kichijōji**
Map 2 A2

Inokashira Kōen Zoo

042 246 1100 | www.tokyo-zoo.net

This hidden gem out in Kichijōji sees few foreign visitors. Situated in a sprawling public park, Inokashira Zoo focuses mainly on Japanese species, with a few other Asian animals thrown in for good measure. Most of the animals are of the smaller variety with amur cats, palm civets and *tanuki* (raccoon dogs) drawing the biggest crowds. Red-crowned crane and the docile Yaku deer roam freely and are very camera-friendly. The zoo is also involved in the preservation and proliferation of endangered animals native to Japan. Next to the main building there's a lovely botanical garden and a cool sculpture museum. Admission is ¥400 for adults and ¥150 for students. It's free for kids. The zoo is closed on Mondays.

Ōshima Kōen Zoo

Ōshima Kōen, Senzu
Ōshima-machi
Ōshima
Map 1 C3

049 922 9111 | *www.tokyo-zoo.net*
On the island of Ōshima, south of Tokyo, this captivating zoo sits smack in the middle of a national park. Ōshima Kōen Zoo has more than 700 creatures of 60 different species. A number of endangered animals are on display, including giant tortoises and Hawaiian geese. The conservationists working here have been successful in breeding the rare Japanese wood pigeon. Ōshima is a volcanic island and the striking Monkey Hill was formed naturally by cooling lava. Other animals include two-humped camels, wallabies and barking deer. Entry is free and it is open daily. Positioned on the western side of the island, there are also hiking paths as well as a decent golf course close by.

Ueno Zoo

9-83 Ueno Kōen
Taitō-ku
🚇 *Ueno*
Map 12 C3 29

03 3828 5171 | *www.tokyo-zoo.net*
The oldest zoo in Japan, Ueno first opened its gates back in 1882. It has a wider mix of animals than any other zoo in the country with nearly 470 different species. Spread out over 36 acres, there is a handy monorail that links its east and west sides. Some of most beloved animals include white tailed eagles, Sumatran tigers and white rhinoceros. But the real superstar is the giant panda. On weekends you may have to queue, as the exhibit is tremendously popular. Recently, some of the dreary cages have been replaced with more civilised habitats. The Gorilla Woods is one such example and the bears will soon be living in swankier quarters as well. Adults get in for ¥600, students for ¥200 and kids under 12 get in for free. The zoo is closed on Mondays.

Ueno's Sad History

Ueno Zoo was infamously the site of one of the darkest days in Tokyo history. During the second world war the municipal government put all the zoo's animals to sleep, for fear they would escape and run wild after Allied bombing. Some of the elephants refused to eat the poisoned food and subsequently starved to death.

Animals in Ueno Zoo

Beach Parks

6-2-1 Rinkai-chō
Edogawa-ku
Map 2 C2

Kasai Rinkai

03 5696 1331 | www.tokyo-park.or.jp

Kasai Rinkai is the best beach park in the Tokyo area. Originally a fishing community, it suffered a major blow in the early 20th century when many villagers were lost during a wicked typhoon. These days it's a quaint place to take in the urban greenery and stare out at Mother Nature. The waters are not so spectacular, but its hushed seashore offers a nice breather from the capital. There's a bird sanctuary that offers avian lovers a chance to see more than the ubiquitous crows. An enormous Ferris wheel and an admirable aquarium make it a good place to head with the kids. The park is surprisingly uncongested and only gets busy at the height of the cherry blossom season.

Mr Crow

One of the few truly menacing aspects of Tokyo existence is the enormous crows that inhabit the city's skies. Diving through the air like jet-black servants of Satan, they are not afraid of humans and have been known to attack children. Japanese portend that the birds have exceptional memories; if you cross them, there will be payback. When relaxing in the park, keep an eye on your snacks to avoid an attack.

Beaches

There are not many remarkable beaches in Tokyo proper, but just outside the city limits there are a number of options. Shōnan in Kanagawa has a chilled out California vibe and attracts surfers with its stellar waves. Chiba's Kujūkuri-hama Beach on the Bōsō-hantō Peninsula has long stretches of pure white sands. And the Izu Islands, south of Tokyo are one of the best-kept secrets in the country. Most of these beaches are dead quiet in the off-season and jam packed in the summer. July and August are the busiest, while June can often be marred by the rainy season. All beaches in the Tokyo area are open to the public. They are relatively clean and safe with little undertow. Women going topless is not acceptable.

South of Tokyo
🚇 *Takeshiba*
Map 1 C3

Izu Islands

www.town.oshima.tokyo.jp

Most residents don't make it down to the Izu Islands, and they are really missing out. These nine volcanic islands stretch south from Tokyo and are a great way to catch some rays. Municipally part of Tokyo, the Izu Islands once served as a place of exile for criminals and other undesirables. Today, they are long gone, it's just sand and surf. All of the islands offer campsites and cheap accommodation during the summer. From September to May, you may have a hard time finding a place to stay, but don't worry: it's acceptable to set up camp right on the beach. As with most Japan beaches, July and August are the busiest, and June is often too rainy. May is a great time to go as all the islands are relatively deserted and you'll be truly isolated. Ōshima and Shikinejima are the most popular, but all of the islands are worth checking out. Get there by catching a ferry from Takeshiba station in Tokyo.

Chiba-ken
🚇 *Inubō-saki*
Map 1 C3

Kujūkuri-hama Beach

www.chiba-tour.jp

A good trek from the city, but well worth the hassle, Kujūkuri-hama Beach is a 60km stretch of white sand that is relatively rock and reef free. It's perfect for swimming and is a family orientated beach where children run wild during their summer holidays. There are many small towns along the beach and getting something to eat or drink is never a problem. One of Kujūkuri-hama's most distinct characteristics is its straight coastline. Most beaches in Japan run along irregular coastlines, yet Kujūkuri provides stunning panoramas. Get the Limited Express JR Sōbu Line for two hours from Tokyo station to Chōshi. Switch to the Chōshi Dentetsu line for about 20 minutes and get off at Inubō-saki.

Kanagawa-ken
Katase Enoshima
Map 2 A4

Shōnan Beach
www.kanagawa-kankou.or.jp
Kanagawa's Shōnan beach is possibly the most popular outside the city. This region has long been a resort town and has a rich history. Many *manga* and films have been set in Shōnan, solidifying its reputation as the place to soak up the summer sun. Watersports are big and you'll see plenty of sailboats as you laze on the shore. Bodyboarding has recently taken off in a big way and boards can be rented everywhere. But surfing is still the main activity. Every summer, surfers from all over head down and tackle the waves. This is a beautiful beach but be prepared for crowds in July or August. It's easy to reach: catch the Odakyū Odawara line to Sagami Ono, and then take the Enoshima line direct to the beach.

Botanical Gardens
The city has some beautiful botanical gardens that are as aesthetically gratifying as they are tranquil. Most charge a small entrance fee, but all the money goes to maintaining the grounds. The Japanese attention to detail is never more apparent than in these mini-Edens. Some are of the European variety, some are distinctly Japanese and some fuse disparate landscaping tenets into an eclectic mix. These gardens have stricter rules than the typical park. Most forbid smoking, eating and drinking, so be sure to check the regulations prior to entering.

5-31-10 Jindaiji-
Motomachi
Chōfu-shi
Kichijōji
Map 2 A2

Jindai Botanical Gardens
042 483 2300 | www.tokyo-park.or.jp
The must-see Jindai Botanical Gardens are in the Chōfu district, in western Tokyo. Regarded by many as the pre-eminent botanical garden in Tokyo, it is a vast expanse and perfect for strolling. The garden was initially a nursery providing trees for a Tokyo beautification project but following the second world war it was formally opened to the public. More a park than a garden, Jindai features 30 disparate sections, each showcasing a different plant life. Some of the most cherished displays include peonies, roses and azaleas. A greenhouse was added in the early 1980s where there is an especially charming lily pond. Jindai Gardens also host agricultural demonstrations and workshops in Japanese. Immediately outside the back entrance there's a spot where visitors can purchase flowers. Admission is ¥500 and it is closed on Mondays. To get there, go to Chōfu station on the Keiō line, take the Odakyū bus to Mitaka or Kichijōji and get off at Jindaiji Shokubutsu Kōen-mae.

3-7-1 Hakusan
Bunkyō-ku
Myōgadani
Map 4 B1 **30**

Koishikawa Botanical Gardens
03 3814 0139 | www.bg.s.u-tokyo.ac.jp/koishikawa/eigo
Maintained by the University Tokyo Graduate School of Science, the Koishikawa Botanical Gardens are conveniently located in midtown Tokyo. This 40 acre spread features more than 4000 plant species as well an arboretum. It helps in the conservation of endangered plants. One of the biggest projects has been cultivating endangered flora native to Japan's Yakushima Islands and returning them to their natural habitat. There is also a massive botanical library on the grounds, though the majority of the books are in Japanese. The gardens feature mostly plants native to Japan, with a healthy dose of vegetation from other east Asian countries. Admission is ¥330. Closed on Mondays.

3-2 Yumenoshima
Koto-ku
 Shin-Kiba
Map 2 C2

Yumenoshima Greenhouse

03 3522 0281 | *www.yumenoshima.jp*

Set in one of Tokyo's more industrialised areas, Yumenoshima Greenhouse is an emerald oasis in an otherwise dreary locale. The complex has a space-age look when approached from the street, but once inside it is a little Eden of greenery. Yumenoshima has a trio of domes. Dome A has a forest theme with a functioning waterfall; Dome B recreates a subtropical environment with many eye-catching flowers and Dome C features foliage from the Ogasawara islands. One of the highlights is a small greenhouse that displays carnivorous vegetation and you can watch condemned insects get gobbled up and digested by these lethal plants. It's popular with schoolchildren. Admission is ¥200 and it's closed on Mondays.

Something To Sit On
If you go out for a day in the park with some Japanese friends, be sure to bring a blanket or a tarp, as most Japanese people find sitting directly on grass to be extremely unsanitary.

Parks

With a reputation for glass, steel and concrete, it might be surprising to find that Tokyo actually has some splendid parks. All within the heart of the metropolis, they are a great opportunity to get away from chaotic big-city life. Parks are generally tremendously tidy and litter is scarcely seen. Drinking alcoholic beverages is perfectly legal, though barbeques are frowned upon. These parks are great places to picnic, but you may want to stock up on provisions before you arrive, as the shops nearby add on a hefty mark-up. Entry to most parks is free, though the elegant Shinjuku Gyōen charges ¥200. For more information and maps to the city's parks, visit www.tokyo-park.or.jp.

Nerima-ku
 Hikarigaoka
Map 2 A2

Hikarigaoka Kōen

This jewel of a park is a bit out of the way, in northern Nerima-ku, but it offers some stunning scenery and is usually dead quiet. It used to be a military headquarters before the municipality turned it into a park in 1973. Its most unique characteristic is its rolling hills, as most of the city's parks are completely flat. One of its quirks is the resident stray cats. Irresponsible pet owners have been leaving unwanted kittens here for years. These ragamuffin kitties keep to themselves, but if you have a love of animals, maybe you can make some feline friends.

Chiyoda-ku
 Tokyo
Map 10 F2 **31**

Imperial Palace East Gardens

Though you can't get inside and see the Imperial Palace up close and personal, its park is well worth a trip. The only section of the palace open to the public, this is as close as you'll get to shaking the Emperor's hand. The park is generally quiet and you'll never have to jostle for picnic space. Park-goers tend to act more reserved here than at other parks – there's never any blaring music or drunken revellers. The garden is very relaxing and there are also many picturesque photo-ops. The Nijūbashi Bridge and Imperial Palace main gate are two of the more celebrated sights.

Imperial Palace East Garden

South of the station
Shinjuku-ku
🚇 **Shinjuku Gyōen-mae**
Map 7 D2 32

Shinjuku Gyōen

www.env.go.jp/garden/shinjukugyoen

Not be confused with Shinjuku Central Park on the west side of Shinjuku-ku (which is a travesty of city planning and mainly only a popular place to live for the city's homeless), Shinjuku Gyōen is one of Tokyo's most beautiful parks, and once you walk through its gates you are likely to agree. It feels more like a gigantic garden than a park. The grounds themselves are immaculate and the staff take serious measures to keep it that way. Incorporating elements of Japanese and western European landscaping techniques, it emanates a sophisticated air that is sometimes absent from other city parks. At almost 60 hectares and with more than 20,000 trees, there's a lot to take in. The greenhouses showcase

Yoyogi Kōen

nearly 2,000 tropical plants and are open from 11:00 to 15:00. The park opens from 09:00 to 16:30 daily, except Mondays. During cherry blossom and chrysanthemum season it is open every day. Admission is ¥200 for adults and ¥50 for children.

West exit of station
Ueno-ku
🚇 **Ueno**
Map 12 C2 33

Ueno Kōen

Urban Ueno Kōen is chock full of things to do and see. Renowned museums, the biggest zoo (p.182) in the city and beautiful temples are just some of the sights worth taking in. While it is comparatively short on grassland, it has lots of lush trees and throughout cherry blossom season it takes on a heavenly atmosphere. Tokyo National Museum (p.177), the National Science Museum (p.176) and the National Museum of Western Art (p.172) are all within walking distance from one another. And Shinobazu Pond is a peaceful spot, its serene perimeter ideal for long romantic walks.

Harajuku
Shibuya-ku
🚇 **Harajuku**
Map 8 A1 34

Yoyogi Kōen

www.tokyo-park.or.jp

Yoyogi Kōen is the big daddy of Tokyo parks. Particularly popular with the expat population, it is the place to be on a sunny weekend afternoon. It opened in 1967 and the spacious park is full of trees. It's large enough for full on football matches and frisbees and baseballs are free to fly through the air. If you don't feel like paying through the nose to hear live music, Yoyogi Kōen is a sensible alternative. Amateur musicians of all genres set up along the periphery of its grounds and play their hearts out every weekend. There are often cultural festivals held here too. Just outside the park, other places worth visiting include Harajuku (p.154) and Meiji Jingū (p.178).

Shortcut To Yoyogi Kōen

Sunny weekends in Yoyogi Kōen are wildly popular. Unfortunately, getting out of the train station on a sun-drenched Saturday or Sunday is a nightmare. People are jammed together getting out of the station's park exit and the mob moves a metre-a-minute. To avoid this human cattle-drive, go out of the Takeshita exit and walk up the hill to the park entrance. You'll save yourself a lot of time and aggravation.

Tours & Sightseeing

Talking Your Talk

All visitors' centres will have maps and brochures in English, Korean and Chinese. However, the JNTO (www.jnto.go.jp) has literature in French, German and Spanish as well. It has two desks conveniently located on the Arrivals floor at Narita Airport and one in central Tokyo. For more, see City Information on p.23.

During Prime Minister Junichiro Koizumi's time in office there was a big push to improve tourist information centres, and launch overseas advertising campaigns to lure tourist dollars to the Land of the Rising Sun. As a result, there are a number of tour and sightseeing options for the adventurous traveller, including those geared towards Anglophones. The staff at information centres, and throughout the services industry in general, tend to be highly proficient in English, but this linguistic ability quickly diminishes the further out you go.

The Japan National Tourist Organization (JNTO) is an excellent resource for foreigners looking to explore (www.jnto.go.jp). It has an office in Narita Airport (both terminals) and in Yūrakuchō in the city centre. There are also three branches of the Tokyo Tourist Information Centre around town. They can provide maps, directions and interesting itineraries. JNTO also has offices in many western capitals, so it may be possible to pick up some literature before arriving in Tokyo. For a full listing of tourist information centres, see City Information on p.187.

The city's main tour companies offer variations of the same itineraries so it's wise to shop around. The majority cover a lot of ground and are very thorough. These often entail big groups and a strict schedule. The Japanese believe that non-Japanese like to travel in the same manner that they do, that is, in large throngs. If this is not your idea of fun, you may want to traipse the city yourself – getting lost is one of the best ways to get acquainted with a new town.

Aside from the stereotypical run round the temples and shrines, there are some more irreverent possibilities. There's everything from *otaku* tours for *manga* maniacs, sneak peaks into the life of sumo wrestlers with a look inside their hallowed training stables to extensive culinary tours for gastronomic connoisseurs. Many tour companies offer pre-planned itineraries. Even old Tokyo-pros are bound to see a new side to the metropolis – there's nothing better to recharge a cynical, long-term expat's batteries than witnessing first-time visitors marvel in the city's majesty.

Activity Tours

Other options **Activities Chapter** p.208

Hiking, rafting and scuba diving tours can all be easily arranged. However, most of them will take you out into the country as the city proper is obviously not the place to immerse yourself in Mother Earth. The Japanese are sticklers for safety and you'll be in more danger crossing the street in Shibuya than going on any of these tours. Be sure to check how strenuous the activities actually are before you book though. For more info on adventure tours, check out *Outdoor Japan's* website (www.outdoorjapan.com) or pick up the excellent magazine at most foreigner friendly pubs and bookstores in town.

Take It Up Takao

If you're dying for a hike and don't have the time to travel to the countryside, consider Mount Takao. This 600 metre high mountain is accessible from Shinjuku using the Chūō and Keiō Takao Lines. The trails are clearly marked and barebones English language maps are available at Takao's main train station.

Various Locations

Gunma-ken

Map 1 C3

Canyons

0278 72 2811 | *www.canyons.jp*

Canyons offers a number of outdoor activities for people who aren't content merely sightseeing. Rafting, caving and snowshoe hikes are conducted by a professional bilingual staff and are good for both novices and seasoned outdoor enthusiasts. It also gives ski and snowboard lessons for first-timers. Many activities can be combined into a multi-day adventure. The four locations take you far out into the wilderness, with two bases in far-off Shikoku and Nagano, and two in Gunma, just two hours from Tokyo.

5-7-20 Asamizodai
Kanagawa-ken
Map 2 A4

Discovery Divers Tokyo

080 5707 3260 | *www.discoverydiverstokyo.com*

Discovery Divers Tokyo organise dive tours in Osezaki, Atami and around the Izu peninsula. They also have indoor pool lessons for fledgling divers near their headquarters in Kanagawa. Prices for dive tours vary, check their website for details, but a weekend tour in Osezaki-with four dives-will cost about ¥25,000. They offer a number of certification programmes that are particularly good for budding dive instructors.

3-30-8 Ikebukuro
Toshima-ku
🚇 *Ikebukuro*
Map 2 B2

Friends of the Earth Japan

03 6907 7217 | *www.foejapan.org*

Friends of the Earth works towards raising environmental awareness in the community and hosts conservation fundraising activities. The Tokyo branch organises hiking tours through the countryside around the city, which are very popular and a great way to meet people. The hikes usually range from easy to moderate level. Afterwards, most hikers stop at a local pub and throw back a few cold ones. The tours are free, though the train fare out to the hills will cost between ¥1,500 and ¥3,000.

3-15-9 Higashi Nakan
Nakano-ku
Map 2 B2

Mar Scuba

090 3851 3901 | *www.marscuba.com*

Mar Scuba has an international staff and offers diving tours around Tokyo to beginners and seasoned pros. It offers a variety of tours including a two day tour diving in Mikomoto, near Shimoda at the tip of the Izu Peninsula. The whole package includes instruction, meals and two nights in a traditional Japanese *minshuku* inn. Tours cost under ¥60,000 with six divers and two dive leaders per group.

Bicycle Tours

Cycling tours are a great way to get around the city and see the sights. Drivers in Japan are rather cautious and you're far safer on the roads than back home. While it is not law to wear protective gear, cycling tour groups often insists that participants wear a helmet to avoid any insurance calamities.

Various Locations

Cycle Tokyo!

http://cycle-tokyo.cycling.jp

Cycle Tokyo is an organisation that puts together group bike trips and promotes the benefits of cycling. Founded in 2005, it schedules one big tour roughly every two months. The website is a wealth of information pertaining to the ins and outs of pedalling round the city. Many of the tours are themed. One tour hits all the big embassies and another heads out to *onsen* country. Members are a mix of Japanese and foreigners and it's a good way to meet new people. Tours are free.

1-6-3 Marunouchi
Chiyoda-ku
🚇 *Tokyo*
Map 13 B4 **35**

Tokyo Great Cycling Tour

03 4590 2995 | *www.tokyocycling.jp*

The professionally-guided Tokyo Great Cycling Tour is great for visitors and longterm residents alike. The tour takes place every Saturday, meeting at the Marunouchi Hotel, and takes you through the centre of Tokyo, visiting many of the city's landmarks such as Tsukiji Fish Market, Tokyo Tower and the Imperial Palace. Tours last for six hours, with a maximum of ten riders. The cost is ¥10,000, which includes bike rental, lunch and a knowledgeable guide.

Boat Tours & Charters

Boat tours are popular with visitors all year-round, but the Japanese only partake during the cherry blossom season or on the most humid of summer nights. The main waterway is the Sumidagawa, which looks a lot better at night. By day the river's murky waters are a bit depressing and the ramshackle buildings that line it are something of an eyesore. Once the sun goes down though, the river takes on a nourishing air, and Tokyo's eerie tranquility is rather intoxicating.

Romance Is Dead?

In summer, many of the Sumidagawa night tours are of the booze cruise variety, where college students regularly go for wild parties and fall about the place. While it's great for carrying-on with the locals, it's not conducive to a romantic night on the river. Always check what kind of tour is being offered before booking.

5-9-16 Higashi-Shinagawa
Shinagawa-ku
 Shinagawa
Map 6 4B **36**

Crystal Yacht Club

03 3450 4300 | *www.crystal-yc.co.jp*

Crystal Yacht Club offers a classy night out with fine French food and romantic views for the starry-eyed. Its sole ship – the Lady Crystal – is an elegant alternative to the more family orientated boats that usually cover the waterfront. Lunch cruises last two hours and cost between ¥6,000 and ¥10,000. Dinner is a more popular option but it will cost you. Set courses range from ¥12,000 to ¥25,000. There is also a children's menu if you want to bring your kids along (but this is ill advised).

Asakusa
 Asakusa
Map 4 E2 **37**

Tokyo Cruise Ship Company

03 3841 9178 | *www.suijobus.co.jp*

This is the most trusted of the river lines and offers a variety of packages. It has a dozen boats, all featuring modern amenities. Many are rather unorthodox looking and are a treat in themselves. The Himiko Water Bus looks like something out of a Jules Verne novel and is great for sightseeing, while the You ship is particularly charming, decked out like a Mississippi riverboat and features a working pipe organ. Ships can also be rented out for private parties. They offer a plethora of tour packages, and prices vary by route and by season. Check the website for more info.

Brewery Tours

4-20-1 Ebisu
Shibuya-ku
 Ebisu
Map 5 F2 **38**

Beer Museum Yebisu

03 5423 7255 | *www.sapporobeer.jp*

Yebisu Beer has a brewery tour that is well worth a look. A short walk from Ebisu station, this tour gives beer lovers an inside guide into the production of this fine Japanese lager. There is also a museum that chronicles the history of beer in Japan and displays classic advertisements. Beer tasting is possible but it will cost a bit extra. One glass goes for ¥200. It's closed Mondays and over the New Year.

View from Takeshiba

Arakawa
Arakawa-ku
Map 2 B2

Tokyo City Sake Brewery Tour
03 6824 6333 | *www.tctour.co.jp*
Tokyo City Tours is an online company that offers a sake brewery tour that will give you the lowdown on the art of making Japanese sake (rice wine). On a two day expedition starting in Nagano, you'll learn about sake brewing from experienced guides. Breakfast and dinner are included, and tour members spend the night in a traditional Japanese *ryokan*. For more information on rice wine, check out the excellent website by the Sake Brewers Association (www.japansake.or.jp). It has maps of all the major breweries in Japan, as well as tips on how to pick the best sake for your own personal taste.

Bus Tours
A number of bus tours take in Tokyo and its surrounding areas. These tend to be more popular with the Japanese than foreigners. Taking a bus tour is a good way to get a feel for the city when you first arrive, but you'll be short changing yourself by not getting out and experiencing the metropolis on your own two feet. That said, these tours are ideal for senior citizens or people with children. The bus tours that take in Kyoto, Mount Fuji and other prime spots across the country are good value for money and are much cheaper than travelling by train.

The Quicksteppers
When getting off a tour bus, watch out for the old-timers. Japanese retirees have an obsession with disembarking as quickly as possible and can be uncharacteristically pushy. When the bus stops, stay in your seat and let the stampede pass before standing up.

5-4-1 Heiwajima
Marunouchi
🚇 *Tokyo*
Map 11 F4 39

Hato Bus
03 3433 1972 | *www.hatobus.com*
The Hato Bus Company has a plethora of tour options and should have something to suit everyone. Half-day, full-day and night tours are all available and feature an English-language guide. The morning tour is good for early birds and the Panoramic Tokyo tour takes in the main religious sights. Full-day and night tours include meals. Check the website for prices for the different packages.

Mitsubishi Building
Marunouchi
🚇 *Tokyo*
Map 14 B1 40

Sky Bus Tokyo
03 3215 0008 | *www.skybus.jp*
See Tokyo in record-breaking time with the Sky Bus. These open-topped double-decker buses are more of a novelty than an all-encompassing expedition into the heart and soul of the city, but on a sunny day it's a lark and the kids will enjoy it. One-hour jaunts take in the Imperial Palace, Ginza and other big sights in the city centre. Tours leave on the hour from the south exit of Tokyo station. Prices are ¥1,200 for adults and ¥600 for children.

Culinary Tours

Various Locations

A Taste of Culture
03 5716 5751 | *www.tasteofculture.com*
Japanese cuisine can be overwhelming and a culinary tour is a good way to learn the basics. Artisans of Leisure (www.artisansofleisure.com) offers a massive week-long food tour that covers Kyoto and Tokyo. Food-obsessed Tokyoites who don't have the time to trek all over the Kantō Plane, should sign up with A Taste of Culture. This culinary school teaches the basics of Japanese cooking as well as offering tours to various markets. Many foreign expats stick to the big name supermarkets for their grocery shopping and these tours are a prime opportunity to get acquainted with the markets that the top chefs swear by. Certain dates are put aside specifically for food tours, but private market excursions can be booked by small parties.

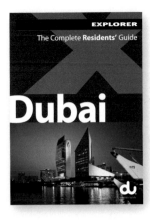
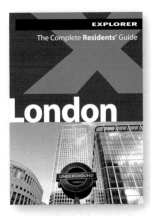
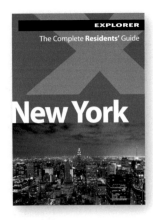

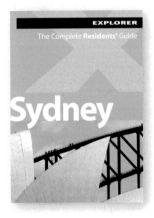

Dolphin & Whale Watching

While whale is somewhat of a delicacy on the restaurant scene, they are equally as popular in their natural habitat, and many people like to do a spot of whale watching when they get the chance. Unfortunately for Tokyoites, most whale watching outfits are way out in Hokkaidō and Okinawa. However, the Ogasawara Whale Watching Association south of Tokyo operates out of the Ogasawara Island archipelago.

Chichi-jima
Ogasawara-mura
Map 1 C4

Ogasawara Whale Watching Association

049 982 3215 | www.h2.dion.ne.jp/~owa/english/index.html

Getting to the Ogasawara Island archipelago is an adventure in itself. There are no airports and a daylong boat ride from Tokyo is your only option. Whale watching costs from ¥8,000 to ¥10,000 for a six-hour trip. Common species sighted are humpback whales, sperm whales and bottlenose dolphins.

Helicopter Tours

To experience the full grandeur of the Tokyo sprawl, consider taking a helicopter tour. More encompassing than the standard rooftop viewpoint, a ride in the sky will give you a more tangible understanding of just how gargantuan the capital truly is. Many tour companies can help set up a whirlybird ride. Prime Travel (www.primetravel.com) and Geo Passage (www.geopassage.com) both offer helicopter tours, either on their own or as part of larger sightseeing packages. These agencies both offer 15 minute sky tours of the downtown area before whisking passengers off to Tokyo Disneyland. For more thorough excursions, try Excel Air (www.excel-air.com) or Asahi Helicopter (www.asahi-heli.co.jp). Both companies have extensive sightseeing tours in Tokyo and Yokohama. Night rides are available, offering far superior vistas than the ones you'll experience during the smoggy, humdrum daytime. These night tours are very popular on Valentine's Day and during Christmas, so be sure to book ahead. Asahi Helicopter also offers flight training for those who want to take to the sky themselves. And if you're looking to purchase a helicopter of your own, Excel Air can help.

Heritage Tours

4-35-9 Arakawa
Arakawa-ku
Map 2 B2

Kamakura Tour

03 6824 6333 | http://tctour.co.jp

A guided trip to enthralling Kamakura can be organised through Tokyo City Tour. Home to the iconic bronze Buddha, no Tokyoite should miss a chance to see this gargantuan deity. Aside from this breathtaking statue there is also the Tsurugaoka Hachimangū shrine and Kenchōji temple. The van ride from Tokyo takes roughly two hours and costs ¥12,000 for adults and ¥9,000 for kids. Lunch is not included but there are many fine traditional Japanese dining options in the area. The tour is conducted on Fridays and Saturdays only.

JTB Building
2-3-11 Higashi-
Shinagawa
Shinagawa-ku
🚇 Shinagawa
Map 2 B3

Nikko Tour

03 5796 5400 | www.japanican.com/sunrisetours

This heritage excursion offered by Sunrise Tours will take you to the enchanting town of Nikko in the Tochigi prefecture. Nobody should miss this beautiful collection of shrines, bridges and historic gates. Picturesque Lake Chūzenji is a great place for a walk and Kegonno waterfall is considered the most stunning in the country. The tour includes an English language guide and a traditional Japanese lunch. It's a one-day tour that will have you back in the city by 20:00. Nikko is traditionally much colder than Tokyo, so dress accordingly. The tour costs ¥13,000 per person.

Island Resorts

1309-13 Mitsune
Hachijō-machi
Map 1 C4

Hachijo Island Tours

049 962 1168 | *www.hachijo.net/index.html*

The Izu island chain south of Tokyo offers a peaceful getaway. Few Japanese come here except for vacationing college students in July and August. Of the nine islands, Ne-jima and Shikine-jima are the most popular with foreigners. Both have plenty of fishing and camping options. However, Hachijō-jima has foreigner friendly tours and accommodation that come highly recommended. Hachijo Island Tours takes travellers on snorkelling, diving and fishing excursions and offers an expedition to see fascinating second world war military tunnels. Small Japanese style inns are available or for the more adventurous, camping grounds.

Novelty Tours

OAK Tower
6-8-1 Nishi-Shinjuku
Shinjuku-ku
Map 7 A1 **41**

H.I.S. Experience Japan

03 5322 8988 | *http://hisexperience.jp*

Sumo runs deep in the Japanese psyche and H.I.S. Experience Japan offers a unique tour that allows you to get up close and personal with wrestlers in training. Normally closed off to the general public, a trip to a sumo stable is a sacred experience and one you won't easily forget. To begin with you get to watch early morning sumo practice. The tour then continues with a chance to talk to the wrestlers (translators will be on hand). The tour finishes with the traditional sumo meal of *chanko nabe* and then a brief lecture by the stable master. It is offered 12 times a year and costs ¥18,000.

Nerd Knowledge

For a more personal tour of the geek contingent, contact resident J-Pop expert Patrick Macias (jaguar@mindspring.com). Macias conducts tours of the Tokyo *otaku* sights and is a walking encyclopedia of nerd knowledge. His blog is worth a look (www.patrickmacias.blogs.com).

Various Locations

Pop Travel Japan

www.popjapantravel.com

If you were a big nerd back in your home country, you'll still be a big nerd in Japan. But, you'll have many more companions. To get a peek into the Tokyo geek universe, sign up for this fun-packed otaku tour. This California-based company offers different tours taking in various aspects of Tokyo dork life. Tours hit the nerd hubs of Akihabara and Harajuku as well as more off-the-beaten-path spots. They also have a tour dedicated to the Gothic Lolita craze. These massive package tours take place periodically throughout the year. Sign up early to save a spot. They're very much geared towards tourists.

Private Tours

A private tour is an excellent option for those who want a more personal experience. Tokyo City Tour (see p.196) runs private tours that hit all the major spots in town. Alternatively, enlist the services of noted travel writer Chris Rowthorn. He has lived in Tokyo for over a decade and offers individual tours throughout the year. He'll steer you away from the tourist traps and into the true heart of the city. Apply online (www.infohub.com/tour_guides/423.html) and plan your own itinerary. Another good private tour operator is Bespoke Tokyo (www.bespoketokyo.jp).

Private Numbers

Be careful when booking private tours. For the Japanese, 'private tour' means less than 20 people. Double check that you and your tour guide will be the only ones trekking around town.

Shopping Tours

4-14-4 Meguro
Meguro-ku
Meguro
Map 2 B3

Tokyo Fashion Tour

090 3680 0836 | www.fashioninjapan.com
Slaves to style will enjoy this tour that hits all the hippest clothing boutiques and brand name shops. Led by fashion connoisseur Loic Bizel, you'll get a first-hand introduction into the consumer crazed world of contemporary Tokyo. Harajuku, Ginza and Aoyama are all covered; as well as lesser known hotspots that only the coolest are hip to. Tours can be anything from two to three days and can be customised to fit individual tastes. Strap on your platform-heels, check your makeup in the mirror and follow these trend-spotters. The tour company is based in 107 Laurel Court, Meguro-ku.

Designer bags

Sightseeing Tours

Shinbashi-Ekimae
Bldg No.1
2-20-15 Shinbashi
Minato-ku
Shinbashi
Map 2 B2

Nippon Travel Agency

03 3614 3066 | www.nta.co.jp
Nippon Travel Agency has an extensive five-day tour that explores Tokyo, Mount Fuji and Kyoto. These tours are tailored towards tourists, but they will interest foreign expats who are new to the country. Covering the most significant sights in the city, it's a whirlwind jaunt that won't leave much opportunity for relaxation or alone time, but it'll check off all the top 'to do' sights and attractions. Prices fluctuate according to the season, but look to pay around ¥130,000 for this mammoth trek.

Walking Tours

Contrary to popular belief, Tokyo is a walkable city. While trekking from Ikebukuro to Odaiba is unadvisable, taking in individual areas in pragmatic chunks is a superb way to experience the capital. A number of unique walking tours exist, each with their own distinctive flavour. Becoming familiar with the city on foot also gives you a more unified image of the lay of the land. Tokyoites that walk or cycle around town have a far better mental map in their heads than those who rely solely on the train system. And they look better naked. For more information, see Walking on p.37 in Getting Around.

Walk This Way

A number of Tokyo scribes have taken a stab at writing self-guided walking tour books. These handy collections offer endless leg-stretching possibilities and can easily be purchased online. Two books worth owning are *Day Walks Near Tokyo* by Gary D.A. Walters and *A Flower Lover's Guide to Tokyo: 40 Walks for All Seasons* by Sumiko Enbutsu and Michiru Unae. One great free option is the *Tokyo Walks* leaflet available from the JNTO Tourist Information Centre (p.23).

Various Locations

Mr Oka Walking Tours

042 251 7673 | http://mroka.homestead.com
If you want to get off the trodden trail and stretch your legs at the same time, drop a line to Mr Oka. An authority on the remnants of old Edo, Mr Oka offers guided excursions throughout the capital in English. A retired professional tour guide, he has a number of walking expeditions to choose from and is an encyclopaedia of Tokyo history. His introductory strolls are perfect for new arrivals and his more specialised treks will show old residents something new. Call between 15:00 and 22:00 to make a booking.

Tours & Sightseeing

1-1-1 Marunouchi
Chiyoda-ku
🚇 **Ōtemachi**
Map 13 A4 42

Tokyo City Guide Club Walking Tours
090 1110 1684 | *http://5.pro.tok2.com/~tcgc/*

If you'd like to see the city on foot and not squander a single yen, get in touch with the Tokyo City Guide Club. You are the guinea pig, as students who have recently become certified tour guides get to try out their newly acquired skills. These excursions hit most of the main tourist destinations, such as Meiji Jingū and the Imperial Palace. Tours take place periodically throughout the year. Check the website for specifics. Reservations are necessary and most treks last between 90 minutes and two hours.

Shrine & Temple Etiquette

There is certain etiquette to follow when attending a Japanese shrine. Firstly, dress with a modicum of couth. Once you've passed under the *torii* (gate), head to the hand-cleansing basin and wash your hands. Pour the water onto your hands, sip a bit, gargle and spit. Once at the altar, put some coins into the allotted receptacle – one of the luckiest is the ¥5 coin. Bow deeply twice. Clap loudly twice, then bow one final time. However at temples, you should never clap. Just put your hands together and bow your head in front of Buddha or the altar.

Tokyo Metropolitan Govt Bldg
8-1-2 Nishi-Shinjuku
Shinjuku-ku
🚇 **Shinjuku**
Map 7 A2 43

Tourist Information Center
03 5321 3077 | *www.tourism.metro.tokyo.jp*

The Tokyo Metropolitan Government has its own tour guide programme and it is reasonably priced. These tend not to fill up to the point where you'll be lost in the crowd but they offer excursions in eight different languages and are exceptionally knowledgeable. Two guides lead the group, giving participants an opportunity to ask questions without disrupting the flow of the proceedings. Costs depend on the number of walkers on board, but expect to pay between ¥1,000 and ¥3,000. The streets of Shinjuku tour is free and covers a lot of ground. Though advertised as walking tours, you may be required to jump on the occasional bus or train.

Tours Outside Tokyo

While truly urbane Tokyoites may never feel the need to leave the concrete, some residents may sporadically want to get away from it all. Fortunately, travel outside the capital is extremely convenient and a number of options are available. Be prepared – English won't be widely spoken so do your homework before setting off. Gunma is often overlooked but it offers skiing, and some of the best *onsen* in the country. Mount Fuji is a painless daytrip and a quasi-painful hike up to the peak. Yokohama is now almost an urban extension of Tokyo but its seafaring vibe and detached charisma are instantaneously tangible.

Minakami
Gunma
Map 1 C3

Forest & Water Gunma Tours
0278 72 8017 | *www.fw-jp.com*

Just north of Saitama prefecture is bucolic Gunma. Possessing a excess of *onsen*, fans of the bubbly mineral baths will have their hands full. The Kusatsu region is especially renowned for its boiling baths. To find the *onsen* that is right for you, check out the region's informative website (www.kusatsu-onsen.ne.jp). Aside from lazily lounging around in your underwear, Gunma has many outdoor activities. In the winter, snowboarding and skiing are popular on the slopes of Mount Tanigawa and in the warmer months, white water rafting is all the rage on the Tonegawa. Adventure seekers should contact the Forest & Water tour company (p.195). It offers an assortment of activities and put together nice package deals. The website is predominantly in Japanese, but the staff speak English.

Asahi
Fujiyoshida-shi
Yamanashi-ken
Map 2 A4

GoRiki Mount Fuji Eco-tour

0555 24 1032 | www.fujitozan.jp/english

Admit it. When you were a kid there were three things that you knew about Japan: ninjas, Godzilla and Mount Fuji. Well, ninjas are ancient history, and Godzilla was killed by Mothra back in 1968, but Mount Fuji is still standing. Towering upwards to nearly 3,800 metres, the majestic Fuji-yama is one of the most distinguished mountains in the world. Bounded by the serene Fuji Five Lakes, it is a trek that every Tokyoite must make at least once. Many climbing tours are available, but the packages offered by GoRiki Mountaineering School are highly recommended. The knowledgeable hike-leaders are proficient in English and can give you insights into the significance of Fuji-yama. Different tours are available, check out their website for prices. Accommodation and meals are included. The most popular months to climb the mountain are from late June to early September, after which date it is not advisable due to bad weather conditions.

18 Yamashita-chō
Naka-ku
Yokohama
Map 2 A4

Yokohama Sightseeing

045 221 2111 | www.welcome.city.yokohama.jp

Even though Yokohama is the second largest city in Japan, it is perceptibly more compact and user-friendly than Tokyo. For foreign Tokyoites, it is a nice daytrip and offers some pleasant views of the Pacific Ocean. For young Japanese it's also a highly romantic dating spot. There's plenty to do in the area and the Yokohama Visitors Bureau has several tour options. They offer full-day or half-day tours in the morning or afternoon. All of these excursions are by bus and cover the main attractions in the city, such as Landmark Tower, the Foreigners Cemetery and Chinatown. Full-day tours are about six hours and half-day tours last around four hours. Prices vary according to the package. A private taxi tour for about twice the price is also available. Check out the website for more information.

Noodles On Show

When in Yokohama pay a visit to one of the most off-the-wall museums in the country. The Shin-Yokohama Ramen Museum (www.raumen. co.jp) offers a detailed history of the much-loved noodles. The evolution and cultural significance of *ramen* is treated with an academic reverence that will boggle the western mind. Best of all, below the museum there's a recreation of a 1950s Japanese town where you can sample *ramen* from all over Japan. They don't get many foreigners here, so don't be offended when they offer you a fork.

Tour Operators

Tour operators generally offer quality packages and often bend over backwards to accommodate foreign travellers. The Japanese are obsessed with attracting tourists, and workers in the service industry take particular pride in their jobs. While not wanting to encourage any jingoistic notions of superior Japanese efficiency, it must be said that the horror stories that you often hear about tour operators in other Asian countries simply don't apply. Prices don't tend to vary much between competing companies, but it's worth shopping around for deals. It's hard to pinpoint a cheap time to travel. In the winter folks are flocking home to be with family, the spring is abuzz with cherry blossom seekers, everyone leaves town in the summer and flights go through the roof, and the autumn sees foliage aficionados heading to any region with a substantial forest. Finding a bargain is really just down to luck.

Tour Operators		
Canyons	0278 72 2811	www.canyons.jp
H.I.S. Experience Japan	03 5322 8988	http://hisexperience.jp
Hato Bus	03 3433 1972	www.hatobus.com
J&Y Travel Japan	042 442 5077	www.jy-travel-japan.com
JAPANiCAN	03 5796 5759	www.japanican.com
Kamikaze Tours	080 5425 4429	www.kamikazetours.com
Kinki Nippon Tourist Co	03 5256 1581	www.knt.co.jp/kokusai
Nippon Travel Agency	03 3614 3066	www.nta.co.jp
Tokyo City Tour	03 6824 6333	www.tctour.co.jp
Tokyo Great Cycling Tour	03 4590 2995	www.tokyocycling.jp

Daytrips

Think of Tokyo and you think of unending urban sprawl, but Japan's superb train network makes it surprisingly easy to get out of the city, putting a variety of natural and cultural attractions within easy reach. All the day-trips listed here can be reached in under two hours by train. Once you arrive you can either explore on foot or by using local transport. A trip out provides welcome respite from Tokyo's relentless bustle, not to mention a very literal breath of fresh air. It is custom to bring back souvenirs or treats such as *senbei* (rice crackers) to friends, family and colleagues, and there will be plenty of shops to choose from.

The Okutama Hills

One of the most popular destinations for a day trip is actually partially within Tokyo, albeit the rural western half of the city's administrative area. The Okutama hills straddle western Tokyo and neighbouring Saitama, and offer a range of day hikes suitable for everyone from the complete beginner to the super fit. The best bet for softies is Mount Takao, conveniently located at the end of the Keiō Line from Shinjuku station (about one hour's travel time, and technically just outside Okutama). Here you can enjoy a cable car ride most of the way up the mountain, and then a gentle stroll down. More challenging hikes in the same area equally well served by train include Mount Mitake and Mount Otake. Both are accessible from Ōme station on the Ōme line (about 90 minutes from Shinjuku).

Kawagoe

It often seems like old Japan has totally disappeared, erased by a tsunami of concrete and steel. Pockets of old-world charm do linger on however, with Kawagoe in Saitama Prefecture one of the closest such relics. Sometimes called 'Little Edo', after the old name for the capital, Kawagoe features a maze of old stores and warehouses. Enjoy period sweets including *senbei* rice cakes, or stop off at one of the town's many traditional tea shops. Take a Japanese speaker with you as the various sights are likely to need an explanation.

Yokohama

Swapping one metropolis for another might seem like a strange day out, but Yokohama offers a distinctively different atmosphere from Tokyo. Head to the Minato Mirai district of the city to enjoy bracing seaside strolls or a rollercoaster ride. Also in the same area is good boutique shopping in the Akarenga Sōko, renovated red-brick warehouses from the early 20th century that now offer a hive of upmarket shops and eateries. End the day with drinks atop the Landmark Tower – currently Japan's tallest building – or with dinner in the city's Chinatown.

Also worth a look in Yokohama is Zoorasia – an attractive landscaped zoo that is far better than its dilapidated Tokyo rival. Anyone with a taste for noodles should head to Yokohama's Ramen Museum (see Noodles On Show on p.196). Tacky but fun, the museum recreates the atmosphere of downtown life in the old days and features different styles of *ramen* from around the country.

Chinese Treats

Yokohama's Chinatown is home to over 500 Chinese eateries and shops. Whether trying out some street food or splashing out for a four-star meal, there are multiple options. Yamashita Park is a choice spot for romantic walks and starry-eyed lovers wander aimlessly.

Kamakura

Flying Food Snatchers

When you head to the beaches of Kamakura, keep a wary eye on the sky. The area's hawks are ruthless scavengers that are famous for taking snacks right out of your hand. The birds consider everything from bento boxes to burgers to be fair game, so keep a tight grip on your lunch.

A Profitable Trip?

Kamakura's quirkiest attraction is the money-washing shrine, tucked away in the hills of the city at the Zeniarai shrine. Legend has it that the spring there will cause any money washed in its magical waters to multiply. Worth a try at least.

Kamakura

Probably the most popular daytrip destination from Tokyo, Kamakura offers an unbeatable mix of countryside and culture. Among the attractions are one of Japan's biggest outdoor Buddha statues, Tsurugaoka Hachimangū shrine, a beautiful bamboo forest, and the rocky island of Enoshima. The latter makes a good place to the end the day, featuring a variety of cheap restaurants set atop vertiginous cliffs. Kamakura is just one hour from Tokyo station on the Yokosuka Line. Travel around the area is an attraction in its own right. The dinky Enoshima Electric Railway, or *Enoden*, features dainty tramcars that weave their way around town and along the seashore. Kamakura also offers a range of a seaside restaurants and a long stretch of beach, but those in search of a dip are probably better off heading a little further down the coast to Zushi and Hayama.

Zushi & Hayama

Just beyond Kamakura on the Yokosuka Line, Zushi and Hayama are the place for a summer swim. In July and August the beaches are crowded with young people enjoying the sun and surf, as well as the temporary beach bars that spring up in the summer months. Expect crowds, fairly brisk water temperatures, and a good day out. And if you need to mix a little culture in, look behind the beach at Hayama. There you will find the excellent Museum of Modern Art Hayama, one of Japan's best private art galleries. If you spot some well-heeled looking types in the area, don't be surprised, Hayama is a popular second-home location for Tokyo's rich and famous. It's also the location of the Imperial family's summer villa.

Monkey Island

After Zushi and Hayama, the Yokosuka line terminates in its titular town. Mainly known as a US naval base, Yokosuka also features some underrated attractions that can be taken in on the same day. Start with a tour of the battleship Mikasa, the flagship of the Japanese fleet that defeated the Russian navy at the decisive Battle of Tsushima in 1905. Then hop aboard a ferry for the five-minute ride to Sarushima, or Monkey Island. The only uninhabited island in Tokyo Bay, Sarushima features a maze of paths through dense undergrowth and crumbling ruins – notably the remains of 19th century fortifications intended to protect Tokyo Bay from intruding western vessels. Sarushima makes a great spot for picnics and barbecues in the summer months.

Omiyage shop

Senbei

Island Hopping

Travellers to the Izu Islands (p.183) should check out Tokyo's little-known third airport. Located in west Tokyo, Chōfū Airport (serviced by New Central Airlines, www.central-air.co.jp) is the only service provider offering flights to these islands, sometimes on planes so small that one person gets to sit up front with the pilot. It's great fun for those who like flying, but terrifying for those who don't.

Weekend Breaks

Japan's high-speed trains and comprehensive air links put much of the country within easy reach when planning a weekend away. With options ranging from a challenging assault on Mount Fuji, to a relaxing soak in a hot-spring bath in Kusatsu, there is something to satisfy everyone. All the options listed can be reached in fewer than four hours by train, or one hour by plane. All offer accommodation options to satisfy every budget, from thrifty to extravagant.

Hakone

Although doable as a day trip, Hakone's many attractions are better appreciated as a leisurely weekend away. Begin by taking the Odakyū Line to Odawara station, just 70 minutes from Shinjuku station. From there your journey continues at a much more sedate pace on the Hakone Tozan line, but there's no need to be frustrated by the decline in speed. Zigzagging its way ever higher into the mountains, the Hakone Tozan line is a breathtaking ride, and really the first of many attractions. The train also delivers you to a variety of other attractions, including the excellent Hakone Open-Air Museum (see table) a world-class sculpture collection that benefits from its picturesque setting on the slopes of a wooded ravine. Continue on to savour some of Hakone's natural marvels, including the bubbling volcanic mud of Owakudani – literally the 'great boiling valley' – and serene Lake Ashi, famous as one of the best spots for an inspiring view of Mount Fuji (if the weather cooperates). End your day with a stay at one of the area's many *minshuku* and *ryokan* traditional inns, many of which feature *onsen* (natural hot-spring baths), or at the Hakone Fujiya, famous as Japan's first western-style hotel. Anyone planning to visit Hakone should get a Hakone Freepass, available from any Odakyū Line station, which covers return rail travel from Tokyo to Hakone, and two or three days unlimited use of public transport in the Hakone area, including cable cars.

Hakone

Fujiya Hotel	359 Miyanoshita, Hakone-machi, Kanagawa	0460 82 2211	www.fujiyahotel.jp	Deluxe hotel
Hakone Lake Hotel	Kojiri Tōgendai, Hakone-machi, Kanagawa	0460 84 7611	www.hakone-lakehotel.com	Budget hotel
Hakone Open Air Museum	Ninotaira, Hakone-machi, Kanagawa	0460 82 1161	www.hakone-oam.or.jp	Attraction
POLA Museum of Art	1285 Kozukayama, Sengokuhara, Hakone-machi, Ashigarashimo-gun, Kanagawa	0460 84 2111	www.polamuseum.or.jp	Attraction

Nikko

If you want to mix natural and cultural wonders, head to Nikko. This area is most famous as the home of Tōshōgū – the sprawling mausoleum complex that houses the remains of legendary *shogun* Tokugawa Ieyasu. A trip to this historic site is a must, and a viable alternative to the usual Kyoto pilgrimage. That's not all that Nikko has to offer; catch a bus up the winding mountain roads to see the lofty Kegon waterfalls, then continue on to explore the shores of Lake Chūzenji and the

Pull A Sicky & Explore

While it might be tricky to get a few weekdays off, Nikko is well worth calling in sick for. It's busy as a beehive on the weekends, even in the bone-chilling winter months. Taking in the sights on a Tuesday or Wednesday will give you the opportunity to keep away from the maddening crowds and appreciate Nikko in splendid isolation.

wetlands of the Oze National Park. Nikko can be reached in about two hours from Shinjuku station. A car is useful for exploring the countryside, but there are buses to all main sites.

Nikko

Senhime Monogatari Inn	Yasukawa-chō 6-48, Nikko, Tochigi	0288 54 1010	www.senhime.co.jp	Mid-range hotel
Tōshōgū	2301 Yamauchi Nikko-shi, Tochigi	0288 54 0560	www.toshogu.jp	Attraction

Kyoto & Nara

If there is one weekend away that is almost obligatory, it is a trip to Kyoto and its neighbour, Nara. Both are former capital cities and both are a treasure trove of historical sites and old-world flavour. Begin by catching the *shinkansen* to Kyoto (about two and a half hours from Tokyo or Shinagawa stations). There you can make your way round the city's numerous sites, including the Golden Pavilion and Kiyomizudera temple, several of the most famous Japanese rock gardens, and the Gion area, home to the city's famous *geishas*.

To maintain the period flavour, spend the night at a traditional Japanese inn, before heading to Nara the following day. There you will find more historical sites, including Tōdai-ji – reputedly the biggest wooden building in the world, and home to a huge and imposing statue of Buddha. If all this culture leaves you in need of something different, Kyoto and Nara can offer that too. In the summer try the popular half-day hike from Kurama to Kibune, just outside Kyoto, ending your day with lunch at one of the many alfresco restaurants set up on platforms over a babbling river. Kyoto and Nara can be easily explored on foot or with public transport.

Kiyomizudera

Shopping for souvenirs

Kyoto & Nara

Budget Inn	295 Aburanokoji-chō, Shimogyō-ku, Kyoto	0753 44 1510	www.budgetinnjp.com	Budget hotel
Kinkaku-ji	1 Kinkaku-ji-chō Kita-ku, Kyoto	0754 61 0013	www.shokoku-ji.or.jp	Temple
Kiyomizu-dera	1-294 Kiyomizu, Higashiyama-ku, Kyoto	0755 51 1234	www.kiyomizudera.or.jp	Temple
Kyoto Hotel Okura	Kawaramachi-Ōike, Nakagyō-ku, Kyoto	0752 11 5111	http://kyoto.okura.com	Deluxe hotel
Hotel Fujita Nara	47-1 Shimosanjō-chō, Nara	0742 23 8111	www.fujita-nara.com	Mid-range hotel
Tōdai-ji	406-1 Zōshi-chō, Nara-shi, Nara	0742 22 5511	www.todaiji.or.jp	Temple

Fuji Off-Peak
Some of the accommodation huts on Mount Fuji are open just before and after the July to August climbing season. Climb at these times and you can avoid the crowds, but you may also face tougher conditions at the summit (snow and ice are possible). Always prepare your trip thoroughly.

Mount Fuji

Gruelling, but very much a must-do, is a climb to the top of Mount Fuji. The official climbing season is July and August, and the standard way to make the ascent is overnight. Stay at one of the huts along the trails, and then get up while it's still dark to reach the summit in time to see the dawn. It is a great experience, and perfectly doable for anyone who is reasonably fit, but it's not to be taken too lightly. At 3,776 metres, Fuji is a proper mountain, not a hill. Some climbers may feel the effects of the altitude, and conditions at the summit can be freezing cold and very stormy, even on the balmiest of summer days. Make sure to bring clothing for hot, cold and rainy conditions. It must also be said that climbing Fuji is not the zen-like, contemplative experience that you might imagine. Make the ascent in season and there will likely be a riotous jam of people all the way up the mountain. The carnival atmosphere is part of the experience, however, and does nothing to detract from the genuinely breathtaking views. Get to the top and you may not be on top of the world, but you are certainly at the top of Japan. There are various possible routes to the top, but the most popular option from Tokyo is to approach from the Fuji Five Lakes area. The nearest station is Kawaguchiko on the Fujikyūko Line (about two hours from Shinjuku), from where buses will take you to the Fifth Station, about 1,500 metres below the summit. The usual climbing time from this point is about five to seven hours, and then three to five hours coming down. Accommodation huts are mainly clustered around the seventh and eighth, not far short of the summit.

Mount Fuji

Fuji Lake Hotel	1 Funatsu, Fujikawaguchiko-machi, Minamitsuru-gun, Yamanashi	0555 72 2209	www.fujilake.co.jp	Mid-range hotel
Hinode-kan	Mt Fuji 7th Station, Kamiyoshida, Fujiyoshida-shi, Yamanashi	0555 24 6522	www10.plala.or.jp/hinodekan	Budget hotel

Izu Islands

Not far from the metropolis, but a world away in terms of atmosphere and pace of life, are the Izu Islands. Stretching from the mouth of Tokyo Bay, these dots of land are a popular destination for short breaks, particularly in the summer, when the decent beaches offer pleasant swimming, surfing and windsurfing. Nearest, biggest and easiest to get to is Ōshima. It offers a variety of attractions, including an interesting hike up Mount Mihara – an active but currently unthreatening volcano. Out beyond Ōshima is Niijima – known as a party island for teens and twenty-somethings in

Onsen

Onsen Etiquette
*Japanese baths are
for relaxing in, not
washing. When visiting
onsen (p.264), first
wash thoroughly at the
showers set beside or
around the bath. Only
when you're sparkling
clean is it time to slip
into the soothing hot-
spring waters.*

summer. Whichever island
you pick, there are various
accommodation options,
ranging from campsites to
small inns and resort hotels.
The islands can be reached
from Tokyo by ferry, jetfoil or
plane (the latter option takes
just minutes). Though they are
mainly known as a summer
destination, try an out-of-
season visit if you really want
to get away from it all. Some
hotels may be shut, but you
will likely have your island all
to yourself. Ōshima Island is
big enough to make renting
a car necessary to thoroughly
explore it. On smaller Niijima,
rent a bicycle instead.

Izu Islands

Oshima Onsen Hotel	3-5 Aza-Kizumiba, Senzu, Ōshima-machi, Ōshima	049 922 1673	www.oshima-onsen.co.jp	Mid-range hotel
Niijima Grand Hotel	371 Yamatsu Yamakawa, Niijima-mura	049 925 1661	www15.ocn.ne.jp/~nghotel	Mid-range hotel

Kusatsu

No stay in Japan is complete without experiencing the country's volcanic hot-spring
baths. Known as *onsen* (p.264), and varying in temperature from soothing to scorching,
this is an experience you can get without leaving Tokyo – try Oedo Onsen Monogatari
in Odaiba (see p.265), but it's much more pleasant to head to one of the hot-spring
resorts. Kusatsu Onsen is reputedly the biggest hot spring in Japan in terms of the
quantity of water gushing forth. It can be reached in just under three hours from Tokyo
using a combination of bus and train, setting out from Ueno station. There are also
direct buses from Shinjuku, taking exactly four hours.

The town offers endless accommodation options at all price levels and it's hard to
beat when it comes to bathing. The highlight is the town's *rotemburo*, or outdoor
onsen. It claims to be the largest in Japan, and is now a more pleasant experience
than before with changing rooms and other facilities all refurbished in 2007. Be
warned: Kusatsu's *onsen* are famously among Japan's hottest. Other attractions of
the area include the beautiful Mount Shirane volcano, atop which sits a crater lake of
uncanny blueness, and a range of other mountains linked by hiking trails. The Kusatsu
area can be explored using a network of bus services, but renting a car will make life
a lot easier.

Kusatsu

Koizumikan Ryokan	379 Kusatsumachi, Agatsuma-gun, Gunma	027 988 2068	na	Mid-range hotel
Osakaya Ryokan	356 Kusatsumachi, Agatsuma-gun, Gunma	027 988 2411	www.osakaya.info	Deluxe hotel

Fashion Boutiques p.123
Financial Advisors p.95

Written by residents, the Shanghai Explorer
is packed with insider info, from arriving
in the city to making it your home and
everything in between.

Shanghai Explorer Residents' Guide
We Know Where You Live

Holidays From Tokyo

When you feel the need for a proper holiday, Japan offers a wealth of options – though it must be said that it isn't as conveniently located as Asian rivals such as Hong Kong and Singapore. Where those cities sit no more than two to three hours' flying time from popular tourist destinations, for Tokyo the flight times are likely to be at least four hours. That said, the country still makes a great base for exploring East Asia and the Pacific.

Flight time: *2.5 hours*
Time Difference: *0*
Best time to visit:
Year round

Okinawa

Okinawa is part of Japan, but doesn't always feel like it. Occupied by US forces until 1972, it retains an American flavour, with many foreigner-friendly bars, restaurants and shops. That's part of the appeal for Americans in search of home comforts, but most people go for the beaches, and Okinawa offers numerous sun and swim options. Temperatures are cooler from November to March, but still pleasant. Cheap packages are available for most of the year, except during the peak holiday season of July and August. Further south, islands such as Ishigaki-jima and Iriomote-jima offer a real back-to-nature feel with superb natural beaches, hikes in the jungle and great diving.

Flight time: *3.5 hours*
Time Difference: *+1*
Best time to visit:
November to August

Guam & Saipan

In contrast to Okinawa, the islands of Guam and Saipan are independent, but feel almost like part of Japan. Both were occupied by the Japanese during the second world war and are now informally occupied by hordes of Japanese tourists. They offer similar attractions to Okinawa, including good beaches and great snorkelling, but feel more like a getaway. Head to small outlying islands such as Tinian and Rota for some real peace and quiet. Cheap packages are available. Temperatures are pleasant year round, but typhoons and heavy rain can be a problem in September and October.

Flight time: *6.5 hours*
Time Difference: *-19*
Best time to visit:
Year round

Hawaii

The closest outpost of America proper, and a hugely popular destination, Hawaii's attractions are almost too numerous to list. It's got beaches, hiking, food, nightlife, sports and outdoors activities. The islands have something for everyone, whether it's to party, play or chill out. The weather is good year round, and the time difference is so huge that it actually isn't too problematic – just subtract a whole day when you head out there. Packages are available year round, but are expensive compared to south-east Asia.

Flight time: *7 hours*
Time Difference: *-2*
Best time to visit:
November to June

Thailand

Perhaps the most popular destination for package trips, Thailand offers something for every budget and taste, from backpacking to five-star hedonism and sun seekers to culture vultures. Try the beaches in Phuket and Ko Samui for sea and sand, head to mountainous Chiang Mai for a cultural retreat or sample the chaos, colour and intensity of Bangkok. The 2006 military coup and ensuing political uncertainty haven't affected tourism at all, but some areas in the south of the country have seen ethnic unrest so check with your embassy before going.

Flight time: *7.5 hours*
Time Difference: *-1*
Best time to visit:
Year round

Malaysia

Overshadowed by Thailand as a tourist destination, Malaysia actually has a lot to offer. It's certainly among the best places in Asia if spotting wildlife is on your list of things to do. The snorkelling is first-rate, and the Borneo half of the country offers the chance to see Orangutans in the wild, and watch turtles come ashore to lay eggs. Malaysia is also among the more developed and most hassle-free of south-east Asian nations, with less of the constant harassment that can be a problem for tourists in some other countries.

Indonesia

Flight time: 8 hours
Time Difference: -2 to 0
Best time to visit:
Year round

Another of Asia's great beach destinations, there's no doubting the number one draw: Bali. Now fully recovered from the terrorist bombings of 2002, Bali once again draws huge numbers of tourists with a mix of cheap, moderate and deluxe accommodation options. Scenery and food is a match for anywhere in Asia but some parts of the country have been experiencing unrest so check with your embassy before travelling.

Vietnam

Flight time: 6.5 hours
Time Difference: -2
Best time to visit:
Year round

Still in the process of opening up to the world, Vietnam boasts some of Asia's most beautiful landscapes, from the misty mountain forests of the interior to the patchwork quilt of rice paddies along the coast. Wherever you go, the food will likely be great. There are beaches to compete with any other destination and weather is good most of the year, though typhoons can be a problem from July to November.

Cambodia

Flight time: 10 hours
Time Difference: -2
Best time to visit:
October to March

The lack of direct flights from Tokyo makes this one a long haul, but it's worth it for the majesty of Angkor Wat. Surpassing the hype, the jungle temples of Angkor are Asia's answer to Machu Picchu or the pyramids. The temples are a short flight from the capital, Phnom Penh, but the adventurous can get there on a fast riverboat up the Tonle Sap. The legacy of the Vietnam War means landmines can still be a problem. Stick to the well-trodden paths, particularly in remote areas.

China

Flight time:
3 to 6 hours
Time Difference: -1
Best time to visit:
March to October

It's impossible to summarise the myriad attractions of a country as vast as China, but the most popular starting points for Tokyo-based travellers are Beijing and Shanghai. The former offers the country's key historical sites – not least the Great Wall and the Forbidden Palace – while the latter is the place to go for a glimpse of modern China as it transforms from poor to rich at breakneck speed. Also popular is Hong Kong, with its beguiling mix of western and Chinese ways.

Australia

Flight time:
7.5 to 10 hours
Time Difference: -1 to +1
Best time to visit:
Year round

Though it's a long flight from Tokyo to anywhere in Australia, the insignificant time difference makes it an easy and popular destination. Sydney tops the list, with its appealing mix of city and sea, but Oz offers a host of alternatives. Visit Uluru (Ayers Rock), explore the jungles of the northern coast, or go diving over the Great Barrier Reef. The weather is generally good year round, though some people will find the midsummer months (December to February) unbearably hot.

Travel Agencies

A'cross Travellers Bureau	03 5795 4727	www.across-travel.com
Hankyu Kotsusha	03 3798 2424	www.hankyu-travel.com
HIS	03 5360 4821	www.his-j.com
JALPAK	03 5520 0550	www.jalpak.co.jp
JTB	0570 019 489	www.jtb.co.jp
Kinki Nippon Tourist	03 6731 1711	www.knt.co.jp
Map Tour	03 3340 6745	www.maptour.co.jp
Nippon Travel Agency	03 3614 3066	www.nta.co.jp
No. 1 Travel	03 3205 6073	www.no1-travel.com
Yomiuri Travel Service	03 5550 0666	www.yomiuri-ryokou.co.jp

Activities

Activities

Further Out ◀

The geography of the Kanto Plains offers plenty of destinations for hiking (p.223), watersports (p.246) and world-class skiing and snowboarding (p.240), just a few hours from the city centre. To meet like-minded people you can head for the hills with at the weekend, see Socially Active on p.242.

Sports & Activities

Most primary school students in Japan are required to select one sports team or club to join. For many, the chosen activity becomes a lifelong hobby. This extracurricular requirement has created a society of people who are passionate about their pastime, and there are many opportunities for others to get out there and join them.

The government does its part by maintaining and subsidising numerous municipal sports centres, outfitted with indoor and outdoor facilities for everything from swimming to sumo. Private gyms and athletics complexes also abound, but costs vary widely depending on activity, area and level of comfort or exclusivity.

While the economic downturn following the burst of the bubble took its toll on Japan's astronomically priced golf courses, long-running upscale establishments like Tokyo American Club (p.254), Yokohama Athletic & Country Club (p.255) and the Tokyo Lawn Tennis Club (p.254) are still prospering. However, organisations like Tokyo Gaijins (www.tokyogaijins.com) put together frequent inexpensive group excursions, while magazines like *Outdoor Japan* (www.outdoorjapan.com), *Metropolis* (www.metropolis.co.jp) and online *Fitness Japan* (www.fitnessjp.com) are great sources of information and help locals with shared interests to link up.

Japan as a nation loves baseball and football, as well as the more traditional pastimes such as martial arts, sumo and flower arranging, meaning there will always be chances to partake in or simply enjoy these cultural mainstays. But today, you are just as likely to meet an avid wakeboarder, ice-hockey player or salsa dancer.

Sports and activities can, for the most part, be enjoyed year-round in Japan. There are five distinct seasons: dry winters, pleasant springs and autumns, humid summers and a rainy season in June and July. The urban jungle is outfitted with multiple fields, rinks,

Activity Finder

swimming pools, courts and arenas, and if the local climate or terrain is less than ideal for your chosen sport (such as for stillwater fishing or rock climbing), it is common to find indoor alternatives.

Aerobics & Fitness Classes

Japan is enjoying a fitness craze, and you'll have no problem finding places to achieve those New Year resolutions. Most of the city's gyms and fitness centres (p.252) offer classes (usually for members only) in everything from tai chi to jazz dance and hip-hop. Contact the relevant club for membership fees and for information on how to join. For budding teachers keen to pass on their knowledge and passion for sport, Tokyo College of Sports and Recreation (03 5696 9090, www.tsr.ac.jp) offers a range of courses in many disciplines, including judo, tennis, swimming, athletics and child sports and nursery teaching.

Aerobics & Fitness Classes

Aerosports	Shinjuku-ku	03 3352 2800	www.aerosports.co.jp	basic, workout, shape up, sports, relaxation, tai chi
Central Fitness Club	Aoyama	03 5468 1191	www.central.co.jp	yoga, qigong, tai chi, stretch, relaxation, pilates, core training, street, jazz and latin dance
The Premier Club	Toranomon	03 5472 0055	www.central.co.jp	yoga, qigong, tai chi, relaxation, pilates, core training, hip-hop and jazz dance, aerobics
Tipness Roppongi	Roppongi	03 5474 3531	http://tip.tipness.co.jp	aerobics, yoga, kickboxing, aqua training
Work Out World	Akasaka	03 5510 4001	www.wowd.jp	kickboxing, hip-hop and jazz dance, tai chi, yoga

American Football

American football was brought to Japan in 1934 by an American teacher, Paul Rusch, who initially put together three college teams. It was not until 1971, however, that the X-League was founded. Today, players can join the Urban Football League and the Japan Private Football Federation.

Various Locations

Japan Private Football Federation

http://jpff.sakura.ne.jp

The Japan Private Football Federation comprises dozens of teams in different divisions across Japan. The majority of players are Japanese, but a few western expats turn out too. See the website (Japanese only) for links to individual teams, many of which are seeking new players.

Various Locations

Urban Football League

www.edogawa-sports.jp/americanfootball

Founded in 1991, this League is not as well known or supported as the JPFF, and has only nine teams. But, that does mean that you can enter a new team of your own. Since it is sponsored by, and based in Edogawa-ku, it is also called the Edogawa League.

Various Locations

X-League

www.xleague.com

The X-League is semi-professional, with teams funded by corporate sponsors. Each is allowed a maximum of four foreign players, and a work visa is necessary to join. Officially, no compensation is offered, but some teams provide free gym membership (valued at about ¥10,000 per month), and a small cash bonus for touchdowns or interceptions. The final game of the season is the Japan X Bowl in Tokyo Dome, and the winner goes on to play the nation's top college team in the Rice Bowl.

Archery

Asahi Archery

3-23-3 Minami-Ōtsuka
Toshima-ku
Ōtsuka
Map 4 A1 **1**

03 3986 2301 | www.asahi-archery.co.jp

Asahi Archery sells equipment for both western (*yōkyū*) and Japanese (*kyūdō*) styles of archery. For the western style, you can choose from compound and recurve bows from brands such as Eastern and Hoyt. The selection of gear includes custom fibreglass, carbon fibre and bamboo bows, accessories, books and DVDs. Arrows for both styles are also sold, and credit cards are accepted.

Edogawa Archery

8-5-10 Minami-Koiwa
Edogawa-ku
Map 2 C4

03 3657 2086 | www26.tok2.com/home/edoarch

Edogawa is an indoor, 12 metre range for western style shooting, just five minutes on foot from Koiwa station on the Sōbu line. Beginners are welcome, and the cost of ¥200 for 12 arrows includes bow rental. Call for details about monthly seminars for higher level shooters. Closed on Thursdays.

Komazawa Olympic Park

1-1 Komazawa Kōen
Setagaya-ku
Komazawa Daigaku
Map 5 C4 **2**

03 3421 6199 | www.tef.or.jp/kopgp/guide/kyudo.html

The Kyūdō Center within Komazawa Olympic Park in Setagaya has seven 28m lanes, changing rooms and free showers. It costs ¥315 for two hours and ¥170 for each additional hour, and roughly half that for children. While no lessons or rentals are offered, the staff maintain a list of local instructors looking for students. It's closed on the first and third Monday of every month.

Art Classes

Other options **Art & Craft Supplies** p.276, **Art Galleries** p.170

Right Brain Research

3-1-23 Moto-Azabu
Minato-ku
Roppongi
Map 11 B3 **3**

03 5770 7401 | www.rbr-art.com

When Dr Betty Edwards released the film *Drawing on the Right Side of the Brain*, she instilled millions of people with the belief that they could draw. Roppongi's Right Brain Research (RBR), New Center for Creative Arts, follows her principles, and offers monthly, five-day seminars (¥95,000) to help people develop their artisitc skills. RBR also hosts three-day acrylic and oil workshops (¥31,500 plus materials) roughly every month.

Badminton

Though less popular than in other parts of Asia, badminton is still widely played. Municipal gyms with indoor courts usually dedicate certain times or zones to badminton nets, and will often lend rackets and shuttlecocks at no extra charge. Several foreigner-friendly clubs get together regularly around town.

Akasaka Badminton Club

4-18-3 Akasaka
Minato-ku
Akasaka-mitsuke
Map 10 B4 **4**

03 5413 2717 | akabado@gmail.com

This club meets every month at the Akasaka Community Plaza on Aoyama Dōri, next to Akasaka Police Station. The fee is ¥300 to ¥500, depending on how many players show up. The club provides feather shuttlecocks, and has a few racquets that it can loan out. Afterwards, players tend to go out for drinks. Occasionally, the ING Badminton Club, which uses the same courts, announces sessions in its monthly newsletter. Email the ING club to be added to the mailing list.

Albatross Badminton Club

3-1-19 Shibaura
Minato-ku
Tamachi
Map 11 E2 **5**

03 3452 4151 | mune2006@hotmail.co.jp

The Albatross Badminton Club usually meets on Friday evenings or on Saturdays at the Minato City Sports Center, near Tamachi station on the Yamanote line. The turnout is generally low, but with enough people to get a few games going, and most players are of an intermediate level. The only costs are the price of using the gym. For those living in the area, the fees are ¥300 for adults, and ¥100 for children. For resident's of other wards, gym use costs ¥700.

Tokyo Badminton Club

Various Locations

http://bad80.hp.infoseek.co.jp

The badminton club meets in school gyms around Setagaya-ku at weekends and on public holidays. The skill levels of this international group range from beginner to advanced, and players can get coaching or draw straws to play pick-up doubles. The organiser requests that players do not wear strong perfumes or colognes or discuss work matters. The cost per session is ¥500 to ¥1,000. Members usually go out to dinner together afterwards.

Baseball

While baseball is Japan's most popular spectator sport, there are not many opportunities for the average Joe to join a team and play on a regular basis. Fortunately, though, children can get a few swings in at places such as the Honmura Club. This is an international team of primary school children

Baseball			
Jingu Gaien	Sendagaya	03 3478 6800	www.meijijingugaien.jp
Kōrakuen Virtual Sports Plaza	Bunkyō-ku	03 3817 6199	www.locomo.co.jp
Leisureland Palette Town	Koto-ku	03 3570 5657	www.leisureland.co.jp

that play at the diamond in Arisugawa Kōen in Hirō. To find out more about practice times and how to join, you can email honmuraclub@mac.com. Otherwise, there are a few batting cages scattered throughout the city (see table). To see some of the local teams in action, try visiting the Yoyogi Oyama Kōen baseball fields in Shibuya-ku (2-53-1 Nishihara, 03 3466 7229) or Sogo Recreation Park in Edogawa-ku (7 Nishi-Kasai to 4 Minami-Kasai, 03 3675 5030).

Tokyo Dome

Basketball

2-17 Kamata
Setagaya-ku
🚇 **Kasai Rinkai**
Map 2 A3

American Basketball Club

090 3062 7379 | sabatokyo@hotmail.com

The American Basketball Club was actually founded by an Aussie, Sam Arnold, in the 1990s. Sunday games take place at You Port Setagaya Rec Center (see p.253). The club charges an initial ¥2,000 sign-up fee, and ¥2,000 per game thereafter. Teams are divided into North American and international squads. Detailed statistics are recorded, and an MVP (Most Valuable Player) is announced at the end of the year. Sam also runs a tennis academy (www.geocities.com/satatokyo) using the same facility.

2-17 Kamata
Setagaya-ku
🚇 **Kasai Rinkai**
Map 2 A3

Fred Fishman

080 5464 0242

At the last count, Fred Fishman had close to 500 prospective players on his basketball mailing list, so when he announces a get-together, the 20 or so spots fill up quickly. Indoor five-a-side games take place at You Port Setagaya Rec Center (see p.253). Games are quite competitive and cost ¥1,000 per person.

Various Locations

Tokyo Gaijins

03 3224 1257 | www.tokyogaijins.com/basketball

This club claims to be the largest basketball club in Tokyo, and it organises hundreds of group trips and sporting events each year. Players of all skills and levels are welcome. Games are usually held at the Minato-ku Labor and Welfare Hall (*Kinrō Fukushi Kaikan*) in Mita, but are also occasionally held at the nearby Minato-ku Sports Center or the Akasaka Community Plaza (see p.255). Visit the website or email for more information or to join the mailing list.

Birdwatching

Other options **Environmental Groups** p.219

Beyond the skyscrapers, Tokyo has a few spots to temp twitchers. Indigenous species include orioles, cormorants, herons, wagtails, sandpipers, turtle doves and woodpeckers. There are also seasonal inhabitants, like mockingbirds (November to April), plovers (April to September) and kingfishers (September to December). To see the most symbolic bird in Japan (the rare red-crowned crane) in its natural habitat, head to the northern island of Hokkaidō. For tips about birdwatching in the Tokyo area, contact the Wild Bird Society of Japan (03 5436 2620, www.wbsj.org).

6-2-1 Rinkai-chō
Edogawa-ku
🚇 **Kasai Rinkai**
Map 2 C2

Kasai Rinkai

03 5696 1331 | www.tokyo-park.or.jp

You can reach Kasai Rinkai by foot from the train station of the same name on the Keiyo line, which departs from Tokyo station. It is also accessible by car, or by boat from Hinode Pier (50 min) or Ryōgoku (80 min). A third of the park is a bird sanctuary (*chōruien*) so you can get your ornithology fix by walking the footpath or from the observation deck. Entrance to the park, which also boasts a large Ferris wheel, is free.

3-1 Tōkai
Ōta-ku
🚇 **Ryutsu Center**
Map 2 B3

Tokyo-ko Yacho Kōen

03 3799 5031 | www.wbsj.org/sanctuary/tokyoko

The Tokyo-ko Yacho Kōen wild bird park is a 15 minute walk from Ryutsu Center station on the Tokyo Monorail. It is also accessible by bus from Shinagawa or Ōmori stations, or by car (free parking). The 25 hectare grounds include wooded areas, marshland, tall grasses and three lakes. There are several viewing areas, as well as a nature centre. The

Ku, Shi, Cho
To help you locate places more easily, it's good to know that ku means ward. Within these ku are cho (neighbourhoods), shi are cities (outside Tokyo) and ken is the Japanese word for prefecture. An exception is Tokyo prefecture, which is known as Tokyo-to, because it is the capital.

park also boasts a high-resolution camera that streams live video and can be controlled remotely (www.birdfan.net) by anyone wanting to eavesdrop on the natural goings on from their cubicle.

Board Games

While there is an active Japan Monopoly Association (monopoly_japan@yahoo.co.jp for details), the most popular board games in Tokyo are usually of the home-brewed variety, including *go* (or *igo*), *shōgi* and *mahjong*. Loyal followers gather weekly in parlours around the city to play.

The game *go* came to Japan from China and has a rich history, and when Tokugawa unified Japan in 1603 he even appointed a 'Minister of *Go*'. There are various schools and styles, including 'speed *go*' and two-on-two games where turns alternate and no communication is permitted. New strategies can be gleaned from newspapers (see Newspapers & Magazines on p.40) and from TV. The Nihon Ki-in (Japan *Go* Association) world headquarters is in Tokyo (www.nihonkiin.or.jp, 03 3288 8727) and enthusiasts flock to the non-descript building in Chiyoda and pay ¥1,000 to play all day. The foreign *go* community has an unofficial headquarters in Ben's Cafe (see p.358). Each Sunday, players gather at around noon to engage in friendly tabletop battle.

Shogi is another popular game. It is often compared to chess, as the objective is to capture the opposing king. There are also bishops, knights and pawns, though they of course have Japanese names. *Shōgi* has recently become popular among a slightly younger crowd. Contact the Japan Shogi Association in Sendagaya at info@shogi.or.jp for a list of parlours in your neighbourhood.

The first *mahjong* world championship was held in Tokyo in 2002, and won by a Japanese woman. Like *go*, the game was developed in China. It was first introduced to the west by Abercrombie & Fitch in 1920. Today, games in Tokyo often involve gambling, and there are hundreds of places to play. To find one, simply keep an eye out for the *kanji* characters (麻雀).

Bowling

Other options **Sports Centres** p.253, **Sports Clubs** p.253, **Country Clubs** p.255

While bowling elsewhere is associated with out-of-shape, balding men in monogrammed team jackets, Tokyo has sexed things up a bit, with DJ booths, low lighting and centres open till the early hours. So don your finest threads, hop off the train at any major stop on the Yamanote line, listen for the sounds of pins crashing over thumping bass lines, and get ready for a long night of drunken strikes.

Bowling			
Brunswick Sports Garden	1-30-1 Higashi-Ikebukuro	Toshima-ku	03 3988 7221
Citizen Plaza	4-29-27 Takadanobaba	Shinjuku-ku	03 3363 2215
EST	1-14-14 Shibuya	Shibuya-ku	03 3409 4721
Leisure Land Palette Town	1 Aomi	Koto-ku	03 3570 5656
The Prince Park Tower Tokyo	4-8-1 Shiba-Kōen	Minato-ku	03 5400 1159

Boxing

Hirose Bldg
2832 Noborito
Tama-ku
🚉 **Mukōgaoka**
Map 2 A3

Nitta Boxing Gym

044 932 4639 | www.nittagym.com

The president of Nitta Boxing Gym, Shosei Nitta, is quick with a smile and a friendly English greeting. He welcomes men and women of all ages to his gym, which is five minutes from Mukōgaoka station on the Odakyū line. The website proudly displays a photo gallery of members from the US, Australia, England, Nigeria, France and Korea. Several pro boxers train at the relatively tiny gym, which has five sand bags and a 4 x 4 metre ring. There are several training courses, ranging from Shape Up and Weight Down to the Professional Boxer and Champion course. The joining fee is ¥18,000 (or ¥9,000 for family of existing members), and monthly dues are ¥12,000. Less frequent visitors can buy five tickets (valid for six months) for ¥12,000. There are ladies only sessions from Monday to Thursday from 10:00 to 11:00.

Ozaki Boxing Gym

5-42-8 Yoyogi
Shibuya-ku
🚇 *Sangūbashi*
Map 8 A1 6

03 3465 5599 | www.oz-gym.com

The guys in this gym, set in the quiet backstreets near Sangūbashi station, really know their workouts. Even first-timers on the ¥1,500 trial day are not spared the routine of stretching, skipping, hitting the sandbag and sparring in the ring for a few friendly rounds. Thankfully, the instructors don't hit back – unless you want them to. The deafening noise from passing trains on the Odakyū line which runs alongside the gym every two or three minutes adds to the experience. There are well thought-out training courses for all levels of skill and fitness. To join costs ¥15,740 and monthly dues are ¥12,600 for men, ¥10,500 for women and young adults, and ¥7,350 for those in their early teens or younger.

Roppongi Fight Club

Torikatsu Bldg
5-2-4 Roppongi
Minato-ku
🚇 *Roppongi*
Map 11 B2 7

03 3408 2039 | http://roppongifightclub.fc2web.com

In a small, wood-floored space on the sixth floor of a building (above the ¥100 shop) on bustling Gaien Higashi Dōri, Roppongi Fight Club seems to rise above the alcohol-fuelled fray down below. RFC focuses on boxing and fitness, offering classes for both men and women. Equipment and facilities include a ring, punching bags, speed bags, Stairmaster, exercise bike, weights and a wall-length mirror. Fees are ¥12,000 for men and ¥8,000 for women. There's an ¥18,000 one-time membership fee, but if you print out the coupon on the website you'll get a discount.

Camping

Other options **Outdoor Goods** p.295, **Campsites** p.30

City folk in desperate need of a night under the stars are surprisingly well served in the Tokyo area. With good facilities and a steady flow of people, it might be a stretch to call the campsites found in western Tokyo and Saitama 'wilderness,' but a visit out this way will get you briefly back to Mother Nature. For more rustic, leafy green campsites in other parts of the country, visit the CampJo website (www.campjo.com – in Japanese only), which allows users to search by area and specific features. Outdoor Japan also has a useful website in English (www.outdoorjapan.com). Most campsites sell everything you could possibly need, including basics such as food, drinks and firewood.

Hikawa Campground

702 Hikawa,
Okutama-machi
Western Tokyo

0428 83 2134 | www.okutamas.co.jp/hikawa/index_hi.html

Hikawa offers a breath of fresh air just three minutes from Okutama station, the terminus of the scenic Ōme train line. In addition to camping sites along the rocky banks of the Hikawagawa, there are log cabins that cost between ¥5,000 and ¥70,000 (for up to 35 people) per night. During the day, families can enjoy barbecues and swimming, while at night the sparklers and beer keep the mood festive. Reservations are required, and must be made well in advance as this is probably the most popular campsite in the Tokyo area. If Hikawa is fully booked, try the equally scenic America Camp Village (www.t-net.ne.jp/~amecamp), just a few kilometres downstream.

Nagatoro Camp

Oaza Ido
Nagatoro-machi
Saitama-ken
Map 2 A1

0494 66 0640 | www.nagatoro-camp.com
There are two riverside campsites at Nagatoro in Saitama, one for tents and one for 4WDs and caravans. Both are less than two hours from Tokyo. To get there by train, take the Takasaki line from Ueno to Kumagaya, and then hop on the Chichibu line to Nogami. Once you're there, activities include swimming, fishing, canoeing and hiking. For those happy to dispense with the tent ordeal, the sites offer Spartan bungalows and cabins for ¥4,000 to ¥25,000 per night. The sites are closed in the winter, usually from mid-December to mid-March. Call or visit the website to make reservations.

Canyoning

Other options **Hiking** p.223

Canyoning with Evergreen (below)

Canyons Outdoor Adventure Experiences

Various Locations

0278 72 2811 | www.canyons.com
Canyons Outdoor Adventure Experiences offers guided excursions to sites in Gunma and Nagano. The staff have scouted some of Japan's best natural water slides and falls, and lead safe but fun tours from April to mid-October. The cost is ¥8,000 to ¥9,000 for a half-day (two to three hours) of shooting rapids, or ¥12,000 to ¥16,000 for a full day including lunch. The group also runs canoeing, kayaking and caving adventures in the warmer months, and skiing and snowboarding trips when the snow starts to fall. Visit the website or email info@canyons.jp for more.

Paddling Up The Gawa

For further information about paddling in and around the Tokyo area, contact the Japan Canoe Federation (www.canoe.or.jp; info@canoe.or.jp). Evergreen (see below) also offer canoeing and kayaking trips in the summer.

Climbing

Unless you plan on attaching suction cups to your hands and becoming Spider-Man, Tokyo has few fresh air options for climbers. There are, however, several indoor gyms with walls, outcroppings and overhangs suited to varying skill levels. These include Pump (www.pump-climbing.com), in Ogikubo, Kawasaki and Yokohama, and T-Wall (www.nona.dti.ne.jp/~t-wall), in Kinshicho and Edogawa. But for the real deal, there are mountains just a few hours away. One of the most popular destinations is Mount Ogawa, on the border of Nagano and Yamanashi in Chichibu Tama Kai National Park, which is easily accessed by car. Further afield are the Three Peaks of Hakuba in Nagano. Tours can be arranged by the Evergreen Outdoor Centre (below). For further information, fax the Japan Free Climbing Association (04 4945 2476, http://homepage2.nifty.com/jfa).

Evergreen Outdoor Center

4683-2 Happo
Hakuba
Nagano-ken
Map 1 B3

0261 72 5150 | www.evergreen-hakuba.com
This is a gateway to all manner of rock climbing experiences, from indoor walls, to boulders and free climbing. There are one day (09:00 to 16:00) programmes for beginners that start with technique training at a gym in the morning, then move outdoors. The cost is ¥8,400 for adults and ¥6,300 for children, which includes instruction, equipment rental and insurance. The centre is popular with foreigners, and runs multi-day tours of the nearby Tateyama Alpine Route and the Three Peaks of

Hakuba for more experienced climbers. It also runs canoeing, kayaking and canyoning sessions in the summer, and skiing and snowboarding in the winter.

Cookery Classes

Various Locations

Kyoko Hattori

090 8961 6216 | ykhatto@ybb.ne.jp

Kyoko Hattori is trained in French, Japanese and Chinese cooking techniques and teaches private classes for men, women and children. These can be tailored to the specific needs of students. She also leads clients on tours of the city's culinary hotspots like Kappabashi (p.310), home to purveyors of the world's finest plastic food, just in case you want some faux sushi or pretend fruit.

1-22-14 Uehara
Shibuya-ku
🚇 *Yoyogi Uehara*
Map 5 D1 8

Living Food Cooking School

03 6421 2925 | www.veggieparadise.jp

As a graduate of the Natural Gourmet Institute in New York and a former instructor at San Francisco's Living Light Culinary Arts Institute, Yuki Itoh has an interesting take on how to bake a cake. For a start, she doesn't use flour, eggs or sugar. Her studio is on the second floor of her restaurant, Veggie Paradise (p.356), in residential Yoyogi-Uehara. Here, she instructs up to eight pupils at a time on how to make veggie burgers and sprout grains so that the nutrients are not destroyed. To get a taste, sign up for a two-hour trial lesson (¥3,150 including materials). Itoh's lessons range from one-time classes for friends to a course for aspiring professional chefs. It's one minute from the south exit of the station.

Various Locations

Mickey Cooks

080 5670 2343 | http://atlierfigo.exblog.jp/i8

Miyuki (Mickey) Horiike teaches in both English and Japanese to classes of around 30 students. She trained in London at Le Cordon Bleu, and while her specialty is Japanese fusion, she can also teach other Asian styles, Italian, French, American and Moroccan cooking. Classes are either held at her home in Setagaya, a community centre in Akasaka or at Tokyo American Club (see p.383), which is temporarily in Takanawa. She will also conduct three-hour lessons at your home for ¥6,000 to ¥8,000 per person (minimum two people).

Cricket

The cricket community in Japan is small but active, with regular matches on the half-dozen pitches in the Kanto area. The nearest to central Tokyo is the matted concrete ground at Koiwa in Edogawa-ku, and the most verdant is at the Yokohama Country & Athletic Club (see p.255), which began 140 years ago as the Yokohama Cricket Club. There are a few leagues and tournaments, and prominent teams include the Tokyo Wombats (www.tokyowombats.com), Indian Engineers (www.ieccjapan.com), Ichihara Sharks (www.ichiharasharks.com) and the British Embassy (http://becc.tmespace.com).

Koshi Bldg (5F), 2-11-14
Minami-Aoyama
Minato-ku
🚇 *Aoyama Itchome*
Map 8 F1 86

Japan Cricket Association

www.cricket.or.jp

This is the only local organisation recognised by the International Cricket Council. It runs two leagues: the premier Japan One Day Championship (J1C) and a friendlier Japan Two Day Championship (J2C). Of the 12 teams in J1C, half of the players are Japanese and the rest are expats. Sign up online for newsletters with the latest bowling and batting action.

4-6-5 Nishi-Koiwa
Edogawa-ku
Map 2 C2

Kanto Cricket Association

090 1057 8787 | *www.geocities.com/nisarhiro/cricket*

The Kanto Cricket Association was established in Edogawa two decades ago, and now oversees the Japan Gold Cup tournament. Though previously a 40 over, one-day league, in 2005 it switched to Twenty20. Games are played at a public pitch in Koiwa, the first and only one within Tokyo's 23 wards.

Cycling

Other options **Bicycles** p.277, **Mountain Biking** p.233, **Bicycle** p.33

Various Locations

Cycle Tokyo Project

http://cycle-tokyo.cycling.jp

This is a non-profit initiative to get residents and tourists out on a two-wheeler and exploring the city. The helpful website lists several recommended routes, and also contains a directory of shops that sell and rent bicycles. The volunteer staff will also lead you on a bike tour of your choosing – with a few weeks' advance notice.

Various Locations

Don's Half-Fast Flash Mob Urban Weekend Bicycle Rides

www.kirin.co.jp/brands/HL/shop/index.html

This club, organised by long-time expat Don Morton, meets every weekend in front of Roppongi's Grand Hyatt, and rides 30km to 70km around the city. Morton's only rules are that members know how to fix a flat (he can teach you), and can keep up with the pack. Rides take anywhere from two to six hours, including breaks for beer. The group gathers every first Wednesday of the month at funky lounge The Pink Cow (p.331) in Shibuya to eat, drink, socialise and plan new rides.

Belly Boogie
Belly dancing is starting to take off and a good way to learn how to do the seductive shimmy is with one of the free, monthly, one-hour workshops taught by Alegra in Shibuya. She teaches dancers of all levels. A single class costs ¥3,500, but packages of classes offer reduced rates. See www.freebellydance. com or email freebellydance@gmail. com for details.

Dance Classes

If weekends are for dancing the night away in nightclubs and salsa joints, weekdays are a time for honing one's skills at one of the city's many dance schools (see table below and the schools on p.218). From ballroom, popularised by movies like *Shall We Dance*, to belly dancing, Tokyo is a city of hip shakers of all stripes. Even pole dancing has become mainstream, with the help of Lu Pole Dance Art Flow Studio (see table). Casino Dance Studio (p.218) also offer a range of disciplines, from ballet to belly dancing. Tokyoites have a fascination with all things Hawaiian, so it should come as no surprise that hula classes are available everywhere you look. According to the *International Herald Tribune* there are over 300 schools in the city, serving over 100,000 students. Try the Expressive Art Studio, just one minute from the east exit of Shibuya station, which offers not only hula but ballet, belly dancing and yoga classes too. For kids, Marsha Grey has been dancing for over 25 years and is a licensed early childhood teacher. She offers Keiki Hula classes for 2 to 4 year olds and over 5s for ¥15,000 per 10 sessions. These take place at The New Center for Creative Arts (RBR) in Moto-Azabu. See the table for contact details.

Salsa

Salsa is hot in Tokyo with men and women in raunchy outfits fervently dancing the night away. Typically devoted, Japanese dancers really know how to work the floor and spend hours perfecting their moves. Areas such as Roppongi have plenty of salsa schools, clubs and bars (see p.364 for some examples), or check out Salsa Hotline Tokyo (www.salsa. co.jp/zzz/index_E.html) for listings.

Dance Classes

Expressive Art Studio	090 8344 0724	www.yogastudiotokyo.com
Lu Pole Dance Art Flow Studio	03 5941 8998	www.lupoledance.com
The New Center For Creative Arts	03 5770 7401	www.rbr-art.com

Casino Dance Studio

Torikatsu Bldg (4F)
5-2-4 Roppongi
Minato-ku
🚇 *Roppongi*
Map 11 B2 9

03 5771 7046 | www.studio-casino.com

While predominantly a salsa school, this large dance school also teaches Latin, ballroom, hip-hop, reggaeton, cha-cha, tango, ballet and belly dancing. Most of the 75 minute classes cost ¥2,500 (excluding the one-off membership fee of ¥3,150). There are free trial lessons for many of the styles, and discount packages are available. The website is loaded with more information including schedule details. Every last Thursday of the month, salsa students and teachers descend on one of the many salsa clubs nearby. Head past Almond from Roppongi Crossing down Gaien-Higashi, the studio is next to Starbucks above a *hyaku-en* (¥100) shop.

Dance in the Town

Rubber Soul (4F)
2-16-14
Minami-machi
Western Tokyo
🚇 *Kokubunji*

www16.ocn.ne.jp/~dittcuba

Those in the Tama region of Western Tokyo can swing their salsa hips two nights a week in Kokubunji. Classes are held on Saturdays and Sundays and the Japanese instructor teaches in English and Japanese, and likes to throw in some Spanish here and there for good measure. Classes range from 55 to 70 minutes, with various levels from beginner to intermediate, and cost ¥2,000.

Salsa Caribe

Reine Roppongi Bldg
5-3-4 Roppongi
Minato-ku
🚇 *Roppongi*
Map 11 B2 10

03 3746 0244 | www.tokyo.to/caribe

A lively, easy-to-dance-to music selection and a popular place to go even during the week. At the weekend, Salsa Caribe attracts many latinos from all over Tokyo, and in the later hours there is a predominance of merengue. Classes are for Japanese and foreigners, but be warned, sometimes it gets too packed to dance!

Diving

Discovery Divers Tokyo

Various Locations

080 5707 3260 | www.discoverydiverstokyo.com

In colder months, DDT organises pool sessions at Yugawara Sports Center in Atami, Shizuoka-ken. Once the mercury starts to rise, the group leads PADI-certified divers to Izu Peninsula, just a few hours south of the city. Note that you need to book dives at least four days in advance.

Mar Scuba

Various Locations

090 3851 3901 | www.marscuba.com

Mar Scuba has been around since 1997, and is the longest running foreign-owned diving operation in the capital. English-speaking guides lead excursions to Izu Peninsula, Okinawa and top dive spots outside Japan. Mar attempts to maintain a safe, friendly and non-competitive environment, so that divers of all ages and experience levels can relax and enjoy the natural beauty of the ocean. Clients are roughly 75% to 25% foreign to Japanese, and occasionally gather for social events.

Drama Groups

New Worlds Theatre

Various Locations

www.newworldstheatre.com

New Worlds Theatre was founded in 2006, and is one of the newest troupes on the block. The president, Alec Harris, is a playwright and hopes to reinvigorate the English theatre scene by taking advantage of the talent and experience among the city's expat community. Shows are staged in places where the atmosphere best adds to the performance and past venues have included an English football pub and the ritzy Yokohama Country & Athletic Club (see p.255).

Various Locations

Tokyo International Players
090 6009 4171 | *www.tokyoplayers.org*

Tokyo International Players has been around since 1896, and is by far the longest-running expat theatre group in town. Located in the Lion's Plaza Ebisu, the all-volunteer group puts on four to five shows a year, running the gamut from comedies to musicals. Auditions for actors, production, dancers and musicians are open to the public. The only requirements are proficiency in English and a willingness to commit the time needed to get the shows up and running and ready for stage night. The group relies on the efforts and financial support of volunteers and sponsors. Theatre tickets cost ¥4,000 for adults and ¥2,500 for students and children.

Environmental Groups
Other options **Voluntary & Charity Work** p.63

Eco-consciousness is sweeping Japan, with cultural movements like LOHAS (Lifestyles Of Health And Sustainability) and an annual Eco-Products Fair that draws crowds of over 150,000. Now that people are finally aware of the toll that humans are taking on the natural environment, the next step is to get out and take action. Beach clean-ups are one of the most popular initiatives in the city. These are organised biannually by the Japan Environmental Action Network (see table below). There are also several government and non-governmental groups that may be looking for volunteers.

Environmental Groups			
Friends of the Earth Japan	03 6907 7217	www.foejapan.org	Against deforestation and global warming Offers development aid to third world countries
Greenpeace Japan	03 5338 9800	www.greenpeace.or.jp	Advocacy group against whaling, deforestation and the dumping of nuclear waste
Japan Environment Association	03 5114 1251	www.jeas.or.jp	Information group that acts as an intermediary between the Ministry of the Environment and eco-conscious groups
Japan Environmental Action Network	042 32 48252	www.jean.jp	Organises annual spring and autumn clean-ups along Japan's coastline
Japan Environmental Education Forum	03 3350 6770	www.jeef.or.jp	Environmental education umbrella group
Japan National Trust for Cultural and Natural Heritage Conservation	03 6303 1110	www.national-trust.or.jp	Conducts independent surveys and researches potential sites of cultural or natural importance
Japan Tropical Forest Action Network	03 5367 2865	www.jatan.org	Drafts and circulates educational newsletters, letters and press releases about deforestation
Konohana Family	0544 58 7568	www.konohana-family.org	Organic, vegetarian, subsistence farming commune
WWF Japan	03 3769 1714	www.wwf.or.jp	Protection of animals and their habitats since 1971

Fencing

Kishi Kinen
Taikukan (4F)
1-1-1 Jinnan
Shibuya-ku
🚇 *Harajuku*
Map 8 C2 87

Federation Japonaise d'Escrime

03 3481 2378 | www.sportsweb.ne.jp/fje

Japanese fencing's governing body, the Federation Japonaise d'Escrime, is housed in the same building in Shibuya as the national headquarters for several other sports. The group also publishes a list of area clubs on its website, as well as a blog called *Fencing Online Japan* (www.sportsweb.ne.jp/foj.htm) with related links and information about upcoming tournaments and activities. Unfortunately, the website is in Japanese only, so the best way to find information may be by drafting a simple English email or enlisting the help of a Japanese-speaking friend.

Taito Fencing Club

www.k3.dion.ne.jp/~taitofc/sub5.html

At meetings on Wednesday (18:30 to 21:30) and Saturday evenings (18:00 to 20:45), the Taito Fencing Club welcomes all ages and levels. The group gathers at the Taitō Ward Riverside Sports Center, 12 minutes on foot from Asakusa station. The cost is ¥450 to ¥500 for adults and ¥100 to ¥200 for children.

Wel-Seta Fencing Club

http://f33.aaa.livedoor.jp/~fencing/

This club meets on Friday evenings between 19:00 and 21:00 at a public gymnasium in Setagaya to practice foil, epee and sabre. The cost per session is ¥1,000. Alternatively, keen swordsmen and women can sign up and pay ¥3,000 a month to become a member.

Fishing

Japan, as an island country with a history of fishing for sustenance, still has a few nostalgic anglers who would rather get out a rod and sit by the water than go to their local supermarket or sushi bar. Tokyo's Tamagawa, Edogawa (a tributary of the mighty Tonegawa) and Arakawa rivers are popular spots for fishermen to try their luck in the slow-moving currents. Among the native species are *ayu* river trout, the fishing of which legally begins on 1 June in Tokyo. Contact the Akigawa Gyokyo governing body (0425 96 2215) for a one-day (¥2,000) or season (¥8,000) licence. Area anglers also take to Tokyo Bay year round, which is especially popular in late autumn for the sea bass and other species that typically inhabit the shallower depths. While outdoor fishing can be done pretty much anywhere, the oh-so-Japanese pint-size indoor pools dotted about the city are what make fishing in this city unique. There are several around town, but one not to missed is Tsuribori Sangenjaya (see entry below).

Lazy days fishing

4-18-1 Taishido
Setagaya-ku
Sangenjaya
Map 5 C2 **90**

Tsuribori Sangenjaya
03 3412 3950

Nestled behind one of Starbucks' coffee emporiums in the backstreets of Setagaya, Tsuribori Sangenjaya hasn't changed much since it first opened in 1963. The signs have accumulated a little rust, and the prices have probably gone up a bit, but it still has the rustic charm (no pun intended) of pre-Olympics Tokyo. The building is a converted house, and the basic facilities include benches around a hole with fish in it. Unsurprisingly, the beverage policy is BYO, and the ageing proprietor will kindly ask that you take your empties with you when you go. The price is ¥800 for the first hour, and a few hundred more for each hour thereafter. This is an experience not to be missed.

Flower arranging at Ohara

Flower Arranging
Other options **Gardens** p.287, **Flowers** p.284

3-8-3 Kita-Aoyama
Minato-ku
Omotesandō
Map 8 D2 **11**

Nicolai Bergmann International School of Floristry
03 5464 0716 | *www.nicolaibergmann.com*

Nicolai Bergman, an artist and entrepreneur from Copenhagen, founded his International School of Floristry to teach European floral arranging with a touch of Scandinavian style. Personalised lessons, taught by Bergmann himself at his Omotesandō studio, cost ¥12,000 to ¥15,000.

5-7-17 Minami-Aoyama
Minato-ku
Omotesandō
Map 8 E3 **12**

Ohara School of Ikebana
03 5774 5097 | *www.ohararyu.or.jp*

Ohara has a rich history of *ikebana* (the Japanese art of flower arranging), which dates back more than 100 years, counting one million students worldwide. Teachers at its white, 10 storey headquarters on Kottō Dōri in the ritzy Omotesandō area offer classes in English on Wednesdays, Thursdays and Fridays. Two-hour lessons cost ¥2,500 to ¥3,000 (plus ¥1,500 to ¥3,000 for materials), depending on the difficulty level and type of flowers used. Reservations must be made at least one day in advance. The website lists dozens of affiliated schools overseas, so there's no need to drop the hobby if you leave Japan.

7-2-21 Akasaka
Minato-ku
Aoyama itchome
Map 10 B4 **13**

Sogetsu Kaikan
03 3408 1151 | *www.sogetsu.or.jp*

The Sogetsu style of Japanese flower arranging was developed by Sofu Teshigawara in the 1920s. Its main office, the Sogetsu Kaikan, is located in Akasaka, and offers a popular introductory class for English speakers most Mondays from 10:00 to 12:00 for ¥3,800 per person (including all materials). There are also regular *Iemoto* classes on Tuesdays, Wednesdays and Thursdays. Finally, those looking to become experts and/or instructors can embark on their journey of learning here. Sogetsu teaches from four textbooks, each containing 20 lessons. Call to confirm class schedules and to make reservations. The website lists contact details for schools worldwide.

Football

After baseball, football is easily the most watched and played sport in Tokyo. The shortage of full-sized pitches is balanced out by an astounding number of smaller futsal (five-a-side indoor soccer) courts. Tucked away in all matter of spaces and even on top of buildings (www.adidas-futsalpark.com/shibuya), the futsal action never seems to stop, from daybreak until midnight. Email futsal@tokyogaijins.com to be put on a mailing list for upcoming friendlies. At weekends, players in the popular two-division Tokyo Metropolis League (www.footyjapan.com/tml) head out of central Tokyo to where the fields are taken over by 11 a side combat. Email info@footyjapan.com to inquire about teams looking for players. Footy Japan also runs the British Football Academy (p.226) for kids.

Frisbee

Every Sunday at 14:00, a few dozen people show up for casual games of ultimate frisbee on the shores of the Tamagawa that divides Tokyo and Kanagawa-ken. There are two fields (one near Futako-Tamagawa station, the other near Futako-Shinchi station), so check out the Tokyo Ultimate forum on Outdoor Japan's website (http://outdoorjapanforums.com) before setting off, or contact Tim on 090 7839 5522 for more information.

Golf

Literally hundreds of golf courses can be found within a two-hour drive from central Tokyo. There are an abundance of mountain courses, but also many along the country's long coastlines – ranging in difficulty from tough championship courses to those geared towards social players with their wide fairways and lack of hazards.

Green fees on weekdays can vary from ¥5,000 to ¥30,000, but expect to pay nearly double that on weekends (and with tee off times far too close to each other for comfort.) Membership is expensive, but many courses allow non-members to play at a slightly lower cost. Prices are geared at foursomes so playing as a pair or a threesome may be more expensive and players must stop for lunch after nine holes on most courses, even if they want to play through. To help you get around the course, there are a plethora of buggies, carts and other devices.

Golf in Japan (www.golf-in-japan.com) is a comprehensive English directory with reviews, contact details and even the occasional bargain. Before you head out, get some tips from the pros at Setagaya's Fairway

Golf Clubs			
Name	Area	Phone	Length
Akabane Golf Course	Tokyo	03 3966 6155	6,237yds
Ishioka Golf Club	Ibaraki-ken	02 9677 2141	7,071yds
Miho Golf Club	Ibaraki-ken	02 9840 0001	7,010yds
Odawara Golf Club	Kanagawa-ken	04 6583 2111	6,626yds
Shishido Hills Country Club	Ibaraki-ken	02 9677 2141	7,005yds
Sohbu Country Club	Chiba-ken	04 7464 7111	7,155yds
Tamagawa Golf Club	Kanagawa-ken	044 411 6227	1,205yds
Tokyo Golf Club	Saitama-ken	04 2953 9111	6,810yds
Tokyu Kenzan Sports Garden	Yokohama	045 901 5211	210m
Wakasu Golf Links	Tokyo	03 3522 3221	6,811yds

Golf (http://fairwaygolf.jp/node/45), or Jingu Gaien (see below). For a list of courses, visit www.travelhost.co.jp. For driving ranges in the city, see City Swingers opposite.

Jingu Gaien Golf Practice Center

03 3401 4359 | www.meijijingugaien.jp/golf

This three-tiered driving range within the Meiji Jingu Gaien (Outer Gardens) athletic complex is popular day and night, with 163 launching pads. Prepaid cards are available for ¥3,000 to ¥20,000 and the price per ball isn't cheap – it varies depending on which area you're hitting from, with the top floors offering the best value – but it's a fun way to complement a Swallows (p.248) home game at Jingu Baseball Stadium next door. Semi-private lessons for up to four people start at ¥4,620 per hour; private instruction will set you back ¥3,465 per half hour. Every Sunday there are two 70 minute group lessons for up to 10 children in elementary or junior high school; the cost is ¥1,680 per golfer. Rental clubs are available for ¥320 each.

856-2 Yanashiro
Chiba-ken
Map 1 C3

Kazusa Monarch Country Club
043 929 3100 | www.giganet.net/kmcc

Designed by Jack Nicklaus, Kazusa Monarch Country Club offers some of the best golf in Japan, just a few hours away in Chiba. The 7,020 yard, par 72 course offers five water hazards, a bunker on nearly every hole, and breathtaking natural surroundings. Rental clubs (¥1,050 to ¥3,150) and soft-spike shoes (free) are available. Non-members can book online for discounted weekday (¥13,500 to ¥14,500) and weekend (¥23,500 to ¥25,500) rates. Lodging rates start from ¥8,660 per person, including breakfast. Billiards and mahjong are available in the clubhouse to pass the times until you can get back out on the links. Tip your hat to the Golden Bear before you tee off.

3473 Shiogo
Shirosato-machi
Ibaraki
Map 1 C3

Windsor Park Golf and Country Club
029 688 2221 | www.wpgcc.com

Windsor Park offers that rare combination of excellent golf and reasonable prices. The course is a favourite among Tokyo expats for breaking with Japanese tradition and allowing golfers to play a straight 18 holes without breaking for lunch – all the while carrying or wheeling their own clubs. Non-members pay ¥5,000 to ¥14,000 for a round on the par 72, 7,007 yard course. Windsor also woos families with an array of services and amenities including a business centre, free babysitting and even a pet hotel.

Hiking
Other options **Canyoning** p.215, **Outdoor Goods** p.295

Tokyo is by and large a flat city, but head in any direction but east and a slew of mountains awaits the casual and dedicated hiker alike. The most popular and accessible destination is Mount Takao (www.takaotozan.co.jp) in western Tokyo, easily reached by train (see p.36 for more). Get on the Chūō or Keiō line from Shinjuku, heading toward Takaozan-Guchi station. Another option is hilly Kamakura (www.kamakura-burabura.com), a religious area home to a giant Buddha statue (see p.198 for more on the area). For other suggestions, email the Japan Walking Association at jwa@walking.or.jp or visit www.walking.or.jp.

Horse Riding
Horse riding in central Tokyo doesn't come cheap. The only option within the limits of the Yamanote line is the Tokyo Riding Club (see p.224). Membership rates are astronomical, but the club is open to non-members. Further out, there are several more affordable (and picturesque) schools. The less densely populated areas of Machida, Hachiōji and Yokohama have riding schools open to the public.

City Swingers
Driving ranges can found in virtually every neighbourhood in Tokyo – from all-mod-con golfing centres to mom and pop 50-yard ranges. There are also several par 3 courses. Nearly all ranges offer classes, many of them indoors, offering computer simulated play. See also Sports & Leisure Facilities on p.252.

Horse Riding			
Avalon Hillside Farm	Yokohama	042 921 7081	www.avalon-hf.com
Crane Riding Club	Western Tokyo	042 737 5600	www.uma-crane.com/map/tokyo.html
Hachioji Riding Club	Funakichō Hachioji	042 691 1915	www.hachioji-rc.co.jp
Kunitachi Riding Club	Western Tokyo	042 572 6802	www5a.biglobe.ne.jp/~kunijoba
La Hacienda Yokohama	Yokohama	045 363 2501	www.la-hacienda-yokohama.com
Malvern Riding Club	Machida-shi	042 770 7582	www.mal-vern.com

If it's ponies that are of interest, head to the Yoyogi Pony Park (03 3373 9996), next to the Tokyo Riding Club stables near Sangūbashi station. Here, your child can ride for free from 15:00 to 16:30 daily (and also from 10:00 to 11:30 on weekends) from March to December. From 11:30 to 11:45 and 16:30 to 16:45 every day, children can feed the animals carrots, cabbages and apples that they've brought from home.

4-8 Kamizono-chō ◀
Shibuya-ku
🚉 *Sangūbashi*
Map 7 B4 **15**

Tokyo Riding Club

03 3370 0984 | *www.tokyo-rc.or.jp*

Joining the Tokyo Riding Club near Yoyogi Kōen will cost you a cool ¥2 million, plus another ¥96,000 per year, and that doesn't even include the riding fees of ¥4,500 to ¥5,500 every time you saddle up. Despite these seemingly prohibitive rates, the club boasts over 450 members. Non-members are also welcome. Experienced riders can go on 45 minute hacks for ¥7,000 to ¥8,000, but beginners are usually required to take 30 minute lessons, which cost ¥13,000 to ¥14,000 all in, including an instructor fee and equipment rental charges. The school is closed on Mondays.

Ice Hockey

Despite Japan not being competitive internationally, ice hockey is booming in Tokyo. The professional Asia League (www.alhockey.com) has four Japanese teams, plus two from Korea and one from China, and games in Yokohama and Higashi-Fushimi are well-attended. The youth and college ice hockey scenes are thriving, and feed into two adult (*shakaijin*) leagues – Tokyo and Kanagawa – each with several divisions and dozens of teams.

Many of the *shakaijin* teams hold open practices for ¥500 to ¥2,500 per skate. Two popular options for visitors are Jinxs (http://ip.tosp.co.jp/i.asp?i=icejinx), who practise at Jingu Skate Arena (see below) typically on Wednesday nights, and the Pirates (http://groups.yahoo.co.jp/group/pirates-icehockey), who practice at 10:00 on Saturday mornings at Citizen Ice Skate Rink (see below). Additionally, the Tokyo Canadians (www.tokyocanadians.com), a group of mostly North American expats who get together weekly and also travel to tournaments around Asia, occasionally open their ice time to experienced players.

There is also a well-organised inline league (www.misconduct-hockey.co.jp) with well over 1,000 players. Games take place at the Amazing Square sports complex (see p.253) near Kita-Senju, and consist of two 20 minute halves, with lines of three plus a goalie. The cost of registering a team is ¥180,000, which guarantees 10 games over five months, plus playoffs.

Ice Skating

Ice skating suffered as the economic downturn of the early 90s forced many rinks to close, but more recently the sport has experienced a boom following Shizuka Arakawa's gold medal in women's figure skating at the 2006 Winter Olympics. These days, many of the arenas are dangerously crowded at weekends and on holidays, but a good time can still be had by aspiring Nancy Kerrigans and Bobby Orrs.

Ice Skating			
Citizen Ice Skate Rink	Takadanobaba	03 3371 0910	www.citizen-plaza.co.jp/iceskate
Dydo Drinko Ice Arena	Western Tokyo	042 467 7171	www.seibu-group.co.jp/rec/fushimi
Higashi-Yamato Skate Center	Western Tokyo	042 566 6411	www.seibu-group.co.jp/rec/bigbox/yamato/skate
Kanagawa Skate Rink	Kanagawa-ken	045 321 0847	http://park2.wakwak.com/~ksr
Meiji Jingu Ice Skating Rink	Sendagaya	03 3403 3458	www.meijijingugaien.jp
Shin-Yokohama Skate Center	Yokohama-shi	045 474 1112	www.princehotels.co.jp/skate/shinyokohama

Karting

With few circuits around, petrol heads of the automobile variety are not so well catered for, but karting on the other hand is easy to come by. Take a look at the table (below) for some handy listings.

Karting			
Circuit Akigase	048 855 7862	Kamiōkubo 1099, Urawa	Saitama-ken
New Tokyo Circuit	043 636 3139	Kaminihonmatsu 249, Hikida, Ichihara	Chiba-ken
Mobara Motor Sports Land	047 525 4433	Daida, Mobara	Chiba-ken
Ōi Matsuda Kart Land	047 525 4433	Nakaimachi, Ashigarakamigun	Kanagawa-ken

Kids Activities

Other options **Mother & Toddler Activities** p.231, **Kids' Items** p.291

Soft-play amusement centres for younger children are not uncommon, but the non-commercial ones might be a bit harder for non-Japanese to find. Throughout Japan there are publicly funded *jidokan* (children's centres), which offer facilities, equipment and information for families with children, for free. The facilities on offer range from the physical, such as a large jungle gym and mazes, to quieter activities, including colouring in, art and crafts and woodwork. The centres also often run lectures on topics such as baby massage and other parent and child activities. A small fee may be requested for some activities where supplies are needed, for example leatherwork. Although the *jidokan* in Shibuya (1-18-24 Shibuya, 03 3409 6361) is particularly large and well-known among foreign and mixed families, more basic facilities are also likely to exist in your neighbourhood. Ask around for locations and advice on where to go, and keep an eye out for posters in your local ward. For more information (in Japanese), visit www.jidoukan.or.jp.

There are also more commercial options, where a small or more significant fee might be payable. The Kodomo no Shiro (Children's Castle) in Shibuya is one such option, see p.232. It's similar to the *jidokan*, but the facilities are a bit more upmarket. Meanwhile, Kidzania (03 3536 2100, www.kidzania.jp) is a fun mini city where children get to dress up and act out their dream job, becoming doctors, firemen, nurses and cabin attendants for the day.

Many of the bigger theme parks (p.180) have activity areas where the little ones can run and play in complete safety. Game centres are another option if you're really at a loose end (see p.168). Once you get over the noise and the flashing lights of the video games, they can be quite good fun. And then there are the usual museums (p.175) and heritage sites that might interest slightly older children, not to mention Tokyo Disneyland, the British Football Academy and Tokyo Dome City (see p.226). For useful information, babysitting, classifieds and discussions, visit www.tokyowithkids.com or www.piqniq.jp.

Kids at play

Various Locations ◀

British Football Academy

www.footyjapan.com

Kids of every nationality are welcome to play at the Academy. Classes are held at four centrally located schools at weekends and on evenings (Tokyo International School, K. International School, Sarugaku Elementary School and Nanzan Elementary School) – visit the Academy's website for directions to each location.

British Football Academy

Classes are in English and cater for children of all ages from 'Pups' (3 to 4 years) to 'Academy Stars' (11 to 15 years). Monthly fees start at about ¥5,250.

Various Locations ◀

I can. gymnastics

03 3440 0384 | www.igcjapan.com

The gymnastics exercises in this programme are designed to build children's confidence, strength and agility. English language instruction is given to Tiny Tots (from walking age to 3 years), Beginners (age 3 to 6) and Advanced Beginners (6 to 12 years). I can. gymnastics has centres in several central locations.

7-20 Ueno Kōen ◀
Taitō-ku
🚇 **Ueno**
Map 12 D2 **16**

National Museum of Science & Nature

03 3822 0111 | www.kahaku.go.jp

This museum has plenty for kids to get their hands on. Fun with Science for pre-schoolers offers a range of activities, while children can carry out their own experiments in the Science Discovery Classroom. The museum also hosts a science school that features experiments that mum and dad can join in but English language guidance is slightly lacking. For more on this area, see Ueno in Exploring on p.160.

3-1-1 Higashi Ikebukuro ◀
Toshima-ku
🚇 **Ikebukuro**
Map 3 F1 **17**

Sunshine City

03 3989 3321 | www.sunshinecity.co.jp

There's something for all the family here (Ikebukuro in Exploring on p.164 for more). You can watch the fish swim by in the Aquarium (p.168), take in the superb view across the city from the Observatory and be transported into space at the Planetarium. When hunger strikes, head to the Namja Town gourmet theme park. English information and explanations are limited.

1-1 Maihama Urayasu ◀
Chiba-ken
Map 2 C3

Tokyo Disneyland

0456 83 3333 | www.tokyodisneyresort.co.jp

Make sure you take your kids to see Mickey and the gang on a weekday when Japanese kids are at school, or you could spend more time queuing for rides than actually on them. This vast area has pretty much everything you would find at Disneyland in the States – only the food here is better. A one-day passport costs ¥5,800 for adults, ¥5,000 for juniors (12-17 years) and ¥3,900 for children (4-11 years). Children under 4 go free. If you've still got the energy afterwards, pop into the more adult-orientated DisneySea next door.

1-3-61 Kōrakuen ◀
Bunkyō-ku
🚇 **Kōrakuen**
Map 9 E2 **18**

Tokyo Dome City

03 5800 9999 | www.tokyo-dome.co.jp

As well as being the home stadium of the Yomiuri Giants (p.248), Tokyo Dome City also contains a bowling alley and theme park. Some of the more thrilling attractions at the theme park include a roller coaster and an 80 metre vertical-drop hair raiser. Rides start at ¥600. If mum and dad can't handle the palpitations, they can sit back and relax in the La Qua spa centre (p.265) that also has numerous shops and restaurants.

Kitesurfing

Other options **Surfing** p.183

This exciting sport, which involves being pulled by the wind as you glide over water, is taking off big time. It is relatively undemanding on the body and is easy to learn – after a few lessons most people should be able to pull off a few jumps and spins. A large community of kiteboarders exists outside Tokyo in places such as Hamamatsu in Shizuoka-ken, Chigasaki, Enoshima, Miura and Yokosuka in Kanagawa-ken, and Katakai and Kemigawahama beach in Chiba. While there are no formal organisations as yet, there are lots of informal groups. International websites like www.windfinder.com and www.kitebeaches.com have listings of schools, board shops and other useful info.

Hamamatsu
Shizuoka-ken
Map 1 B3

Kiteboarding Japan

053 464 9911 | *www.kiteboardingjapan.com*
This foreign-owned boardshop and school has been up and running for about six years. It's an approved International Kiteboarding Organisation school, and although it is one hour out of the city by *shinkansen*, it has a great reputation and many students make the trip all the way to Hamamatsu for lessons. The website is currently only in Japanese, but will be launched in English soon.

Language Schools

Other options **Language** p.14, **Learning Japanese** p.138

While English is big business in Japan, many schools have also been set up in the city for foreigners wanting to study Japanese. These vary enormously from cheap schools crammed with young Chinese and Korean students, to professional outfits specialising in business Japanese. It's worth sitting in on classes before joining because complaints have floated about in relation to some of the cheaper schools, mainly that students hear more Mandarin and Korean than Japanese. Many of these classes are also preparatory courses for university, so make sure you select one that suits your needs. Full or part time study in groups or with private tutors is available, with some schools also offering flexible lessons to fit in with individual's schedules. Keep an eye out for volunteer classes that teach Japanese on the cheap or for free in the different ward offices. These classes are worth looking at, but the quality of teaching can vary. Another (cheaper) option is to set up a 'language exchange' with a local, or take up one of the free offers of tuition found in magazine classifieds, but watch out as some of these teachers may be more interested in improving their own English than teaching you Japanese. Visit www.aikgroup.co.jp/j-school for a comprehensive list of schools, courses, and other details.

1-6-9 Shibuya
Shibuya-ku
🚉 *Shibuya*
Map 8 C3 **19**

ARC Academy Shibuya Ekimae School

03 3409 0391 | *www.arc-eg.com*
ARC is a major language centre that not only teaches Japanese, but trains Japanese teachers. Branches can also be found in Ikebukuro, Shinjuku and Yokohama. Full-time, part-time, general, corporate and intensive courses are offered and it uses its own material. Private lessons over 10 hours will set you back ¥56,000, and three months worth of group lessons (twice a week) costs ¥64,000.

Association for Japanese-Language Teaching

3-25-2 Toranomon
Minato-ku
🚇 *Kamiyachō*
Map 11 D3 **20**

www.ajalt.org

AJALT is a reputable organisation that wrote the excellent *Japanese for Busy People* series of textbooks. A huge array of courses are available, ranging from kids classes to everyday communication classes and even classes for diplomats and other bigwigs. Group lessons start at ¥2,100 per hour and hour-long private lessons cost ¥6,510.

Shinjuku International Exchange School

1-22-25
Hyakunin-chō
Shinjuku-ku
🚇 *Okubo*
Map 3 E3 **21**

03 5348 6591 | www.sie-s.com/index.htm

A traditional school for full-time learners of the Japanese language, with students from many countries. Students can take courses lasting from 15 months to two years. The centre is open Monday to Friday from 09:00 to 16:15. The total cost of lessons and materials for the first year is ¥680,000. Dormitory rooms are available for students who wish to stay there, but a valid visa is required.

Libraries

Other options **Second-Hand Items** p.297, **Books** p.278

Look around you when taking a train in central Tokyo and you will notice that those who are not taking a nap have their nose in a book. The country's high literacy rate (99%) may seem surprising given the number of *kanji* (Chinese characters that are used in Japanese writing) but this, combined with an excellent network of libraries, means access to a good book is fairly easy. The starting point for bookworms should be the main library in your ward – your local ward office will have information on this. Most of these libraries have a wide selection of books in English and other languages. You'll also be able to read the local English papers, borrow CDs, DVDs and videos, and check out noticeboards giving information on language lessons, lectures, concerts and many other matters. The libraries are simple to join and usually only an alien registration card (p.55) is needed as identification. In most cases, you will only be able to use the libraries in the ward where you live, but some allow you to take books out from libraries in the ward where you work. In addition to the ward libraries, a number of institutions also house an impressive range of English language reading material, see below. For more information on reading, see also Books on p.40.

Japan Foundation Library

1-23-32 Akasaka
Minato-ku
🚇 *Tameike-Sannō*
Map 11 D1 **22**

03 5562 3527 | www.jpf.go.jp

This place is a veritable Mecca for Japanophiles. Scholars of Japanese culture and history and those whose interest pushes them to delve more deeply can take advantage of the 25,000 or so books, magazines, reference materials and theses housed here. It also contains English translations of novels and other materials. Join up with your alien registration card (p.51) to use the cleverly put together facilities, borrow books or enjoy the views. It's open Monday to Friday from 10:00 to 19:00 and is closed Sundays, public holidays and most Saturdays.

JETRO Business Library

2-2-5 Toranomon
Minato-ku
🚇 *Tameike-Sannō*
Map 11 D1 **23**

03 3582 1775 | www.jetro.go.jp

The Japan External Trade Organization is a government-related organisation established to promote trade and investment with Japan. As its name suggests, this is a place where you will find economic and business information and statistics for pretty much any country. The helpful staff will help you with anything you need. This impressive reference library has about 150,000 titles in many languages and is a good place to source business opportunities. It's open Monday to Friday from 09:00 to 17:00.

National Diet Library

1-10-1 Nagata-chō
Chiyoda-ku
🚇 *Nagatacho*
Map 10 D4 24

03 3581 2331 | www.ndl.go.jp
This is the main library in the country (the *Diet* being the parliament) and it archives a copy of everything ever published in Japan, as well as foreign language books and materials. It's a tad straightlaced and you need to fill out a form just to go in, but it is worth it for the huge selection of reading material. Much of the foreign-language material is not on the shelves and you have to go through catalogues to get books fetched for you from the stacks. Over 1,500 newspapers and periodicals are also available in this reference only library. It's open Monday to Friday from 09:30 to 19:00 (closing at 17:00 on Saturdays). The library is closed on Sundays and on public holidays.

Tokyo Metropolitan Art Museum Reading Room

8-36 Ueno Kōen
Taitō-ku
🚇 *Ueno*
Map 12 C2 25

03 3823 6921 | www.tobikan.jp
This small library is an art lover's delight, with about 30,000 books devoted solely to the subject. It has a number of foreign books and magazines on its shelves. All material is for reference purposes only and cannot be signed out. It's open from 10:00 to 17:00 and is closed the third Monday of the month and on public holidays. For more on the museum, see p.172.

Tokyo Metropolitan Library

5-7-13 Minami-Azabu
Minato-ku
🚇 *Hirō*
Map 11 A4 26

03 3442 8451 | www.library.metro.tokyo.jp
While not on the scale of the National Diet Library, the Tokyo Metropolitan Library has about 240,000 books on its open shelves, and holds as many as 1,480,000 volumes in total, including many foreign publications. Although the books here are purely for reference, the library is departmentalised into four subject floors – General Reference, Social Sciences, Humanities and Natural Science. The fifth floor holds 43,500 volumes of historical material on Tokyo. It also has sister libraries in Hibiya and Tama. It's open Monday to Friday from 10:00 to 21:00 and on Saturdays, Sundays, and public holidays it closes at the earlier time of 17:30.

Shorinji Kempo

Martial Arts

Many people come from all over the world to study martial arts in Japan. Known collectively as *budo*, literally the 'the way of stopping two spears' (without actually having to go that far), martial arts offer participants the opportunity to develop both mentally and physically, improving their health, fitness, confidence and discipline. The ability to kick-ass should a situation arise is certainly also a benefit. *Dōjō* can be found all over Tokyo – from large purpose-built training centres to small extensions of teachers' homes. Those interested in taking up a martial art should be aware of what is involved in each art. Aikido is non-competitive in that it teaches defensive techniques and is very much about personal growth. Judo is split into two forms, traditional and sport, so make sure you take up the style that suits you. Karate has many forms and schools, and tends to be more aggressive and competitive than other arts. *Shorinji Kempo* (p.230) is a relative newcomer to the scene and has only been around for about 60 years. It is a non-competitive art focussed on pair work and combines elements of karate, aikido, boxing, wrestling and other arts. *Kendo* is the 'way of the sword,' or a Japanese version of fencing. *Kyūdō*, while not technically a martial art, is traditional Japanese archery and is said to be very difficult to master, but great fun. Also, while not listed below, Tokyo has many Dōjō for other fighting forms such as taekwando, jujitsu, kickboxing and MMA (mixed martial arts), not forgetting more ancient arts such as *kenjutsu* (the art of the sword), *battojutsu* (the art of drawing a sword) and *laido* (the art of mental presence and immediate reaction). *Sojutsu* is another art form that leads back to the spear issue and actually using them this time, it translates as 'spear fighting'.

Aikikai Foundation (Aikido)

17-18
Wakamatsu-chō
Shinjuku-ku
🚇 **Wakamatsu-Kawada**
Map 3 F3 **27**

03 3203 9236 | www.aikikai.or.jp

What better place to learn Aikido than at Aikikai – the world headquarters of Aikido. Classes for all levels are held several times a day – seven days a week – with special classes for women. Membership fees are ¥10,500, and students will need to buy a uniform at extra cost.

Japan Karate Association

2-23-15 Kōraku
Bunkyō-ku
🚇 **Iidabashi**
Map 9 D2 **28**

03 5800 3091 | www.jka.or.jp

The Japan Karate Association is the largest and most prestigious karate organisation in the world, with members in over 100 countries. Its mission is to 'promote the soul and spirit of the art of karate, based on the ancient Japanese tradition of *bushidō*. Training is available at the headquarters in Bunkyō-ku, but contact the association for details of other *Dōjō* and lessons.

Kodokan Judo Institute

1-16-30 Kasuga
Bunkyō-ku
🚇 **Kasuga**
Map 9 F2 **29**

03 3818 4172 | www.kodokan.org

The Kodokan institute has been around since 1882, and is the world headquarters of judo. Courses for men, women and children of all abilities are available here, as are special international courses. The *Dōjō* is open daily between 15:30 and 20:00 for members to practise freely. The site also has a memorial hall, a library and scientific laboratories and study rooms. It's located next to exit A1 of Kasuga station.

Seidokan Aikido of Tokyo

Higashi Itabashi
Gymnasium
Itabashi-ku
Map 2 B2

03 5994 1185 | www.tokyoseidokan.com

This *Dōjō* is affiliated with the Aikido Institute of America. Classes are held on Saturdays and Sundays in English and are led by Chris Koprowski, a fourth-dan practitioner. Beginners are welcome to attend. For the most part, classes are held at Higashi Itabashi Gymnasium, opposite the Family Mart, about 600 metres from Itabashikuyakusho-mae station, but check with them beforehand.

Shiseikan – Meiji Jingu Budojo

1-1 Yoyogi
Shibuya-ku
🚇 **Harajuku**
Map 7 B3 **30**

03 3379 9137 | www.meijijingu.or.jp

A number of foreigners practice *kyūdō*, *judo* and *kendo* here in a *Dōjō* set amid beautiful surroundings in the grounds of the Meiji Jingū. A place for serious practitioners, only those who are committed to studying an art should join up here.

Shorinji Kempo

Various Locations

www.shorinjikempo.or.jp

This relatively unknown but inspiring art was begun in Japan in 1947, and focuses on personality development through a series of mastered techniques and a rather unique education system.The website has information in English detailing the history and origins of *shorinji kempo*, which is a good way to learn more about this art. There is also a *Dōjō* search option so you can find out where the nearest training facilities are located.

Tokyo Kyumeikan Kendo Dojo

2-1 Akatsukashin-Machi
Itabashi-ku
🚇 **Akatsuka**
Map 2 B2

03 3930 4636 | www.bekkoame.ne.jp/~kyumeikan

English language instruction is available at this well known *Dōjō* in Itabashi. Classes are available for beginners, experts, adults and children and *Iaido* (the art of mental presence and immediate reaction) instruction is included in the price. The *Dōjō* has many international links and a sister *Dōjō* in Yantai, China. The atmosphere is supportive and there is a good post-practice social scene and outings are organised regularly. It may be better to call rather than send an email if trying to get in touch with them. Directions to the *Dōjō* can be found on the website.

Mother & Toddler Activities

Mother (or father) and child activities are a great way to bond with your child and are also a means of socialising outside the home. Many classes such as music, yoga and gymnastics are said to aid development and to improve motor skills. For baby swimming classes, check with your local swimming pool (see Swimming on p.245).

Azabu Music Together

Various Locations

www.azabumusictogether.com

Music Together is a music group that caters to babies and toddlers up to pre-school age. The internationally renowned programme aids in child development and creates music awareness through song, and the use of drums, flutes, triangles and other various creative instruments. The interactive parent-child sessions are held at various locations across the city under the supervision of experienced teachers. Fees include a songbook and CD, and a parent guide. A 10 week course costs ¥26,000. Visit the website for online registration and class locations. For instruments, there's an online store at www.musictogether.com.

Blue Sky

Tsurumaki
Setagaya-ku
Map 2-A3

www.blueskytokyo.com

Blue Sky organises a series of English-language programmes for new and expectant mothers (and fathers). Workshops on breastfeeding and parenting, as well as mother and baby groups, toddler music and activity groups, picnics and social parties are all held regularly. The group is headed by Iona Macnab, an Australian mother of three and long-term Tokyo resident. She also has a blog: http://babycafejapan.blogspot.com. Contact them for further information, directions and maps.

Gymboree

Motoazabu Crest Bldg, 2-3-30 Moto-Azabu
Minato-ku
🚇 **Hirō**
Map 11 A4 31

03 5449 2311 | www.gymboree.jp

Gymboree's catch phrase is 'growing young minds', and it offers play, music, art, fitness and communication classes with the emphasis on fun, in seven levels for newborns to five-year-olds. Members can use the play gyms for free when they are not used for classes. Sessions are 45 minutes to one hour long, and enrollment is accepted on a rolling basis. Gymboree is located about 10 minutes walk from Hirō station next to the Qatar Embassy opposite Aiiku Hospital.

Itsy Bitsy Yoga

Various Locations

www.itsybitsyyoga.com

The first Itsy Bitsy Yoga centre was set up in 1999 in the United States by Helen Garabedian, a parent with a passion for yoga. Today, there are schools around the world, with several centres in the Tokyo area. The classes are led by professionals specialising in yoga for babies and toddlers up to the age of four. Visit the website for details of sessions near you.

Gymboree play group

National Children's Castle

5-53-1 Jingū-mae
Shibuya-ku
🚉 *Shibuya*
Map 8 D3 32

03 3797 5666
www.kodomono-shiro.or.jp

The Castle opened in 1985 as a place where children can develop healthy, happy, energetic and sound minds and bodies. Facilities include a gym, pool, gallery, arts studio, play room, video library, a roof garden and a clinic. Admission for the whole day is just ¥400 for children and ¥500 for adults. From Shibuya station walk up Miyamasu-zaka past Shibuya Post Office, then along Aoyama Dōri towards Aoyama University. The castle is on your left. Days and opening times vary, check on the website.

Tumble Tots

1-7-17 Tsunashima-
Higashi,
Kohoku-ku
Yokohama
🚉 *Tsunashima*
Map 2 A4

045 547 5140 | *www.tumbletotsjapan.com*

The Tumble Tots programme and equipment were designed by a former coach of the British Olympic Gymnastic team and is aimed at developing the physical abilities, coordination, balance and language skills of kids aged from 6 months to seven years. Lessons are 45 minutes long, with instruction in English, and there is a good mix of Japanese and foreign children. Costs range from ¥12,600 to ¥19,950 a month.

Motorcycling

Honda, Kawasaki, Suzuki, Yamaha – Japanese names are known all over the world as makers of high quality motorbikes. The Japanese are also massive fans, with millions of *ōtobai otaku* (motorbike geeks) having big arguments as to why their bike of choice is superior to any other. There are hundreds of motorcycle clubs dedicated to certain types of bikes. To find one, simply ask at the shop where you bought your machine. If you have yours shipped over, try asking at parts shops or mechanics that deal with your model. While Tokyo's roads are not quite Route 66, tours around the five lakes of Mount Fuji, Nikko, the Japan Alps or the Izu Peninsula offer spectacular scenery.

Lord's Angels

Wakō
Saitama-ken
Map 2 A1

www.gospeljapan.com/arthur/angels/

Headed by Arthur Hollands, a Harley-riding priest born in Osaka of American and Japanese descent, the Lord's Angels is a group of Christian bikers. The group meets once a month in Wakō, Saitama.

Women's International Motorbike Association

Various Locations

www.wima.gr.jp

Launched in 1996, WIMA Japan has a membership of around 70 women from many countries, including Japan. The group regularly travels to Europe for WIMA international rallies and holds spring and autumn meetings in the Japan Alps and other locations.

Mountain Biking
Other options **Cycling** p.217

Various Locations

International Adventure Club Tokyo
www.iac-tokyo.org

The IAC has a membership of around 350 of various nationalities, and offers outdoor activities such as mountain biking, cycling, hiking, camping, climbing and winter sports. The club organises rides around Tokyo and has a very active social calendar. The website features forums, lists of events and how to join. Annual membership is only ¥1,000.

21-41 Daikyū-chō
Shinjuku-ku
🚇 *Yotsuya-*
Sanchōme
Map 7 E2 **33**

Japan Mountain Bike Association
03 5363 3200 | www.japan-mtb.org

The JMBA administers races, tournaments and all other mountain biking events across Japan. The lack of English on their website is a drawback, but you can call or email them (admin@japan-mtb.org) for further information and to get in touch with fellow like-minded bikers.

Various Locations

Outdoor Club Japan
www.outdoorclubjapan.com

This fast growing club started in 2007 and has picked up more than 150 members in its first year. It offers mountain biking, cycling, hiking, climbing, winter sports, water sports, Ultimate Frisbee, drinking, social trips and much more. The website has more information on the club's activities, a calendar of all forthcoming events and details of how to join. Membership costs ¥1,500, after which all events are free.

Music Lessons
Other options **Dance Classes** p.217, **Singing** p.240

1-38-7 Akatsutsumi
Setagaya-ku
🚇 *Kyōdō*
Map 5 A2 **34**

Araya Piano Studio
03 5809 1305 | www.arayapianostudio.com

Yuko Araya is a piano instructor with 20 years experience teaching in the US. He offers lessons in both English and Japanese. Lessons can be arranged at the teacher's or student's home. Rates vary depending on the length of the class. Detailed directions to his home can be found on the website.

37-10-6
Udagawa-chō
Shibuya-ku
🚇 *Shibuya*
Map 8 B3 **35**

Music Instructors Corporation in Tokyo
0120 31 9355 | www.mic-tokyo.co.jp/music

Music Instructors Corporation (MIC) brings high quality music lessons, with original materials, to your home. Instruction can be arranged in various languages, including English, French, German and Spanish. While not cheap – fees start at ¥12,000 for twice-monthly classes, MIC is extremely flexible and has a good reputation. The school operates Monday to Friday from 09:30 to 18:30, and until 19:00 on Saturdays.

Setagaya
Setagaya-ku
Map 2 A3

Nagauta Shamisen
03 3412 6096 | http://shamisen.freehostia.com

Makoto Nishimura offers reasonably priced lessons in *nagauta* style music that is often used in *Kabuki* theatre. The *shamisen* and other traditional instruments such as the *shinobue* flute and *kotsutsumi* drum also feature. All classes are taught in English and are by appointment only. Makoto is a lovely lady who has a passion for music, and she has strong ambitions to spread the knowledge and playing of *nagauta* music across the world. Visit the website or contact her directly for more details.

Various Locations

Shimamura Music

03 5600 3888 | www.shimamura.co.jp

Shimamura Music offers lessons in many musical instruments at various locations across the city (see the website for listings of schools and shops). It caters to players of all levels and abilities, and even offers crash courses on learning a new piece. There's a music salon in which members can book a room for practice at any time. Trial lessons are free and monthly fees range from ¥5,000 to ¥10,000. They also have a massive music shop selling sheet music, gadgets, software and instruments.

Orchestras & Bands

Other options **Singing** p.240, **Music Lessons** p.233

1-7-1 Uchi-Kanda
Chiyoda-ku
Kanda
Map 14 C1 36

Big Wing Jazz Orchestra

www.bigwingjazz.com

This 18 piece big jazz band has been around since 1978. The music is centred around the usual (US) chart favourites, with some original compositions thrown in the mix. The band regularly plays live and makes occasional tours overseas, including regular visits to the Manly International Jazz Festival in Australia. Several non-Japanese play in the band, which gets together on Thursday evenings at the HMVP Otemachi Studio next to UFJ Bank, about five minutes walk west of JR Kanda station. They also cater to weddings, garden parties and other events. Visit the website for more details and for links to other amateur big bands and jazz sites in Japan.

Ro-on Jujo
Kaikan
Kita-ku
Higashi-Jūjō
Map 2 B2

New Symphony Orchestra

www.shinkyo.com

The 'Shinkyo' Orchestra is an amateur group comprised of all kinds of people that rehearses and performs under the banner of 'music is for anyone and everyone'. Practices take place on Saturday evenings from 18:00 to 21:00 at the Ro-on Jujo Kaikan, about seven minutes walk from the south exit of JR Higashi Jūjō station. The orchestra even provides a baby-sitting service during rehearsals. The English website is not kept as up-to-date as the Japanese version, but does have a lot of info on it, including how to join.

3-20-2 Nishi-
Shinjuku
Shinjuku-ku
Hatsudai
Map 3 D4 37

Tokyo Philharmonic Orchestra

03 5353 9521 | www.tpo.or.jp

The Tokyo Philharmonic is one of the major orchestras in the city. A highly professional outfit, competition to join is fierce and only those who are truly masters of their instrument will be considered. Details of events, performances and auditions are available on the website. The orchestra is based in the huge Tokyo Opera City building attached to Hatsudai station.

Photography

Photography is a popular hobby here and the stereotype of the Japanese tourist abroad, snapping away from morning to night also holds true in the motherland. Head to the area east of Shinjuku station and you'll find camera superstores such as Yodobashi, Bic Camera and Sakuraya as well as dozens of small independent specialist and second-hand stores – shop around, and talk with the very knowledgeable staff and you should be able to pick up some real bargains (see Camera Equipment on p.278 in Shopping). Also check out bookshops (p.278) for the huge range of photography books on Tokyo – an especially interesting purchase is a book detailing the provocative work of Nobuyoashi Araki. For inspiration, try the Tokyo Metropolitan Museum of Photography (p.176).

Tradtional dancers and drummers

Various Locations
Nikon Salon
03 3769 7953 | www.nikon-image.com/eng/activity/salon

Nikon's contribution to encouraging photography, if you feel that the world should see your snaps, you can put them on display at the Nikon Salons in Shinjuku or Ginza. Book in advance and the salon will give you free exhibition space for about a week. To apply, take your pictures to one of the salons and fill out the application form.

Zushi
Kanagawa-ken
Map 2 A4
Photospace B
046 873 2775 | http://photospace_b.tripod.com

Andy Barker, from the United States, has a photography school in Zushi on the southern coast of Kanagawa-ken, about an hour south of Tokyo. The first foreign photographer to produce a photography book on Kamakura, he offers 21 hour group courses and private lessons. He teaches at his school or can travel to students' houses, and for 2008 he is offering a discount to celebrate 10 years of teaching photography in Japan.

Pottery

Japan has a wide range of regional ceramic styles, and some are considered to be among the world's finest. Surprisingly, there are a number of foreign practitioners who excel at these styles, which are often considered to be exclusively Japanese. If you travel to any of the great regional ceramic centres that produce styles such as *Bizen-yaki*, *Satsuma-yaki*, *Raku-yaki* or *Tobe-yaki*, you will find small shops where you can try your hand at making a pot or a plate. While such places will have traditional kilns, many places around Tokyo use electric ovens. There are, however, a number of places that offer good classes for potential potters out there. Ask at your local ward office (p.88) for information on *tōgei kyōshitsu* (pottery schools).

1-71-2 Motomachi,
Naka-ku
Yokohama
Map 2 A4
Agape Ceramic Studio
045 212 5002 | www.acsjapanesepottery.com

Tom and Kae Morris run the Agape Ceramic Studio and Retreat House in Yokohama, which offers hands-on classes on the basics of pottery in English and Japanese. The three-month courses offer you the chance to make a variety of ceramic items. The history of ceramics is also taught in lessons, which are very reasonably priced at ¥12,000 for a nine-hour per month course.

2-9-4
Dōgenzaka
Shibuya-ku
🚇 *Shibuya*
Map 8 B3 38
JIC Ceramic Studio
03 3461 8902 | www.jicceramic.com

Located less than a minute from Shibuya station (Inokashira line) in the Kato Building, this small school offers lessons in English, French or Japanese. Courses range from a 12 session programme with two hour lessons for beginners, up to intermediate and advanced classes. Costs are ¥31,500, with additional fees charged for materials and firing.

2-15-4
Nishi-Waseda (105)
Takadanobaba
🚇 *Takadanobaba*
Map 3 F2 39
Karakuri Nendo
070 6552 4354 | www.potterytokyo.com

For a good budget option, try the reasonably-priced pottery classes at Karakuru Nendo. Courses of three-hour lessons twice a month cost ¥5,000, four times a month are ¥8,000, and drop-in classes and trial lessons are available for ¥3,000 per session. Lessons can also be arranged at student's homes. For more details, call or visit the website.

Rowing

Many companies and universities have rowing crews, but as they are not accessible to the general public, it is quite hard to find facilities for rowing in Tokyo. The most popular training place is the Toda Olympic Rowing Course that was used in the 1964 Tokyo Olympics and is located near Toda Kōen station in Saitama.

Japan Rowing Association

Kishi Memorial Hall,
1-1-1 Jinnan
Shibuya-ku
🚇 *Harajuku*
Map 8 C2 **40**

03 3481 2326 | www.jara.or.jp

JARA oversees rowing clubs and competitions across the country. Founded in 1920, it is the definitive contact point and source of information for rowers in Japan. The website is entirely in Japanese, but you can call or email (jara@japan-sports.or.jp) to find a club near you.

Tokyo Dragon Boat Club

Sakurabashi
Edogawa-ku
🚇 *Higashi-Ōshima*
Map 2 F2

www.tokyo-dragon.jp

The Tokyo Dragon Boat Club is a social team of paddlers in a sport that is becoming increasingly popular in Japan. Besides boating, club members take part as volunteers in a range of community events around Edogawa-ku. This friendly club competes in races and offers classes to beginners. Head from Higashi-Ōshima station past the 'ampm' convenience store to the club located at Sakurabashi bridge.

Rugby

As many as 126,000 people play rugby in Japan, giving it one of the biggest pools of players in the world. At the top of the game is the professional Big League, followed by university and amateur rugby. Tokyo has four mostly foreign amateur teams, the Tokyo Gaijin RFC, the Yokohama Country and Athletic Club, Tokyo Crusaders RFC and the All France Rugby Club. All four teams play in local amateur leagues and play friendlies against each other. Tens rugby is very popular in Asia and all four teams regularly attend tournaments in places such as Manila, Bangkok, Guam and Hong Kong. Amid Tokyo's 'old school tie' rugby scene, union is king, but there are also a smattering of league clubs. The Tokyo 13 Warriors is a spin off of the Tokyo Gaijins – see the Japan Rugby League website for details: www.geocities.jp/japaneserugbyleague/e/info.html.

All France Rugby Football Club

Various Locations

www.allfrance-rugby.com

Of all the expat rugby clubs in Tokyo, All France is probably the best for inexperienced players as it plays in relatively low leagues and its players are more into fun and fitness than serious competition. Despite its name, it has players from a number of countries and is open to anyone to try out with them. It plays in the Shuto and Construction leagues, the Sugadaira Rugby Festival, competitions in Asia and holds an annual tour.

Komae Touch Rugby Club

Ryokuchi Kōen
Tamagawa
Map 2 A3

http://homepage3.nifty.com/hashimo2/touch/index-e.htm

Keep fit playing rugby without the bruises with the Komae Touch Rugby Club on Saturday and Sunday afternoons. With several teams and various levels of players ranging from 60 year old vets to youngsters and women, the group welcomes anyone along. See the website above for more info, or email quilpie@sun-inet.or.jp.

Tokyo Crusaders RFC

Various Locations

www.tokyocrusaders.com

Patty Foley's pub in Roppongi is the headquarters of the Tokyo Crusaders, which may give you an indication of how highly it values the social aspect of the game. The team plays three weekends a month in spring and autumn leagues, and goes on tour every year, usually to play in international 10s tournaments. For more on the club, email info@tokyocrusaders.com.

Various Locations

Tokyo Gaijin Rugby Football Club
www.tokyogaijin.com
Tokyo Gaijins play nine months of the year in the Tokyo Cup, Shuto League and Ichihara League. It was started up by drinking pals 16 years ago, but it takes its rugby very seriously. The team trains weekly and plays at several locations throughout the city, including Akigase, Chiharadai, Yanokuchi and Yawatajuku Kōen.

11-1 Yaguchidai,
Naka-ku
Yokohama
🚇 **Yamate**
Map 2 A4

YCAC Rugby Club
www.geocities.com/ycac_rugby
The Yokohama Country & Athletic Club was founded by British expats and played in the first rugby match, in Japan, against Kao University, in 1900. It does not play in leagues, but is the only one of the four big foreigners' teams that has its own pitch, and it plays friendlies against teams from across Japan and visiting foreign sides. It is one of the best amateur teams in Japan, with several ex-pros playing there, including one former All Black. The club is 10 minutes from Yamate station, for directions see the website.

Running
By far the best run in the city is a few laps round the Imperial Palace East Gardens (p.185). Head there any day of the week and you'll see joggers of all abilities making their way around the scenic five kilometre course. Tokyo's rivers have wide grassy banks with running tracks and are excellent places to run without having to stop for traffic. Yoyogi Kōen is another hot spot for people who run plugged into their iPods ignoring the sounds of nature around them. The Oda Field track, next to Yoyogi Kōen, is open on Wednesday nights for those worried about running on the streets. Meanwhile, the clubs listed below are friendly and cater to all ages and abilities. See also http://tokyohash.org.

Various Locations

Harriers
03 5284 8335 | www.harriers.jp
This club trains on Tuesday evenings from 19:00 to 21:00 and holds longer distance runs at weekends. Do not be put off by the website, which is entirely in Japanese, as this is a friendly club with several foreign members. The club charges various levels of monthly fees depending on when you want to train.

Various Locations

Namban Rengo
www.namban.org
This club is a group of serious, international runners who train to run in competitive races and *ekiden* (relay races), but also welcomes fun runners. The club trains on Wednesdays, with about 20 to 30 people doing 6km runs. It also does long runs in Yoyogi Kōen (p.186) every Sunday morning, starting at around 09:00. Participation is free.

Sailing
Other options **Boat Tours & Charters** p.188

6-16-37 Zaimokuza
Kanagawa-ken
Map 1 B3

Be-Winds
0467 24 9401 | http://bewinds.blogspot.com
This exciting club, based in Kamakura, has several easy-to-sail boats that can take between one and four persons. Sailing is possible year round here, within the Sagami Bay area. It also hosts events such as informal club races for novices and veterans. The club offers trial sailing experiences from ¥4,000 for half a day, and a large range of classes and courses for sailors of all levels. For more information (in English) see the website above, or email be-winds@d4.dion.ne.jp.

Enoshima
Kanagawa-ken
Map 2 A4

Enoshima Yacht Club

www.enoshima-yc.jp

This large club is located next to the marina in Enoshima (south of Tokyo and Yokohama in Kanagawa-ken). Non-members can hire three or four types of dinghy at a range of prices, and members have access to a number of different craft. The club also runs a sailing school for kids on Sundays and courses that run over the Japanese school holidays.

Various Locations

Tokyo Sail & Power Squadron

www.tspsjapan.org

This branch of the United States Power Squadrons (an non-profit organisation for leisure sailing) offers English-language services to anyone interested in getting out on the water, and offers boating courses, weekend cruises for members, Japanese boat licence test preparation, monthly get-togethers, beach parties and crew networking opportunities. Social meetings are held on the first Wednesday every month at different bars in Tokyo. Check the website for details of the next meet and for information on upcoming events.

Yumenoshima
Marina
Koto-ku
Shin-Kiba
Map 2 C2

Tokyo Yacht Club

www.tyc.gr.jp

Located at a 650 berth marina in Koto-ku, the Tokyo Yacht Club has about 300 members sailing on a mix of 120 yachts and 40 power boats. The club has easy access out into Tokyo Bay and is popular for sailing and fishing. It organises 10 races a year for more than 50 yachts which are split into four classes. The clubhouse is open every weekend. Regular family events are held throughout the year to encourage an interest in sailing for children.

Scouts & Guides

Other options **Kid's Activities** p.225

With over 160,000 boy scouts and 60,000 girl scouts, Japan has a wide network of troops and is looking to host the 2015 World Scout Jamboree. For more information on scouting in Japan and contact details of troups near you, check out the Scout Association of Japan (www.scout.or.jp) or the Girl Scouts of Japan (www.girlscout.or.jp). For two of the most popular international options in Tokyo, see below.

1-7-8 Gotenyama
Kichioji
Kichijōji
Map 2 A2

St Mary's Boy & Girl Scouts

www.stmaryscout.com

Kichijoji Catholic Church is home to the 1st and 2nd Musashino Troop of Boy Scouts and the Girl Scout Tokyo 18 Troop. Boys aged from 6 to 19 years of age are welcome to join the beavers, cubs, scouts, ventures and rovers, and girls can join as a tenderfoot, a brownie, junior, senior or ranger. To join, get a registration form from the church. For more information check the website, or email boyscout@stmaryscout.com or girlscout@stmaryscout.com.

4-25-46 Takanawa
Minato-ku
Shinagawa
Map 6 A4 **41**

Tokyo American Club

03 4588 0670 | www.tokyoamericanclub.org

Scouting is one of the few activities at the TAC open to non-members. Children from international schools, and home-schooled children, attend the cubs and scouts here and do all the typical scouting activities. Cubs go out to events such as sumo, baseball games, camping, ice skating, bowling and hiking. Scouts also do more outdoor activities such as camping. Annual fees start at ¥26,000 per year.

Singing

Other options **Music Lessons** p.233

St Alban's Church
3-6-25 Shiba-Kōen
Minato-ku
🚇 *Kamiyachō*
Map 11 D3 **42**

The British Embassy Choir Tokyo

www.bec.ac
Although an amateur choir, many members have a formal musical background. The choir plays twice a year, at Christmas and during the spring or summer. Styles range from ballads to light opera, folk and popular songs. Membership is free.

3-1 Yoyogi
Kamizono-chō
Western Tokyo

Tokyo International Singers

044 833 9258 | *www.tokyo-singers.org*
Tokyo International Singers is an independent choir founded in 1980, that sings both great choral works and lighter music for summer concerts. It is a truly international group that plays at a range of venues across the Kanto region. Rehearsals are held on Saturday and Monday evenings at Yoyogi Olympics Memorial Youth Center and new members are welcome to visit any rehearsal.

Skiing & Snowboarding

With the mountains as close as 90 minutes away, Tokyo is a great place to live if you like a piste of the action. The season lasts from around November to early May and the quality of the snow is generally good, although it has been getting worse in recent years. A fantastic website for winter sports fans is www.snowjapan.com, which has details on snow conditions, accommodation, forums, video clips and much more, all in English. The 'Japan Ski Town Guides' section is a valuable part of the site, with information on the most popular resorts in Japan, including those in Hokkaidō, Nagano in the Japan Alps, and a couple close to Tokyo.

Weekend packages for skiing or snowboarding are often available for about ¥25,000. Check with travel agents and keep an eye on the press for deals. Many expats go through groups such as Canyons Outdoor Adventure Experiences (p.217) and Tokyo Gaijins (www.tokyogaijins.com). When your knees can't take any more of the slopes, jump into a steaming Jacuzzi in the mountains and soak your cares away (see *Onsen* p.264).

Yuzawa
Niigata-ken
Map 1 B3

Gala Yuzawa

025 785 6543 | *www.galaresort.jp*
This is neither the biggest nor best of resorts, but it is connected directly to the Gala Yuzawa *shinkansen* station which is a major advantage. Cheap and easy day trip packages are available from around ¥10,000. Its convenient location means it gets crowded quickly. Parking is limited so it's best to travel by *shinkansen*. Most accommodation is found in nearby Yuzawa.

Karuizawa
Nagano-ken
Map 1 B3

Karuizawa

026 742 5588 | *www.town.karuizawa.nagano.jp*
Karuizawa is where the well-heeled hit the slopes. While the skiing is good, it can be a more of a fashion parade than other resorts, especially with the huge shopping mall at the *shinkansen* station. Accomodation packages include the Prince Snow Resort, which starts at about ¥11,500 per night (www.princehotels.co.jp). Click on the Japanese language website for a ¥1,000 discount on lift passes.

Naeba
Niigata-ken
Map 1 B3

Naeba

025 789 2211 | *www.welovesnow.com*
This is a huge resort with more than 50 slopes and lots of off-piste fun, only two hours from Tokyo. The chair lifts can carry up to 50,000 people per hour, and the resort boasts

the massive Prince Hotel (www.princehotels.co.jp). Plenty of other accommodation is available in the nearby village. Many young people come for the excellent and foreigner-friendly apres-ski, especially at the Snodeck bar and restaurant. Take the Jōetsu *shinkansen* to Echigo Yuzawa station in Niigata-ken, then a highway express bus to the resort. Lift passes vary in price depending on the time of year and cost from ¥2,000 to ¥5,000.

Snooker & Pool

Snooker is far less popular than pool (there are only about 50 tables in the country). Pool (*biliyardo* in Japanese) is more common, and thre are many pool halls around that allow you to play a quiet game at reasonable rates. Unlike in other countries, snooker and pool halls tend to be in small, dedicated spaces rather than in sports bars. See also Big Box Takadanobaba on p.253 and Yokohama Country Club on p.255.

2-16-6 Nakahara
Higashiyamato-shi
🚉 *Ogawa*
Map 2 B2

Roots
042 2566 8575 | www.roots2000.jp
There is a bar-style atmosphere in this small venue with one snooker table and 10 pool tables. A game of snooker costs ¥420, but if there is a queue, just warm up with a game of pool or have a glass of something cold. This place is little out of the way from central Tokyo, but can be a fun trip out.

4-13-9 Higashi-Ogu
Arakawa-ku
🚉 *Tabata*
Map 2 B2

SnookerClub.Net
03 3893 9933 | www.snookerclub.net
With only three snooker tables in the place, you'll have to become a member to play here and reserve a table in advance by telephone. The club has numerous tournaments and offers free play for those chalking up big breaks. Play costs ¥840 per hour, but serious snooker players can fork out ¥20,000 a month for unlimited time.

Humax Pavilion (5F)
1-20-1 Kabukicho
Shinjuku-ku
🚉 *Shinjuku*
Map 3 E3 44

Sometime
03 3208 0127 | www.sometime-billiards.com
This venue is popular with hardcore players. Sometime oozes class and takes you back to days gone by. It has three snooker tables and 40 pool tables. 30 minutes play will set you back ¥650, so make sure you have been to the cash machine if you are banking on a long stint. It is next to the Koma Theater close to Seibu Shinjuku station.

Social Groups
Other options **Support Groups** p.131

Various Locations

Australia Society Tokyo
www.australiasocietytokyo.com
Hosting gala balls, ski weekends, barbecue parties, coffee mornings and cricket matches, the Australia Society has a strong focus on social life. Australians, New Zealanders and anyone else with a strong association to the Antipodean is welcome to join. One year membership costs ¥3,000.

Yūrakuchō Denki
North Building (20F)
Chiyoda-ku
🚉 *Yūrakuchō*
Map 14 A2 45

The Foreign Correspondents' Club of Japan
03 3211 3161 | www.fccj.or.jp
Members of The Foreign Correspondents' Club of Japan (FCCJ) include journalists, photographers and writers, and it is also regularly frequented by salarymen and diplomats. The club has a member's bar, restaurant, sushi bar and business facilities such as workrooms, a well-stocked library and internet connections. The club's monthly calendar is filled with press conferences held by the major shakers in the fields of business, politics, the arts and many other sectors.

Various Locations ◀ ## Indian Community Activities Tokyo
www.manicat.org

A voluntary association that provides cultural and business information and support for the Indian community, and for people with a connection to India, in Tokyo and the Kanto region. Free yoga classes are offered at the Indian Culture Centre at the Indian Embassy. Membership is free. Check out the website, especially the Useful Info section, for more.

Various Locations ◀ ## Irish Network Japan
www.inj.or.jp

A staff of Irish and Japanese volunteers run this non-profit organisation, whose main aims are to promote Irish culture, and encourage an exchange between Japan and Ireland. Regular events include sports days, *hanami* parties (cherry blossom viewing), Christmas and Halloween festivities, and a huge St Patrick's Day Parade.

Various Locations ◀ ## Japan Africa-American Friendship Association
www.jafa.org

JAFA is an organisation dedicated to supporting cultural and ethnic groups and promoting a positive image of African-American people, their heritage and their culture, to bring about greater understanding between the Japanese and African-Americans. The association hosts events, business and cultural promotions and is open to everyone.

Mejiro Kubo Bldg ◀ ## Japan Australia New Zealand Society
1-7-14 Mejiro
Toshima-ku   *03 3590 8581* | *www.janz.jp*
🚇 *Mejiro*   With the aim of promoting mutual understanding and friendship between Japan,
Map 2 B2   Australia and New Zealand, this society hosts business and academic lectures, parties, food festivals, cultural and sporting exchanges, and a host of individual exchanges and activities. Membership is ¥8,000 per year.

Fuji Building ◀ ## Japan-British Society
3-2-3 Marunouchi
Chiyoda-ku   *03 3211 8027* | *www.japanbritishsociety.or.jp*
🚇 *Nijūbashi-mae*   This thriving body has over 2,000 members and is supported by over 100 Japanese
Map 14 A1 46   and British companies. Functions such as an annual dinner, gala party, tours and outings are available for the main body of membership. Events such as pub nights, barbecues and film nights are held for members under 30. Ordinary annual membership costs ¥10,000.

4-25-46 Takanawa ◀ ## Tokyo American Club
Minato-ku
🚇 *Shinagawa*   *03 4588 0670*
Map 6 A4 41   *www.tokyoamericanclub.org*

The Tokyo American has been a Tokyo institution and retreat from city life since 1928. It offers world-class entertainment and recreation facilities along with a library, scores of activities for children and women, and hosts a long list of events. About one-third of its members are American, another third are Japanese and the rest hail from various other countries. Membership is pricey, starting at ¥1 million, with foreign firms often stumping up the fees for expats.

Socially Active?

Tokyo has a club for everyone. Some of the sports clubs have active social scenes, with evening meetings and get togethers in bars and other venues. Outdoor Club Japan (p.233), International Adventure Club Tokyo (p.233) and Tokyo Gaijins (www.tokyogaijins.com) have a lively social contingent. For women, International Women in Communication (www2.gol.com/users/iwic), Being-A-Broad (www.being-a-broad.com) and Foreign Executive Women (www.fewjapan.com) are worth checking out.

Are you always taking the wrong turn?

Whether you're a map person or not, these pocket-sized marvels will help you get to know the city – and its limits.

Explorer Mini Maps
Fit the city in your pocket

1-1 Ichigaya
Sadoharacho
Shinjuku-ku
🚇 *Ichigaya*
Map 10 C1 **47**

Tokyo Toastmasters Club
03 3260 8621 | http://tokyotmc.freetoasthost.info

This club holds its meetings and events in the Ichigaya Lutheran Center. Members get a chance to practise their public speaking skills at club meetings (held two or three times a month), training seminars and speech competitions. Meetings consist of sessions for business and 'table topics', speeches, evaluation and critique. Guests can attend three meetings free-of-charge, after which they can sign up. Fees are ¥9,000 per six-month term (plus a registration fee of ¥4,500).

11-1 Yaguchidai
Yokohama
Map 2 A4

Yokohama Country & Athletic Club
045 623 8121 | www.ycac.or.jp

The YC&AC was founded in 1868, as Yokohama Cricket Club, by a small group of English merchants, and it has flourished to become one of the most extensive leisure complexes to be found in Japan. The club has programmes for more than 20 sports including lawn bowls, yoga, rugby, cricket and field hockey, and holds many social events in its two restaurants and three bars. Membership does not come cheap though, with initial fees of ¥600,000 and monthly payments of ¥29,000.

Squash
Other options Sports & Leisure Facilities p.252

While there are plenty of places to play squash in Tokyo, most courts tend to be in private sports centres and gyms (see Sports & Leisure Facilities on p.252). Some wards have well-priced courts available for public use – for example the Shinagawa Kenko Center (www.kenko.shinagawa.tokyo.jp) but ask at your ward office for details. The Japan Squash Association (www.squash-japan.com) has a list of courts across the country and is a good resource on squash in Japan.

Surfing
Other options Kitesurfing p.227, Beaches p.183

The best surfing conditions are usually during the typhoon season, between August and October. Howver, the season runs from the spring right through to autumn, when the cold weather brings out only the most dedicated. Head to a surf beach around the Kanto region during this time and you'll be met with streets lined with board shops, deeply tanned surfy types wearing shorts and flip-flops and chilled summer reggae sounds. And the only thing on everyone's mind will be *naminori* (riding the waves).

While there's little happening around Tokyo proper, there's plenty of wave action just a few hours away, in places such as Kujyūkuri, Ichinomiya, or Kamogawa in Chiba-ken. The latter all have strong beach breaks, monstrous reefs and offer some of the best surfing in the region.

The waves are small on the beaches of Kanagawa-ken, but this does little to diminish its popularity. These beaches are within easy reach of Tokyo, and Shonan, Enoshima and Shichirigahama draw big crowds. Meanwhile, north of Tokyo, Ibaraki-ken, Oarai and Kashima pull out some big waves.

Boards and wetsuits can be rented from surf shops in the area for about ¥5,000 a day. Serious boarders often pay these shops to store their boards and equipment to avoid lugging the gear with them every time they come. Lessons are usually advertised and are available through these shops too. For more information on surfing in Japan, a good English-language source is www.japansurf.com, while www.surf-reps.com and www.namidensetsu.com have more detailed info in Japanese.

Swimming

Other options **Sports & Leisure Facilities** p.252, **Beaches** p.183

Pools in many shapes and sizes can be found across Tokyo. Most private sports clubs, gyms and hotels have their own heated indoor pools and offer lessons or activities like aqua aerobics. Ward-run pools are great value, only costing about ¥500 for good facilities. Swimming caps are mandatory in both these kinds of pools.
Newcomers to Japan might be surprised to see lanes filled with elderly people walking and swinging their arms through the water.
Between late June and the end of August many wards open up outdoor pools. For some reason September onwards is not included, despite temperatures over 30°C and searing humidity. Serious swimming can be done in these pools, but they are more geared to fun and serious showing off in bikinis or tight-fitting Speedos. Every 30 minutes or so the lifeguards bizarrely call a five-minute 'break' and everyone has to get out the pool.

Swimming

Edogawa Pool Garden	8-17-1 Nishi Kasai	Edogawa-ku	03 3687 1721	Outdoor
Hikarigaoka Gymnasium Pool	4-1-4 Hikarigaoka	Nerima-ku	03 5383 6611	Indoor
Komazawa Olympic Park Outdoor Swimming Pool	1-1 Komazawa Kōen	Setagaya-ku	03 3421 6121	Outdoor
Meguro Ward Center Pool	2-4-36 Meguro	Meguro-ku	03 3711 1139	Outdoor
Meiji Jingu Swimming Pool	9 Kasumigaoka	Shinjuku-ku	03 3403 3458	Outdoor
National Yoyogi Field Indoor Pool	2-1-1 Jinnan	Shibuya-ku	03 3468 1176	Indoor
Nishi Ikebukuro Heated Pool	4-7-5 Nishi-Ikebukuro	Ikebukuro-ku	03 3981 6468	Indoor
Setagaya Sogo Undojo Indoor Pool	7-9-1 Funabashi	Setagaya-ku	03 3789 3911	Indoor
Shinjuku Cosmic Sports Centre	3-1-2 Okubo	Shinjuku-ku	03 3232 7701	Indoor
Showa Kinen Kōen Rainbow Pool	3173 Midori-machi	Tachikawa-shi	042 528 1751	Outdoor
Tokyo Gymnasium	1-17-1 Sendagaya	Shibuya-ku	03 5474 2111	Indoor

Table Tennis

Other options **Sports & Leisure Facilities** p.252

Japan dominated world table tennis in the 1950s and 1960s, but despite the world centre moving to China, it is still up there with the best. Most Japanese players use a pen-shaped grip, which allows them to get greater spin on the ball, and once mastered it can greatly improve your game. *Takkyū* is popular in schools and many wards have reasonably-priced tables where you can play. Your local ward office (p.88) should have information on table tennis venues, see also listings at www.exist.net/pingpong.html (in Japanese only). Shibuya Higashi-Guchi Kaikan (www.shibuyaest.com/9floor.html), Shinjuku Copabowl (www.jp-l.co.jp/copabowl) and Brunswick Sports Garden (30-1-1 Higashi Ikebukuro, Toshima-ku, 03 3988 7221) are open for public play. The Japan Table Tennis Association's website (www.jtta.or.jp) has lots of information on the sport, but in Japanese only. For a game and a beer, check out Nakame Takkyu Lounge (p.368), a quirky bar hidden in the backstreets of Meguro-ku with it's very own ping pong table.

Tennis

Other options **Sports & Leisure Facilities** p.252

Securing court time can be frustrating for the casual tennis player in Tokyo and you often need to book ahead – sometimes at considerable cost. Public courts are cheap and therefore popular so the wards that run them sometimes use a lottery system to ensure fair allocation of playing time. These courts are usually found in municipal parks.

More serious players should shell out extra cash and head to courts at hotels or private courts at locations including the Shinjuku Hilton, Shinagawa Prince, Meguro Tennis Club, Meiji Jingu Tennis Club and Tokyo Lawn Tennis Club (see p.254). A list of venues to play at can be found at www.tokyotennis.com. Those wanting to see the likes of Roger Federer and other ATP stars should head to the AIG Open (p.250) at the Ariake Colosseum, near Kokusai Tenjijyō station in Odaiba, in early October.

Tennis

Hilton Tokyo	6-6-2 Nishi-Shinjuku	Shinjuku-ku	03 3344 5111	www1.hilton.com
Meguro Tennis Club	5-12-20 Kami-Meguro	Meguro-ku	03 3711 4551	www.como.ac/tc
Meiji Jingu Tennis Club	2-1-15 Kita-Aoyama	Aoyama	03 3401 0389	www.meijijingugaien.jp
Shinagawa Prince	4-10-30 Takanawa	Shinagawa-ku	03 3441 0020	www.princehotelsjapan.com
Tokyo Lawn Tennis Club	5-6-41 Minami-Azabu	Minato-ku	03 3473 1545	www.tltc.jp

Various Locations
Krissman International Tennis School
03 3325 0924 | www.krissmantennis.com
Australian and North American coaches teach tennis at various locations across Tokyo for both adults and juniors. Adults can learn in locations such as the British Embassy (p.19) and Roppongi (p.156) while children's lessons are held at international schools and places like the Tokyo American Club (p.254). There are a range of packages available, but bank on paying about ¥4,000 for a 90 minute lesson.

Futako-Tamagawa
Sports Center
Setagaya-ku
Map 2 A3
Sam Arnold Tennis Academy Tokyo
03 3062 7379 | www.geocities.com/satatokyo
The Sam Arnold Tennis Academy offers weekend practice and game sessions for intermediate and advanced players at Futako-Tamagawa Sports Center in Setagaya-ku (see website for directions). Two-hour sessions, which include practice followed by a 90 minute doubles game with umpires, cost ¥4,000 and personal instruction is provided for intermediate players. Membership is ¥2,000.

Volleyball

Volleyball is hugely popular is Japan with massive television ratings for international matches. Japan has hosted the Men's and Women's FIVB World Cup every four years since 1976 (men) or 1977 (women), and Japan also has its own professional V.League. The sport is played in many schools and universities and there are more than 100 private clubs in the Tokyo area. See www.volleyball.gr.jp for a list. You can also contact the Japan Volleyball Association (www.jva.or.jp) for more information.

3-1-2 Okubo
Takadanobaba
Takadanobaba
Map 3 F2 48
Tokyo International Volleyball Club
090 8451 8682 | http://multidou.com/intervoll
Players from a score of nations have been getting together for friendly games here for over a decade. All skill levels are welcome, but the players are said to be 'motivated'. Court hire is ¥1,500 per person and lockers cost ¥100. Contact Yann for information in French, English or Japanese.

Watersports

Edogawa
Chiba-ken
Map 1 C3
Flying High Wakeboarding
090 7271 6115 | www.flyinghighwakeboarding.com
Tokyoites who miss riding the surf should head out to Chiba to skim across Edogawa behind the Flying High Wakeboarding powerboat. Members (who pay ¥7,000 a year) can ride two 20 minute runs on weekdays for an additional ¥7,000, or weekends for

¥8,000. Equipment rental is included in the fees.

Canoeing with Evergreen (p.215)

Lake Yamanaka-ko
Hakone
Map 1 B3

Tokyo Waterski Club

www.geocities.co.jp/
Athlete-Olympia/4191

Enjoy the thrills of waterskiing while gazing at the majesty of Mount Fuji on a weekend getaway to Lake Yamanaka. These light-hearted trips are a great way to get to know people and enjoy the natural beauty found outside the concrete jungle.

Zushi Beach
Kanagawa-ken
Map 2 A4

Zushi Windsurf School

046 873 2863 | www.j-wind.com/zushi

Providing one-day lessons, the Zushi Windsurf School serves Zushi Beach in Yokohama. Rates begin at ¥8,000 for beginners' classes and ¥10,000 for intermediate windsurfers. Lessons start at 10:00 and board rental is only ¥2,500. Take the Yokosuka line from central Tokyo to Zushi station (less than an hour away). The school is less than 10 minutes walk from the station.

Wine Tasting

4-19-17 Shirokanedai
Minato-ku
🚇 **Shirokanedai**
Map 6 A3 49

French Wine Tasting Club

03 3442 5588 | www.winetestingtokyo.com

Learn about wines from across the globe in sessions where you taste three wines from one particular region. These cultural gatherings are lively and cost ¥9,900 including a gourmet dinner at the Stellato restaurant. Most participants have little background in wines, but are thirsty to learn more.

1-4-4 Jōmyōji
8232 Kamakura
Kanagawa-ken
Map 2 A4

Sake World

http://sake-world.com

Ohio-native John Gaunter is recognised as the world's leading non-Japanese sake authority, or 'The Sake Guy'. John writes regular articles for magazines and newspapers, holds seminars in English each month for expats, and runs intensive educational courses in sake every winter in a brewery.

Various Locations

The Tokyo Wine Society

03 3441 6718 | www.tokyowine.org

This group of enthusiasts does blind tastings each month. People of varying experience and nationalities gather to sample nine or more wines and enjoy a slap-up dinner at a central Tokyo restaurant in a relaxed atmosphere. Usually about 30 people attend the tastings, which range in price from ¥11,000 to ¥13,000. Reservations are necessary and there is a ¥8,000 cancellation fee if you don't show.

Oops!

Did we miss anything? If you have any thoughts, ideas or comments for us to include in the Activities section, drop us a line, and if your club or organisation isn't in here, let us know and we'll give you a shout in the next edition. Visit www. explorerpublishing.com and fill us in.

Spectator Sports

The Japanese are keen sports fans. Three grand sumo tournaments are held in Ryōgoku every year for traditional sport lovers, while many of the world's greatest golfers, tennis players and athletes come to show off their skills to their Japanese fans. Other sports such as ice-skating, volleyball and K1 (mixed martial arts) are massive televised hits that make the primetime spots. Rugby is still very old school in Japan, perhaps even more so than in Britain, and its elite players go through the ranks of rugby universities such as Waseda (www.waseda.jp), Kanto Gakuin (www.kanto-gakuin.ac.jp) and Meiji (www.meiji.ac.jp). Meanwhile, horseracing in Ōi and Fūchū attracts thousands of punters who are happy to while away a Sunday afternoon at the races.

None of these, however, can hold a match to the insane popularity of baseball and football. The rapid emergence of football in Japan is starting to threaten baseball's number one spot as the country's favourite spectator sport, but you'll still find baseball stadiums packed to the rafters with families munching on *yaki-soba* noodles and guzzling beer.

American Football

American football was brought to Japan in 1934 by an American teacher, Paul Rusch, who initially put together three college teams. It was not until 1971, however, that the X-League was founded. Today, players can join the Urban Football League and the Japan Private Football Federation.

Various Locations

American Football X-League
www.xleague.com

American Football has a small but passionate following in Japan. The X-League is a four-division, 60 team professional league, split into east, west and central divisions. Teams in the east division of the top flight include Asahi Silver Star, Obic Seagulls, Fujitsu Frontiers, Renesas Hurricanes and ROCBULL. The latter play games in and around Tokyo, Yokohama and Kawasaki each autumn. With hundreds of universities also fielding teams, the Rice Bowl is the biggest game in Japanese American Football, when the collegiate champs take on the X-League winners in the battle for the title.

Baseball

Baseball is Japan's favourite spectator sport. Professional baseball is split into two divisions: Central League and Pacific League, with six teams competing for the top spot. The winners of each group go into the play-offs for the Japan series each autumn.

Meiju Jingu Stadium
3-1 Kasumigaoka
Minato-ku
Gaiemmae
Map 8 E1 52

Tokyo Yakult Swallows
03 5470 8915 | www.yakult-swallows.co.jp

Compared with the across-town Giants, the Swallows are the perennial underdogs and have a budget to match, forcing them to develop their own young stars and to ship in players past their prime from overseas or bought from other Japanese teams. Despite this, Swallows games are always fun and they have a lively set of supporters.

1-3 Tokyo Dome
Bunkyō-ku
Kōrakuen
Map 9 E2 18

Yomiuri Giants
www.giants.jp/top.html

The Manchester United or the New York Yankees of Japanese baseball, the Giants or *Kyojin* are owned by the Yomiuri media giant and are the biggest and most successful ball club in the country. Pretty much every game the Giants play is televised, much to the chagrin of fans of other teams. Despite this, tickets are relatively easy to come by, going on sale after 10:00 on game days. They can also be purchased beforehand during the presales. The best games are when their biggest rivals, the Hanshin Tigers, come to town from Osaka.

Football

Football has been on the up in Japan since the formation of the professional J.League in 1992. The extraordinarily successful 2002 World Cup (co-hosted with South Korea) added momentum to this newfound popularity. The country has also hosted the FIFA World Club Cup. In addition to league matches, teams play for the Nabisco Cup and the Emperor's Cup – an end of season tournament similar to the English FA Cup.

F.C. Tokyo

Ajinomoto Stadium
Nishi 376-3
Chōfu-shi
🚉 *Tobitakyū*
Map 2 A2

03 3635 8985 | www.fctokyo.co.jp

The 'Gas Men' were originally that, starting life in 1935 as the Tokyo Gas Football Club. In recent years the club has consolidated in J1 and is now settled at Ajinomoto Stadium. The club is looking to expand and make a push for the top so watch this space.

Tokyo Verdy 1969

Ajinomoto Stadium
Nishi 376-3
Chōfu-shi
🚉 *Tobitakyū*
Map 2 A2

www.verdy.co.jp

Verdy moved from its base in Kawasaki in 2001 due to competition from nearby Kawasaki. It shares Ajinomoto Stadium with Frontale and FC Tokyo. They regained top-flight status in 2007 and are looking forward to a long stint in J1. Check out www.brilliantomiya.blogspot.com, an informative English language blog, for more information on the team.

Urawa Red Diamonds

Nakanoda
Saitama-ken
🚉 *Urawa Misono*
Map 2 A1

048 812 1001 | www.so-net.ne.jp/urawa-reds/index_e.html

The country's biggest team attracts attendances of up to 60,000, with dedicated fans raucously cheering for the full 90 minutes. 'The Reds' won the Asian Champions Cup in 2007 and became the first Japanese team ever to win the tournament. They also made an appearance in the World Club Cup later that year. Despite having the largest fan base in the country, they didn't win a title until 2006. After narrowly missing the chance to become champs in 2007, they are on the up and look set to make their mark on Japanese football in the years to come.

Horse Racing

Tokyo Racecourse

1-1 Hiyoshi-chō
Fūchū
Western Tokyo
🚉 *Fūchū Keiba*
Seimon Mae

042 5785 7373 | http://japanracing.jp

Tokyo Racecourse has a capacity for over 200,000 and is the Japan Racing Association's longest course, with three tracks – the main course, a dirt course and a steeplechase course. It hosts Grade 1 races such as the Japan Cup in November and the Tenno Sho (Japanese St Ledger) earlier in the autumn. At only ¥200 for an entry ticket, it's a cheap day out – unless of course you're a keen gambler and it's not your lucky day.

Rugby

Chichibunomiya Stadium

2-8-35 Kita Aoyama
Minato-ku
🚉 *Gaiemmae*
Map 8 F1 **50**

03 3401 3881 | www.rugbyjapan.com

This is the place to watch rugby in Tokyo. The headquarters of the Japan Rugby Football Union seats 27,188 and hosts the 'Brave Blossoms' national team, as well as many games in the Top League (www.top-league.jp), which kicked off in 2003. The

Toshiba Brave Lupus are the current league champs, and have been for the past three years. Other teams include Toshiba's Fūchū-based rivals Suntory Sungoliath and the Ricoh Black Rams.

Sumo

1-3-28 Yokozuna
Sumida-ku
🚇 *Ryōgoku*
Map 4 E3 **51**

Kokugikan (Sumo)
03 3622 1100 | www.sumo.or.jp
For an authentic Japanese sporting experience head over to the Kokugikan Stadium in Ryōgoku for one of the three annual *basho* (15 day grand tournaments) held in January, May and September. Among the crowds outside the arena, you'll find many oversized men in tight fitting *yukata* shuffling around in their *geta* slippers. Tournament days last from 09:00 to 18:00, but unless you are a real sumo nut, just head over around 14:00 or 15:00 and kick back with a *bento* box and a glass (or two) of *sake* and watch the big boys at it. Tickets are hard to come by at weekends, or on the opening and final days, so book in advance. Alternatively, weekday cheap seats cost around ¥2,000. To get a ringside or *masu-seki* (box seats), you'll need to be well connected.

Tennis

Ariake Tennis
Forest Park
2-2-22 Ariake
Koto-ku
Map 6 D3 **93**

AIG Japan Open Tennis Championships
03 3481 2511 | http://aigopen.jp
Early October sees many of the world's top male and female players making the trip to Tokyo for the Japan Open. Past winners on the hard courts here include Roger Federer, Pete Sampras, Monica Seles and Maria Sharapova. Tickets for the semi-finals and final are hard to come by, so book early.

Beach wrestling *Budokan stadium*

Kendo

Small but indispensable…

Perfectly proportioned to fit in your pocket, this marvellous mini guidebook makes sure you don't just get the holiday you paid for but rather the one that you dreamed of.

Los Angeles Mini Visitors' Guide
Maximising your holiday, minimising your hand luggage

Bodymode pilates studio

Sports & Leisure Facilities

With the frenetic pace of life in the city, finding the time to get out and exercise can be a challenge. There's a variety of public and private fitness and relaxation facilities dotted throughout Tokyo, ranging from quaint, no-frills community gyms to upscale members-only sports and country clubs. The Tokyo American Club (p.255) and Yokohama Country & Athletic Club (p.254) are two of the most popular with expats who can afford them. Despite Tokyo's proximity to the sea, the concept of an oceanfront sports centre hasn't taken off, probably due to its lack of anything resembling a white, sandy beach.

The most common facilities at public gyms are machine and free weights, and there's usually a multipurpose indoor court that can be used for basketball, volleyball, badminton, martial arts and table tennis. Private health centres often have a weights room with exercise machines, possibly a swimming pool, and almost certainly studio space for aerobics, yoga, dance and other guided classes. The main difference between public and members-only clubs, besides the price, is the availability of showers and other add-ons like saunas, Jacuzzis, steam rooms, tanning beds and relaxation salons offering extra services including massage, reflexology and aromatherapy.

A few sports clubs, like the You Port Setagaya Rec Center (opposite), allow non-members to take advantage of the facilities, but this is rare. To use the popular chain gyms like Tipness, Central Sports Club, Work Out World or Gold's Gym (see below), you'll have to jump through the membership hoops and fork out an average of ¥8,000 to ¥10,000 a month. Otherwise, stick to the public gyms or Community Centres (p.255) in your ward, which will cost a more wallet-friendly ¥200 to ¥500 per session.

Health Clubs

Joining a health club is one of the easiest ways to keep those fitness-related resolutions. There are several popular gym chains in town, and the vast majority are clean, well-equipped and affordable. Most offer various membership plans, with discounts for students or those who plan to visit at weekends only or at certain times of the day. Towel rental and lockers are not usually included with standard membership, and are available for an additional ¥3,000 a month or so. While gyms in western countries often double as places to socialise and meet new people, in Tokyo it seems, people are there by and large to sweat, not to chat. Other budget options include the government run Community Centres, see p.255 for more information on these. For personal trainers see the Nutritionists & Slimming table on p.129.

Health Clubs	
Central Sports Club	www.central.co.jp
Gold's Gym	www.goldsgym.jp
Konami Sports Club	www.konamisportsclub.jp
Tipness	www.tipness.co.jp
Tokyu Sports Oasis	www.sportsoasis.co.jp
Work Out World	www.wowd.jp

Sports Centres

19-1 Senju Sekiyachō
Adachi
🚉 **Keisei-Sekiya**
Map 2 C2

Amazing Square

Amazing Square has undergone several changes in recent years, and has been an amusement park and a giant maze in its time. Today the complex offers batting cages, an adjacent games arcade and indoor fishing centre (03 3882 2770), a go-cart track (03 3882 0027), inline skating and skateboard park (03 3882 8011), indoor and outdoor futsal courts (www.mfpsc.com/snj.htm), and an indoor inline hockey rink (www.misconduct-hockey.co.jp). Paid parking is available.

1-35-3
Takadanobaba
Shinjuku-ku
🚉 **Takadanobaba**
Map 3 E2 53

Big Box Takadanobaba

03 3208 7171 | www.seibu-group.co.jp/rec/bigbox/baba/sports
This place is exactly what it says on the tin – literally a giant blue box, located just outside the station. As the area is home to several colleges including Waseda University, the facilities are geared towards a younger crowd – but don't let that put you off. The nine-storey complex houses Seibu Fitness Club (03 5272 5203), which offers weights and exercise machines, a 25 metre pool, 100 metre running track, studio, sauna, Jacuzzi and massage room. Big Box also boasts 30 bowling lanes, a billiards room with two dozen tables, a Culture School (03 5272 5205) that offers yoga and dance classes, an internet cafe (03 5291 4323) with comics, karaoke and dart boards, a video arcade and three dining and drinking establishments. In a nutshell, you could spend weeks here and never get bored.

4-7-1 Ōkura
Setagaya-ku
🚉 **Soshigaya-Ōkura**
Map 2 A3

Wel Sunpia Tokyo (Tokyo Kosei Nenkin Sports Center)

03 3416 2611 | www.kjp.or.jp/hp_56
Wel Sunpia Tokyo is a huge, publicly funded complex complete with outdoor tennis courts, a driving range, an indoor multi-use gymnasium, fitness facilities and a water park. Instructors are on hand to coach tennis, golf, youth basketball, women's volleyball, yoga and qigong. Adult education courses are also offered. Western and Japanese restaurants are on hand when hunger strikes, and you can even stay overnight at the traditional inn.

2-17-1 Kamata
Setagaya-ku
🚉 **Futako-Tamagawa**
Map 2 A3

You Port Setagaya Rec Center

03 3709 0161 | www.central.co.jp/club/kampo-tokyo
You Port Setagaya Rec Center (formerly the Kanpo Rec Center), is just 10 minutes by bus from both Futako-Tamagawa and Seijo Gakuen-mae stations. Sports facilities include a pool and fitness centre (run by the Central Sports gym group), 21 tennis courts, squash courts and a driving range. Use of the tennis courts is open to non-members and costs ¥3,150 to ¥3,360 on weekdays and ¥4,200 to ¥5,400 at weekends for a two-hour session. To swim, work out, use the driving range or play squash, it is necessary to either join (membership costs from ¥5,775 to ¥9,450 per month) or to buy a one-day pass for ¥1,890. Squash courts cost an additional ¥315 for 20 minutes). The centre opens daily, but operating hours depend on the activity. Free parking is available for up to three hours.

Sports Clubs

If you prefer exercising and socialising with the upper crust, and you have a few million yen lying around, you may want to consider joining one of the city's exclusive luxury sports clubs. In addition to all of the standard (top of the range) facilities, these typically offer heated pools, squash courts, spas and saunas and other luxury treats. Restaurants and cafes are par for the course, and some places even have adjacent inns and hotels for those who are keen to make a weekend of it. See also the Yokohama

Country & Athletic Club on p.255, an equally exclusive country club that has myriad activities to chase boredom away.

3-26-6 Yakumo
Meguro-ku
🚇 *Jiyugaoka*
Map 5 C4 **54**

Liberty Hill Club

03 5731 5731 | *www.libertyhill.co.jp*

The name of this club refers to its location, on Liberty Hill, in the upscale, foreigner-friendly suburb of Jiyugaoka. Facilities include two outdoor tennis courts, an indoor 25m pool, a golf driving range, and a gym with free weights, weight machines and exercise equipment. There's also a fitness studio, spa and an Italian restaurant. General members pay a ¥315,000 joining fee. plus ¥231,000 per year for up to 10 years. For foreigners and Japanese who frequently travel overseas, Associate membership is also possible, with no joining fee and an annual fee of ¥283,500. Parking is available.

3-3-3 Minami-Aoyama
Minato-ku
🚇 *Gaiemmae*
Map 8 E2 **55**

Riviera Sports Club Minami-Aoyama

03 5474 8000 | *www.riviera-s.jp*

The focus at Riviera Sports Club is on fitness and relaxation. On the fitness side, facilities include a studio, 25m indoor pool, squash court, free weights and exercise machines, as well as a golf practice bay. For those in need of some pampering, the relaxation wing offers sports massage, reflexology, organic germanium bathing, manicures and pedicures, Endermologie, facials and more. Membership costs ¥105,000 plus ¥25,200 per month or ¥252,000 per year. A one-off trial is possible for ¥3,150. Members also receive 10% discount at the attached Riviera Aoyama restaurant. Parking is available.

4-25-46 Takanawa
Minato-ku
🚇 *Shinagawa*
Map 6 A4 **41**

Tokyo American Club

03 4588 0670 | *www.tokyoamericanclub.org*

The Tokyo American Club is the city's most exclusive sports and recreation facility. This social club has moved from its usual home base in Azabudai due to extensive renovation work, and will be in Takanawa until 2010. The temporary site has no bowling alley, driving range or tennis courts, but still has a gym, fitness studio, squash courts, and a 25m outdoor pool. Dining facilities and a new spa and manicure bar are also onsite. There are several types of membership options, from corporate to resident and non-resident. Those residing outside the Greater Tokyo area are quite fortunate as fees involve a mere one-off payment of ¥200,000, plus ¥3,000 to ¥4,000 monthly. This pales in comparison to what those living in the area pay, which is well upwards of ¥2,000,000 annually. All members must also pay a refundable ¥200,000 deposit. The club has more than 3,500 high-rolling members, from over 50 different countries. Valet and self-parking is available.

5-6-41 Minami-Azabu
Minato-ku
🚇 *Hirō*
Map 11 A4 **56**

Tokyo Lawn Tennis Club

03 3473 1545 | *www.tltc.jp*

Tokyo Lawn Tennis Club was established in 1900 and used to sit in the same spot that the *Diet* (Japanese parliament) now holds. It moved to its Azabu location in 1940 and managed to survive the tumultuous years that followed. The club maintains 10 clay tennis courts, five of which are floodlit from sun until 21:00. Locker rooms, showers and the small cafe stay open until 22:00. Membership is quite exclusive and requires two club recommendations and an interview, as well as a hefty annual fee. There are two categories: term regular membership (valid for up to five years), costing ¥100,000 as a one-time payment plus ¥30,000 per month, and permanent membership which costs ¥1,200,000 as a one-off payment, plus ¥13,000 per month. Guests accompanied by a member can volley back and forth over the net for ¥4,000 on weekdays, ¥7,000 at weekends and ¥3,000 in the evenings. The club gets pretty crowded at weekends, especially if the weather is good. Doubles play is rotated regularly though. Parking is available. The club is open Tuesday to Sunday from 06:30 to 22:00. It's closed on Mondays.

Community Centres

The Tokyo Metropolitan Government (www.metro.tokyo.jp) does a fine job of providing recreation facilities that offer everything from badminton courts and archery lanes to cooking areas and sumo rings. The cost of using a municipal sports facility is inexpensive, and prices start at around ¥150 for adults, and half that for children. Each ward normally has one main public gym, and some charge lower prices for area residents. Shibuya Sports Center is only open to those who live, work or study within the ward. Many local governments now list their facilities online, with some even providing the information in English.

Community Centres			
Akasaka Community Plaza	4-18-3 Akasaka	Minato-ku	03 5413 2717
Bunkyō Ward Gymnasium	4-7-13 Yushima	Bunkyō-ku	03 3814 4271
Chiyoda-ku Sports Center	2-1-8 Uchi-Kanda	Chiyoda-ku	03 3256 8444
Chūō-ku Sports Center	2-59-1 Nihonbashi-hamacho	Chūō-ku	03 3666 1501
Edogawa Ward Gymnasium	4-2-20 Nishi-Kasai	Edogawa-ku	03 3653 7441
Meguro-ku Chūō Gymnasium	5-22-8 Meguro Honchō	Meguro-ku	03 3714 9591
Minato Ward Gymnasium	3-1-19 Shibaura	Minato-ku	03 3452 4151
Nakano Ward Gymnasium	4-11-14 Nakano	Nakano-ku	03 3389 3151
Setagaya Sports Center	4-6-1 Ōkura	Setagaya-ku	03 3417 4276
Shibuya Sports Center	1-40-18 Nishihara	Shibuya-ku	03 3468 9051
Shinagawa-ku Sports Center	2-11-2 Higashi-Gotanda	Shinagawa-ku	03 3449 4400
Shinjuku Cosmic Sports Center	3-1-2 Okubo	Shinjuku-ku	03 3232 7701
Shinjuku Sports Center	3-5-1 Okubo	Shinjuku-ku	03 3232 0171
Taito Riverside Sports Center	1-1-10 Imado	Taitō-ku	03 3872 3181
Tokyo Gymnasium	1-17-1 Sendagaya	Shibuya-ku	03 5474 2111

Country Clubs

11-1 Yaguchidai
Naka-ku
Yokohama
Map 2 A4

Yokohama Country & Athletic Club
045 623 8121 | www.ycac.or.jp

The Yokohama Country & Athletic Club (YCAC) is situated on The Bluff, an area south of Yokohama. It was founded in 1868 by a group of foreign traders as a cricket club and has grown over the years to include a bowling alley, fitness centre and outdoor swimming pool, and squash and tennis courts. It's a social club, and members hail from over 40 different countries. While the club has no golf course, it does have a putting green, practice bunker and three short driving bays, and organises regular trips to nearby courses. YCAC also boasts field hockey, cricket and rugby teams and has a football team in the Tokyo Metropolis League (see p.222). Various classes are offered in disciplines such as yoga, *ikebana* and martial arts, as well as coaching in basketball and table tennis. For the less active, there's a library and video centre. Parking and child care facilities are available. Various membership options are possible, ranging from associate membership for terms of six months to two years, with no joining fee, a refundable ¥100,000 deposit and monthly rates of ¥27,800 (single) to ¥43,600 (including family members up to age 19). Weekly joining fees start at ¥10,000, while monthly rates go from ¥37,000 (single) to ¥46,000 (family). Email membership@ycac.or.jp for more information.

Well-Being

Japan is the birthplace of the holistic healing traditions of shiatsu and reiki, and Japanese society has long realised that there is more to the body, health and well-being than what the eye can see. Working with a person's energy is not such an abstract concept and many forms of alternative therapies focus on the spiritual rather than the physical.

However, mind-body pursuits like yoga and tai chi are also popular and many new studios have opened up across the city over the past few years, attracting young Japanese women with a range of classes, including power and bikram yoga.

For those after a more luxurious facial or spa treatment there are a host of pampering palaces. Hotel spas are at the higher end of the spectrum and many only cater to guests and club members. Private salons offer a similar range of treatments, but are better value, although perhaps less up-market. Happily, some treatments can be found for much cheaper rates than you'll find abroad. Coveted beautifying treats such as eyelash extensions (see Ren p.257) are much cheaper than in salons in the US. Appearance is important in the city and maintaining one's look is essential. Happily, Tokyo residents will never be short of places to get their hair elegantly coiffed or their nails buffed, shaped and polished.

Salon Solutions

To find out more about the city's salons, visit www.spinshell.tv or pick up a copy of Metropolis *(www.metropolis.co.jp) or women's magazine* Being-A-Broad *(www. being-a-broad.com/ babmagazine).*

Beauty Salons

Other options **Perfumes & Cosmetics** p.296, **Health Spas** p.258

A bit of self-indulgent pampering is a popular Tokyo pastime and there are plenty of hip spots to indulge at. In general, the quality of service is high, with good hygiene standards. Most beauty salons offer a blend of eastern and western treatments, including facials, waxing, hand and foot nail care, make-up, and eyelash tinting and perming. Facials start at around ¥8,000 at the lower end of the spectrum and go up to around ¥30,000. Standard treatments, like eyelash tinting cost around ¥4,000 and the price of a wax varies between ¥3,000 to ¥13,000. Boudoir (p.257) offers Brazilian waxes (a service that is sometimes hard to find) and they are well known among foreigners for their decadent array of treatments. If you really want to splurge, hotel spas (see Health Spas on p.258) offer similar primping and polishing services, in a more upmarket setting, although with a higher price tag. If you prefer to be pampered at home, Aya Omi offer a mobile waxing, manicure, and pedicure service (see below).

Beauty Salons		
Beaute Absolue	Dream Anzai (2F), 5-5-7 Minami-Azabu	03 3444 2120
Beauty Carmel	1001 Maison House, 5-13-14 Azabu	03 3584 1885
Boudoir	101 Maison Kawai, 2-25-3 Jingū-mae	03 3478 5898
Ren	Maison de Ramia (4F), 5-1-25 Minami Aoyama	03 5469 6339

Various Locations

Aya Omi

090 4728 3885 | *ayaomi6@yahoo.co.jp*

Beautician Aya Omi provides a range of services all in the comfort of your own home. Manicures, pedicures, and waxing come at very attractive prices, with manicures starting from as low as ¥3,500, and pedicures from ¥6,500. Her transport fee is ¥500 but if there is a group of you in one location she usually doesn't charge.

Dream Anzai (2F)
5-5-7 Minami-Azabu
Hirō
🚇 *Hirō*
Map 11 A4 94

Beaute Absolue

03 3444 2120 | *www.beauteabsolue.net*

Situated in a large expat area, Beaute Absolue's staff have no problem conversing in English and most of their clientele are from overseas. Whether you're looking for a facial, manicure, pedicure, eyelash extensions, or a wax, they cover it all. They also offer a unique treatment for nails, called a Bio Sculpture Gel overlay. This popular treatment involves applying a special gel over a person's natural nails to help strengthen and condition them. It leaves a glossy finish that doesn't chip or smudge.

Beauty Carmel

03 3584 1885 | *www.beautycarmel.com*

Beauty Carmel offers a broad selection of body and facial treatments specifically targeting specific skin problems such as acne, age spots, or scaring. The treatment plans tend to be long-term to get the best results, and they have many repeat visit clients. In addition to the above, they also do eyelash extensions and perming, as well as permanent make up and brow shaping. If you're planning to have your special day in Tokyo, the bridal plans start as far back as three months prior to the big day.

1001 Maison House
5-13-14 Azabu
Roppongi
Azabujuban
Map 11 C3 **57**

Boudoir

03 3478 5898 | *www.boudoirtokyo.com*

This Australian-owned and operated day spa is the perfect pampering spot for girls in need of some TLC. Tired skin will be thankful of one of the rescue remedy facials and ladies planning their next beach holiday will be happy to know there's a place nearby which provides reputable Brazilian waxes. Prices tend to be on the higher side, but if you visit the website they often advertise special promotions combining a range of services in a more wallet-friendly package.

101 Maison Kawai
2-25-3 Jingū-mae
Shibuya-ku
Harajuku
Map 8 D1 **58**

Ren

03 5469 6339 | *www.eyelash.jp*

For sexy long eyelashes or an innocent lash flutter, Ren can change your look with the well-placed addition of a few extra fake lashes. These semi-permanent eyelash extensions last up to 90 days, if cared for properly. Prices are cheaper than in many countries where the trend has taken off. They also offer beauty treatments such as the collagen bio lift – a natural alternative to plastic surgery that reduces under eye bags and wrinkles.

Maison de Ramia
5-1-25 Minami
-Aoyama
Minato-ku
Omotesandō
Map 8 E3 **59**

Hairdressers

Tokyo has a number of high quality hairdressers that cater to the foreign community. Costs are dependent on who trims your hair. A cut with a stylist starts at around ¥6,000, while for the same with the director you can expect to pay double that. Colours average at ¥10,000 and highlights at around ¥15,000. Prices vary between salons and it's best to shop around for a good deal.

Sin Den (see table) is a popular salon with foreigners and Watanabe is another popular choice. Foreigners tend to go to hairdressers that speak English rather than top Japanese salons to make sure they'll get exactly what they want. If you're looking for a cheaper alternative, the chain QB House offers ¥1,000 cuts where customers can just drop in, buy a ticket and wait their turn for a quick trim. Some hairdressers, such as A Cut Above, offer special discounts for children and students.

In addition to the standard services you would expect, salons like Watanabe have a manicurist and pedicurist who can work away on your hands and tootsies while you're being fashionably coiffed. An additional treat that is also part of the Japanese salon experience is a hedonistic head massage included with your treatment at no extra charge.

Hairdressers		
A Cut Above	Hirō	03 3441 7218
Essensuals	Ginza	03 3563 6336
Hayato New York	Aoyama	03 3498 9113
Jennifer Hair and Beauty International	Roppongi	03 5770 3611
Shape	Akasaka	03 3568 3666
Sin Den	Jingū-mae	03 3405 4409
Toni & Guy	Jingū-mae	03 3797 5790
Watanabe	Jingū-mae	03 3405 1188

Health Spas

Other options **Massage** p.259, **Sports & Leisure Facilities** p.252

Most upscale hotels have decadent spas with a price tag to match. Treatment costs average at around ¥20,000 per hour for a facial, body, or massage treatment. Oozing with indulgence, special packages include a mix of treatments such as a body polish, massage, and body wrap, and are perfect when the city rush starts wearing you down. Don't be surprised to find that natural, Japanese ingredients such as sake, rice, green tea, and black sesame have made it into the lotions and potions being used. Claudia offers unique treats such as a chocolate spa and a wine spa where you'll be coated head to toe with either chocolate or a grape mix. Stone therapy is another popular option. Meanwhile, sauna-like in nature, Bagus customers lay on hot stone slabs that are great for a relaxing detox. Men are usually welcome at spas, but for those in want of a bit of privacy, The Refinery in Tokyo Midtown is a male only spa, which offers your typical range of spa treatments, including a facial shave for ¥12,500. For steamy dips in the good old outdoors, see Onsen and Sento on p.264.

1-9-2 Azabu-Juban
Minato-ku
🚇 *Azabu-juban*
Map 11 C4 60

Bagus

03 3568 8310 | *www.bagus-spa.com*

If you've tired of traditional saunas, a visit to Bagus may reignite your passion for a good detoxifying sweat. Their Hot Slab Therapy involves relaxing on a hot stone slab in order to work up a sweat and purge toxins from the body – a process that is also believed to help with weight loss. To further unwind you can also try the geranium bath, which improves circulation and helps boost metabolism. The spa is three minutes on foot from exit 5 of Azabujuban station, next to Jomo.

5-1-2 Minami-Azabu
Minato-ku
🚇 *Hirō*
Map 11 A4 102

Claudia

03 5793 3931 | *www.claudia.co.jp*

If you're looking for something a little out of the ordinary then a visit to Claudia may be in order. With a chocolate spa and a wine spa on the menu, it seems women can get their naughty fix in a healthy form. The chocolate spa is exactly as the name implies, and clients are coated head to toe in the sweet stuff. The procedure has both mental and physical benefits and is said to stimulate metabolism. The spa also offers facials but it is their body wraps that make them stand out of the crowd.

1-8 Yūrakuchō
Chiyoda-ku
🚇 *Hibiya*
Map 14 A2 61

The Peninsula Spa

03 6270 2299 | *http://tokyo.peninsula.com*

Located in the Peninsula Hotel, this spa combines the best of European, Asian, and Indian (Ayurvedic) traditions in order to create treatments that are enjoyable and

The Spa

The Peninsula Spa

beneficial both spiritually and physically. Their Ayurvedic treatments include volcanic stone massages, chakra balancing, and a full day 'Ayurvedic Experience,' providing healing on a range of levels. They also offer a good selection of facials and massages designed specifically for men. After clients have finished their treatment, they can enjoy the spa's saunas, steam rooms, relaxation space and a thermal suite, which includes lifestyle showers, ice fountains and saunas.

The Refinery

9-7-4
Akasaka
Minato-ku
Roppongi
Map 11 B2 **62**

03 5413 7207 | *www.the-refinery.jp*
London's men-only day spa, The Refinery, has opened up a branch in the ritzy Tokyo Midtown Complex, providing a welcome relief for men about town. Offering services tailored to professional males, The Refinery has found their niche in the spa scene and the exclusivity of the place is as much of a draw as the services they provide. Try the 45 minute 'Shave Experience,' the ultimate in facial shaves and the de-stress massage to unwind after a hard day at the office.

The Spa

2-1-1 Nihonbashi
Muromachi
Chūō-ku
Nihonbashi
Map 14 C1 **63**

03 3270 8300 | *www.mandarinoriental.com*
Situated 36 floors above the city, The Mandarin Oriental's spa rises above the concrete jungle below to create a calming space. The Spa boasts five VIP treatment suites with their own private facilities, as well as a vitality pool, amethyst crystal steam room, sky view sauna, and rain shower. Their treatments fuse Asian and western inspired traditions and the delectable list includes half-day packages like the Art of Relaxation – an Arabian body treatment, a calming facial, and foot ritual. Five hour packages include options such as the Art of Indulgence – a collection of therapies which involve four hands working on your body simultaneously.

Spa Christina

6-3-18 Akasaka
Minato-ku
Akasaka
Map 11 C1 **64**

03 5545 7111 | *www.sky-gate.co.jp*
Situated in the swanky Akasaka district in the Chisun Grand Akasaka Hotel, Spa Christina retains the class but offers a slightly lower price tag than other spas in the city. In addition to the typical list of treatments, Spa Christina includes such services as Thalassotherapy, seaweed wraps and massage. The geranium bath followed by a body massage is really nice and is designed to refresh and detoxify. The range of massages is extensive with foot, scalp, hand, face, full-body and back all on the menu.

Yu

2-10-8 Sekiguchi
Bunkyō-ku
Mejiro
Map 4 A2 **65**

03 3943 2222 | *www.fourseasons.com/tokyo/spa.html*
Spanning over 2,000 square metres, the Four Season's Yu spa provides a place to truly relax in an overcrowded city. Alongside their six treatment rooms, they have two double rooms that consist of an indoor area combined with an outside Japanese garden and bath. The next level in luxury is their 115 square metre VIP spa suite, which balances the elements by fusing indoor and outdoor facilities. They also have a heated swimming pool that can be used year round. Yu uses their own signature blend of oils in all their treatments, and each blend varies with the season.

Massage

Other options **Health Spas** p.258, **Sports & Leisure Facilities** p.252

Whether you're looking for a relaxing aromatherapy massage or to rebalance your energy through shiatsu, there's a broad range of skilled massage practitioners at the ready to lend a hand. Unlike some other Asian nations, massages in Tokyo are not cheap

The Peninsula Spa

and an hour-long massage will typically cost around ¥7,000. Depending on the type of massage this price will vary, and if you choose to partake in a treatment at a hotel spa, expect to pay more than double that. Getting a massage at home can work out cheaper than going to some of the really upmarket spots. Egbok offers in-home massages for ¥2,000 to ¥3,000 more than their salon prices.

Many therapists who practice a foreign form of massage have completed their training abroad and their credentials will be listed on the company's website. For those who are interested in getting certified in Japan, places like the Kimura Institute (see p.260) offer shiatsu courses in English.

Bali 24 Relax

Rokuei Bldg
7-14-11 Roppongi
Minato-ku
🚇 **Roppongi**
Map 11 B2 **66**

03 3796 2411 | *www.balirelax24.jp*
Open 24 hours a day, 365 days a year, Bali 24 Relax is a mainstay when you're in need of some serious relaxation. Situated in the busy Roppongi area, the Indonesian decor and friendly staff provide an oasis of calm away from the surrounding rush. Massages last from 20 minutes to 120 minutes and prices average ¥105 per minute. Check out their website for updates about cheaper, off-peak specials that are offered in the early morning and around midday.

Egbok

Roppongi Five Bldg
5-18-20 Roppongi
Minato-ku
🚇 **Azabujuban**
Map 11 C3 **67**

03 3586 8909 | *www.egbok-massage.com*
The collective skills of Egbok's team of specialists cover acupuncture, Swedish, aromatherapy, *shiatsu*, reflexology and oil massages. Clients can book in for an individual treatment or combine two complimentary services such as acupuncture and *shiatsu*. Most massages cost just over ¥7,000 for 60 minutes. For home treatments, prices start upwards of ¥8,000. The at-home service is only available for couples or women.

Iyogi

101 Beagle House
2-6-15 Minami
Yukigaya
Ōta-ku
🚇 **Yukigayaotsuka**
Map 2 B3

03 3728 1027 | *www.iyogilomi.com*
Healer Yoko Iyogi's traditional Hawaiian massages work in two ways, by relaxing the entire body whilst improving a person's flow of energy. Iyogi typically combines this rather spiritual form of massage with a Hopi ear candle treatment, where candle wax is used painlessly to help draw impurities out of the ear. She has also extended her services to man's best friend and, with the help of a professional dog trainer, provides ear candling for dogs (see p.108 for more on Pet Grooming).

Kimura Shiatsu Institute

1-48-19 Sasazuka
Shibuya-ku
Map 3 C4 **68**

03 3485 4515 | *www.shiatsu-k.com*
The ancient tradition of *shiatsu*, which literally means finger pressure, helps to restore a person's natural flow of energy by applying pressure to different points on the body. If you would like to try this technique, Susumu Kimura has over 25 years of experience and offers *shiatsu* treatments just outside of Shinjuku. For those who want to learn more, the institute also offers *shiatsu* courses in English.

We're all over Asia

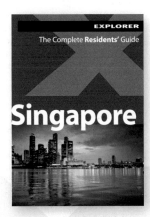

When it's time to make the next stop on your expat Asian adventure, be sure to pack an Explorer Residents' Guide. These essential books will help you make the most of your new life in a new city.

Explorer Residents' Guides – We Know Where You Live

Shimizu Bldg (501)
1-28-9 Shirokane
Minato-ku
🚇 **Shirokane-
Takanawa**
Map 6 A2 69

Salon Axis
090 7639 2021

Rolfing, also known as structural integration, is a form of massage that works with a person's soft tissue, with the intention of correcting posture and thereby reducing pain associated with incorrect alignment. At Salon Axis, practitioners apply this method of treatment, alongside Japanese and Swedish forms of massage. All healers have completed their rolfing training overseas and are dedicated to creating individual healing plans for each individual client.

5-15-10
Minami-Azabu
Minato-ku
🚇 **Hirō**
Map 11 A4 70

Shingen Japon
03 3441 4117 | *www.shingenjapon.com*

Shingen Japon may be predominately known as a hair salon but their massage services make them worth a mention. They work with a select few local therapists, to provide Reiki, aromatherapy, reflexology, and Hawaiian lomi-lomi massage services to help rebalance the body. The trained practitioners also have a few additional skills up their sleeves, including EMF balancing and herbal counselling services.

Meditation

The practice of *zazen* meditation is common throughout Japan and Tokyo has a host of traditional temples where you can get in touch with your spiritual side. Some temples welcome foreigners to their Japanese sessions, whilst others hold special English gatherings throughout the month. Kirigaya-ji has an English practice session the second Saturday of each month at 18:30. When visiting a temple it is best to call ahead to determine the level of English spoken and the best time to come.

Other English friendly places that offer guided meditation are Sahaja Yoga, held every Sunday in Harajuku, and the Dharma meditation classes on Tuesdays in Yoyogi (p.186). Some yoga studios such as FURLA yoga have meditation sessions, whilst others incorporate it into their yoga classes. Studios such as Sun & Moon and Yogajaya have meditation workshops during the year and retreat centres, like the Vipassana Center in Kyoto have monthly 10 day courses that are open to beginners.

Regular meditation is said to bring clarity to the mind and a greater sense of calm into daily life. There are various forms so trying out a few different traditions will help you determine what works best for you.

Patio Oyama 302,
36-35 Oyama-chō
Shibuya-ku
🚇 **Yoyogi uehara**
Map 5 D1 71

Dharma Japan
www.dharma-japan.org

Meditation teacher John Munroe offers Dharma teaching and meditation practice each Tuesday from 19:30 until 21:00. Drawing on his studies, learnt from a broad range of teachers, Munroe is able to guide students down the path towards inner peace and compassion for themselves and those around them. The form of meditation practiced blends eastern and western traditions, although the main focus is on Tibetan and Theravadin Buddhist practices. Dharma Japan also has classes in Kyoto and hosts retreats around the globe.

FURLA Aoyama
3-5-20 Kita-Aoyama
Minato-ku
🚇 **Omotesandō**
Map 8 E2 72

FURLA Yoga
www.furla.co.jp

Learn the basics behind meditation at FURLA Yoga's 'Beauty of the Heart: First Steps in Meditation' class. Held each Friday, the aim of the class is to get in touch with your inner self in order to bring greater meaning and vitality into your life and to make general improvements. The hour-long session is open to everyone and is a good option for those interested in the practice but who are daunted by the thought of visiting a temple.

7-12-22 Kinuta
Setagaya-ku
🚇 **Seijō Gakuen-mae**
Map 2 A3

Kuonji

03 3416 1735

Although foreigners are welcome at Kuonji, it's best to call first to check the schedule and let them know that you're planning a visit. They typically welcome newbies to their session on Saturdays from 19:00 to 21:00 and a ¥400 donation is required to participate in this evening class. The morning *zazen* practice, starts at 06:00 and is free, but beginners are advised to join the night practice.

Jingū-mae Kumin
Kaikan,
6-10-4 Jingū-mae
Shibuya-ku
🚇 **Meiji Jingū-mae**
Map 8 C2 🔢

Sahaja Yoga

03 3409 4565 | *www.t3.rim.or.jp/~hitoshii*

Remaining focused on the present moment is no simple feat. Meditation such as Sahaja Yoga teaches participants to maintain a centred state, and helps them to stay in the present, balanced, and focused. The Sahaja Yoga method is a form of meditation that focuses on self-realisation through an experience known as Kundalini rising. They offer free weekly classes to help people learn to meditate at home and learn simple clearing techniques to overcome daily stress. Classes are sometimes held in another centre close by, contact them before you go to check the location.

4-5-18 Yutaka-chō
Shinagawa-ku
🚇 **Akebonobashi**
Map 2 B3

Toshoji International Zen Center

03 3781 4235 | *www.toshoji.com*

Foreigners can try the ancient Buddhist practice of *zazen* at this centre. Unlike some forms of meditation, the details of the practice are intricate and training under a master is important, especially when you are first starting out. The temple offers group meditation in the morning from 05:00, Monday to Saturday, followed by chanting and cleaning. For those who can't make the early start there is a Saturday Zen training meeting from 18:00. Both the morning and evening sessions are free. If you wish to deepen your practice they also offer five-day training sessions twice a year and serious followers can stay in the dormitory, for a fee.

Dhamma Bhanu,
Funai-gun
Kyoto
Map 1 B3

Vipassana Center

075 7186 0765 | *www.bhanu.dhamma.org*

If you're serious about starting meditation, a Vipassana meditation retreat is a good way to kick start regular practice. Taking part in a retreat involves 10 days of meditation, which can be a rather demanding experience. Although attendees may find the course difficult at first, once familiar with the practice it is usual to arrive at a deeper level of consciousness and a clearer state of understanding. The meditation taught over the 10 days is an ancient Indian technique that focuses on breathing and bodily sensations in order to help people experience each moment fully (see website for full address and registration details).

Nail Bars

The city is inundated with nail bars and having a well-manicured set of tips is standard amongst city fashionistas. Even on a night out, girls can stop to get a quick touch up or a full manicure as some clubs set up makeshift nail bars in order to attract a female crowd. Many nail bars will accept walk-ins, but for the more popular salons, reservations are essential. Beauty salons (p.256) typically offer manicures for anywhere between ¥2,000 to ¥6,000 and Boudoir (p.257) is well-known for its designer styles.

3-12-13 Kita-Aoyama
Minato-ku
🚇 **Omotesandō**
Map 8 D3 🔢

Dashing Diva

03 5774 0266 | *www.dashingdiva.co.jp*

It comes as no surprise that Japan's largest nail salon is located in the swanky Aoyama neighbourhood – the fashion capital of the city. Although this popular New York nail salon has a number of locations throughout Tokyo, its Aoyama flagship store is the one to visit. Their fake nails stand the test of time, lasting approximately three weeks, and if you've ever struggled to find the right fit, they have over 160 different nail sizes to choose from. They also provide great manicures and pedicures.

ViensViens

5-14-14 Hirō
Shibuya-ku
Hirō
🚇 *Hirō*
Map 11 A4 75

03 5798 2020 | www.viensviens.com

It may come as a surprise to learn that, like many things, fashion trends also affect nails. If you're feeling rather clueless in this department, the knowledgeable staff at ViensViens can help advise before adorning your innocent nails. This chic salon offers some decadent nail art options alongside more standard manis and pedis, and if you really want nails people will talk about, it's worth booking in. It's a two minute walk from exit 2 of Hirō station. Go down the main shopping street towards Starbucks and take the first left.

Onsen & Sento

Onsen are natural hot springs that can be found all over Japan (not to be confused with *sento*, which are artificial indoor public baths, filled with steaming tap water). You will recognise an *onsen* or *sento* by the ゆ character for hot water on the sign outside. Popular with tourists and locals alike, people pack onto trains, buses and cars to get out of the city for a relaxing dip in *onsen* in places such as Izu, Hakone, Tochigi and Gunma. Facilities can range from a simple indoor or outdoor bath to massive complexes with baths, saunas, massage and beauty treatment centres, restaurants, karaoke, and relaxation rooms. The facilities at *sento* are often superior, but be warned, the water can be piping hot. Many of these are cheap ¥400 joints, which many people use for their daily wash down.

There are a few basic rules when entering *onsen* or *sento*. First remove your shoes at the entrance, always wash thoroughly before getting in a bath, and don't take your towel into the water. Many places frown upon people with tattoos, so it's best to check the policy beforehand. Most *onsen* and *sento* have separate baths for men and women, but some have mixed *konyoku* bathing for which swimwear is required.

Many locals are said to say they're happy to be Japanese as they soak in the mineral-rich hot water, and you too will be glad that you came to Japan once you've tried it. The experience can be further enhanced if followed by a nice, cold local brew when you're done.

Heiwajima Kurhaus

1-1-1 Heiwajima
Ōta-ku
🚇 *Heiwajima*
Map 2 B3

03 3768 9013 | www.heiwajima-onsen.jp

Located in the Big Fun leisure complex, this centre has outdoor stone baths, several indoor baths and saunas, all of which can be enjoyed for the ¥1,700 admission price. For an extra fee you can add on a Thai massage, foot treatments, Indian massage, shiatsu, Bali beauty treatments or even a full body scrub. Another section of the complex has exercise facilities. Kurhaus has all the usual restaurant options, but what makes it stand out is its cinema, where you can watch (nearly) new releases after a soak.

Hinode Mitsuzawa Tsuru-tsuru Onsen

4718 Oguno
Nishi-Tama-gun
Western Tokyo
🚇 *Heiwajima*

042 597 1126 | www.tourism.metro.tokyo.jp

This is a great spot out in the wilderness that is popular with hikers after they have climbed Mount Hinode. It's one of the more traditional venues, set in a wooden building with outdoor baths in clean country air. Visitors need to take a bus from the station to Tsuru-Tsuru Onsen. Entry is ¥800.

La Qua

1-1-1 Kasuga
Bunkyō-ku
🚇 *Kasuga*
Map 9 F2 95

03 3817 4173 | *www.tokyo-dome.co.jp*
La Qua's central location in Tokyo Dome City means that bathing facilities are limited, crowded and expensive at ¥2,565 per person. However, for an extra ¥525 you can go into the Healing Baden Zone, a tropically themed mixed gender area of low temperature saunas which is a lovely environment in which to unwind. The hot water here comes from a spring deep underground.

Oedo Onsen-Monogatari

2-57 Aome
Odaiba
🚇 *Yurikamome*
Map 6 D4 96

03 5500 1126 | *www.ooedo-global.jp*
More of a theme park than an *onsen*, this is a great place for newcomers to the city or to take visitors. In addition to the usual range of bathing and healing facilities, there's a recreation of a traditional downtown Edo street where you can chow down on a range of goodies and play traditional games. One highlight is that you can pick your own colourful *yukata* to walk around in. General admission is ¥2,827, but it's cheaper after 18:00 when it costs just ¥1,987. There's a complimentary shuttle bus to the *onsen* from a number of locations, visit the website for more details.

Seta Onsen Sanganoyu

4-15-30 Seta
Setagaya-ku
🚇 *Futako-tamagawa*
Map 5 A4 97

03 3707 8228 | *www.setaonsen.co.jp*
This is a completely natural hot spring with views of Mount Fuji on a clear day. Inside the facility are lie-down baths, Jacuzzis, saunas and an open-air bath. Massage and other health and beauty treats are also available. At night, pretty lighting creates a wonderful atmosphere. A trip to this *onsen* will set you back ¥2,300, but you can print off a discount ticket from the website that will save you ¥500.

Takaido Natural Spa – Utsukushi no Yu

2-3-45 Takaido-Nishi
Suginami-ku
🚇 *Takaido*
Map 2 A2

03 3334 0008 | *www.nafsport.com/utsukushi/*
A relatively cheap and small facility not far from central Tokyo, this *onsen* is a more typical bath than those usually found in and around the city. Entry costs ¥800. Despite its small size, it has several indoor and *rotenburo* outdoor baths and a sauna. A distinct feature is the 25 metre warm water swimming pool. The restaurant serves typical fare such as *soba*, *udon*, *ramen* and set meals.

Toshimaen Niwanoyu

3-25-1 Mukoyama
Nerima-ku
🚇 *Toshimaen*
Map 2 A2

03 399 4126 | *www.toshimaen.co.jp/niwa-yu/niwanoyu.html*
This is a large and impressive complex with several zones – open air, bath, sauna and a mixed bathing area where swimwear is required. There's a large pool, a Dead Sea bath, Finnish sauna and a beautiful garden. There are also a range of restaurants, a relaxation area, and a body care centre. Daytime entry costs ¥2,250, but this drops to ¥1,260 in the evenings.

Pilates

Other options **Yoga** p.268

Pilates is a body conditioning method that helps strengthen and tone muscle without adding bulk. It works the deep postural muscles to bring the body back to its correct alignment, while helping to create a lean shape. Over 500 movements are included in the pilates repertoire and as each position needs to be exact (in order to get the most benefit), it is important to work with a trained professional. Machine and mat classes are available. There are a number of pilates studios that offer classes, as well as instructor training. Some modern health clubs, like Tipness in Hibiya (p.209), have specialised equipment, while others offer mat classes as part of their gym schedule. Private lesson machine classes start at around ¥8,000 per hour and mat classes are a little bit cheaper. Group classes are also available at some studios and are about half the price of a private lesson.

Body Arts & Science International (BASI)

2-20-14 Aobadai (3F)
Meguro-ku
Ikejiri-Ohashi
Map 5 E2 76

03 6805 6044 | www.basipilates.jp
With spacious, bright studios in Roppongi and Naka Meguro, and a reasonable price structure, BASI has made an impact on the pilates scene. The BASI form of pilates retains the core principles of pilates whilst introducing additional academic knowledge that the founder of BASI has acquired through years as an athlete, dancer and yoga instructor. Certified instructors teach private, semi-private, and group mat or machine classes. The membership fee is ¥10,500.

Bodymode

6-33-14 Jingū-mae
Shibuya-ku
Meiji Jingū-mae
Map 11 A2 77

03 6419 3748 | www.bodymode.jp
Bodymode offers personalised workouts with a one-to-one pilates training session that covers 20 different pieces of pilates equipment over the course of an hour. Along with Bodymode's individual classes, they also offer group classes. For those who want to take their practice to the next level, pilates instructor training is offered in English.The studio is a licensed training centre of Stott Pilates, a globally recognised pilates method.

Pilates Movement Space

4-15-2 Komazawa
Setagaya-ku
Komazawa
Daigaku
Map 5 B3 78

03 5430 3434 | www.4.ocn.ne.jp/~pilates/
Pilates is suitable for all, regardless of your age or flexibility. Unlike some pilates studios which rigidly stick to set sequences, the experienced director Rie Sakai and her dedicated team tailor each session specifically to the special needs of each client. Classes must be booked, and both private and small group sessions are available, either at the studio or in the clients' home. The more experienced the trainer, the higher the lesson fee.

Yoga Studio Tokyo

Shinmen Bldg (8F),
2-22-14 Shibuya
Shibuya-ku
Shibuya
Map 8 C2 98

090 8344 0724 | www.yogastudiotokyo.com
This offers more than it's name suggests. With an array of classes available, they also offer private pilates lessons each Wednesday for a very competitive price. Located only a few minutes from Shibuya station,this roomy studio is a great place to start your pilates training. Reservations are a must.

Reiki

This age-old Japanese healing technique involves transferring energy through the practitioner's hands to the client's body. During a typical session the healer will place their palms on various points of the body and hold them there for two minutes or more. Working with a person's energy, reiki is believed to heal both the body and mind on a spiritual level. Sessions help reduce stress, enhance well-being and encourage physical, mental, spiritual and emotional development. The number of sessions a person requires is dependent on the problem and the individual, although results may be seen in as little as one session. Japan, being the birthplace of the practice, has a number of skilled reiki healers. If you don't speak Japanese it's best to work with someone who speaks English as practitioners typically discuss the problems their patient wants to address. A few foreigners offer reiki alongside other holistic therapies.

Various Locations

Kate Brady

03 3398 1909 | *www.spiritgatehealings.com*

Kate Brady has a rather varied holistic background with qualifications in acupuncture, aromatherapy, reiki and Chinese herbal medicine, along with the more modern energy healing approaches like Barbara Brennan healing. Her therapeutic methods combine a mixture of these holistic techniques and once an initial assessment is completed, she will determine which method of therapy is best suited to each individual.

1308 Forme Yotsuya
Gaien Higashi
14-61 Samoncho
Shinjuku-ku
🚇 **Shinanomachi**
Map 7 F2 **79**

Lifeforces

03 3357 2067 | *www.lifeforces.org*

Lifeforces offer reiki sessions, treatments and workshops, which draw upon techniques from the original Japanese reiki form, along with more modern variants. In addition to reiki, they also offer a range of holistic therapies, and energy and personal development training sessions. If you have any questions concerning spirituality, healing, or complementary practices, you can call or email them for free. They also have a branch in Shinagawa (03 3472 1714, hari@lifeforces.org).

302 Villa Holonica
3-46-17 Ogikubo
Suginami-ku
🚇 **Hamadayama**
Map 3 A3 **80**

Unicorn Center

090 4962 3640 | *www.unicorncenter.com*

Situated a short distance from Shinjuku, the Unicorn Center is a calming space that offers a variety of holistic therapies and workshops. They offer 60 or 90 minute reiki sessions, as well as 12 hour reiki training courses. For more advanced practitioners, they also teach Reiki I and Reiki II, and master classes.

Stress Management

Other options **Support Groups** p.131, **Counselling & Therapy** p.130

Stress relief can be sought in various forms, from taking up more active pursuits to relaxing through yoga or having a gentle massage. If you're feeling a little out of sorts a visit to an alternative healer like Sainoor Premji (www.healthizarnaturalhealing. ca, healthizar@gmail.com) may help you to rebalance. Her list of skills spans such therapies as hypnosis, reiki, Bach flower, and colour therapy. Premji also holds parenting workshops, offering valuable advice for what is sometimes a difficult and stressful role. Other healers (see reiki on p.266) provide a range of treatments to help release built up tension, while disciplines such as yoga (see p.268), tai chi (see p.267), or meditation (see p.262) will promote a general state of well-being.

If you need someone to talk to, the Tokyo English Life Line (p.131) is a good place to start (03 5774 0992). They operate a free helpline daily from 09:00 to 23:00 and offer advice and face-to-face counselling. Counselling fees are set in line with each individual's income.

Tai Chi

The slow fluid movements that are executed during a tai chi session are a form of moving meditation that help a person to align body and mind. The ancient practice originated in China but has become popular worldwide for its ability to improve health and vitality. One of the most popular places to practice tai chi in the city is Yoyogi Kōen (p.186). Here early risers can join in a foreign-led class on the weekends and on some weekday mornings. If you can't make it to the park, many gyms offer classes (see Central Fitness Club Minami Aoyama on p.209) and typically combine it with the practice of *qigong*. As with any practice, the length of time taken to see results varies, but starting the day surrounded by nature is therapeutic in itself, and busy Tokyoites are likely to benefit from taking time out of their schedules to slow down for a while.

2-1 Yoyogi
Kamizono-chō
Shibuya-ku
🚇 *Harajuku*
Map 8 B1 **81**

Barbara Ferretti Matsuura

03 337 4692 | integratedhealingarts@yahoo.com

Each Saturday between 10:00 and 12:00, Barbara Matsuura holds a combined *qigong* and tai chi class in Yoyogi Kōen. During the practice participants learn meditation, *ba duan jin*, eight *qigong* exercises and tai chi, followed by a short lecture. Reservations are essential, after which Barbara will send you a map of the exact location in the park.

2-1 Yoyogi
Kamizono-chō
Shibuya-ku
🚇 *Harajuku*
Map 8 B1 **82**

Guang Ping Yang Tai Chi Chuan Japan

03 3485 4160 | www2.gol.com/users/ddh/index.html

What better way to start the day than surrounded by nature while taking part in a practice that brings balance to mind, body and spirit? Each week Dan Harington leads students through tai chi classes in Yoyogi Kōen. You'll find this tai chi group practising these slow fluid movements on Tuesdays, Thursdays, and Saturdays from 07:30 to 09:30, and on Sundays between 09:00 and 11:00.

Serene Meals
Yaffa Organic Cafe (p.362) and Nabi (p.350) hold an all inclusive lunch and yoga set once a month, typically on a Sunday. Veggie Paradise Yoga (p.269) also does special meal deals for yogis.

Yoga

Other options **Pilates** p.265

From the outside, yoga appears to be a complicated sequence of stretches. In reality though, this age-old practice has further reaching benefits than just improved flexibility. Linking the body and mind through various breathing techniques, poses (known as asanas), and meditation, a student of yoga aims to integrate the physical and spiritual body.

Many people initially become interested in the practice through its ability to keep the body supple and toned, help with weight loss, and relieve various physical and mental ailments, but after studying it for a while many find they also benefit from a greater sense of calm, both during and after the class. Results differ from person to person, but committing to a regular practice (at least twice a week) will give the best results. There are a number of studios in the city, and a handful offer English or bilingual classes. Bikram yoga is popular among Japanese ladies but the foreign-operated studios focus on the Vinyasa Flow, Ashtanga, Hatha, and Sivananda disciplines. Expect to pay ¥3,000 for a 90 minute session. If you're planning on sticking at it, most places offer discounted pass cards that can bring the price down to about ¥1,800 per lesson.

5-2-37 Minami
Azabu
Minato-ku
🚇 *Hirō*
Map 11 A4 **100**

Be Yoga Japan

080 1001 6154 | www.beyogajapan.com

This peaceful place, a short walk from Hirō station, was Japan's first ISHTA yoga school. As no two people are the same, ISHTA is a yoga philosophy that aims to help students develop a personalised approach to yoga, at their own pace. The Hatha classes are taught in either Japanese or English and the language is clearly marked on the schedule. Lessons last 75 minutes, slightly shorter than the average 90 minutes common at other studios.

FURLA Aoyama
3-5-20 Kita-Aoyama
Minato-ku
🚇 *Omotesandō*
Map 8 E2 **72**

FURLA Yoga

www.furla.co.jp

FURLA Yoga offers a host of small classes open to everyone, but many are specifically aimed at women. Hatha, Anusara, prenatal, postnatal, and meditation are all offered here. Reservations are recommended as classes fill up quickly. Students can register online after becoming a member (which is free). Lessons are held in Japanese and English (or both) – check the schedule before the class to make sure you're attending the right one.

International Yoga Center

5-30-6 Ogikubo
Suginami-ku
Map 2 A2

03 5397 2741 | *www.iyc.jp*

IYC holds over 150 classes weekly at various locations in the city. Classes taught are primarily Ashtanga, although they do have some gentle yoga classes scattered throughout the busy schedule. The main Ogikubo studio is bright and spacious but if you go at the weekend be prepared for it to be a bit more crowded. Mysore classes are offered during the week at the Kudanshita and Roppongi locations. They also have studios in Roppongi, Kudanshita, Aoyama and Shibuya, visit the website for details.

SHIZEN Yoga

Entopia Kichijoji
2-5-9 Kichijōji
Musashino-shi
Map 2 A2

090 3814 4488 | *www.shizenyoga.com*

Mothers will be delighted with SHIZEN, as not only do they hold prenatal and postnatal classes, they also have baby yoga, and yoga for kids. Besides these unique classes, they teach Hatha, Anusara, gentle yoga, and series classes (short term yoga courses designed to help individuals deepen their practice). Instructors can also partake in specially designed classes, which are aimed at helping teachers deepen their knowledge. There's a second studio, SHIZEN Yoga Studio B at Unius Kichijoji Office One, 2-13-4 Kichijōji Minami-chō, Musashino-shi.

Sun & Moon Yoga

3-1-5 Kami Osaki
Meguro-ku
🚉 *Meguro*
Map 5 F3 83

03 3280 6383 | *www.sunandmoon.jp*

This warm and welcoming space in the Higashi Guchi Building (Meguro Eki Mae Manshon) is a favourite among foreign yogis. Many non-Japanese instructors teach classes here and all lessons are either taught in English or in Japanese and English. The schedule includes a mix of Hatha, Vinyasa Flow, Ashtanga, Kripalu, Restorative and Sivananda classes. Sun & Moon also offer various yoga and meditation workshops throughout the year.

Tokyo Yoga Circle

Aoyama Dancing
Square (8F),
2-14-6 Kita-Aoyama
Minato-ku
🚉 *Azabu-juban*
Map 11 C3 84

03 3582 3505 | *www.rajay.org*

Instructor Rajay Mahtani has been teaching yoga in Tokyo since 1987 and has a wealth of experience in the practice. Her classes follow the Iyengar tradition, a rather modern style of yoga that focuses on *pranayama* (breathing exercises) and *asanas* (poses) in order to help students work towards the deeper meaning of yoga. Most lessons are suitable for beginners. Mahtani also teaches prenatal yoga classes on Tuesdays, by appointment only. She also teaches classes in Roppongi.

Veggie Paradise Yoga

1-22-14 Uehara
Shibuya-ku
🚉 *Yoyogi Uehara*
Map 5 D1 101

03 6421 2925 | *www.veggieparadise.jp*

This grassroots yoga studio is situated above Veggie Paradise (p.269), a raw food vegetarian restaurant. With its community atmosphere, students typically come for a class and then relax afterwards over a smoothie or the special yogi dinner or breakfast sets. Vinyasa Flow and Hatha yoga classes are on offer, and most lessons are in English (with some bilingual ones). Bookings should be made by email.

Yogajaya

1-25-11 Ebisu
Nishi (2F)
Shibuya-ku
🚉 *Ebisu*
Map 5 F2 85

03 5784 3622 | *www.yogajaya.com*

This progressive studio is a popular spot for aspiring yogis. Strength and stamina are key elements in the classes offered and the comprehensive schedule is predominantly Hatha focused with some Sivananda, and Ashtanga classes. Yogajaya frequently hosts workshops with visiting yoga teachers, as well as holding retreats overseas. Yogajaya's owner, Patrick Oanicia, is also becoming well known on the international yoga scene.

Shopping

Shopping

Shopping

Tokyoites love their shopping, and on any given day you'll see thousands of people milling about the various department stores, shopping streets and areas. Virtually everything you can dream of is available, from traditional antique ceramics to the most cutting-edge fashion.

Prices can be much steeper than in many other countries, and commodities such as shoes and clothing can be shockingly expensive. Brand items can cost up to 60% more due to import taxes, but domestic brands only carry a 5% consumption tax. However, there are often sales, discounts and one-off deals to be had. Bi-annual sales, usually held around New Year and again in the summer also bring bargains, with up to 80% off the marked price. The New Year's sales often include *fukubukuro* (a surprise bag of items that can be purchased at various price increments). Electronic items can be cheaper, although CDs and DVDs are likely to be more expensive than elsewhere. In general, the Japanese are reluctant to buy second-hand goods, but there are still a surprising number of second-hand shops selling designer clothing and vintage furniture in good condition.

Shopping used to be confined to the local shops and department stores lining the streets in each neighbourhood. However, with the introduction of the shopping mall to Japan, one-stop shopping complexes where you can shop, eat, get a massage, and ship everything back home before you leave the building are springing up everywhere. Old-fashioned markets still exist, especially in the temple yards and parks, but you'll need to seek them out.

Shopping by area is another way of life, with high concentrations of vendors selling a certain type of goods, such as the multitude of electronics stores in Akihabara, high-end boutiques on Omotesandō and Shibuya's penchant for teenage fashion. Outside the city, Gotemba Premium Outlets, and Costco are worth the trip for cut-price goods.

Ginza is the traditional shopping centre, although Shibuya, Harajuku, Omotesandō and Shinjuku are all popular too. In recent years Roppongi has had a shopping revolution and Roppongi Hills and Tokyo Midtown are getting in on the action. Odaiba is a man-made island with sprawling malls (Venus Fort p.313 and Palette Town 03 5500 2655, www.palette-town.com), and is a true testament to the enthusiasm of Tokyo shoppers. On a smaller scale, try the Sunshine Building (p.177) in Ikebukuro.

Open & Shut

Tokyo is switched on 24 hours a day. Most convenience stores are 24 hour, and many larger supermarket chains such as Seiyu (p.314) have 24 hour branches. Most shops open from around 10:00 to 20:00 or 22:00. Department stores generally operate from 10:00 to 20:00 daily. Over big holiday periods such as New Year, large supermarkets and many department stores remain open but most stores close for a few days from 1-4 January.

What & Where To Buy – Quick Reference

Alcohol	275	Electronics & Home App	282	Lingerie	291	Second-Hand Items	297
Art	275	Eyewear	283	Luggage & Leather	292	Shoes	298
Art & Craft Supplies	276	Flowers	284	Maternity Items	292	Souvenirs	300
Baby Items	276	Food	284	Medicine	293	Sports Goods	300
Beachwear	277	Gardens	287	Mobile Phones	294	Stationery	302
Bicycles	277	Gifts	288	Music, DVDs & Videos	294	Tailoring	302
Books	278	Handbags	288	Musical Instruments	295	Textiles	302
Camera Equipment	278	Hardware & DIY	289	Outdoor Goods	295	Toys & Games	303
Car Parts & Accessories	279	Hats	289	Party Accessories	296	Wedding Items	303
Carpets	279	Home Furnishings	290	Perfumes & Cosmetics	296		
Clothes	280	Jewellery & Watches	290	Pets	297		
Computers	282	Kids	291	Photographers & Artists	297		

Louis Vuitton

Clothing Sizes

Japanese clothing sizes tend to be smaller, and tall people may find it difficult to get sizes that fit, although most of the larger malls and department stores will stock larger sizes. To find your equivalent Japanese size, visit www.onlineconversion. com/clothing. Shoe sizes are a bit trickier as they are measured in centimetres (see table below).

Shoe Size Conversion Chart

Ladie's Shoe Sizes									
British	4	4.5	5	5.5	6	6.5	7	7.5	8
European	37	37.5	38	38.5	39	39.5	40	41	42
American	6.5	7	7.5	8	8.5	9	9.5	10	10.5
Japanese(cm)	23	23.5	24	24	24.5	25	25.5	26	26.5
Men's Shoe Sizes									
British	8	8.5	9	9.5	10	10.5	11	11.5	12
European	42	42.5	43	44	44.5	45	46	46.5	47
American	8.5	9	9.5	10	10.5	11	11.5	12	12.5
Japanese(cm)	26.5	27	27.5	28	28.5	29	29.5	30	30.5

Online Shopping

Online shopping has experienced a renaissance in the last few years, and Tokyoites do much of their shopping this way for the sake of convenience. For books, music and movies, Amazon, Tower Records, and HMV all have online shopping services. Many foreign companies also ship to Japan, although you may have to pay an arm and a leg for import duty and shipping. eBay and Yahoo! auctions are popular for hard-to-find items. You can even order groceries over the net from most major supermarket chains (p.314), with same-day delivery, while international foodie heaven can be found at The Foreign Buyer's Club (see table below for details).

Online Shopping

http://oohjapan.com	Fashion, electronics, cosmetics, sports equipment & household goods
http://pages.ebay.com/jpbridge.html	Online auctions
www.amazon.jp	Books, CDs, DVDs, household goods
www.fbcusa.com	International food, household goods, gifts
www.the-seiyu.com	Groceries
www.themeatguy.jp	Meat & grocery items
www.towerrecords.jp	Books, magazines, DVDs & CDs
www.tsutaya.co.jp	CD & DVD rental

Refunds & Exchanges

Refund and exchange policies vary greatly. Most retailers display their policy in the store (usually by the checkout desk), and it should also be printed on the receipt. Sometimes this may be in English. Often a shop will say it doesn't give exchanges or refunds but when faced with an item in returnable condition and a receipt, they usually will. Make sure you keep the receipt and do not remove any tags (keeping the original packaging helps too). However, street vendors are unlikely to issue refunds or exchanges. Sometimes store credit will be offered in lieu of a refund. If you have trouble getting the service you need, asking for the manager or going to the customer service desk usually does the trick.

Consumer Rights

The National Consumer Affairs Center of Japan (NCAC) is the regulating body for consumer affairs. It drafts the regulations on consumer affairs and mediates between vendors and consumers in the case of grievances. Visit its website for more information (www.consumer.go.jp). A consumer is entitled to cancel a services contract, without penalty, within two weeks of signing.

Shipping

Many shops will ship items to your home for a small fee, especially if you are buying over a certain amount. Domestic shipping outfits like Kuroneko-Yamato, Sagawa-kyubin and Pelican-bin will sometimes do same-day delivery. These companies are also often used to ship online purchases, and orders can be tracked with the shipping number via the company's website. Many people also ship heavy or awkward items through a domestic shipping company's local branch to their home or onward holiday destination. These can include anything from items purchased at a local convenience store to luggage and sports equipment. Foreign shipping companies like FedEx, UPS and DHL are also available, albeit on a more limited basis than the services offered by domestic shipping companies. FedEx is available in most Kinko`s locations (www.english.fedexkinkos.co.jp).

Shipping Companies	
DHL	www.dhl.co.jp
Kuroneko-Yamato	www.kuronekoyamato.co.jp
Sagawa-kyubin	www.sagawa-exp.co.jp
Pelican-bin	www.nittsu.co.jp/pelican
FedEx	www.fedex.com
UPS	www.ups.com

How To Pay

It's always best to pay with cash in Japan, although credit cards and e-cash are slowly becoming more widely accepted. Many shops accept gift cards that can be used in a variety of establishments. Some of the larger electronics outlets will offer a small discount, often 5%, if you pay cash for certain larger purchases.

There are many ATMs located all over the city near banks and in convenience stores, but they sometimes close early. Most major credit cards such as Visa, MasterCard and American Express are accepted, and retail outlets will often have a list of other international and domestic cards they accept. For online purchases, cash on delivery or 'convenience payment' (where you make your order and pay at the convenience store before the items are shipped) are popular methods of payment. For more on money, see p.38.

Bargaining

There is not much opportunity to bargain in Japan and price tags are usually taken at face value. However, in places such as electronic shops you have a bit of leverage and can try to get a discount on big purchases. Street vendors are more likely to be open to some haggling.

Edible Appreciation

There's a very welcome custom in Japan to courier or ship food baskets as gifts. Most shops have catalogues where you can choose from the useful (gift sets of oils and salad dressings), to the unique (specialities like fish eggs), or the downright indulgent (think kilos of premium Wagyu beef). You can find cakes, coffee, jellied desserts, fruit, fish, rice crackers, imported biscuits, or just about anything to say thank you, congratulations or simply that you care.

Sake barrels

Alcohol

Other options **Drinks** p.363, **On The Town** p.363

The legal age for purchasing alcohol is 20 in Japan. Everything from beer to wine and spirits can be found at local convenience stores and groceries, while there are some specialist shops for sake, *umeshu* and imported wines. Beer and chūhai (an alcopop drink) can be brought for a few hundred yen from street vending machines, and many people stop off for a sneaky drink between bars. Imported spirits are incredibly cheap, but drinks such as champagne can cost up to 20% more than what you'd pay abroad. A bottle of decent wine will cost about ¥3,000 but there are some good deals to be had for around ¥1,500. *Shōchū*, a strong domestic liquor, is probably the cheapest alcohol available, and blends with just about anything. In general, domestic brands will be cheaper than imports. Airport prices are duty free, allowing for good savings, so it's worth stocking up when passing through. If wine is your tipple of choice, YaMaYa Wine Cellars are scattered across the city, and they have a good selection of wines at reasonable prices.

Alcohol

Costco	3-6-1 Oyamagaoka	Machida-shi	042 798 6001	www.costco.co.jp
Hasegawa	Omotesando Hills (3F), 4-12-4 Jingū-mae	Shibuya-ku	03 5785 0833	www.hasegawasaketen.com
Seijo Ishii	Atre Ebisu (3F), Ebisu station	Shibuya-ku	03 3448 1070	www.seijoishii.co.jp
YaMaYa	Various Locations	See p.321		www.yamaya.co.jp

Art

Other options **Art & Craft Supplies** p.276, **Art Classes** p.210, **Art Galleries** p.170

Art is a big business and there are hundreds of small galleries dotted all over the city (see p.170). If you take a stroll around some of the more fashionable neighbourhoods, like Daikanyama, Omotesandō, Aoyama or Ginza, you'll stumble across many, each filled with various different styles. Traditional Japanese art and modern works are both popular and most galleries will sell the work being displayed. To commission an artist for a one-off piece, it's best to talk to the gallery owner or a representative. Ceramics are of particular interest to locals, due to the country's rich pottery history, and calligraphy and woodblock prints are both perennial favourites. In fact, modern calligraphy and woodblock printing are the hot mediums to have at the moment, so it's a good time to invest in some up-and-coming, talented local calligraphers and print artists.

Art

Carre MOJI	5-11-24 Minami-Aoyama	Minato-ku	03 5766 7120	www.carremoji.jp
Galerie 412	Omotesando Hills	Shibuya-ku	03 5410 0388	na
Uchida Art Co	International Arcade, 1-7-23 Uchisaiwai-chō	Chiyoda-ku	03 3593 8383	www.e-loec.com
Utsuwa	3-5-5 Minami Aoyama	Minato-ku	03 3402 8110	http://tsuwa-takede.com

Art & Craft Supplies

Other options **Art Classes** p.210, **Art Galleries** p.170, **Art** p.279

Art and crafts supplies are easily come by: most stationery shops stock the basics, while for more technical tools Sekaido is a good bet. This huge art-supply megastore has several locations in the city and is well known for its 'surprised Mona Lisa' mascot. Discounts are available though the company's 'point card'. It stocks everything from paints and crayons to canvases and plaster casting supplies. Tokyu Hands has a great art department with doll-making supplies, as well as random parts of just about anything you might want to make. Okadaya, TOA and Yuzawaya round out the fabric arts categories, and also carry leather and other accessory making items. Loft and Ito-ya have a more limited supply but are always a good bet for rubber stamps (inkan and hanko) and the basics.

Ukiyo

Ukiyo-e is a form of Japanese woodblock print. These iconic woodblocks were extremely popular between the 17th and early 20th centuries. They commonly featured scenes of the countryside, historic battles or fables, and beautiful women. *Ukiyo* means 'floating world', the freewheeling Japanese culture that once flourished in cosmopolitan Tokyo and Osaka. And *ukiyo-e* are revered remembrances of these roaring times. The prints were accessible for working-class people as they were mass-produced and cost very little. The New Otani Art Museum (03 3221 4111) has many Ukiyo-e worth checking out.

Art & Craft Supplies

Ito-ya	2-7-15 Ginza	Chūō-ku	03 3561 8311	www.ito-ya.co.jp
Loft	21-1 Udagawachō	Shibuya-ku	03 3462 3807	www.loft.co.jp
Okadaya	3-23-17 Shinjuku	Shinjuku-ku	03 3352 5411	www.okadaya.co.jp
Sekaido	3-1-1 Shinjuku	Shinjuku-ku	03 5379 1111	www.sekaido.co.jp
TOA Textile World	1-19-3 Jinnan	Shibuya-ku	03 3463 3351	na
Tokyu Hands	Various Locations		See p.320	www.tokyu-hands.co.jp
Yuzawaya	Various Locations		See p.321	www.yuzawaya.co.jp

Baby Items

There are hundreds of small boutiques and international chains that cater to new mums and dads, not to mention the bigger stores. Most major department stores like Isetan (p.307) and Mitsukoshi (p.307) have a separate children and baby section with basic clothing, cold weather wear and bedding. Barneys (p.306) carry great baby shower gifts, such as Kate Spade diaper bags. Takashimaya (p.308) have a particularly good baby section, popular with mums for their eclectic mix of clothes and imported toys – they have a particularly extensive section of wooden, German and Scandinavian brands. For toys, clothes, and other items, check out Toys R Us, which has a companion store, BabiesRUs. Gap has reliable children and baby clothing with international sizing,

Baby Items

Akachan Honpo	7-22-17 Nishi Gotanda (5F)	Shinagawa-ku	03 3779 0365	www.akachan.co.jp
Barneys New York	3-18-5 Shinjuku	Shinjuku-ku	03 3352 1200	www.barneys.co.jp
The Gap	Various Locations		See p.320	www.gap.co.jp
IKEA	Various Locations		See p.317	www.ikea.com
Isetan	Various Locations		See p.318	www.isetan.co.jp
Loft	21-1 Udagawachō	Shibuya-ku	03 3462 3807	www.loft.co.jp
Mitsukoshi	1-4-1 Nihombashi Muromachi	Chūō-ku	03 3241 3311	www.mitsukoshi.co.jp
Takashimaya Times Square	5-24-2 Sendagaya	Shinjuku-ku	03 5361 1122	www.takashimaya.co.jp
Tokyu Hands	Various Locations		See p.320	www.tokyu-hands.co.jp
Toys R Us	Various Locations		See p.321	www.toysrus.co.jp
Yuzawaya	Various Locations		See p.321	www.yuzawaya.co.jp

in many convenient locations across the city. Loft (p.307) and Tokyu Hands (p.308) offer an ever-changing range of stationery, baby albums, memory books, home-proofing items, and skincare. Loft also has a small imported toy department packed with popular Australian and American brands.

For more sturdy basics, Yuzawaya does a great line of baby bowls, cups and cutlery, as well as nursery wares, and nursing bras for mum. They also carry a large range of stuffed animals. Akachan Honpo is the source for diapers, formula, baby food, strollers and items like breast pumps, highchairs, furniture and bassinettes. IKEA stock really versatile highchairs, childproofing gear, bedding, and a limited range of toys.

Baby food, cereals, and snacks can be found at grocery stores and natural food and organic stores, see Supermarkets on p.314 and Food on p.284 for more.

Beachwear
Other options **Sports Goods** p.300, **Clothes** p.280

Swimwear is available year-round due to the fact that many spas allow mixed bathing with swimsuits. For cute bikinis, one-pieces, and surf-worthy trunks, Oshman's and Yuzawaya have a nice selection in many colours, sizes, and styles. Oshman's also has a large surf department too. For something sportier, check out The Sports Authority or Victoria. Most department stores have a swimwear department but the selection may be limited out of season. Barneys and Isetan carry resort collections though. Department stores tend to be pricier but offer more glamorous choices.

Beachwear

Barneys New York	3-18-5 Shinjuku	Shinjuku-ku	03 3352 1200	www.barneys.co.jp
Isetan	Various Locations		See p.318	www.isetan.co.jp
L-Breath	4-1-14 Shinjuku	Shinjuku-ku	03 3354 8311	www.victoria.jp
Murasaki Sports	1-7-2 Jingū-mae	Shibuya-ku	03 3479 5571	www.murasaki.co.jp
Oshman's	Various Locations		See p.319	www.oshmans.co.jp
The Sports Authority	Palette Town 1-chōme, Aomi	Koto-ku	03 3599 2101	www.sportsauthority.jp
Takashimaya Times Square	5-24-2 Sendagaya	Shinjuku-ku	03 5361 1122	www.takashimaya.co.jp
Yuzawaya	Various Locations		See p.321	www.yuzawaya.co.jp

Bicycles
Other options **Art Classes** p.210, **Art Galleries** p.170

Most neighbourhoods have a local bike shop where you can buy a bike, get it repaired, and get kitted out in accessories. Second-hand shops are also a great way to go, and some local shops offer both new and used models. Outdoors shops like Oshman's and L-Breath have a good selection that are less run of the mill. Kids' bikes are easy to come by and most larger toy chains, like Toys R Us, and bike shops carry them. Tokyu Hands and Loft have a great selection of accessories to personalise your new wheels.

Bicycles

BicCamera	Various Locations		See p.316	www.biccamera.co.jp
L-Breath	4-1-14 Shinjuku	Shinjuku-ku	03 3354 8311	www.victoria.jp
Loft	21-1 Udagawachō	Shibuya-ku	03 3462 3807	www.loft.co.jp
MDS	6-8-10 Minaminagasaki	Toshima-ku	03 3953 4314	www.mds.co.jp
OD BOX ANNEX	6-2-6 Ueno	Taitō-ku	03 3836 1055	www.odbox.com
Oshman's	Various Locations		See p.319	www.oshmans.co.jp
Tokyu Hands	Various Locations		See p.320	www.tokyu-hands.co.jp
Toys R Us	Various Locations		See p.321	www.toysrus.co.jp

Manga

MDS specialises in (pricey) mountain bikes and also offers a maintenance and pick-up service. Check out OD BOX Annex in Ueno if road racers or touring bikes are more your style. Prices go from mid-range and up.

Books
Other options **Libraries** p.228

Tokyo is a city of readers, and you often see people on trains with their nose in a book. Small neighbourhood bookshops stock a wide selection of Japanese books, magazines and comics. For foreign language reads, online stores like Amazon.co.jp will have the biggest selection but there are some good local options. Kinokuniya next to Takashimaya Times Square is a favourite with expats. It has some English-speaking staff, an electronic search system, a huge section of books on Japanese culture and translated comics. Maruzen and Libro have good children's books sections, and Junkudo carries most big sellers. The top floor of the mammoth Ikebukuro branch is full of English language books and magazines. It has more of a library astrosphere and the staff won't bother you if you simply want to leaf through some periodicals. Tower Records and HMV tend to be a bit cheaper than other shops for foreign magazines as they import them directly. They also have a good selection of music and photography books. The area around Jimbōchō and Kanda is known as 'Book Town', and there are close to 200 used and antique bookshops (try Sanseido for new English-langauge books).
Blue Parrot is a good place to start for second-hand English books. The books are in good condition, there's a large selection and the stock changes frequently. It also has a buy-back system. Good Day Books is the city's other beloved English used bookstore. It has a great selection and hosts sporadic book readings and signings.

Books

Aoyama Book Center	Various Locations		See p.316	www.aoyamabc.co.jp
Blue Parrot Books	2-14-20 Takadanobaba	Shinjuku-ku	03 3202 3671	www.blueparrottokyo.com
Good Day Books	1-11-2 Shibuya	Shibuya-ku	03 5421 0957	na
HMV	Takagi Bldg, Udagawachō	Shibuya-ku	03 5458 3411	www.hmv.co.jp
Junkudo	2-15-5 Minami-Ikebukuro	Ikebukuro	03 5956 6111	www.junkudo.co.jp
Kinokuniya Bookstore	Various Locations		See p.318	www.kinokuniya.co.jp
Libro	Kichijōji Parco (B2F)	Musashino-shi	042 221 8122	www.libro.jp
Maruzen	Various Locations		See p.318	www.maruzen.co.jp
Sanseido	1-1 Kanda Jimbōchō	Chiyoda-ku	03 3233 3312	www.books-sanseido.co.jp
Tower Records	Various Locations		See p.320	www.towerrecords.jp

Camera Equipment
Other options **Electronics & Home Appliances** p.282

Many of the major camera brands are Japanese, so it's no surprise that it's easy to find a great camera. The easiest way to get one is to head over to the large electronics chains like Yodobashi, Bic, or Sakuraya, which offer a wide range of Polaroids, digital cameras and film cameras, as well as all the film and accessories to go with them. Most large outlets provide film processing services. Akihabara is also worth a look, but you may find that the prices are not quite as competitive. If you're looking for something more technical, Lemon Camera and Fujikoshi Camera stock new and used Leica, Hassleblad, and Rollei cameras. Most of these shops are online too, so you can browse before heading down there. In general, digital cameras have dropped in price, and some cameras, such as medium formats, are slightly cheaper in Japan. Film processing is more expensive than in other countries. National Photo specialises in professional processing in addition to the basic services. Most large outlets also provide film-processing services. Guarantees for items bought in Japan are generally only valid in Japan.

Camera Equipment

BicCamera	Various Locations		See p.316	www.biccamera.co.jp
Fujiya Camera	5-61-1 Nakano	Nakano-ku	03 3388 0848	www.fujiya-camera.co.jp
Fujikoshi Camera	Nihonbashi Muromachi 3-3-1	Chūō-ku	03 3241 1635	www.fujikoshi-camera.com
LAOX	Various Locations		See p.318	www.laox.co.jp
Lemon Camera	Ginza Kyōkai-dō Bldg 4-2-1 Ginza	Chūō-ku	03 3567 3131	www.lemonsha.com
National Photo Harajuku	NP Bldg, 6-13-11 Jingū-mae	Shibuya-ku	03 3486 7761	www.nationalphoto.co.jp
Sakuraya	3-19-2 Shinjuku	Shinjuku-ku	03 5269 3030	www.sakuraya.co.jp
Yodobashi Camera	Various Locations		See p.321	www.yodobashi.com

Car Parts & Accessories

Autobacs is by far the largest automobile repair and parts dealer in Japan. There are plenty of local shops who buy parts wholesale from the garages. Auto Square operates the USS car auctions every Thursday at various locations. Many people source spare parts online through sites like *Craigslist* (http://tokyo.craigslist.jp/) or magazines like *Metropolis* (www.metropolis.co.jp) and *Tokyo Notice Board* (www.tokyonoticeboard.co.jp). Visit a local garage and ask around; the guys who hang out there may be willing to share their favourite hole in the wall shop with you. Costco carries a selection of car accessories and tyres.

Car Parts & Accessories

Auto Square Car Auctions	4-39-9 Tsurumi-chō	Yokoyama-shi	na	www.auto.co.jp
Autobacs	5-18-10 Adachi	Adachi-ku	03 3848 0189	www.autobacs.com
Costco	3-6-1 Oyamagaoka	Machida-shi	0427 98 6001	www.costco.co.jp
Yellow Hat	Various Locations		See p.321	www.yellowhat.jp

Carpets

There are hundreds of interior shops in Tokyo, and the majority offer some form of carpeting or rugs. If you are in the market for Persian carpets, it's best to consult the

Carpets

Afternoon Tea	Various Locations		See p.316	na
Agito	Roppongi Hills West Walk	Minato-ku	03 5770 4434	na
Apadana Co. Ltd	4-25-9 Ogikubo	Suginami-ku	03 3392 3500	www.karuizawa-ginza.org
FrancFranc	Various Locations		See p.317	www.francfranc.com
IDC Otsuka	TFT Bldg, 3-1 Ariake	Koto-ku	03 5530 4321	www.idc-otsuka.co.jp
IKEA	Various Locations		See p.317	www.ikea.com
Loft	21-1 Udagawachō	Shibuya-ku	03 3462 3807	www.loft.co.jp
The Persian Carpet Association in Japan	AB Akasaka Bldg 8-1-5 Akasaka	Minato-ku	03 3478 3168	www.carpet-association.jp
Tokyu Hands	Various Locations		See p.320	www.tokyu-hands.co.jp

Persian Carpet Association in Japan. It can provide you with a list of reputable and knowledgeable importers and retailers that deal in authentic and quality carpets. Carpeting can be rather pricey as most houses do not have it. Area rugs and mats can be quite affordable and are more common. IKEA has some great options, as has FrancFranc and IDC. Agito has a large carpeting department specialising in avant-garde finishes, along with other fashionable household items.

Clothes

Other options **Beachwear** p.277, **Lingerie** p.291, **Shoes** p.298, **Tailoring** p.302

Japan is one of the world's major fashion centres, and big name global brands from Gap to Louis Vuitton can be found. Fashion's heavy hitters, like Chanel, Tods, Prada and Dior can be found in Roppongi, Omotesandō, and Ginza, as well as in small boutiqes in upmarket department stores like Isetan and Barneys. Isetan in particular is a treasure trove of men's and women's labels, including Donna Karan, Takeo Kikuchi, Chloe, and Ralph Lauren. Mitsukoshi carries labels such as Diane Von Furstenburg, Jil Sander, and Banana Republic. Barneys does vintage Von Furstenburg, Rick Owens, and its signature house brands.

More budget-friendly British brands like Next and Topshop (in La Foret Harajuku) have also taken a hold here, as has Spanish giant Zara. Benetton is popular and brings a welcome splash of colour.There are also some wonderful high-street Japanese brands such as Uniqlo and Muji. Jeans Mate is a casual staple that has some exciting budget threads. Inside you'll find loads of jean styles, most in the ¥3,000 to ¥8,000 range, casual shirts, T-shirts, fleeces, and sweatpants. Other favourites are the select Tomorrowland, Ships, and United Arrows, that do both a men's and women's range. Adelaide is an edgy favourite with the Aoyama crowd, and Index is great for less formal work clothes. If you're looking for street fashion, there's no place better than Takeshita-Dōri in Harajuku. Hundreds of trend hunters prowl this heaving lane looking for the next hottest thing, before it catches on and prices rocket.

Sizes tend to run small, especially for Japanese brands, and larger sizes sell out quickly. Most shops will do alterations such as hemming and men's shops will make any necessary adjustments to suits. In general, expect prices to be higher than abroad. That said, if you shop around there are always bargains to be had, especially in second-hand shops, see p.297, and the bi-annual sales are a steal.

Various Locations
See p.319

RAG TAG
www.ragtag.jp

With various locations in Tokyo, RAG TAG specialises in designer consignment. They will take your old designer clothes, carefully inspect them and value them. The showrooms are filled with Japanese brands such as Frapbois, Hysteric Glamour, Sunao Kurihara, and Issey Miyake, as well as international designer labels such as Yves Saint Laurent, Chanel, Dior, Martin Margiela, and Balenciaga. It also often sells a nice selection of vintage watches, costume jewellery, sunglasses and shoes. Some of the shops specialise in certain items, such as designer labels, haute-couture or suits. Visit the website for details and store locations.

Various Locations
See p.320

Tomorrowland
www.tomorrowland.co.jp

Tomorrowland may be a young clothing company, but it has gained momentum thanks to the rising popularity of select shops. Featuring men's and women's departments with everything from formal wear to shoes, the selection verges on the ultra trendy, and is recognisable for its classically stylish, edgy flavour. Expect to find high-quality items here, with knowledgable staff and a personalised service. Prices are reasonable considering what you get for your money. There are several locations in the central Tokyo area.

Various Locations
See p.321

Uniqlo
www.uniqlo.com

Often referred to as the 'Japanese Gap', this casuals shop is famous for its fashion-forward clothes and wallet-friendly prices. In addition to its signature fleeces, it carries a selection of very affordable jeans (starting from ¥3,000), tops, yoga and workout clothes, underwear and basics, cashmere and merino wool knits and accessories. From time to time it does special edition lines by international, up-and-coming designers. Check out the popular cheap and chic *yukata* robe sets, available in the summer collections.

Clothes

ABC Mart	1-12-1 Dōgenzaka	Shibuya-ku	03 3476 5650	www.abc-mart.com
Adelaide	3-6-7 Minami-Aoyama	Minato-ku	03 5474 0157	www.adelaide-addition.com
Adidas	YM Sq Harajuku 4-31-10 Jingū-mae	Shibuya-ku	03 5785 2600	www.adidas.jp
American Apparel	Various Locations		See p.316	www.americanapparel.net
Anna Sui	Various Locations		See p.316	www.annasui.com
Banana Republic	Various Locations		See p.316	na
Barneys New York	3-18-5 Shinjuku	Shinjuku-ku	03 3352 1200	www.barneys.co.jp
Benetton	Various Locations		See p.316	www.benetton.com
CABANE de ZUCCA	Various Locations		See p.316	www.a-net.com/top/
Comme Ca Du Mode	Various Locations		See p.317	www.taido.co.jp
DIESEL	Roppongi Hills	Minato-ku	03 5413 9830	na
Escada	Various Locations		See p.317	www.escada.com
Index	Various Locations		See p.318	na
Isetan	Various Locations		See p.318	www.isetan.co.jp
J Crew	Various Locations		See p.318	www.jcrew.com
Jeans Mate	Various Locations		See p.318	www.jeansmate.co.jp
Louis Vuitton	Various Locations		See p.318	www.louisvuitton.com
Marithé + François Girbaud	Various Locations		See p.318	www.girbaud.com
Mitsukoshi	1-4-1 Nihonbashi Muromachi	Chūō-ku	03 3241 3311	www.mitsukoshi.co.jp
MUJI	Various Locations		See p.319	www.muji.net
Next	Jiyūgaoka	Meguro-ku	na	www.next.co.uk
Oshman's	Various Locations		See p.319	www.oshmans.co.jp
Parco	Various Locations		See p.319	www.parco.co.jp
Puma	1-13-14 Jingū-mae	Shibuya-ku	03 3401 6400	www.puma.jp
RAG TAG	Various Locations		See p.319	www.ragtag.jp
Ralph Lauren	Various Locations		See p.319	www.ralphlauren.com
Takashimaya Times Square	5-24-2 Sendagaya	Shinjuku-ku	03 5361 1122	www.takashimaya.co.jp
The Gap	Various Locations		See p.320	www.gap.co.jp
The Suit Company	Various Locations		See p.320	www.uktsc.com
Tomorrowland	Various Locations		See p.320	www.tomorrowland.co.jp
Topshop	La Foret, 1-11-6 Jingū-mae	Shibuya-ku	03 3475 0411	www.topshop.com
Uniqlo	Various Locations		See p.321	www.uniqlo.com
United Arrows	Various Locations		See p.321	www.united-arrows.jp
Zara	Various Locations		See p.321	www.zara.co.jp

Computers
Other options **Electronics & Home Appliances** p.282

Tokyo's computer shops are at the cutting-edge of technology, and all the latest equipment and accessories can be found. Akihabara is noted for it's speciality computer shops, especially if you like building your own from scratch. The area around the station is full of shops where you'll find everything from new and used parts to shells, and all the other bits needed to build a computer. The selection can be overwhelming, so the more typical computer user can just head over to any of the larger electronics outlets. Prices are pretty much set across the board, however point-card schemes and discount schemes may differ, favouring one retailer over another. Both PC and Mac are easy to find, however foreign warranties may not be valid here. Repairs can be done through private companies or items can be sent back to the manufacturer. In the case of the latter, it can take months to get back to you. Manufacturers such as Dell and Apple have several shops around the city and can also be shopped online.

Computers

Apple	Various Locations		See p.316	www.apple.com
BicCamera	Various Locations		See p.316	www.biccamera.co.jp
Dell	Various Locations		See p.317	www1.jp.dell.com
Kojima Denki	Various Locations		See p.318	www.kojima.net
LAOX	Various Locations		See p.318	www.laox.co.jp
Sakuraya	3-19-2 Shinjuku	Shinjuku-ku	03 5269 3030	www.sakuraya.co.jp
Sofmap	Various Locations		See p.320	www.sofmap.com
Yodobashi Camera	Various Locations		See p.321	www.yodobashi.com

Electronics & Home Appliances
Other options **Camera Equipment** p.278, **Computers** p.282

Electronics are easy to come by, and pretty much everything is state of the art. Most major electronics companies are Japanese, and brands like Panasonic and Sony are well-known. Most electronic items can be found in major chain outlets like Bic Camera, Yodobashi Camera, and Sakuraya. Yodobashi chains usually don't have any English-speaking staff, but they have the biggest selection, at slightly lower prices. Smaller outlets like Best Denki (on the top floor of Takashimaya, p.308), LAOX, Sofmap and Kojima Denki are easy to find around most stations. LAOX and Sofmap have English-speaking staff. If you're short on time, check out what's on offer in your neighbourhood shop. Although they are gradually disappearing, there are still some small independent electronics dealers where you can pick up last minute batteries or light bulbs. To check for the cheapest prices, visit www.kakaku.com.

Electronics & Home Appliances

Best Denki	Various Locations		See p.316	www.bestdenki.ne.jp
BicCamera	Various Locations		See p.316	www.biccamera.co.jp
Don Quijote	1-16-5 Kabuki-chō	Shibuya-ku	03 5291 9211	www.donki.com
Kojima Denki	Various Locations		See p.318	www.kojima.net
LAOX	Various Locations		See p.318	www.laox.co.jp
Sakuraya	3-19-2 Shinjuku	Shinjuku-ku	03 5269 3030	www.sakuraya.co.jp
Sofmap	Various Locations		See p.320	www.sofmap.com
Takashimaya Times Square	5-24-2 Sendagaya	Shibuya-ku	03 5361 1122	www.takashimaya.co.jp
Yodobashi Camera	Various Locations		See p.321	www.yodobashi.com

Promo girls in Akihabara

Akihabara is the centre for serious techno-junkies. The streets surrounding the station are lined with small electronics shops dealing in both new and used items, hard-to-find video games, computer-building materials and parts, and even retrofitted computers and vintage devices. If you're looking for used goods or parts, *Metropolis* or *Tokyo Notice Board* have hundreds of classified ads for cheap or free items for the picking. If you buy from a major outlet, shipping is free for some large items. If you have a problem with anything you have purchased, take take it back to the shop where you bought it, with the original packaging, paperwork and receipts. Guarantees are usually standard, and you should have a certificate stamped by the store which will allow you to return it in the event of faults and problems. Most large outlets have point-card programmes that offer up to 5 to 10% back on purchases. The high concentration of shops in Akihabara means that prices here are competitive and many offer big discounts. Bargain Don Quijote has multiple branches throughout the city and is a good place to buy household goods when you first arrive in Japan (see p.104 for more on Setting Up Home).

Eyewear
Other options **Sports Goods** p.300

Glasses are a real fashion statement in Tokyo, and most places have prescription glasses and contact lenses, as well as fashion glasses frames and sunglasses. Most opticians will do eye tests for free, and places like Sakuraya will do a basic eye exam every three months for contact lens wearers (for a nominal fee). Contact lenses are especially popular, and prices are competitive. Around most stations you'll see promotion girls handing out flyers advertising a local retailer's latest discounts. For sunglasses, it doesn't get any cheaper than around Takeshita Dōri. You can get pairs for under ¥1,000 in this area, and though they may not last long, they'll be fashionable for a time. For a more substantial investment, check out the sunglasses section of most department stores. Isetan (p.307) and Takashimaya (p.308) carry Gucci, Dior, Oliver Peoples, Louis Vuitton, and Chanel. Washin Optical is an upmarket chain that sells nice one-of-a-kind handmade frames.

Eyewear				
alook	Various Locations		See p.316	www.alook.jp
Isetan	Various Locations		See p.318	www.isetan.co.jp
LUNETTES du JURA	Omotesando Hills	Shibuya-ku	03 3401 3858	na
Megane Super	Various Locations		See p.319	www.meganesuper.co.jp
Paris Miki	Various Locations		See p.319	www.paris-miki.co.jp
Sakuraya	3-19-2 Shinjuku	Shinjuku-ku	03 5269 3030	www.sakuraya.co.jp
Takashimaya Times Square	5-24-2 Sendagaya	Shibuya-ku	03 5361 1122	www.takashimaya.co.jp
Washin Optical	Various Locations		See p.321	www.washin-optical.co.jp
Zoff	Various Locations		See p.321	www.zoff.co.jp

Flowers

Other options **Gardens** p.287

Japan has a long tradition of flower arranging. Magazines on the subject of floral arranging can be found in most bookshops alongside manuals on how to make intricate arrangements. For classes on the art of flower arranging, see p.221.

The cheapest and easiest place to buy flowers is at your local convenience store (*combini*). They might not last long, but they won't put a dent in your wallet. Local florists will ship anywhere in Japan and Hana-Yoshi is a reliable online shop that has a good variety of fresh, seasonal flowers that tend to last well. International shipping is costly and is not common, so if you're sending flowers abroad it's best to go through a local florist in that country. Yuzawaya (see table below) has a great flower section and often offers big discounts. Aoyama Flower Market (p.284) is a more fashionable option; the flowers come in unusual colours, arranged in minimalist glass vases. Market-brought bouquets start at ¥1,000. Department stores are expensive for flowers as they employ professional florists, often with specialised *ikebana* (traditional Japanese flower arranging) training. Larger arrangements and plants can be shipped to your home for a small fee, usually by one of the more popular shipping companies like Yamato-Kuroneko-Yamato or Sagawa-kyubin (see p.114 for more). To get the most out of your flowers, cut the stems diagonally under running water, replace the water regularly, and keep them out of direct sunlight.

Flowers

Aoyama Flower Market	Various Locations		See p.316	www.aoyamaflowermarket.com
Hana-Yoshi	Various Locations		0120 158 744	www.hana-yoshi.co.jp
Isetan	Various Locations	Shinjuku-ku	See p.318	www.isetan.co.jp
Takashimaya Times Square	5-24-2 Sendagaya	Shinjuku-ku	03 5361 1122	www.takashimaya.co.jp
Yuzawaya	Various Locations	Ōta-ku	See p.321	www.yuzawaya.co.jp

How Many?

Japan tends to sell goods in small portions, and avoids selling them in certain numbers because it is considered bad luck. Vegetables are usually sold per piece, or in pre-packaged bags that are rather uniform in volume. The weight is not marked (for example, one bag of potatoes contains five potatoes). Prices for fish vary according to type and season and are sold per unit, not by the kilogram.

Food

Other options **Supermarkets** p.314, **Department Stores** p.306, **Convenience Stores** p.306, **Markets** p.309

The food culture in Tokyo is second to none – the freshness, quality and range on offer is fantastic. Aside from local greengrocers, butchers and fishmongers, there is a huge variety of convenience stores (*combini*) and supermarkets to choose from. Most carry similar stock, including vegetables, meat, fish, dairy and domestic products. Most of the smaller shops stock predominantly Japanese food and can be quite bewildering for those new to the country, with indecipherable packaging and unfamiliar items. The larger supermarkets and department store food halls are good for western products – Isetan (p.307) and Mitsukoshi (p.307) have particularly expansive food halls where you can sample gourmet treats before you buy.

Independent shops (see table on p.286) like YaMaYa are good for western food. The latter is a foreign food and alcohol shop with bargain prices. It also does delivery for large orders. Carnival sells items like English marmelade and Mexican tortillas. Dean & Deluca, New York's famous deli, sells gorgeous ready-made US style foods, while Viron is the place to go for French pastries and quiches and Trois Grois is an excellent bakery. See also the company entries on p.286 for favourite speciality goods.

The vegetable shops and fish markets in Tokyo are particularly good. Tsukiji Fish Market (p.310) is a must-do for the freshest fish and a wild shopping experience. Isetan's (p.307) fish market also has a dazzling selection of fresh, colourful seafood. Radish Boya and Crayon House (see table p.286) are excellent for organic vegetables.

International Food

While the vast selection of Japanese food available should be sufficient to keep the wolves at bay, there are times when nothing will satisfy like a taste of home. Fortunately, Tokyo has a number of international supermarkets and imported food stores that stock western favourites such as Weetabix, Vegemite and Heinz baked beans – unfortunately they cost almost double what they would at home. Some supermarkets also have sections with food from around the world such as Italian, Mexican, Chinese, Indian and Thai shelves. National Azabu (p.315) and Kinokuniya International (p.314) are the two best-stocked supermarkets for western food, but those looking to buy cheaper items in bulk should take the long trip out to Costco (p.314) or order their imported goods online at The Flying Pig (www.theflyingpig.com). One Italian emporium worth a visit is Ferrarini. It sells great Italian meats, cheeses, pasta, oils and vinegars, and there's a cool Milanese restaurant there too. Of the Japanese supermarkets, Seijo Ishii (p.315) and Daimaru Peacock (p.306) have the best selections of international food, but these are on the more expensive side. As well as a good selection of wine at reasonable prices, YaMaYa also carry a wide range of foods from across the world. The Kaldi coffee chain is also a good place to pick up items not normally found on the shelves of Japanese supermarkets. In the past, it used to be hard to get decent bread in Japan, but things are much better now, with excellent bakery chains located in or around most stations that bake baguettes, loaves and some slightly stranger items you might not have seen in a bakery before. Favourite bakeries include Kyle's Good Finds (p.287) and Kobeya Kitchen (www.kobeya.co.jp) which can be found at many of the city's train stations.

Health Food

Although not quite as advanced as the organic food movement in the west, Tokyo is in the middle of a health food revolution, and there are a growing number of choices. Gruppe has been a long-time leader in organic foods in the Tokyo area, but newer providers like the online delivery services from Tengu Natural Foods and Radish Boya are quickly gaining popularity. Natural House (p.315) offers healthy, organic alternatives to the usual supermarkets, while shops such as Brown Rice Deli Cafe and Crayon House (see table p.286) are also popular for the popular vegetarian cafes attached.

Vegetarian Food

Despite its Buddhist roots, vegetarianism is rare in Japan. However, you can find veggie items at most health food stores (see above). Tōfu is popular, but it's usually cooked in a fish or meat stock. Many things that are labeled or described on menus as 'vegetarian' often come with the hidden surprises of pork or beef extract, so when in doubt, ask (you may need some Japanese help if your language skills are not advanced). Two shops worth trying are Natural House (p.315) and the online Foreign Buyers Club (p.314).

Sushi

Onigiri

Food

Brown Rice Deli	Green Bldg (1F) 5-1-17 Jingū-mae	Shibuya-ku	03 5778 5416	www. www.brown.co.jp
Carnival	2-10-12 Kichijōji Honchō	Kichijōji	042 222 3303	na
Crayon House	3-8-15 Kita-Aoyama	Omotesandō	03 3406 6409	na
Dean & Deluca	Various Locations		See p.317	www.deandeluca.co.jp
Ferrarini	2-14-1 Comodio Shiodome	Minato-ku	03 6430 0486	www.ferrarini-ifp.jp
Godiva Chocolatiers	Various Locations		03 5351 2310	www.godiva.co.jp
Miuraya	Various Locations		See p.319	www.miuraya.com
Radish Boya	Online Shopping			www.radishbo-ya.co.jp
Tengu Natural Foods	185-2 Komahongō Hidaka-Shi	Saitama-ken	042 982 4811	www.alishan.jp
The Garden	Various Locations		See p.320	na
Trois Grois	Odakyu Department Store 1-3 Nishi-Shinjuku	Shinjuku-ku	03 3342 1111	na
Viron Shibuya	33-8 Udagawachō	Shibuya-ku	03 5458 1770	na
YaMaYa	Various Locations		See p.321	www.yamaya.co.jp

1-8-7 Asagaya
Suginami-ku
Asagaya
Map 3 B2 34

Buon'Italia
03 5327 5531
www.buonitalia.jp
Buon'Italia's shady location in the quiet residential area of Asagaya is a refreshing site for an extensive collection of olive oils pressed from a wide range of olives, processed at different temperatures and from different *terroirs*. The selection of olives and oils are elevated to the level of fine wines and tastings are available.

Various Locations
See p.217

Cheese Oukoku
www.cheese-oukoku.co.jp
With 10 locations in the Tokyo area, this chain of cheese shops sells a reasonably-priced range of international cheeses to fit the needs of any party or meal. The friendly staff are always ready to make a suggestion if you need help choosing something and are happy for you to taste any of the selections. To complete the expereince, they also sell cheese planes, crackers, olives, dried tomatoes and assorted dried fruit and nuts to go with your cheese. The creamy garlic and herb brie and heavenly cumin gouda are a must-try.

Online Shopping

The Foreign Buyer's Club
078 857 9001 | *www.fbcusa.com*
This online shop has been thriving in various forms for the last 21 years and is a favourite among North Americans and other expats looking for a taste of home. It not only stocks a large range of food and snack items, but also baking goods, novelty and frozen foods, and health and beauty products. Prices are a bit steeper than at international supermarkets but it's worth it as many of the items available are hard to find elsewhere. Home delivery is possible.

5-27-5 Ogikubo
Suginami-ku
Ogikubo
Map 3 A2 35

Gruppe
03 3393 1224 | *www.gruppe-inc.com*
This local favourite is one of Tokyo's longest established organic shops, and is still central to the organic foods community. It stocks basic vegetables, grains and packaged goods, as well as snack foods and spices. If you're looking for organic meats, however, they are a little on the sparse side. The Ogikubo branch also has an organic restaurant upstairs. There are other branches in Kichijoji and Mitaka.

What & Where To Buy

Jean-Paul Hevin

**Isetan
3-14-1 Shinjuku**
Shinjuku-ku
🚇 *Shinjuku
Sanchōme*
Map 7 C1 **31**

03 3351 7882 | www.jph-japon.co.jp
The fabled master of chocolate delights romanced Tokyoites in 2005 with the arrival of a boutique in Shinjuku Isetan's extensive food hall. Visiting the boutique is an experience in luxury. A doorman ushers in just a limited number of shoppers at a time to maintain the precisely perfect temperature for the chocolate, the decor is beautiful, and the chocolates are masterpieces. Delights include everything from a simple square of dark bitter chocolate to delicate truffles dusted in cocoa powder, delectable hot chocolate, chocolate cake, macaroons and chocolate dipped chestnuts. Expect luxury chocolates at luxury prices.

Cocoa Culture

Chocolate seems to be going through a mini revolution in Tokyo. Most department store food halls boast a selection of chocolatiers including Jean-Paul Hevin (p.287) and the glorious Belgian Godiva Chocolates (p.286), who have an ever-widening number of department store counters, in addition to independent boutiques. For great sweet gifts, visit La Maison du Chocolat (p.287).

Kaldi Coffee Farm

2-31-8 Daita
Setagaya-ku
🚇 *Shinjuku*
Map 7 C1 **33**

03 3412 5640 | www.kaldi.co.jp
Kaldi is the place to stop when you need something sweet. It has a good range of savoury produce, but it is the freshly brewed coffee that has made them a name. There's also a wide range of teas and generously sized chocolate brownies. Cookies, American cheesecake, Canadian maple syrup and a host of baking supplies make this a great place if you want to buy the ingredients to make your own sweet treats.

Kyle's Good Finds

2-7-10 Arai
Nakano-ku
🚇 *Nakano*
Map 3 C2 **34**

03 3385 8993 | www.kylesgoodfinds.com
This bakery and catering outfit makes delectable cakes, mouthwatering brownies, and made-to-order birthday cakes with speciality decoration (perfect for childrens' birthday parties). Choose from a wide selection of pies, muffins and bread. The carrot cake is a popular favourite, as is the health-conscious apple sauce spice cake. Catering is available upon request.

L'abeille

Various Locations

03 3398 1778 | www.labeille.jp
This collection of shops all over Japan has a cluster of garden-like, aeries in Tokyo devoted to all forms of honey. From clover and acacia, to honeys flavoured with coffee, chocolate, orange essence, and vanilla delight your tastebuds with small tastes of their golden and delicious products before you buy.

La Maison du Chocolat

3-4-1 Marunouchi
Chiyoda-ku
🚇 *Tokyo*
Map 14 A2 **32**

03 3201 6006 | www.lamaisonduchocolat.com
A steadfast favourite with Tokyo residents, this long-established titan of the chocolate world has a strong foothold with chocolate lovers in Japan. It offers a wide range of sweet somethings from basic milk and dark pastilles, to fruit and champagne flavoured truffles. The candied orange peel dipped in dark chocolate is a hit with the locals and makes a simple and tasteful gift.

Gardens

Other options **Hardware & DIY** p.289, **Flowers** p.284

DIY centres are the main places to get plants for your garden or terrace. Simachu has a big variety of orchids, small trees, boxed plants, and hanging plants. It also stocks soils, gardening supplies, supplements, insecticides, and a large variety of pots, ceramic borders, and grass seed. Costco stocks garden furniture and a limited variety of plants. It has a reliable delivery service. Many florists will do some kind of plant order, particularly those associated with larger department stores (see Flowers on p.284 and Department Stores on p.306). Tokyo has a relatively mild climate, so native plants like camelia bushes and pines do particularly well. Many people plant short decorative grass called *Ryūhige* (dragon's beard), as ground cover. Jasmine and morning glory are popular for the warmer weather, and many locals keep meticulous rose gardens.

Gardens				
Costco	3-6-1 Oyamagaoka	Western Tokyo	042 798 6001	www.costco.co.jp
IKEA	Various Locations		See p.317	www.ikea.com
Simachu	2-10-11 Nakano	Nakano-ku	03 5342 6311	na

Cultural Taboos
Be sure not to give a couple anything that's equally divisible (for example, eight cakes) or four of anything, as even numbers and the number four symbolise divorce and death in Japan and are considered extremely bad luck.

Gifts

Other options **Souvenirs** p.300

Gifts are a wonderful way to show your appreciation, and this is a welcome custom in Japan, where people often give food or fruit as small tokens of thanks. The food is usually a cake or a selection of chocolates from a well-known shop, or fancy fruit baskets. The food halls in department stores such as Isetan (p.307) and Takashimaya (p.308) are perfect places to shop. Chocolate shops are also a hit, see Cocoa Culture on p.287 and the table on p.286 for ideas. Gifts are traditionally brought back for family, friends and even work colleagues from business trips or holidays – small souvenirs such as keychains or sweets are popular choices. Tokyu Hands (p.308) and Loft (p.307) are good shops for presents. For more personal gifts, items for the home, such as scented candles or nice teacups are a good choice. Utsuwa has lovely handmade pieces of ceramic for a range of different prices. Watashi no Heya carries Demeter room scents, little ceramic pieces, and the infamous French Diptyque candles.

Gifts				
Barneys New York	3-18-5 Shinjuku	Shinjuku-ku	03 3352 1200	www.barneys.co.jp
Loft	21-1 Udagawachō	Shibuya-ku	03 3462 3807	www.loft.co.jp
Oriental Bazaar	9-13-5 Jingū-mae	Shibuya-ku	03 3400 3933	www.jyohoo.net
Takashimaya Times Square	5-24-2 Sendagaya	Shinjuku-ku	03 5361 1122	www.takashimaya.co.jp
Tokyu Hands	Various Locations		See p.320	www.tokyu-hands.co.jp
Utsuwa	3-5-5 Minami Aoyama	Shibuya-ku	03 3402 8110	http://utsuwa-kaede.com
Watashi no Heya	Various Locations		See p.321	www.watashinoheya.co.jp

Handbags

For modest and functional bags at a good price, the first place to look is the department stores (p.306). Most higher end department stores will have a Prada, Coach, Louis Vuitton or Hermès boutique. Places like Marui and Parco will have less expensive options than Isetan or Takashimaya. For something more everyday, Tokyu Hands and Loft have selections of nylon and cotton bags for heavy use. Accessorize, Topshop and Zara do cute, casual, flirty bags, while Gap is a bit plainer. Expect to pay more than you would at home, especially for imported brands. For him, the men's department in Isetan (p.307) has a very nice selection of portfolios, briefcases, shoulderbags and overnight cases. These are at the more expensive end of the range but they are well made and will last a lifetime. For more ideas, see Luggage & Leather on p.292.

Handbags

Accesorize	1-13-18 Jingū-mae	Shibuya-ku	03 5414 0068	www.accessorize.jp
Barneys New York	3-18-5 Shinjuku	Shinjuku-ku	03 3352 1200	www.barneys.co.jp
Coach	Various Locations		See p.317	www.coach.com
Hermès	Isetan Shinjuku	Shinjuku-ku	03 3225 2514	www.hermes.com
Loft	21-1 Udagawachō	Shibuya-ku	03 3462 3807	www.loft.co.jp
Louis Vuitton	Various Locations		See p.318	www.louisvuitton.com
Samantha Thavasa	Various Locations		See p.320	www.samantha.co.jp
The Gap	Various Locations		See p.320	www.gap.co.jp
Tokyu Hands	Various Locations		See p.320	www.tokyu-hands.co.jp
Topshop	La Foret, 1-11-6 Jingū-mae	Shibuya-ku	03 3475 0411	www.topshop.com
Zara	7-9-19 Ginza		03 5537 1491	www.zara.co.jp

Hardware & DIY

Other options **Outdoor Goods** p.295

DIY is a bit of an undiscovered activity in Tokyo, as most people don't have much space and can't renovate their apartments. In addition to the smaller local shops that sell nails, hammers and cut keys, there are some larger DIY outlets such as Simachu in Nakano-ku. Both offer home items, garden tools, building materials, plumbing supplies, and some outdoor goods. Costco is a bit more limited but is good for garden furniture and all-in-one tool sets. IKEA sells items such as shelving and rails and racks, and other general home improvement items. Tokyu Hands is a bit of an 'everything' shop that also sells general hardware items.

Hardware & DIY

Costco	3-6-1 Oyamagaoka	Western Tokyo	042 798 6001	www.costco.co.jp
IKEA	Various Locations		See p.317	www.ikea.com
Simachu	2-10-11 Nakano	Nakano-ku	03 5342 6311	na
Tokyu Hands	Various Locations		See p.320	www.tokyu-hands.co.jp

Hats

As expected, most department stores and boutiques carry a wide range of hats and hat-related accessories such as hatpins. Hats are available throughout the year, and selections vary with the seasons. Isetan has a particularly good selection on the first floor of the Shinjuku men's department (by designers like Takeo Kikuchi or Paul Smith) and the accessories floor of the main Shinjuku building. The hats are a bit pricey, so you might want to look at some of the high-street brands in department stores such as Parco, Tokyu Hands (p308) or 01CITY (Marui City).

Loft also carries hats in the accessories and bags section. Many of these are knitted caps and are less formal, and are friendlier on the wallet. If you have something specific in mind, Mama's Parade custom-make fabulous hats – allow at least two weeks. Prices vary, but expect to pay ¥10,000 and upwards for your new hat, depending on the work involved and materials used.

Hats

Isetan	Various Locations		See p.318	www.isetan.co.jp
Loft	21-1 Udagawachō	Shibuya-ku	03 3462 3807	www.loft.co.jp
Mama's Parade	1-35-7 Yoyogiuehara	Setagaya-ku	03 3469 8681	na
01CITY	6-15-1 Ueno	Taitō-ku	03 3836 1414	www.0101.co.jp
Parco	15-1 Udagawachō	Shibuya-ku	03 3464 5111	www.parco.co.jp
Tokyu Hands	Various Locations		See p.320	www.tokyu-hands.co.jp

Home Furnishings & Accessories
Other options **Hardware & DIY** p.289

There are plenty of furniture shops in Tokyo, with varying ranges of prices and styles.
There are new design shops opening up every day, and there is one for every budget.
Agito in Roppongi Hills is on the more luxurious and expensive side with large
couches that are bigger than some modest apartment rooms. IDC Otsuka offers a
straightforward styles and clean lines for the mid-priced budget. Watashi no Heya and
In the Room are slightly more muted, and FranFranc represents a younger and quirkier
sense of style – its selection of plates are emblazoned with edgy prints, and many
of the items in store come in bright colours. Afternoon Tea in Ginza is popular with
trendy mums. Meanwhile, IKEA does great kids' furniture and cheap steals for students.
Don Quijote has multiple branches across the city and is good for cheap household
goods. The most modest shops are the second-hand recycle shops that surround many
stations. Here you can find a mix of cast-off everyday furniture and traditional antiques.
Flea markets are also a great place to look for antique furniture (see Kappabashi, Oedo
Antique Fair, Togo Jingu Antique Market on p.310).

Home Furnishings & Accessories				
Afternoon Tea	Various Locations		See p.316	www.afternoon-tea.net
Agito	Roppongi Hills West Walk	Minato-ku	03 5770 4434	na
Don Quijote	Various Locations		See p.317	www.donki.com
FrancFranc	Various Locations		See p.317	www.francfranc.com
IDC Otsuka	TFT Bldg, 3-1 Ariake	Koto-ku	03 5530 4321	www.idc-otsuka.co.jp
IKEA	Various Locations		See p.317	www.ikea.com
In the Room	Various Locations		See p.318	www.intheroom.jp
Watashi no Heya	Various Locations		See p.321	www.watashinoheya.co.jp

Jewellery & Watches

Most department stores carry a range of jewellery and watches from basic gold
necklaces to more elaborate pieces, including engagement and wedding rings. Luxury
jewellery has always been popular and perennial favourites are Cartier and Tiffany's,
which have several branches across the city (both have a bridal consultation service).
Japan is famous for pearls, and Mikimoto is the best known dealer. However if you're
looking for something more affordable, Zara and Accesorize always have good options
made from plastic, wood and other cheaper materials. Carese and Barneys specialise
in vintage watches and jewellery, and Isetan men's department has a notable watch
selection. Diesel clothing company offers some more affordable timepieces. Go to
Ginza and have a walk about; there are hundreds of small jewellers lining the quiet
back streets. Many of the parks and streets in Shibuya play host to street vendors
hawking their ethnic wares.

Jewellery & Watches				
Accesorize	1-13-18 Jingū-mae	Shibuya-ku	03 5414 0068	www.accessorize.jp
Barneys New York	3-18-5 Shinjuku	Shinjuku-ku	03 3352 1200	www.barneys.co.jp
Carese	Omotesando Hills	Shibuya-ku	03 6912 0316	na
Cartier	Various Locations		See p.317	www.cartier.jp
DIESEL	Roppongi Hills	Minato-ku	03 5413 9830	na
Isetan	Various Locations		See p.318	www.isetan.co.jp
Mikimoto	Various Locations		See p.319	www.mikimoto.com
Tiffany & Co.	Various Locations		See p320	www.tiffany.co.jp
Zara	Various Locations		See p.321	www.zara.co.jp

Kids

Tokyo kids are rather fashionable, thanks to the big selection of children's stores and fashion-conscious mums. Matching coordinates are big news, and shops tend to be one-stop answers for everything needed to create a look, with matching separates, full outfits, and a range of shoes. The Gap, Comme Ca Du Mode, Uniqlo, and Muji are particularly notable for their affordable clothing and footwear. The Gap and Uniqlo do a well-known selection of contemporary casuals, semi-formals, beachwear, playwear, cold-weather gear, shoes and accessories. Take advantage of Uniqlo's signature kids fleeces and lower prices, with T-shirts starting as low as ¥500. Muji takes a more understated track with basics such as cotton undergarments and plain T-shirts, sandals, rubber wellingtons, coats, scarves, sweaters, and playsuits in neutral colours and comfortable cuts. Comme Ca Du Mode goes for a more fashion forward approach with complete outfits, hats, accessories, and semi-formal wear at mid-range prices. Petit Bateau is limited to smaller children aged 1 and under, but also sells lounging clothes and nice fitting T-shirts for mums too. Mothercare is another good option for children's clothing.

Miki House is a better bet for older kids, from age 2 to 10, but also stocks clothing for younger children. Most outlets boast a shoe section as well, though they are considerably pricier than other high-street shops. For dressier clothes, try the department stores, which often carry miniature suits and velvet dresses. Barneys and Takashimaya have a formal wear section for children with items such as christening robes. Most department stores will carry kids shoes to match, and Parco in Kichijōji has a whole floor dedicated to children's clothes, carrying French brand Du Pareil au Meme (DPAM) as well as local brands like Sense of Wonder and Baby!. For quirky accessories for teenage girls, Claire's is very affordable, while Accessorize may appeal to those with a slightly edgier or bohemian sense of style.

Kids

Akachan Honpo	T.O.C. Bldg,			
	7-22-17 Nishi Gotanda	Shinagawa-ku	03 3779 0365	www.akachan.co.jp
Barneys New York	3-18-5 Shinjuku	Shinjuku-ku	03 3352 1200	www.barneys.co.jp
Claire's	Various Locations		See p.317	www.clairesn.co.jp
Comme Ca Du Mode	Various Locations		See p.317	www.taido.co.jp
Gap	Various Locations		See p.320	www.gap.co.jp
Miki house	Various Locations		See p.319	www.mikihouse.co.jp
Mothercare	6-4-5 Shinozaki	Edogawa-ku	03 5666 3403	www.mothercare.co.jp
Parco	Various Locations		See p.319	www.parco.co.jp
Petit Bateau	Various Locations		See p.319	www.petit-bateau.co.jp
Toys R Us	Various Locations		See p.321	www.toysrus.co.jp

Lingerie

Other options **Clothes** p.280

Department store lingerie sections are a good place to start, and they usually offer a selection of everyday basics and lace naughties from brands such as La Perla, Wacoal, Vivienne Tam, Calvin Klein and many other high-fashion brands. Barneys carries a very high-end selection of trousseau-style lingerie. Yuzawaya and Okadaya have large lingerie sections too, and there you'll find lesser known brands like Body Wild that are pretty but won't break the bank. If you want cute, go for Peach John, whose motto is 'Lingerie is Love Jewellery'. Amos Style rounds out the bunch as the cheapest option, popular with students and high-school girls. Une Nana Cool is an affiliate of Wacoal where young ladies can choose bra straps and have small decorations sewn on for a nominal fee. MUJI and Uniqlo have great plain cotton basics, with camisoles costing as little as ¥1,000.

Lingerie

Amo's Style	Various Locations		See p.316	www.amostyle.com
Barneys New York	3-18-5 Shinjuku	Shinjuku-ku	03 3352 1200	www.barneys.co.jp
Isetan	Various Locations		See p.318	www.isetan.co.jp
MUJI	Various Locations		See p.319	www.muji.net
Okadaya	3-23-17 Shinjuku	Shinjuku-ku	03 3352 5411	www.okadaya.co.jp
Peach John	Ryōshin Harajuku (4-8F)			
	6-17-11 Jingū-mae	Shibuya-ku		www.peachjohn.co.jp
Une Nana Cool	Various Locations		See p.321	www.une-nana-cool.com
Uniqlo	Various Locations		See p.321	www.uniqlo.com
Yuzawaya	Various Locations		See p.321	www.yuzawaya.co.jp

Luggage & Leather

Small luggage shops can be found on the shopping streets around most stations. The locals often use wheelie cases to transport belongings and shopping on the train. Tokyu Hands has a large selection of luggage and travel bags, which is similar to the selection in Loft. It stocks a combination of hard and soft shell wheel bags, as well as accessories, locks and decorations that will help to identify your bag. Ranges include small name brands up to the international bigwigs like TUMI and Samsonite. Hunting World in Takashimaya deals exclusively in leather items, and there is also a Louis Vuitton boutique close by. Leather sofas are popular and come in all shapes and prices. IDC Otsuka has some of the most popular ones, and Agito does a nice selection of Italian imports.

Luggage & Leather

Agito	Roppongi Hills West Walk	Minato-ku	03 5770 4434	na
IDC Otsuka	TFT Bldg, 3-1 Ariake	Koto-ku	03 5530 4321	www.idc-otsuka.co.jp
Loft	21-1 Udagawachō	Shibuya-ku	03 3462 3807	www.loft.co.jp
Louis Vuitton	Various Locations		See p.318	www.louisvuitton.com
Tokyu Hands	Various Locations		See p.320	www.tokyu-hands.co.jp

Maternity Items

Many of the general clothing shops like MUJI, Uniqlo and Gap carry a maternity range and Mothercare is also worth a look. Most department stores can offer a more glamorous

Maternity Items

Akachan Honpo	T.O.C. Bldg (5F),			
	7-22-17 Nishi Gotanda	Shinagawa-ku	03 3779 0365	www.akachan.co.jp
Barneys New York	3-18-5 Shinjuku	Shinjuku-ku	03 3352 1200	www.barneys.co.jp
Comme Ca Du Mode	Various Locations		See p.317	www.taido.co.jp
Gap	Various Locations		See p.320	www.gap.co.jp
Loft	21-1 Udagawachō	Shibuya-ku	03 3462 3807	www.loft.co.jp
Mothercare	6-4-5 Shinozaki	Edogawa-ku	03 5666 3403	www.mothercare.co.jp
MUJI	Various Locations		See p.319	na
Petit Bateau	Various Locations		See p.319	na
Takashimaya Times Square	5-24-2 Sendagaya	Shinjuku-ku	03 5361 1122	www.takashimaya.co.jp
Tokyu Hands	Various Locations		See p.320	www.tokyu-hands.co.jp
Uniqlo	Various Locations		See p.321	www.uniqlo.com
Weleda	Various Locations		See p.321	www.weleda.jp

selection of evening and resort wear. For T-shirts and simple basics, Petit Bateau offers a wide selection for mother and child. Shops like Loft (p.307) and Tokyu Hands (p.308) carry some maternity-related items, such as skin creams and nursing pillows. Meanwhile, Weleda and Jurlique (in Takashimaya, see table) have an excellent selection of creams and beauty products that are especially good for expecting and nursing mums. For Toys (p.303) and other nursery items such as furnishings, see p.260.

Oops!

Did we miss anything? If you have any thoughts, ideas or comments for us to include in the Shopping section, drop us a line. If your shop isn't in here, let us know and we'll give you a shout in the next edition. Just visit www.explorerpublishing.com and fill us in.

Medicine

Other options **General Medical Care** p.116

Most prescriptions are dispensed at local pharmacies, which can be found next to the clinic or hospital. Your doctor will direct you to the closest one, but you are entitled to have your prescriptions filled by the pharmacy of your choice. The majority of medicines that would be 'over the counter' in other countries (such as panadol, aspirin or cold medications) are kept behind the counter in Japan, and you must first consult the pharmacist before you can purchase them. Foreign prescriptions can usually be dispensed, but you must first visit a Japanese doctor to have the prescription confirmed and approved. Medicines dispensed may sometimes be the Japanese generic brand rather than the name you're used to back home but the make up will be the same. Pseudoephedrine and the cold and congestion medications that contain it are banned in Japan. These may be confiscated on arrival at the airport (see Moving Services on p.104 for more). Medicines, particularly painkillers, are manufactured in smaller doses in Japan, so you may find yourself taking doses more often than you might at home.

For more daily needs, pharmacies like Matsumoto Kiyoshi and Sundrug are stocked with creams, powders, vitamins, feminine items, first-aid supplies, contraceptives and the usual medications and prescription items. Pharmacies generally fill prescriptions from about 10:00 to 19:00, Monday to Friday, with shorter hours on Saturdays. Most open around 09:00 and some may be open as late as 21:00 or 22:00, depending on the location and the chain. At a pinch, your local convenience store should offer very basic items such as aspirin, bandages and condoms, if not more.

Medicines

American Pharmacy	2-4-1 Marunouchi	Chiyoda-ku	03 5220 7716	na
Matsumoto Kiyoshi	Various Locations		See p.318	www.matsukiyo.co.jp
Sundrug	1-38-1 Wakamatsu-chō	Fuchū	042 369 6211	www.sundrug.co.jp
The Medical Dispensary	32 Mori Bldg (1F),			
	3-4-30 Shiba-kōen	Minato-ku	03 3434 5817	na
Tomod's	Various Locations		See p.320	www.tomods.jp

2-4-1 Marunouchi
Chiyoda-ku
🚇 *Tokyo*
Map 14 B1 🔳

American Pharmacy

03 5220 7716

Located in the Marunouchi Building in Chiyoda-ku, the American Pharmacy is a one-stop shop and long-time favourite for more familiar, mostly American brands, like Bufferin, Advil, Johnson&Johnson, and Benadryl, as well as health and beauty products that may be hard to find such as the Burt's Bees range. American prescriptions can be filled here (once confirmed by a Japanese doctor). It is open Monday to Friday from 09:00 to 21:00 and from 10:00 on Saturdays. It opens from 10:00 to 20:00 on Sundays and on holidays.

Mobile Phones

Other options **Telephone** p.111

In Tokyo it's all about the latest and best, and people frequently update their phone. As a result, mobile phone shops are everywhere, from the small corner shops to large electrical retailers such as Yodobashi and BicCamera (see table below), who usually also offer an English language service. Visit the showrooms of the different service providers to see what's available, as they will have sample models and can clue you in about options and extras. For the most part though, all shops tend to have the same stock, and the choice is really of the service provider. Once you've decided who to go with, the service provider will take care of

Mobile phones

everything for you, from set-up to repairs.

Most phones come with a guarantee, as well as a service plan (for a nominal fee). For more information on getting connected and an idea of monthly costs, see Mobile Phones (Residents Chapter) on p.112.

Mobile Phones

au by KDDI	Various Locations		See p.316	www.au.kddi.com
BicCamera	Various Locations		See p.316	www.biccamera.co.jp
NTT DoCoMo	Various Locations		0120 605 250	www.nttdocomo.co.jp
SoftBank Mobile	Various Locations		See p.320	http://mb.softbank.jp/mb
WILLCOM Inc	3-4-7 Toranomon	Minato-ku	0120 921 157	www.willcom-inc.com
Yodobashi Camera	Various Locations		See p.321	www.yodobashi.com

Music, DVDs & Videos

There are a wealth of music and DVD stores to browse and buy from. For music, Tsutaya is a small, locally run CD shop that also does rentals. Disk Union deals in new and used items, and is a good bet when seeking out discontinued and hard-to-find items. The ubiquitous international chains HMV and Tower Records carry a good range similar to what you'd find abroad, including a good international film selection.

In general, prices are higher than you'd pay abroad, whether the goods are imported or not. Expect to pay about ¥3,500 for a new release CD, ¥1,600 for an older release, and between ¥1,800 to ¥5,000 for a DVD. Prices for DVDs vary depending on release dates,

Music, DVDs & Videos

Disk Union	Various Locations	Shinjuku-ku	See p.317	www.diskunion.co.jp
HMV	Takagi Bldg, Udagawachō	Shibuya-ku	03 5458 3411	www.hmv.co.jp
Tower Records	Various Locations		See p.318	www.towerrecords.jp
Tsutaya	Gate Tower, 6-11-1 Roppongi	Minato-ku	03 5411 2667	www.tsutaya.co.jp

edition, and the country of origin. Videos can usually only be found second hand or at the rentals sales at Tsutaya for around ¥500 a piece. Be sure to check the region of the DVD when ordering online – Japan is region 2, as are all DVDs sold domestically. Amazon.com is great for UK or US versions, while with Japanese counterpart Amazon Japan (www.amazon.co.jp) you can pay COD (cash on delivery).

Musical Instruments
Other options **Music Lessons** p.233, **Music, DVDs & Videos** p.294

The area around Ochanomizu station is the place to go for musical instruments. There are dozens of guitar shops, violin showrooms and piano stores, as well as quite a few sheet music and music book outlets that offer new and used wares in various languages. Electric keyboards and pianos can be found at most of the big electronics chains such as BicCamera and Yodobashi, and in some department stores. Shimamura Music is probably the country's biggest music emporium, with multiple stores. It sells everything from sheet music to software and instruments. You can also arrange lessons (see p.233) here if you haven't quite mastered your piece yet. For a more retro touch, the area in and around Kichijōji station has a few vintage guitar shops.

The most popular traditional Japanese instruments are the *taiko* drum, Japanese flute, and shamisen (a three-stringed guitar-like instrument). Most guitar shops also stock *shamisen* and will give you a demo. It's worth looking in the 'Classifieds' section of magazines like *Metropolis* as used guitars, amps, and other equipment is often advertised at cut prices.

Musical Instruments

BicCamera	Various Locations		See p.316	www.biccamera.co.jp
Bottom's Up Guitars	2-4-11 Denenchōfu	Ōta-ku	03 3721 1721	www.buguitars.com
Kawai Omotesandō	5-1 Jingū-mae	Shinagawa-ku	03 3409 2511	http://shop.kawai.co.jp
Shimamura Music	Seibu, Shinjuku Pepe	Shinjuku-ku	03 3207 7770	www.shimamura.co.jp
Steinway Tokyo	1-5-1 Yūrakuchō	Chiyoda-ku	03 3539 1711	www.h-matsuo.co.jp
Yodobashi Camera	Various Locations		See p.321	www.yodobashi.com

Outdoor Goods
Other options **Camping** p.214, **Sports Goods** p.300, **Hardware & DIY** p.289

The Ochanomizu area, including parts of Bunkyō-ku and Chiyoda-ku is famous for its multitude of camping and outdoor gear and is worth a wander. L-Breath in Shinjuku is a leading outdoor shop that sells everything from hiking boots to canned oxygen for mountain-climbing. It has an especially good selection of mountain climbing accessories and cold weather gear for trekking and hiking. Oshman's provide much less technical fare, with basic hiking boots and clothing. The Sports Authority do some camping equipment and tents, as well as camping accessories. Basic survival gear, earthquake survival gear and camping miscellany can be found at Tokyu Hands (p.308), and Loft (p.307). Costco (p.314) carries a variety of tents, flashlights, outdoor furniture, barbecues and packaged food for camping.

Outdoor Goods

Costco	3-6-1 Oyamagaoka	Western Tokyo	042 798 6001	www.costco.co.jp
L-Breath	4-1-14 Shinjuku	Shinjuku-ku	03 3354 8311	www.e-victoria.jp
Loft	21-1 Udagawachō	Shibuya	03 3462 3807	www.loft.co.jp
Oshman's	Various Locations		See p.319	www.oshmans.co.jp
The Sports Authority	Palette Town, Aomi	Koto-ku	03 3599 2101	www.sportsauthority.jp
Tokyu Hands	Various Locations		See p.320	www.tokyu-hands.co.jp

Party Accessories

Other options **Party Organisers** p.383, **Caterers** p.383

The best places to get party accessories are Tokyu Hands and Loft, which offer a dizzying selection of party poppers, party games, decorations, masks, board games and paper plates. Tokyu Hands stocks wigs and costumes all year round, along with a great selection of stage makeup. Its rubber masks are particularly amusing.
Other costume accessories, wigs and makeup can be found at Okadaya and Yuzawaya, which also carry Halloween costumes in season. Meanwhile, the Keio Plaza Hotel has a costume hire service.

Party Accessories				
Keio Plaza Hotel	2-2-1 Nishi-Shinjuku	Shinjuku-ku	03 3344 0111	www.keioplaza.com
Loft	21-1 Udagawachō	Shibuya-ku	03 3462 3807	www.loft.co.jp
Okadaya	3-23-17 Shinjuku	Shinjuku-ku	03 3352 5411	www.okadaya.co.jp
TOA Textile World	1-19-3 Jinnan	Shibuya-ku	03 3463 3351	na
Tokyu Hands	Various Locations		See p.320	www.tokyu-hands.co.jp
Yuzawaya	Various Locations		See p.321	www.yuzawaya.co.jp

Perfumes & Cosmetics

The selection of cosmetics and perfumes in the city is amazing, and you can find virtually anything you want. Basic cosmetic needs can be met at most local pharmacies, while for brand name cosmetics, try department stores like Takashimaya, Mitsukoshi, Tokyu Hands and Isetan, and Daimaru, which sells a massive range of brands. It offers most major international brands like Chanel, Dior, Clinique, MAC, NARS, Helena Rubenstein and Napoleon Perdis. It will also have a good number of domestic brands, the most internationally famous being Shiseido and Shu Uemura. Again, prices are a bit steeper than abroad, and you might be able to get some items cheaper in duty free.
Shu Uemura is particularly famous for its lash products, sold at the company's trademark 'lash bar'. The cleansing oils range, which sometimes feature limited edition packaging by famous Japanese artists are also coveted.
Products sold at spas and salons are usually highly marked up and are much more expensive. Isetan has an excellent perfume counter in both the main building and in its men's department in Shinjuku, as has Barneys. They carry brands such as Marc Jacobs, Creed, Demeter, and most other big names. Takashimaya has a custom perfume-blending salon, where you can sample the different notes and design your own signature scent. Weleda does an excellent selection of products for sensitive skin and pregnant mothers.

Perfumes & Cosmetics				
ainz & tulpe	Harajuku Quest Bldg (B1-1), 1-13-14 Jingū-mae	Shibuya-ku	03 5775 0561	www.harajuku-quest.com
Isetan	Various Locations		See p.318	www.isetan.co.jp
Loft	21-1 Udagawachō	Shibuya-ku	03 3462 3807	www.loft.co.jp
MAC	Various Locations		See p.318	www.maccosmetics.com
Mitsukoshi	1-4-1 Nihombashi Muromachi	Chūō-ku	03 3241 3311	www.mitsukoshi.co.jp
Shu Uemura	1-5-3 Jingū-mae	Shibuya-ku	03 3486 0048	www.shu-uemura.co.jp
Takashimaya Times Square	5-24-2 Sendagaya	Shinjuku-ku	03 5361 1122	www.takashimaya.co.jp
The Body Shop	Various Locations		See p.320	www.thebodyshop.com
Tokyu	3-3-7 Kita-Aoyama (101)	Minato-ku	03 3403 0109	na
Weleda	Various Locations		See p.321	www.weleda.jp

Pets

Other options **Pets** p.107

Tokyoites may not have much space, but they love their pets. In general, pets sold in shops are pedigree, and come with a certificate. However, there is often no way to be sure if they haven't come from a puppy mill, so asking a friend about breeders, or consulting a pedigree association, is the best way to go about it. Ask about any vaccinations the pet may have had or will need. Depending on your home country, you may need to have your pet microchipped, and vets (p.107) can tell you more about this. Popular pets include cats, dogs, fish and reptiles. A big hit with kids are stag beetles, and you can see a dazzling and possibly stomach-turning array of them in most pet shops. Most pet shops will also carry supplies and accessories. Tokyu Hands and Loft also have a wide range of stylish dog fashions, and Costco carries pet supplies imported from the States.

There are many strays looking for homes in Tokyo, so it's worth checking with your local ward office about animal rescue programmes in your area. Sadly, pet abandonment is a growing problem, although more and more animal rescue organisations are springing up to meet the growing demand. These organisations are mostly grassroots and are spread out all over the country, but there are some in the Tokyo area. Check out http://angelswithfurjapan.wordpress.com for more information on organisations, volunteering, and animals who are looking for homes, or see Pet Refuge on p.108.

Pets				
Costco	3-6-1 Oyamagaoka	Western Tokyo	042 798 6001	www.costco.co.jp
Kojima Pet	Various Locations		See p.318	http://pets-kojima.com
Loft	21-1 Udagawachō	Shibuya-ku	03 3462 3807	www.loft.co.jp
Pet Forest Roppongi	6-7-6 Roppongi	Minato-ku	03 5770 3011	www.petforest.co.jp
Tokyu Hands	Various Locations		See p.320	www.tokyu-hands.co.jp

Portrait Photographers & Artists

Digital cameras are standard these days, so many people can take pretty good snaps of their own. However, if you want something more professional, you can hire a professional. Most major department stores have photo studios that do portraits, although be prepared to pay for this service. For wedding photos, wedding halls usually contract a photographer on the couple's behalf, but if there's a particular photographer you'd like to use, say so. Pencil-drawn portraits and sketches are rare. Your best bet for finding an artist is to head to some of the city's parks, such as Yoyogi Kōen (p.186) or Inokashira Kōen (p.181).

Portrait Photographers & Artists				
Isetan	Various Locations		See p.318	www.isetan.co.jp
Martin Richardson Photography	Various Locations			www.mrp-images.com
Takashimaya Times Square	5-24-2 Sendagaya	Shinjuku-ku	03 5361 1122	www.takashimaya.co.jp

Second-Hand Items

Other options **Books** p.278

Despite the Japanese love of all things new, second-hand goods are starting to gain popularity and second-hand and recycle shops are starting to multiply. Many sell everything from simple furniture to home decorations and sports equipment, and

Second-hand shops in Ikebukuro

some will also do buyback, so if you are looking to unload unwanted goods it's worth paying one a visit. Second-hand or recycle shops are easily recognisable as they'll have signs saying 'used' or 'recycle' hung in the window, and many will have eye-catching street side racks. The Pink Cow (www.thepinkcow.com), a popular expat haunt in Shibuya, regularly holds clothing swaps.

Second-hand books and music are easily come by. Shops like Disk Union, Blue Parrot Books and Good Day Books are a good place to start. Second-hand threads are less common but are gaining popularity. For designer cast-offs, browse the shops between Meguro-ku and Ebisu on Komazawa Dōri – RAG TAG is a great outlet for designer pieces. Santa Monica does great clothes and accessories such as hats and bags.

For electronics and household goods, check out the ads in *Metropolis* (www.metropolis.co.jp) or *Tokyo Notice Board* (www.tokyonoticeboard.co.jp). Akihabara is another great area for used electronics such as computer parts. There are several flea markets in the city, which are good places to find second-hand kimono and other goods (see Markets on p.309 for more). Also, antique markets are held at many of the city's shrines, usually on a Sunday.

Second-Hand Items

Blue Parrot Books	2-14-20 Takadanobaba	Shinjuku-ku	03 3202 3671	www.blueparrottokyo.com
Disk Union	Various Locations		See p.317	www.diskunion.co.jp
Good Day Books	1-11-2 Ebisu	Shibuya-ku	03 5421 0957	na
RAG TAG	Various Locations		See p.319	www.ragtag.jp
Santa Monica	1-11-5 Jinnan	Shibuya-ku	03 3409 5017	na

Shoes

Other options **Clothes** p.280, **Sports Goods** p.300

Shoes can be tricky in Japan, not least because of the small sizes (see the size chart on p.273). Prices vary depending on the store, but a good pair of leather shoes or heels can cost upwards of ¥20,000. Department stores (p.306) tend to do a bigger range than boutiques, with more sizes and varying prices. Isetan in Shinjuku has a big ladies' shoe section in the main building and an upmarket men's department with labels like Ermenegildo Zegna. 01CITY is good for affordable footwear. For the runway collections, head to Barneys – just a block from Shinjuku station. It has most big name designers, including Manolo Blahnik and Jimmy Choo. Oshman's sell flip-flops all year round. Loft and Tokyu Hands have a selection of insoles and other foot and shoe care items.

Shoes

Barneys New York	3-18-5 Shinjuku	Shinjuku-ku	03 3352 1200	www.barneys.co.jp
Isetan	Various Locations		See p.318	www.isetan.co.jp
Loft	21-1 Udagawachō	Shibuya-ku	03 3462 3807	www.loft.co.jp
Mitsukoshi	1-4-1 Nihombashi Muromachi	Chūō-ku	03 3241 3311	www.mitsukoshi.co.jp
01CITY	6-15-1 Ueno	Taitō-ku	03 3833 0101	www.0101.co.jp
Oshman's	Various Locations		See p.319	www.oshmans.co.jp
Takashimaya Times Square	5-24-2 Sendagaya	Shinjuku-ku	03 5361 1122	www.takashimaya.co.jp
Tokyu Hands	Various Locations		See p.320	www.tokyu-hands.co.jp

Written by residents, the Kuala Lumpur Explorer is
packed with insider info, from arriving in the city to
making it your home and everything in between.

Kuala Lumpur Explorer Residents' Guide
We Know Where You Live

Souvenirs
Other options **Second-Hand Items** p.297,
Markets p.309

It's customary to bring back a small souvenir
(*omiyage*) to your friends and co-workers when
you go on a trip or holiday. There are small
souvenir shops in many of the main stations like
Tokyo station. These often sell a mix of knick-
knacks and speciality food items, although these
are mostly sweets. Some even stock goods from
other regions, in case you only remember to buy
something when you get back.
Keyrings and mobile phone straps are popular, as
are specialty food items like jams, pickles, sweets
and biscuits. Loft and Tokyu Hands have a wide
selection of the latter, as well as handkerchiefs

Hyaku-en Heaven
Hyaku-en (¥100) shops are a
great way to stock up on small
everyday items, as well as wallet-
friendly souvenirs to take back
home. Everything from stationery
to ceramics and kitchen-related
items are on sale. The ceramic
figurines depicting traditional
figures in Japanese culture are
popular souvenirs and gifts. A 5%
consumption tax is added to all
marked prices. *Go Hyaku-en* (¥500)
yen) shops also exist and sell larger
items, but these are rare.

and fans. If you're looking for cheap, authentic Japanese items you don't really have
to look much further than your local *Hyaku-en* (100 yen) shop. As the name implies,
everything is ¥100 (¥105 with consumption tax) and they stock a staggering array of
home, garden, household and decorative items. Oriental Bazaar is a perennial favourite,
though some of the items might seem a bit tacky. It has a nice selection of used
kimono in the basement that's worth a look.
For more upmarket souvenirs, Kiddyland, just down the street from Oriental Bazaar,
is a Mecca for plush toys and one-of-a-kind character items. The area just inside the
Kaminarimon Gate of Sensōji is also an ideal souvenir spot as the path leading to the
temple (known as Nakamise) is the main shopping strip and is lined with vendors.
Some of the quality may be iffy, but they're good for Japanese kitsch, small statues,
incense and burners and traditional *washi* paper.

Souvenirs

Kiddyland	6-1-9-Jingū-mae	Harajuku	03 3409 3431	www.kiddyland.co.jp
Loft	21-1 Udagawachō	Shibuya-ku	03 3462 3807	www.loft.co.jp
Oriental Bazaar	9-13-5 Jingū-mae	Shibuya-ku	03 3400 3933	www.jyohoo.net
Tokyu Hands	Various Locations		See p.320	www.tokyu-hands.co.jp
Yuzawaya	Various Locations		See p.321	www.yuzawaya.co.jp

Sports Goods
Other options **Outdoor Goods** p.295

The Jimbōchō area in Chūō-ku has a cluster of sports shops catering to everything
from ski equipment to baseball kits, with everything in between. Victoria and L-Breath
are actually two different shops owned by the same company, with outlets all over
the city. Victoria has some branches that specialise in just golf or tennis. The Jimbōchō
branch is spread out over several floors and stocks items related to most sports. If
you're in the market for fitness equipment, try The Sports Authority in Palette Town in

Sports Goods

L-Breath	4-1-14 Shinjuku	Shinjuku-ku	03 3354 8311	www.e-victoria.jp
Oshman's	Various Locations		See p.319	www.oshmans.co.jp
The Sports Authority	Palette Town 1-chōme, Aomi	Koto-ku	03 3599 2101	www.sportsauthority.jp
Victoria Golf	4-1-10 Shinjuku	Shinjuku-ku	03 3352 5281	www.victoria.jp

Colourful souvenirs

Odaiba. This superstore has just about any sports equipment you can think of, from treadmills and weight lifting paraphernalia to outdoor goods. Prices tend to be a bit cheaper and it's worth the trip out there.

For watersports goods, Oshman's is the place to go. It has an annual wetsuit fair where you can order tailor-made wetsuits at reasonable prices, as well as a surfing department that sells boards and equipment, and does repairs and maintenance.

Stationery

There are an abundance of stationery shops in each area, stocking everything from basic ballpoint pens to clever staplers. Ito-ya in Ginza is a must-visit if you want something a bit classier. It carries a lovely selection of greeting cards, postcards, and Japanese paper. It also has a department for leather book covers. Meanwhile, Yuzawaya stocks all the supplies necessary to make personalised stationery. Reliable favourites Loft and Tokyu Hands can cover all your everyday needs, and they can also personalise items if required. Tokyu Hands also does nameplates and excellent business cards. Any of the above will also do custom New Year cards starting as early as late October. For stylish writing, there's a Montblanc showroom in Ginza and for pen connoisseurs, Euro-Box is practically a museum of fine writing instruments, with many collectors' items. See also Art & Craft Supplies p.276.

Stationery

Euro-Box	1-9-8-407 Ginza	Chūō-ku	03 3538 8388	www.euro-box.com
Ito-ya	2-7-15 Ginza	Chūō-ku	03 3561 8311	www.ito-ya.co.jp
Loft	21-1 Udagawachō	Shibuya-ku	03 3462 3807	www.loft.co.jp
Montblanc	Montblanc Ginza Bldg, 7-9-11 Ginza	Chūō-ku	03 5568 8881	www.montblanc.com
Tokyu Hands	Various Locations		See p.320	www.tokyu-hands.co.jp
Yuzawaya	Various Locations		See p.321	www.yuzawaya.co.jp

Tailoring

Other options **Clothes** p.280, **Souvenirs** p.300, **Tailors** p.105, **Textiles** p.302

Tailoring isn't popular in Japan and tailors are few and far between. Some supply their own material, or others will allow you to bring your own. Prices vary greatly depending on the job and the tailor. The best way to find one is to get a recommendation from a friend or through word of mouth. Many dry-cleaning shops will do basic repairs and hemming, and may be able to recommend a good tailor for bigger jobs. Most tailors will also do alterations.

Tailoring

Eikokuya	Sumitomo Seimei Kachidoki Bldg, 5-3-6 Kachidoki	Chūō-ku	03 3532 6833	www.eikokuya.co.jp
Smiley Tailor	Smiley Bldg, 7-4-1 Roppongi	Minato-ku	03 3408 5141	na
Tailor Iwanaga	6-1-6 Minami-Aoyama	Minato-ku	03 3400 5540	na
Taka-Q	3-29-12 Shinjuku	Shinjuku-ku	03 3352 3761	www.taka-q.com

Textiles

Other options **Tailoring** p.302, **Souvenirs** p.300

The Nippori area on the Yamanote line is the centre for fabrics in the city. The main street is lined with dozens of shops catering to all price ranges. If you're looking for upholstery fabric, IKEA is a cheap, reliable option. Yuzawaya has two floors dedicated to all kinds of fabrics, and Okadaya has a whole building filled with every type and finish imaginable. TOA has three locations (Shibuya, Ikebukuro and Nakano) selling basics, with a few surprises thrown in for good measure.

Textiles

IKEA	Various Locations		See p.317	www.ikea.com
Okadaya	3-23-17 Shinjuku	Shinjuku-ku	03 3352 5411	www.okadaya.co.jp
TOA Textile World	1-19-3 Jinnan	Shibuya-ku	03 3463 3351	na
Yuzawaya	Various Locations		See p.321	www.yuzawaya.co.jp

Toys & Games

Tokyo is a wonderland for toys. Toys R Us has stuffed toys and barbies and the like, while Takashimaya Times Square has a charming toy department, which includes smart Scandinavian and wooden toys and early learning items. For a fun experience, go to Kiddyland and Snoopytown across the road from Harajuku station. Both shops carry an up-to-the-minute range of character items, clothes, plushes, and other small treats. Akihabara is the best place to go for video games, new or old, though the major electronics outlets like BicCamera, Yodobashi Camera, and Sakuraya will have them too. Just take a walk around Akihabara, especially around the station, and you will be able to find everything from the latest instalment of *Final Fantasy* to the newest Wii accessory, and even vintage Nintendo and Atari games.

Toys & Games

BicCamera	Various Locations		See p.316	www.biccamera.co.jp
Kiddyland	6-1-9 Jingū-mae	Harajuku	03 3409 3431	www.kiddyland.co.jp
Loft	21-1 Udagawachō	Shibuya-ku	03 3462 3807	www.loft.co.jp
Sakuraya	3-19-2 Shinjuku		03 5269 3030	www.sakuraya.co.jp
Snoopy Town	1-14-27 Jingū-mae	Harajuku	03 5770 4501	www.snoopy.co.jp
Takashimaya Times Square	5-24-2 Sendagaya	Shinjuku-ku	03 5361 1122	www.takashimaya.co.jp
Toys R Us	Various Locations		See p.321	www.toysrus.co.jp
Yodobashi Camera	Various Locations		See p.321	www.yodobashi.com

Wedding Items

Getting married in Tokyo is a big business and there are plenty of shops and services available to help make your day special. Most shops will have a variety of dresses off the rack, but will also offer some design options. Belle Mariee is a great choice if you're not sure which way to go and it also offers a comprehensive menu of wedding services right down to flowers, the cake and the hall. Novarese has beautiful Italian designer dresses, which work well for bridesmaids too. For other necessities, Tokyo's comprehensive department stores offer formal outfits, cards and gifts. Most major department stores also have gift registries. In recent years it's become more fashionable to add a personal touch to your invitations, so head to Loft or Toyku Hands for lovely paper, stamps and a range of items for invitations and centrepieces. (also see Stationery p.302).

Wedding Items

A LILIALE	3-28-11 Shinjuku		03 3341 3018	www.a-liliale.jp
Belle Mariee	1-15-3 Jingū-mae	Shibuya-ku	03 5775 1226	www.belle-mariee.com
Isetan	Various Locations		See p.318	www.isetan.co.jp
Loft	21-1 Udagawachō	Shibuya-ku	03 3462 3807	www.loft.co.jp
Mitsukoshi	1-4-1 Nihombashi Muromachi	Chūō-ku	03 3241 3311	www.mitsukoshi.co.jp
Novarese	5-3-10 Aoyama	Minato-ku	03 5468 6633	www.novarese.co.jp
Tokyu Hands	Times Square Bldg, 5-24-2 Sendagaya	Shibuya-ku	03 5489 5111	www.tokyu-hands.co.jp
Vive la mariee!	7-12-13 Aoyama	Minato-ku	03 5774 5635	www.vivelamariee.net

Places To Shop

Since as early as the 1600s when the Mitsukoshi department store was just a humble kimono shop, Tokyoites have had a fondness for shopping. As the years have passed that penchant has only got stronger – expanding and diversifying to meet the eclectic mix of shopping subcultures here.

Time To Shop
If you're the kind of shopper who likes to get an early start it may pay to sleep in a little when planning your Tokyo shopping excursion. Things don't get started in the city until around 10:00 or 11:00 and shops close at around 20:00 or 21:00.

Cosplay

Cosplay is a popular pastime and subculture. It involves dressing up as a character from manga, anime, video games, *and sometimes even TV personalities and characters from shows, fantasy movies, pop groups and novels.*

The department stores of Ginza (see p.306) still retain a soft spot in the older generation's hearts but younger crowds are moving away from this scene – seeking the latest looks from the streets of Shibuya (p.305) and Harajuku (p.304). Designer brands are popular and shopping malls (see p.312) in areas like Roppongi and Omotesandō (p.305) have opened up to provide one-stop shopping for a wealthy crowd.

Those looking for a bargain are still well catered for. On weekends, at various locations in the city, vendors set up temporary stands selling second-hand goods at flea markets, or antiques at one of the antiques fairs (see p.310). Permanent markets like Ameyoko (see p.309) also offer some cheaper clothing and food finds. You'll quickly find that each district within this urban sprawl has a distinct character of all its own.

Areas To Shop

Whether you enjoy haggling with market stall vendors or prefer a more sophisticated shopping experience, Tokyo offers both extremes – throughout the city you'll find areas catering for different shopping needs. The streets of Harajuku (namely Takeshita Dōri) are a haven for Japanese youth, while Omotesando Hills, only a five-minute walk away, houses Yves Saint Laurent, Dolce & Gabanna and other top brands. Akihabara is an electronics Mecca with numerous department stores selling the latest gadgets (see p.282) and the Ochanomizu and Jinbochō areas have a concentration of sports shops (see p.300).

Chūō-ku
🚇 **Ginza**
Map 14

Ginza

This swanky neighbourhood boasts some of the most expensive retail real estate in the world and the calibre of shops reflect the exorbitant rent. The main shopping follows Chūō Dōri with department stores Wako (p.308) and Mitsukoshi(p.307) in the centre of it all. Apple's flagship store is also situated in the area and the six-storey building is instantly recognisable by its famed logo. Uniqlo has followed suit, opening a flagship store down the road. This budget clothing chain may provide a stark contrast to the surrounding shops but it has done well to secure a presence in the area.

A visit to the Sony Building is a must for the techno-savvy, and it would be easy to spend a day there trying out the latest goods. Near the Sony Building, Giorgio Armani, has decided to take shopping to the next level. In November 2007 he opened a 12 level Armani building at 5-5-4 Ginza, which contains a range of his collections along with an Armani Spa, and an Armani Restaurant (03 6274 7000, www.armaniginzatower.com). Ginza also has some of the top Japanese restaurants in the city (see Kojyu p.345) as well as traditional coffee houses to enjoy a warm brew (see Ginza Fugetsudo p.360). Leave your car at home for this shopping trip – take heed of the inflated rent prices when considering the cost of parking here.

Jingū-mae
Shibuya-ku
🚇 **Harajuku**
Map 8

Harajuku

Cross the road from Harajuku station and embrace the thriving crowds of Japanese youth looking for bargains on Takeshita Dōri. Amid the cheap clothing, accessory and shoe shops here you'll find cosplay stores (see Tipbox above) with gothic, Lolita-style clothing on display. If you make it through the hordes of people and cross the road into Urahara, which literally means 'backstreets' of Harajuku, you'll find a host of smaller boutiques and private labels selling the latest fashion. There are a number of men's clothing shops here, as well as good quality second-hand vintage clothing outlets located on Harajuku Dōri. Funky cafes are dotted throughout the area, such as Yaffa (see p.362), and Bape (see p.358). Parking here is pricey and given the excellent train access it's best to leave your car at home.

Omotesando & Aoyama

Minato-ku
Omotesandō
Map 8

This sophisticated shopping strip may only be a short walk away from the extreme youth culture of Harajuku, but both the shops and the clientele seem worlds apart. Designers such as Ralph Lauren and Gucci have opened up elegant stores here and the 2006 opening of Omotesando Hills (p.313) has acted as an even greater draw for well-heeled fashionistas. The Oriental Bazaar (p.300), a multi-level antique and souvenir shop, is a popular destination for tourists and is instantly recognisable by its red and green Japanese facade. Tucked away further up the hill is the Hanae Mori Antique Market, a collection of small shops selling western and Japanese antiques (see p.300). Over the hill you'll find the striking glass-fronted Prada building and on the same road on the opposite side, the shopping emporium Loveless (3-17-11 Minami Aoyama, map 8-E3), which sells an eclectic mix of fashionable items. Aoyama also has a number of design stores and Cibone in the basement of Bell Commons (Aoyama Bell Commons, B1, 2-14-6 Kita-Aoyama, 03-3475-8017, map 8-E2) is worth a visit. Shoppers can take a break at a number of cafes and restaurants located in the shopping area, but after the shops shut for the day things quieten down around here.

Roppongi

Minato-ku
Roppongi
Map 11

Over the years the Roppongi district has been known for many things – some more pleasant than others. But with the 2007 opening of Tokyo Midtown (see p.313) and the longer established Roppongi Hills (see p.312) the area is attracting a different crowd. These two stylish malls offer the latest clothes, quality dining and entertainment. In the surrounding areas you'll find a number of foreign-friendly bars and clubs and at night the place draws in both foreigners and Japanese looking for a fun night out.

Shibuya

Shibuya-ku
Shibuya
Map 8

Situated in the heart of Shibuya, Shibuya 109 (Map 8-B3) is a haven for fashionable teens. It's loud, bright, and bustling – be prepared to be a bit overwhelmed by it all. The mall spans 10 levels and covers anything an avid shopper could wish for. If it becomes a bit too much the eighth floor has a good sushi restaurant to take a break in. The surrounding area has a number of shopping malls including O1CITY (O1 is pronounced 'marui') and O1O1 JAM (see p.307). These two malls stick to the main O1O1 style while O1O1 JAM also includes a range of sports clothes from leading labels like Puma, Nike and Adidas. O1CITY offers a greater selection of men's clothing. Tower Records and HMV also have multi-level stores in the area. Shibuya is the place to go for emerging and unique trends in fashion. Overall Shibuya has a little bit of everything, with cinemas, karaoke rooms, and numerous cafes, restaurants, *izakaya*, bars and clubs. The easiest way to get here is by train but if you do want to drive, there are some carparks on the outskirts of the area.

Shimokitazawa

Another great area for shopping and exploring is the quirky Shimokitazawa (see p.166 for more). As well as just browsing through the funky winding streets, one shop worth a visit is Village Vanguard (03 3460 6145, 2-10-15 Marche Shimokitazawa). It is part of a chain with over 200 stores across Japan, but this branch is funkier and windier than the town itself, and has more novelty items than you ever thought you'd need. Postcards, sunglasses, coffee table books, squeaky toys, sofas, alarm clocks, watches, CDs, inflatable sofas and even Mickey Mouse garlic crushers are crammed into this offbeat Tardis-like labyrinth.

Combini

Convenience Stores

While the British often give directions using pubs as landmarks, the Japanese use convenience stores (*combini*). Most corners in Tokyo have a Lawson, 7-Eleven, Family Mart, Circle-K, or Am-Pm open 24 hours a day.

Combini offer a massive range of items, mostly of the unhealthy, processed variety. Instant food is cheap and easily come by, with options such as sandwiches, *onigiri* rice balls, instant noodles, *oden* (vegetables such as radishes, boiled eggs and fish cakes in a soupy broth, popular in winter), fried chicken, Chinese dumplings, *bentō* lunch boxes, salads, beer snacks, icecream and confectionary. Alcohol such as beer, wine, sake and other spirits is also available. These stores also have ATMs, machines selling tickets to sports events and concerts, postal services, photocopying, faxing and digital photograph printing. You can also pay your bills, pick up a newspaper or magazine, or browse the latest DVD or video game releases. Cosmetics and basic medicines also feature, and many shops have public toilets.

Recently, some *combini* have started selling fresh fruit and vegetables, and the Natural Lawson chain markets a healthier range of items.

Department Stores

The department store shopping experience is the epitome of Japanese service. Inside these spacious emporiums the number of staff sometimes rivals the number of customers. With their polite bows, chants of *irrashimase* (welcome), and strong focus on customer service, a visit can be a rather regal experience. Stores like Mitsukoshi (p.307) and Takashimaya (p.308) have grown from humble beginnings and expanded beyond Japan. Many of these chains are owned by railway groups and have prominent locations near major stations. There are also a number of department stores – like Loft (p.307) and O1CITY (p.307) – that target trendy kids in hip fashion districts.

More traditional department stores all tend to follow the same formula: a supermarket in the basement, and several floors of clothing, furniture, kitchenware, toys, sporting goods, and restaurants at the top. Places like O1O1 however, have a number of different stores under the company umbrella. All these department stores have baby-changing facilities.

6-8-7 Ginza ◀
Chūō-ku
🚇 *Ginza*
Map 14 A3 2️⃣

Barneys New York

03 3289 1200 | *www.barneys.co.jp*

The plush Ginza neighbourhood provides a suitable backdrop for this upmarket department store, and Japan's love of foreign elite brands has also led to stores opening in Shinjuku and Yokohama. This three-floor building has top names in fashion as well as skincare, jewellery, luggage, fragrances, baby goods and golf kit. If you're looking to splurge on a pair of Jimmy Choos or Manolo Blahniks then you have come to the right place. The Yokohama store also has a hairdresser, restaurant and cafe.

9-1-1 Marunouchi ◀
Chiyoda-ku
🚇 *Ochanomizu*
Map 13 B1 3️⃣

Daimaru

03 3212 8011 | *www.daimaru.co.jp*

The Daimaru chain was once the largest retailer in Japan, and the first Japanese supermarket to open abroad. Daimaru operate a number of department stores which have delicatessens. These sell everything from souvenirs (for which it is particularly good) to fashion accessories, and there are a massive range of cosmetics, with many international brands. The supermarkets are under the name Daimaru Peacock and have a wide selection of international foods, but they can sometimes be pricey, especially in comparison with the Japanese food on offer.

Various Locations
See p.318

Isetan

www.isetan.co.jp

This is a department store aimed at fashionable men. The main building has more feminine products, including women's clothing (in larger sizes), accessories, beauty products and homewares. But there is a separate building, with goods and services specifically for men, which spans 10 floors. There is also a rooftop golf school and a men's spa. Women shouldn't feel left out though. The nearby Isetan Beauty Park is somewhere to take a rest, have a bite to eat, and get pampered.

21-1 Udagawachō
Shibuya-ku
🚇 **Shibuya**
Map 8 C3 **4**

Loft

03 3462 3807 | www.loft.co.jp

Loft sells funky household goods at reasonable prices. The Shibuya store spans seven floors, two of which are dedicated to interiors. On these you'll find bed linen, curtains, lights, furniture, kitchen equipment and bathroom accessories. The other floors cover health and beauty, stationery, party supplies, jewellery and travel gear. There is also a Chinese tea shop, should you want a rest. With a few teas blended with alcohol on the menu, the place also caters for those in need of a stiff drink. Unlike its big brother, the Seibu department store (p.308), Loft is aimed at a younger crowd.

3-6-1 Ginza
Chūō-ku
🚇 **Matsuya**
Map 14 B2 **5**

Matsuya

03 3567 1211 | www.matsuya.com

Matsuya reflects its elite surroundings in the plush Ginza district. This multi-storey building is home to top-label men's and women's fashions, accessories, children's clothes and toys, household goods, and some beautiful, traditional Japanese items such as kimono. There is a golf school on the roof. If all the shopping has left you famished, the eighth floor has a number of restaurants offering varied Japanese cuisine (sushi, soba, tempura and eel) as well as western and Chinese options. There is also an overseas shipping service.

1-4-1 Nihombashi
Muromachi
Chūō-ku
🚇 **Mitsukoshimae**
Map 13 C4 **6**

Mitsukoshi

03 3241 3311 | www.mitsukoshi.co.jp

You know a shop is important when it has its own subway station. This multi-level emporium was originally a kimono shop, and first opened its doors in 1673. By the 1960s it had expanded to carry clothes, accessories, and household goods. These days, the 12 floor building sells much more, including sporting equipment and craft and hobby goods. The upper floors house Japanese and international restaurants, while the basement levels are worth a visit for free treats from the deli section. Shopping here is not cheap.

6-15-1 Ueno
Taitō-ku
🚇 **Ueno**
Map 12 D3 **7**

O1CITY (Marui City)

03 3833 0101 | www.0101.co.jp

Marui is marketed to a young crowd, with up-to-date fashion, reasonable prices and prominent locations. It's innovative approach includes tailoring stores to the people who frequent the surrounding area (see Areas To Shop: Shibuya p.305). In each store you'll find men's and women's clothing, accessories, bags and cosmetics. Some branches, like Marui City in Ueno, have restaurants on upper levels. The Marui Young Shinjuku branch (3-18-1 Shinjuku, Shinjuku-ku) is worth visiting for the crazy, Gothic-

Lolita fashion. For those who can't make it to a store, you can also shop online (and in English) at http://maruione.jp.

15-1 Udagawachō
Shibuya-ku
🚇 *Shibuya*
Map 8 B3 **8**

Parco
03 3464 5111
Parco has three sections in adjacent buildings, Parco Part 1, Parco Part 2 and Parco Part 3. Part 1 is designer all the way, with international labels such as Vivienne Westwood, Anna Sui and Japanese designers Yohji Yamamoto and Tsumori Chisato. Part 2 is devoted to the home and Part 3 kits out the young fashionistas in stylish clothing. There is also a cosmetics section, music and book department and a food hall.

21-1 Udagawachō
Shibuya-ku
🚇 *Shibuya*
Map 8 C3 **9**

Seibu
03 3462 0111 | www.seibu.co.jp
The first Seibu store opened in 1949 and the chain is still going strong today. The Shibuya store is 12 storeys high and is split into two parts, Annex A and Annex B, which sit on opposite sides of the road. The former is brimming with all the latest in women's fashion, while the latter has a men's department, children's clothes section and an accessories department. Two basement floors make up foodie heaven, with many international products and numerous tasting stands. And there's even an art gallery to unwind if the shoppers get on your nerves. Loft (p.307) is the homeware branch of the store and can be accessed by an underground passage.

5-24-2 Sendagaya
Shinjuku-ku
🚇 *Shinjuku*
Map 7 C2 **10**

Takashimaya Times Square
03 5361 1122 | www.takashimaya.co.jp
Since its inception in 1922, Takashimaya has opened stores in New York, Singapore, Taiwan and throughout Japan. The expansive Takashimaya Times Square first opened in 1996. Reaching 14 floors, it retains a prominent position in an area famed for its skyscrapers. This upmarket spot has many high-class brands, and the third floor – Salon le Chic – boasts Dolce & Gabbana, Fendi and Prada. Parents with a penchant for labels will be happy to know there are baby-changing facilities on several floors. You'll also find a Tokyu Hands and an HMV music store sharing the space. There's a second branch in Nihonbashi (2-4-1 Nihonbashi, 03 3211 4111).

Various Locations
See p.320

Tokyu Hands
Tokyu Hands is Tokyo's 'general store', and even those not keen on shopping will find something to interest them here. From homeware to car parts and hardware, it has it. The store is especially big on Japanese lifestyle products. Unfortunately the rest of the population is also privy to this fact and the crowds can be trying. Take a deep breath, dive in, and dare to come out empty handed. There are other branches in Shibuya and Ikebukuro.

4-5-11 Ginza
Chūō-ku
🚇 *Ginza*
Map 14 B3 **11**

Wako
03 3562 2111 | http://shop.wako.co.jp
This is a well-known shopping spot for affluent followers of fashion. Wako's prominent position, innovative window displays, and famous clock tower make it stand out from the crowd. It is situated where the Hattori Clock Tower once stood. The tower was destroyed in the great Kanto quake and when Wako was built, the store was fitted with the clock as a symbol of remembrance. It has a range of quality jewellery, homewares, clothing and gifts. It also stocks a delectable range of cakes, chocolate and sweet treats. There are also traditional Japanese crackers and condiments, for those who want a more authentic present. A French restaurant can be found in the basement, and a cafe sits on the second floor. Wako is also in Hirō.

Places To Shop

Sayonara Sales

If you want to pick up some low cost second-hand goods check out *Tokyo Notice Board* (www.tokyonoticeboard.co.jp) or *Metropolis* (www.metropolis.co.jp) for a list of 'sayonara sales'. These happen when people leaving the country sell their household items cheaply or give them away for free.

Markets

This may be a city of towering skyrises and high-tech gadgets, but it hasn't lost its traditional charm. Markets appear every weekend, and some – like Ameyoko – are permanently set up. Flea and antique markets are most common, and some beautiful traditional treasures – such as artwork, ceramics and kimono – can be found at these spots. The vibe is relaxed and you are welcome to browse without being pestered to make a purchase. If you do want to buy, bargaining is acceptable, but there are no real set standards and some places may be unwilling to budge on their marked price. The whole process is done rather politely, with none of the theatrics seen in other parts of the world. Makeshift markets normally start at dawn and run until mid afternoon. Shops within permanent markets tend to open from around 09:00 and close sometime between 17:00 and 19:00.

Ameyoko

Ueno
Taitō-ku
🚇 *Ueno*
Map 12 C4 🔟🔢

Following the train tracks between Ueno and Okachimachi, this permanent site retains some of its old-school charm from the days when it was a black market after the second world war. A range of food – dried fruit, fish and sweets – is sold, as well as a good range of larger men's clothing, cheap bags, and some well-priced sporting labels. It's usually bustling and the crowd here is slightly older – mainly due to the location. There are a number of hole-in-the-wall eateries where you can grab a beer with the locals and try some *yakitori*.

Best Flea Market

3-5-1 Marunouchi
Chiyoda-ku
🚇 *Yūrakuchō*
Map 14 A3 🔢

03 3287 5386 | *www.recycler.org*

Second-hand goods line the pavement of the Tokyo International Forum every second Sunday for bargain hunters to sift through. Items range from clothes to artwork, and you never know what you'll find. But don't expect anything valuable, as antiques aren't allowed to be sold here. The market was created to help bring a festive vibe to the Marunouchi area and is jointly organised by the OMY Area Management Association, the Tokyo International Forum, and the Citizen's Recycling Society.

Yoyogi Sunday Flea Market

Nishi Asakusa
3-chōme
Taitō-ku
🚇 **Inaricho**
Map 12 F3 **14**

Kappabashi

www.kappabashi.or.jp

Many foreigners are amazed by the number of ornate plastic food displays that line restaurant windows. Kappabashi Dōri is where Tokyo's restaurants (and interested tourists) come to buy these plastic models, along with chinaware, tableware, bulk food and kitchen equipment. The website www.bento.com has a good introduction to the stores and one place worth a visit is Propack (03 3843 2341), a six-floor maze of supplies from stationery, serving bowls and party supplies to international food. To find the market, take exit three of Tawaramachi station, and walk towards Ueno. At the second set of traffic lights you'll see a giant statue of a chef on top of the building on the far right corner. Turn into that street.

Asakusa 1 chōme
Taitō-ku
🚇 **Asakusa**
Map 4 E2 **15**

Nakamise Dōri

www.asakusa-nakamise.jp

The bustling street leading from the Kaminarimon gate to Sensōji temple is a hive of activity. You'll find a range of traditional Japanese souvenirs – such as Yukata – and some more modern ones – like fridge magnets and posters of pop stars. Stroll the lane, taking in the sights from the 90 different shops, and sample some freshly baked rice crackers and green tea icecream along the way. This market may seem overly touristy, but it does have a rich heritage and has been here since 1685.

3-5-1 Marunouchi
Chiyoda-ku
🚇 **Yūrakuchō**
Map 14 B2 **16**

Oedo Antique Fair

03 5444 2157 | *http://antique-market.jp*

Around 250 licensed antique dealers set up shop here twice a month, in the courtyard of the Tokyo International Forum. It can be a bit of a treasure hunt, but you're likely to find some interesting novelty items. Antiques include jewellery, calligraphy sets, ceramics, artwork and kimono. Since starting in 2003, the fair has gained momentum and a large number of tourists and locals now visit. On a sunny day this a great spot to meander through, while sampling fare from one of the food vendors.

1-5-3 Jingū-mae
Shibuya-ku
🚇 **Harajuku**
Map 8 C1 **17**

Togo Jingu Antique Market

One of the largest antique fairs in the Kanto region, this is worth taking the time to meander through. Both western and Japanese antiques are sold and you'll find a collection of interesting knick-knacks, artwork, ceramics and Japanese yukata and kimono. The shrine market is popular among Tokyo's foreign community and a mixed crowd is always looking for bargains in the stalls. The setting also provides a stark contrast from the neighbouring Takeshita Dōri.

5-2 Tsukiji
Chūō-ku
🚇 **Tsjukiji-shijō**
Map 14 C4 **18**

Tsukiji Fish Market

www.tsukiji-market.or.jp

This market is something of an institution. The market operates nearly 24 hours a da and the cramped, bustling inner section where the wholesale auctions take place comes alive around 03:00. The main draw is the tuna auction, with masses of huge bluefin tuna on slabs of ice and the buzz of haggling from potential buyers. Meat, fruit, vegetables and flower auctions. The markert is busiest between 08:00 and 10:00, with shoppers and tourists milling about and buyers loading their auction wins. The outer section of the market has wider alleys and sells an array of food-related products, and kitchenware. It's a great place to stop and refuel as it has a selection of restaurants. If you haven't had your fill of fish, try the sushi – it's the freshest in the city.

The market opens daily, apart from Sundays and national holidays. Bear in mind that it's a working market so it can be a bit grubby – it might be best to keep good clothing for more special occasions.

Tsukiji Fish Market

Shopping Malls

With shopping being a popular pastime for many, malls have started sprouting up all over the city. The two latest additions – Omotesando Hills and Tokyo Midtown – boast both stunning innovative architecture and a host of international shops and restaurants.

Shopping Malls			
Artre	Ebisu	03 475 8500	na
Garden Walk Makuhari	Chiba-ken	043 212 8200	na
Laforet	Harajuku	03 3475 0411	na
Roppongi Hills	Roppongi	03 6406 6000	www.ropongihills.com
Ebisu Garden Place	Ebisu	03 5423 7111	na

Most malls target a fashionable crowd, with a range of women's and men's boutiques and cafes, restaurants, hair and nail salons. There are also lifestyle and accessory shops. Despite having excellent facilities for mothers with babies, the major malls (especially in the centre of the city) are lacking in play facilities to keep young children entertained. Parking is available within the complex and the rate is often discounted or free on presentation of a purchase receipt, depending on how long you stay. By far the easiest option is to catch a train in. Most malls open around 10:00 or 11:00 and close at around 21:30. Visit the individual websites for store listings.

1312 Fukasawa
Gotemba-Shi
Shizuoka
 Gotemba
Map 1 B3

Gotemba

0550 81 3122 | www.premiumoutlets.co.jp

This sprawling mall situated an hour and a half out of Tokyo is a bargain hunter's dream. The hundreds of brands with shops here include Armani, Banana Republic, Gucci, Escada, French Connection, Adidas, and Diesel to name just a few. After being trapped in the city, the open space of this outdoor mall is a welcome relief, and despite the crowds (including tour buses of shoppers) it still feels spacious compared to the malls of the city. Parking is not a problem and mothers will also find the service to be family friendly with free strollers, baby-changing facilities and baby rooms equipped with microwaves and hot water facilities. To keep the kids entertained, there is a ferris wheel. When hunger strikes, the food bazaar – with its international cuisine – has something to keep everyone happy.

2-4-9 Toyosu
Koto-ku
 Toyosu
Map 6 E2 19

Lalaport

03 6910 1234 | http://toyosu.lalaport.jp

This sprawling complex has more to offer than the staggering 190 shops and restaurants within it. It also contains the Ukiyo-e museum (see Ukiyo-e on p.276 for more), featuring Japanese prints from the Edo period, has an idyllic garden designed by Belgian flower artist Daniel Ost, a 12 screen cineplex, and is the site of Kidzania – a career role-playing theme park for children. The selection of shops covers men's and women's fashion – with a large range of foreign brands, kids' clothes and toys, accessories and home and lifestyle goods. Mothers will be happy to know they have baby rooms for breastfeeding and diaper changing, as

Venus Fort

well as hot water facilities, drinks for children and if you accidentally left your stroller at home you can borrow one. Ladies should also visit on 'Ladies day' on a Wednesday as there are certain deals just for women. Parking is plentiful, and may even be free, depending on how much you spend.

Omotesando Hills

4-12-10 Jingū-mae
Shibuya-ku
🚇 *Omotesandō*
Map 8 D2 **20**

Omotesando Hills
03 3497 0310
www.omotesandohills.com
After much anticipation, Omotesando Hills finally opened its doors in 2006 to a well-heeled crowd. Offering one-stop shopping in the centre of Tokyo, it has 12 floors of designer stores and restaurants and is a veritible haven for Aoyama's fashion-conscious shoppers. Besides clothing stores, the mall also contains nail and hair salons, restaurants, and cafes. Designed by world-renowned architect Tadao Ando, the interior spirals around, gradually sloping upwards to follow the street's natural gradient. Each shop is on the small side, and window shopping is brought to new levels with only a quick glance needed to take in some of the store's selections. Mothers are catered for with a nursing room and two baby-changing facilities. Drivers can park in the car park underneath.

6-10 Roppongi
Minato-ku
🚇 *Roppongi*
Map 11 B2 **21**

Tokyo Midtown
03 6406 6000 | *www.tokyo-midtown.com*
One of the latest additions to Tokyo's shopping scene is Tokyo Midtown, an urban lifestyle space in the Roppongi district. This multi-faceted complex contains fashion boutiques, design stores, fine dining, bars, a 24 hour supermarket, medical facilities, apartments, an art museum (see p.156 for more) and a world-class hotel, The Ritz-Carlton (p.28). Designed with the aim of creating a high standard of 'everyday life' facilities for local city dwellers, the place contains a broad spectrum of facilities, while maintaining a sophisticated sense of style. It has a modern design and green spaces throughout are a calming breath of fresh air. Parking is available.

Palette Town
Koto-ku
🚇 *Aomi*
Map 6 D4 **22**

Venus Fort
03 3599 1735 | *www.venusfort.co.jp*
Get transported back to 18th century Europe in this theme park of a shopping mall. You won't find any rollercoasters here, but the bubbling water fountains, European architecture, and a blue sky that changes throughout the day (with the sun setting in the evening) does make it unique. There are approximately 170 shops – most of which are women's fashion stores – but you will also find jewellery, makeshift stalls selling trinkets, various beauty shops (including a day spa and nail salon), as well as international restaurants and a food court. The child facilities are exceptional with private nursing rooms, large baby-changing areas and wide bathrooms designed to make it simple to bring a stroller in. The staff are helpful – keep an eye out for attendants wearing a badge emblazoned with an English flag. Parking is available.

Supermarkets & Hypermarkets

Grab A Bargain
As closing time approaches, pre-packaged food such as sushi and ready-to-eat salads go on sale and can be picked up for up to 50% less than the original price.

Supermarkets are often located in the basements of department stores, with dedicated food halls selling fresh produce, bakery goods, meat and other essential food items. The Tokyu department store at Shibuya station is a prime example of this and a range of foreign products are stocked here. Department store shopping does tend to be pricier though and it's often best to take a walk around your neighbourhood to see if there is a local vendor selling fruit and vegetables. Purchasing from these small, sometimes makeshift shops, works out a lot cheaper than shopping in store. Besides department stores, you can find some supermarkets around Tokyo. In Minato-ku, National Azabu and Nissin (see right) cater to the foreign community and stock a range of international brands. Other chains, such as Seiyu (www.seiyu.co.jp), have branches all over town, but while they are good for Japanese goods and fresh food, they aren't so hot for international food. You can also shop online through the Foreign Buyers Club (p.286), The Flying Pig (www.theflyingpig.com) and Spinshell (www.spinshell.tv) which will allow you to buy foreign food and have it delivered directly to your door. Flying Pig also allows you to buy bulk items from Costco (www.costco.co.jp), which is helpful as its locations are a little too far out of the city for some shoppers. A number of organic supermarkets, such as Natural House, have recently opened up to meet the needs of a more health-conscious crowd. Supermarkets mainly sell food and if you're looking for other products such as household goods and toiletries you will have to visit a pharmacy. Baby-changing facilities and entertainment areas for children are limited.

Supermarkets & Hypermarkets			
Food Magazine	6-11-1 Roppongi	Minato-ku	03 5410 5445
The Garden	Various Locations	See p.320	
Tokyu	3-3-7 Kita-Aoyama	Minato-ku	03 3403 0109

Costco

3-6-1 Oyamagaoka
Western Tokyo

042 798 6001 | www.costco.co.jp

For those who have visited a Costco, they know it is no ordinary supermarket. Alongside the great range of fresh meat, fish, fruit and vegetables they sell DVDs, office supplies and home furnishings. International foods are well stocked, with branded goods and Costco's own-label products. It is also a great place to go if you are throwing a party, as there are a number of ready-prepared platters and lots of items are packaged in bulk so nobody will go without a chocolate muffin.

Hanamasa

Ginza Nine Bldg
8-5 Ginza
Chūō-ku
🚇 **Shimbashi**
Map 14 A3 23

03 3571 1571 | www.hanamasa.co.jp

Shop as much as you like, 24 hours a day, at this cheap bulk food supermarket. The food here is a mix of Hanamasa's own store brand and foreign foods. Items are sold in bulk and the more you buy the bigger the discount you'll receive. They have a large range of frozen food items and confectionary as well as seasonings and sauces. The food tends to cover different cuisines and Japanese, Thai and Italian ingredients are just some of the available items. Fresh produce and meat are also on sale and you'll struggle to get through the huge bunches of bananas. Hanamasa has various branches throughout the city, but the Ginza branch has no parking.

Kinokuniya International

Various Locations
See p.318

03 3409 1231 | www.e-kinokuniya.com

Perhaps the most well known of the international supermarkets, there is a good selection of meats, pastries, cheeses and even ready-made meals should you want a day off from cooking. The bakery here is worth a visit for sweet and savoury goods and

Kinokuniya also sells magazines and newspapers printed in English. Bear in mind that there is a bookshop in Shinjuku that has the same name (see Kinokuniya on p.314).

Hirō Plaza (1F)
35-6-6 Hirō
Shibuya-ku
🚇 Hirō
Map 5 F2 25

Meidi-ya

03 3444 6221 | www.meidi-ya.co.jp
The large selection of international foods at good prices make this a regular haunt for both expats and locals. The imported fruit can sometimes be pricey, but is often made into fruit baskets for a healthy (and welcome) gift. There's a dedicated wine cellar with a good selection of wines. Some locations offer free parking.

4-5-2 Minami Azabu
Minato-ku
🚇 Hirō
Map 6 A2 26

National Azabu Supermarket

03 3442 3181 | www.national-azabu.com
National Azabu Supermarket is a haven if you're hankering for some food from home. There is a good selection of western food, meat, cheese, and fresh fruit and vegetables, baking goods as well as a good wine selection. Brands here cost a little more than local items but you may find it's worth it to be certain of quality ingredients. parking is free and a home delivery service is also available (for purchases of least ¥5,000). Do check whether or not they will deliver to your area before loading up your cart if you don't come by car. On the second floor, there is a range of stationery, books, magazines and toiletries. Around Christmas and other festive holidays, it sells home decorations. To find it, go out Exit 1 and walk around the corner past Kobeya Kitchen heading towards Prince Arisugawa Memorial Park. Walk past Segafredo on the corner and cross the road at the next set of lights and you are there.

3-6-18 Kita Aoyama
Minato-ku
🚇 Omotesandō
Map 8 E3 27

Natural House

03 3498 2277 | www.naturalhouse.co.jp
This organic supermarket offers fresh natural bread, meat, juices and a range of non-perishable items, as well as some healthy takeaway lunch sets. Vegetarians will love this supermarket as it sells a range of soy-based products, fake meats and tempeh. The portions here tend to be a bit small and the prices higher but still reasonable. They have a good selection of medicinal teas, natural beauty products, natural healing products (such as essential oil blends) and health supplements. At the back of the store there's some yoga equipment and books in Japanese for sale. It's just a short walk from Exit B4 of Omotesandō station on Aoyama Dōri.

2-34-2 Higashi Azabu
Minato-ku
🚇 Azabu-juban
Map 11 C4 28

Nissin World Delicatessen

03 3583 4586 | www.nissinham.co.jp
Nissin spans over many levels, offering both foreign and domestic products. Alongside dairy products, frozen food, meat, bread and fruit and vegetables, there are also general household goods, barbecue tools and a flower shop. The alcohol selection is impressive and you can buy a range of quality foreign wines. Free parking is available on the first floor, but if you're on foot and spend over ¥10,000 they will do home delivery – just check they deliver to your area before you shop.

Atre Ebisu (3F)
Ebisu Station
Ebisu
🚇 Ebisu
Map 5 F2 29

Seijo Ishii

03 3448 1070 | www.seijoishii.co.jp
The reputation of this supermarket has seen it mentioned in international press for its selection of food and drink. A fantastic range of Japanese and international foods, you can spend a long time browsing the shelves. The prices can be a little on the expensive side, but it does stock well-known brands. This is a good place to go if you fancy a culinary treat.

Afternoon Tea — Flags 3F, 3-37-1 Shinjuku (03 3225 6075), Ginza Namiki Bldg 1F, 2-3-6 Ginza (03 5159 1652)

Agito — Roppongi Hills West Walk (03 5770 4434)

Alook — 3-29-10 Shinjuku, Opp Kinokuniya (03 5369 2408), 4-9-15 Ueno (03 5812 3878)

American Apparel — 1-22-8 Shibuya (03 3409 2890), 15-5 Hachiyamacho (03 3464 1880), 2-3-9 Azabujuban (03 5765 3051)

Amo's Style — Ginza INZ1 1F (03 3538 5411), Odaiba Aquacity 3F (03 3599 5321), Shinjuku Alta B2F (03 3350 6220)

Anna Sui — Ikebukuko Sunshine, Sunshine City Alpa B1F, 3-1-2 Higashi-Ikebukuro (03 3989 3321), Omotesandō Store, 1F Garden Terrace, 6-1-4 Jingū-mae (03 3486 1177), Roppongi Hills Side B1F, 6-10-1 Roppongi (03 3403 2337), Shibuya Parco Part 1 (3F), 15-1 Udagawachō (03 3464 7870)

Aoyama Book Center — Cosmos Aoyama Garden, Jingū-mae (03 5485 5511), Maru Bldg 4F, 2-4-1 Marunouchi (03 5221 8860), Roppongi Denki Bldg 1F, 6-1-20 Roppongi (03 3479 0479), West Walk (4F), Roppongi Hills, 6-10-1 Roppongi (03 5775 2151)

Aoyama Flower Market — Shibuya Tokyu B1F (03 3477 3787), Yūrakuchō Marui 1F (03 3211 0580), Mitsukoshi Ebisu B2F (03 5421 4687), Seibu Ikebukuro B1F (03 5953 2687), Shinjuku Mitsukoshi Alcott B2F (03 3358 2987)

Apple — 1-20-9 Jinnan, Shibuya-ku (03 6415 3300), 3-5-12 Ginza Chūō-ku (03 5159 8200), Best Denki, Takashimaya Times Square 11F (03 5366 4141), Biccamera, 1-11-1 Yūrakuchō (03 5221 1111)

au by KDDI — 5-6-6 Minami-Aoyama, Minato-ku (03 5485 5557), Nokia store Narita Terminal 1 (4F Central Bldg), 1-1 Aza-Goryobokujo, Sanrizuka (047 632 7636), Nokia store Narita Terminal 2, B1 Main Bldg, 1-1 Aza-Furugome, Furugome (047 634 6666), Yaesu Chikagai, Tokyo Station (03 5201 3161)

Banana Republic — Printemps Ginza 1F-B1F (03 5524 3306), Shinjuku Mitsukoshi Alcott 2F (03 5363 9621)

Benetton — Omotesandō Bldg, 4-3-10 Jingū-mae (03 5474 7155), Livin Hikarigaoka 3F, 5-1-1 Hikarigaoka (03 3977 4555), Nakano Broadway 1F, 5-52-15 Nakano (03 3385 8593), Shinjuku Tohkai Bldg, 3-27-4 Shinjuku (03 3341 5995), Tokyo Dome City (03 3868 7011)

Best Denki — Daiei Akabane 3F, 2-5-7 Akabane, Kita-ku (03 5249 3336), Matsuya Asakusa 6F, Asakusa (03 3847 4500), Shinjuku Takashimaya Times Square 11F, Shinjuku-ku (03 5366 4141)

BicCamera — Camera-kan, 1-1-3 Higashi-Ikebukuro (03 3988 0002), Daiei Akabane 3F, 2-5-7 Akabane (03 5249 3336), Ikebukuro Main Store, 1-41-5 Higashiikebukuro (03 5396 1111), Matsuya Asakusa 6F (03 3847 4500), Pasokon-kan, 1-6-7 Higashi-Ikebukuro (03 5956 1111), Shibuya Hachikoguchi, 2-5-9 Dōgenzaka (03 3477 0002), Shinjuku Nishiguchi, Odakyu Halc (03 5326 1111), Takashimaya Times Square 11F (03 5366 4141), Yūrakuchō Store, 1-11-1 Yūrakuchō (03 5221 1111)

CABANE de ZUCCa — Roppongi Hills Hillside B1F (03 3404 7733), Shibuya Parco Part 1, 3F (03 3477 8817), Yūrakuchō Seibu 6F (03 3213 3910)

Cartier 1-28-1 Minami-ikebukuro (03 3981 0111), 1-4-1 Nihonbashi-Muromachi (03 3241 3311), 5-3-2 Minami Aoyama (03 5464 6400), 5-5-15 Ginza (03 3289 5871), Isetan, 3-14-1 Shinjuku (03 3352 1111)

Cheese Ōkoku Kichijoji Lonlon1F, Kichijoji (042 222 9844), Ikebukuro Seibu B1F, Ikebukuro (03 5949 5037), Ginza Matsuya B1F, Ginza (03 3535 9844)

Claire's Akabane store BIBIO, 1-6-1-202 Tokyo Kita Akabanenishi, Akabane (03 5993 7263), Harajuku station shop, 1-20-9 Shibasaki, Jingū-mae (03 5785 1605), Ikebukuro Sunshine Stores (03 5952 4830), IMA shop Hikarigaoka (03 3977 0089), Shimokitazawa shop north wing, 2-24-6 Sawa, Setagaya (03 3485 6018)

Coach Ikebukuro Tobu 2F (03 5951 6501), Nihonbashi Mitsukoshi 1F (03 3274 8429), Odaiba Aquacity 3F (03 5564 0631), Shinjuku Odakyu Honkan 3F (03 3342 6524)

Comme Ca Du Mode Ginza Mitsukoshi 3F (03 3567 7660), Shinjuku Takashimaya 6F (03 5361 1111)

Dean & Deluca 2-24-1 Shibuya, Shibuya-ku (03 3477 4795), 2-18-1 Atre Shinagawa, 2F. Konan, Minato-ku (03 6717 0935), Corti Seijo 1F, 6-5-34 Seijo, Setagaya-ku (03 5429 1451), Tokyo Midtown B1, 9-7-4 Akasaka, Minato-ku (03 5413 3580)

Dell Biccamera, Shibuya-higashiguchi (03 5466 1111), Sofmap, Akihabara Pasokon, Sogo-kan (03 3253 9190)

Disk Union 2-1-12 Kanda-surugadai (03 3295 1461), 3-31-4 Shinjuku (03 3352 2691), Antena 21 Bldg, 30-7 Udagawachō (03 3476 2627)

Don Quijote 1-12-6 Okubo (03 5292 7411), 1-16-5 Kabuki-chō (03 5291 9211), 3-14-10 Roppongi (03 5786 0811)

Escada Hotel Imperial, Imperial Plaza 1F, 1-1-1 Uchisaiwai-chō (03 3503 2450), Matsuya Dept. Store, Ginza Head Shop 4F, 3-6-1 Ginza (03 3567 2981), Nihonbashi Takashimaya Dept. Store, Nihonbashi 4F, 2-4-1 Nihonbashi (03 3273 0200), Odakyu Dept. Store, Shinjuku Head Shop 6F, 1-1-3 Nishi-Shinjuku (03 5323 4936), Roppongi Hills, 6-12-1 Roppongi Keyakizaka (03 5772 2071), Seibu Dept. Store, Ikebukuro Head Shop, 1-28-1 Minami Ikebukuro (03 5928 1988), Tokyu Dept. Store, Shibuya Head Shop 3F, 2-24-1 Dōgenzaka (03 3477 3795)

FrancFranc DECKS Tokyo Beach 3F, 1-6-1 Daiba (03 3599 6577), Ikebukuro PARCO 5F, 1-28-2 Minami-Ikebukuro (03 5953 8421), LUMINE Shinjuku 14F, 1-1-5 Nishi-Shinjuku (03 5325 6375), ALCOTT B3F, 3-29-1 Shinjuku Mitsukoshi (03 5919 1341), Shinjuku Southern Terrace, 2-2-1 Yoyogi (03 5333 7701)

Godiva Chocolatiers 2-24-1 Shibuya (03 3477 3111), 4-6-16 Ginza (03 3562 1111), Isetan, 3-14-1 Shinjuku (03 3352 1111)

HMV Takagi Bldg, Udagawachō (03 5458 3411)

IKEA 2-3-30 Hamacho, Funabashi, Chiba-ken (047 436 1111), 201-1 Orimoto-chō, Tsuzuki, Kanagawa (045 470 7500)

In the Room　3-1-13 Shinjuku (03 3354 0101), Marui City Kichijoji, 1-7-1 Kichijoji-Minami
(042 248 0101), Marui City Kinshicho, 3-9-10 Kotobashi (03 3635 0101)

Index　Atre Ueno 1F, 7-1-1 Ueno (03 5826 5859), Bigbox 1F, 1-35-3 Takadanobaba
(03 5287 3518), INDEX-SOLITAIRE 2F, 2-24-1 Shibuya (03 3477 4656), Lumine Est
Shinjuku 3F, 3-38-1 Shinjuku (03 5368 0608), Odaiba Venusfort 2F (03 3599 2205)

Isetan　1-11-5 Kichijoji-honmachi, Musashino (03　221 1111), 2-5-1 Akebono-chō, Tachikawa
(03　525 1111), 3-4-1 Shinjuku (03 3352 1111), 6F Main Bldg, Isetan Shinjuku
Store (03 3225 2514)

J Crew　Guranduo Tachikawa 5F (042 54 0224), Isetan, Kichijoji Shinkan 1F (042 23 0904)

Jeans Mate　AD Bldg 1F, 3-1-22 Shinjuku (03 3350 6870), Ameyoko Kouki Bldg B1-2F, 4-2-8 Ueno
(03 3836 2735), Oak Ikebukuro Bldg 1F, 1-21-11 Ikebukuro (03 3988 0612), Shibazaki
Bldg 1F, 1-20-9 Jingū-mae (03 3746 3168)

Kinokuniya (Books)　3-17-7 Shinjuku (03 3354 0131), Shibuya Tokyu Plaza 5F, 1-2-2 Dōgenzaka
(03 3463 3241), Takashimaya Times Square, 5-24-2 Sendagaya (03 5361 3301)

Kinokuniya (Food)　3-11-13 Minami-Aoyama, Aoyama (03 3409 12310, Shibuya Tokyu Honten (B1F),
Shibuya-ku (03 3477 3111), Takashimaya (B1F), Shinjuku (03 5361 1111), 3-7-3 Kichijōji-
Honmachi, Kichijōji (042 221 7779)

Kojima Denki　1-34-24 Zenpukuji (03 5310 3500), 5-41-20 Wakabayashi (03 5779 3600)

Kojima Pet　3-60-21 Kameido (03 3681 5545), 5-1-18 Nishi-shinjuku (03 5358 4521), Odaiba Palette
Town 1F (03 5564 0170)

LAOX　1-15-3 Soto-Kanda (03 3255 5301), 1-2-9 Soto-Kanda (03 3255 9041)

Louis Vuitton　Matsuya Ginza, 3-6-1 Grinza (03 3567 1211), Mitsukoshi Ikebukuro, 1-5-7 Higashi-
Ikebukuro (03 3987 1111), Mitsukoshi Nihonbashi, 1-4-1 Nihonbashi Muromachi
(03 3241 3311), Mitsukoshi Shinjuku Alcott, 3-29-1 Shinjuku (03 3354 1111), Roppongi
Keyakizaka Dōri, Roppongi Hills, 6-12-3 Roppongi (03 3478 2100), Seibu Shibuya, 21-1
Udagawa-chō (03 3462 0111)

MAC　2-5-1 Yūrakuchō, Chiyoda-ku (03 6252 3280), Odakyu, 1-1-3 Nishi Shinjuku (03 5339
3134), Seibu, 1-28-1 Minami Ikebukuro (03 5391 3457), 3-6-1 Ginza (03 3538 0613),
Omotesando Hills West Wing, 4-12-10 Jingū-mae (03 5410 1122), Seibu, 21-1 Udagawa-
chō, Shibuya-ku (03 3462 3409), Isetan, 3-14-1 Shinjuku (03 3352 0516), Daimaru, 1-9-1-
Marunouchi, Chiyoda-ku (03 5208 8811)

Marithé + François Girbaud　1-12-13 Jinnan 8F (03 3476 8018), 1-35-5 Ebisu-Nishi, Sibuya (03 5728 6130), 15-1
Udagawachō (03 3477 5724), 3-1-1 Minami-Aoyama (03 3401 4177), Printemps 6F, 3-2-1
Ginza (03 3564 0395)

Maruzen　3-10 Nihonbashi 2 (03 3272 7211), Yūrakuchō-Denki Bldg, 1-7-1Yūrakuchō (03 2014 1451)

Matsumoto Kiyoshi　1-16-7 Jingū-mae (03 3423 5115), 1-30-2 Asakusa (03 3845 6918), 22-3 Udagawa-chō
(03 3463 1130), 5-5-1 Ginza (03 3289 5321), 6-1-26 Roppongi (03 3470 6244), Ameyoko,
4-10-16 Ueno (03 3837 5326), Kitasenju station (03 3870 0604)

Megane Super 1-15-9 Soto-kanda (03 5298 8001), Diamond Bldg 1F, 5-9-12 Ginza (03 3571 8037), K3 Bldg 1F, 3-27-5 Shinjuku (03 3355 0653), Tokyodo Bldg 1F, 4-4-2 Ueno (03 3835 6025)

Miki House Tobu Department Store Ikebukuro 7F, 1-1-25 Nishi Ikebukuro Toshima-ku (03 3981 5040), Tokyu Department Store Head Store 7F, 2-24-1 Dōgenzaka Shibuya (03 3477 3820), Isetan Shinjyuku Main Office 6F, 3-14-1 Shinjyuku (03 3225 0781), Matsuzakaya Ginza 7F, 6-10-1 Ginza, Chūō-ku (03 3571 5303)

Mikimoto 1F Shinhankyu Bldg, 1-12-39 Umeda (06 6341 0247), 2-1-24 Shinsaibashisuji, Chūō-ku (06 6212 3227), 3-120 Motomachi, Naka-ku, Kanagawa (045 681 3801), Landmark Plaza, 2-2-1-2 Minatomirai Nishi (045 222 5155), 4-5-5 Ginza (03 3535 4611), Imperial Hotel Store, 1-1-1 Uchisaiwaicho (03 3591 5001)

Miuraya 3-7-1 Izumi. Eihuku-chō station North Exit (03 5300 8011), Central Plaza Ramla 1F (03 5225 1188)

MUJI 1F Aoyama Bldg, 2-12-28 Kita Aoyama (03 3478 5800), 1F, TIP'S Nishi Kasai Bldg, 6-16-1 Nishi Kasai (03 5674 7482), Infos Yūrakuchō, 3-8-3 Marunouchi (03 5208 8241), Keihan City Mall, 1-1, Kyomachi, Tenmabashi (06 4790 0511), 7F Hanshin Dept. Store, 1-13-13 Umeda (06 6348 8708), 7F Lumine Kitasenju, 42-2 Senjuasahi-chō (03 5813 8520), Ario Kameari, 3-49 Kameari (03 5629 1815), Marui City Ueno, 6-15-1 Ueno (03 3836 1414)

Next 5-7-14 Jingū-mae, Harajuku (03 5778 3881), Mosaic Ginza Hankyu (B1F), Ginza (03 3575 2025), Aquacity Odaiba, Odaiba (03 3599 5560), 2-9-17 Jiyūgaoka, Meguro-ku (03 5731 2227), Sunshine City Alpa (2F), Ikebukuro (03 5953 0150)

Oshman's 1-14-29 Jingū-mae, Shibuya-ku (03 3478 4888), Flags, 3-37-1 Shinjuku (03 3353 0584), Kichijoji-honcho 2-11-2, Musashino-shi (042 228 7788), Tips Machida Bldg, Harada-machi, 6-7 Machida-shi (042 728 4888)

Parco Shibuya Parco Part3 6F,14-5 Udagawa-chō, Shibuya-ku (03 3477 8830), 1-28-2 Minami Ikebukuru, Toshima-ku (03 5391 8000), 15-1 Udagawachō, Shibuya-ku (03 3464 5111)

Paris Miki Hankyu Oicho 2F (03 3778 2296), New Melsa Ginza 2F (03 5537 3764), Sangenjaya Tokyu 2F (03 5430 3318), Shinjuku Centre Bldg B1F (03 3348 5476)

Petit Bateau 2-25-7 Kitazawa (03 5790 5464), 5-1-3 Lamia Bldg, Minami-Aoyama (03 5468 2471), Hillside Terrace B-2, 29-18 Sarugakucho (03 5784 3570), K-2107 Bldg 1F, 2-10-7 Kichijojihoncho, Musashino-shi (03 2228 7140), Stella Jiyūgaoka 1F, 1-26-4 Jiyūgaoka (03 5731 5730)

RAG TAG 1-17-7 Jinnan (03 3476 6848), Shinjuku Chūōguchi Bldg 4-5F (03 5366 6722), Suns Bldg 2F, 1-7-2 Jingū-mae (03 3478 0287)

Ralph Lauren 1-6-10 Ginza (03 3562 1500), 1-9-33 Yukinoshita Kamakura-shi, Kanagawa (046 724 7272), 4-25-15 Jingū-mae (03 6438 5800)

Samantha Thavasa — Ikebukuro Parco 1F (03 5951 1733), Odakyu Myload 1F (03 3349 5742)

Sofmap — 1-18-5 Koushin Bldg (03 3346 9651), 3-13-12 Sotokanda (03 3253 9190)

SoftBank Mobile — 1F Alteka Plaza, 1-13-9 Jingū-mae (03 6406 0711), Bank of Tokyo-Mitsubishi UFJ Roppongi Bldg 1F, 4-9-7 Roppongi (03 5775 5011), Kiyama Building, 27-4 Udagawa-chō, Shibuya-ku (03 5459 6625), Nissei Murase Bldg 1F, 3-25-11 Nishiki, Naka-ku, Nagoya-Shi (052 957 8050), The Diamond B1F, 1-4 Minamisaiwai, Nishi-ku, Yokohama-shi, (045 324 6671), Tokyo station, 1-9-1 Marunouchi (03 3284 1177)

The Body Shop — Odaiba Aquacity (03 3599 5265), 1-1-24 Kichijoji Minami-machi (042 229 7641), 1F Keihan Mall Higashinoda, Miyakojima-ku (03 5215 6129), 2 Jiyūgaoka (03 3725 0806), 2F Mosaic Mall, Ginza Hankyu (03 3576 8058), 4F Atre Omori (03 5753 8585), 5F Tachikawa Lumiine (042 548 8108), 623 Takane, Mizuho-Machi, Nishitama-gun (03 42568 4125), Ark Hills, 1 Akasaka (03 3356 7869), Chiba Parco, 2-2-2 Chūō-ku (03 202 1890), Ginza 5-chōme, Ginza (03 3575 9883), Ginza Micalady, 1 Ginza (03 3356 6325), Hibiya Chanter, 1 Yuraku-chō (03 5157 5292), Kitasenju Lumine, 42 Asahi-chō, Senju (03 5813 1425), Musashi Murayama Mu, 1-1-3 1F Diamond City Mu (03 4259 0395), Ogikubo Lumine, 1-7-1 Kamiogi (03 5347 0915), Shinjuku Lumine Est, 3-38-1 (03 35369 3275), Tama Centre, Mitsukoshi, 1-46-1 Ochiai (03 355 6355), Tokyo Station, 1 Marunouchi (03 3284 1738)

The Gap — 19-3 Udagawa-chō (03 3770 5411), 4-30-3 Jingū-mae (03 5414 2441), Aqua City Odaiba, 1-7-1 Odaiba (03 3599 5333), MAST Bldg, 5-26-16 Okuzawa (03 3724 8311), Shinjuku Flags, 3-37-1 Shinjuku (03 5360 7800), 3-29-1 Shinjuku Mitsukoshi (03 5363 2411), Shinjuku-Isetan Department Store, 6F Main Bldg, 3-14-1 (03 3225 4311), Sukiyabashi Hankyu Department Store (B1), 5-2-1 Ginza (03 3571 7211), Sunshine City, 1-2 Higashi Ikebukuro (03 3980 3600)

The Garden — 2F Artre, 2-16-9 Kami Osaki, Shinagawa-ku (03 6408 8429)

The Suit Company — 4-5-10 Ueno (03 5846 5657), 5-2-1 Ginza (03 5568 3035)

Tiffany & Co. — 1-1-25 Nishi Ikebukuro (03 3981 2211), 1-5-7 Higashi Ikebukuro (03 3987 0347), 2-6-1 Fujimi, Chiba-ken (043 224 0791), 6-10-1 Ginza (03 3572 1111), International Terminal Haneda Airport (03 5756 4811)

Tokyu Hands — 1-28-10 Higashi Ikebukuro (03 3980 6111), Takashimaya Times Square complex Shinjuku-ku (03 5361 3111), Marronnier 5-9F, 2-2-14 Ginza (03 3538 0109)

Tomod's — Ebisu Gardenplace Office Tower B1F (03 5423 1189), Lumine Shinjuku1 (B2F) (03 5324 5789), Shinagawa Intercity 2F (03 5782 8889)

Tomorrowland — Shibuya Seibu A-kan 3F (03 3496 3094), Yūrakuchō Seibu Fashion-kan 4F (03 3213 6623)

Tower Records — 1-22-14 Jinnan (03 3496 3661), Ikebukuro Parco 5-6F (03 3983 2010), Kinshichō Olinas Mall (4F) (03 3621 8601), Yodobashi Akiba Bldg 7F (03 3251 7731), Yodobashi Kichijoji (6F), 1-19-1 Kichijojihonmachi (042 229 1010)

Toys R Us Shimura Shopping Centre, 3-26-4 Shimura (03 3967 3372), Sunshine City, 3-1 Higashi-Ikebukuro (03 3983 5400), Sunstreet 1F, 6-31-1 Kameido (03 3638 1511), 1-1-1 Toshimaen, Kasuga-chō (03 3998 0114)

une nana cool 16-14 Udagawa-chō (03 5784 0250), Ikebukuro Parco 3F (03 5954 5318), Shinjuku Myload 3F (03 3349 5694)

Uniqlo 3-13-3 Shinjuku (03 5369 0731), 5-7-7 Ginza (03 3569 6781), ABAB 6F, 4-8-4 Ueno (03 5812 3871), Atre Kameido 4F, 5-1-1 Kameido (03 5836 3271), JR Tokyo station Bldg, Yaesuminami-guchi (03 3214 6317), JR Ueno station Bldg 3F (03 5246 6872), Kichijoji Lonlon 2F (042 223 7210), Nakano Sunmall (03 5318 3301), Sunshine City Alpa B1F (03 5956 3901)

United Arrows Ikebukuro Parco 3F (03 5979 3735), Yūrakuchō Seibu Fashion-kan 3F (03 3286 5580)

Washin Optical 3-28 Shinjuku (03 3354 5588), Opp Shibuya 109 (03 5489 4521)

Watashi No Heya Lumine Est Shinjuku B2F (03 5379 1130), Shin Marunouchi Bldg 4F (03 3211 6131)

Weleda Aoyama (03 5468 0031), Ebisu (03 5768 9577), Kichijoji (042 220 5888)

YaMaYa 2-68-5 Ikebukuro, Toshima-ku (03 5950 1321), 1-43-6 Higashi-Ikebukuro, Toshima-ku (03 3980 2977), 1-6-2 Kouji-machi, Chiyoda-ku (03 3511 2501), 1F 11-26 Hikarigaoka MK Bldg, 5-chōme Takamatsu (03 5372 6077), 8-10 Palazio Himonya Bldg, 2-chōme Minami (03 5728 3321), 1F Dai-ichi Ginza Bldg, 12-18 Ginza 7-chōme (03 3524 8780), 1F Onoko Shinjuku Bldg, 3-2-7 Nishi-Shinjuku (03 3342 0601), 1F Oomori NM Bldg, 2-1-1 Oomori-kita (03 5753 6228), 2-25-14 Kameido, Koto-ku (03 5858 0057), Akasaka Mita Bldg, 2-14-33 Akasaka (03 3583 5657), Aoyama Tower Place 1F, 8-4-14 Akasaka (03 5474 8761), Shibuya Square A, 1-9-5 Dōgenzaka (03 5728 3321)

Yellow Hat 2-12-6 Kasuga-chō, Nerima-ku (03 3825 1680), 794-1 Utsugi-chō, Hachioji-shi (042 692 3511), 2-19-10 Aobad, Meguro-ku (03 5773 3700)

Yodobashi Camera 1-11-1 Nishi-Shinjuku (03 3346 1010), Bee-One Mall, B1 (043 224 1010), Ekimae Honchō 21-12, Kawasaki-ku (044 221 1010), 1-1-11 Hara Machida, Machida-shi (042 721 1010), 7-4 Higashi-Machi, Hachioji-shi (042 643 1010), 1-5-10 Minami Saiwai, Nishi-ku (045 313 1010), 3-26-8 Shinjuku (03 3356 1010), Termina Bldg 1F, 3-14-5 Koto-bashi (03 3632 1010), 4-9-8 Ueno (03 3837 1010)

Yuzawaya 4-12-8 Nishikamata (03 3734 4141), 7-2, 4 Minami-Senju (03 5811 4141) 7-2- 4 Minami-Senjyū, Ōta-ku

Zara 7-9-19 Ginza (03 5537 1491), 1-6-4 Higashi-Ikebukuro (03 5957 5010), 2-13 Kichijoji Honchō (042 228 7340), 3-27-10 Shinjuku (03 3354 1133)

Zoff Akasaka Biz Tower B1F, 5-3-1 Akasaka (03 5574 8550), Odakyu Department Store Shinjuku 2F, 1-1-3 Nishi-Shinjuku (03 3345 2622)

Going Out

Going Out

As the working day draws to a close, the city comes to life with droves of workers making the move from office to *izakaya* (Japanese-style pubs). Every night of the week you'll find Tokyo's restaurants, bars and *izakaya* draw in a crowd that stays till the last train home, while at the weekend the party continues well into the early hours. Bawdy booze-fuelled fights are rare. Over the years, more international restaurants targeting both foreigners and locals have opened up across the city. In areas with a large foreign contingent you'll even find Japanese restaurants that target a more international crowd (See Rainbow Roll Sushi p.345). Karaoke (p.382) has also gone upscale to keep up with the times, and places like Lovenet (p.368) have opened to attract more well-heeled patrons. This and similar establishments, as well as a host of western restaurants, have opened in the Roppongi area and Tokyo's expat nightlife scene tends to focus around this district.

Eating Out

Whether you're looking to spend ¥20,000 on delectable raw fish or slurp cheap noodles from a vending machine, the city caters to all culinary persuasions. With the number of eateries in Tokyo estimated at over 200,000, the variety of restaurants is astounding. Alongside the mix of international food (see the Cuisine List below), and the usual *sushi* and *sashimi*, there is a range of Japanese food that is not well known outside Japan, see Japanese Cuisine on p.327 for more. For a selection of the city's restaurants to get you started, see the restaurant listings on p.330, read on. To explore the culinary options further, try websites like www.bento.com, www.metropolis.co.jp or www.sunnypages.jp, or restaurant guides such as the *Michelin Guide Tokyo* and the *Good Food Guide* by Rob Satterthwaite.

Restaurant Opening Hours

Many restaurants open around 11:00 for lunch and then re-open for dinner – closing as the last train leaves the station around midnight. The day is split into a set lunchtime, normally from around 11:00 to 14:00, late afternoon tea, and dinner from 17:00 or 18:00. Restaurants and *izakaya* located in business districts often close completely over the weekends and holiday periods or else reduce their hours, while those in entertainment areas stay open, some until the early hours of the morning. On Sundays and holidays opening hours are typically reduced, especially during Golden Week at the end of April, when many smaller restaurants close.

Delivery & Takeaways

Knowing Japanese will expand your delivery options, but even if you don't know the local lingo there are still a few places you can call upon. Burger joints like Homeworks (p.330) deliver to central Tokyo, as do more upscale pizzerias like Pizzakaya (p.340) and Pizza Salvatore Cuomo (www.salvatore.jp) and the well-known pizza chains. Pizza and Chinese food delivery has really taken off recently, with multiple options and reasonable prices. Indian restaurant Moti (p.338) has branches throughout Tokyo and has a takeaway

Cuisine List – Quick Reference

Cuisine	Page	Cuisine	Page	Cuisine	Page
African	330	Indian	336	Middle Eastern	351
American	330	Indonesian	338	Nepalese	352
Brazilian	332	Italian	339	Pacific Rim	354
Chinese	333	Japanese	341	Portuguese	354
Far Eastern	334	Korean	350	Seafood	354
French	335	Mediterranean	350	Thai	355
German	336	Mexican	351	Vegetarian	356

and delivery service. The Earl (www.thearl.com) delivers gourmet sandwiches to hungry office workers in the city and also provides catering services. For more on ordering in, see Caterers on p.383.

Hygiene

Hygiene standards in restaurants in Tokyo are generally high, leaving little cause for worry. However, if you do have any concerns the Food Safety Commission is an independent organisation within the food industry that is dedicated to assessing food risks. It also makes recommendations to the relevant ministries and responds to food-borne incidents in the city. It can be reached on 03 5251 9220. Random checks of restaurant hygiene standards do happen, but it is uncommon to hear of places being closed down due to poor sanitation.

Nomikai

Group binge drinking is a cultural phenomenon that takes on different names depending on the occasion: *nijikai* (post-wedding party), *bōnenkai* (end of year party), *shinnenkai* (New Year), *oirashikai/ owakarekai* (joining or leaving a company): and *gokon* (matchmaking parties). When the alcohol starts flowing, guards are let down and relationships are forged. These parties are usually held at traditional bars called *izakaya (p.327)*, which offer set courses and inexpensive two or three hour bottomless booze deals (*nomihōdai*). Social hierarchy governs who pours drinks for whom – so impress your host by keeping their glass topped up, while uttering a self-deprecating 'maa, maa, maa'.

Discounts

A relatively recent introduction to the drinking scene is the happy hour – but the 'hour' part was evidently lost in translation and many bars, like the 30 odd branches of Hub (p.367), serve up heavily discounted drinks for several hours, several days of the week. Savings can also be had by printing out coupons from the bar or restaurant's website, or online restaurant and bar directories like Gourmet Navigator (www.gnavi.co.jp).

Special Deals & Theme Nights

Traditional holidays like Christmas and Thanksgiving bring with them a slew of dining specials. Most involve a set menu and special deals are advertised in local publications like *Metropolis* (www.metropolis.co.jp) and *The Weekender* (www.weekenderjapan.com), as well as on each restaurant's webpage.

At Halloween, local bars and clubs host parties and information on these events can also be found in the publications mentioned above. Irish pubs come to life on St Patrick's Day and a parade is held in the Omotesandō area around this time.

During the week, many specials are targeted towards ladies, with a number of bars in Roppongi offering free drinks for women on certain nights. Some restaurants, such as Leroux (p.335) and Bakery Cafe 632 Harajuku (p.357), offer set meal deals for ladies every day. Alternatively, some outlets, such as The Pink Cow (p.331), do monthly 'all you can eat' buffets open to everyone. Places like Ben's Cafe (p.358) also host a range of events which are listed on their websites. All-you-can-drink specials are common in *izakaya* (p.327), as well as in some restaurants – just check the days they are available before you go. Weekday hours tend to be up until the last train, to help intoxicated patrons to make their way home.

Tax & Service Charges

Tax is an additional 5% and it is compulsory for restaurants to show their prices with tax, rather than just add it on to your bill at the end. Some restaurants will do this by showing both prices (before and after tax) by each menu item. In more upscale restaurants it is common for a 10% service charge to also be added to your bill.

Tipping

Tipping is not a standard practice in Japan. People rarely tip and in many situations offering a tip could cause embarrassment so it is best avoided (unless you absolutely feel the service was exemplary). Service staff in Japan do not depend on tips to live (as is the case in some other countries) so you shouldn't feel bad about not leaving one. One exception to the rule is taxis. It's common practice to round your fare up to an easy-to-handle amount to avoid the driver searching for change. Some restaurants add a 10% service charge onto the bill.

Dress & Door Policy

Despite boasting some truly world-class establishments, Tokyo by and large does not ascribe to a discriminatory door policy system, and perhaps owing to the world-famous eccentricities of Japanese fashion, prescribed dress codes are also rare. Only the strictest nightclubs and hotel bars prohibit jeans; a few more will refuse entry to men wearing shorts or sandals. Women can get away with much more – or less. Cloakrooms are not as common as in other places. That said, a few of the classier establishments do oblige and most clubs have paid lockers (usually ¥300) to stash your valuables in. Just don't lose your key, or you'll be stuck with a hefty replacement charge at best and an empty locker at worst.

Independent Reviews

All of the venues in this book have been independently reviewed by food and drink writers based in Tokyo. The entries aim to provide informative, engaging and unbiased views of each outlet. If any of the reviews in this section have led you astray, or if your favourite local eatery doesn't grace these pages, then drop us a line at info@explorerpublishing.com.

Restaurant Listing Structure

The Going Out section features reviews of a few hundred restaurants, bars, cafes and nightclubs to start you on your way eating and drinking around the city. Each review gives an idea of the food, service, decor and atmosphere, while those venues that really excel earn the coveted 'Explorer Recommended' star. Restaurants have been categorised by cuisine and are listed in alphabetical order. The On the Town section (p.363) covers bars, pubs, nightclubs, and gay and lesbian venues.

Vegetarian Food

Being a vegetarian in Japan is not easy. One fundamental element of Japanese cooking is *katsuobushi dashi*, a soup stock made from dried fish flakes. You'll find this is the base for most soups and broths, even if they look vegetarian. *Konbu dashi*, made from a type of seaweed, is the alternative but is not as common. Fish and meat extracts make their way into many sauces here and having a Japanese-speaking friend to help decipher labels, or ask at restaurants, can be a great help. It will vary how much the staff know about what goes into each dish and you may just be told an answer, yes or no, regardless of whether it's the right one. There also may be meat in even what seem like purely vegetable dishes, so double check everything before ordering.

However, things are slowly getting more vegetarian friendly and a range of restaurants have opened up to cater specifically for vegetarians, see p.356. Aside from these, Indian (p.336), Mexican (p.351) and western-style restaurants, run by foreigners or Japanese who have lived abroad, are good vegetarian-friendly options. Japanese food (p.341) does offer a range of choices, particularly Shōjin Ryōri (p.341).

Quick Reference Icons

🌄	Alfresco Option
👔	Dress Code
€€€	Expensive
👶	Kids Welcome
⊘	Unlicensed
€	Cheap

Street Food

Street Food in Tokyo is typically safe to enjoy and the city provides an array of options. Makeshift stalls at festivals, near temples, and at other spots with ample foot traffic serve up greasy fare like *takoyaki* (fried octopus balls) and *okonomiyaki* (savoury pancakes, see p.328) as well as *wagashi* (Japanese sweets). Traditional *yatai* may be dwindling in size, but some entrepreneurial vendors have changed their fare to reach a younger crowd. If you visit the Tokyo International Forum (p.44) during the week you'll find a collection of vendors serving up modern cuisine from the side of their vans. Others have stuck with tradition, like the *yaki-imo* (sweet potato) men who drive small trucks through the streets or park up outside train stations. Established vendors, offering crepes and kebabs are a popular street side dining choice, for those on the go. The numerous creperies on Takeshita Dōri in Harajuku typically have long queues at the weekend – indicating how good they are. Just around the corner on Meiji Dōri, boisterous staff wearing cowboy hats at Kebab Box J (03 3470 0706, 1-8-8 Jingū-mae) target those looking for a meaty fix.

The Safe Choice

When confronted with a machine selling fast-food noodles, take CNN personality Richard Quest's advice: 'When in doubt, keep to the buttons toward the top left' – this is where you'll find the most familiar options.

Brunch

If you're craving a lazy Sunday brunch, visit one of the western-style restaurants in the city, such as Beacon (p.354), Ben's Cafe (p.358), Fujimamas (p.354), Good Honest Grub (p.330), Suji's (p.332) or West Park Cafe (p.361). High-class hotels are also a good choice. French Kitchen in the Grand Hyatt in Roppongi offers a delectable buffet assortment for ¥6,000 (including a glass of champagne). Be wary of places that advertise brunch, without seeing the menu, as some cafes and restaurants serve up typical dishes under the guise of 'brunch'. Prices are similar to what you would expect to pay at lunch and most restaurants don't start serving until 11:00 or 11:30.

Fujimamas and Suji's are great spots to take the kids and Suji's offers a separate menu for children.

Japanese Cuisine

Japanese people take pride in their regional delicacies and throughout the country you'll find both a local take on popular Japanese dishes like *okonomiyaki*, as well as specialities unique to each area. Tokyo is the birthplace of *edomae* sushi (also known as *nigiri*), which is well known abroad. Back in the 17th century Matsumoto Yoshiichi introduced vinegar into the sushi rice mix, cutting down the once lengthy preparation process, starting sushi's evolution into what we know it as today. This local delicacy is best appreciated fresh from the sea, straight from an early morning sale at the Tsukiji fish market (p.310), where visitors and locals can enjoy a fresh, raw fish breakfast at one of the many sushi restaurants.

Strong importance is placed on the seasons in Japan and this is reflected in the food available. During the cooler months it's popular to share *nabe* – a hotpot of various meat, vegetables and tofu with friends and family. The Ryōgoku area is a good spot to try *chanko nabe*, a heartier version of the dish which is popular among sumo wrestlers. During summer, when the city feels as if it is melting, *unagi* (grilled eel) is a common choice and is believed to provide some much needed stamina.

Izakaya

These informal spots are a mix of both restaurant and bar. The main focus is typically on drinking, but a visit to one will almost always involve eating as well as drinking, and they are a great place to start an evening out or to enjoy a few beers after work. They cater to all spectrums of the market and you'll find everything from the traditional Japanese styled Yozakura Bijin (p.348) to the rowdy Andy's (p.346). The standard of food varies, but most include a selection of seafood and meat dishes, salads, fried food, pizza, pasta, and the popular drinking snack *edamame* (soybeans). All dishes are to be shared among the group and at least one dish should be ordered per head. A small starter, known as *otōshi*, is often served on arrival. The cost of the dish is added to the bill and is thought of as a kind of table charge. It can be turned down and taken off the bill.

As well as those reviewed (see table, p.328), there are a number of good chains with branches in popular areas like Roppongi, Shibuya, and Shinjuku, which are generally cheap and cheerful.

Izakaya	
Doma Doma	www.doma-doma.com
Watami	www.watami.co.jp
Who's Food's	www.whosfoods.com
Tsubohachi	www.tsubohachi.co.jp
Wan	www.oizumifoods.co.jp/wan
Tengu	www.teng.co.jp
Hakkenden	www.marche.co.jp/contents/hakkenden
Shoya	www.daisyo.co.jp/gyoutai/shoya
Yarukijaya	www.daisyo.co.jp/gyoutai/yaruki

Japanese Cuisine

Japanese (General)	Chanko Tomoji	341
	Daichi	342
	Inakaya (West Shop)	343
	Kojyu	345
Izakaya	Gaya	342
	Gonpachi	342
	Janken	344
	Shin Hinomoto (Andy's Izakaya)	346
	Yozakura Bijin	348
Kaiseki	Kitcho	344
Okonomiyaki (& Monjayaki)	Sakura-tei	328
Ramen	Ippudo	343
	Kohmen	344
	Shin-Yokohama Ramen Museum	347
Regional	Ai Ai	341
	Mikura	345
Shabu Shabu	Shabuzen	346
	Zakuro	348
Shōjin Ryōri	Bon	341
Soba & Udon	Hinaya	343
	Yabu Soba	348
Sushi	Rainbow Roll Sushi	345
	Sukiyabashi Jiro	347
	Sushi no Midori	347
Tempura	Kobikichō Tenkuni	344
Teppanyaki	Yasaiya	348
Tonkatsu	Maisen	345
	Tonki	347

Kaiseki

This traditional form of Japanese cuisine is as much a work of art as it is a delight to the tastebuds. Each seasonal dish is delicately prepared and presented one by one over the course of an hour or more. Serving sizes are small and dishes cover different forms of preparation such as fried tempura, broiled fish, steamed sesame tofu, and raw fish. Prices start at around ¥5,000 for a bentō and skyrocket upwards from there. Visit www.bento.com for more options.

Okonomiyaki (& Monjayaki)

This savoury pancake varies slightly with each region. Hiroshima's *okonomiyaki* style is well known throughout the country and the generous layers of cabbage, batter, *yaki soba* noodles, topped off with an egg and a sprinkling of green onions, make for a filling meal. *Monjayaki* is a Tokyo speciality, enjoyed straight off the hotplate you cook it on, and is a slightly runnier version of *okonomiyaki*. Besides restaurants like Sakura-tei (p.346) you'll also find *okonomiyaki* being served up by street side vendors at major festivals and outside busy temples.

Ramen

This noodle dish typically comes in four varieties: salt, soy sauce, pork, and miso. Each type is combined with a chicken or pork based broth, fresh noodles, and slithers of meat. You'll find *ramen* chains throughout the city (see Ippudo, p.343) as well as select restaurants dedicated to serving up the perfect blend. A quick online search for 'Tokyo ramen' will reveal a number of blogs reviewing the best places around town. You'll soon discover how committed Japan is to perfecting this steaming noodle broth from China.

Regional

Regional cuisines are also represented in Tokyo. Okinawan restaurants like Ai Ai (p.341) tend to be brightly decorated emitting an island vibe. The food typically contains spam and *gōya* (a bitter vegetable that may take a while to get used to). The Kyoto region is famous for its fresh vegetables and the beautiful presentation of its *kaiseki* cuisine. Places like Mikura (p.345) serve up healthy dishes sourcing ingredients like *kamo-nasu*, a fleshy eggplant; and *kujo-negi*, green onion, from the area.

Shabu Shabu & Sukiyaki

Shabu Shabu involves dipping thinly sliced meat into a boiling pot of water and swishing it around to cook before dipping each portion in sauce. *Sukiyaki* is similar, with diners gathering around a steaming broth filled with meat slithers, vegetables and tofu chunks. Once cooked, the meat is dipped in a side bowl of raw egg. There are a number of all-you-can-eat *shabu shabu* and *sukiyaki* places which have a set price of ¥1,500 upwards for around 90 minutes. Prices will vary depending on your meat of choice, and places like Zakuro (p.348) offer high quality cuts with a fee tag to match. Try www.bento.com for more options.

Shōjin Ryōri

Shōjin Ryōri (Buddhist temple cuisine) is as ornate as *kaiseki*, but unlike the former it is 100% vegetarian. Your cheapest option for trying this style of cooking is to check each restaurant's website for specials. Bon (p.341) has a great weekday lunch special for ¥5,000. Bon's dishes are *fucha ryori*, a distinct style of *Shōjin Ryōri* with Chinese influences. Websites for vegetarians in Tokyo are the best source for finding *Shōjin Ryōri* places worth visiting.

Soba & Udon

Soba is a type of buckwheat noodle that is enjoyed cold and dipped in soy sauce or a fish-based stock in summer, and in winter is dished up in a hot broth. *Udon* is *soba's* larger counterpart. The noodles are made with wheat flour and are served in a soup with a range of toppings from *tempura* to *natto*. At Hinaya (p.343) you'll find the complete selection, including the popular curry *udon*. The *Sunny Pages* (www.sunnypages.jp) list a selection of *soba* and *udon* restaurants with reviews and ratings.

Sushi

These bite-sized pieces of fish wrapped in rice and seaweed are what Japan is most famous for and you'll never be short of a place to sample this raw delicacy. One popular option is to visit the Tsukiji fish markets and have a sushi breakfast. If you're on a budget, the Kappa Sushi chain (www.kappa-create.co.jp) offers *kaiten zushi* (conveyor belt style) with each dish at ¥105. Rainbow Roll Sushi (p.345) has added a western touch to their sushi creations and is a popular spot with expats.

Tempura

Tempura consists of vegetables and seafood battered and deep fried to crisp perfection. There are restaurants dedicated just to *tempura* dishes (see Kobikichō Tenkuni, p.344) as well as places serving up *tempura* as a side dish or on top of noodles. Bento.com has a selection of tempura restaurants worth trying.

Family Restaurants

Family restaurants are a big part of life outside the central city. Easy parking and kids' menus make them a popular choice for families. They all offer a blend of western and Japanese dishes for a low price. Popular options include Royal Host (www.royalhost.jp) and Skylark (www.skylark.co.jp). American breakfast food chain Dennys (03 5565 9708, www.dennys.co.jp) falls under this category, but don't expect to find your old favourites. Staples such as pancakes have been replaced with dishes like seaweed and fish egg rice bowls, which target Japanese tastes. Saizeriya (www.saizeriya.co.jp) is one of the most common options and serves up cheap Italian dishes.

Teppanyaki

Teppanyaki is a definite crowd pleaser as diners enjoy fine cuts of meat and vegetables being cooked in front of them on a teppan grill. Sit by the counter at Yasaiya (see p.348) to enjoy the action. Search for *teppanyaki* restaurants in Tokyo on google to find a range of other options.

Tonkatsu

Pork cutlets are covered in flour, dipped in egg and coated with breadcrumbs before being deep-fried to create a crisp outside and tender inside. Each cut is generally served with cabbage or on top of rice, with a thick savoury sauce. *Tonkatsu* is a popular choice with the locals and both Tonki (p.347) and Maisen (p.345) attract a hungry crowd.

African

1-3-1
Higashiyama
Meguro-ku
🚇 *Naka-Meguro*
Map 5 E2 1

Queen Sheba

03 3794 1801 | *www.queensheba.jp*

A night feasting on deep fried samosas, goat and chicken kebabs, couscous, injera (a slightly sour bread loaded with various meats) and dabo (seasoned traditional bread), will be sure to provide a break from the norm in Japan. Large tabletop candles light up this basement eatery, shedding light on the various wall hangings, ethnic trimmings and animal skins draping the walls. Foreign food like french fries sneak on to the menu, but the excellent set menus cover a range of ethnic flavours, leaving you more than satisfied. Set-menus start at ¥2,000 and include a selection from the a la carte menu – such as lentil stew, kebabs, bread, and samosas. The beverage menu offers another glimpse of the African continent with an original blend of drinks, honey wine and African beer. The restaurant is a short walk from Naka Meguro station, head along Yamate Dōri, away from Meguro, and it's just past the Honda bike shop.

10-7 Wakamiyachō
Shinjuku-ku
🚇 *Iidabashi*
Map 9 C3 2

Tribes

03 3235 6699 | *www.tribes.jp*

From its earthy decor to its contemporary blend of African and French cuisine, Tribes is quite distinct from other places in the city. Fried crocodile with ham, cheese and eggplant, and ostrich with ginger sauce sit alongside tamer options like koftas and lamb couscous. Its broad selection is a delight for meat lovers, the service is friendly and the owner, who once lived in Africa, is only too happy to share his stories and discuss his creations as you peruse the menu. Its assortment of African beer is worth a try and the wine selection includes high quality South African wines starting at around ¥4,000 a bottle. The tribal decor adds character, as do the music videos and African promotional videos that are played on a screen at the back. Expect to pay around ¥4,000 or more per head for dinner. Walk up Kagurazaka Dōri and turn left just before Bishamonten Temple, and Tribes is instantly recognisable by the African mural on its outer wall.

American

2-20-8 Higashi
Shibuya
Shibuya-ku
🚇 *Shibuya*
Map 8 D4 3

Good Honest Grub

03 3797 9877 | *www.goodhonestgrub.com*

Tucked away in a quiet back street, Good Honest Grub's new location is a far cry from the busy spot it once held just off Omotesandō. The new hangout fits the owner's intention to allow patrons to linger over the fine food in a more relaxed setting, and its homely feel complements its delicious creations. The popular weekend brunch menu includes french toast, fruit drizzled with maple syrup, scrambled eggs with smoked salmon, bacon or ham, hash browns and toast. Lunch focuses mainly on sandwiches, but vegetarian lasagne and caesar salad are also options. The 'bean me up', a blend of spices, beans and onions wrapped in tortilla, is a popular choice. Dinnertime brings a greater selection of dishes including pan-seared salmon and stuffed chicken breasts. You'll find this restaurant on a side street off Meiji Dōri. From Shibuya, walk along the side opposite the station, pass the post office and turn left just after Shop 99.

Shichiseisiya Bldg (1F)
5-1-20 Hirō
Shibuya-ku
🚇 *Ebisu*
Map 5 F2 148

Homework's

03 3444 4560 | *www.homeworks-1.com*

If you're hankering for a decent burger fix then pop by Homework's to satisfy your craving. Its Hirō location is popular with both locals and expats. Here you can sit at the counter and watch as your juicy patty is fried up in front of you, or take a seat in the sun when they fold back the doors at the front. Their burgers start at ¥900 and vary in price depending on the size – their super size is 150 grams. You'll find the usual favourites like cheeseburgers as well as Italian or Polynesian burgers and seasonal specials like a cranberry turkey burger feature on the menu. A range of sandwiches and some basic salads are also on offer. Vegetarian-friendly, golden veggie burgers and chickpea sandwiches, among other meat free dishes, can also be ordered. Local delivery is available.

Park Hyatt Tokyo
3-7-1-2 Nishi
Shinjuku
Shinjuku-ku
🚇 Shinjuku
Map 7 A2 **4**

New York Grill

03 5322 1234 | *http://tokyo.park.hyatt.com*
You can't find better spot to impress guests than The New York Grill on the 52nd floor of the Park Hyatt. The surreal city scene, viewed through floor to ceiling windows, is coupled with some stunning epicurean creations, bringing the best cuts of meat and seafood from around the world. You may find New Zealand lamb, Australian tenderloin, Hokkaidō scallops and Kōbe beef on the menu, but their selection changes every three months. It does however retain its focus on fresh seafood and meat with the main menu divided by cooking method: grill, oven, and rotisserie. Vegetables are ordered as a side dish and range between ¥1,000 and ¥1,500, a tiny fraction of the cost of a main meal. The drinks selection is extensive, especially if you consider its wine cellar filled with 1,600 bottles of wine. Relive memories from *Lost in Translation* after your meal at the New York Bar (p.370) next door.

1-3-18 Shibuya
Shibuya-ku
🚇 Shibuya
Map 8 D3 **5**

Pink Cow

03 3406 5597 | *www.thepinkcow.com*
There's never a dull moment at this expat hangout. From non-profit fundraisers, book release parties and knitting groups, to live house music, improvisation comedy nights, Middle Eastern buffets and business networking events – the place has something for most. Its funky out-of-the-box decor includes shared sofa seating before the stage. Tables at the back are a step away from the action but will still allow you to enjoy the night's festivities while feasting on fresh Californian cuisine. Grilled chicken burritos, turkey burgers and daily pasta specials are items typical to the menu that starts at around ¥1,200. It is also one of the few places in Tokyo that really knows how to serve a salad as a main dish and their avocado, tomato, and tofu salad is a good option for vegetarians. Available for both venue hire, or to cater for your party at home, the Pink Cow can satisfy a range of culinary needs.

Tribes

New York Grill

Faro Nishi-Azabu (1F)
1-15-4 Nishi-Azabu
Minato-ku
 Roppongi
Map 11 A2 **6**

Porterhouse Steak

03 5771 5322 | www.porterhouse.jp

Foreign food in Tokyo can often come at a higher price and a good old-fashioned juicy steak is no exception. If you're after a tender meat selection, and you're willing to pay a premium for the pleasure, then Porterhouse Steak in Nishi-Azabu provides an elegant setting to enjoy your meal. Their top-notch steaks range from ¥7,500 for a 16oz New York strip sirloin up to ¥21,000 for the prized 32oz Porterhouse 'jumbo' cut. All of their beef is dry aged for 40 days, a process used to enhance the flavour. Porterhouse is also known for its fresh seafood dishes. Their comprehensive international wine selection, candle-lit tables, stylish decor and high-class cuisine all lend themselves to a romantic evening out.

3-1-5 Azabudai
Minato-ku
Roppongi
Map 11 C3 **7**

Suji's

03 3505 4490 | http://sujis.net/japan

The hearty American fare served up at Suji's can cure the cravings of those looking for a slice of home. Favourites like meatloaf, juicy burgers and shepherd's pie fill the dinner menu, and there are some slightly smaller options for kids. Dinner is well priced with the majority of main dishes at under ¥2,000. The brunch menu offers a few tasty specials, such as a New York omelette with smoked salmon, green onion and cream cheese, or country style pancakes with banana and walnut. Prices range from ¥1,100 to ¥2,400 and brunch can also be enjoyed throughout the day. The modern interior, lined with portraits of the New York skyline, leads to an open terrace that's perfect for people watching during the summer months. Suji's is a great spot for a family meal with all the trimmings. Walk down Gaien Higashi Dōri towards Kamiyachō station and it's situated on Iikura Katamachi crossing.

Brazilian

B1 Evergreen Bldg
4-3-24 Jingū-mae
Shibuya-ku
Omotesandō
Map 8 D2 **8**

Barbacoa Grill

03 3796 0571 | barbacoa-grill@wondertable.com

With the closing of Copa Tokyo in 2007, this is the most authentic Brazilian restaurant in town. Vegetarians need not shy away from this joint, as even though the place is known for its meaty all-you-can-eat beef and chicken course, featuring 15 kinds of churrasco cuts, it also has an extensive salad and dessert bar and, if you wish, you can opt for just the salad buffet. The traditional Brazilian method of barbecuing the cuts of meat is clearly a crowd favourite and everyone, from office workers to celebrities, seems to want a slice of the action. Barbacoa continues its Brazilian theme throughout the restaurant with its Latin soundtrack and Portuguese speaking staff. Its caipirinha is worth a try, or if you want to indulge you can partake in the all-you-can-drink along with the all-you-can-eat option. Expect to spend ¥3,000 to ¥7,000 per person, depending on the course you choose.

Shibuya Fhontis
Bldg (B1)
2-23-12 Dōgenzaka
Shibuya-ku
Shibuya
Map 8 B3 **9**

Tucanos

03 5784 2661 | www.pjgroup.jp/tucanos/e_tucanos/index.html

This lively basement dining spot offers both an all-you-can-eat and an all-you-can-drink menu. A range of pork, chicken and beef cuts, a salad bar (with 30 different salad style options), cheese bread, fries, rice and Brazilian dishes like *feijoada* (a pork and bean stew) and dessert are included in their ¥4,000 set menu. Add an extra ¥2,000 if you want the 'all-you-can-drink' option (¥3,000 if you want caipirinhas as well). The large location attracts a festive bunch and the nightly samba shows at 19:00 and 21:00 contribute to the Brazilian vibe. Lunchtime sets on weekdays are excellent value. At weekends, lunch is slightly more expensive and all-you-can-drink is also available.

Chinese

Other options **Far Eastern** p.334

3-2-13 Nishi Azabu
Minato-ku
🚇 *Roppongi*
Map 11 A3 **10**

Chinese Cafe Eight

03 5414 5708 | www.cceight.com

If you're looking for a truly authentic Chinese dining experience then this is the right place. This spot is a hit for its low prices and large servings, but don't expect any special treatment from the staff, especially during the lunch and dinner rush. It has some pretty unique decor consisting of male and female genitalia displayed over the walls, and it is open 24 hours a day, so it attracts a broad mix of people, including many Japanese and Chinese youth. The menu is extensive and among the array of typical dishes like peking duck, dumplings and shark fin soup are options for more daring diners – scorpion anyone? It is situated straight across the street from the Grand Hyatt. They also have locations in Ebisu (03 3717 2858) and Akasaka (03 6234 9788).

Hill Side in
Roppongi Hills (2F)
6-10-1 Roppongi
Minato-ku
🚇 *Roppongi*
Map 11 B3 **11**

Hong Kong Tea House Restaurant

03 5413 9588 | www.soho-s.co.jp

Located in the plush Roppongi Hills area, this restaurant serves up cuisine to match the calibre of its location. The restaurant's sleek lines, modern decor and multi-level dining are a far cry from some of the long-established dim sum restaurants of the east. But the contemporary decor and dim sum served all day (traditionally it is served at lunchtime) have made it popular. Dim sum set menus are offered throughout the week accompanied by roasted pork or duck with rice. The sets are good value at ¥1,500 during the week and ¥2,500 at weekends (with the addition of dessert and an extra dim sum). The extensive a la carte menu features steamed *yuba* with beef and shitake mushrooms and steamed barbecue pork rolls, as well as Hong Kong style peking duck. The drinks selection is relatively standard with a mixture of wine, beer and liqueurs, some of which are from China.

4-1-9 Kinshi
Sumida-ku
🚇 *Kinshichō*
Map 2 C2
ⓔ

Ling Ling Saikan

03 3625 1245

Also known as 'It's Vegetable', this simple organic Taiwanese vegetarian restaurant offers a daily lunch buffet brimming with dishes that are also available a la carte at dinner time. The cosy family feel, friendly staff and low prices keep patrons coming back for more. During the lunchtime rush, customers take advantage of an all-you-can-eat option for less than ¥1,500, piling their plastic plates high with seasonal dishes like soy and vegetable in black bean paste and vegetable chunks and tightly bound parcels of bean protein coated in a sweet and sour sauce. Mild curry with brown rice and spicy tofu dishes are also served, alongside a sweet seasonal fruit or bean dessert. You can find it by turning left from the north exit of the JR Kinshichō station and follow the tracks across the road until you see their colourful signs.

Odakyū Hotel
Century Southern
Tower (19F)
2-2-1 Yoyogi
Shinjuku-ku
🚇 *Shinjuku*
Map 7 C2 **12**

Xenlon

03 3374 2080 | www.xenlon.com

Xenlon makes a stunning first impression as you walk over an arched bridge and are faced with a menacing silver dragon, staring down from above. This sight is quickly followed by another memorable scene – Tokyo's city sprawl. Situated on the 19th floor of one of Shinjuku's towering skyscrapers, this Chinese grill offers stunning views and upscale cuisine. A range of course options are presented, with the lunch sets starting at ¥3,500 and dinner sets at ¥5,000. With stir-fried dishes straight from the wok, freshly steamed dumplings and peking duck, the selection covers the best of foreigner-friendly Chinese cuisine which is matched with an extensive wine list and Chinese beer.

Far Eastern

Other options **Chinese** p.333, **Japanese** p.341, **Thai** p.355, **Korean** p.350

Dear Nishi-Azabu
Bldg (1F)
3-1-20 Nishi-Azabu
Minato-ku
🚇 *Roppongi*
Map 11 A3 **13**
🚫

Charleston Cafe Oriental

03 3404 4745 | *www.charlestoncafe.com*

This lively spot, just a stone's throw from Roppongi Hills, dishes up a blend of cuisine from the east and west, and refreshing fruit cocktails to wash it down with. Thai favourites like phad thai, papaya salad and Thai curry make up a large portion of the menu, with other dishes like seafood pho, nasi goreng and Italian pastas and pizzas also making an appearance. Most dishes fall under ¥1,500, making dining here a cheap option, but if you want to indulge in their extensive selection of drinks, your meal price will quickly double – large drinks are around ¥1,000 each. Charleston's decor breaks away from the norm and is reminiscent of a beachside hut with some additional decorations to match seasonal events. Photos of famous diners, such as Rod Stewart, are plastered on the walls. The service here is friendly and the owner is genuinely concerned that everyone enjoys the time spent at this tropical oasis.

T's Harajuku (3F)
Jingū-mae 4-30-4
Shibuya-ku
🚇 *Meiji Jingū-mae*
Map 8 D2 **14**

Elephant Cafe

03 3478 2233 | *www.elephant-cafe.tokyo.walkerplus.com*

Elephant Cafe may not be able to promise authentic cuisine but it does promise an enchanting place to enjoy your meal. Concealed from the busy street, it's hard to tell that this expansive late night dining spot has the capacity for 400 diners. On first entering this dimly lit venue your waiter or waitress will lead you through the scattered tables to the welcoming clap of the other attentive staff nearby. A grand Buddha resting on a bed of elephants is the focal point of the room and the whole place has a distinct south-east Asia vibe to it. The menu comprises meals scented with coriander and other typical spices. Menu items include nasi goreng, tom yum kung, Vietnamese pho noodle soup, and some interesting takes on foreign cuisine such as tom yum kung pizza. Well-priced dishes fall under ¥1,000, but there is a small table charge. They also have a selection of exotic cocktails in addition to the usual tipples.

Zoe Ginza (B1)
3-3-1 Ginza
Chūō-ku
🚇 *Ginza*
Map 14 B2 **15**

My Humble House

03 5524 6166 | *www.mhht.jp*

My Humble House in Ginza serves up modern Singaporean cuisine in a classic plush setting. With its classy decor, delectable menu and central location it would be natural to assume that this restaurant has prices that are anything but humble – however that is not the case. Dishes are priced at around ¥1,000 upwards and include such treats as a crab, avocado and grapefruit salad, an aromatic laksa (coconut curry), fresh spring rolls with salmon, avocado and mango and the famous Singapore dish, Hainanese chicken rice served in a clay pot. My Humble House has succeeded at taking the melting pot of cuisines typical to Singapore and transforming them into artistic creations to delight the taste buds of Tokyoites. For a great deal, reserve one of the excellent value dinner sets.

Ryuo Bldg (2F)
1-8-12 Ebisu Minami
Shibuya-ku
🚇 *Ebisu*
Map 5 F2 **16**

Sin Tong Kee

03 3713 2255 | *www.sintongkee.jp*

Tucked away on the second floor on a quiet street, it's easy to miss this gem. The restaurant's decor doesn't make it stand out, but the crowds that swarm this humble place at lunchtime are an indication of the quality of food on offer. Singaporean food is known to be culturally diverse, with influences from China, Malaysia and India, and after scanning the menu you'll quickly realise there are lots of flavours to be savoured here. The house speciality is Chinese-inspired Hainanese chicken rice – steamed chicken dipped in chili, soy, and ginger sauce (also offered in a children's set menu for nearly half the price). Pork Bak Kut Teh and laksa are slurped up while Singaporean chili crab, chicken or fish head curry and various vegetable dishes are also offered. Fresh juices and beers complement meals or you can try a Singapore sling from the cocktail selection. Finish with one of their fruity desserts.

Nice Bldg (2F)
5-29-9 Daizawa
Setagaya-ku
🚇 *Shimokitazawa*
Map 5 C1 **17**

Tibet Tibet

03 5433 1565 | *www.livemedia.co.jp/wwc*

Tibet Tibet's decor seems as full of contrasts as its menu. The peaceful Buddha statue from Nepal gazing out, the stylish leather sofa seating and white floor cushions against low tables and a DJ booth resting in the corner, all make for a rather eclectic mix against the restaurant's overriding white colour scheme. The menu blends modernity with tradition through its serving of well-known favourites in a fresh and contemporary way. From all over the Golden Triangle and beyond, rich curries, Japanese influenced Vietnamese spring rolls, tempura and spicy Thai soups are dished out by the staff. Some original cocktails, various beers from abroad and local sakes are also on offer. Dishes average between ¥600 and ¥1,000 and it's best to order a few to be shared.

French

7-5-5 Ginza
(nr House of Shiseido)
Chūō-ku
🚇 *Ginza*
Map 14 A3 **18**
€€€

L'Osier

03 3571 6050 | *www.shiseido.co.jp/e/losier*

Professional service and superb cuisine have led head chef Bruno Menard and restaurant L'Osier to international culinary fame. After attaining three stars in the *Michelin Guide Tokyo 2008*, and since being voted best eatery in the 2008 edition of the Zagat guide to Tokyo, you can be sure your meal is the creme de la creme of French fare available in the city. The beautifully presented dishes cover a selection of fresh seafood, like lobster with a rich pistachio pate consomme of artichoke and spinach with a citrus confit, meat dishes and decadent desserts. Meals can be ordered a la carte or you can try the set seasonal dinner for ¥18,000, which includes an appetiser, two mains and dessert. Even if you don't get a set you can still expect to pay around ¥10,000 a head at lunch and over ¥20,000 per head at dinner.

1-16-3 Tomigaya
Shibuya-ku
🚇 *Yoyogi Kōen*
Map 8 A2 **19**

Leroux

03 3467 1247 | *www.leroux.jp*

Between Yoyogi Kōen and Shibuya station, this cosy find is a welcome break from some of the more crowded dining spots in the area. Although warm and welcoming, the minimalist interior isn't exactly a topic of conversation, but happily the food is. Not quite traditional, the two-man Leroux team blends French and Italian cuisine, while adding a contemporary touch. They take pride in using the freshest (mainly organic) vegetables and ingredients. Their passion to please is also reflected in the ornate dishes served up in their set menu for ¥3,500. Four different meal sets are available, including one especially for ladies for a slightly cheaper price of ¥2,800. You can order a la carte and their assortment covers pastas, sauteed meat and fish, fresh vegetable dishes and daily specials.

Leroux

Barbizon 25 Bldg (1F)
5-4-7 Shiroganedai
Minato-ku
🚇 *Shirokanedai*
Map 5 F3 **143**
€€€

Quintessence

03 5791 3715 | www.quintessence.jp

Quintessence oozes style, from its sleek minimalist entrance through to its dark, chic interior. The finest details create the ambience here; Italian leather is used to craft their chairs and low couches, private rooms are decorated in silk and every detail is sophisticated. Luxury comes at a price and dining at this three star restaurant, the highest rating given by the *Michelin* guide, will cost ¥8,000 for lunch and ¥18,000 for dinner (per person) for a set menu. A 10% service charge is also added here. Each visit to this restaurant is unique; the daily menu, selected by the chef, depends on which seasonal items are available and dishes tend to be delicate in nature. The selection of French wine is extensive with around 600 varieties ranging from ¥10,000 to ¥40,000 a bottle. It's a 10 to15 minute walk from Exit A1 of Shirokanedai station down Gaien Nishi Dōri on your left.

German

Pure Roppongi (2F)
5-18-1 Roppongi
Minato-ku
🚇 *Roppongi*
Map 11 C3 **20**

Bernd's Bar

03 5563 9232 | www.berndsbar.com

Popular with German expats, this bar and restaurant is a home away from home and the perfect spot to indulge any meat cravings you may have. With its good meat selection – from schnitzel to garlic steak – and an entire portion of the menu dedicated to sausages, you're in for a hearty meal. It's also worth trying their special flammkuchen, a German style pizza topped with sour cream, onions, bacon, garlic, cheese and Bernd's Bar's secret ingredient. This establishment wouldn't be complete without a fine range of German beers and Bernd's provides patrons with a selection of altbier (pale ales), pils(the most popular kind of German beer), schwarzbier (dark lagers) and weizenbier (wheat beers), as well as some top German wines. Located in an area that often draws a transient crowd, Bernd's friendly service helps it retain a loyal following.

Roppongi 1st Bldg (B1F)
1-9-9 Roppongi
Minato-ku
🚇 *Kamiyachō*
Map 11 D2 **21**

Zum Einhorn

03 5563 9240 | www.zum-einhorn.co.jp

This intimate dining spot provides a contrast to the bustling Bernd's bar in the same vicinity, offering a quieter location to linger over your meal. Their menu is seasonal and includes well-known favourites like frankfurters with sauerkraut and flammkuchen, as well as more succulent fare – braised scallops with white wine sauce, and roasted lamb with mushrooms. The mains here range between ¥2,000 and ¥5,000, with most falling under ¥3,000. Zum Einhorn's selection of German microbrews is worth trying and they are all reasonably priced. The open dining area contains a scattering of tables, with one private dining room available for special occasions.

Indian

Roppongi Hills (B1)
6-10-1 Hillside
Minato-ku
🚇 *Roppongi*
Map 11 B3 **22**

Diya

03 6438 1177 | http://r.gnavi.co.jp/b822100/

Sophisticated and elegant, Diya is a far cry from some of the Indian places in the city. Its authentic cuisine includes dishes like tender ukhara lamb chops marinated in ginger, garlic and Indian rum and spices, Goan sesame prawns, kabuli nan stuffed with cashew nuts and raisins, and spinach and cheese sag paneer. Their dinner menus are great value, starting at ¥3,500, and can be combined with an all-you-can-drink wine, beer and cocktail set menu (¥1,500 for 90 minutes). The service is swift and friendly and they do their best to accommodate everyone. The decor is sleek and uncluttered with tables bordering the edge of the room and some spread out in the centre.

Not big, but very clever…

Perfectly proportioned to fit in your pocket, this marvellous mini guidebook makes sure you don't just get the holiday you paid for but rather the one that you dreamed of.

Tokyo Mini Visitors' Guide
Maximising your holiday, minimising your hand luggage

Hama Bldg (3F)
6-2-35 Roppongi
Minato-ku
🚇 *Roppongi*
Map 11 B2 23

Moti

03 3479 1939

For reliably good Indian food visit any of the Moti restaurants located throughout Tokyo and Yokohama. Having first opened their doors back in 1978, Moti has stood the test of time in Tokyo's dining scene and if you visit, you'll quickly learn why. Besides staple Indian dishes like samosas, kofta, tandoori, naan, vindaloo and korma, Moti has a delicious chicken zanjri, a warm curry which blends chicken, cashew nuts, cottage cheese, peas and raisins. For vegetarians, their alu gobi is a good choice. The service here is generally prompt and friendly. The decor is plush gold and red and the carpeted floors make a nice change from the wooden settings of some restaurants. Set lunches and dinners are available, and if you want to order a la carte most dishes are ¥1,000 to ¥2,000.

Ginza Kosaka
Bldg (7-9F)
6-9-4 Ginza
Chūō-ku
🚇 *Ginza*
Map 14 B3 24

Nataraj

03 5537 1515 | *www.nataraj.co.jp*

With branches throughout the city, this vegetarian Indian restaurant chain is a popular choice if you're looking for a healthy curry. Traditional meaty favourites like tikka masala and keema are prepared with soybean meat substitute, while other dishes on the menu are rich in seasonal vegetables. The rich green palak paneer with chunks of cottage cheese and the navratan korma are good choices and best mopped up with buttery naan bread. For vegans, dishes that contain milk or eggs are clearly marked and those interested in macrobiotic cuisine can choose from the macrobiotic menu. The weekday lunch buffet is great value and their dinner menu will leave you pleasantly satisfied. The Ginza location is elegantly decorated with Indian sculptures and a water fountain bubbling away in the centre as diners enjoy their meal. Nataraj's prices are reasonable, despite being situated in the heart of this upmarket district.

Garden Side
Tokyo Midtown
9-7-4 Akasaka
Minato-ku
🚇 *Roppongi*
Map 11 B2 25
🚫

Nirvana New York

03 5647 8305 | *www.nirvana-newyork.jp*

The upscale Nirvana New York, situated in Tokyo Midtown, provides a modern take on traditional Indian dishes. Plentiful portions are replaced with ornately presented dishes where style matches taste. Customary favourites are offered alongside contemporary dishes like marinated mustard shrimps and Tasmanian salmon salad. The dimly lit romantic interior overlooks the city and despite being situated on the first floor of Midtown Nirvana, it manages to capture a clear view of the Tokyo skyline. Its vegetable and mushroom biriyani, which comes brimming with cashews, peas, okra, mushrooms, carrots, baby corn and paneer cheese, is a top menu item and their deep-fried roti flatbread, beautifully presented with a selection of chutneys, also hits the spot. The lunchtime buffet is excellent value, especially when you consider the dinnertime prices and you can enjoy a cocktail or two relaxing on the restaurant's wooden terrace. It's pretty popular, so reservations are necessary to secure a spot.

Indonesian

Roppongi Hills
Hillside (B1)
6-10-1 Roppongi
Minato-ku
🚇 *Roppongi*
Map 11 B3 26
🚫

Bali Cafe Putri

03 5786 7795 | *www.jbm-gr.com*

This stylish spot in Roppongi Hills is a great place to spend an evening admiring the view. The outdoor terrace overlooks Roppongi while the indoor dining area offers views of a beautiful garden. Typical Balinese dishes like gado gado (a vegetable salad coated in peanut sauce) and sambal goreng daging (stewed beef in a spicy sauce of chili paste, spices and coconut milk) are served up by friendly Balinese staff. Desserts also retain their traditional island touch and fried bananas with icecream, mango sorbet and coconut icecream are on the list. Most of their dishes are under ¥1,000 and set lunches are only ¥1,050. Expect to spend around ¥3,000 for dinner here, or slightly more if you get a set course. Courses start at ¥3,000 and for this price each person can try eight dishes.

Ginza Corridor (2F)
7-2 Ginza
Chūō-ku
Ginza
Map 14 A3 **27**

Lime
03 5537 1455
This restaurant is a little out of the ordinary and both the decor and menu have an innovative touch. Dishes like cold noodles mixed with salmon, avocado, and fish eggs, or spicy scallop and vermicelli salad, are a sample of the chef's Balinese fusion creations. Nasi goreng remains on the menu, as well as an assortment of satays and more typical desserts like mango pudding. Despite the swanky location, most of the dishes are great value, being priced around ¥1,000. It also has a long cocktail menu and their alcoholic drinks (wine, beer, and cocktails) start from ¥620. However, what makes this restaurant really worth a visit is the decor; the restaurant is home to 2,000 tropical fish swimming in a brightly lit, 15 metre long tank.

Italian
Other options **Mediterranean** p.350

Ebisu-Fort (2F)
1-24-2 Ebisu Minami
Shibuya-ku
Ebisu
Map 5 F2 **28**

Bergamo
03 5725 2555 | *bergamo@non-piu-fame.com*
A recent addition to Tokyo's Italian restaurant scene, Bergamo is a trendy place to hang out with friends over fine Italian food. The stylish international vibe was carefully crafted by the owner – right down to employing some foreign staff to serve Bergamo's well-heeled patrons. A small DJ box overlooks a cavernous main dining area, which is separate from the sleek bar area at the entrance. En route to the restaurant, patrons get a glimpse of the fresh fare in the open kitchen. The menu is typically Italian with a selection of pizzas including the Bismark (with an egg on top) and calzone. Pastas include many tomato-based options, but overall the menu is a delight for cheese lovers with choices like gnocchi with four kinds of Italian cheese and asparagus cream sauce and a scrumptious Italian cheese risotto.

1-9-19 Tomigaya
Shibuya-ku
Yoyogi Kōen
Map 8 A2 **29**

Life
03 3467 3479 | *www.s-life.jp*
Life's warm, rustic charm provides respite from busy Tokyo life. Attracting a young crowd and with a young team running the show, Life manages to create a cool vibe in a natural country-style setting. Typical fare like pizzas, pasta, risotto and antipasti are on offer, along with some sweet treats. A range of cocktails, foreign beer and wine can be found on the menu, including unique creations like mango beer. Its 'slow food' theme makes it easy to unwind, as does the soft jazz playing in the background. The service is prompt and flexible, and the set menus from ¥2,700 to ¥3,900 are a good option if you are contemplating a few dishes. Only eight pizzas are made a day from their special dough mix, so you'll need to get in quick. To get there, take the exit for Yoyogi Hachiman station and turn left. Follow the road around and it is a few minutes walk away.

Barbazon 25 (2F)
5-4-7 Shirokanedai
Minato-ku
Shirokanedai
Map 5 F3 **144**

Luxor Ristorante
03 3446 6900 | *www.luxor-r.com*
Stylish design, professional staff and top-quality cuisine help to justify this eatery's high prices. The contemporary menu attracts a sophisticated crowd seeking something a little bit different and by matching his menu to the season, Chef Mario Frittoli ensures his Italian dishes are always the freshest available. Creative dishes are the order of the

day: try the filet mignon housed in slithers of chestnut crepes, ricotta cheese and a red wine sauce or the Japanese-influenced sauteed bonito with mushrooms resting on a creamy black sesame paste with polenta. Each beautifully presented plate focuses on quality rather than quantity – allowing you enough space to finish with one of their petite desserts. Luxor also offers Italian cooking lessons and outside catering. Its romantic setting is perfect for a wedding party. A second branch has opened in Marunouchi (2F Tokyo Bldg, 2-7-3 Marunouchi, Chiyoda-ku, 03 6212 6900).

5-6-24 Minami-
Aoyama
Minato-ku
🚇 **Omotesandō**
Map 8 E2 **30**

Napule
03 3797 3790

A large brick oven, visible through a large street-level window, and the smell of freshly baked pizzas, invite passersby

Pizzakaya

into Napule. The head pizzaiolo picked up top honours at the World Pizza Cup 2007 and the Japanese media has been abuzz ever since. The newer location in Tokyo Midtown is very popular, but it is still possible to show up for dinner at the original Omotesandō location without a reservation. For lunch, ask to be seated on the third floor where the large windows allow sunlight to stream in on very satisfied diners. The selection includes four lunch menus starting from ¥1,000 for pasta, salad and coffee, to ¥2,000 for antipasto, salad, a fish or meat option and coffee. The dinner set menus start at just under ¥4,000 per person, or you can dine a la carte. If you are walking from Omotesandō crossing towards Shibuya, it is before the Spiral building, near the station.

203 Koyama Bldg
3-1-19 Nishi Azabu
Minato-ku
🚇 **Roppongi**
Map 11 A3 **31**

Pizzakaya
03 3479 8383 | www.pizzakaya.com

When Brendan Murphy couldn't find a decent pizza in Tokyo in 1996, he decided to solve the problem by opening his own pizza parlour. His recipe was a clear success and the place has been going strong ever since. The selection is broad, from 'the love pizza', a spread of artichoke hearts, red onions, portabella and mitake mushrooms, to the bacon cheeseburger pizza, coated in beef chunks, bacon, mushroom, onion, mozzarella and cheddar cheese. Pizzas range from around ¥1,500 to ¥3,500, but if you're feeling extra hungry the all-you-can-eat deal, priced at ¥3,150 for two hours (¥5,250 with drinks) is great value in a city where pizza is expensive. Their menu also includes delicious sides, pastas and salads, including items like honey soy sauce chicken wings, basil pesto penne and caeser salad. Pizzakya's tiled floor, booth seating and bright colour scheme all add to its authenticity. Be prepared for a bit of a wait for your meal at busy periods and weekends.

1-3-1 Kanda-Kajichō
Chiyoda-ku
🚇 **Kanda**
Map 13 C3 **32**

Pizzeria Bar D'Oro
03 3252 1620 | www.metius-foods.com

Situated in a neighbourhood of overworked businessmen and some slightly questionable establishments (near the train tracks close to the station), this is not the kind of place you would expect to find good quality Italian cuisine. But, providing an oasis amid its surroundings, this pizzeria radiates with the rich scent of Italian cooking and cheerful banter from a post-work crowd unwinding over fine wine. The communal table spanning the length of one side of the room adds a social touch to the dining area, while the tables near the floor-to-ceiling windows are suitable for a more intimate affair. The backstreet view doesn't lend itself to romantic endeavors, but it is likely to provide interesting dinner conversation throughout the evening. Wood fired pizzas, gnocchi, pasta, bruschetta and typical Italian favourites are included on the well-priced menu and served throughout the day. Branches of this chain are located throughout the city – including Ginza, Shinjuku, Ebisu and Kouzimati.

Japanese
Other options **Far Eastern** p.334

2-31-8 Jingū-mae
Shibuya-ku
🚇 **Meiji Jingū-mae**
Map 8 D1 **46**

Ai Ai
03 3403 5575
Hidden away from the bustling nearby Harajuku neighbourhood in a basement, Ai Ai's unremarkable entrance is deceiving. Inside, the island decor, sturdy wooden tables and miniature rooms with low entrances help to distinguish it from typical *izakaya*. Among other Asian dishes, typical Okinawan cuisine like taco rice (ground beef on a bed of rice and lettuce), and *gōya chanpuru* (stir-fried seasonal vegetables with *gōya*, tofu chunks and spam) make the list. The bar also serves delicious cocktail blends and Orion beer straight from Okinawa's sunny shores. It is frequented by a young crowd, foreign and Japanese, for post-work drinks or after a day of shopping. From Meiji Jingū-mae station walk down Meiji Dōri (on the same side as Gap) until you reach the overpass with Diesel on the far corner. Turn down the road on the right and at the first pedestrian crossing, cross over towards the convenience store and it's about a minute away on the left side of this street.

1-2-11 Ryūsen
Taito-ku
🚇 **Iriya**
Map 12 F1 **49**
€€€

Bon
03 3872 0375 | *www.fuchabon.co.jp*
In life's hustle and bustle, food is often gone before you have the opportunity to savour it. Pleasing to the eye and the palette, Bon's vegetarian Shōjin Ryōri cuisine, based on a form of Zen vegetarian cooking known as Fuchū, helps remind customers that food should be lingered over. The meal is served in a traditional Japanese setting, complete with attentive staff, tatami mat flooring and private rooms. Prices start at ¥3,800 for a lunch box and range up to ¥10,000 per head for a full course including two different soups and eight different seasonal vegetable dishes (reservations are required). Take Exit 3 from Iriya station, turn left off the main road and follow this street until you reach the fourth set of traffic lights. Then turn left and head towards Saitokuji. Walk past Otori jingu and turn left at the traffic lights, take the first right and it's on your left just before Saitokuji.

3-24-4 Ryōgoku
Sumida-ku
🚇 **Ryōgoku**
Map 4 E3 **33**

Chanko Tomoji
03 3631 4889 | *www.tomoji.co.jp*
The exterior of this unassuming venue is simple, with traditional wooden doors and Japanese curtains, and is in the heart of the sumo wrestler district, Ryōgoku (just a short walk from the station). Its signature dish, *chanko nabe,* is fittingly described as a sumo wrestlers hot pot, blending fresh meat, fish, tofu and vegetables, including 18 types of shellfish, in a tasty *miso*, sesame oil and citrus broth. The restaurant hardly seems large enough to feed a troupe of sumo wrestlers, but it churns out some suitably hearty proportions. Prices start at ¥2,730 per serving. A selection of fresh *sashimi*, Japanese salads, pickled dishes and other fishy finds are also available. Meals here are typically accompanied with sake, *shōchū*, whiskey or beer and the sake list includes a number of famed brews from throughout the country.

Kamiyachō Prime Place (2F)
4-1-17 Toranomon
Minato-ku
🚇 *Kamiyachō*
Map 11 D2 **34**

Daichi

03 3433 8318 | www.yasaiya-daichi.jp

Lunchtime deals are generous here, considering the organic nature of the restaurant, ranging from ¥1,000 to ¥1,500. Options include Korean bibimbap – soft vegetables and egg mixed with rice in a heated stone bowl, and a beautifully presented seasonal vegetable curry. During the lunchtime rush, chatty office workers crowd around the open counter in the centre of the restaurant, or tuck themselves away at tables on the slightly raised second level. Staff remain attentive despite the rush and hover nearby, ready to fill your glass. At dinner, enjoy hearty meals like skewers of pork wrapped in bacon and mushrooms stuffed with meat. The drinks menu is very Japanese but continues the healthy trend with veggie cocktails. Traditional items such as rice cake do not go amiss on the dessert list. Skewers are inexpensive and average around ¥400; vegetables cost ¥500 and above and you'll probably need to order a few.

Sugitomo Bldg (B1)
3-11-6 Nishihara
Shibuya-ku
🚇 *Yoyogi Uehara*
Map 5 D1 **37**

Gaya

03 3481 5255 | www.gaya.co.jp

Sushi crafted with brown rice is rare in the city and even more so at an *izakaya*. Then again most dishes on Gaya's organic menu may come as a surprise. Classified as an *izakaya*, cuisine here is in a different league than most: crisp salads, delectable dressings, root vegetable pancakes and the crowd favourite – fried soy meat balls that resemble chicken – are just some of the offerings. The dessert menu is also a cut above the rest with homely apple pie, chocolate cake and soy icecream. Although not entirely vegetarian, it follows macrobiotic principles with a healthy, seasonal menu that's focused on vegetables as the foundation of its fresh cuisine – even the organic beer and wine list matches the theme. More funky than hippy, their Yoyogi Uehara main branch provides counter style seating overlooking the kitchen, as well as private tables to the side. Since first opening in 1987, they have expanded and now have branches in Aoyama, Tachikawa and Sendai, as well as two branches in Los Angeles.

B1-13-11
Nishi-Azabu
Minato-ku
🚇 *Roppongi*
Map 11 A3 **38**

Gonpachi

03 5771 0170 | www.gonpachi.jp

Gonpachi is well known for being Quentin Tarantino's inspiration behind the House of Blue Leaves restaurant in *Kill Bill Vol. 1*, as well as being a presidential dining spot when George Bush paid a visit to the capital. Its unassuming door opens up to an expansive restaurant where glowing lanterns are strung together overhead lighting up the dark wooden tables below, in a scene reminiscent of old Japan. In the open kitchen, chefs prepare juicy *yakitori* such as grilled chicken meatballs, tomato wrapped in bacon and tiger prawns, as well as fresh *soba* and crispy *tempura*. The floor above offers private booth seating and a view of the festivities below. The genuinely friendly and accommodating staff shuffle along hastily to the sound of the *shamisen* playing in the background. Considering this restaurant's rich atmosphere, it has managed to keep its prices reasonable; *soba* and *yakitori* are generally under ¥1,000 each unless you go for more expensive meats. With a lot of space and a good selection of beer, *shōchū* and sake, this is a great place to gather a group of friends. Find it on the corner of the crossing on Nishi-Azabu.

Gonpachi

2-14-7 Akasaka
Minato-ku
🚇 **Akasaka**
Map 11 C1 **50**

Hinaya
03 3583 0178
http://akasakahinaya.blogspot.com
Cheap, delicious and with free extra servings of *udon*, you won't leave hungry from this lunchtime gem. Popular with local workers it's best to visit between 13:00 and 15:00 to avoid the lunchtime rush. You can then take some time to enjoy your meal in Hinaya's traditional wooden setting. Their Sanuki *udon* noodles are served in a tasty broth which is a

Udon

combination of Rishiri *konbu* – kelp from Rishiri Island off northern Hokkaidō – and *iriko* (dried white-back sardines) from the Seto Inland Sea. The lunch set includes *udon*, *kayaku-gohan* (mixed rice) and two small side dishes. The most popular option is their curry *udon*, but it's worth trying their more traditional selection like *umejiso* (sour plum and basil leaf) or for the more game the *neba-neba sanshu-mori* includes *natto* (fermented soy beans), okra, and grated yam. Dishes start from ¥900. Hinaya is three minutes from Exit 2 of Akasaka station. It is situated up a small side alley and has a natural wooden exterior.

4-10-11 Roppongi
Minato-ku
🚇 **Roppongi**
Map 11 B2 **35**

Inakaya (West Shop)
03 5775 1012
The festive spirit that resonates throughout this popular expat hangout, coupled with its quality food, make this well worth a visit. The food here is reminiscent of upscale *izakaya* fare, but the prices are a lot higher. Grilled meat, seafood and fresh vegetables are eaten straight from large wooden paddles making a unique dining experience. The restaurant's boisterous, *yukata*-clad waiters shouting orders loudly over the constant chatter of diners also adds to the experience, as does watching the chefs grill up your order before your eyes. Touristy for some, the restaurant has been known to have a few Hollywood celebrities pop by for a bite. From Roppongi Crossing, walk down Gaien-Higashi Dōri towards Tokyo Midtown and take the second right. There is also another branch nearby which stays open until 05:00 at East Shop, 5-3-4 Roppongi, 03 3408 5040.

Nakayama Bldg (B1F)
3-11-14 Ginza
Chūō-ku
🚇 **Higashi-Ginza**
Map 14 B3 **44**
€

Ippudo
03 3547 1010 | *www.ippudo.com*
This basement *ramen* shop draws in hungry office workers for its rich-tasting, cheap *ramen*. Be prepared to wait, as the queue reaches all the way up the well-trodden staircase, out on to the street. Once you do make it inside, the communal dining area includes a large central wooden table to your right and a few smaller tables. If you secure a spot to yourself with a vacant seat, don't be surprised if you suddenly have unannounced fellow diners. The house speciality is Hakata *ramen*, with a creamy pork broth originating from the Hakata region of Fukuoka city. Efficient waiters swiftly present each bowl and your order may have already been taken while waiting in the queue. Patrons can help themselves to additional toppings including ginger, crushed garlic cloves and bean sprouts mixed with sesame seeds in chili oil. You can also pay an extra ¥100 for a second helping of noodles if you're hungry. Unless you want a beer or some *gyōza* to go with your meal, you can leave here satisfied, having spent less than ¥1,000. Branches of this chain are located throughout Japan.

Nishimura Bldg (B1) ◀
22-2 Udagawa-chō
Shibuya-ku
🚇 *Shibuya*
Map 8 B3 **39**
€

Janken

03 5784 2432

In a crowded field and facing cut-throat competition, this *izakaya* manages to stay above the fray, offering cheap drinks and tasty food in a fun atmosphere, just seconds from the main Hachikō meeting spot (see Top Dog on p.95). What makes it unique is the popular rock, paper, scissors game – known as *janken* in Japanese – that is taken to a new level by using it to determine the size of your portion of *edamame*, a popular drinking snack. Upon ordering, the friendly staff will challenge you to a match and your serving is dependent on whether you win or loose. The food here is typical of an *izakaya,* and is very cheap. Dishes such as *gyōza* dumplings and *mochi* potato pancakes (all around ¥500) are delicious, especially when washed down with a crisp beer.

1-11-2 Ginza ◀
Chūō-ku
🚇 *Ginza itchōme*
Map 8 C2 **42**

Kitcho

03 3535 1177 | *www.seiyo-ginza.com*

In the basement of the luxury Hotel Seiyo in Ginza, Kitcho is a well-concealed gem that many pass by. The food here is some of the best in Tokyo and the seasonal *kaiseki* cuisine they serve is an elegantly presented treat. Despite the hotel's regal decor, its star restaurant retains a traditional Japanese atmosphere, with an earthy colour scheme and a simple interior. However, luckily for foreigners, it is not entirely traditional and you can enjoy your meal sat at a table, served by English speaking staff. Kaiseki should be tried at least once, but it's an experience which does not come cheap – lunch ranges from ¥8,000 to ¥21,000 and dinner can be anything from ¥25,000 per head. Reservations are essential.

Takashimaya ◀
Times Square
5-24-2 Sendagaya
Shinjuku-ku
🚇 *Shinjuku*
Map 7 C2 **55**

Kobikicho Tenkuni

03 5361 1875

This quaint restaurant serves delicious, crispy tempura in a traditional setting. The decor is minimalist and there is a tiny rock garden. The assortment available is comprehensive with an array of vegetables including mushrooms, pumpkin, potatoes and fresh seafood such as shrimps, squid and scallops on the list. The menu offerings come with rice, miso soup and Japanese pickles and all items can be ordered a la carte for around ¥260 to ¥1,260. If you're feeling hungry you can opt for one of their set courses; options are tailored to either fish or vegetable lovers. The drinks menu caters to Japanese tastes, with cold beers and sake brews being among the most popular choices.

1-9-5 Ebisu ◀
Shibuya-ku
🚇 *Ebisu*
Map 5 F2 **45**
€

Kohmen

03 5475 0185 | *www.kohmen.com*

With 12 branches scattered throughout Tokyo's major districts, Kohmen is your best bet for a satisfying bowl of noodles. Each branch is distinct in its design, while the flavour remains the same. The Ebisu branch spans two floors with a long wooden counter across its lower level. Its counter seats fill up with a variety of ramen lovers and upstairs the area centres on a 61 inch plasma television screen. Its stylish and clean interior and the prompt service (excluding lunchtime), doesn't affect the price, which stays below ¥1,000. Tuck into a rich pork broth with eight toppings, grilled pork and noodles and choose from salt, sesame and soy sauce based *ramen*, as well as plump *tsukemen* (dipping noodles). You can also savour side dishes like salty, plum-flavoured *toroniku* (fatty pork) or opt for almond tofu jelly for dessert. Beer costs an inexpensive ¥530 and *oolong* tea and soft drinks are less than ¥500. Kohmen is only a minute away from the east exit of the JR Ebisu station, go down the road with Sunkus on one corner and UFJ bank on the other and it's to your left.

Kojyu

8-5-25 Ginza
Chūō-ku
 Ginza
Map 14 A3 **36**

03 6215 9544

Hidden in the backstreets of Ginza surrounded by numerous hostess clubs (in the Daini Sanyu Building), it would be easy to pass Kojyu without even noticing it was a place to dine. Its humble, narrow entrance does little to distinguish it as one of Tokyo's best restaurants (as voted by *Michelin*), but that's exactly what it is. Once inside it might take a while to register that what you see is all there is. A few booth seats line the counter and there are two private tatami mat rooms, suitable for an intimate party, with a sole Japanese scroll and vase of flowers used to decorate each. The owner, Toru Okuda, is as humble as the decor, but the seasonal cuisine is not. Seafood lovers will delight in the array of elaborate dishes including eel roasted in a sweet soy sauce and charcoal grilled crabs. To accompany your meal there are a range of wines and Japanese sake. As there is no English menu, it may help to go with someone who's fluent in Japanese.

Maisen

4-8-5 Jingū-mae
Shibuya-ku
Omotesandō
Map 8 D2 **57**

03 3470 0071

Maisen has become a bit of an institution in Tokyo for its *tonkatsu*. Ask around and you'll be informed that this is one of the top *tonkatsu* places in the city. The vast setting for this pork cutlet shop was once a public bathhouse and some of the initial design details are still intact, including the original high ceilings. The menu includes a selection of crunchy pork, as well as other meat and seafood options, breaded or deep-fried and served with cabbage, rice, soup and pickles. Their menu also contains some lighter options, all at reasonably low prices. It's near Omotesandō station; go out of Exit A2 and take the next street on your right, walk past FCUK and Barbacoa and follow the road until you see the restaurant.

Mikura

1-6-10 Ginza (B1)
Chūō-ku
Ginza itchōme
Map 14 C2 **47**

03 3564 3921 | *www.fukunaga-tf.com/mikura*

Minimalist natural decor creates a refined ambience at Mikura, with sleek wooden counter seating, low chairs and a traditional floor seating arrangement. The low-key design allows visitors to concentrate on the quality, Kyoto-inspired cuisine. The multi-course menu ranges in price from ¥2,800 up to ¥7,600. Ingredients are typical of the region and tend to vary depending on the season. Local vegetables, seafood and meat are lightly seasoned and beautifully presented. Individual tofu *nabe* pots, nutty mushrooms, omelettes folded over seafood, charcoal grilled crab, *teriyaki* dishes, cod basted in *miso*, warm chestnut rice and *udon* are just a sample of the options available here. For dessert, try not to pass up the sweet *mochi* cake – it's delicious. Mikura is an exemplary example of Kyoto cuisine, doing its hometown proud. It's a few minutes walk from Exit 6 of Ginza Itchōme station, in the block next to the Mizuho Bank.

Rainbow Roll Sushi

Monteplaza (2F)
1-10-3 Azabu-Jūban
Minato-ku
Azabu-Jūban
Map 11 C4 **52**

03 5572 7688 | *www.wdi.co.jp*

This is a rather ironic place, serving up a western take on sushi in the country from which the dish came. But the American-style mix is popular among the foreign community and includes some ingredients that are shunned in more traditional places. The *ikura* and smoked salmon roll is one such example, with cream cheese and cucumber added to the mix. Other original options include sauteed pork with an apple and sour cream sauce. Each sushi roll ranges between ¥950 and ¥1,600, and side dishes are in a similar price range. The setting is refined, with shared marble tables and private booths.

Sakura-tei

03 3479 0039 | *www.sakuratei.co.jp*

This artistic hotspot in the backstreets of Harajuku is popular with Japanese youth and the foreign community. It is a sensual cocktail, from the funky art adorning the walls to the smoky savoury pancake scent rising up from each table. Patrons enjoy the process as much as the outcome, mixing and cooking the batter with their own choice of toppings. Diners can choose from *okonomiyaki*, *monjayaki*, or *teppanyaki* options or a mix of all three. The restaurant's special *Sakura-Yaki*, which combines pork, squid, shrimp, onions, mushrooms and egg for ¥1,000, is the most popular menu item. If you visit during the cherry blossom season take a seat outside to understand why the Japanese relish in the beauty of cherry blossom trees, known as *sakura* in Japanese. Sakura-tei is situated at the back of the Design Festa Gallery, but the main entrance is just around the corner, off Cat Street.

Shabuzen

03 3485 0800 | *www.gnavi.co.jp/shabuzen*

This restaurant's claim to fame is its debut in the film *Lost in Translation*. On visiting you may be left wondering, just like Bill Murray and Scarlett Johansson, what cut of meat to choose, as the selection looks very similar. The cheapest find on the menu is an all-you-can-eat imported beef or pork *shabu shabu* or *sukiyaki* set. Their premium superior *Ōmi* beef, which is recognised throughout Japan for its quality, will set you back ¥12,800 per person. *Kaiseki*, *shabu shabu* and *sukiyaki* are also available and the typical meal is served with side dishes of delicately prepared seasonal food. Diners can choose from a booth seat or private *tatami* room. Once here they will be served by accommodating, kimono-clad waitresses. A 10% service charge is added to all bills.

Shin Hinomoto

03 3214 8021

More commonly known as Andy's, this Japanese style *izakaya* is perfect for after work drinks or a party with friends. Situated under the Yamanote line tracks it wins no extra points for its views, but promises to be fun especially as the beers continue to flow throughout the evening. Its speciality is seafood and British owner Andy knows what's best to order each day. Many patrons leave the selection up to him and are pleased with the array of dishes he brings out during the night. A range of salads, a selection of vegetables (the mushrooms with mayonnaise are appetising) and typical *izakaya* fare like deep fried chicken are also on the menu. The jugs of beer go down a treat with the boisterous crowd here. Andy's is opposite the Yūrakuchō Denki building and is right underneath the train tracks. Look out for the large red lantern out the front and the noisy crowd inside.

Okonomiyaki chef

Rainbow Roll Sushi

Shin-Yokohama Ramen Museum

2-14-21 Shin-Yokohama
Kōhoku-ku
🚇 *Shin-Yokohama*
Map 2 A4

045 5471 0503 | *www.raumen.co.jp*

It can be surprising to stumble upon a museum dedicated to a sole item of food. But just a short trip out of Tokyo, in neighbouring Yokohama, the Ramen Museum is every noodle lover's dream. Visitors to the first floor can learn about the history of *ramen* and how the popular noodle dish is made, and they can also stock up on numerous *ramen* themed souvenirs. Underground, there is a replica of Tokyo's backstreets 50 years ago, when Tokyoites first started to embrace this warming noodle broth. *Ramen* restaurants representing regional takes on the dish can be found here, as well as other shops representing the era. Each place offers a mini ramen option for around ¥550 and a full bowl for approximately ¥1,000. Admission is ¥300 for adults and ¥100 for children. This well-known spot is only a three minute walk from the station.

Sukiyabashi Jiro

Tsukamoto Bldg (B1F)
4-2-15 Ginza
Chūō-ku
🚇 *Ginza*
Map 14 B2 **53**

03 3535 3600

Sukiyabashi Jiro shot to international culinary fame after receiving three stars in the *Tokyo Michelin Restaurant Guide* for 2008. This simple basement dwelling, with room for only 23 people, may seem like an unlikely spot for some of Tokyo's best sushi. Here, the focus is on the meal not the setting, and head chef Jiro Ono and his son delicately prepare the freshest raw fish. The environment in which the sushi is made is strictly controlled and the fish and rice are kept at different temperatures. Sushi places like this can be a little daunting, especially with the lack of prices on display. Come prepared with a lot of cash (at least ¥20,000), because although you may leave feeling full, you're sure to have an empty wallet.

Sushi no Midori

Ginza Corridor
7-6-12 Ginza
Chūō-ku
🚇 *Ginza*
Map 14 A3 **54**

03 5568 1212 | *http://homepage2.nifty.com/sushi_no_midori*

Sushi in Ginza isn't known for being a cheap meal option, especially if you're after the best. But if you take a walk away from the central strip you'll stumble upon a queue of people who already know about this treasure. Lacking the price tag of some of the neighbouring sushi restaurants, Sushi no Midori offers fresh, delicious fish at excellent prices, especially if you choose one of its sets. Always busy (there are no reservations), the predictable queue validates its quality and the friendly patrons inside are clearly happy about their dining choice. Customers can choose whether they want to sit at the counter overlooking the skilled sushi chefs or at a table (being flexible about where you sit will speed up your waiting time.) Located on the Ginza Corridor, follow the tracks towards Shinbashi and you'll see the queue near the end of the strip.

Tonki

1-1-2 Shimo-Meguro
Meguro-ku
🚇 *Naka-Meguro*
Map 5 F3 **58**

03 3491 9928

Hungry crowds of locals and interested foreigners flock daily to this long-established joint to get their fill of some of Tokyo's most prized *tonkatsu*. Customers choose from a selection of different pork cuts, which are then breaded and deep-fried in consecutive vats of oil – a process used to create a crispy exterior that is moist inside. Be sure to order a set, which includes rice, miso soup, pickles and a drink all for only ¥1,650. Watching the production line in the large open kitchen is all part of the fun as chefs in prim white uniforms bustle about. Queues here tend to be long, so be prepared for a bit of a wait. Find it a few minutes away from the west exit of the JR Meguro Station in the block to the left, across the road from the station. Look for an entrance with blue curtains over glass doors

2-10 Kanda Awajichō
Chiyoda-ku
🚇 *Awajichō*
Map 13 B2 **51**

Yabu Soba

03 3251 0287 | www.yabusoba.net

Step back in time at this rustic soba shop and sample noodles the way they're supposed to taste. With a wealth of experience, this traditional shop has survived through six generations and first opened its doors back in 1880. A quaint courtyard with a wooden fence leads into a historic building and the serene, welcoming scene offers respite from the surrounding city. The focus here is on lovingly prepared *seiro* style *soba* noodles and the extensive menu includes both hot and cold noodles with eel, tempura, mushrooms, aubergine and an array of seasonal ingredients. If the season is right, it's worth sampling the imaginative conger eel *soba*. Other traditional dishes can be ordered on the side, like sushi, sashimi, grilled eel and Japanese sweets like *manjū*. Most noodle options cost between ¥1,000 and ¥2,000 as do the various side dishes. Beer and sake provide the basis for the drinks menu. Located only two minutes from Exit A3 of Awajichō station, it is in the same block as Hotel New Kanda.

Kishida Bldg (1F)
7-18-8 Roppongi
Minato-ku
🚇 *Roppongi*
Map 11 B2 **56**

Yasaiya

03 5775 5335 | www.vegedinning.com

Despite being located in Tokyo's somewhat rowdy entertainment district, Yasaiya still manages to retain a sophisticated vibe with its warm Japanese wooden interior and welcoming chefs who are happy to discuss the menu. The daily selection covers farm fresh vegetables, tender cuts of meat and seafood dishes cooked before your eyes on a hot plate. Watching the chefs cook is all part of the fun and taking a counter seat is a good idea for diners who like to get involved with their meal. Yasaiya focuses on retaining the natural flavour of each dish and with vegetables sent direct from the farm to the restaurant you're in for a natural treat here. The alcohol list covers a good selection of *shōchū*, beer and wine. Dinner with drinks will cost around ¥5,000 a head.

1-21-2 Minami
Ikebukuro (4F)
Toshima-ku
🚇 *Ikebukuro*
Map 3 F1 **41**

Yozakura Bijin

03 5952 5860 | www.diamond-dining.com/yozakura

Classically charming and romantic, this themed izakaya is what you may imagine old Japan to be like with its paper lanterns, ornate rock gardens, delicate cherry blossom trees and shrine for patrons to make prayers for love. But the restaurant's theme, inspired by the love affair between a prostitute and her customer, may seem strange to foreign ears. Traditional tatami rooms come in varying sizes, with some suitable for large parties. Whether you are in a big group or dining alone, polite, *yukata*-clad waitresses will lead you through the menu, which isn't available in English. The immense selection of vinegar-based drinks normally requires some extra explanation. The upscale fare features authentic Japanese favourites and roll your own sushi which is a fun way to try your hand at the craft. It is reasonably-priced at around ¥3,000 to ¥4,000 per head. Located a minute away from the south exit of Ikebukuro station, cross the road and walk along Meiji Dōri past the Resona Bank. It's on the same block just before the next corner.

3-14-13 Nishi Nippori
Arakawa-ku
🚇 *Nippori*
Map 2 B2

Zakuro

03 5685 5313 | http://zakuro.oops.jp

Zakuro knows what it's doing when it comes to *shabu shabu* and the restaurant was the first in Tokyo to add the dish to their menu, back in 1955. The simple cooking method involves dunking paper-thin slices of beef into a bubbling pot of water, and creates succulent melt-in-the-mouth meat morsels. Other authentic meals such as tempura, *sukiyaki* and *teppanyaki* also feature on the menu, but the *shabu shabu* is a must here. Zakuro's decor is rather simplistic, especially when you consider its premium prices. Its in the basement of the Nipporikonishi Building, and quite large,

PlanetTokyo.com

Because you'll need more than a passport

though certain areas have been sectioned off into smaller rooms containing a few tables for a more private setting. The faint sound of laughter that floats in from distant rooms gives the impression that the restaurant is bigger than it actually is. The selection of alcohol is extensive, ranging from local sake brews to expensive French wine.

Korean

Other options **Far Eastern** p.334

Accorder Jingū-mae (B1)
2-31-20 Jingū-mae
Shibuya-ku
🚇 *Meiji Jingū-mae*
Map 8 D1 **59**

Nabi

03 5771 0071 | *www.nabi-tokyo.com*
This sleek dining spot, decorated by the Idee Shop, provides both a stylish atmosphere and a fine selection of Korean dishes. Their organic menu covers five taste sensations: salty, sweet, sour, hot, and bitter. Traditional favourites are abundant, like bibimbap, mixed rice with seven kinds of vegetables and a fried egg, dak hanmali which is a whole chicken cooked in soup, or seasoned pork, beef, chicken or seafood served with fresh salad greens to wrap around each meaty morsel. Their dishes are supported by unique cocktail blends and a comprehensive bar selection. Only a few minutes from the bustling streets of Harajuku, this expansive basement restaurant is suitable for either a group dinner with friends in their raised middle section or a cosy candlelit dinner in one of their comfy booth seats bordering the room.

3-24-22 Nishi-Azabu
Minato-ku
🚇 *Roppongi*
Map 11 A3 **60**

Toraji

03 5786 1771 | *www.ebisu-toraji.com*
Toraji's Nishi-Azabu branch of this chain offers a higher level of sophistication than its other locations. It's a short walk down Roppongi Dōri towards Nishi Azabu Crossing, on the left. The dark wooden interior, sleek open kitchen and minimalist decor help create a chic setting. The menu covers a range of red meat, presented raw then cooked to your liking over a gas burner. Meat options cost around ¥1,000, but if you're looking for the finest of cuts expect to pay ¥3,000 or more. Seafood and fresh vegetables can also be grilled to your taste and national dishes like kimchi, bibimbap and nang myun, can be ordered on the side. For a change, try the ginseng wine or *soju* (the Korean equivalent to sake). Otherwise, well-known brews are around ¥600 each. Three different courses are available for ¥4,000, ¥6,000 and ¥8,000 and each combine soup, kimchi, bibimbap and dessert. The meat offered for each course varies with the price.

Mediterranean

Other options **Italian** p.339, **Spanish** p.355

5-2-40 Minami-
Azabu
Minato-ku
🚇 *Hirō*
Map 11 A4 **61**

Cicada

03 5447 5522 | *www.tyharborbrewing.co.jp*
Cicada's spacious setting, natural floors and polished wooden tables, highlighted by the soft glow of candles, make a perfect spot for a relaxed drink over tapas. Spanish, Moroccan, and Mediterranean fare influence the chef's creations and spicy crab cakes, horiatiki salad with feta and kalamata olives or the cheese platter will leave you struggling to limit your selection. Those who appreciate olive oil will also enjoy the hand-picked oils from around the world that have found their own section on the menu. Cicada's extensive range of wines is also available by the glass and the full menu is available at the bar if you can't secure a table. Cicada provides weekday lunch sets and a set menu that allows you to try a range of dishes from their dinner menu. Dinner can be pricey, especially since you'll want to try it all. From Exit 3 of Hirō station turn right. It's on the same side of the road a few minutes walk away.

Spyros

Morikawa Bldg (2F)
3-15-24 Roppongi
Minato-ku
🚇 *Roppongi*
Map 11 C3 62

03 3796 2677 | *www.spyros.jp*

Located just off Roppongi's main drag, this restaurant is a change of pace from the surrounding establishments. Its crisp white and blue interior is overtly reminiscent of the Greek islands and offers a multitude of Mediterranean treats. Spyros does its homeland proud with plump olives, fresh Greek salads with feta, tzatziki, fava and taramosalata dips ready to be mopped up with warm pita, rice wrapped in vine leaves and souvlaki all on the menu. Dine a la carte or from the good value set menus from ¥2,800 per person. For an extra ¥2,100 all the beer and wine you can drink will be served up from the bar. Spyros also has good value lunch sets with their chicken or salmon gyros only costing ¥650. Service is attentive and polite, but without the lively Greek touch. Overall, this is a great spot when you're after some well-priced, tasty Greek fare.

Mexican

Fonda de la Madrugada

Villa Bianca (B1)
2-33-12 Jingū-mae
Shibuya-ku
🚇 *Harajuku*
Map 8 D1 63

03 5410 6288 | *www.fonda-m.com*

Restaurants in Tokyo love to recreate an authentic setting – transporting patrons from the humdrum of daily life and into the locale of a chosen theme. Fonda de la Madrugada has gone as far as to import its furniture and tiles from Mexico. On entering, you'll step into a lively old Mexican courtyard, complete with a live Mariachi band. The spicy menu is a mix of quesadillas, cheesy nachos, meaty tortillas, tacos and a good selection of fish dishes. Reasonably priced seafood dishes start at ¥2,000, while well-known Mexican favourites are less than ¥2,000. Drinks can be enjoyed at the bar or at your table and diners can also choose to order food at the bar. Fonda de la Madrugada strives to provide its patrons with all the ingredients for an enjoyable evening and has been doing so since it first opened its Mexican doors back in 1993.

Junkadelic

4-10-4 Kamimeguro
Meguro-ku
🚇 *Naka-Meguro*
Map 5 F3 64

03 5725 5020 | *http://junkadelic.jp*

Big servings, tasty fare and a casual, fun vibe make Junkadelic worth the trip to Naka Meguro. The hodgepodge of furniture, colourful flags and religious decor scattered within its walls enhance the restaurant's informal feeling. Diners can glimpse the fajitas, enchiladas, or chimichangas being cooked up in the open kitchen, but most are too busy contemplating the truly extensive tequila and rum selection. If you're out for a big night then the jugs of frozen margarita are a good way to start your evening. Among the authentic Mexican and Tex-Mex dinner selection are some of the owner's unique creations, like Mexican pizza. Reserve early if you plan to visit at the weekend as this is a popular spot with Tokyo's young, hip crowd. Follow the train tracks (heading away from the river) up until you come to a T junction. You'll see Junkadelic just off to your right.

Middle Eastern

Harem

CI Plaza (B1)
2-3-1 Kita-Aoyama
Minato-ku
🚇 *Gaienmae*
Map 8 F1 65

03 5786 2929 | *www.harem.co.jp*

This lively restaurant in the upscale Aoyama neighbourhood offers a change of pace from the average Turkish eatery in the city. Harem has forged away from the well-trodden path offering some delightful Turkish tastes such as balik bugulama – a salmon stew with vegetables in a spinach sauce and harem sarma – an almond and hazelnut stuffed chicken roll, as well as some old favourites like spicy lamb kebabs and dolma. Some of the portions may be on the smaller side and going for a set will allow you to sample more food for a good price. The course menu has three options for ¥4,000, ¥5,000, or ¥7,000. Each covers an appetiser, salad, main and dessert as well as some warm ekmek bread. If you're planning on having a few drinks, alongside the regular array of cocktails, there are original blends like the vodka-based Turkish sunrise and the blue Mediterranean sea breeze, for ¥850 each.

Nipporikonishi
Bldg (B1F)
3-14-13 Nishi Nippori
Arakawa-ku
🚇 *Nippori*
Map 2 B2

Zakuro

03 5685 5313 | *http://zakuro.oops.jp*
Delicate portions and beautiful presentation are thrown out of the window at this basement dining spot. Here, it's all hearty kebabs, slow roasted lamb shanks with rice and beans and other filling Turkish delights. Dishes are served up to diners sprawled out on Persian rugs. Visiting Zakuro is a novelty, especially as the evening draws on and drunken diners reach for the Aladdin costumes piled high in the corner. Meat eaters may love it here, but the service is variable. The ¥2,000 set menu is a popular dinner choice and when you consider that some a la carte options nearly match this price it is great value. If you want to join the weekend rush, be sure to reserve a spot and don't be late for your booking without calling ahead to let them know. The level of service can vary – more so at the weekends when Zakuro's carpets become crammed with diners smoking shisha and eagerly looking around for their next dish.

Nepalese

Caeser Bldg (B1F)
1-2- 22 Shimo Meguro
Meguro-ku
🚇 *Meguro*
Map 5 F3 **66**

Katmandu Gangri

03 3493 4712
Blends of authentic Tibetan and Nepalese dishes are served up at this long established ethnic dining spot. Rich in herbs and spices, Katmandu's dishes span further than just their popular curry selection. Options like momo dumplings, alu tama – a richly seasoned soup of potatoes, bamboo shoots and beans, heavily stuffed samosas and spicy chicken and vegetable stir fries can be washed down with a creamy lassi. Some not so traditional concoctions are on the menu and, like some other restaurants in the city, Tibetan flavours have been turned into a 'Tibet pizza' option. Dishes are excellent value at ¥3,000 per head for dinner and a basic selection of beer and wine. Katmandu's modest location hardly seems fitting for the tasty cuisine served here and if you're in the neighbourhood it's worth popping by to sample it for yourself. Follow the main road downhill towards Naka Meguro and it is on your left.

Meguro Business
Mansion (5F)
2-15-2 Kamiōsaki
Shinagawa-ku
🚇 *Meguro*
Map 5 F3 **67**

Madal

03 3442 3566 | *www.madal.jp*
Dining traditional Japanese-style – at low tables sitting on the floor – can quickly lose its novelty. Madal, however, has brought the fun back into dining by providing a relaxed atmosphere with comfortable colourful cushions on the floor and against the wall to unwind on. With curtains draped from the ceiling and natural textured walls, Madal does well at creating an authentic dining space. The food is traditional and spans further than just their delicious curry menu. Depending on the time of year you visit, you may be able to enjoy *gyakok* (a Tibetan hotpot of meat, vegetables and tofu), tandoori chicken, momo (meat and vegetable filled half moon dumplings served in a hot tomato soup), Tibetan-style chow mein and other exotic dishes. Expect to pay around ¥3,000 a head at dinner and anywhere between ¥780 and ¥1,050 for the curry lunch sets. The drinks menu is limited but includes some foreign beers from India, Mexico, The Philippines and Nepal, as well as sweeter non-alcoholic drinks such as chai and lassi.

Fujimamas

Pacific Rim

Lights Ebisu (1F)
1-21-18 Ebisu
Shibuya-ku
⊛ Ebisu
Map 5 F2 68

Aotea Rangi
03 3447 1496
www.unitedf.com/aotea_rangi
This quaint dining spot, only a short walk from Ebisu station, boasts succulent green-lipped mussels from New Zealand's shores. Plump and juicy, the mussels come fresh from the pot coated in sauces like bacon, chili and tomato, or buttery garlic and herb. Once the mussels are done you can mop up the remains with chunks of fresh bread. The menu choices include pastas, seafood, New Zealand lamb, venison, and oysters. If you're looking for some kiwi cuisine they really do have a comprehensive choice of both authentic dishes and New Zealand wine and beer. Come early or be sure to reserve a spot as this cosy place, with only 16 seats inside and eight on the terrace, fills up fast.

1-2-5 Shibuya
Shibuya-ku
⊛ Shibuya
Map 8 D3 69

Beacon
03 6418 0077 | *www.tyharborbrewing.co.jp*
Beacon's sleek, hip interior attracts a crowd to match the setting – a host of young sophisticated socialites in search of some fine wine and cuisine. Its menu, heavy on meat and seafood, mixes east and west with dishes like blue fin tuna steak with a citrus soy sauce and wasabi mash, and scallops with Brussels sprouts and chive cream. Their high-quality Australian beef dishes bring out the meat's natural succulence and can be matched with a glass or bottle from the wine selection, many of which hail from Australia, New Zealand and California. Those with a sweet tooth can sample the creme brule and assorted cakes. Set courses and an a la carte menu are available at both lunch and dinner and each week the lunch specials change. If you want to visit during the weekend reservations are essential. Just off Aoyama Dōri, across the road from the children's castle.

6-3-2 Jingū-mae
Shibuya-ku
⊛ Meiji Jingū-mae
Map 8 D2 70
⊛

Fujimamas
03 5485 2283 | *www.fujimamas.com*
This is modern Asian fusion cuisine tailored to a foreign crowd. Open from brunch to dinner, it regularly fills with a good mix of people. On entering you'll notice their delicious cake selection in front of an open bar, lined with a range of tipples. Spanning two floors, the wooden downstairs area has a rustic feel to it, while upstairs is more intimate with private *tatami* rooms that are perfect for a party. The dinner menu depends on what seasonal ingredients are available and may include interesting seafood dishes like pan seared salmon with wasabi cream, or mama's Thai style caesar salad with calamari croutons. The lunch menu includes hearty salads and sandwiches and there are also lunchtime menus for kids. All meals are reasonably priced and brimming with flavour. Turn right before Kiddyland and it's to your right off Omotesandō Dōri.

Portuguese
Other options **Mediterranean** p.350

1-25-6 Shōtō
Shibuya-ku
⊛ Shibuya
Map 8 4A 71

Manuel
03 5738 0125 | *www.pjgroup.jp/manuel*
A haven away from the crowds in the neighbouring Dōgenzaka area, Manuel's is a quaint place to while away an evening. The warm interior is enhanced by terracotta tiled floors

and deep maroon tablecloths covering the few tables throughout the room. Low ledges along the wall house a collection of fine ports and wines, hinting at its comprehensive Portuguese wine list. The menu includes authentic Portuguese dishes like Carne de Porco a Alentejana, a tasty blend of pork, clams and vegetable chunks and Arroz de Polvo (octopus rice), as well as some dishes from other nations like Feijoada Vegetariana, a hearty winter stew with black beans. All mains are less than ¥2,000. Reservations are recommended. Walk in the direction of the Shōtō museum. When you see the Lawson convenience store on your left, take the diagonal right and it's on the right.

Seafood

2-36-11 Kameido (2F)
Koto-ku
🚇 **Kameido**
Map 2 C2

Zauo
03 5858 1288 | *www.zauo.com*
You can't do much better than this novelty restaurant when it comes to fresh fish. Diners here have to catch their own. On arrival, patrons are seated in a specially designed wooden boat surrounded by water. Seats are available, but part of the fun is being with the boisterous crowd onboard. Armed with rods, nets, buckets and bait, diners start the hunt for their dinner in fishing tanks that vary in contents and cost. Customers decide what kind of fish they would like before dropping their line. There is a wide selection to choose from and when you do get a bite, which won't take long, the friendly staff and excited customers will commend your catch. The fish is then whisked away and prepared to your liking – grilled, sashimi or BBQ are just some of the options. Set courses are available starting from ¥5,800 and each course includes two 'all-you-can-drink' hours from a selection of 40 beverages. Arrive before the post-work crowd if you want to look around. The restaurant is located three minutes walk from Kameido station.

Thai
Other options **Far Eastern** p.334

Roppongi Loa Bldg (13F)
5-5-1 Roppongi
Minato-ku
🚇 **Roppongi**
Map 11 B2 **72**

Erawan
03 3404 5741 | *www.erawan-jp.com*
Looking over the sprawling metropolis below, Erawan provides panoramic views of the city, and cuisine at a great price, successfully offering a sense of calm. The expansive menu includes traditional Thai favourites and a great curry spectrum: red, yellow and green. Dishes are full of flavour (expect some to be spicy) and some have an extra zesty punch. Menu items include deep-fried spring rolls, salads with a tropical touch, fresh seafood (including succulent prawns) and coconut based soups. Erawan's stunning decor also raises its profile, with bamboo trimmings, polished wooden tables, chiseled carvings and other authentic extras. Private rooms are available for more intimate evenings as well as a roomy main dining area perfect for large groups to share delectable dishes. And just as Thailand is known as the land of smiles, you can expect the waiters to follow suit with welcoming grins.

2-4-1 Marunouchi
Chiyoda-ku
🚇 **Tokyo**
Map 14 B1 **73**
💶

The Mango Tree
03 5224 5489 | *www.mangotree.jp*
Following on from its success in Bangkok and London, Mango Tree has opened a branch in central Tokyo. Picking the perfect location on the 35th floor of the Marunouchi building, Mango Tree offers an elegant setting and a bird's-eye backdrop of the concrete jungle below. The tasty Thai cuisine served here is beautifully presented and prepared with a modern touch. The appetisers include an array of seafood delicacies, like deep-fried spicy fish cakes seasoned with curry and kaffir lime leaves and sweet chili sauce. Mains include various curries and stir-fries seasoned with sweet

chili, tamarind and fish sauce. The frozen fruit drinks are also reminiscent of Thailand's sunny shores. Prices here are high with entrees averaging around ¥4,000. If you want to sample their full selection at a lower price, their lunchtime buffet for ¥2,625 for adults and ¥1,575 for children is the best option.

Vegetarian

2-2-5 Azabu-Jūban
Minato-ku
🔲 *Azabu-Jūban*
Map 11 C4 **74**
🚫

Eat More Greens

03 3798 3191 | *www.eatmoregreens.jp*

Tokyo is slowly catching on to creative vegetarian fare and Eat More Greens is one place that has got the mix right. Their menu features a range of tapas, salads, pizzas and rice and pasta dishes with a breakdown of what ingredients may cause an allergic reaction and whether the dish is vegan or not. Some top picks include the creamy pumpkin moussaka and the avocado and sprouts salad pizza, consisting of a thin crust piled with greens. The floor-to-ceiling windows spread sun over the natural interior, booth seats line an open kitchen and tables for two are placed side by side, making the most of the natural light. When the weather is good, diners can enjoy the terrace seating. Considering its location, the prices are excellent value at around ¥1,000 a dish. Take Exit 4 and head down the road to the left of Wendy's. You'll see Eat More Greens on your right.

2-21-26 Hyakuninchō
Shinjuku-ku
🔲 *Ōkubo*
Map 3 E3 **75**

Saishokukenbi

03 5332 3627 | *www.daisho-kikaku.com*

Tucked away in Koreatown, in a large Buddhist temple, this vegetarian buffet is a delectable find. The selection is comprehensive and includes skewered fake meat, vegetarian dumplings, pasta, tempura, a range of salads and warm vegetables with soy meat, vegetarian desserts and tea and coffee. Many of the dishes here are fried and, although not as healthy as other vegetarian spots in the city, Saishokukenbi is a safe bet if you're looking for a hearty feed. Many dishes are vegan and if they contain dairy products, are clearly labelled. The buffet lunch is ¥1,200 on weekdays and ¥1,500 on Saturday and Sundays and their buffet dinner is ¥2,000. Make sure you take a look at the giant Buddha housed inside a nearby building. This is located in a large Buddhist meeting place a few minutes from Ōkubo station, near the tracks.

1-22-14 Uehara
Shibuya-ku
🔲 *Yoyogi Uehara*
Map 5 D1 **76**

Veggie Paradise

Veggie Paradise

03 6421 2925 | *www.veggieparadise.jp*

The innovative raw cuisine offered here includes *daikon* dumplings filled with shitake mushrooms, and soy protein chunks that bear a striking resemblance to deep-fried chicken. Both lunch and dinner are set menus and patrons can choose between 'living food' or a combination (raw and macrobiotic) course that includes soup (hot or chilled), salad, brown rice or natural yeast bread. A dessert is offered at dinner. With unique creations like a rich kiwi avocado tart with a crust of blended almonds and dates, you'll be pleasantly surprised at how delicious sugar-free desserts are. Organic wine and beer are available but the fresh smoothies, power drinks and herbal teas are a better match for the menu. There's also a yoga studio and a cookery school (lessons are available in English). From the east gate of Yoyogi Uehara station, turn right, walk up the hill and it's the third street on your right a few minutes from the station.

Cafes & Coffee Shops

Other options **Internet Cafes** p.362

Having dessert at well-to-do cafes has become popular among affluent women. As a result, cafes catering to this upmarket crowd have opened throughout the city, each offering beautifully crafted treats. Celebrity pastry chef Toshi Yoroizuka's shops in Ebisu and Tokyo Midtown (p.313) are a prime example; expect a crowd if you visit at the weekend.

But those in need of a caffeine fix will not be short of cheaper options. The smoky Doutor (www.doutor.co.jp) chain has branches throughout the city, but foreign firms are penetrating the market and Starbucks (www.starbucks.com) has become a hit with the younger crowd. Dean & Deluca (p.359) and Segafredo (www.segafredo.it) can also be found in the city, but are less common. These places tend to open early in the morning and close at around 21:00 or 22:00.

Privately owned spots offer a more unique experience. Both Cafe Heavens (p.358) and Frames (p.360) cater for a late night crew – only closing a few hours before others are getting ready to open. Retro cafes like Shichimencho (p.361) and One's Diner (p.360) retain individual style, as does Calico Cat Cafe (p.359), where patrons can play with one of the moggies in residence. The quality of coffee varies between cafes, but places like Asuka (p.359) have come to realise the importance of a good brew and offer a quality cup – complete with latte art.

Food varies from sandwiches to hot meals, but typically a set lunch of a main plus soup, salad, and coffee will be offered. If you visit late in the afternoon a coffee and cake set may be available.

12-34-1 Sarugaku-chō
Shibuya-ku
🚇 *Daikanyama*
Map 5 F2 **77**

Asuka

03 3464 0125 | *www.asukaone.jp*

Nestled in the backstreets of Daikanyama, this is not the easiest place to find, but is well worth the hunt. It feels healthy without being too earnest, with a modern natural decor and hip jazz music setting the scene. The menu is inventive vegetarian, with dishes such as soy nuggets with fresh lemon juice, soy cheese and tomato toasted sandwiches and onion with seaweed and tahini sauce. Lunch sets vary, but typically include a soup, sandwich or Japanese-style option – such as brown rice with soy meat and veggies, miso soup and pickles. The comprehensive coffee menu includes decaffeinated as an option – a rare find in the city. Asuka is about a 10 minute walk from the station, following many twists and turns. It's best to print out the map from the website and have their phone number at the ready. The owner speaks fluent English.

6-32-10 Jingū-mae
Shibuya-ku
🚇 *Meiji Jingū-mae*
Map 8 C2 **78**
🚫

Bakery Cafe 632 Harajuku

03 3498 0632 | *www.piazza.co.jp*

This eclectic bakery offers fresh bread, *bentō* boxes, outdoor dining and a full bar. The music tends to be sweet J-pop and hip-hop, a taste which is reflected in the selection of magazines available for customers to flick through. A towering wall, covered in vines, shelters the courtyard from the nearby noise and jostling crowds, while floor to ceiling windows create an airy space indoors. Smoking is permitted both indoors and out. The cafe is open for breakfast, lunch, and dinner. The menu includes pasta, pizza, and rice dishes such as *nasi goreng*. The lunch sets start at around ¥1,000 and come with a soup and salad or bread, and a set drink. Choices include western standards such as grilled chicken and caesar salad or vegetable curry. The ladies' set includes dessert, and you can upsize your meal for an extra ¥100. The aromatic teas are worth checking out. Bakery Cafe 632 is just off Omotesandō. Go up the side street behind Condomania and turn right.

Bape Cafe

3-27-22 Jingū-mae
Shibuya-ku
🚇 *Harajuku*
Map 8 D1 **79**

03 5770 6560

Nigo is the designer behind hip-hop fashion label A Bathing Ape. His cafe draws a young hip crowd, just like his colourful designs do. American fare is the mainstay of this Harajuku hangout, and most dishes cost less than ¥1,000. The shrimp red curry at ¥800 is a popular choice, as are the waffles with banana and maple syrup. Burgers, steaks and beef curry are also available. The drink selection is limited, and prices average ¥500, including the beer. The sunny space below has floor-to-ceiling windows and is a bit smoky, while the upstairs booths are reserved for non-smokers. To find it, walk down Meiji Dōri towards Sendagaya. Turn right when you reach the overpass with Diesel on the corner. Bape is down the second street on your right.

Ben's Cafe

1-29-21 Takadanobaba
Shinjuku-ku
🚇 *Takadanobaba*
Map 3 E2 **80**

03 3202 2445 | www.benscafe.com

Ben's breaks the chain coffee house mould by creating an arty space with a community vibe. Reminiscent of a backpackers' cafe, it offers many ways to make new international friends. Poetry nights are held on the third and fourth Sundays of the month, and there are open mic nights every third Thursday, as well as a sprinkling of other events. The coffee menu and list of microbrewed beers is extensive. Weekend brunch is popular, and the English breakfast (eggs, bacon, baked beans, fried tomatoes and toast) is a bargain at ¥1,000. Typical cafe fare, like sandwiches, quiche, muffins, pies, and cakes, is also available. Take the main exit from the station and walk across the rotary system towards Waseda University. Turn right into the narrow street after the Yoshinoya fast food restaurant. Head up the hill, past the post office and Ben's cafe is on the right.

Benugo

Ebisu Garden Place
1-24-16 Ebisu
Shibuya-ku
🚇 *Ebisu*
Map 5 F2 **81**

03 3440 1237 | www.benugo.co.jp

This healthy lunch bar has a good selection of western food. Sandwiches include the California (filled with salmon, crab mayonnaise, avocado, and cucumber) and salmon and cheese bagels. There are also salads, paninis, burritos and croissants, along with muffins and sweeter delights for afterwards. There is a selection of fresh coffee and tea, and soymilk is available. Small round tables are clustered together, surrounded by high-backed chairs, or there is counter seating that overlooks Ebisu Garden Place.

Cafe 246

1-2-6 Minami-Aoyama
Minato-ku
🚇 *Aoyama Itchōme*
Map 11 A1 **147**

03 5771 6886 | www.246cafe-book.com

This is a classy space to enjoy great coffee and well-priced food. It has a retro charm, rich colour scheme, spacious layout, and outdoor seating. The extended opening hours and range of special events attract a mixed crowd, from office workers to fashionable locals. The menu varies through the day. On weekdays, lunches include curry, pasta, or sandwiches. At dinner, there is more hearty fare like seafood pasta, grilled chicken or nicoise salad. Wireless internet is also available.

Cafe Heavens

1-16-15 Ebisu-Nishi
Shibuya-ku
🚇 *Ebisu*
Map 5 F2 **82**

03 5428 3399 | http://cafe-heavens.com

The natural, wooden decor here is brightened by vibrant, colourful paintings on the walls. The country-style tables and chairs, some still containing natural wooden grooves, add to the homely feel. The food is Spanish influenced, ranging from small tapas to paella. Lunch sets vary and include meat, salad, pasta, or soup options – each one for less than ¥1,000. This is a good spot to linger over coffee and cake and there is a selection of Japanese treats, like mung bean and sesame pudding. There are also more indulgent items, like chocolate gateaux.

Caffe Antologia

03 3485 7865 | *caffeantologia@yagyu-shouten.com*

This cosy cafe has soft jazz playing in the background, dark wooden tables and a slightly smoky atmosphere. The collection of quality coffee marks it out from the chain venues throughout the city, and alongside the cappuccino you'll find green tea latte and Vietnamese brews. There are a selection of snacks available and the daily lunch sets cost ¥850. Tea or coffee can be included for an extra ¥150. Lunchtime paninis come with a green salad, potato mash, and a cup of warming vegetable soup. The menu is only in Japanese, but the pleasant staff are happy to translate. The well-priced drink selection includes cocktails – like mimosa and bellini – for around ¥700. It's not overly busy, and if you're struggling to find it, the police box opposite is a good marker.

Calico Cat Cafe

042 2229 8353 | *http://homepage3.nifty.com/calico*

Snuggling up with a cup of tea and a feline companion can be a heart-warming experience. But in Tokyo, where it's hard to own a pet, such encounters are not so common. Calico Cat Cafe is trying to change that, by providing a chance for people to mingle with moggies. The cafe is home to 14 cats who wander freely around, playing and dozing in the trees. Visitors can play with the cats or just relax and watch, and the experience is odour free, thanks to a number of air fresheners. A visit costs ¥800 for one hour or ¥600 for 30 minutes. At weekends and on holidays, every extra 10 minutes is an additional ¥120. Basic drinks are ¥150, and there is a three-hour weekday special for ¥2,000, including two drinks. The cafe is 30 seconds from the park exit.

Dean & Deluca

03 3284 7071 | *www.deandeluca.co.jp*

This trendy New York cafe chain has been a hit with busy Tokyoites with its gourmet treats, quality coffee, and great on-the-go lunches. Sleek marble counters house pastry, doughnut, and muffin displays and their delectable cinnamon rolls will have you coming back for more. If you're looking for something a bit more substantial you can pick up sandwiches filled with salad greens and meat slices in fresh focaccia or ciabatta breads. Lasagne, quiche and salads, as well as weekday pasta lunch sets are also available. There is a comprehensive selection of coffees, with the 'red eye' (blended coffee with a shot of espresso inside) being a good fit for this bustling city. With a number of locations in the heart of Tokyo, be prepared for the lunchtime rush here, as local office workers come looking for their caffeine fix.

Fresh coffee beans

Flamingo Cafe

03 6418 5020

With its quiet courtyard, this cafe is a lovely spot to escape the crowds. The seating is shrouded with greenery, but still lets some sun through. The lunchtime crowd can choose from Japanese, or Italian pasta options such as *omu raisu* (mixed fried rice covered with an omelette) or creamy fettuccini. Lunch sets are ¥1,000, but if you're hungry they can be upsized for an extra ¥100. The standard set includes an all-you-can-eat salad bar (including drinks). The dinner menu is affordable and includes thin-crust pizzas for around ¥1,500, creamy risottos for around ¥1,200, and a selection of fish and meat entrees. From Exit A5 of Omotesandō station, turn right after the Prada building and it's on this street.

Hikawa Bldg (B1)
2-11 Sarugakachō
Shibuya-ku
🚇 *Daikanyama*
Map 5 F2 86

Frames

03 5784 3384 | *www.frames-tokyo.info*

If you're looking for a late night feast then you can't pass by Frames in Daikanyama. Taking orders until 03:00, Frames is suited to Tokyo's hip night-time crowd. The menu includes options like New Zealand lamb chops with mustard, Indonesian nasi goreng, and raw spring rolls with shrimp and avocado served with a sweet chili dipping sauce. They have a fruity cocktail selection, with mixes averaging around ¥1,000, as well as a range of coffees and teas. The crisp white decor contributes to the stylish modern vibe and the cafe provides the perfect backdrop for a catch up with friends. Follow the road on the right of the train tracks (JR line heading from Shibuya to Ebisu). You'll pass a Sunkus and then a Lawson, Frames is to your right just before Namiki bridge. Other branches of Frames can be found in Shibuya and Naka Meguro.

1-40-10 Shimouma
Setagaya-ku
🚇 *Sangenjaya*
Map 5 D3 87

Fungo

03 3795 1144 | *www.fungo.com*

Located near the park in Setagaya, this American style cafe serves up a mix of hearty salads, sandwiches and burgers. The retro diner setting – complete with jukebox – adds fun to the dining experience. There are hot and cold sandwich menus offering Japanese flavours (such as teriyaki chicken), and western choices like bacon, lettuce and tomato. The list is comprehensive, including an option for kids. Hamburgers average around ¥1,200 to ¥1,400. Sweeter choices include New York cheesecake and fresh banana smoothies. There are three different lunchtime sets and a separate dinner menu.

6-6-1 Ginza
Chūō-ku
🚇 *Ginza*
Map 14 A3 88

Ginza Fugetsudo

03 3571 5000

It can be hard to find a place which still retains some old world charm. Places like Fugetsudo, a traditional *kissaten* (down Namiki Dōri), are becoming rare as the younger crowd head to hip coffee spots. You won't find an extensive coffee selection at this old school coffee shop and the menu, just like the decor, is distinctly 70s. A visit is like stepping back in time, and a stark contrast to the frantic chains nearby. Watch the world go by through the floor-to-ceiling windows while enjoying some traditional Japanese sweets and some refined green tea or freshly brewed coffee. This simple pleasure is relatively cheap with drink prices around ¥500.

2-28-4 Sendagaya
Shibuya-ku
🚇 *Sendagaya*
Map 8 D1 89

One's Diner

03 5772 6760 | *www.freshnessburger.co.jp*

Freshness Burger is known throughout the city but One's, part of the same corporate chain, is a much more secluded spot. A short distance from the busy streets of Harajuku, the place retains its sense of individuality. After travelling through America, the owner returned to Japan with a collection of authentic decorations and a clear idea of what a real diner should look like. The menu – like the setting – is typically American, with burgers and milkshakes a popular choice. It also does a good vegetable wrap with french fries. The prices are fair.

5-5-21 Minami Aoyama
Minato-ku
🚇 *Omotesandō*
Map 8 E3 90

Pure Cafe

03 5466 2611 | *http://pure-cafe.com*

Stylish decor, T-shirt clad waitresses, and the soft scent of essential oils from the neighbouring Aveda shop add to the modern ambience of Pure Cafe. But, it is the food that really sets it apart. Vegans will delight that in this fish-loving city there is a place where they can freely choose from the menu. Creative, seasonal ingredients are combined to make organic salads, sandwiches served on thick natural bread, and warming soups. The selection of sweet treats includes bread pudding, tofu cheesecake, baked apple with tofu cream, and other rich, yet healthy, desserts. It also sells a range of breads and foreign grocery items from couscous to rice milk. The crowd is predominately young women. Organic coffee, wine and beer are also available.

Shichimencho Cafe (Comfort Foods and Music)

5-16-1 Minami-Aoyama
Minato-ku
🚇 **Omotesandō**
Map 8 E3 **91**

03 5467 3939 | *www.try-to-fly.com*

Located next to the Blue Dog Gallery on Kotto Dōri, Shichimencho's jumbled decor provides a stark contrast to the prim Aoyama neighbourhood. Thousands of vinyl records line the cafe's wall, while a mix of comics and old musical equipment decorates the expansive window overlooking the coffee chains below. The seats are also mismatched, adding to the place's eclectic charm. The orange handwritten menu is only in Japanese and includes dishes like avocado don, tofu lasagne, and a prawn coconut green curry. The serving sizes are ample, especially when upsized for an additional ¥100. You can also add ¥200 for your choice of tea, coffee, or juice, and ¥300 for beer. Smoking is permitted and during busy times this rustic joint can become consumed by tobacco scents.

Smooch

Ebisu Garden Place
Shibuya-ku
🚇 **Ebisu**
Map 5 F2 **92**

03 5795 2727 | *www.smooch.co.jp*

Finding a fresh fruit smoothie in Tokyo can be difficult. For those on the go, Smooch's innovative creations are good low fat, high nutrient snacks. The banana, peanut butter, granola, low fat yogurt and milk smoothie is a comforting blend, while the fig, prune, and almond will do wonders for digestion. The strawberry cheesecake – a mixture of strawberries, bananas, and cream cheese with cookie crunch, low-fat yogurt and milk – appears decadent, but is 99% fat free. For an additional ¥60, vitamin booster shots can be thrown into the mix. If you want to enjoy your drink on site, the hot pink cafe in Ebisu Garden Place is a great spot for relaxing outdoors, but tables inside are limited. Some 16 different drinks are on offer and prices range from ¥460 to ¥590. Open daily from 08:00 to 21:00.

Toshi Yoroizuka

Tokyo Midtown East
9-7-2 Akasaka
Minato-ku
🚇 **Roppongi**
Map 11 B2 **93**

03 5413 3650 | *www.grand-patissier.info/ToshiYoroizuka*

Join the 'ladies who lunch' at this gourmet pastry shop and pick up a delectable treat to take home or to enjoy in the outdoor seating area. The sleek shop's sole focus is these delicate creations, and if you've got a sweet tooth it is well worth a visit. Treats include Assiette Mont-Blanc Cygne (a rich chocolate mouse with a crispy cream meringue resting on top), Monica (a crisp cake base with custard, wrapped in cream with strawberries), and Crème Brulée Pistache (lavender icecream with a pistachio sauce). Expect to pay between ¥1,000 to ¥2,000, depending on what takes your fancy.

West Park Cafe

23-11
Motoyoyogi-chō
Shibuya-ku
🚇 **Yoyogi Kōen**
Map 5 D1 **94**
🚫

03 5478 6065 | *www.maysfood.com*

A grand spot for a sunny day, this cafe has an open-air terrace overlooking a quiet residential street. The chalk blackboard and food display may conjure memories of cafes back home, and the generous portions may make you question whether you really are still in Japan. It offers sets at lunch, including hearty burgers, pastas, pizzas, sandwiches, filling salads, and herb rotisserie chicken. The dinner menu is similar but with options such as cajun-style roasted atlantic salmon added. Lunch sets are around ¥1,500 and mains at dinnertime are roughly the same price. The broad drink selection includes world beers, which are best enjoyed while catching the last rays of sun during their weekday happy hour.

4-26-5 Jingū-mae
Shibuya-ku
🚇 *Meiji Jingū-mae*
Map 8 D2 95
🚫

Yaffa Organic Cafe
03 5772 6388 | *www.yaffa.jp*
A sunny spot away from the shopping crowds below, located on the third floor of M's Building, this quaint cafe serves up plentiful portions of healthy food. The daily lunch sets average around ¥1,000 and include brown rice, sandwiches, pasta and quiche options. The lattes, served in a bowl, hit the spot with coffee lovers, and beside the organic tea selection there is a range of natural beer and wine. The permanent wooden blinds let the sunlight trickle through but, if you really want some sun, the bright wooden deck area is the best place. Funky electronic beats jazz the place up. Between 15:00 and 18:00, Yaffa offers a special menu of cake plus coffee or tea for only ¥900. Other menu options range from garlic and cheese pizza to a Japanese *natto* rice bowl.

6-1-27 Yanaka
Taito-ku
🚇 *Nishi-Nippori*
Map 12 B1 96

Yanaka Bossa
03 3823 5952 | *www.yanakabossa.jp*
Situated in a sleepy old neighbourhood, this quaint coffee house with its mismatched retro furniture and old Singer sewing machine feels a lot like grandma's house. This hidden gem attracts a mix of people, from curious tourists to creative types from the neighbouring university campuses, and the people who call this charming town home. There is a good selection of coffees from Brazil, Mexico and Ecuador, with refills at a discounted price. Light meals like quiche, curry, and toasted sandwiches are available, as well as chocolate cake and cheesecake. But the relaxed vibe is the main selling point.

Internet Cafes
From businessmen to teenage couples, people from all walks of life enjoy a visit to their local internet cafe – and often it's not just to do a bit of web surfing. With internet cafes in Japan typically being places which combine small manga (Japanese comics) libraries and computers to access the internet, a whole host of people drop in to curl up with their favourite comic, surf the net, or even snuggle up with a loved one in a private booth.

There are a number of independent cafes as well as major chains scattered throughout the city and they are easy to find in the major centres – like Shinjuku, Shibuya, and Roppongi. The larger chains are typically open 24 hours a day, seven days a week, and its not unusual for overworked businessmen who miss their last train home to make the most of the cafe's reclining chairs. With many places having a late night rate of just over ¥1,000 for about six hours, bunking here works out to be cheaper than a capsule hotel. If you visit during the day most places offer private booth seats for around ¥300 to ¥400 per hour, some also have open seats for slightly less. Drinks in many of the larger chains are free of charge and a range of soft drinks, coffee, tea and maybe even corn soup are available at the touch of a button from vending machines. This little touch varies in the smaller cafes, some offer free soft drinks and some don't. Two normal cafes who offer free internet access are Marunouchi Cafe (see table below) and Ben's Cafe (p.358).

Internet Cafes

Gran Cyber Cafe	6F, 2-28 Udagawa-chō	Shibuya-ku	03 5428 3676	www.bagus-99.com
	ROI Bldg 12F, 5-5-1 Roppongi	Minato-ku	03 5786 2280	
J-Net Cafe	7F, 34-35 Udagawa-chō	Shibuya-ku	03 5458 5935	www.cafejnet.ne.jp
Manga Manboo	1-13-11 Higashi-Ikebukuro	Toshima-ku	03 5911 4344	www.manboo.co.jp
	2-10-13 Yoyogi	Shibuya-ku	03 5304 7911	
Marunouchi Cafe	Shin Tokyo Bldg, 3-3-1 Marunouchi	Chiyoda-ku	03 3212 5025	

On The Town

Tokyo appears to cater to its every dweller, and certainly doesn't slight the drinkers. The city of 33 million has a bar or nightclub for virtually any persuasion, and whether it's great nightscapes, a thriving party scene or a pint of cold Guinness you're after, you'll find it in Tokyo.

Most bars are open six or seven days a week, from 17:00 or 18:00 until either the last train or well into the morning. Nightclubs tend to get going after midnight, which weeds out last-train-home types. Different areas of town are known for distinct traits and perhaps even a stereotypical bar patron: the hostess-chasing executives in Ginza, the foreign tourists or business people in Roppongi, tanned and wild-haired youths in Shibuya.

Special drinks deals can also be found on 'Ladies Day,' in places like the Tokyo Sports Café (see Sports Bars above) – the day differs from bar to bar so check in advance when to go.

Sports Bars

If you want to watch international sports, most of the sports bars are in Roppongi. Tokyo Sports Cafe (www.tokyo-sportscafe.com) shows major games on their multiple plasma screens and offers free pool tables. The abundance of underage females however, makes for a somewhat awkward viewing experience. The bar was actually shut down by police a few years ago – but resurfaced as 'Lime'. Around the corner Brainbuster (www.brainbuster-tokyo.com) shows MMA (mixed martial arts) events live on their eight screens. For a traditionally western experience, the most popular option is Legends Sports Bar (p.368), located at street level on Roppongi's main drag (Gaien Higashi Dōri). Fans often show up in team colours and big games, broadcasting live can draw a good crowd.

There are also a few football pubs around town, the most popular being the two branches of The Footnik (www.footnik.net) in Ebisu and Ōsaki.

Drinks

Other options **Alcohol** p.275

Sake

Alcohol could be called the lifeblood of Tokyo. Drinks are offered (and consumed) just about everywhere, from bath houses to train station platforms. Business arrangements are inked in sake. Alcohol-fuelled matchmaking parties do their part to boost Japan's flagging birth-rate. The government has announced that the drinking age will be lowered from 20 to 18 – although ID checks are rare anyway. Efforts to curb underage drinking and drink driving (p.140) have been effective, but public drunkenness is still a fact of life.

While domestic drinks like *nihonshu*, *shōchū* and beer from Japan's big four – Kirin, Asahi, Sapporo and Suntory – have always been widely available, it is increasingly easy to seek out the finest Old and New World wines (WW, p.372), imported beers (Billy Barew's, p.365) and even domestic microbrews (Popeye, p.371). Finely crafted cocktails are also becoming more common (p.365).

For a no-frills beer, cocktail or glass of wine, expect to pay around ¥700. Prices vary more by establishment than area – as seen in places like Ginza's bargain-basement Three Hundred Bar (p.371).

Bars & Pubs

Tokyo Midtown East
9-7-2 Akasaka
Minato-ku
🚇 *Roppongi*
Map 11 B2 97
🚫

A971 Garden
03 5413 3210 | *www.a971.com*
Following in the footsteps of Heartland (www.heartland.jp) at the foot of Roppongi Hills, A971 Garden arrived with the birth of nearby Tokyo Midtown in March 2007, to the delight of singles in the area. Bottles of Carlsberg are just ¥500 (a throwback to the ¥500 bottles of Heartland's eponymous beer) and fresh orange juice cocktails start at ¥700. There's a restaurant upstairs – A971 House – just in case you meet someone you want to start up a conversation with. Internet terminals and a light cafe menu make A971 a nice place to hang out during the day as well.

7-15-10 Roppongi
Minato-ku
🚇 *Roppongi*
Map 11 B2 98

Agave
03 3497 0229 | *www.agave.jp*
Where can you find 400 varieties of tequila and mescal outside of Mexico? Tucked away in the basement of the Glover Building, just steps from the main Roppongi intersection, Agave has been serving up a fantastic selection for the better part of a decade. Favourites include the Patron Perfect Margarita (¥1,800), while tequila-friendly snacks like nachos (¥1,400), chicken taquitos (¥1,200) and even cactus and smoked salmon salad (¥1,400) top the menu. This is a connoisseur's paradise so don't ask for lime and salt.

1-16-3 Kabukichō
Shinjuku-ku
🚇 *Roppongi*
Map 7 C1 99

Asia de Cushion
03 5292 5547 | *www.kitanokazoku.co.jp/cushion*
It might seem odd that the people behind prison-themed *izakaya* Lockup (www.kitanokazoku.co.jp/lockup) are also responsible for Shinjuku's relaxing retro lounge Asia de Cushion. As the name suggests, the decor at this spacious eighth-floor bar in the Shinjuku Square Building features hundreds of soft pillows to lean up against while plopped down at one of the low tables. Candles soften the atmosphere, while white curtains are used to create semi-private enclaves in which to enjoy fantastic drinks and food. Highlights include the grilled aubergine steaks (¥780 for three), as well as the Burmese palata flatbread and accompanying delicious dips (¥980). The friendliness of the staff justifies the 10% service fee.

1-1-10 Kabukichō
Shinjuku-ku
🚇 *Shinjuku*
Map 7 D1 100

Bar Plastic Model
03 5273 8441 | *www.plastic-model.net*
It can be argued that what makes an 80s bar truly great is not only the music it plays, but how well it transports its customers back to the glory days of the decade. In Japan the era is remembered for a skyrocketing economy and a little red and white Nintendo with the words 'Family Computer' on it. Located in the heart of Shinjuku's Golden Gai district (a great, but Japanese-only, guide to the area can be found at www.goldengai.net/shop), Bar Plastic Model embodies the spirit of the surrounding area by transporting revellers back to an age of innocence – while simultaneously getting them blitzed on sake bombs. Look for the blue sign.

7-13-13 Minami-Aoyama
Minato-ku
🚇 *Omotesandō*
Map 8 F4 101

Bar Rage
03 5467 3977 | *www.mixologist.co.jp/bar_rage*
Bar Rage was the first of a recent slew of bars that offer drinks under the banner of 'mixology,' crafted only with all-natural ingredients and top-shelf spirits. But while the fresh fruit cocktails are great – if pricey, starting around ¥1,600 a pop – that's not the only reason to visit this little-known bar. It's hidden on the third floor of the unmarked Aoyama Jin & IT Building within the triangular no man's land between Shibuya, Nishi-

Azabu and Hirō. The bartender attributes the lack of a sign outside to not being able to afford it – but plush decor tells a different story. Upon entering, you can either go left to the wooden rooftop terrace, or right, along the bar, where nine leather armchairs replace the standard stools. Further along are three private rooms, each with a different theme but still lavishly appointed. The food is top-notch, as is the service, making Bar Rage one of Tokyo's best-kept secrets. All it needs now is customers.

Belgo

3-18-7 Shibuya
Shibuya-ku
🚇 *Shibuya*
Map 8 C4 **102**

03 3409 4442 | *www.eurobeer.net/belgo*

Some pubs are good for socialising, while others are known for their selection of good brews. One of four sister bars in Tokyo specialising in Belgian beers, Belgo is more the latter. Located on Meiji Dōri, across from Shibuya Police Station in the Shibuya Ichigokan building, the venue is dungeon-like, fitted with dark wooden furniture and devoid of any dart boards or billiards tables that might distract from the beer-consuming experience. The clientele is mostly men in their 30s to 50s – any older and the steep staircase leading to the tiny loft might prove too hazardous. So what makes this place such a treat? The answer is the whopping 120 varieties of Belgian beer on display in the eerily glowing refrigerators by the bar. While the Hoegaarden and monk-brewed Chimay White on tap might be tempting – by all means, have a few – just don't be afraid to seek recommendations from the knowledgeable staff.

Billy Barew's Beer Bar

1-6-3 Shibuya
Shibuya-ku
🚇 *Shibuya*
Map 8 C3 **103**

03 5778 2808 | *www.bbj.ne.jp/bbbb*

There are five branches of this beer-lovers' paradise scattered around the Yamanote line, and all have English-language menus of more beer than you could drink in a week, categorised by country. The one with the most seating and largest selection is in Shibuya, just a five-minute trek from the station, toward the United Nations University – an appropriate location for a world beer bar. Live music nights and English-speaking staff make this branch quite approachable. If it's a livelier crowd you fancy, check out the Ebisu and Shinjuku outlets, which are open daily from 18:00 until late. One point to note, though, is that while the menu may be broad, the stock is rarely deep. Attempts to order a round of one brew or another may well prove a challenge.

The Cluriaune

1-14-3 Kabukichō
Shinjuku-ku
🚇 *Shinjuku*
Map 7 C1 **104**

03 5287 2908 | *www.0352872908.com*

Two attributes of The Cluriaune make it stand out among the city's dozens of Irish pubs. The first is that the tiny bar (located on the fifth floor of the grungy Dai 103 Tokyo Building in the heart of Shinjuku's Kabukichō district, is open 12 hours a day (17:00 to 05:00) every day of the year. The second is the imperial gallon-sized beer glass that sits on the counter, calling out your name. For just ¥6,400, the genial bartender will fill this majestic mug with smooth, black Guinness – and perhaps even take a Polaroid to record the misadventure on which you are about to embark.

Cocktail Bars

Mixology, the art of skilfully creating cocktails, has arrived in Tokyo on the back of the healthy eating trend. A good example is the lineup of vegetable-based cocktails at Japanese restaurant Daichi (p.342). For fruit-based creations, try the two branches of Bar Rage (p.364), where patrons order by selecting from the day's fresh fruit – which adds a nice citrus aroma to the bar. If you're in the Ginza area, stop by the historic Old Imperial Bar within the Imperial Hotel (p.27), it was designed by Frank Lloyd Wright and you should order its signature drink, the Mount Fuji. For quantity over quality, you can't go wrong with the cocktail selection – which is 50% off before 19:00 – at the 30 plus branches of Hub (p.367).

Coins Bar

Noah Shibuya Bldg ◀
36-1 Udagawa-chō
Shibuya-ku
🚇 *Shibuya*
Map 8 B3 **105**
€

03 3463 3039 | *http://gourmet.suntory.co.jp/shop/0334633039*

The vast majority of food and drinks at Coins Bar, (in the Noah Shibuya Building across from Tokyu Hands), costs just ¥315, making it a good place to fuel up before a big night of clubbing in the neighbouring Dōgenzaka 'love hotel' district. The basement bar attracts a mixed crowd of foreigners and Japanese, making it a productive place to socialise. Lots of fried options are counter-balanced by healthy fare like *edamame* and veggie sticks with assorted miso dipping sauces – and despite the prices, most of the dishes aren't half bad. It's a good idea to call ahead, as Coins Bar is often closed for private parties. But with a DJ booth and deals like seven food dishes and bottomless drinks for ¥2,500 a head, it's a wonder the place isn't fully booked nightly.

Cool Train

7-7-4 Roppongi ◀
Minato-ku
🚇 *Roppongi*
Map 11 B2 **106**

03 3401 5077 | *www.cooltrain.jp*

Art gallery by day and live music bar by night, Cool Train is one of the city's undiscovered gems – regardless of whether or not you're a jazz fan. It is in the basement of the Harrington Garden building on a quiet backstreet near 7-Eleven, within the Art Triangle Roppongi (p.87), a term coined to link the Mori Art Museum, the Suntory Museum of Art and The National Art Centre, Tokyo. Sisters Eriko and Minako manage both the art in the daytime and book bands for the evenings, while the masterful bartender creates stiff drinks. The kitchen, despite its size, turns out truly sublime dishes like grilled veggies dressed with a basil puree. Most food and drink items are affordably priced at around ¥1,000, which makes the music charge (¥1,000 Tuesday to Wednesday; ¥2,000 Thursday to Sunday) much more reasonable. Impress a date before the word gets out.

Costa Rica

2-23-4 Jingū-mae ◀
Shibuya-ku
🚇 *Meiji Jingū-mae*
Map 7 D4 **107**
€

Costa Rica is hard to pass by without stopping in for a drink. The easy going proprietor, Motoki-san, welcomes one and all into his funky street-corner bar with standing room for perhaps five people. Foreigners and Japanese alike frequent this neighbourhood dive bar (opposite Yamazaki), and it's not unusual to see crowds gathered around the entrance every night of the week. Drinks are ¥500, except on Thursdays, when they are even cheaper for women. Costa Rica is also a gateway to another bar, hidden in the back of the dilapidated yet charming building. Bonobo attracts an equally diverse crowd, who come to chill out on the couches while local DJs man the decks. For an even more relaxing experience, take your drinks upstairs and relax on *tatami* mats while dreaming of Tokyo 40 or 50 years ago.

Enoki

Nonbei Yokochō ◀
1-25-9 Shibuya
Shibuya-ku
🚇 *Shibuya*
Map 8 C3 **108**
€

03 3407 5320 | *www.enoki.cc*

Nonbei Yokocho is a sight to behold. This street of unbelievably tiny bars near Shibuya station was built immediately after the second world war, and hasn't changed much since. Enoki is one of these establishments (north of Shibuya station, between the Yamanote line tracks and Meiji Dōri), and is run by Chizuru Doi (many of her roughly 4,000 customers just call her Mama). The bar accommodates only eight people, which makes friendliness a necessity. Most of the bars in this 'Drunk's Alley' will let you in only with a referral; if you arrive unannounced, don't be surprised at a less-than-warm welcome (or a less-than-fair bill). Doi, however, issues an open invitation to all comers on her website, which she updates regularly with photos of her faithful patrons. The bar's name, a type of mushroom, hints at the proprietor's emphasis on healthy foods, which she serves up arbitrarily throughout the night. There is no menu, per se. Just trust yourself in the able hands of a true master of her trade. Saturday night is the least busy, but the seats still fill up fast.

7-9-3 Roppongi
Minato-ku
🚇 **Roppongi**
Map 11 B2 **109**

Fiesta

03 5410 3008 | *www.fiesta-roppongi.com*

If you're prone to stage fright, Japan's many karaoke complexes offer respite in the form of private rooms in which to sing, drink and dance the night away. But if you're more into the western concept – that is, belting out tunes in a room full of strangers – there are a few places in Tokyo vying for your yen. Fiesta in Roppongi joins Smash Hits (www.smashhits.jp) in Hirō as the two most popular options for English speakers. Fiesta holds up to 40, and rather than the pay-by-the-hour system favoured by Japanese karaoke bars, it charges a flat ¥3,150 (¥2,000 for ladies on Thursday) for three drinks and unlimited songs. Additional drinks are available for ¥800 to ¥1,000, while bottles of wine and champagne start at ¥5,000. Only songs in English are allowed from Thursday to Saturday, and the selection is impressive: over 10,000 tunes, updated monthly. If it doesn't have the particular anthem your act relies on, make a request and the management promises to try to get it by your next visit.

Iwata Bldg (B1)
1-33-4 Nishi-
Ikebukuro
Toshima-ku
🚇 **Ikebukuro**
Map 3 F1 **110**

Hub

03 3989 8682 | *www.pub-hub.com*

The Hub is a Tokyo institution, with the city's best-known happy hour (half-price drinks before 19:00). The kitschy chain of English pubs boasts more than 30 locations in Greater Tokyo. The Ikebukuro Nishiguchi branch is one of four within a short walking distance of the station, and stands out from the pack, with a crew of top-notch cocktail-makers behind the bar. There is a cash on delivery system: order, pay, drink… repeat. If you consider Hub's spicy fried potatoes (¥380) and a one-litre beer tower (¥1,350) among the finest meals money can buy, chances are you'll become a regular. Check the website for the locations of the other branches.

Ikushin Bldg
26-5 Udagawa-chō
Shibuya-ku
🚇 **Shibuya**
Map 8 B3 **111**

Insomnia Lounge

03 3476 2735 | *http://r.gnavi.co.jp/g069807*

Shibuya's Insomnia Lounge is officially the best second-date spot in town. Its late opening hours make it easy to gab the night away, getting all those burning questions off your chest before the trains start running again in the morning. The crimson walls and flashy decor (think lots of mirrors) are sufficiently romantic for a follow-up encounter – but the vibe might be over the top for a first meeting. To confidently bring someone here right off the bat, you'd have to be able to suggest that the candles and wall-to-wall red carpeting are simply design elements, rather than a subtle (or not so subtle) way of announcing 'I'm game if you are'.

Hinode Pier
2-7-104 Kaigan
Minato-ku
🚇 **Hamamatsuchō**
Map 15 A3 **112**

Jicoo

0120 049 490 | *www.jicoofloatingbar.com*

There are a few 'booze cruise' options in town, but none nearly as classy as Jicoo. The exterior of the futuristic-looking boat was designed by manga artist Leiji Matsumoto to resemble a tear drop, with lots of teal windows dotting the long, curvy, silver frame. The vessel looks like it could dive at any moment. Stepping inside, you'd be forgiven for mistaking the cabin for a disco club. The glass dancefloor continually changes from red, to blue, to green – and silver poles, funky white chairs and a piano complete the decor. The views of Odaiba to the east and the Tokyo skyline to the west are fantastic from any seat in the house. Jicoo isn't a particularly cheap night out, given the ¥2,500 entry fee and cocktails that start at ¥1,000; but it's a great way to impress a client or a date. Jicoo picks up passengers on the hour from Hinode Pier (near Hinode station on the Yurikamome line, or Hamamatsuchō on the Yamanote line). If you're throwing a party, contact the staff about hiring out Jicoo or the company's smaller, open-air boat, for gatherings of up to 130 people.

367

E Space Tower (15F)
3-6 Maruyamachō
Shibuya-ku
🚇 *Shibuya*
Map 8 B4 `113`

Legato

03 5784 2121 | *www.legato-tokyo.jp*

Named best overall restaurant in town by Tokyo lifestyle magazine *Metropolis* in 2007, Legato is also known for its classy lounge, offering fantastic views from its 15th floor perch. It is clear that at least as much consideration went into the wine list as the menu of fusion cuisine. Keep this in mind when you browse through the selection of mostly Old World bottles, every one of which is priced to sell at ¥4,000. There are two seating areas: the stylish almond-shaped island bar, and tables closer to the floor-to-ceiling windows. At night the venue comes alive, with lights cast down from the star-shaped fixtures. If Insomnia Lounge (p.367) down the road is the best second-date spot in town, this is one of the best for making that crucial first impression.

Aoba Roppongi Bldg
3-16-33 Roppongi
Minato-ku
🚇 *Roppongi*
Map 11 C3 `114`

Legends Sports Bar

03 3589 3304 | *www.legendsports.jp*

Feeling homesick? Miss watching your team on the TV? You'll find strength in numbers at this Roppongi institution. In summers, the mostly foreign crowd gathers outside on the spacious patio; in colder months, the action shifts inside, where sporting equipment bedecks the walls and the multiple TVs show the best in football, basketball, baseball and ice hockey, beamed in from around the world. For another taste of home, experience the Legends Burger (¥1,600), piled gloriously high with cheese, bacon, tomato, avocado, lettuce, onion and a fried egg – or take the healthier route with a plate of hummus and pita (¥1,000). On weekdays from 17:00 to 19:00, Legends and sister pub Hobgoblin (www.hobgoblin.jp) next door offer a popular buy-one-get-one-free drink deal. Check the English website for the broadcast schedule, and call or email before you go, just to double check you'll be wearing the right colours.

7-14-4 Roppongi
Minato-ku
🚇 *Roppongi*
Map 11 B2 `115`
🆒

Lovenet

03 5771 5511 | *www.lovenet-jp.com*

With the popularity of karaoke diminishing since its peak in the 90s, the industry was faced with a choice: adapt or perish (well, maybe not perish, but the need for a change in direction was clear). Lovenet is the flagship of a new breed of luxurious karaoke joints that have cropped up in recent years. It is located just steps from Roppongi crossing, occupying the third and fourth floors within the Hotel Ibis. The 33 rooms feature themes and statement designs; the most popular are the cosy, earthy Morocco Suite (¥4,000 per hour) and the Aqua Suite (¥25,000 per hour), which comes equipped with a hot tub.

Line House (2F)
1-3-13 Kamimeguro
Meguro-ku
🚇 *Naka-Meguro*
Map 5 E2 `116`

Nakame Takkyu Lounge

03 5722 2860 | *www.mfs11.com*

Residents will be the first to admit that navigating Tokyo is a feat best attempted with as many aids as possible. The king of all these, of course, is the GPS-guided map. So when even a navigation system can't find a bar, you know someone doesn't want you to find it. Such is the case, it would seem, with Nakame Takkyu (*takkyu* is Japanese for ping-pong) Lounge, which is so well hidden that even many of its neighbours have no idea such an excellent bar exists in their midst. Use a printed map to get close, and look for an alley to the left of a parking garage. Follow it to the end, walk up the flight of stairs, and ring the buzzer. With any luck you'll be let in to enjoy the glory of this spacious, carpeted establishment with a well-stocked bar, genial staff – and a ping-pong table as the piece de resistance. A second branch is tucked into an unmarked apartment in Omotesandō, 201 From Five, 3-17-1 Minami-Aoyama (03 3401 7979).

Nighttime hotspots

3-7-1-2 Nishi-
Shinjuku
Shinjuku-ku
🚇 *Shinjuku*
Map 7 A2 **117**
€€€ 🍸

New York Bar

03 5323 3458 | *http://tokyo.park.hyatt.com*

The people at New York Bar on the 52nd floor of Shinjuku's Park Hyatt are well aware that many of the foreigners who visit their bar are there for one reason: to see a movie set. The long bar at the back was where Bill Murray pulled off one of the biggest mismatches of all time when he chatted up Scarlet Johansson in *Lost in Translation*. Mismatched would describe what most people feel as they the step out of the lift and are greeted with a 'how may we help you?' from three black-suited staff. If you don't feel a little out of place then, wait until you see the bill. For two standard cocktails in the evening expect a five-figure bill. But it's fun to pretend you're just in Tokyo to nonchalantly film a whiskey commercial and do the media circuit (for which you'll be paid a cool two million). For those on a budget, stop by any day except Sunday around 19:00 – you'll be able to see the nightscape but avoid the ¥2,000 per person seating charge, which kicks in at 20:00. The attached New York Grill (p.331) offers fine dining with the same exhilarating views.

6-10-3 Roppongi
Minato-ku
🚇 *Roppongi*
Map 11 B3 **118**

The Oak Door Bar

03 4333 8784 | *http://tokyo.grand.hyatt.com*

Want to do business over a stiff drink? The Oak Door Bar within the labyrinthine Grand Hyatt Tokyo is the place to do it. The mostly English-speaking crowd is an interesting mix of moneyed hotel guests, well-dressed singles and business people from the investment banks housed in the attached Roppongi Hills complex. Still, there's no cover charge and a Bombay Sapphire gin and tonic will cost you ¥1,200 – only slightly more than you'd pay at most other bars in the area. If hunger sets in, ask for a menu from the attached restaurant or China Room lounge. Both offer delicious haute cuisine, which tastes even better when someone else is paying.

1-8-1 Yūrakuchō
Chiyoda-ku
🚇 *Hibiya*
Map 14 A2 **119**
€€€

Peter

03 6270 2763 | *http://tokyo.peninsula.com*

A seat at the bar of French restaurant Peter, perched atop the five-star Peninsula Tokyo Hotel overlooking the grounds of the Imperial Palace, could well be the most sought-after location in town. A dedicated lift takes would-be diners and drinkers straight from the opulent lobby to the 24th floor – at which point it's not uncommon to hear a few gasps of delight. Designers spared no expense when 'planting' rows of chrome trees, which beautifully reflect the ambient purple mood lighting. A bar this smooth calls for a martini, which will set you back ¥1,600. It's not cheap, but thankfully there's no seating charge.

The Oak Door Bar

Peter

2-18-7 Ryōgoku
Sumida-ku
🚇 **Ryōgoku**
Map 4 E3 **120**

Popeye

03 3633 2120 | *www.40beersontap.com*

Tatsuo Aoki is something of a godsend for Tokyo's beer lovers. When deregulation in the mid 90s paved the way for micro-breweries to start churning out beer, Aoki opened a bar and started serving them to curious Tokyoites. Today, his joint near the sumo stadium in sleepy Ryōgoku (near the Hotel Belle Grande) has over three dozen domestic craft beers on tap – a fact he trumpets in the name of his website. Offering everything from stouts to pilsners to pale ales, Popeye's menu is unrivalled. The bar snacks aren't bad either.

6-28-10 Okusawa
Setagaya-ku
🚇 **Jiyūgaoka**
Map 2 A3

Saraba

03 3703 7323 | *www.saraba.jp*

When the management changed at Jiyūgaoka Irish pub O'Carolan's (www.o-carolan. co.jp) many regulars went looking for a new watering hole in the area. They found it in Saraba, a combined bar and art gallery run by a Senegalese man and his Japanese wife in a converted house. Upstairs, the minimalist space exhibits works by local artists, who are often friends of the owners. Downstairs, a mix of Japanese, Senegalese and other nationalities gather to enjoy the cool African vibe. Menu items include specialities like *yass* lime-mustard chicken (¥1,000) and *fataya* fried fish pies (¥600). In addition to expat standards Corona and Guinness, Saraba also carries a Kenyan beer called Tusker, and the wine list includes selections from South Africa and Tunisia. Though the Jiyūgaoka suburb is only 15 minutes from Shibuya by train, its prices are noticeably lower and its people noticeably more laid back, making it a worthwhile trip. It's the house with the red facade along the Oimachi line tracks.

Fazenda Bldg (B1)
5-9-11 Ginza
Chūō-ku
🚇 **Ginza**
Map 14 B3 **121**

Three Hundred Bar

03 3572 6300 | *www.300bar.com*

In business since 1992, the original branch of Three Hundred Bar has long attracted foreign and Japanese visitors alike with its extensive menu of drinks, cocktails and surprisingly good food – with nothing priced at over ¥300 (¥315 with tax), as the name implies. A second branch opened a few blocks away (8-3-12 Ginza, 03 3571 8300) in 2005 to accommodate the growing number of patrons. This newer space has also attracted its own faithful regulars, who come for the free DJ sets on Friday and Saturday nights. Pick up a book of tickets and use them at either Three Hundred Bar location.

4-1 Kioichō
Chiyoda-ku
🚇 **Nagatachō**
Map 10 C3 **122**

Trader Vic's

03 3265 4707 | *www.newotani.co.jp*

Hidden away in Akasaka's New Otani Hotel since 1974, Tokyo's branch of the worldwide Trader Vic's chain only gets better with age. For those who aren't familiar with the story of the establishment's founder, here's a brief recap: the proprietor at the original bar in California, Victor Bergeron would allow customers to barter personal effects to pay their tab, hence the moniker. While few could afford to get drunk on the stellar cocktails on offer here (bartering or not) the decor alone warrants a visit. The popular Sunday brunch buffet (¥6,600 adults, ¥3,300 children) features many of the menu's highlights, as well as free-flowing sparkling wine. Note the dress code prohibits jeans, T-shirts or sports shoes.

2-1 Higashi-Shinagawa
Shinagawa-ku
🚇 **Shinagawa**
Map 6 B4 **123**

TY Harbor Brewery

03 5479 1666 | *www.tyharborbrewing.co.jp*

TY Harbor Brewery is operated by TY Express, the company behind two well-regarded eateries popular among Tokyo's foreign community: Cicada (p.350) in Hirō and Aoyama's Beacon (p.354). The waterfront restaurant and microbrewery is especially pleasant in the summer, when the wooden terrace is expanded to accommodate up to 130 people. Customers more often than not tend to be well-dressed business people – but the casual beer-guzzler shouldn't let that keep them from enjoying the five craft brews on offer. Start with the ¥980 tasting set, then pick a favourite and choose from five serving sizes, ranging from a 250ml glass (¥480) to a half-gallon pitcher (¥3,000). To get there, either hop in a taxi from Shinagawa station, or take either the Tokyo Monorail or Rinkai line to Tennozu Isle, and then it's a five-minute walk.

Urban Bldg (1F)
3-14-4 Taishido
Setagaya-ku
🚇 *Sangenjaya*
Map 5 C2 **124**
€

Voco
03 5779 6023 | *www.voco.co.jp*
Let King Kong point the way to this popular if little-known Sangenjaya pizza, beer and DJ bar. The iconic reminder of a bygone era hangs off the roof of a three-storey building along the laid-back Chazawa Dōri, which merges into Route 246 near the metro station. Voco is a street-level bar built around a brick oven along Chazawa Dōri, just before the giant King Kong. The space in front of the U-shaped bar is narrow, but makes for easy access to the drinks and food. A great vibe, turntables for hire, and party plans starting at just ¥2,500 a head also make Voco one of the best spots in town to throw a party.

1-5-1 Marunouchi
Chiyoda-ku
🚇 *Tokyo*
Map 14 B1 **125**

W.W
03 5288 7829 | *www.pjgroup.jp/ww*
Stretching from Tokyo Station to the west and the Imperial Palace to the east, the Marunouchi area has undergone a stunning renovation in recent years. Reopened in 2007, the Shin-Marunouchi Building (Shin-Maru Biru for short) offers some of the classiest shopping and dining destinations in Tokyo. Drinks connoisseur hangout W.W is located on the sixth floor of this sparkling skyscraper. Despite the elegant surroundings, the drinks menu remains surprisingly affordable. On weekdays from 14:30 to 18:30, glasses of beer and wine are just ¥500 – with free house-spiced nuts. At other times, choose from the menu of bottles organised by country. France is by far the most well represented, with over 100 options, but Italian (36), Australian (32) and American (30) wineries have a decent presence. There are even half a dozen Japanese wines on offer. Proceed with caution. The smiling, smartly dressed staff know their vino (so you don't have to). Ditch the stools at the semi-circular bar and instead grab a seat on the couch in the attached lounge. The views of the red-brick Tokyo Station and Ginza further along are the same, but you'll enjoy your drinks in more relaxed seating.

4-9-23 Ayase
Adachi-ku
🚇 *Ayase*
Map 2 B2
€

Wongwenyai
03 3620 2581
For a country with a pacifist constitution, Japan loves its fighting sports. Even more than the traditional Japanese martial arts, it seems to be the imported styles that spark the greatest interest. Muay Thai kickboxing is one of the most popular of these foreign sports, and Wongwenyai (or Ōenjai in Japanese) is the place to see it on Saturday nights. Competitors fight in a ring that takes up half of the restaurant's dining room. Saturday night is the time to see the boys in action, while gorging on authentic Thai food and washing it down with bottles of Singha Beer. Located in far-flung Adachi Ward, this ramshackle establishment offers Tokyoites a little taste of south east Asia. Reservations should be made at least a week in advance – if you show up without a booking and there are no empty seats, you may find yourself a little closer to the action in the ring than you'd like. Note, the ¥2,000 seating charge on fight nights. The bar is next to the pharmacy, one minute from the west exit of the station.

Gay & Lesbian

Other options Gay & Lesbian p.373

Japan has an interesting take on homosexuality. While the numbers of gay men and women who are open about their sexual orientation are still small, popular culture is full of not-so-subtle references. In *kabuki* productions, men play both male and female roles, while at the hugely popular *takarazuka* shows, women dressed as male characters attract legions of female fans. Then there's the long-running transvestite cabaret at Roppongi's Kingyo (p.374).

In 2005, television audiences couldn't get enough of actor Masaki Sumitani, better known by his stage name Hard Gay, whose trademark act involved donning a black leather Village People costume and humping things. While some would argue this widespread infatuation with Hard Gay signals the readiness of the public to accept homosexual activity, some gay organisations decried the behaviour, noting that his overt sexuality was clearly just a mockery. Indeed, his popularity faded when he was spotted on a date with a woman. Ask any Tokyo resident where to find a gay-friendly bar or party, and undoubtedly you'll be directed to Shinjuku's Nichōme district. The relatively tiny neighbourhood is said to be home to over 200 gay bars, and this number may not be an exaggeration. Virtually every building is stacked from top to bottom with businesses catering to the GLBT community. Many of the bars are men only and a minority are women only, but many popular establishments are open to all comers, regardless of gender or sexual orientation.

Barely beneath the surface, the gay and lesbian clubbing scene is thriving. Some of the city's biggest and most popular nightclubs regularly host events marketed to the gay and lesbian community under the 'Gay Mix' or 'All Human Mix' banners. The

The city at sundown

most popular of these parties are The Ring at the Warehouse in Azabu-Jūban (p.377), Glamorous at Shibuya's Rock West (www.rockwest.jp) and Shangri-La at far-flung super club Ageha (p.375). Gold Finger (www.goldfingerparty.com) is one of the most popular all-girl parties.

Nichōme's clubs also see a steady stream of gay and lesbian clientele every night of the week. Promoter Tokyo Gay Night (www.tokyogaynight. net) throws occasional blow-outs at Shinjuku's cavernous Club Code (p.376) that attract upwards of 2,000 (mostly Japanese) men.

Generally, 'competing' event organisers and DJs within the gay scene tend to help each other out with mentions and links on their websites. A good place to start investigating what's going on is Ageha's Shangri-La page (www.ageha.com/gn/ja/ links). Also check out the clubbing listings in the weekly magazine *Metropolis* (www.metropolis.co.jp). Finally, two annual events bring homosexuality into the public eye. The Tokyo International Lesbian and Gay Film Festival (www.tokyo-lgff.org) in July showcases works by local auteurs, while the Tokyo Pride Parade (http://parade.tokyo-pride. org/6th/english) draws thousands of participants and spectators and culminates in a celebration in Yoyogi Kōen near Harajuku station.

2-18-1 Shinjuku
Shinjuku-ku
🚇 *Shinjuku*
Sanchōme
Map 7 D1 127
€

Advocates Cafe

03 3358 8638 | *www.advocates-cafe.com*

Advocates Cafe beckons one and all with its location on a street corner in the heart of Nichōme. Those who come early can take advantage of the unbeatable drinks deal to kick off the night: three hours of bottomless Suntory beer for ¥1,000, every day from 18:00 to 21:00. The staff are friendly and the customers are a mix of foreigners and Japanese. Once you've mingled and drunk your fill, continue on to one of the many dance clubs in the area like Arty Farty and GB (below), Dragon (2-14-4 Shinjuku, 03 3341 0606) or even the associated Advocates Bar around the corner.

2-11-6 Shinjuku
Shinjuku-ku
🚇 *Shinjuku*
Sanchōme
Map 7 D2 128

Arty Farty

03 3356 5388 | *www.arty-farty.net*

Voted 'Best Gay Bar' by Tokyo lifestyle magazine *Metropolis*, Arty Farty continues to draw in crowds of all sexual persuasions. Really the only differences from a 'straight' club are the free condoms on the bar, and the white Cupid suspended from the ceiling, aiming his bow at the dance floor—oh, and maybe the shirtless foreign guy in the corner. The lack of a cover charge makes Arty Farty and its sister establishment, The Annex, among the most popular for foreigners checking out the Nichōme district.

Shinjuku Plaza Bldg
2-12-3 Shinjuku
Shinjuku-ku
🚇 *Shinjuku*
Sanchōme
Map 7 D2 129

GB

03 3352 8972 | *www.techtrans-japan.com/GB*

The long-running GB is a large basement-level club that attracts men (and men only, except for at Halloween) from around the world. There is no cover charge, with beer and cocktails around ¥700 a pop, making this one of the cheapest nights out in Tokyo. The venue is quite spacious, but fills up on Fridays and Saturdays. GB is occasionally closed on Mondays, so be sure to call ahead if you're planning to start the week here.

3-14-17 Roppongi
Minato-ku
🚇 *Roppongi*
Map 11 C2 130

Kingyo

03 3478 3000 | *www.kingyo.co.jp*

Kingyo's transsexual cabaret is a must-see in Tokyo, and packs in a diverse crowd of both GLBT and straight individuals, and even the occasional bachelorette party. The 50 minute revue combines traditional Japanese aesthetics with poignant political commentary, for one of the most interesting regular stage events around. Even the stage itself is a sight to behold, as it constantly changes shape thanks to a backstage technician. Reservations can be made on the website for the two nightly shows starting at 19:30 and 22:00 (with a third show from 01:30 on Fridays and Saturdays). Following the performance, the dancers come to mingle with the audience in typical Tokyo 'hostess' fashion. For couples, the ¥20,000 'First Class Course' includes two of the best seats in the house for the second show, as well as a fresh fruit plate and a full bottle of Moët & Chandon. A three-minute video trailer is available to download from the website.

2-15-10 Shinjuku
Shinjuku-ku
🚇 *Shinjuku*
Sanchōme
Map 7 D1 131

Kinswomyn

03 3354 8720

Kinswomyn is the most famous women-only bar in Tokyo. It's situated on the third floor of an apartment building (Dai-ichi Tenko Building) that has seen better days, but don't let that put you off. The best way to guarantee a warm reception at this cosy, one-room venue is to arrive with someone who has already been and can show you around. But fear not, if you're new in town, this is a great place to meet (and practise your Japanese on) fellow lesbian ladies. At weekends the bar can get a little boisterous – consider yourself warned!

Nightclubs

The recession hasn't had much of an impact on the quality of clubbing opportunities in Tokyo. The biggest names in house, trance, techno and hip-hop still stop by on a regular basis. Local legends like DJ Krush, Mike McKenna and Ken Ishii also continue to do the rounds, to the delight of area punters. In addition to dance clubs, Tokyo also has a selection of live jazz joints. The stars play at Aoyama's Blue Note Tokyo (p.380), Marunouchi's Cotton Club (www.cottonclubjapan.co.jp) or Roppongi's Billboard Live (www.billboard-live.com), but fine sets can also be heard at smaller venues like Cool Train (p.366) and Birdland (3-10-3 Roppongi, 03 3478 3456). To find schedules and information, Japanese language websites like Cyber Japan (www.cyberjapan.tv) or Clubberia (www.clubberia.com) are very switched on. For English speakers, *Metropolis* (www.metropolis.co.jp) publishes a bi-weekly clubbing column and also compiles an upcoming schedule of concerts, parties and DJ sets.

Drinking & Driving

The Metropolitan Police Department has begun a campaign to crack down on drink driving, following harsher laws implemented in September 2007 increasing maximum fines and jail terms for driving under the influence – sometimes by a factor of three. There are three categories of inebriation used to mete out punishment: tipsy, faded and wasted (for lack of an official translation). 'Tipsy' is anyone who registers between 0.15 and 0.25mg per litre of breath, 'faded' would be anyone over 0.25mg. It is up to the discretion of the police officer to determine who is legally 'wasted'. The officer may utilise a sobriety test to determine this and could take into consideration body weight and age.
Keep in mind that punishment isn't solely for the driver. The establishment that provided the alcohol and even the passenger(s) could be liable, whether they're drunk or not. A recent news item reported that dozens of passengers on a bus were fined ¥300,000 each for 'allowing' their bus driver to drive under the influence. See the MPD website (www.keishicho.metro.tokyo.jp) or call 03 3581 4321 for more information.

2-2-10 Shin-Kiba
Koto-ku
🚇 *Shin-Kiba*
Map 6 F2 **132**
🔣 🚫

Ageha

03 5534 2525 | www.ageha.com

Despite its location on one of the man-made islands in Tokyo Bay, clubbers flock to Ageha (aka Studio Coast) for its massive parties headlined by top house and techno DJs like Junior Vasquez, Armand Van Helden and Paul Van Dyk. To get there, take the Yūrakuchō metro line to Shin-Kiba, or catch a ride on the free shuttle bus from Shibuya. The bus stops on Roppongi Dōri across from Shibuya Police Station, under the pedestrian overpass. The website has a schedule. In summertime, a popular pastime is jumping into the pool on the outdoor deck, which boasts a DJ booth and its own bar, and is a great place to watch the sunrise before the long trek home. Entry ranges from ¥3,500 to ¥5,500, and don't forget your photo ID.

2-11 Sarugakuchō
Shibuya-ku
🚇 *Daikanyama*
Map 5 E2 **133**

Air

03 5784 3386 | www.air-tokyo.com

Tucked away in a quiet residential part of trendy Daikanyama, Air is located in the Hikawa Building below Frames (p.360), a cafe that's open until 04:00. Even though it was featured in Sophia Coppola's *Lost in Translation*, its reputation as one of the city's best clubs is due more to the high-profile product and media release parties it hosts and the big-name house, techno and drum 'n' bass DJs who stop by on a regular basis. As with most similar establishments, Air normally doesn't start filling up until after midnight. To get there from Shibuya station, take the east exit, turn left, cross the pedestrian overpass, and walk alongside the Yamanote line toward Ebisu for about 15 minutes. You'll know you're getting close when the club's staff start telling you to keep it down.

1-19-2 Kabukichō
Shinjuku-ku
🚇 *Shinjuku*
Map 7 C1 **134**

Code

03 3209 0702 | *www.clubcomplexcode.com*

Code is perhaps the largest of central Tokyo's clubs, with room for 2,000 people. Located on the fourth floor in Shinjuku Tōhō Hall, above a movie theatre in the Kabukichō district, the space is divided into three areas, all cleverly named. Barcode and Decode are smaller lounges (and are available for private parties), that are attached to the main Encode dancefloor, where a steady stream of house, trance and Euro beat keeps punters moving. Code throws a weekly Morning Party on Sundays from 06:00 to early afternoon in homage to Japan's anitquated 'morality laws' that prohibited dancing between midnight and sunrise. The cavernous club also occasionally hosts huge men-only parties that beckon gay revellers out of the nearby Nichōme neighbourhood.

3-8-40 Minami-
Aoyama
Minato-ku
🚇 *Omotesandō*
Map 8 E2 **135**

Le Baron de Paris

03 3408 3665 | *www.lebaron.jp*

Not to be confused with Nishi-Azabu's The Baron (www.thebaron.jp), Le Baron de Paris is the Tokyo branch of the French nightclub. As one of the only clubs in Aoyama (in the Aoyama Center), Le Baron tends to attract many of the area's fashion industry. Although it's not necessary, the queue behind the velvet rope adds an air of exclusivity to the proceedings. Once inside, order a bottle of Belvedere (¥8,000) and party like a rock star to a soundtrack of thumping house and electro.

7-13-7 Roppongi
Minato-ku
🚇 *Roppongi*
Map 11 B2 **136**
🚇

Midas Cafe

03 5785 3262 | *www.midascafe.com*

Following the closure of giant Roppongi clubs Velfarre and Vanila, the venues within the Grace Building (www.grace-roppongi.com) have enjoyed a boom in business. Entry to Midas Cafe (normally between ¥2,000 and ¥4,000) on the second floor includes entry to Feria in the basement and Crystal Lounge upstairs. While not known for its sound system, decor or even music selection (which is mostly Top 40 hip-hop and R&B), Midas is popular for all-you-can-drink events like the Christmas-themed 'Pimps and Ho-Ho-Hos' party. Note that the strict door policy prohibits entry to men wearing shorts or sandals.

4-1-1 Nishi-Azabu
Minato-ku
🚇 *Roppongi*
Map 11 A3 **137**
€

Muse

03 5467 1188 | *www.muse-web.com*

At one point, Muse was an undiscovered diamond in the rough. Located just far enough from the bustle of Roppongi, Muse was one of the best singles clubs in town. The crowd came to have a good time, and the DJs or music – which is mostly Top 40 hip-hop – was never the big draw. The recently renovated space features two dancefloors, each with a bar, billiards, electronic darts and even ping-pong. The best feature, however, may be the hanging swing. Over the years, though, Muse has become known as a haven for foreign guys and the Japanese women who follow them. Entrance for men is ¥2,000 and includes two drinks. Ladies get in free.

Za House (B1F)
1-34-17 Ebisu-Nishi
Shibuya-ku
🚇 *Daikanyama*
Map 5 E2 **138**

Unit

03 5459 8630 | *www.unit-tokyo.com*

Unit is a cosy, basement-level club between Daikanyama and Nakameguro, at the junction of Kyū-Yamate Dōri and Komazawa Dōri. Although at the weekend Japanese DJs and live acts typically provide the soundtrack, Unit is also an all-genre concert venue for big-name overseas artists like Talib Kweli, Spoon and Ozomatli. Don't miss the attached lounge (Saloon) and cafe (Unice), which offer respite from the sweaty dancefloor.

Fukao Bldg (B1)
1-4-5 Azabu-Jūban
Minato-ku
🚇 **Azabu-Jūban**
Map 11 C4 **139**

Warehouse

03 6230 0343 | *www.a-warehouse.net*

Located in the international neighbourhood of Azabu-Jūban, Warehouse manages to attract a slightly more sophisticated crowd than clubs just up the road in central Roppongi. While big-name DJs appearances are rare, locals spin hip-hop and house for the clubbers who generally pack the place at weekends and for two regular parties. The Ring, held monthly, draws an out and proud crowd, while ladies come out for the free entry to the weekly AZ Wednesday parties. Sign up as a member on the website for discounts.

2-16 Maruyamachō
Shibuya-ku
🚇 **Shibuya**
Map 8 B4 **140**

Womb

03 5459 0039 | *www.womb.co.jp*

Womb is perhaps the most popular club on Shibuya's famed Love Hotel Hill. It made a cameo appearance in the movie *Babel* as the spot where Japanese teens experiment with drugs and let loose – and the reality isn't far off. The main floor is usually packed with twenty-something Japanese who know their music, with a few foreign faces here and there. All attention is focused on the stage, where top hip-hop, drum'n'bass, house and breakbeat DJs keep a tight grip on their audience. If dancing in a sardine can (albeit one with a 10 metre high ceiling) isn't really your thing, check out the attached Obi Lounge near the entrance. It's all chilled beats and stiff drinks in here, and the floors above it overlook the dance floor so you're sure not to miss out on any of the action. Bring photo ID.

Oops!

Did we miss anything? If you have any thoughts, ideas or comments for us to include in the Going Out section, drop us a line, and if your cafe, bar, club or restaurant isn't in here, let us know and we'll give you a shout in the next edition. Visit www.explorerpublishing.com and fill us in.

Womb

Cabaret & Strip Shows

Shinjuku and Roppongi are the main areas for strip clubs in Tokyo. They are not quite as elaborate as establishments in the west, nor are they as down and dirty as the notorious clubs in neighbouring south-east Asia. Shinjuku's red-light district (Kabukichō) is home to many clubs. If you are not Asian, you will undoubtedly be asked by hawkers if you are interested in ogling some dancing girls. Make sure you know the entry fee before waltzing in, not all of these establishments are trustworthy. The clubs in Roppongi are far more professional and no such precautions will be needed here. Most places have a payment system that will include a drink or two. Many of the Kabukichō clubs are engaged in other salacious activities and are not for the timid. The ones in Roppongi are far more pedestrian and interested females will also be comfortable. A must-see is the transexual cabaret at Kingyo (p.374)

Gambling

Casinos are theoretically prohibited in Japan, but there are a number of other gaming options offered. Betting on horse, motorboat, bicycle and motorbike races is permitted. State-sponsored lotteries (*takarakuji*) are also common and all major cities have them. Pachinko parlours are everywhere in Japan and even backwater towns will have a few. These pinball and slot machine hybrids pay out small silver balls which can either be used to continue playing or cashed in for prizes. The prizes are then taken to an adjoining, officially unaffiliated exchange centre where hard cash can be procured. Betting on the Chinese game of mahjong is also a prevalent in Japanese society.

Cabaret & Strip Shows

Climax	No 2 Rene Bldg (4F), 5-3-1 Roppongi Minato-ku		03 3796 5539	www.climax-r.com
Marbles	Imperial Building B-1, Roppongi	Minato-ku	03 5570 4428	www.marbles-tokyo.com
Seventh Heaven	7-14-1 Roppongi	Minato-ku	03 3401 3644	www.seventh-heaven.com
Tantra	Zeches Baum (B2), 3-9-5 Roppongi	Minato-ku	03 5775 4468	www.tantra-mensclub.com

Cinemas

The Japanese are movie crazy and cinemas are abundant in Tokyo. Every major area has theatres, though Shinjuku, Shibuya and Ikebukuro have the lion's share. Western films usually arrive a few months after their initial releases back home. Almost all foreign films have Japanese subtitles and preserve the original audio. However, animation and children's films will often be dubbed into Japanese, so be sure to check before you buy your ticket. Japanese films with English subtitles are almost non-existent. Tokyo cinemas are immaculate and you won't be stepping on any sticky stuff walking down the aisles. Ticket prices are expensive, usually between ¥1,500 and ¥2,000. Matinees do exist and in many large chains women can take advantage of Ladies Days, typically Wednesdays, where admission is half price. Most cinemas show blockbuster Hollywood films. There are also a few independent art houses which show underground and independent releases. Uplink Factory, Image Forum and Cinema Rise all offer up engaging, unconventional films. The Tokyo International Film Festival (see oppostite) takes place in late October and is well worth checking out.

Movie Munchies

Bringing outside food into a Japanese cinema is entirely acceptable. Cinema-goers will often bring in bags full of snacks and even *bentō*. Tokyo cinemas don't have the assortment of munchies available that westerners are accustomed to, though the extortionate prices will unfortunately be familiar.

Cinemas

Cinema Rise	13-17 Udagawa-chō	Shibuya-ku	03 3464 0051	www.cinemarise.com
Cinema Sunshine	Sunshine Building, 1-14-3 Higashi Ikebukuro	Toshima-ku	03 3982 6101	www.cinemasunshine.co.jp
Eurospace	Tōbu Fuji Building, 24-4-201 Sakuragaoka-chō	Shibuya-ku	03 3461 0211	www.eurospace.co.jp
Image Forum	2-10-2 Shibuya	Shibuya-ku	03 5766 0116	www.imageforum.co.jp
National Film Center	3-7-6, Kyobashi	Chūō-ku	03 3561 0823	www.momat.go.jp
Shin-Bungeiza	Maruhan-Ikebukuro Building, 1-43-5 Higashi-Ikebukuro	Toshima-ku	03 3971 9422	www.shin-bungeiza.com
Toho Theatre	Roppongi Hills, 6-10-2 Roppongi	Minato-ku	03 5775 6090	www.tohotheater.jp
Uplink Factory	Totsune Building, 37-18 Udagawa-chō	Shibuya-ku	03 6821 6821	www.uplink.co.jp

Various Locations ◀

Tokyo International Film Festival

www.tiff-jp.net

The Tokyo International Film Festival has been going strong for 20 years and has gradually become more and more celebrated. Held in October every year, it is one of the largest film festivals in Asia. While open to film makers the world over, there is specific attention paid to other auteurs of the orient. Venues and prices vary; check the website for specifics.

Comedy

There is a thriving expat comedy scene in Tokyo. Although there are no actual comedy clubs, there are troupes that perform at various venues around town. The popular Tokyo Comedy Store and Tokyo Cynics (www.tokyocomedy.com/tokyo_cynics) get the locals laughing at different clubs, including The Crocodile (in Jingū-mae), The Baron (in the Emerald Nishi Azabu Garden in Minato-ku) and The Pink Cow (in Shibuya-ku). The humour here primarily focuses on the trials and tribulations of expat life in Japan. Most of the comedy is in English, but the Tokyo Comedy Store has occasional events solely in Japanese. Both groups feature improvisation as well as stand-up comedy. Newcomers are encouraged and regular auditions are held. Twice a month, Harajuku's Pizza Express transforms itself into the Punchline Comedy Club. Up-and-coming foreign comedians always include a stop here when touring the Asian expat comedy circuit.

Comedy Clubs

The Baron	Emerald Nishi-Azabu Garden, 1-8-21 Nishi-Azabu	Minato-ku	03 6406 4551	www.thebaron.jp
Crocodile	6-18-8 Jingū-mae	Shibuya-ku	03 3499 5205	www.music.co.jp/~croco
Pink Cow	1-3-18 Shibuya	Shibuya-ku	03 3406 5597	www.thepinkcow.com
Tokyo Comedy Store	Various Locations		na	www.tokyocomedy.com

4-30-3 Jingū-mae ◀
Shibuya-ku
🚇 *Meiji Jingū-mae*
Map 8 C2 141

Punchline Comedy Club

03 5775 3894 | www.punchlinecomedy.com

Harajuku's Pizza Express transforms itself into the Punchline Comedy Club twice a month. Up-and-coming and underground comics (together with a few famous names) will have you rolling in the aisles. These touring performers are also a nice alternative to the expat comics who tend to focus solely on life in Japan. For ¥8,500 you get an all-you-can-eat pizza buffet and three comics. The comics come from every English speaking country, with heavy doses of British performers. Recent performers to appear include Bill Bailey, Ron Vaudry and Simon Bligh.

Concerts & Live Music

Live music is huge in Tokyo and venues of every size can easily be found. Big name rock and pop acts from North America and Europe frequently sell out venues here. Tickets are far more expensive than back home, often five times what you would pay to see a foreign performer in their native land. However, local Japanese musicians can be seen for a lot less and the numerous music open-mic nights around town are another option for the budget minded. Jazz aficionados will have their work cut out for them. The Blue Note and Cotton Club (0570 030 033, www.cottonclubjapan. co.jp) are two high-end venues that host some of the biggest names in the genre. The more down-to-earth clubs such as Pit Inn and B flat (03 5563 2563, www.bflat.jp) showcase local stars and fledgling foreign jazz musicians. Barebones punk and rock clubs are hidden all over Shibuya, Kōenji and Shimokitazawa. Sufferers of claustrophobia beware as these tiny venues don't leave much elbow room. Superstar rock and pop acts hit larger venues such as Nippon Budōkan (www. nipponbudokan.or.jp), Tokyo Dome (www.tokyo-dome.co.jp) and Saitama Super Arena (www.saitama-arena.co.jp). Expect to pay through the nose if seeing shows here, the cheapest tickets being about ¥7,000 for foreign acts.

What's On?

To find out about upcoming gigs around town, check *Metropolis* (www.metropolis.co.jp) or *Japanzine* (www.seekjapan.jp). Both of these English-language periodicals have up-to-date listings on live music happenings. For fans of more unconventional sounds, logon to the Tokyo Gig Guide (www. tokyogigguide.com). This has listings of underground music events as well as detailed directions to every noteworthy venue in Tokyo.

New Wave Harajuku
4-32-12 Jingū-mae
Harajuku
🚇 *Meiji Jingū-mae*
Map 8 D1 `142`

Astro Hall

03 5738 2020 | *www.astro-hall.com*

You could walk past Astro Hall a hundred times and not even know that it was there. On a bustling Harajuku shopping street, it is buried deep in the bowels of the city. This tiny space is a great venue to check out young Japanese indie bands and western acts on the verge of success. Shows are usually reasonably priced and the crowd is hip yet down-to-earth. The Horrors, Tegan and Sara, and The Switches have all played here recently.

5-13-3 Minami-
Aoyama
Minato-ku
🚇 *Omote Sandō*
Map 8 E3 `143`

Blue Note Tokyo

03 5485 0088 | *www.bluenote.co.jp*

Blue Note Tokyo is the city's premier jazz club. An offshoot of the original Blue Note in New York City, it draws the genre's biggest acts from North America and Europe. Seeing big names here means paying big bucks. Lesser known acts cost around ¥8,000 and living legends will set you back at least ¥10,000. Some jazz aficionados complain about the exorbitant prices and the inattentive audiences, who seem more interested in their caviar than the music. But the Blue Note is extremely intimate, a great place for a date, and the staff are very courteous. The venue mainly showcases bebop, smooth jazz and vocalists. Recent performers include Branford Marsalis, Hank Jones and David Sanborn. Fans of more esoteric sounds may need to look elsewhere.

2-12-4 Shinjuku
Shinjuku-ku
🚇 *Shinjuku*
Sanchōme
Map 7 D1 `144`

Pit Inn

03 3354 2024 | *www.pit-inn.com*

The Pit Inn holds a special place in the hearts of the Tokyo music community. While advertised as a jazz club, this moniker does not do it justice. Avant-garde experimentalists, Japanese yodellers and freeform beboppers can share the stage on any given night. The entry is usually quite reasonable and the crowd is a mix of the old and the young. The venue is very basic and the only cocktails available come in cans. There is also a matinee that showcases fledgling musicians, between 14:30 and 17:00.

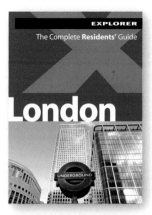
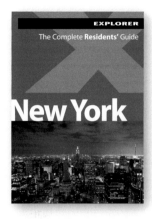
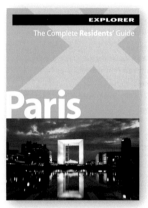

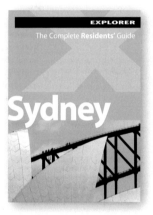

2-6-10 Senda Bldg
Shimokitazawa
🚇 *Shimo-Kitazawa*
Map 5 C1 **145**

Shelter

03 3466 7430 | *www.loft-prj.co.jp/SHELTER*

Shelter is Tokyo's equivalent to New York's CBGB (country, blue grass and blues) club. This isn't just because of its dinginess and raucous atmosphere, it's also got rock'n'roll history to boot. Every great Tokyo punk band has tried their luck at this venerable institution. At the weekend, it often feels like it has been oversold and patrons are crammed together like commuters on a rush-hour train. However, the quality of the bands that play here, and the intensity of the crowd, make this only a minor nuisance.

3-1-25 Nishi Azabu
Minato-ku
🚇 *Roppongi*
Map 11 A3 **146**

Super Deluxe

03 5412 0515 | *www.super-deluxe.com*

Just outside the heart of Roppongi, Super Deluxe is different things to different people. One night it hosts DJ events and the next night it will have free jazz. One weekend there will be an underground film festival and the next weekend there will be *koto* players. A spacious underground studio, it also has a good selection of micro-brews.

Karaoke

Daisuke Inoue had no idea his little music-playing contraption would launch the worldwide karaoke craze. But nearly four decades since Inoue's invention (which he never patented), the pastime is still a mainstay of Japanese nightlife. In 2007 alone, the country's estimated 130,000 karaoke rooms attracted 47 million customers. Tokyo has more than its fair share of venues in which to practise the art of the 'empty orchestra'. There are two bars offering the publicly humiliating style of singing popular in karaoke bars in the west: Fiesta (p367) and Smash Hits (see table). The vast majority of karaoke establishments, however, rent out private rooms offering the bare essentials: TV, mics and room service. The largest chains are Karaoke-kan (www.karaokekan.jp), with more than 100 branches in central Tokyo, and Big Echo (www.clubdam.com/be), with over 70.

Karaoke

Aria Blu	T-Wing (7-9F), 1-6-2 Kabukichō	Shinjuku-ku	03 5155 5633	www.ariablu.com
Fiesta	Crest Roppongi (3F), 7-9-3 Roppongi	Minato-ku	03 5410 3008	www.fiesta-roppongi.com/en
Lovenet	Hotel Ibis (3-4F), 7-14-4 Roppongi	Minato-ku	03 5771 5511	www.lovenet-jp.com
Smash Hits	M2 Bldg (B1), 5-2-26 Hirō	Shibuya-ku	03 3444 0432	www.smashhits.jp

While there are countless options vying for your yen, those with comfortable cashflow looking for a memorable night of crooning should try Roppongi's Lovenet, which offers 20 poshly appointed private suites (two to 100 people) with a hefty price tag. Aria Blu in Shinjuku has similarly lavish rooms with similarly large rates.

Karaoke Bar

Kabuki-za theatre

Theatre

Other options
Drama Groups p.218

Tokyo's theatre scene is often overlooked by expat residents as they assume that everything is only in Japanese. While this is true of the bigger shows, there are still plenty of options. The Tokyo International Players is an expat acting troupe that stages three or four plays a year. Recent productions have included Anton Chekhov's *The Cherry Orchard* and Neil Simon's *Plaza Suite*. Along with operas and ballets, The New National Theatre stages the occasional play in English. Those looking to experience traditional Japanese *kabuki* should head to Kabuki-za Theatre in Ginza. Headsets with an English language interpretation of the dramas are available, and don't be ashamed of relying on them. Even the Japanese use them because the Japanese spoken in *kabuki* drama is no longer understood.

Theatre

Kabuki-za	4-12-5 Ginza	Chūō-ku	03 3541 3131	www.shochiku.co.jp/play/kabukiza/theater
New National Theatre	1-1-1 Hon-machi	Shibuya-ku	03 5351 3011	www.nntt.jac.go.jp
Tokyo International Players	807-42 Lion's Plaza Ebisu 3-25-3 Higashi Shibuya	Minato-ku	090 6009 4171	www.tokyoplayers.org

Party Organisers

Other options **Party Accessories** p.296

Party Organisers

Brain Busters	www.brainbusters.info	Techno
Manas	www.sfaira.net/manas	Trance
Psy16	www.psy16.com	Trance
Space Gathering	www.spacegathering.net	Ambient
Trance Cafe	www.trancecafe.com	Trance

Tokyo is a party town and there are many organisers who can help you put together your own shindig. The majority of these event planners are of the techno-rave variety and can be guaranteed to provide a rocking good time. The organisers listed here are run by native Tokyoites, so speaking a bit of Japanese might be required. Some of them provide the space, while others leave finding a location up to you. The New Year and late summer are their busy seasons, so plan ahead if booking anything during these times.

Caterers

Corporate Gourmet	www.corporategourmet.net
The Earl	www.thearl.com
Fujimamas	www.fujimamas.com
Good Honest Grub	www.goodhonestgrub.com
Kiwi Kitchen	www.kiwikitchen.com
Mandarin Oriental	03 3270 8800
To the Moon and Back	www.tothemoonandback.jp
Tokyo American Club	www.tokyoamericanclub.org
Tokyo Catering	03 5459 7811
Tokyo Wedding Catering	www.tokyoweddingcatering.com

Caterers

Entertaining at home is not all that common, as apartments and houses can be rather cramped. However, if you have the space, there are plenty of catering options. All companies listed in the table offer quality food, and many are associated with upmarket hotels or restaurants. Some specialise in Asian fusion, while others have authentic western food that will have you thinking that you are back home. Another option is to check with your favourite eatery and ask if they offer delivery (see also Delivery & Takeaways on p.324).

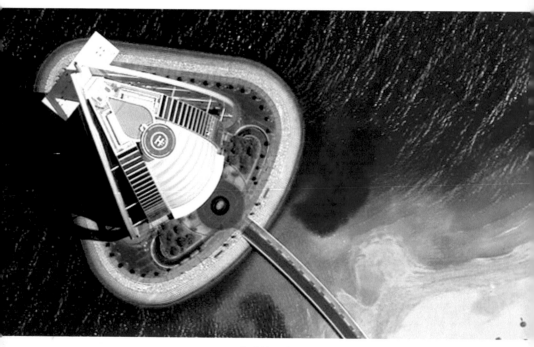

Maps

Maps

User's Guide

For new arrivals, Tokyo can appear a daunting city. Its size, congestion and sheer foreignness are significant obstacles, but they should not stop you from exploring. The maps that begin on p.390 cover the city on two scales. The outer areas are covered on a scale of 30,000 to one (30,000:1). This means that 1mm on the map is equivalent to 30,000mm (or 30 metres) on Tokyo's streets. The more central areas are covered in more detail, on a scale of 15,000:1 (so 1mm is equal to 15m). The sheet cut index, on p.390 shows exactly where is covered.

Ku, Shi, Cho

To help you locate places more easily, it's good to know that ku *means ward. Within these* ku *are* cho *(neighbourhoods),* shi *are cities (outside Tokyo) and* ken *is the Japanese word for prefecture. An exception is Tokyo prefecture, which is known as Tokyo-to, because it is the capital.*

There are also coloured annotations on these maps. They mark places that are mentioned in the book, and the different colours correspond to different chapters. So, on Map 8 E2 is the Napule restaurant (see p.340 for review) in Going Out. On Map 7 B4 is Meiji Jingū (p.178) in Exploring. If you're near a cluster of annotations and want to know what they are, simply turn to the relevant chapter and count through the icons in the margin.

Until your Japanese gets up to scratch, keep your destination written in Japanese on a piece of paper to show to taxi drivers and when asking for directions. Once you're out of hotels and into your own home, you can use the street and area index (p.388).

To help orientation, it's worth noting that addresses in Japan don't usually use street names and numbers (although in Tokyo some of the main streets do actually have names). Instead, they use a complicated system of wards *ku* (区), cities *shi* (市) and areas (or towns) called *chō* (町). In addresses, numbers are used to represent each part: the area within that *chō* (*chōme*, 丁目), the block and then the building. So the address 8-10-5 Udagawa-chō, Chūō-ku refers to the 8th chōme of Udagawa, and the 5th building of the 10th block in that area in Udagawa town in Chūō ward.

A useful tool for figuring out these addresses (and the best bilingual map on Tokyo) is the *Tokyo City Atlas* by Kodansha, which shows the boundaries of *ku* and sub areas, and the blocks within them. For a bigger picture, p.355 gives an overview of the city's outer lying areas, and opposite is a map of Japan.

Online Maps

If you can read (and type) Japanese, http://maps.google.co.jp shows Tokyo, and the rest of Japan, in great detail. You can search by address or business name (and it will find a lot of places if you use English), or you can zoom in and look around manually. You can also see the city in three different ways: the standard view is a vector map with landmark icons shown, there is a satellite image, and the hybrid view is a blend of the two. Google's international page allows more searching in English, but isn't in quite the same detail as the Japanese site.

Map Legend

Hotel	Highway
Education	Major Road
Park/Garden	Secondary Road
Hospital	Other Road
Shopping	Tunnel
Heritage/Museum	Hibiya Line
Industrial Area	Yūrakucho Line
Built up Area/Building	Marunouchi Line
Land	Tozai Line
Pedestrian	Toei Shinjuku Line
A10 Station Exits	Toei Asakusa Line
Airport	Toei Mita Line
	Ginza Line
	Toei Oedo Line
	Chiyoda Line
	Namboku Line
	Railway Line
	Ku Border

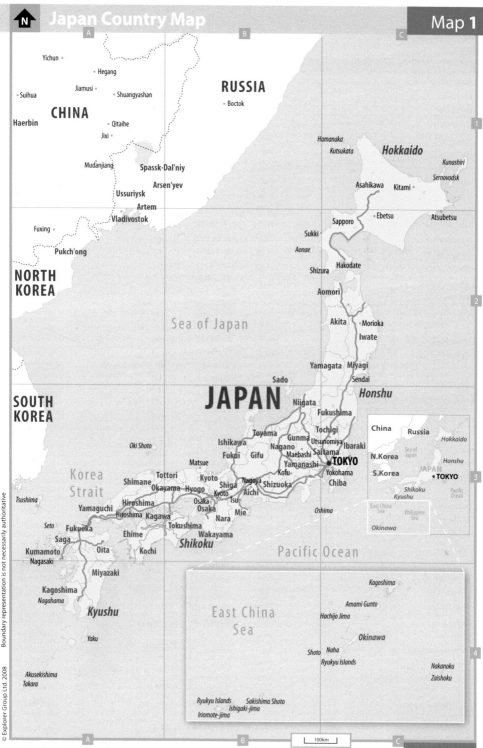

Street Index

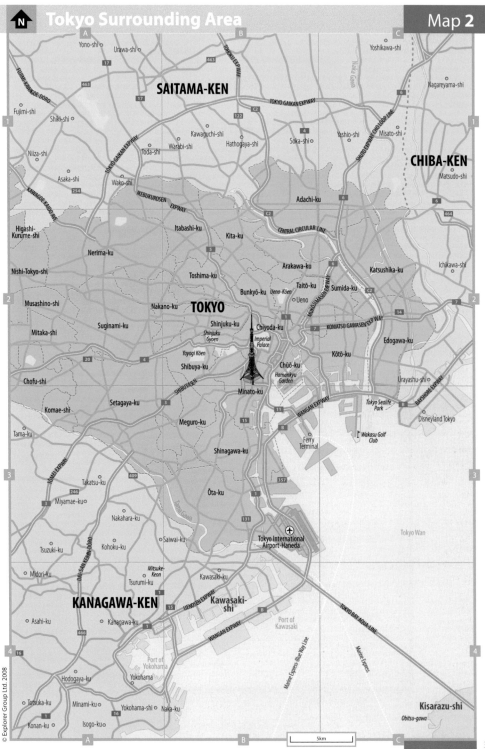

Yono-shi
Urawa-shi
Yoshikawa-shi

SAITAMA-KEN
Nagareyama-shi

Fujimi-shi
Shiki-shi
Kawaguchi-shi
Yashio-shi
Misato-shi

CHIBA-KEN

Niiza-shi
Toda-shi
Warabi-shi
Hathogaya-shi
Sōka-shi

Matsudo-shi

Asaka-shi
Wako-shi

Higashi-Kurume-shi
Itabashi-ku
Kita-ku
Adachi-ku

Nishi-Tokyo-shi
Nerima-ku
CENTRAL CIRCULAR LINE

Musashino-shi
Toshima-ku
Arakawa-ku
Katsushika-ku
Ichikawa-shi

Mitaka-shi
Nakano-ku
Bunkyō-ku
Ueno-Kōen
Taitō-ku
Sumida-ku

Suginami-ku
TOKYO
Ueno

Shinjuku-ku
Shinjuku Gyoen
Chiyoda-ku
Edogawa-ku

Chofu-shi
Yoyogi Kōen
Imperial Palace
Kōtō-ku

Komae-shi
Shibuya-ku
Chūō-ku
Hamarikyu Garden
Urayashu-shi

Tama-ku
Setagaya-ku
Minato-ku
Tokyo Sealife Park
Disneyland Tokyo

Meguro-ku
Ferry Terminal
Wakasu Golf Club

Shinagawa-ku

Takatsu-ku
Miyamae-ku
Ōta-ku

Nakahara-ku
Tama Gawa

Tsuzuki-ku
Kohoku-ku
Saiwai-ku
Tokyo Wan

Midori-ku
Mitsuke-Keon
Tsurumi-ku
Kawasaki-shi
Tokyo International Airport-Haneda

KANAGAWA-KEN
Kawasaki-shi

Asahi-ku
Kanagawa-ku
Port of Kawasaki

Port of Yokohama
Marine Express

Hodogaya-ku
Yokohama
Kisarazu-shi

Totsuka-ku
Minami-ku
Yokohama-shi
Naka-ku
Obitsu-gawa

Konan-ku
Isogo-ku

© Explorer Group Ltd. 2008

5km

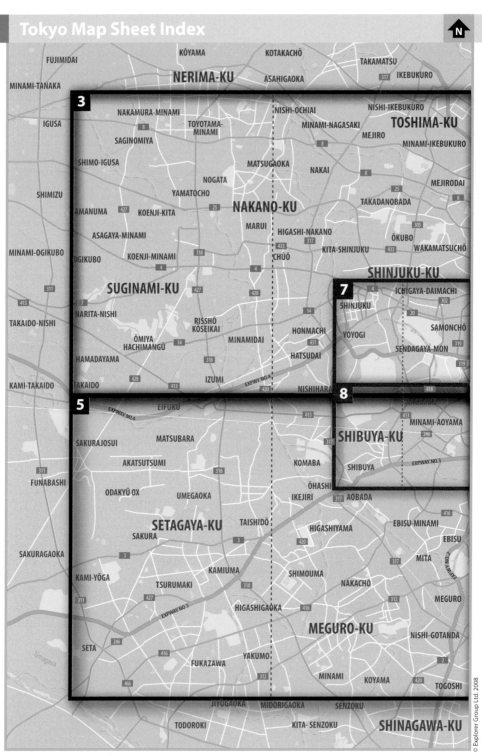

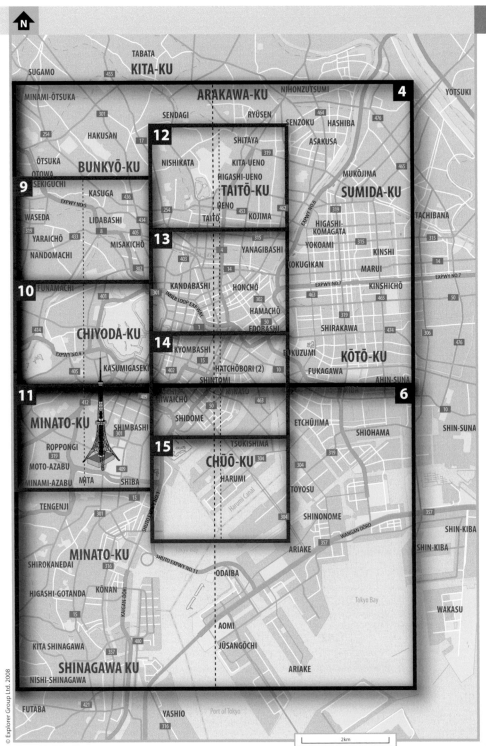

SUGAMO

TABATA

KITA-KU

MINAMI-ŌTSUKA

ARAKAWA-KU

NIHONZUTSUMI

4

YOTSUKI

SENDAGI

RYŪSEN

SENZOKU

HASHIBA

476

254

HAKUSAN

17

12

SHITAYA

ASAKUSA

464

ŌTSUKA

BUNKYŌ-KU

NISHIKATA

KITA-UENO

319

MUKŌJIMA

465

OTOWA

HIGASHI-UENO

9

SEKIGUCHI

KASUGA

436

TAITŌ-KU

SUMIDA-KU

TACHIBANA

WASEDA

IIDABASHI

434

254

UENO

453

462

HIGASHI-KOMAGATA

319

319

YARAICHŌ

433

8

405

TAITŌ

KOJIMA

YOKOAMI

315

315

NANDOMACHI

MISAKICHŌ

13

315

YANAGIBASHI

KOKUGIKAN

KINSHI

14

302

403

MARUI

EXPWY NO.7

10

FUNAMACHI

401

4

14

KANDABASHI

HONCHŌ

463

KINSHICHŌ

465

50

301

302

414

CHIYODA-KU

INNER LOOP EXP WAY

HAMACHŌ

50

SHIRAKAWA

474

306

476

1

EDOBASHI

319

14

KYOBASHI

FUKUZUMI

KŌTŌ-KU

EXPWY NO.4

KASUMIGASEKI

402

15

FUKAGAWA

405

HATCHŌBORI (2)

10

SHINTOMI

AHIN-SUNA

11

409

IWAICHŌ

50

463

6

MINATO-KU

412

SHIMBASHI

SHIDOME

ETCHŪJIMA

SHIOHAMA

SHIN-SUNA

301

ROPPONGI

319

TSUKISHIMA

10

MOTO-AZABU

409

15

304

319

MINAMI-AZABU

MITA

SHIBA

CHŪ̄O-KU

304

SHIN-KIBA

15

HARUMI

TOYOSU

TENGENJI

301

Harumi Canal

SHINONOME

357

SHIN-KIBA

MINATO-KU

SHUTO EXPWY NO.11

304

SHIN-KIBA

SHIROKANEDAI

316

ARIAKE

357

HIGASHI-GOTANDA

KŌNAN

ODAIBA

WANGAN DŌRO

WAKASU

15

Tokyo Bay

KITA SHINAGAWA

480

AOMI

357

SHINAGAWA KU

JŪSANGŌCHI

ARIAKE

NISHI-SHINAGAWA

FUTABA

421

YASHIO

Port of Tokyo

316

© Explorer Group Ltd. 2008

Map **3**

KAMI-SAGINOMIYA

Nanzō-in

NAKAMURA-MINAMI

NERIMA-KU

Shin Egota

Jiseikai

Eroda

Musashino Ryōen

Nakano-kita Post Office

Shimo-Igusa

Nogata Fire Station

SHIN-ŌME KAIDŌ

SAGINOMIYA

Saginomiya

Toritsu-Kasei

Numabukuro

SHIMO-IGUSA

NOGATA

Nogata

WASEDA DŌRI

SHIRASAGI

NAKANO-KU

Heiwano -mori Park

Arai-Yakushimae

HON-AMANUMA

NOGATA

ARAI

Arai-yakushi

YAMATOCHO

Toy Museum

Asagaya Library

Mabashi Park

BROADWAY

AMANUMA

KŌENJI-KITA

Nakano Sun Plaza

Kawatika General

Selyū

Nakano Ward Office

Nakano

Asagaya

Kōenji

Ogikubo

KŌENJI-MINAMI

Central Library

Nakano General Hospital

Minami-Asagaya

Suginami Ward Office

Shin-Kōenji

Higashi-Kōenji

Shin-Nakano

OGIKUBO

Suginami Tax Office

UMEZATO

Sanshinomori Park

WADA

Ogikubo Danchi (Apts)

Asagaya Danchi (Apts)

Narita Library

MATSUNOKI

Myōhō-ji

Nakano-Fujimichō

Zenpukujigawa Park

ITSUKAICHI KAIDŌ

SUGINAMI-KU

Salvation Army

NARITA-NISHI

Folk Museum of Suginami

HŌNAN DŌRI

Hōnanchō

MINAMIDAI

Hamadayama

HŌNAN-DŌRI

Dai-en-ji

HŌNAN

HAMADAYAMA

Nishi-Eifuku

HOTOMY KAIDŌ

IZUMI

Eifukucho

SHUTO EXPWY

Sasazuka

General Information p.1   Residents p.49   Exploring p.145   Activities p.207   Shopping p.271   Going Out p.323

© Explorer Group Ltd. 2008

392

Map **3**   **Tokyo** Explorer 1st Edition

Map **3**

N

NAGASAKI

Higashi-Nagasaki

NISHI-OCHIAI

Keiain

Shinamachi

Ochiai-Minami-Nagasaki

MINAMI-NAGASAKI

110

Ikebukuro   Tōbu

Toshima
Ward Office

Higashi-
Ikebukuro

Tokyo
Met Space   Ikebukuro   Mitsukoshi

Sunshine City

NISHI-IKEBUKURO   Seibu   172

41   5   18

Higashi-Ikebukuro   435

TOSHIMA-KU

Tetsugakudō
Park

Kawai

440

NAKA-OCHIAI

317   6
Seibo
Int'l Catholic
Hospital

8

MEJIRO DŌRI   8

Mejiro

Kishimojin

Zōshigaya
Cemetery

305

TAKADANUBADA   Zōshigaya

8

KAMI-TAKADA

Nakai

Yakuō-in   Otomeyama
Park

Shimo-ochiai

Stamp Museum

MEJIRO

Nakai   Shimo Ochiai

Takadanobaba

P

Nakai   KAMI-OCHIAI

Ochiai
Central Park   Big Box   25

53

H 72

Ringa Royal   8

Plaza Citizen   80

39

NISHI-WASEDA

Ochisi
Post Office   Braille Library

25   48

WASEDA DŌRI   92

317

Higashi-Nakano

F   Toyama Park   Toyama

Waseda

HIGASHI-NAKANO   SHINJUKU-KU   Cosmic Centre

Umewaka
Noh Theatre   433   OKUBO DŌRI

Yodobashi
Wholesale Market   75   ŌKUBO   305

Toyama Park

Int'l Medical
Center of Japan

F   Hōsen-ji   302   21   Shin-Ōkubo   433   Statistics
Center

Aikido World
Head Quarters

Nakano-Sakaue   Shinjuku
Tax Office   Higashi-Shinjuku Tokiwa

302   27   Wakamatsu-Kawada

HONCHŌ   Okubo   H

44   Tokyo Women's
Medical College Hospital

Nakano-Shimbashi   Shinjuku
Ward Office

Map
7   Nishi-Shinjuku

Hanazono-Jinja

Akebonobashi

Nishi-Shinjuku Gochōme   Tokyo Medical
College

Hilton H   SAN'EICHŌ

432   Tochōmae   Shinjuku

Yotsuya

YAYOICHŌ   414   20

14   Shinjuku-Gyoemmae   Yotsuya-Sanchōme

317   Ōkido-mon   P

HONMACHI   New Nat'l
Theatre   15   Shinjuku   Shinjuku Gyoen
National Garden

431   37   YOYOGI   Yoyogi   Tōden

Hatsudai   Minami-Shinjuku   305   Sendagaya   418   319   Keiō

HATSUDAI   Japanese
Sword Museum   4   Kokuritsu-Kyōgijō   Shinanomachi

Hatagaya   Harajuku
Police Station   SENDAGAYA   Meiji Meml
Picture Gallery

Sangūbashi   Nat'l Olympic
Meml Youth Centre   Meiji-jingū Outer
Gardens (Jingū Gaien)

HATAGAYA   Yoyogi Park

Sakura   HATAGAYA

SHIBUYA-KU   79   Jica   36 E Vietnam

Map
8   Yoyogi Park   Jingu Stadium   414

© Explorer Group Ltd. 2008

1000 m

Map 4

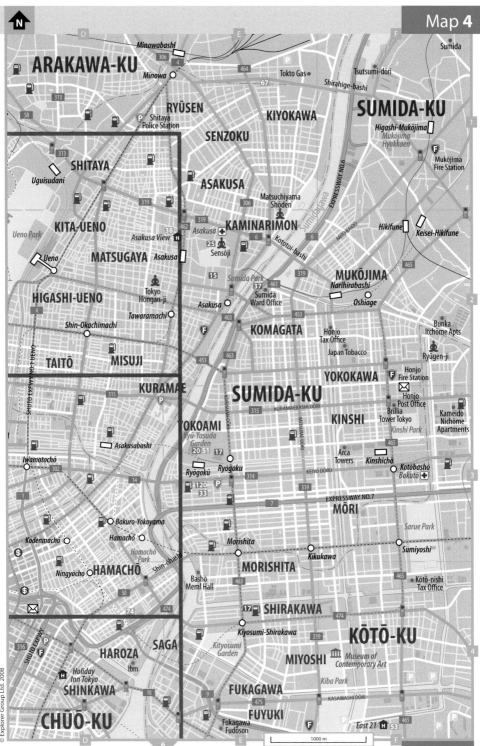

Map **4**

ARAKAWA-KU

Minowabashi
Minowa

Tokto Gas
Shirahige-bashi
Tsutsumi-dōri

SUMIDA-KU

RYŪSEN
Shitaya
Police Station

KIYOKAWA

Higashi-Mukōjima
Mukōjima
Hyakkaen

SENZOKU

SHITAYA
Uguisudani

Mukōjima
Fire Station

ASAKUSA

Matsuchiyama
Shōden

KITA-UENO

Asakusa
KAMINARIMON

Hikifune
Keisei-Hikifune

Asakusa View
Sensōji

Kototoi-bashi

Ueno Park
Ueno

MATSUGAYA
Asakusa

MUKŌJIMA
Narihirabashi

HIGASHI-UENO
Tokyo
Hongan-ji

Sumida Park

Asakusa
Sumida
Ward Office
Oshiage

Bunka
Itchōme Apts

Tawaramachi

Shin-Okachimachi

Asakusa

KOMAGATA
Honjo
Tax Office

Ryūgen-ji

TAITŌ
MISUJI

Japan Tobacco

Honjo
Fire Station

KURAMAE

YOKOKAWA
Honjo
Post Office

SUMIDA-KU

KURAMAEBASHI DŌRI

KINSHI
Brillia
Tower Tokyo

Kameido
Nichōme
Apartments

YOKOAMI
Kyū-Yasuda
Garden

Asakusabashi

Kinshi Park

Iwamotochō

Arca
Towers
Kinshichō

Kotōbashō
Bokutō

Ryōgoku
Ryōgoku

KEIYŌ DŌRI

Bakuro-Yokoyama
Hamachō

MŌRI
Sarue Park

Kodenmachō

EXPRESSWAY NO.7

Hamachō
Park

Shin-ōhashi

Morishita

Kikukawa
Sumiyoshi

Ningyōchō
HAMACHŌ

MORISHITA

Kōtō-nishi
Tax Office

Bashō
Meml Hall

SHIRAKAWA

SAGA

Kiyosumi-Shirakawa

KŌTŌ-KU

HAROZA

Kiyosumi
Garden

MIYOSHI
Museum of
Contemporary Art

Holiday
Inn Tokyo
Ibm

SHINKAWA

FUKAGAWA
Kiba Park

KASAIBASHI DŌRI

CHŪ-KU

FUYUKI
Fukagawa
Fudōson
East 21

1000 m

© Explorer Group Ltd. 2008

Map 5

SUGINAMI-KU IZUMI

Kami-Kitazawa

428

Sakurajōsui

SHUTO EXPWY

Daitabashi

Meidaimae

4

Shimo-Takaido

318

Higashi-Kitazawa

SAKURAJOSUI

MATSUBARA

Matsubara

Hanegi

Shin-Daita

145

Higashi-Matsubara

Shimo-Kitazawa

AKATSUTSUMI

Kitazawa
Police Station

Hanegi Park

DAITA 17

DAIZAWA

Umegaoka

Setagaya
Daita

ODAKYŪ OX

34

Yamashita

318

Nat'l Ctr For
Child Health
& Development (Res.inst.)

Kyōdo

Gōtokuji

UMEGAOKA

11

Chitose-Funabashi

Chitose
Post Office

Gōtoku-ji

WAKABAYASHI

Shōin Jinja

TAISHIDŌ

124

Miyanosaka

Setagaya
Ward Office

Wakabayas

Nishi-Taishidō

90

Sangejaya

SAKURA

Setagaya

Shōin Jinjamae

Carrot Tower

Sangenjaya

Kamimachi

SETAGAYA DORI

3

Komadome
Hachiman

TAMAGAWA DORI

Agricultural
Museum

Kantō Chuō

Baji Kōen

Central Library

SETAGAYA-KU

TSURUMAKI

Komazawa

NAT'L ROAD NO.246

Komazawa Daigaku

318

St. francisco

311

89

YŌGA

Tokyo Den'en Line

Sakura-Shinmachi

Hasegawa Machiko
Art Museum

3

78

Komazawa
Olympic Park

2

Gym

HIGASHIGAOKA

Nat'l Hospital
Organization Tokyo
Medical Centre

426

2

TAMAGAWADAI

Yōga

SETA

Tamagawa

97

427

246

KOMAZAWA DORI

416

FUKAZAWA

YAKUMO

Tōkō-ji

466

KAMI-NOGE

Yakumo

Kinokuniya

54

Tamagawa
Takashimaya

20

Futako-Tamagawa

Kami-Noge

F

General Information p.1   Residents p.49   Exploring p.145   Activities p.207   Shopping p.271   Going Out p.323

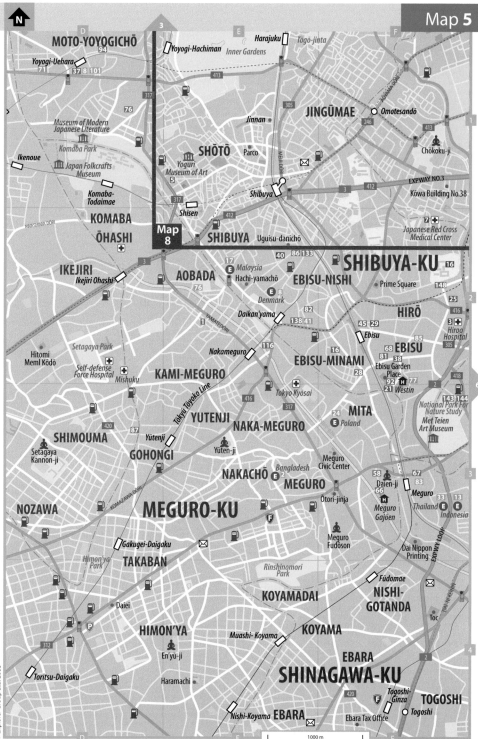

Map **5**

N

MOTO-YOYOGICHŌ
94

Yoyogi-Uehara
71 37 8 101

Yoyogi-Hachiman

Harajuku
Tōgō-jinta
Inner Gardens

413

305

JINGŪMAE

Omotesandō

246

413

Chōkoku-ji

EXPWAY NO.3

Kōwa Building No.38

Museum of Modern
Japanese Literature

Komaba Park

Jinnan

Museum of Modern
Japanese Literature

Ikenoue

Japan Folkcrafts
Museum

76

317

Komaba-
Todaimae

KOMABA
ŌHASHI

AWASHIMA DŌRI

SHŌTŌ

Yoguri
Museum of Art
5

Parco

Shibuya

Map
8

SHIBUYA

Shisen

Uguisu-danichō

412

Japanese Red Cross
Medical Center

7

IKEJIRI

Ikejiri Ohashi

AOBADA

76

17
Malaysia
Hachi-yamachō

40 86 133

SHIBUYA-KU 16

148

Prime Square

EBISU-NISHI

25

Denmark
8

HIRŌ

Hitomi
Meml Kōdo

Setagaya Park

Self-defense
Force Hospital

Mishuku

KAMI-MEGURO

YAMATE DŌRI

1

Daikan'yama

82

138 41

Nakameguro

116

416

Tokyo Kyōsai

YUTENJI

Tokyu Tōyōko Line

317

Ebisu

45 29

16

EBISU-MINAMI

28

68 EBISU
81 38
Ebisu Garden
Place
92 H 77
21   Westin

85

Hiroo
Hospital
305

3

418

2

National Park For
Nature Study
Met Teien
Art Museum

6

SHIMOUMA

420

87

Yūtenji

GOHONGI

Setagaya
Kannon-ji

Yūten-ji

NAKA-MEGURO

Bangladesh

NAKACHŌ

MEGURO

MITA

24
Poland

Meguro
Civic Center

58
66
Daien-ji
H
Meguro
Gajōen

Meguro

67
83

33 13
Thailand   Indonesia

NOZAWA

MEGURO-KU

KOMAZAWA DŌRI

F

Ōtori-jinja

Meguro
Fudoson

Dai Nippon
Printing

EXPWAY LOOP

Gakugei-Daigaku

Himon'ya
Park

TAKABAN

Daiei

P

Rinshinomori
Park

KOYAMADAI

Muashi- Koyama

KOYAMA

Fūdomae

NISHI-
GOTANDA

Toc

312

HIMON'YA

En'yū-ji

EBARA

SHINAGAWA-KU

2

4

Toritsu-Daigaku

Haramachi

Nishi-Koyama EBARA

Ebara Tax Office

Togoshi-
Ginza
F

Togoshi

TOGOSHI

420

1000 m

© Explorer Group Ltd. 2008

D   E   F

Map **6**

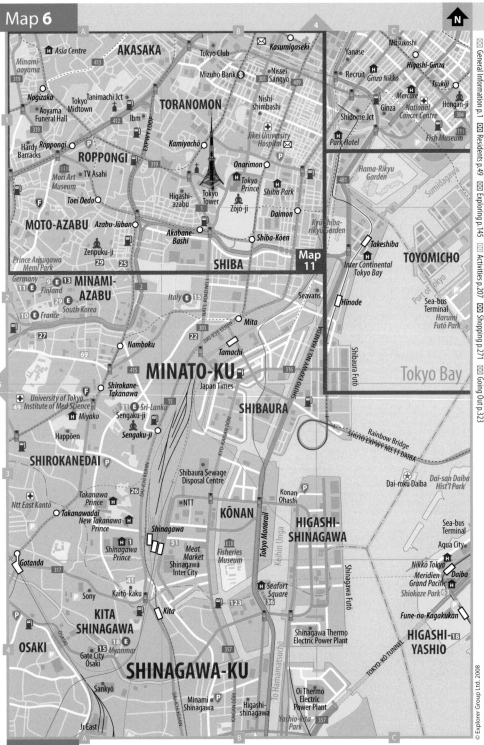

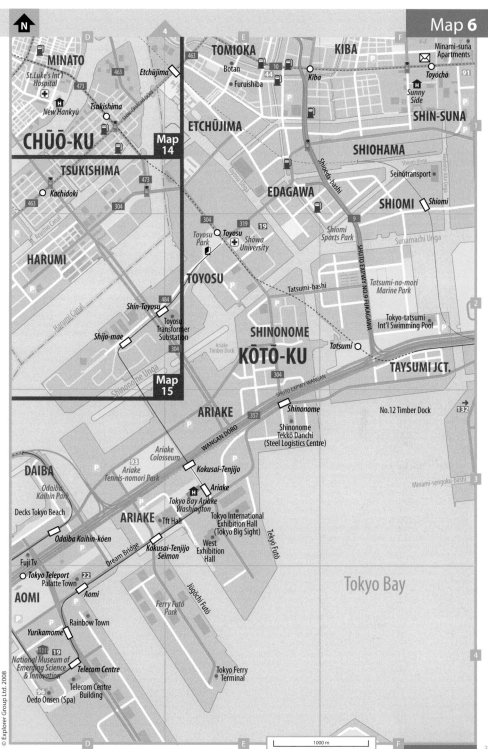

Map **6**

© Explorer Group Ltd. 2008

MINATO

St. Luke's Int'l Hospital

New Hankyū

Tsukishima

Etchūjima

CHŪŌ-KU

Map **14**

TSUKISHIMA

Kachidoki

HARUMI

Shin-Toyosu

Shijo-mae

Toyosu Transformer Substation

Map **15**

TOMIOKA

Botan

• Furuishiba

KIBA

Kiba

Minami-suna Apartments

Toyōchō

Sunny Side

SHIN-SUNA

ETCHŪJIMA

SHIOHAMA

Seinōtransport

EDAGAWA

SHIOMI

Shiomi

Shiomi Sports Park

Toyosu Park

Toyosu

Shōwa University

TOYOSU

Tatsumi-bashi

Tatsumi-no-mori Marine Park

Tokyo-tatsumi Int'l Swimming Pool

SHINONOME

KŌTŌ-KU

Tatsumi

TAYSUMI JCT.

Ariake Timber Dock

No. 12 Timber Dock

ARIAKE

Shinonome

Shinonome Tekkō Danchi (Steel Logistics Centre)

Minami-sengoku-bashi

DAIBA

Odaiba Kaihin Park

Decks Tokyo Beach

Ariake Colosseum

Ariake Tennis-nomori Park

Kokusai-Tenjijo

Ariake

Tokyo Bay Ariake Washington

ARIAKE

• Tft Hall

Tokyo International Exhibition Hall (Tokyo Big Sight)

West Exhibition Hall

Odaiba Kaihin-kōen

Kokusai-Tenjijo Seimon

Dream Bridge

Fuji Tv

Tokyo Teleport

Palatte Town

AOMI

Aomi

Rainbow Town

Yurikamome

National Museum of Emerging Science & Innovation

Telecom Centre

Telecom Centre Building

Ōedo Onsen (Spa)

Ferry Futō Park

Tokyo Ferry Terminal

Tokyo Bay

SHUTO EXPWY NO.9 FUKAGAWA

SHUTO EXPWY WANGAN

WANGAN DŌRO

Harumi Canal

Arashio Canal

Toyosu Unga

Shinonome Unga

Sunamachi Unga

Shiomi Unga

Jūgo-hri Futō

Tekyō Futō

1000 m

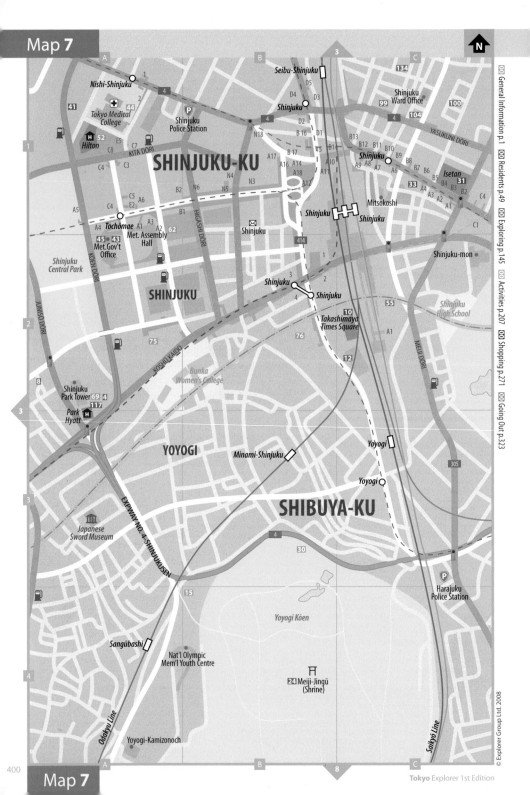

Map **7**

N

General Information p.1 | Residents p.49 | Exploring p.145 | Activities p.207 | Shopping p.271 | Going Out p.323

Nishi-Shinjuku 1

4

41

44

Tokyo Medical
College

Shinjuku
Police Station

52

Hilton

E5

C7 C8

KITA DORI

SHINJUKU-KU

C4 C3

C5 A6

E2

C4

A5

A4 A1 A3 A2

Tochōmae

45 43
Met.Gov't
Office

62

Met. Assembly
Hall

HIGASHI DORI

B2

B1

N6 N5

N4 N3

A17

A16 A14

A18

A12

A10

A11

Seibu-Shinjuku

D5

D4 D3

Shinjuku

D2

N18 B 16 D1

B 17

B13

B12 B11 B10

Shinjuku

A9 A8 A7 A6

99

104

4

100

134

Shinjuku
Ward Office

YASUKUNI DORI

B9 B8

B7 B6 B5

33 A4 A3 A2 A1

Isetan
31

C4

Mitsokoshi

C1

Shinjuku

Shinjuku

Shinjuku-mon

Shinjuku

Shinjuku

Shinjuku
High School

414

SHINJUKU

Shinjuku

3

4

2

1

Shinjuku

Shinjuku

10

Takashimaya
Times Square

A1

55

76

12

MEIJI DORI

Shinjuku
Central Park

KŌEN DORI

JUNISO DORI

2

8

75

Bunka
Women's College

Shinjuku
Park Tower 69 4

117

Park
Hyatt

3

YOYOGI

Minami-Shinjuku

Yoyogi

Yoyogi

SHIBUYA-KU

305

3

EXPWAY NO. 4 SHINJUKU SEN

Japanese
Sword Museum

4

30

15

Harajuku
Police Station

Odakyu Line

Sangūbashi

Yoyogi Kōen

Nat'l Olympic
Mem'l Youth Centre

24 Meiji-Jingū
(Shrine)

Saikyo Line

Yoyogi-Kamizonoch

Map **7**

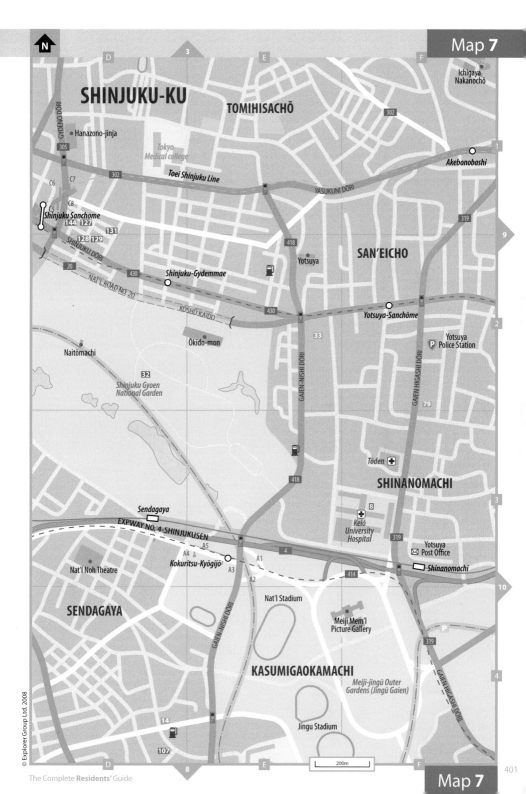

Map 7

N

SHINJUKU-KU

TOMIHISACHŌ

Ichigaya
Nakanochō

302

Hanazono-jinja

305

Tokyo
Medical college

Akebonobashi

1

C6 C7

302

Toei Shinjuku Line

YASUKUNI DORI

319

C5 C8

Shinjuku Sanchome

144 127

131

128 129

SHINJUKU DORI

20

430

NAT'L ROAD NO 20

KOSHŪ KAIDO

Shinjuku-Gydemmae

Yotsuya

SAN'EICHO

9

430

Yotsuya-Sanchōme

2

Naitōmachi

Ōkido-mon

33

Yotsuya
Police Station

32

Shinjuku Gyoen
National Garden

GAIEN-NISHI DORI

GAIEN HIGASHI DORI

79

418

SHINANOMACHI

Tōden

3

Sendagaya

EXPWAY NO. 4-SHINJUKUSEN

8

Keiō
University
Hospital

319

Yotsuya
Post Office

A5

Nat'l Noh Theatre

A4

Kokuritsu-Kyōgijō

A3 A1

A2

4

414

Shinanomachi

10

SENDAGAYA

GAIEN-NISHI DORI

Nat'l Stadium

Meiji Mem'l
Picture Gallery

GAIEN HIGASHI DORI

P

319

KASUMIGAOKAMACHI

Meiji-jingū Outer
Gardens (Jingū Gaien)

4

14

107

Jingu Stadium

200m

© Explorer Group Ltd. 2008

Map **8**

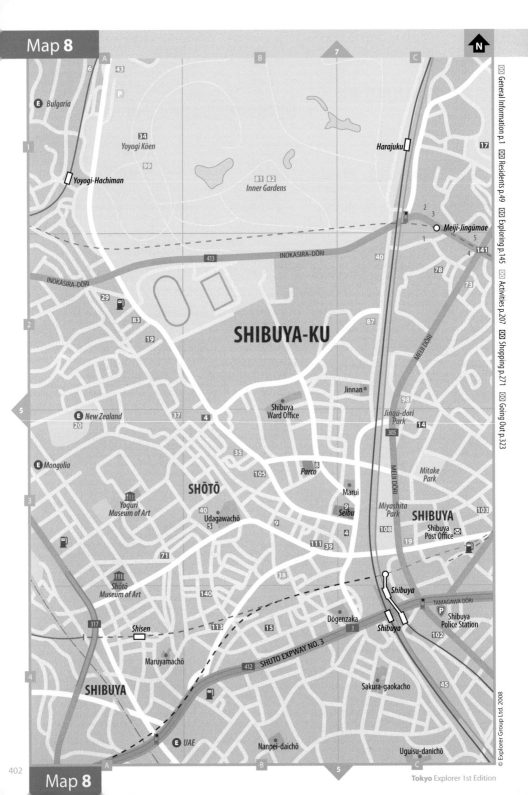

E Bulgaria

Yoyogi Kōen

Yoyogi-Hachiman

Inner Gardens

Harajuku

Meiji-Jingūmae

INOKASHIRA-DŌRI

INOKASHIRA-DŌRI

SHIBUYA-KU

MEIJI DŌRI

E New Zealand

Jinnan

Jingū-dori
Park

E Mongolia

Shibuya
Ward Office

Mitake
Park

SHŌTŌ

Parco

Yoguri
Museum of Art

Marui

Udagawachō

Seibu

Miyashita
Park

SHIBUYA

Shibuya
Post Office

Shōtō
Museum of Art

Shibuya

Shisen

Shibuya

TAMAGAWA DŌRI

Shibuya
Police Station

Dōgenzaka

Shibuya

Maruyamachō

SHUTO EXPWAY NO. 3

SHIBUYA

Sakura-gaokachō

E UAE

Nanpei-daichō

Uguisu-danichō

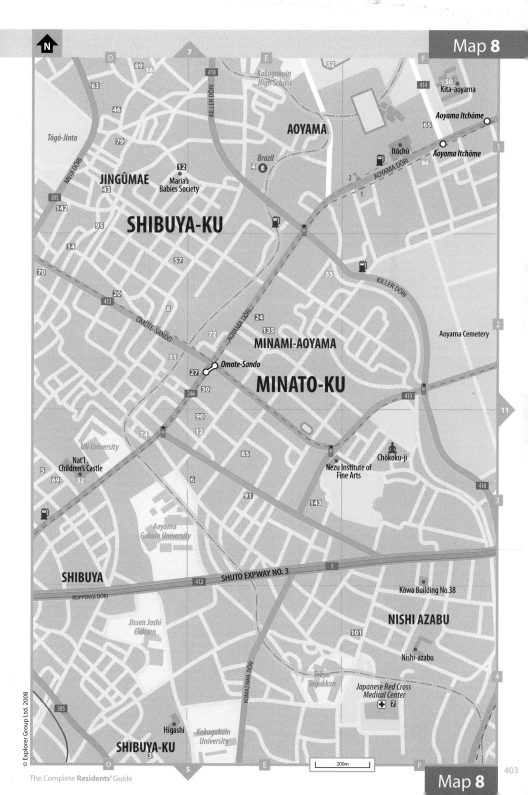

Map **8**

N

AOYAMA

Kita-aoyama

Aoyama Itchōme

Itōchū

Aoyama Itchōme

AOYAMA DŌRI

Tōgō-Jinta

JINGŪMAE

Maria's
Babies Society

Brazil

SHIBUYA-KU

Kokugakuin
High School

KILLER DŌRI

MEIJI DŌRI

KILLER DŌRI

Aoyama Cemetery

OMOTE-SANDO

AOYAMA DŌRI

MINAMI-AOYAMA

Omote-Sando

MINATO-KU

UN University

Nat'l
Children's Castle

Chōkoku-ji

Nezu Institute of
Fine Arts

Aoyama
Gakuin University

SHIBUYA

SHUTO EXPWAY NO. 3

ROPPOVGI DŌRI

Kōwa Building No.38

NISHI AZABU

Jissen Joshi
Gakuen

KOMAZAWA DŌRI

Nishi-azabu

Tōkyu
Jogakkan

Japanese Red Cross
Medical Center

Higashi

Kokugakuin
University

SHIBUYA-KU

200m

Map **9**

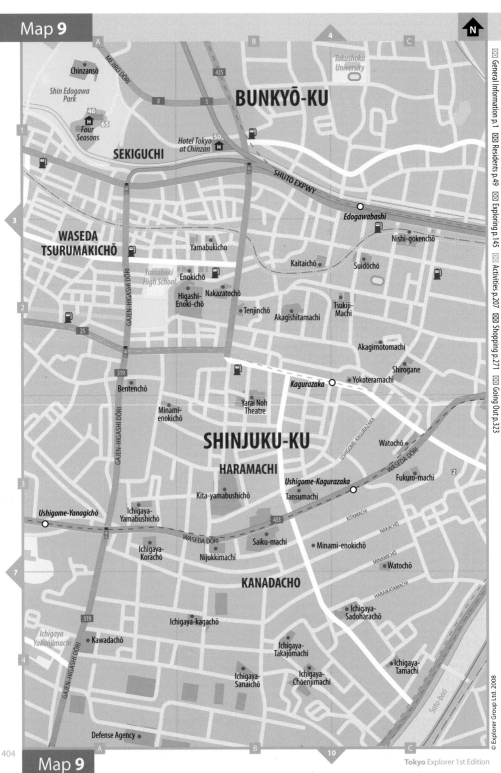

BUNKYŌ-KU

Takushoku University

Chinzansō

Shin Edogawa Park

MEIJIRO DORI

435

8   5

46
65
Four Seasons

SEKIGUCHI

Hotel Tokyo at Chinzan   50

SHUTO EXPWY

Edogawabashi

Nishi-gokenchō

WASEDA TSURUMAKICHŌ

Yamabukicho

Kaitaichō

Suidōchō

Yamabuki High School

Enokichō

GAJEN-HIGASHI DORI

Higashi-Enoki-chō

Nakazatochō

25

Tenjinchō

Akagishitamachi

Tsukiji-Machi

Akagimotomachi

Shirogane

319

Bentenchō

Kagurazaka

Yokoteramachi

Minami-enokichō

Yarai Noh Theatre

SHINJUKU-KU

HARAMACHI

Watochō

USHIGOME-KAGURAZAKA

WASEDA DORI

Fukuro-machi

2

Kita-yamabushichō

Ushigome-Kagurazaka

Tansumachi

KITAMACHI

NAKACHO

Ushigome-Yanagichō

Ichigaya-Yamabushichō

433

MINAMICHO

Watochō

Ichigaya-Korachō

Saiku-machi

Nijukkimachi

Minami-enokichō

KANADACHO

HARAIKATAMACHI

Ichigaya-Sadoharachō

Ichigaya-kagachō

Ichigaya Yakuōjimachi

319

Kawadachō

Ichigaya-Takajōmachi

Ichigaya-Tamachi

GAJEN-HIGASHI DORI

Ichigaya-Sanaichō

Ichigaya-Chōenjimachi

Soto-bori

Defense Agency

© Explorer Group Ltd. 2008

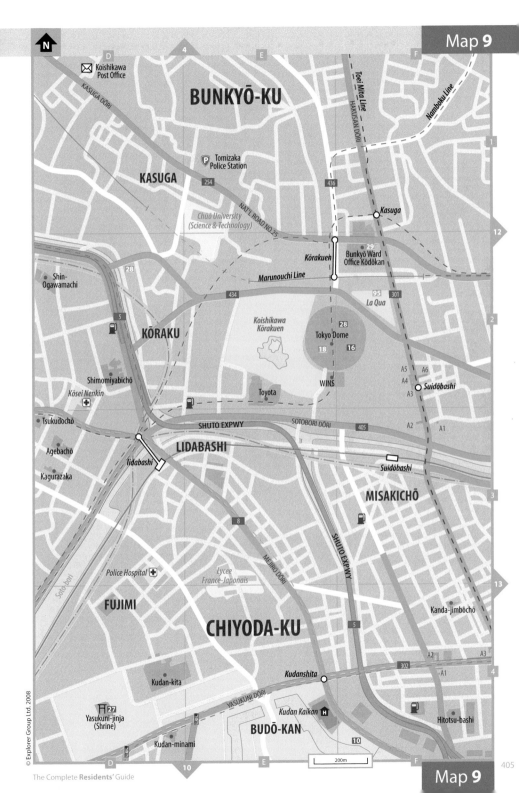

Map 9

N

✉ Koishikawa
Post Office

BUNKYŌ-KU

KASUGA DORI

Toei Mita Line

HAKUSAN DORI

Namboku Line

KASUGA

254

NAT'L ROAD NO.25

436

Ⓟ Tomizaka
Police Station

Chūō University
(Science & Technology)

○ *Kasuga*

12

Shin-
Ogawamachi

28

Kōrakueh

29
Bunkyō Ward
Office Kōdōkan

434

95 **301**
La Qua

5

KŌRAKU

Koishikawa
Kōrakuen

28

Tokyo Dome

18 **16**

2

Shimomiyabichō

Kōsei Nenkin ✚

Toyota

WINS

A5   A6
A4
A3

○ *Suidōbashi*

Tsukudochō

SHUTO EXPWY

SOTOBORI DORI

405

A2   A1

Agebachō

LIDABASHI

⬜ *Iidabashi*

Kagurazaka

Suidōbashi

MISAKICHŌ

3

Soto-bori

8

MEIRO DORI

SHUTO EXPWY

13

✚ Police Hospital

Lycée
France-Japonais

Kanda-jimbōchō

FUJIMI

CHIYODA-KU

5

A2   A3

302

A1

Kudan-kita

○ *Kudanshita*

4

⛽

Hitotsu-bashi

Ħ**27**
Yasukuni-jinja
(Shrine)

Kudan Kaikan Ⓗ

BUDŌ-KAN

10

Kudan-minami

YASUKUNI DORI

200m

Map 9

Map **10**

N

Ⓖ General Information p.1 Ⓡ Residents p.49 Ⓔ Exploring p.145 Ⓐ Activities p.207 Ⓢ Shopping p.271 Ⓞ Going Out p.323

Ichigaya
Hachimanchō

47

Ichigaya

302

YASUKUNI DORI

302

Namboku Line

Soto-bori

405

3

Shinjuku
Hist'l Museum

SAN'EICHŌ

GOBANCHŌ

YONBANCHI

SHINJUKU-KU

21

ROKUBANCHŌ

Chūō Line

SHINJUKU DORI

NTV
Kojimachi

Green Palace

Israel Ⓔ

Portugal Ⓔ
25

NIBANCHŌ

CHIYODA-KU

WAKABA

26

SHINJUKU DORI

Yotsuya

Zenkyoren

23
24

Kōjimachi
50

Sophia
University

414

405

Ⓔ India 12

HIRA-KAWACHŌ

Minami-
Motomachi

4

Shimizudani
Park

Toshi Centre

Zenkyoren

South Africa Ⓔ
28

State
Guesthouse

55 Ⓗ 12
New Ōtani

123

Kioicho

Akasaka
Prince Ⓗ

9b

Tōgō Gosho

9a

6

Suntory
Museum of Art

Residence of
Speaker, House
of Rep.

Akasaka-Mitsuke

Sudan, Lebanon & Jordan

8

Excel Tokyu Ⓗ

B

MOTO-AKASAKA

Toyokawa 卍
Inari

NATIONAL ROAD NO.246

Mexico Ⓔ
Prudential
Tower

Mansion of
Prince Chichibu

Akasaka
Fudōson

Hibiya
High School

405

Hanzōmon Line

13

Akasaka
Police Station

Yamawaki
Gakuen

Hie Jinja
(Shrine)

319

Canada Ⓔ 6

0   2

MINATO-KU

1

4

Akasaka
Post Office

1

Akasaka

5   3

3   2

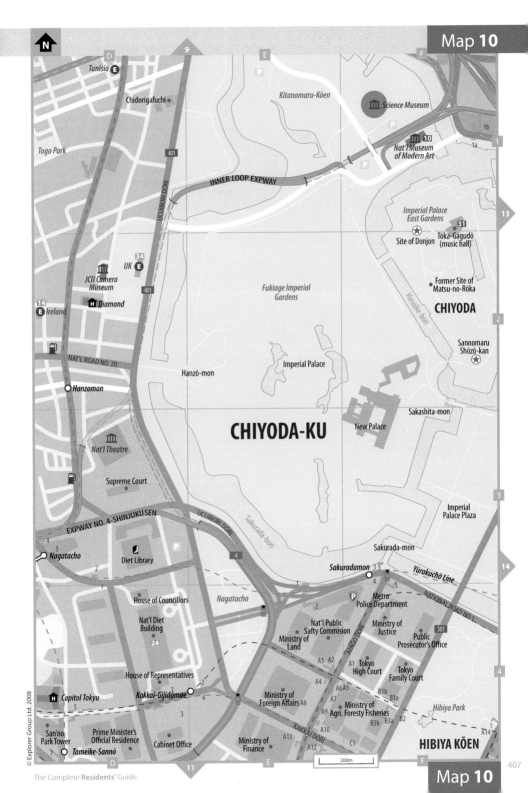

Map **10**

N

Tunisia E

Chidorigafuchi

9

Kitanomaru-Kōen

P

E

Science Museum

F

Togo Park

401

401

INNER LOOP EXPWAY

P

P

Nat'l Museum
of Modern Art

10

1b

1a

1

JCII Camera
Museum

34

UK E

13

*Imperial Palace
East Gardens*

Site of Donjon

31

Tōka-Gagudō
(music hall)

14

E Ireland

H Diamond

*Fukiage Imperial
Gardens*

Former Site of
Matsu-no-Rōka

CHIYODA

Sannomaru
Shōzō-kan

2

NAT'L ROAD NO. 20

Hanzō-mon

Imperial Palace

Hanzomon

New Palace

Sakashita-mon

Nat'l Theatre

CHIYODA-KU

Supreme Court

3

*Imperial
Palace Plaza*

EXPWAY NO. 4-SHINJUKU SEN

UCUIBORI DORI

Sakurada-bori

Nagatacho

4

3

2

1

Diet Library

P

4

Sakurada-mon

Sakuradamon

3

4

Yūrakuchō Line

14

UCUIBORI DORI

House of Councillors

1

Nagatacho

2

Metro
Police Department

P

NATIONAL ROAD NO. 1

Nat'l Diet
Building

24

Nat'l Public
Safty Commision

Ministry of
Land

Ministry of
Justice

Public
Prosecutor's Office

301

ATAGO DORI

A3 A2

A1 Tokyo
High Court

Tokyo
Family Court

House of Representatives

A4

A6 A5

B1b

B1a

H Capitol Tokyu

5

Kokkai-Gijidōmae

1

2

4

Ministry of
Foreign Affairs A8

A7

Ministry of
Agri. Foresty Fisheries

A9

B3b

B3a

B2

Hibiya Park

San'no
Park Tower

Prime Minister's
Official Residence

3

Cabinet Office

Ministry of
Finance

KAKKAI DORI

A10

A13

A12

C1

A14

7

Tameike-Sannō

D

11

E

200m

F

HIBIYA KŌEN

Map **11**

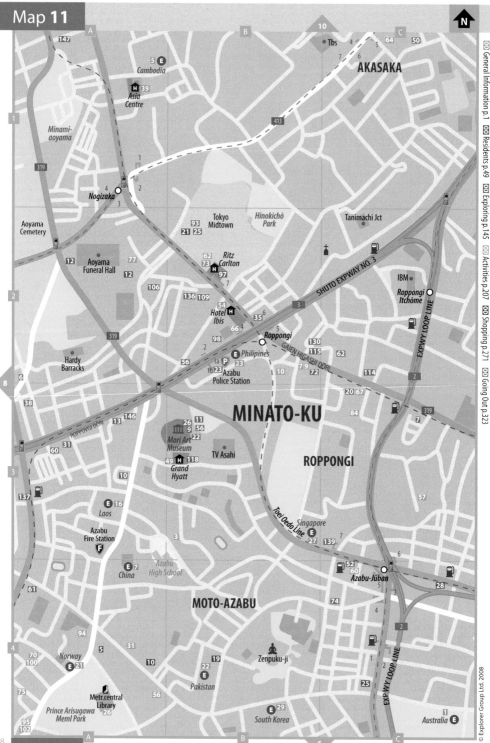

General Information p.1   Residents p.49   Exploring p.145   Activities p.207   Shopping p.271   Going Out p.323

147

5 Cambodia

39 Asia Centre

10

Tbs   4   64   50
7   6
5

AKASAKA

Minami-aoyama

319

413

Nogizaka

Aoyama Cemetery

1
2
3
4

Tokyo Midtown

93
21 25

Hinokichō Park

Tanimachi Jct

12

Aoyama Funeral Hall

77
12

106

136 109

62
73   Ritz Carlton
97

7

SHUTO EXPWAY NO. 3

IBM

Roppongi Itchōme

EXPWY LOOP LINE

319

54
Hotel   66   4
Ibis   35   6
5

98

Roppongi

2

56

1a   P
1b   23   23   Azabu
Police Station

Philipines

130
115

GAIEN HIGASHI DORI

62

7 9
72

10

114

2

20 67

84

MINATO-KU

38

13   146

ROPPOVGI DORI

60   31

10

137

26   11
9   56
22

Mori Art Museum

49   118
Grand Hyatt

TV Asahi

ROPPONGI

57

Toei Oedo Line

Singapore
27   139

7

16
Laos

Azabu Fire Station

3

52
60

Azabu-Jūban

6

28

61

7
China

Azabu High School

MOTO-AZABU

74

2

94

31

5

10

19

22
Pakistan

Zenpuku-ji

25

70
100
Norway

21

75

95
102

Metr.central Library

26

56

South Korea

29

Australia

Map **11**

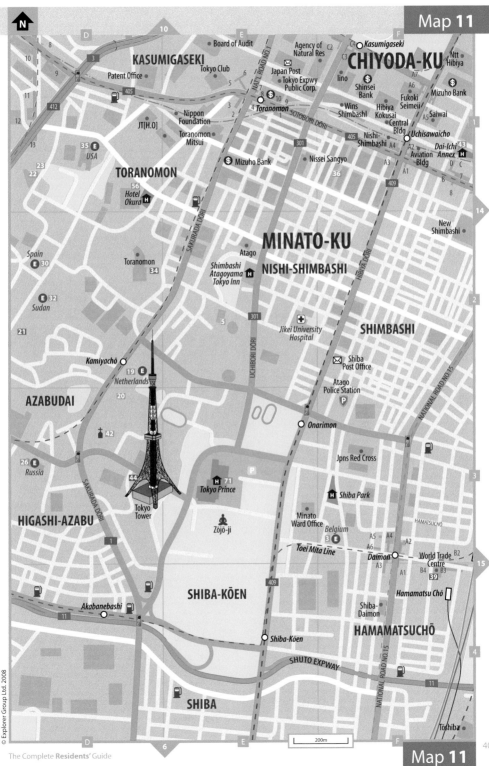

KASUMIGASEKI

• Board of Audit

Agency of
Natural Res

• Kasumigaseki

CHIYODA-KU

Ntt
Hibiya

Patent Office •

Tokyo Club

Japan Post
Tokyo Expwy
Public Corp.

Iino

Shinsei
Bank

Fukoki
Seimeii

Mizuho Bank

405

Toranomon

Wins
Shimbashi

Hibiya
Kokusai

Saiwai

Nippon
Foundation

SOTOBORI DORI

Nishi-
Shimbashi

Central
Bldg

Uchisawaicho

JT[H.O]

Toranomon
Mitsui

301

405

Dai-Ichi
Annex

Aviation
Bldg

TORANOMON

Mizuho Bank

Nissei Sangyo

36

409

New
Shimbashi

35 USA

Hotel
Okura

56

SAKURADA DORI

Atago

MINATO-KU

Spain
30

Toranomon
34

Shimbashi
Atagoyama
Tokyo Inn

NISHI-SHIMBASHI

HIBIYA DORI

32
Sudan

UCHIBORI DORI

301

SHIMBASHI

21

5

Jikei University
Hospital

Kamiyachō

19
Netherlands

Shiba
Post Office

AZABUDAI

20

Atago
Police Station

42

26
Russia

Onarimon

Jpns Red Cross

NATIONAL ROAD NO.15

Tokyo
Tower

44

Tokyo Prince

H 71

Shiba Park

HIGASHI-AZABU

1

Zōjō-ji

Minato
Ward Office

Belgium
E

HAMATSUCHO

A5   A4

A2

Toei Mita Line

A6

Daimon

A3   A1

World Trade B2
Centre

B4 B3

39

15

Akabanebashi

11

SHIBA-KŌEN

409

Shiba-
Daimon

Hamamatsu Chō

HAMAMATSUCHŌ

Shiba-Kōen

SHUTO EXPWAY

NATIONAL ROAD NO.15

11

SHIBA

Toshiba

© Explorer Group Ltd. 2008

200m

Map **12**

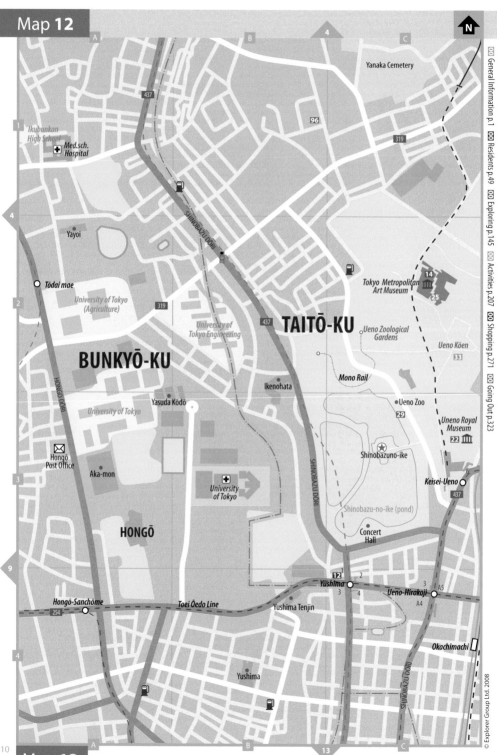

Yanaka Cemetery

437

96

319

Ikubunkan
High School
Med.sch.
Hospital

Yayoi

SHINOBAZU DORI

Tōdai mae

University of Tokyo
(Agriculture)

319

University of
Tokyo Engineering

437

TAITŌ-KU

Tokyo Metropolitan
Art Museum

14

25

Ueno Zoological
Gardens

Ueno Kōen

33

BUNKYŌ-KU

HONGO DORI

University of Tokyo

Yasuda Kōdō

Ikenohata

Mono Rail

Ueno Zoo

29

Uneno Royal
Museum

22

Hongō
Post Office

Aka-mon

SHINOBAZU DORI

Shinobazuno-ike

Keisei-Ueno

437

University
of Tokyo

Shinobazu-no-ike (pond)

HONGŌ

Concert
Hall

9

12

Yushima
2

Hongō-Sanchōme

Toei Ōedo Line

Yushima Tenjin

3   4

Ueno-Hirakoji

3   A5

A4

254

Okachimachi

Yushima

SHINOBAZU DORI

4

13

General Information p.1   Residents p.49   Exploring p.145   Activities p.207   Shopping p.271   Going Out p.323

© Explorer Group Ltd. 2008

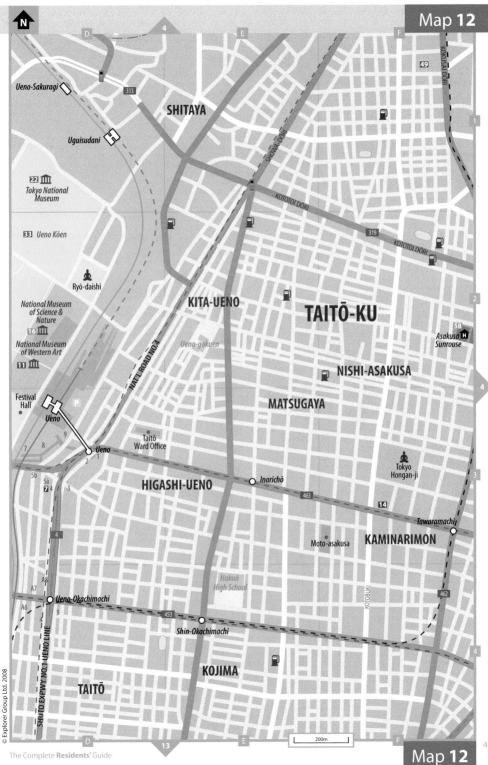

Map **12**

Map **13**

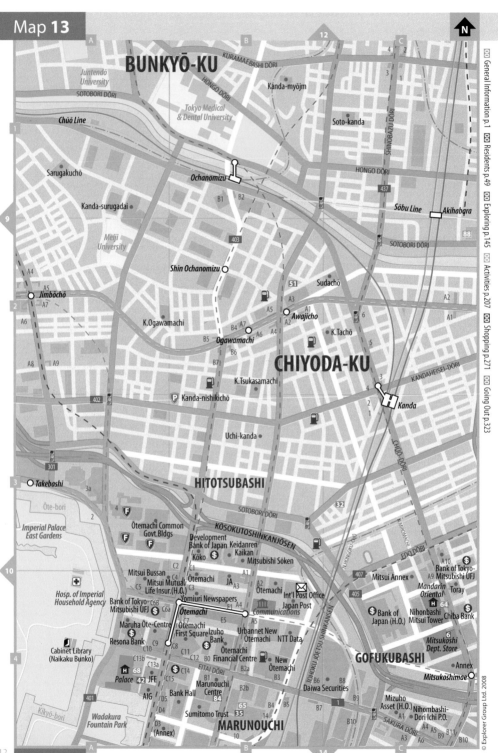

BUNKYŌ-KU

Juntendo University

SOTOBORI DŌRI

Chūō Line

KURAMAEBASHI DŌRI

Kanda-myōjm

Soto-kanda

HONGO DŌRI

Tokyo Medical & Dental University

Sarugakuchō

Ochanomizu

B1　B2

437

Sōbu Line　*Akihabara*

Kanda-surugadai

Meiji University

Shin Ochanomizu

88

SOTOBORI DŌRI

A4

A5

A7

Jimbōchō

A6

403

51

Sudachō

A2

A3

Awajicho

K.Ogawamachi

A5

A1

A2　A1

6

A2

A1

K.Tachō

A8　A9

B4　A7

Ogawamachi

A6　A4

5

B5

CHIYODA-KU

KANDAHEISEI-DORI

B7

B6

3

K.Tsukasamachi

4

2

H

Kanda

P Kanda-nishikichō

1

402

CHŪŌ-DŌRI

Uchi-kanda

Takebashi

301

HITOTSUBASHI

32

3a

Ōte-bori

2

SOTOBORI DŌRI

Imperial Palace East Gardens

KŌSOKUTOSHINKANJŌSEN

Ōtemachi Common

F

Govt.Bldgs

Development

Bank of Japan Keidanren

Kaikan

Kōko $

Mitsubishi Sōken

EDO DŌRI

C2

NIHONKOKU-CHO

A10 $ Bank of Tokyo-

Mitsui Bussan

C4

C1

A1

Ōtemachi

JA

Mitsui Annex

A9 Mitsubishi UFJ

Hosp. of Imperial Household Agency

Mitsui Mutual

C3

A3

A2

407

Mandarin Oriental Toray

Life Insur.(H.O.)

Ōtemachi

Int'l Post Office

C5

405

H 64

Bank of Tokyo-

C6B

Yomiuri Newspapers

C6a

F1 A4

Japan Post

$ Bank of

Nihonbashi

Chiba Bank

Mitsubishi UFJ $

Ōtemachi

Communications

Japan (H.O.) Mitsui Tower

6

Maruha Ōte-Centre

C7

Izuho

Urbannet New

Mitsukoshi Dept. Store

Resona Bank

Ōtemachi

Bank

Ōtemachi NTT Data

C9

First Square

E5

GOFUKUBASHI

Cabinet Library (Naikaku Bunko)

C10

C8

C11

Ōtemachi

Annex

C13b

C12 B0

Financial Centre

New

Mitsukoshimae

H 68

C13a

$

C14

Ōtemachi

Palace 42 JFE

C15

EITAI DŌRI

B1

B2a

B3

Mizuho

AIG

D5

Marunouchi

Asset (H.O.) Nihombashi-

Kikyō-bori

D4

Bank Hall

Centre

B2b

B9

Dori Ichi P.O.

Wadakura Fountain Park

401

Sumitomo Trust

65

B4 B5

SAKURA DŌRI

O3

35

14

B7

1

(Annex)

MARUNOUCHI

B10

A3 A4 A5 B11

10

A6

B10

Map **13**

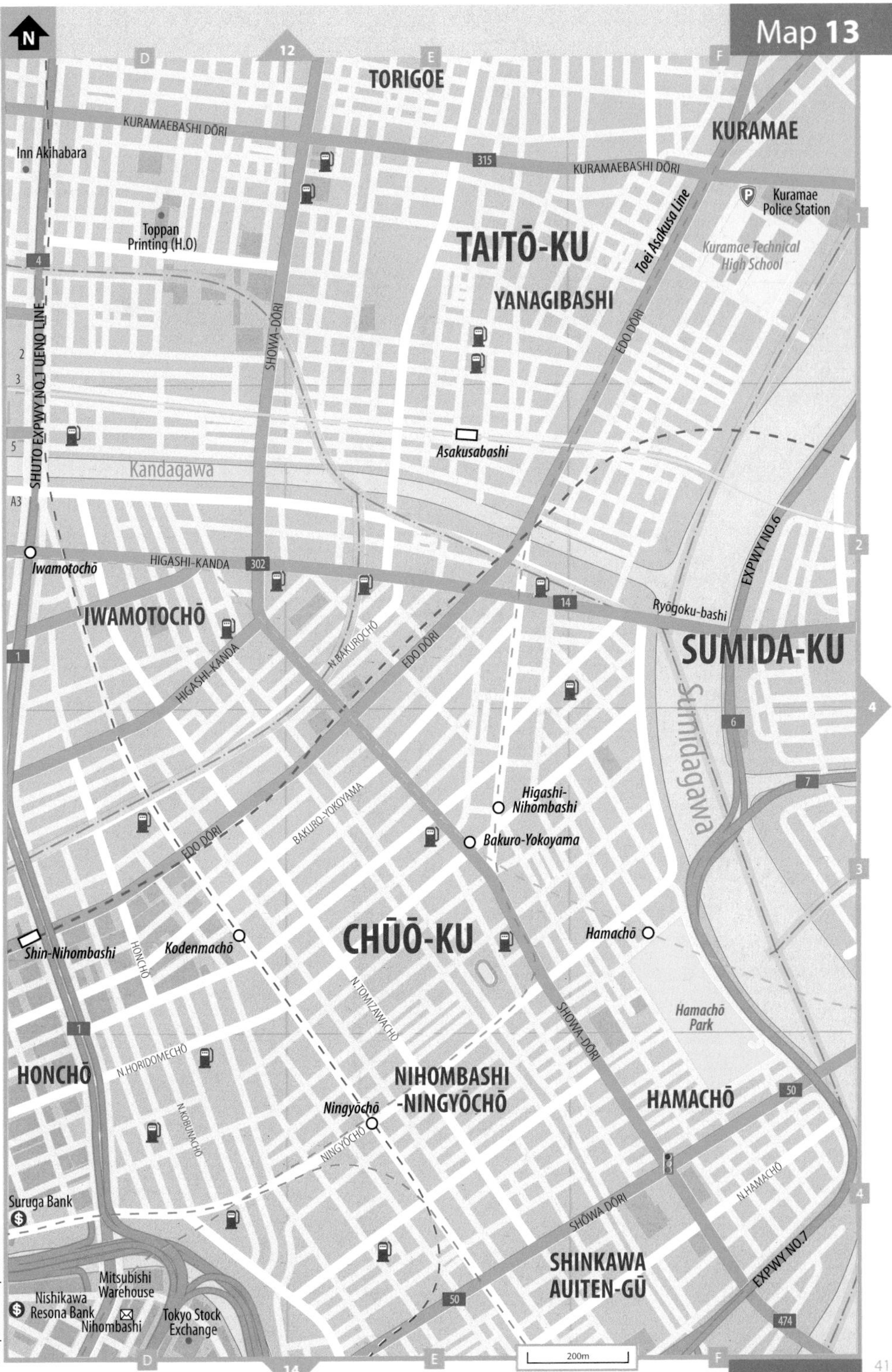

TORIGOE

KURAMAE

KURAMAEBASHI DŌRI

Inn Akihabara

KURAMAEBASHI DŌRI

315

P Kuramae
Police Station

Toppan
Printing (H.O)

TAITŌ-KU

Kuramae Technical
High School

YANAGIBASHI

SHUTO EXPWY NO.1 UENO LINE

Kandagawa

Asakusabashi

EDO DŌRI

Toei Asakusa Line

EXPWY NO.6

Iwamotochō

HIGASHI-KANDA 302

14

Ryōgoku-bashi

IWAMOTOCHŌ

SUMIDA-KU

HIGASHI-KANDA

N.BAKUROCHŌ

EDO DŌRI

6

Sumidagawa

7

EDO DŌRI

BAKURO-YOKOYAMA

Higashi-
Nihombashi

3

Bakuro-Yokoyama

Shin-Nihombashi

Kodenmachō

CHŪŌ-KU

Hamachō

HONCHŌ

N.TOMIZAWACHŌ

Hamachō
Park

HONCHŌ

N.HORIDOMECHO

1

Ningyōchō

**NIHOMBASHI
-NINGYŌCHŌ**

SHŌWA-DŌRI

HAMACHŌ

50

N.BUNACHŌ

NINGYŌCHŌ

N.HAMACHŌ

Suruga Bank

$

SHŌWA-DŌRI

Mitsubishi
Warehouse

Nishikawa
Resona Bank
Nihombashi

$

Tokyo Stock
Exchange

**SHINKAWA
AUITEN-GŪ**

50

EXPWY NO.7

474

200m

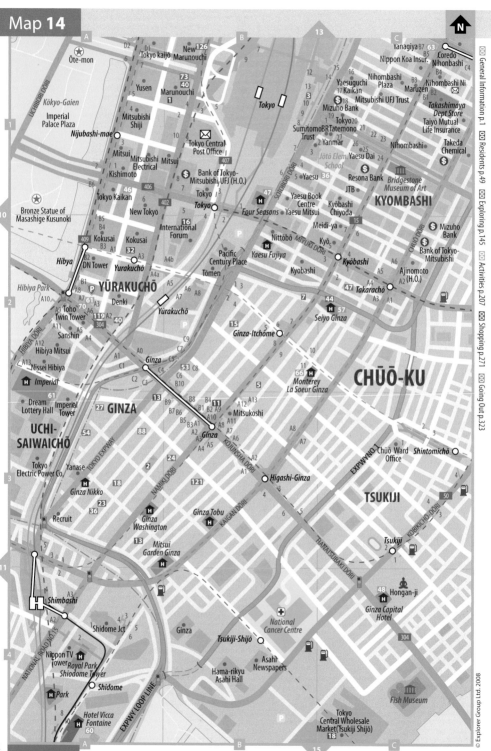

Map **14**

[14] General Information p.1 [14] Residents p.49 [14] Exploring p.145 [14] Activities p.207 [14] Shopping p.271 [14] Going Out p.323

Map **14**

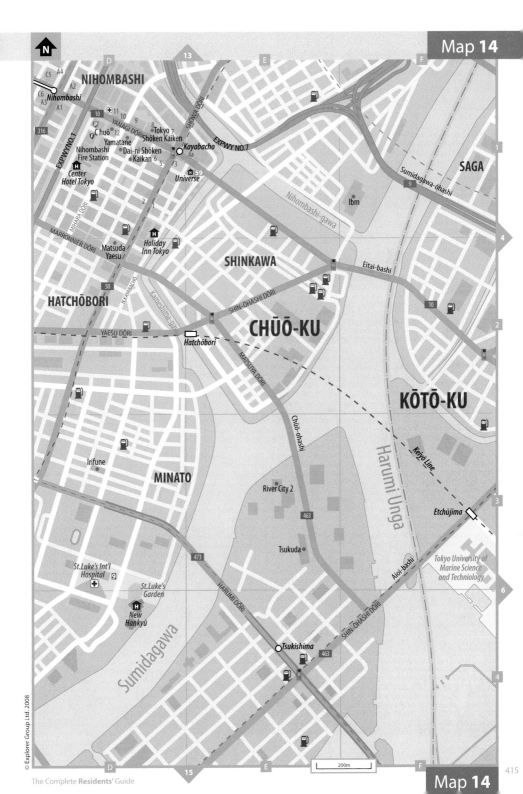

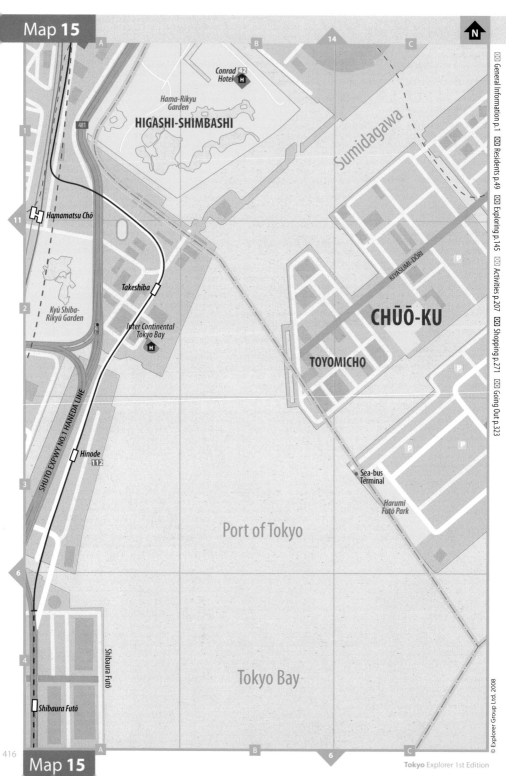

Map **15**

N

Conrad
Hotel 42 H

Hama-Rikyu
Garden

HIGASHI-SHIMBASHI

Sumidagawa

481

1

14

C

B

A

Hamamatsu Chō

11

Kyū Shiba-
Rikyū Garden

2

Takeshiba

Inter Continental
Tokyo Bay
H

KIYASUMI-DŌRI

P

CHŪŌ-KU

TOYOMICHO

P

SHUTO EXPWY NO.1 HANEDA LINE

Hinode
112

3

P

Sea-bus
Terminal

Harumi
Futō Park

P

P

Port of Tokyo

6

Shibaura Futō

4

Tokyo Bay

Shibaura Futō

General Information p.1   Residents p.49   Exploring p.145   Activities p.207   Shopping p.271   Going Out p.323

Map 15

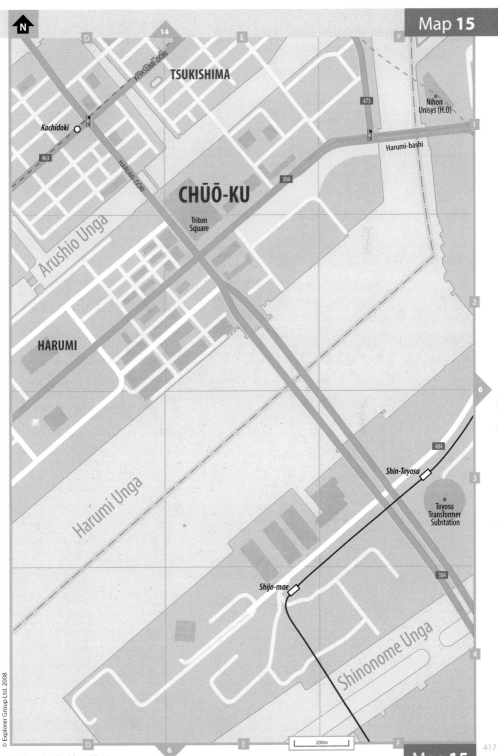

© Explorer Group Ltd. 2008

Is getting lost your usual excuse?

Whether you're a map person or not, this
pocket-sized marvel will help you get to know
the city like the back of your hand – so you
won't feel the back of someone else's.

Tokyo Mini Map
Fit the city in your pocket

EXPLORER

Index

Index

Index

Index

Index

Residents' Guides

All you need to know about living, working and enjoying life in these exciting destinations

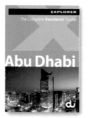   

Coming in 2008/9: Bangkok, Brussels, Mexico City, Moscow, San Francisco, Saudi Arabia and Taipei

Mini Guides
The perfect pocket-sized
Visitors' Guides

Coming in 2008/9: Bangkok, Brussels, Mexico City, Moscow, San Francisco and Taipei

Mini Maps
Wherever you are,
never get lost again

Check out www.explorerpublishing.com/products

Photography Books
Beautiful cities caught through the lens

Calendars
The time, the place, and the date

Maps
Wherever you are, never get lost again

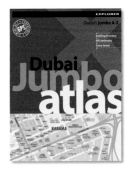

Activity and Lifestyle Guides
Drive, trek, dive and swim... life will never be boring again

Retail sales
Our books are available in most good bookshops around the world, and are also available online at Amazon.co.uk and Amazon.com. If you would like to enquire about any of our international distributors, please contact retail@explorerpublishing.com

Bulk sales and customisation
All our products are available for bulk sales with customisation options. For discount rates and further information, please contact corporatesales@explorerpublishing.com

Licensing and digital sales
All our content, maps and photography are available for print or digital use. For licensing enquiries please contact licensing@explorerpublishing.com

Check out www.explorerpublishing.com/products

Ahmed Mainodin
AKA: Mystery Man
We can never recognise Ahmed because of his constantly changing facial hair. He waltzes in with big lambchop sideburns one day, a handlebar moustache the next, and a neatly trimmed goatee after that. So far we've had no objections to his hirsute chameleonisms, but we'll definitely draw the line at a monobrow.

Andrea Fust
AKA: Mother Superior
By day Andrea is the most efficient manager in the world and by night she replaces the boardroom for her board and wows the pants off the dudes in Ski Dubai. Literally. Back in the office she definitely wears the trousers!

Ajay Krishnan R
AKA: Web Wonder
Ajay's mum and dad knew he was going to be an IT genius when they found him reconfiguring his Commodore 64 at the tender age of 2. He went on to become the technology consultant on all three Matrix films, and counts Keanu as a close personal friend.

Bahrudeen Abdul
AKA: The Stallion
Having tired of creating abstract sculptures out of papier maché and candy canes, Bahrudeen turned to the art of computer programming. After honing his skills in the southern Andes for three years he grew bored of Patagonian winters, and landed a job here, 'The Home of 01010101 Creative Freedom'.

Alex Jeffries
AKA: Easy Rider
Alex is happiest when dressed in leather from head to toe with a humming machine between his thighs – just like any other motorbike enthusiast. Whenever he's not speeding along the Hatta Road at full throttle, he can be found at his beloved Mac, still dressed in leather.

Ben Merrett
AKA: Big Ben
After a short (or tall as the case may have been) career as a human statue, Ben tired of the pigeons choosing him, rather than his namesake, as a public convenience and decided to fly the nest to seek his fortune in foreign lands. Not only is he big on personality but he brings in the big bucks with his bulk!

Alistair MacKenzie
AKA: Media Mogul
If only Alistair could take the paperless office one step further and achieve the officeless office he would be the happiest publisher alive. Wireless access from a remote spot somewhere in the Hajar Mountains would suit this intrepid explorer – less traffic, lots of fresh air, and wearing sandals all day – the perfect work environment!

Cherry Enriquez
AKA: Bean Counter
With the team's penchant for sweets and pastries, it's good to know we have Cherry on top of our accounting cake. The local confectioner is always paid on time, so we're guaranteed great gateaux for every special occasion.

Annabel Clough
AKA: Bollywood Babe
Taking a short break from her successful career in Bollywood, Annabel livens up the Explorer office with her spontaneous dance routines and random passionate outpouring of song. If there is a whiff of drama or a hint of romance, Annabel's famed vocal chords and nifty footwork will bring a touch of glamour to Al Quoz.

Claire England
AKA: Whip Cracker
No longer able to freeload off the fact that she once appeared in a Robbie Williams video, Claire now puts her creative skills to better use – looking up rude words in the dictionary! A child of English nobility, Claire is quite the lady – unless she's down at Rock Bottom.

Darwin Lovitos
AKA: The Philosopher
We are firm believers in our own Darwinism theory at Explorer – enthusiasm, organisation and a great sense of humour can evolve into a wonderful thing. He may not have the big beard (except on weekends) , but Darwin is just as wise as his namesake.

Hashim MM
AKA: Speedy Gonzales
They don't come much faster than Hashim – he's so speedy with his mouse that scientists are struggling to create a computer that can keep up with him. His nimble fingers leave his keyboard smouldering (he gets through three a week), and his go-faster stripes make him almost invisible to the naked eye when he moves.

David Quinn
AKA: Sharp Shooter
After a short stint as a children's TV presenter was robbed from David because he developed an allergy to sticky back plastic, he made his way to sandier pastures. Now that he's thinking outside the box, nothing gets past the man with the sharpest pencil in town.

Helen Spearman
AKA: Little Miss Sunshine
With her bubbly laugh and permanent smile, Helen is a much-needed ray of sunshine in the office when we're all grumpy and facing harrowing deadlines. It's almost impossible to think that she ever loses her temper or shows a dark side... although put her behind the wheel of a car, and you've got instant road rage.

Derrick Pereira
AKA: The Returnimator
After leaving Explorer in 2003, Derrick's life took a dramatic downturn – his dog ran away, his prized bonsai tree died and he got kicked out of his thrash metal band. Since rejoining us, things are looking up and he just found out he's won $10 million in a Nigerian sweepstakes competition. And he's got the desk by the window!

Henry Hilos
AKA: The Quiet Man
Henry can rarely be seen from behind his large obstructive screen but when you do catch a glimpse you'll be sure to get a smile. Lighthearted Henry keeps all those glossy pages filled with pretty pictures for something to look at when you can't be bothered to read.

Enrico Maullon
AKA: The Crooner
Frequently mistaken for his near-namesake Enrique Iglesias, Enrico decided to capitalise and is now a regular stand-in for the Latin heartthrob. If he's ever missing from the office, it usually means he's off performing for millions of adoring fans on another stadium tour of America.

Iain Young
AKA: 'The Cat'
Iain follows in the fine tradition of Scots with safe hands – Alan Rough, Andy Goram, Jim Leighton on a good day – but breaking into the Explorer XI has proved frustrating. There's no match on a Mac, but that Al Huzaifa ringer doesn't half make himself big.

Firos Khan
AKA: Big Smiler
Previously a body double in kung fu movies, including several appearances in close up scenes for Steven Seagal's moustache. He also once tore down a restaurant with his bare hands after they served him a mild curry by mistake.

Ieyad Charaf
AKA: Fashion Designer
When we hired Ieyad as a top designer, we didn't realise we'd be getting his designer tops too! By far the snappiest dresser in the office, you'd be hard-pressed to beat his impeccably ironed shirts.

Grace Carnay
AKA: Manila Ice
It's just as well the office is so close to a movie theatre, because Grace is always keen to catch the latest Hollywood offering from Brad Pitt, who she admires purely for his acting ability, of course. Her ice cool exterior conceals a tempestuous passion for jazz, which fuels her frenzied typing speed.

The Team

Ingrid Cupido
AKA: The Karaoke Queen
Ingrid has a voice to match her starlet name. She'll put any Pop Idols to shame once behind the mike, and she's pretty nifty on a keyboard too. She certainly gets our vote if she decides to go pro; just remember you saw her here first.

Ivan Rodrigues
AKA: The Aviator
After making a mint in the airline market, Ivan came to Explorer where he works for pleasure, not money. That's his story, anyway. We know that he is actually a corporate spy from a rival company and that his multi-level spreadsheets are really elaborate codes designed to confuse us.

Jake Marsico
AKA: Don Calzone
Jake spent the last 10 years on the tiny triangular Mediterranean island of Samoza, honing his traditional cooking techniques and perfecting his Italian. Now, whenever he returns to his native America, he impresses his buddies by effortlessly zapping a hot dog to perfection in any microwave, anywhere, anytime.

Jane Roberts
AKA: The Oracle
After working in an undisclosed role in the government, Jane brought her super sleuth skills to Explorer. Whatever the question, she knows what, where, who, how and when, but her encyclopaedic knowledge is only impressive until you realise she just makes things up randomly.

Jayde Fernandes
AKA: Pop Idol
Jayde's idol is Britney Spears, and he recently shaved his head to show solidarity with the troubled star. When he's not checking his dome for stubble, or practising the dance moves to 'Baby One More Time' in front of the bathroom mirror, he actually manages to get some designing done.

Johny Mathew
AKA: The Hawker
Caring Johny used to nurse wounded eagles back to health and teach them how to fly again before trying his luck in merchandising. Fortunately his skills in the field have come in handy at Explorer, where his efforts to improve our book sales have been a soaring success.

Joy Tubog
AKA: Joyburgh
Don't let her saintly office behaviour deceive you. Joy has the habit of jumping up and down while screaming 'Jumanji' the instant anyone mentions Robin Williams and his hair sweater. Thankfully, her volleyball team has learned to utilize her 'uniqueness' when it's her turn to spike the ball.

Juby Jose
AKA: The Nutcracker
After years as a ballet teacher, Juby decided on mapping out a completely different career path, charting the UAE's ever-changing road network. Plotting products to illuminate the whole of the Middle East, she now works alongside the all-singing, all-dancing Madathil brothers, and cracks any nut that steps out of line.

Kate Fox
AKA: Contacts Collector
Kate swooped into the office like the UK equivalent of Wonderwoman, minus the tights of course (it's much too hot for that), but armed with a superhuman marketing brain. Even though she's just arrived, she is already a regular on the Dubai social scene – she is helping to blast Explorer into the stratosphere, one champagne-soaked networking party at a time.

Kathryn Calderon
AKA: Miss Moneypenny
With her high-flying banking background, Kathryn is an invaluable member of the team. During her lunchtimes she conducts 'get rich quick' seminars that, she says, will make us so much money that we'll be able to retire early and spend our days reading books instead of making them. We're still waiting...

Katie Drynan
AKA: The Irish Deputy
This Irish lass is full of sass, fresh from her previous role as the four leaf clover mascot for the Irish ladies' rugby team. Katie provides the Explorer office with lots of Celtic banter and unlimited Irish charm.

Kelly Tesoro
AKA: Leading Lady
Kelly's former career as a Korean soapstar babe set her in good stead for the daily dramas at the bold and beautiful Explorer office. As our lovely receptionist she's on stage all day and her winning smile never slips.

Matt Farquharson
AKA: Hack Hunter
A career of tuppence-a-word hackery ended when Matt arrived in Dubai to cover a maggot wranglers' convention. He misguidedly thinks he's clever because he once wrote for some grown-up English papers.

Kiran Melwani
AKA: Bow Selector
Like a modern-day Robin Hood (right down to the green tights and band of merry men), Kiran's mission in life is to distribute Explorer's wealth of knowledge to the fact-hungry readers of the world. Just make sure you never do anything to upset her – rumour has it she's a pretty mean shot with that bow and arrow.

Mathew Samuel
AKA: Mr Modest
Matt's penchant for the entrepreneurial life began with a pair of red braces and a filofax when still a child. That yearning for the cut and thrust of commerce has brought him to Dubai, where he made a fortune in the sand-selling business before semi-retiring at Explorer.

Laura Zuffa
AKA: Travelling Salesgirl
Laura's passport is covered in more stamps than Kofi Annan's, and there isn't a city, country or continent that she won't travel to. With a smile that makes grown men weep, our girl on the frontlines always brings home the beef bacon.

Michael Samuel
AKA: Gordon Gekko
We have a feeling this mild mannered master of mathematics has a wild side. He hasn't witnessed an Explorer party yet but the office agrees that once the karaoke machine is out, Michael will be the maestro. Watch out Dubai!

Lennie Mangalino
AKA: Shaker Maker
With a giant spring in her step and music in her heart it's hard to not to swing to the beat when Lennie passes by in the office. She loves her Lambada… and Samba… and Salsa and anything else she can get the sales team shaking their hips to.

Mimi Stankova
AKA: Mind Controller
A master of mind control, Mimi's siren-like voice lulls people into doing whatever she asks. Her steely reserve and endless patience mean recalcitrant reporters and persistent PR people are putty in her hands, delivering whatever she wants, whenever she wants it.

Mannie Lugtu
AKA: Distribution Demon
When the travelling circus rode into town, their master juggler Mannie decided to leave the Big Top and explore Dubai instead. He may have swapped his balls for our books but his juggling skills still come in handy.

Mohammed Sameer
AKA: Man in the Van
Known as MS, short for Microsoft, Sameer can pick apart a PC like a thief with a lock, which is why we keep him out of finance and pounding Dubai's roads in the unmissable Explorer van – so we can always spot him coming.

Maricar Ong
AKA: Pocket Docket
A pint-sized dynamo of ruthless efficiency, Maricar gets the job done before anyone else notices it needed doing. If this most able assistant is absent for a moment, it sends a surge of blind panic through the Explorer ranks.

The Team

Najumudeen Kuttathundil
AKA: The Groove
If it weren't for Najumudeen, our stock of books would be lying in a massive pile of rubble in our warehouse. Thankfully, through hours of crunk dancing and forklift racing with Mohammed T, Najumudeen has perfected the art of organisation and currently holds the title for fastest forklift slalom in the UAE.

Noushad Madathil
AKA: Map Daddy
Where would Explorer be without the mercurial Madathil brothers? Lost in the Empty Quarter, that's where. Quieter than a mute dormouse, Noushad prefers to let his Photoshop layers, and brother Zain, do all the talking. A true Map Daddy.

Pamela Afram
AKA: Lady of Arabia
After an ill-fated accident playing Lawrence of Arabia's love interest in a play in Jumeira, Pamela found solace in the Explorer office. Her first paycheque went on a set of shiny new gleamers and she is now back to her bright and smiley self and is solely responsible for lighting up one half of the office!

Pamela Grist
AKA: Happy Snapper
If a picture can speak a thousand words then Pam's photos say a lot about her - through her lens she manages to find the beauty in everything – even this motley crew. And when the camera never lies, thankfully Photoshop can.

Pete Maloney
AKA: Graphic Guru
Image conscious he may be, but when Pete has his designs on something you can bet he's gonna get it! He's the king of chat up lines, ladies – if he ever opens a conversation with 'D'you come here often?' then brace yourself for the Maloney magic.

Rafi Jamal
AKA: Soap Star
After a walk on part in The Bold and the Beautiful, Rafi swapped the Hollywood Hills for the Hajar Mountains. Although he left the glitz behind, he still mingles with high society, moonlighting as a male gigolo and impressing Dubai's ladies with his fancy footwork.

Rafi VP
AKA: Party Trickster
After developing a rare allergy to sunlight in his teens, Rafi started to lose a few centimeters of height every year. He now stands just 30cm tall, and does his best work in our dingy basement wearing a pair of infrared goggles. His favourite party trick is to fold himself into a briefcase.

Richard Greig
AKA: Sir Lancelot
Chivalrous to the last, Richard's dream of being a medieval knight suffered a setback after being born several centuries too late. His stellar parliamentary career remains intact, and he is in the process of creating a new party with the aim of abolishing all onions and onion-related produce.

Roshni Ahuja
AKA: Bright Spark
Never failing to brighten up the office with her colourful get-up, Roshni definitely puts the 'it' in the IT department. She's a perennially pleasant, profound programmer with peerless panache, and she does her job with plenty of pep and piles of pizzazz.

Sean Kearns
AKA: The Tall Guy
Big Sean, as he's affectionately known, is so laid back he actually spends most of his time lying down (unless he's on a camping trip, when his ridiculously small tent forces him to sleep on his hands and knees). Despite the rest of us constantly tripping over his lanky frame, when the job requires someone who will work flat out, he always rises to the editorial occasion.

Shabsir M
AKA: Sticky Wicket
Shabsir is a valuable player on the Indian national cricket team, so instead of working you'll usually find him autographing cricket balls for crazed fans around the world. We don't mind though – if ever a retailer is stumped because they run out of stock, he knocks them for six with his speedy delivery.

Shan Kumar
AKA: Caped Crusader
Not dissimilar to the Batman's beacon, Explorer shines a giant X into the skies over Al Quoz in times of need. Luckily for us, Shan battled for days through the sand and warehouse units to save the day at our shiny new office. What a hero!

Steve Jones
AKA: Golden Boy
Our resident Kiwi lives in a nine-bedroom mansion and is already planning an extension. His winning smile has caused many a knee to weaken in Bur Dubai but sadly for the ladies, he's hopelessly devoted to his clients.

Shawn Jackson Zuzarte
AKA: Paper Plumber
If you thought rocket science was hard, try rearranging the chaotic babble that flows from the editorial team! If it weren't for Shawn, most of our books would require a kaleidoscope to read correctly so we're keeping him and his jazz hands under wraps.

Tim Binks
AKA: Class Clown
El Binksmeisterooney is such a sharp wit, he often has fellow Explorers gushing tea from their noses in convulsions of mirth. Years spent hiking across the Middle East have given him an encyclopaedic knowledge of rock formations and elaborate hair.

Shyrell Tamayo
AKA: Fashion Princess
We've never seen Shyrell wearing the same thing twice – her clothes collection is so large that her husband has to keep all his things in a shoebox. She runs Designlab like clockwork, because being late for deadlines is SO last season.

Tom Jordan
AKA: The True Professional
Explorer's resident thesp, Tom delivers lines almost as well as he cuts them. His early promise on the pantomime circuit was rewarded with an all-action role in hit UK drama Heartbeat. He's still living off the royalties – and the fact he shared a sandwich with Kenneth Branagh.

Sobia Gulzad
AKA: High Flyer
If Sobia's exam results in economics and management are anything to go by, she's destined to become a member of the global jet set. Her pursuit of glamour is almost more relentless than her pursuit of success, and in her time away from reading The Wealth of Nations she shops for designer handbags and that elusive perfect shade of lipgloss.

Tracy Fitzgerald
AKA: 'La Dona'
Tracy is a queenpin Catalan mafiosa and ringleader for the 'pescadora' clan, a nefarious group that runs a sushi smuggling operation between the Costa Brava and Ras Al Khaimah. She is not to be crossed. Rival clans will find themselves fed fish, and then fed to the fishes.

Sunita Lakhiani
AKA: Designlass
Initially suspicious of having a female in their midst, the boys in Designlab now treat Sunita like one of their own. A big shame for her, because they treat each other pretty damn bad!

Zainudheen Madathil
AKA: Map Master
Often confused with retired footballer Zinedine Zidane because of his dexterous displays and a bad head-butting habit, Zain tackles design with the mouse skills of a star striker. Maps are his goal and despite getting red-penned a few times, when he shoots, he scores.

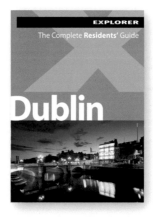

Flick back a few pages and ask yourself…
…would you like to see your face?

Explorer has grown from a one-man operation a decade ago to a 60+ team today and our expansion isn't slowing down. We are always looking for creative bods, from PR pro's and master marketers to daring designers and excellent editors, as well as super sales and support staff.

So what are you waiting for? Apply online at www.explorerpublishing.com

The *Tokyo Explorer* Team

Lead Editor Tim Binks
Deputy Editor Katie Drynan
Editorial Assistants Mimi Stankova, Kathryn Calderon
Designer Shawn Jackson Zuzarte
Cartographers Mohammed Faisal, Mohammed Illyas,
Sudeer Mekkatu, Sunita Lakhiani
Photographers Victor Romero, Pamela Grist, Tim Binks,
Florian Lumperda, Nick & Hitomi O'Connell, Andy Sharp
Proofreader Jo Holden MacDonald
Translators Miki Binks, Nozomi Okuyama-Smith

Publishing
Publisher Alistair MacKenzie
Associate Publisher Claire England
Assistant to Associate Publisher Kathryn Calderon

Editorial
Group Editor Jane Roberts
Lead Editors David Quinn, Katie Drynan,
Matt Farquharson, Sean Kearns, Tim Binks, Tom Jordan
Deputy Editors Helen Spearman, Jake Marsico,
Jenny Lyon, Pamela Afram, Richard Greig
Senior Editorial Assistant Mimi Stankova
Editorial Assistants Grace Carnay, Ingrid Cupido

Design
Creative Director Pete Maloney
Art Director Ieyad Charaf
Design Manager Alex Jeffries
Senior Designer Iain Young
Junior Designer Jessy Perera
Layout Manager Jayde Fernandes
Designers Hashim Moideen, Rafi VP, Shawn Jackson Zuzarte
Cartography Manager Zainudheen Madathil
Cartographers Juby Jose, Noushad Madathil, Sunita Lakhiani
Traffic Manager Maricar Ong
Production Coordinator Joy Tubog

Photography
Photography Manager Pamela Grist
Photographer Victor Romero
Image Editor Henry Hilos

Sales & Marketing
Media Sales Area Managers Laura Zuffa, Stephen Jones
Corporate Sales Executive Ben Merrett
Marketing Manager Kate Fox
Marketing Executive Annabel Clough
Marketing Assistant Shedan Ebona
Digital Content Manager Derrick Pereira
International Retail Sales Manager Ivan Rodrigues
Retail Sales Coordinators Kiran Melwani, Sobia Gulzad
Retail Sales Supervisor Mathew Samuel
Retail Sales Merchandisers Johny Mathew, Shan Kumar
Sales & Marketing Coordinator Lennie Mangalino
Senior Distribution Executives Ahmed Mainodin, Firos Khan
Warehouse Assistant Najumudeen Kuttathundil Ismail
Drivers Mohammed Sameer, Shabsir Madathil

Finance & Administration
Finance Manager Michael Samuel
HR & Administration Manager Andrea Fust
Admin Manager Shyrell Tamayo
Junior Accountant Cherry Enriquez
Accountants Assistant Darwin Lovitas
Administrators Enrico Maullon, Kelly Tesoro
Drivers Rafi Jamal, Mannie Lugtu

IT
IT Administrator Ajay Krishnan
Senior Software Engineer Bahrudeen Abdul
Software Engineer Roshni Ahuja

Contact Us

Reader Response
If you have any comments and suggestions, fill out
our online reader response form and you could win prizes.
Log on to **www.explorerpublishing.com**

General Enquiries
We'd love to hear your thoughts and answer any questions
you have about this book or any other Explorer product.
Contact us at **info@explorerpublishing.com**

Careers
If you fancy yourself as an Explorer, send your CV
(stating the position you're interested in) to
jobs@explorerpublishing.com

Designlab & Contract Publishing
For enquiries about Explorer's Contract Publishing arm
and design services contact
designlab@explorerpublishing.com

PR & Marketing
For PR and marketing enquries contact
marketing@explorerpublishing.com
pr@explorerpublishing.com

Corporate Sales
For bulk sales and customisation options, for this book or
any Explorer product, contact
sales@explorerpublishing.com

Advertising & Sponsorship
For advertising and sponsorship, contact
media@explorerpublishing.com

Explorer Publishing & Distribution
PO Box 34275, Dubai, United Arab Emirates
www.explorerpublishing.com

Phone: +971 (0)4 340 8805
Fax: +971 (0)4 340 8806

Emergency Numbers

Ambulance	119
Coast Guard	118
Fire	119
Police	110

Useful Numbers

KDDI Directory Enquiries (English)	0077
NTT Directory Enquiries	104
Japan Helpline	0120 461 997
Tokyo Metropolitan Police Lost & Found	03 5285 8181

Transport Information

Haneda Airport

Flight Information	03 5757 8111
Lost Property	03 57578107

Narita Airport

Flight Information	047 634 8000
Lost Property	047 632 2105
All Nippon Airways (ANA)	0120 02 9709
Japan Airlines (JAL)	03 5460 0511
Japan Rail	www.japanrail.com
Route Planner	www.jorudan.co.jp
Tokyo Metro	www.tokyometro.jp

Landmark Hotels

Cerulean Tower	03 3476 3000
Conrad	03 6388 8000
Four Seasons Hotel Tokyo at Chinzanso	03 3943 2222
Four Seasons Hotel Tokyo at Marunouchi	03 5222 7222
Grand Hyatt	03 4333 1234
Hilton Tokyo	03 3344 5111
Hotel Okura	03 3582 0111
Imperial Hotel	03 3504 1111
Mandarin Oriental	03 3270 8800
Palace Hotel	03 3211 5211
Park Hyatt	03 5322 1234
The Peninsula	03 6270 2888
Rihga Royal	03 5285 1121
The Ritz-Carlton	03 3423 8000
The Westin	03 5423 7000

Hospitals

Government

National Center for Child Health & Development	03 3416 0181
National Hospital Organization Tokyo Medical Center	03 3411 0111
Tokyo Metropolitan Hiro Hospital	03 3444 1181
Tokyo Metropolitan Otsuka Hospital	03 3941 3211

Private

Aiiku Hospital	03 3473 8321
International Catholic Hospital	03 3951 1111
Japan Red Cross Medical Center	03 3400 1311
Keio University Hospital	03 3353 1211
St Luke's International Hospital	03 3541 5151

Tourist Information

Asakusa Cultural & Sightseeing Center	03 3842 5566
JNTO Tourist Information Center	03 3201 3331
Odakyu Sightseeing Service Center	03 5321 7887
Tokyo Tourist Information Center	03 5321 3077

Area Codes

Tokyo Area Code	03
Japan Country Code	+81
Chiba	043/047
Hakone	0460
Kawaguchiko	0555
Kobe	078
Kusatso	0279
Kyoto	075
Nagano	0261
Nara	0742
Nijima Island	04992
Nikko	0288
Osaka	06
Oshima Island	04992
Western Toko	042
Yokohama	045

Embassies & Consulates

Australia	03 5232 4111
Belgium	03 3262 0191
Brazil	03 3404 5211
Cambodia	03 5412 8521
Canada	03 5412 6200
China	03 3403 3388
Denmark	03 3496 3001
Finland	03 5447 6000
France	03 5798 6000
Germany	03 5791 7700
India	03 3262 2391
Indonesia	03 3441 4201
Ireland	03 3263 0695
Italy	03 3453 5291
Malaysia	03 3476 3840
Netherlands	03 5776 5400
New Zealand	03 3467 2271
Norway	03 3440 2611
Philippines	03 5562 1600
Poland	03 5794 7020
Portugal	03 5226 0614
Russia	03 3583 4224
Singapore	03 3586 9111
South Africa	03 3265 3379
South Korea	03 3452 7611
Spain	03 3583 8531
Sri Lanka	03 3440 6911
Sweden	03 5562 5050
Thailand	03 3441 1386
UK	03 5211 1100
USA	03 3224 5000
Vietnam	03 3466 3313